GILBERT BAYES
Sculptor 1872-1953

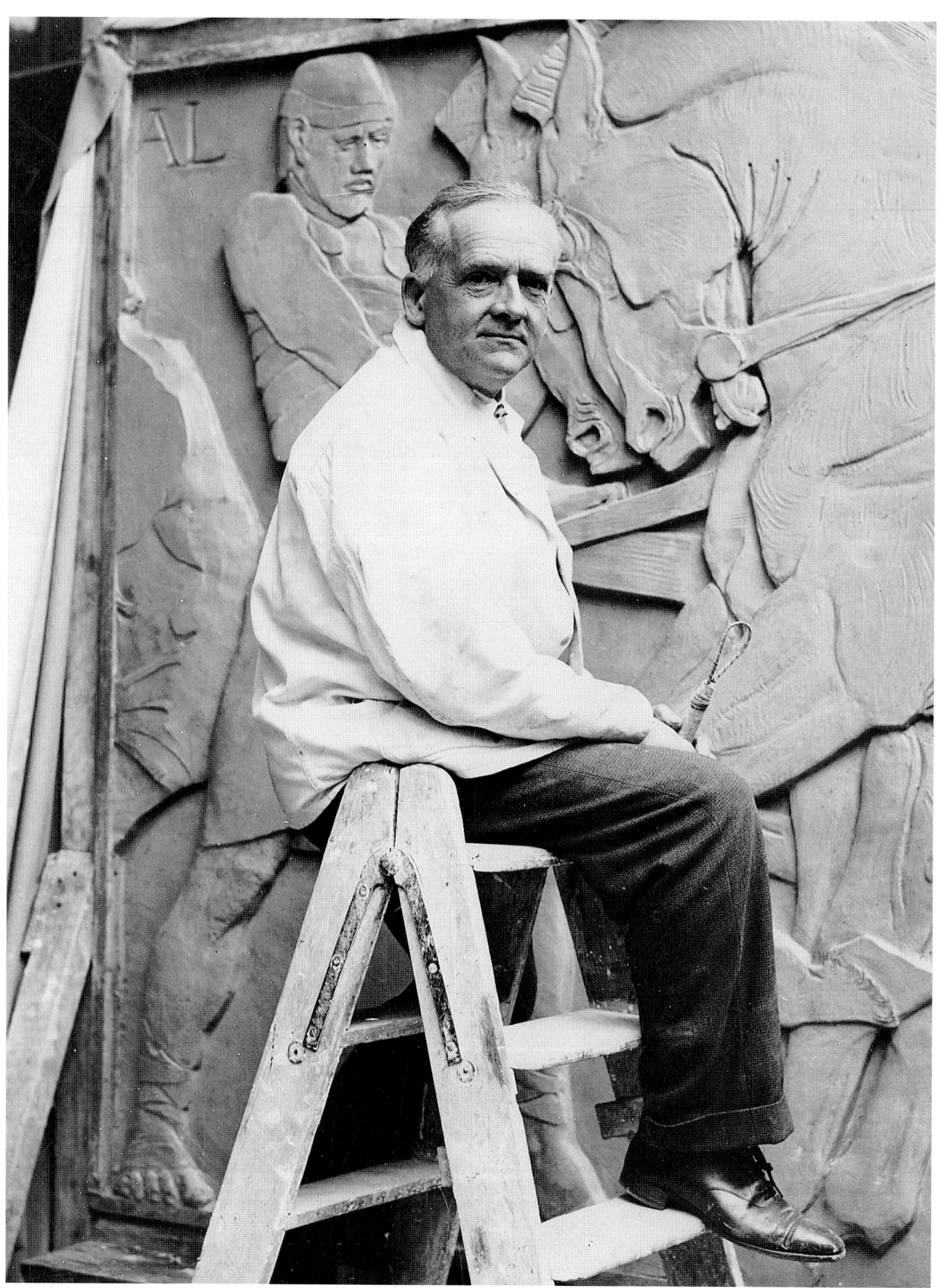

Gilbert Bayes in his studio in 1930 with the full-size plaster for part of the Saville Theatre frieze.

GILBERT BAYES
Sculptor 1872-1953

Louise Irvine & Paul Atterbury

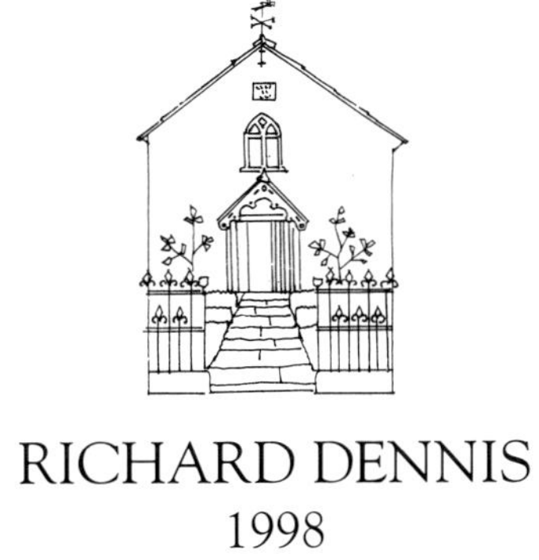

RICHARD DENNIS
1998

Written and produced by Louise Irvine and Paul Atterbury, in conjunction with Peyton Skipwith.
Additional contributions by Philip Attwood, Michael Barker and Benedict Read.

Published to coincide with two exhibitions: Gilbert Bayes, Fine Art Society, New Bond Street, London W1;
Gilbert Bayes, Henry Moore Centre, Leeds 12th October to 6th November 1998.

Publication of this book has been made possible by the support of the Bayes Trust.

ACKNOWLEDGEMENTS

Our interest in the life and work of Gilbert Bayes was initially stimulated by the research for the Doulton Story exhibition, held at the Victoria & Albert Museum, London, in 1979. For the first time we met Jean and Geoffrey Bayes, Gilbert's daughter and son, and since then they have been unhesitantly kind, cooperative and generous with their time and the family material in their care. It is due to their patience, interest and steady support that this book, and the exhibitions devoted to their father's work, have finally come about, and for that we shall always be in their debt. Many other people and institutions have been helpful during the long period of Bayes research, and we should like to thank the following for both information and photographs:

A&B Photographic Services, London; Amber Amerlinck, Canadian National Exhibition Archives; A.J.D. Anstee, Bentalls; Dr J.B. Baker, Hythe; Stella Beddoe, Brighton Art Gallery; John A. Bennett, Birmingham; Bob Bell, St Mark's Church; Conrad Biernacki, Toronto; Bonham's, London; Alison Brown, Aberdeen Art Gallery; Carpenter's Hall; Michael Cates, East Kent Maritime Trust; Philip Chapman; Christie's, London; Lottie Clark, Sue Cox, Hythe Library; G.R. Cowie, Queens University; M. Croal, Manchester City Art Gallery; Martin Cruise, Sun Alliance Insurance Group; Phil Dracket; Rhoda Edwards, St Olave's School; Dr Mark L. Evans, National Museums and Galleries of Wales; J.J. Fitzpatrick; Sgt. Chris Forrester, Metropolitan Police; Albert Gallaghan; Trevor Graham, Glasgow University; Julian Gravett, Lewisham College; Stephen Green, Marylebone Cricket Club; Deborah Greenhalgh, Nevill Keating Pictures; Noelle Guibert, Comédie Française; Nick Hewitt, National Inventory of War Memorials; Virginia Hewitt, Royal Numismatic Society; Ray James, New Zealand; Anthony Jarvis; Ed Judd, California; Alex Kader; C. Kelly, Royal Geographical Society; Dan Klein; Michael Lang, Bayes Trust; George Large, Royal Institute of Painters in Watercolours; Bruce Lindsay, Jonathan Harris; Arvind Mambro, Tata Central Archives; Pauline McMaster, ICI Technology; H.W. Meech, Devonian Group; Janette Moir, Morris Singer Ltd; Edward Morris, Walker Art Gallery; Phil Mortimer, London Fire Brigade; Ann Norbury, Ealing Library; Joan Oaksmonger, Radlett; Jennifer Opie, Victoria and Albert Museum; Sally Lloyd Pearson, Sotheby's; Phillips, London; Alan Powers; A.W. Potter, Royal Academy of Arts; W.L.C. Price, The Law Society; Anthony Rae, Lancashire Constabulary; Paul Reeves; Nell Rhys-Williams, London; P.M. Rogers, Palace of Westminster; Geoffrey Roper, The Free Churches Council; Joanna Soden, The Royal Scottish Academy; Sheena Stoddard, Bristol Art Gallery; Fred Redding, Selfridge's Archive; Neil Roberts, Robert McDougall Art Gallery; Pamela Robertson, Hunterian Museum; Peter Rose; Royal Regiment of Fusiliers; Patti Ryan, Provincial Archives of Newfoundland and Labrador; Jennie Salter, St Pancras Housing Association; H. Sharpe, Society of Motor Manufacturers; Philip Smith; Phil Smyth, Queens University, Belfast; Joanna Soden, Royal Scottish Academy; Sotheby's, London; Roy Still, London Fire Brigade Museum; Donald Sykes, Wye College; John Timmins, Dunedin Public Art Gallery; Alistair Tough, University of Glasgow; Philip Ward-Jackson, Conway Library, Courtauld Institute; Rev Roger Watts, St Nicholas' Church, J. Williamson, Royal Automobile Club.

Finally, particular thanks are due to our contributors, Philip Attwood, Michael Barker and Ben Read, for our editors, Sue Gordon and Sue Evans, to Wendy Wort and Richard Dennis, and to Chrissie Bursey and all the staff at Flaydemouse, who have the patience of saints, especially when confronted by yet more Bayes photographs. We would also like to thank George Hawthorn for his help in establishing a Bayes data base.

LI, PA & PS

Print, design and reproduction by Flaydemouse, Yeovil, Somerset, England
Published by Richard Dennis, The Old Chapel, Shepton Beauchamp, Somerset TA19 0LE

ISBN 0 903685 64 7

CONTENTS

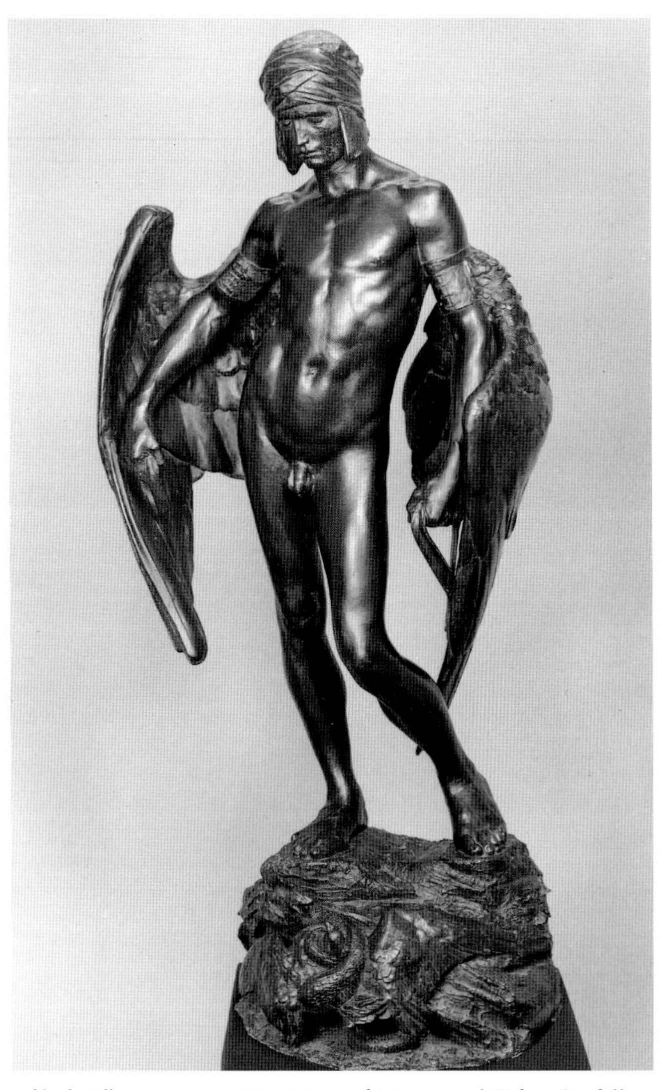

Alfred Gilbert, Icarus, 1884, National Museum of Wales, Cardiff.

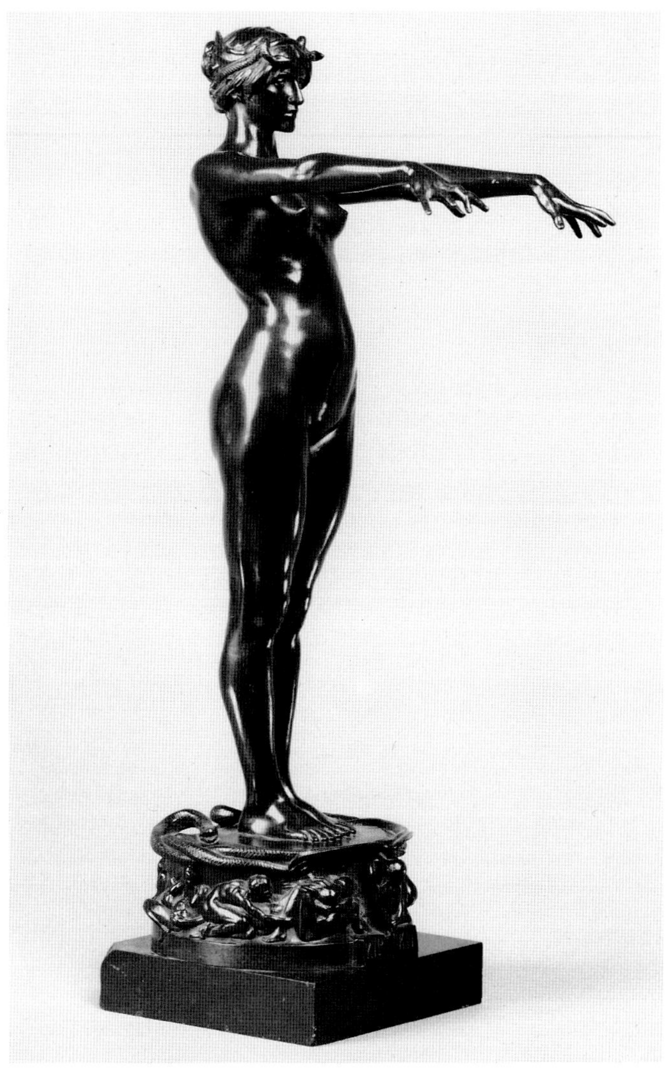

Bertram Mackennal, Circe, 1893, private collection.

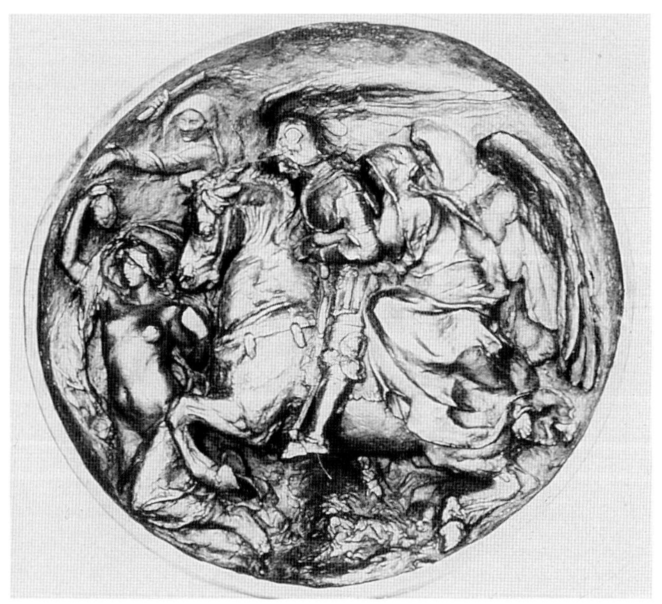

Alfred Gilbert, Post Equitem Sedet Atra Cura, 1887, private collection.

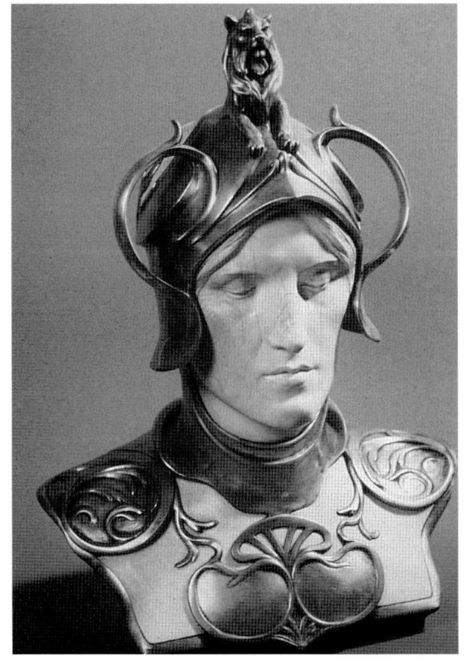

Paul Dubois, La Liberté/De Vrijheid, c.1893, Musées Communaux/Stedelijke Musea, Brussels.

INTRODUCTION
BAYES AND HIS CONTEXT
Benedict Read

In an important assessment of Gilbert Bayes' work at a relatively early stage in his career (Bayes would have been thirty-six years old when the article appeared), Rudolf Dircks writes in *The Art Journal* of 1908: 'The modern movement in English sculpture is one of the most interesting phases of contemporary art, and the work of Mr Gilbert Bayes is an engaging feature in the movement.' As we shall see, Dircks goes on to define this 'engaging' quality in Bayes' work, but whatever one may think about the appropriateness of this actual word to describe the very individual character of Bayes' output, there is little doubt that he can be placed securely within the boundaries of that movement that affected British sculpture from the 1880s onwards and which has generally been termed 'The New Sculpture'.

Possibly the most spirited and concise description of this movement's status was that given by the painter Millais in his 'Thoughts on Our Art of Today': 'So fine is some of the work our modern sculptors have given us, that I firmly believe that were it dug up from under oyster-shells in Rome or out of Athenian sands with the *cachet* of partial dismemberment about it, all Europe would fall straightaway into ecstasy and give forth their plaintive wail – 'We can do nothing like that now.' By the time this was cited by Marion Spielmann in his definitive account of *British Sculpture and Sculptors of Today* of 1901, such a view had become, with some elaboration and variation, almost a critical commonplace, with both contemporary accounts and more recent reassessments – again with varied emphases – picking out certain features of the movement and their origins and analogies. These had been defined in the critical literature of the time. The formal revolution in modelling and casting, which enabled subtler detailing of surfaces and a greater scope for the handling of three-dimensional form, was seen to be inspired partly by France, where a much more thoroughly sophisticated culture of sculpture existed. Millais in his brief critique mentioned Carpeaux and Dalou as influences, and the latter was particularly important through his presence in England as a practitioner and more significantly as a teacher at both the South London Technical Art School and the South Kensington School (later the Royal College of Art) in which role he was able to communicate to British students a new language of sculpture, and this continued after his return to France in 1880 through the continued presence in London as

teachers of Legros and Lanteri. A heightened attraction to Europe led to a sea-change to where young sculptors travelled if they had the desire and opportunity. Rather than going to Rome to view works of Antiquity and the Renaissance which had been culturally almost *de rigueur* before, although Chantrey and Foley disavowed this, now aspirants went to France and Italy to experience contemporary work. Bates, Drury, Frampton, Gilbert, Lee and Pomeroy all went to Paris, Gilbert and Lee to Italy also. Quite apart from new, different ideologies of making sculpture, they would in addition have been made aware of the different plastic formalisations made possible in these countries by the currency in both of the lost-wax methods of casting bronze.

Who first introduced lost-wax cast bronze in England is uncertain. Gilbert, Onslow Ford and Lee were certainly party to its use in the mid 1880s, but it is likely that George Simonds, first Master of the Art Workers' Guild in 1884, was at the same time, and independently, aware of the technique. It was nevertheless Gilbert who, in a work such as *Icarus* from 1894, first demonstrated emphatically the potential of the process: veins, feathers, thongs are all scrupulously rendered in bronze, as well as the rippling musculature of the flesh. At this stage of his career he was still living in Italy, where he had the statue cast. Its impact though was such that the commissioner of the work, Leighton, took it upon himself as President of the Royal Academy successfully to lure Gilbert back to England for the benefit of the nation's sculptural life.

Having said this, it was also true that a new formal language and ideology of sculpture had already been adumbrated in England. Two painter-sculptors of the previous generation, Watts and Leighton, had begun demonstrating that different formulae of physical handling were possible in sculpture, from the 1860s in Watts' case with *Clytie* 1867, and 1877 in Leighton's, when he exhibited his *Athlete Wrestling with a Python*. In addition to these two inspirational godfathers of the new movement there lurked in the background, if not the presence of the painter-decorator and occasional sculptor Alfred Stevens, who died in 1876, certainly his reputation as an artist who embraced all the arts, sculpture, architecture, painting, ornament, design without hierarchical distinction and who, occasionally, painfully produced incomplete masterpieces of such all-in-artworks as the Dining Room of Dorchester House, London which he began c.1855 and the Wellington Memorial in St Paul's Cathedral, London begun in 1856. There were also other sculptors of the previous generation who had made individual, substantial efforts to develop out of the general formal blandness of the age such as Foley and Woolner.

There were also sources and analogues both at home and abroad for the new use of unusual materials and the production of coloured sculpture, the two features often being combined. Some earlier prototypical efforts were without effect or impact. There was an idea expressed in *The Art Journal* of 1861 that the main feature of a *Memorial to the 1851 Exhibition* should be a figure of Queen Victoria of heroic proportions, with gilt ornamental work on the statue, possibly coloured enamel, and 'the dove on the sceptre is to be cast in the newly introduced metal, aluminium; and the globe is to be of crystal.' When Baron Marochetti was working on his commission for the colossal statue of Prince Albert to go at the centre of the Albert Memorial, he proposed at one stage to include some silver as surface covering of the figure, as well as the designated gold, this addition aimed at avoiding monotony. Both these instances may have been slightly one-off ideas; more substantial at this time was the strong commitment of certain other sculptors to polychrome work in imitation of what they argued was antique (i.e. Greek and Roman) practice. John Gibson was the foremost champion of this, and his *Tinted Venus* of 1851-56 the classic exemplar. But he tinted some other works to varying extents, and John Bell made an attempt to persuade those in charge of the Albert Memorial, after Marochetti's death, to substitute for Marochetti's ultimately rejected seated figure a kneeling figure of the *Prince as The Christian Knight* in 'crysoelephantine' mode, as he described it.

It would be a mistake to see these earlier attempts at colouring sculpture in England as in any way influential. Far more significant was what was going on in Europe. France had a rich and varied tradition of colour in sculpture. In addition to a stricter archaeological approach paralleling Gibson and Bell, there was a market in industrially-produced bronzes available in four different colours (green, yellow, black and red) quite apart from nine different patinas. By the end of the century other countries were active: in Belgium, the king's monopoly of ivory from the Congo was directed towards artists, resulting in works like Dubois' *La Liberte/De Vrijheid* of c.1893. The Central European sculptor Tilgner, from Pressburg, now Bratislava, was hailed in his obituary in the local paper *Pressburger Zeitung* 1986 as the founder, no less, of modern polychromy in the art of sculpture. It is possible to locate the coloured sculptures of Bates,

Frampton and Reynolds-Stephens within this pan-European context – Frampton's *Dame Alice Owen* of 1897, a life-size historic portrait figure of the Elizabethan foundress of the Dame Alice Owen School in Islington, London, in bronze, marble and coloured inlays, is a match for any international artwork of the time. One should also remember, especially with the two latter artists, their immersion from an early stage in the mentality and practice of the Arts and Crafts movement, with its relatively different approach to materials and permissible colour combinations from these materials. No analogous context, however, in art can explain Gilbert's use of colour. His *Fawcett Memorial* of 1887 in Westminster Abbey, London, employs gold and silver plating as well as inset turquoises and garnets, while his *Duke of Clarence Memorial* at Windsor Castle 1892-99, mingles and fuses bronze, marble, aluminium, ivory and brass, as well as coloured paintwork. Sources for Gilbert's work, if any, lie in late mediaeval metal memorial sculpture together with contemporary Pre-Raphaelite painting such as that of Burne-Jones.

The new movement in sculpture developed its own specifics in subject matter. In Ideal work, that is subject pieces, the previous generation had portrayed figures and topics from mythology, literature and incidental genre, often with little specificity, using these areas almost literally as excuses for especially the naked, or near naked, human body. One contemporary critic, W.M. Rossetti remarked about the average sculptor's production line: 'Saint, king or hero, Eve, Venus, nymph, shepherd, baby or allegory, he is ready enough.' Another, F.T. Palgrave, commented: 'It is difficult to think of... everybody's Venus with due decorum – one fancies one healthy modern laugh would clear the air of these idle images.' In response the younger generation created a specialised area of subject matter relating to Fate, Life, Love, Enchantment and, occasionally, Death, sometimes coupled together, sometimes also suggestive of another world. Gilbert was a major proponent of such subjects – his bronze relief roundel *Post equitem sedet atra cura* translates as 'Behind the horseman sits dark care'. Others produced works such as *Fate-led* (Toft, 1890), *Love and Fate* (Reynolds-Stephens, 1893). Mackennal's *Circe* of 1894 was not just the legendary enchantress from Homer, she is also practising mesmerism, which was then in the news, while Onslow Ford provided a series of female statuettes (*Folly, Peace* and *The Singer*) of a different mood, what were characterised as giddy creatures, waving and oscillating in their foolish nudity. For about fifteen years after the death of Tennyson in 1892, a distinct phase of Arthurian subject-matter materialised, knights in armour sometimes merging in character with figures designated as St George; their artistic origins owe

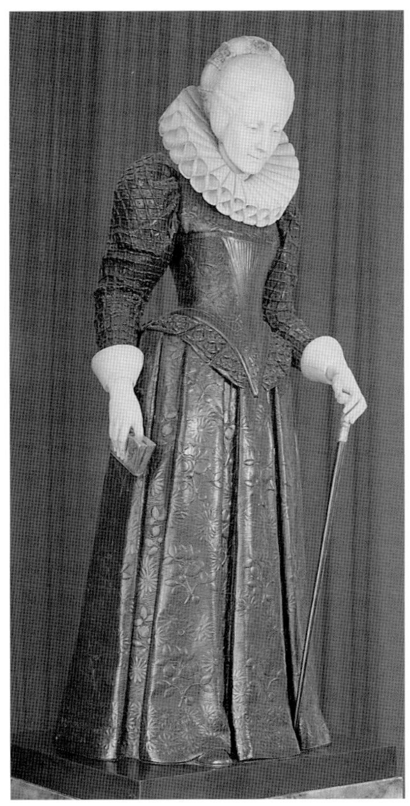

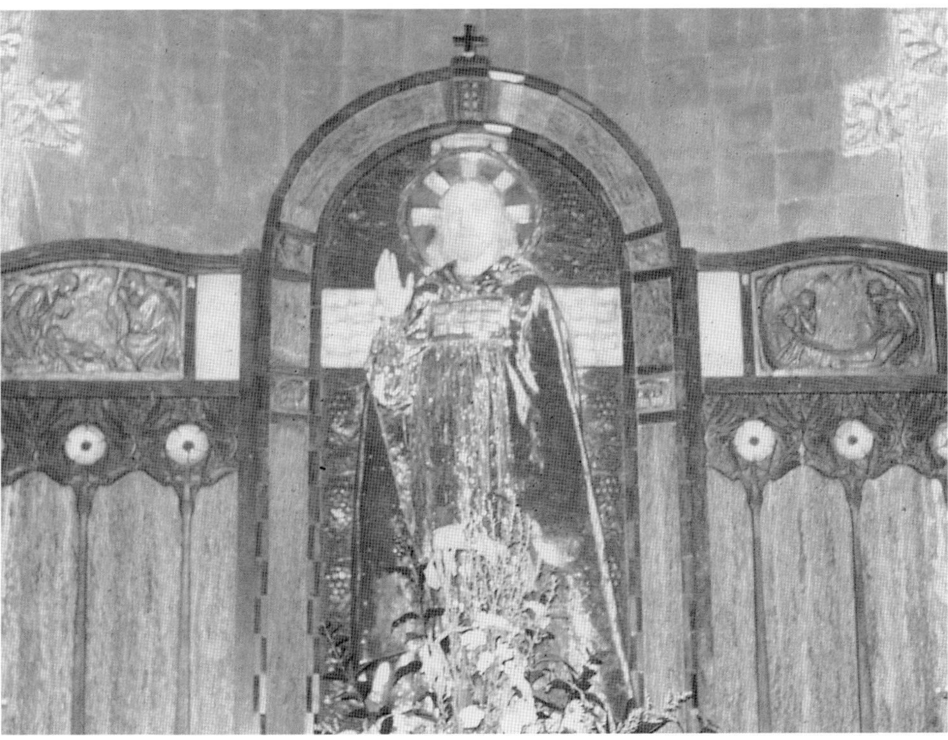

Above: William Reynolds-Stephens, Reredos, 1902-04, Church of St Mary, Great Warley, Essex.
Left: George Frampton, Dame Alice Owen, 1897, Dame Alice Owen School, Potter's Bar.

much, again, to Burne-Jones' painted work.

Attempts were also made to revolutionise the physical context of sculpture. 'Gradually', wrote Spielmann for The Fine Art Society exhibition catalogue in 1902, 'sculptor and public have come to realise that the modeller, like the painter, has his place in the home as well as in the hall and gallery. They are beginning to understand that although statues in life- or heroic-size, like great decorative paintings, are very well for palaces – statuettes, little works of art, and *bibelots*, may take their places in less pretentious rooms along with cabinet pictures, miniatures, and the like.' A parallel effort had been made the generation previously, with Parian ceramic replicas and Art-Union reduced bronzes reproducing at domestic scale major Ideal works by Foley, Bell, Calder Marshall and others. But the new sculptors tried to go one better, to produce and market reduced scale versions in bronze of major works, which they would carefully edit themselves, so to speak, supervising the individual casts and thus retain for these multiples the status of originality. Other works were created as unique casts at this scale.

Another particular feature of the new movement that some have identified was a special notion and practice governing architectural sculpture. It is possible to identify the work of Thornycroft and Bates adorning Belcher's Institute of · Chartered Accountants building in London of 1889-93 as a manifesto of the Arts and Crafts movement; both Belcher and Thornycroft were founder members of the Art Workers' Guild in 1884. It is not just the sculpture

and architecture that form part of an integrated design, the narratives that bedeck the building carry social and political messages too. Other sculptors practised other manners on buildings with a range of functions: Frampton figures and reliefs in bronze and stone on Kelvingrove Art Gallery, Glasgow, 1897-1900, Frampton again with figures and reliefs in bronze and stone on the exterior of Lloyd's Registry of Shipping, London, 1899-1901, while the interior was decorated in bronze, marble and polychrome metal by Lynn Jenkins. At Harrison Townsend's Church of St Mary, Great Warley in Essex, Reynolds-Stephens fitted out a major part of the interior in full colour. Again one might cite precedent analogies for this integrated collaboration between architect and artist; George Gilbert Scott trained up and employed sculptors such as Redfern, Armstead and Philip in the 1860s and 1870s as part of an aesthetic of decorative teamwork that parallels Morris and the Arts and Crafts movement, while some might posit the decorative artist and sculptor John Thomas as a prototype craftsman sculptor who could produce relief and figure work in neo-Gothic or neo-Renaissance styles to suit any particular building or architect.

This then was the context in which the career of Gilbert Bayes established itself and came to flourish. Born in London in 1872, Bayes studied at the City & Guilds School in Finsbury. The City & Guilds at this time were responsible for a distinctive artistic education, particularly as taught by Sparkes and Frith at the South London Technical Art School. In

Sculpture of Today from 1921, Kineton Parkes explains that sculpture was seen as 'but a part of a larger entity, a manifestation in certain required directions to one single end in art. It was a true principle, especially in the case of the industrial arts, and the decorative ones in particular.'

Bayes began exhibiting at the Royal Academy at the fairly early age of seventeen in 1889. His first works were groups and reliefs with titles such as *A Lancashire Milk-horse*, *The Pet of the Ring* and *An Arab Fantasia*. Some were in wax, a relatively unusual medium to use for exhibited work, though its use was more common for sketch models; Leighton was working on his original wax model for *Needless Alarms* in about 1885. In the first twenty years of his exhibiting career Bayes showed some eighteen reliefs and these earned him a special critical acclaim. In an article about Bayes in *The Studio* of 1902, Shaw Sparrow indicated the potential problem about this genre; teachers gave their students frankly pictorial subjects for a low relief panel; 'the pitfall thus opened at their feet invites caution, yet most of them fall into it one by one, exaggerating all the pictorial incidents, and turning out a realistic picture modelled in clay, as if that could do duty for a decorative panel in bas-relief.' Bayes, Sparrow continued, was one of the few sculptors of the youngest school to have talents 'of the right sort' to overcome the pitfalls, and Bayes certainly developed a reputation in this field, not just for his technical expertise in it, but also for a quite distinctive and individual tone in his handling of subject matter – 'a certain feeling of artistic gaiety and lightness of touch, a free handling of romantic and lyrical ideas, decorative animation.' Bayes' work 'is certainly never dull, it never bores you.'

In 1896, sponsored by Frampton, Bayes entered the Royal Academy Schools. He won the Armitage prize in 1897, a Silver Medal in 1898 for a set of models from life, and in 1899 was, we are told by Sparrow, the 'easy winner' of the Gold Medal and travelling scholarship.' Apart from the influence and guidance of Frampton, Bayes was also apparently affected by Brock and Bates. It is hard to determine quite what Brock's impact might have been, as we as yet know so little about his life and work (though this is currently under investigation). Bates, though, we know more about. Again coming from a decorative sculpture background he had developed from the 1880s into a major creator of classical subjects, sometimes in relief, as well as certain key works of polychrome sculpture (*Pandora*, 1890; *Mors Janua Vitae*, 1899). Bates' election as Associate of the Royal Academy in 1892, no doubt through the support of Leighton, would have brought him into the teaching programme at the Royal Academy Schools, and one can certainly identify from about the time of Bayes' study at

the Schools a deepening involvement in classical, as opposed to more playful, genre-type subject matter.

With his travelling scholarship, Bayes spent three months in Italy, followed by nine months in Paris. According to Sparrow, the time in Paris 'kept him abreast of the most potent influences of present-day sculpture', for instance via the International Exhibition of 1900 and its extensive display of masterpieces by French sculptors, as well as a general critical exposure to the work of such French artists as Frémiet, Gérome, Dampt and Bartholdi, in which one can find some equivalences for aspects of Bayes' own output. After his return to London there is a developing maturity in his work, due no doubt to his experience of sculpture in the immediately preceding years of study. *Amor Victor* of 1907 confirms his supreme handling of relief sculpture, as well as epitomising many constituents of his oeuvre. Dircks describes it as 'a large relief in which we have the unbonneted figure of a mounted knight, in the act of charging, his lance shattered, a happy victim to the laughing cupid at his back holding him by a chain of roses. The whole relief is conceived in a rollicking decorative spirit, and would seem to be almost the last note in animation.' The figure of the medieval knight on horseback inevitably invites comparison with Gilbert's *Post equitem...* but the spirit is entirely different, more in line with the possible skittishness of Pegram's *Ignis Fatuus* of 1889.

Bayes' figure groups were also seen to reveal a capacity for three-dimensional handling in bronze – the Irish Elk, which features in *Artemis*, was singled out by Dircks as being 'an animal which lends itself to the intricacies of dexterous modelling,' while in *Sigurd* and *Artemis* Marriott sees a sympathy with the material, bronze, still more happily expressed: 'There is full enjoyment of the plasticity of bronze and its capacity for extension, but everything is articulated and not merely fumbled into shape.' Bayes was praised by Sparrow for his compositions involving horses: he 'likes a horse for its own sake;' in *At the Crest of the Hill* he properly distributes the weight between horses and riders and, we should take it as read, renders this effectively in bronze. This applied to animals in relief too: in *Jason Ploughing the Acres of Mars* Dircks claimed 'the bulls of brazen feet and horns, vomiting forth clouds of fire and smoke, are an excellent instance of Mr Bayes' skill in modelling.' His material competence though was no longer limited to the use of bronze. The memorial relief to *Henry Sidgwick* of 1905 is in bronze, silver and lapis lazuli, *Sigurd* of 1910 is in bronze, marble and enamel, *The Fountain of the Valkyries* of 1912 used bronze, marble and mosaic, all in their ways reflecting possibly the work of Gilbert and Bates at home, and the wider European context he would have witnessed in his time abroad.

A particular vein of comment on Bayes' work does focus on its implicit physical context. 'Its real *forte* is a fanciful distinction that is most attractive in sculpture of a small size; in household sculpture, more effective in homes than in public galleries.' In the context of *A Knight on his War Horse*, Sparrow continues 'statuettes may be placed in any home, whereas large statues require such a scheme of room-decoration as prevents their appeal from being aggressive.' Marriott later develops this: Bayes has an imaginative grasp of all the circumstances and conditions for which the work is intended. These are not just physical but social as well. 'In everything that he designs, useful or ornamental, there is a tacit recognition of the house'; in effect not just the house but every sort of building, sacred or secular, public or private, even the garden as an architectural feature. Marriott continues that Bayes is not merely a sculptor in the sense of making statues and busts but in the sense of 'working in plastic materials with some definite relation to the useful or ornamental purposes of contemporary life in view. Bayes' virtue is his artistic organisation – everything is considered, not only the nature of the material and the character of the particular setting, but also the climate, the conditions of life, even the artistic perceptions of the people most likely to be in contact with the work.'

This developed aesthetic of functional sculpture, a combination and expansion of the various ideologies of the New Sculpture relating to sculpture and architecture, as decoration, as home object, is borne out in Bayes' work in quite distinct, specific areas. He produced nude female statuettes such as the *Greek Dancer, Fate* 'reflecting in her mischievous expression the symbol which is suggested by the title as well as by the two little puppets on a string with which she is playing', and *The Top Spinner*. He also executed what one might categorise as more 'standard' architectural sculpture. His statues of the architects *Chambers* and *Barry* form part of the Pantheon of English Art commemorated in sculpture along the Cromwell Road facade of the Victoria & Albert Museum, a scheme first adumbrated by the architect of this part of the museum, Aston Webb, early in 1905. In 1906 Bayes completed a large relief in bronze of *Assur-Natsir-Pal*, King of Assyria, for the exterior of the National Gallery of new South Wales in Sydney, Australia. The subject of the relief is the King of Assyria present with his queen at the opening of a new building. Before his reign 'Assyria had been reduced to comparative powerlessness, but under him the boundaries of the empire were extended, splendid palaces, temples, and other buildings raised, whose elaborate sculptures and rich painting bear witness to the fact that in his day culminated the first period of Assyrian art. The theme of the relief is, then, most appropriate.' Bayes' relief was the second of a series of four affixed to the building – the others were Percival Ball, Feodora Gleichen and William Reid Dick, installed between 1900 and 1931. Bayes' design had been selected in 1903 at the request of the Trustees of the Art Gallery by the painter Alfred East and significantly, the sculptor George Frampton, who had been Bayes' sponsor for the Royal Academy Schools. Later Bayes was to execute two large equestrian figures for the gallery grounds. Other standard genres Bayes worked in included memorial sculpture and a series of medals.

The first twenty-five years of Bayes' professional career as a sculptor show him to have been a fully-fledged member of the New Sculpture movement. He participated in most of the characteristic stylistic and ideological markers of the movement, the new attitudes to modelling, materials and subject matter. At the same time his contribution was distinctive in mood and subject, in technical supremacy particularly of relief and in a very personal approach to colour in sculpture. Indeed he brought a particular originality of his own to the movement which is summarised poetically, perhaps, but no less validly by one of his contemporary champions, in words already quoted in part: 'to the general current he comes as a sort of contributory rivulet, through pleasant country of hill and dale, romantic country which bears its tale of fantasy and legend', his work 'contributing a certain feeling of artistic gaiety and lightness of touch, a free handling of romantic and lyrical ideas' and 'decorative animation'.

Descriptions of Gilbert Bayes' work are mainly quoted from three contemporary articles:
R. Dircks 'Mr Gilbert Bayes' *Art Journal*, 1908
W.S. Sparrow 'A Young English Sculptor: Gilbert Bayes' *The Studio* March 1902 Vol 25
C. Marriot 'The Recent Work of Gilbert Bayes' *The Studio* 1917 Vol 72

For further reading on Victorian and 'New Sculpture' see the bibliography.

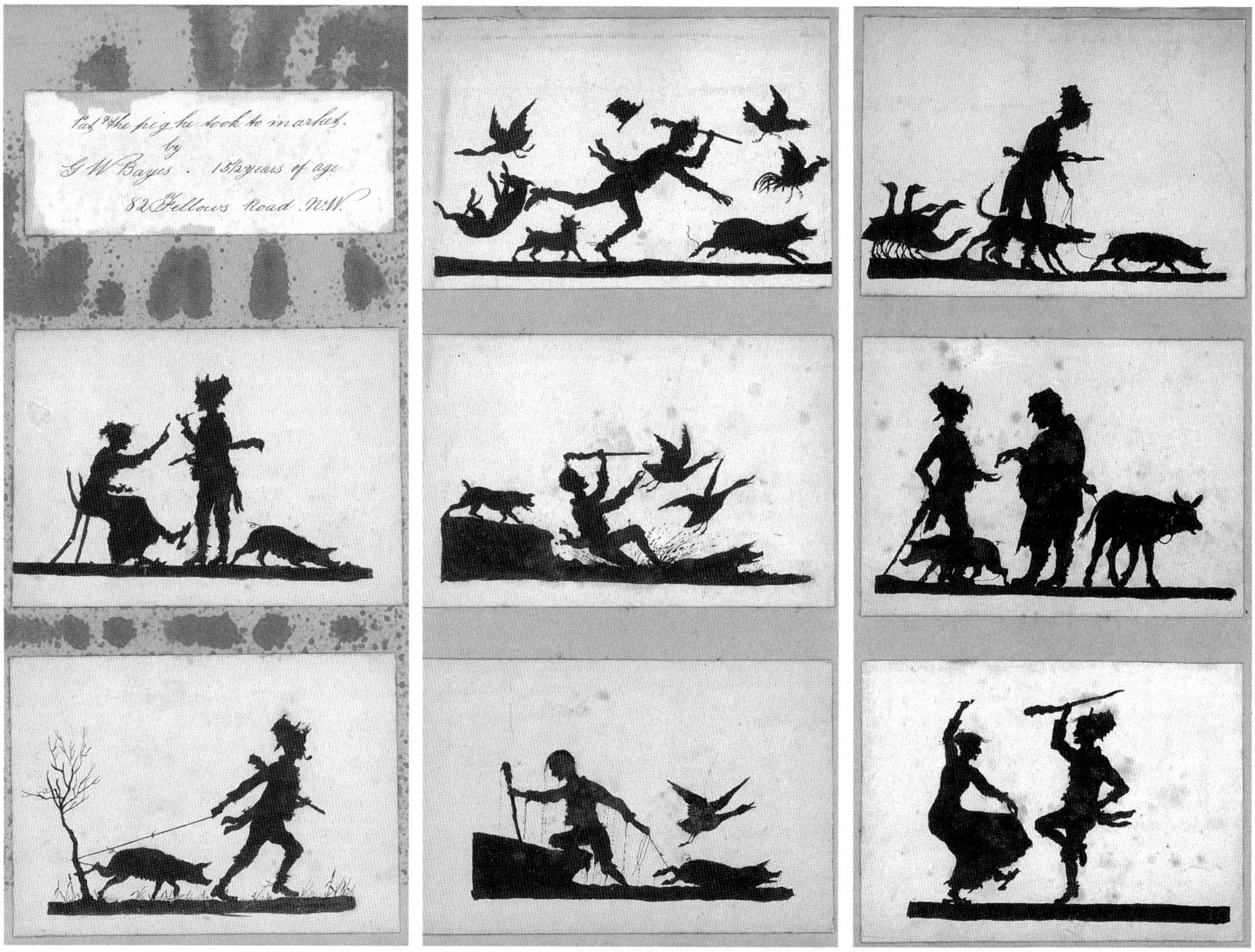

Pat and the Pig, a silhouette story drawn by Bayes aged fifteen, 1888.

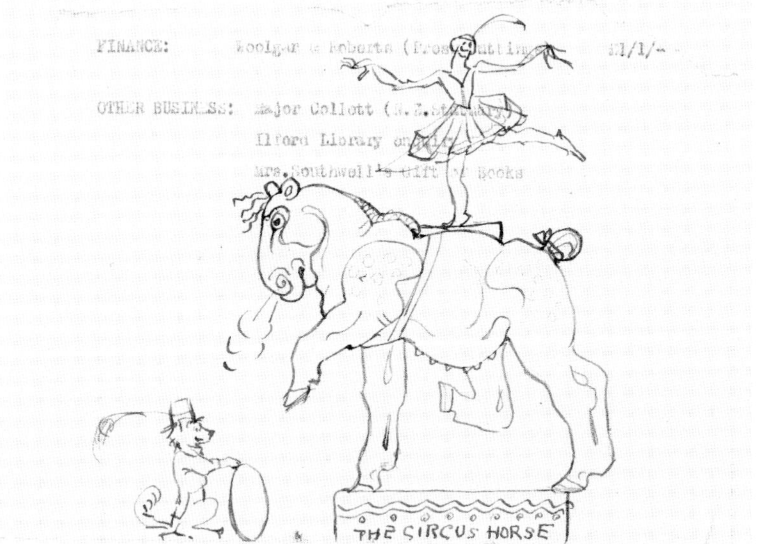

The Circus Horse, comic sketch by Bayes, 1920s.

FAMILY AND BACKGROUND
Peyton Skipwith

Gilbert Bayes was born on 4 April 1872, the son of Alfred Walter Bayes, a professional artist who was born in the remote village of Lumbutts, high in the Pennine Hills. He married Emily Ann Fielden from Todmorden in Yorkshire, and settled in North London in 1863. Alfred's income was always precarious, although he exhibited regularly at the Royal Academy from 1858 until 1908. During his early years in the capital he moved frequently, but remained mostly in the St John's Wood area, giving addresses at 89 Stanhope Street, 20 Eton Street, 2 Gloucester Place, 42 Wellington Terrace, 6 Oval Road and 21 Adelaide Road before finally settling at 82 Fellows Road in 1884, where he remained until his death in 1909. *The Bayes Saga*, a memoir typewritten by his younger daughter, Jessie, who was born in Adelaide Road, tells us all we know of this period. She recalls it dimly as 'a twilight lit by gentle points of candle light touching dear remembered things – the rickety conservatory where we kept our toys; the mettlesome rocking horse with eloquent eyes and a hole where his tail used to hang; the eighteenth century sedan chair which served impartially as castle battlement, dungeon, royal throne or pirates' lugger. Then the tin bath before the kitchen fire when hot water was poured down my back and inevitably rubbed in my eyes; mouse-traps brought to father to kill the poor prisoner; kittens brought him to drown – cruel tasks to inflict on the gentlest of souls just because harder hearts didn't like the job'. She speculated about her mother's early life in London. 'I often wonder what those first years must have been like for her – living in two or three rooms in Kentish Town (assuredly with nothing better than a tap on the landing) after the generous stone-flagged kitchen, complete with baking oven and copper, of her Todmorden home – for the Fieldens had standing – and background'. Jessie's clear implication was that although the two families were already linked by blood, Emily Ann had married beneath her.

Four children survived from Emily Ann's eight pregnancies. Emmeline, born in 1867, Walter (1869-1956), Gilbert (1872-1953) and Jessie (1878-1970). Three were destined to become artists, Emmeline alone falling into what her sister called 'the groove of dedicated house-wifery', which kept her tied to home until her belated marriage in 1912 to Jack Aumonier. Walter was sent away to the Quaker School at Saffron Walden, which he hated, then had a spell in a solicitor's office, which was even less congenial, before

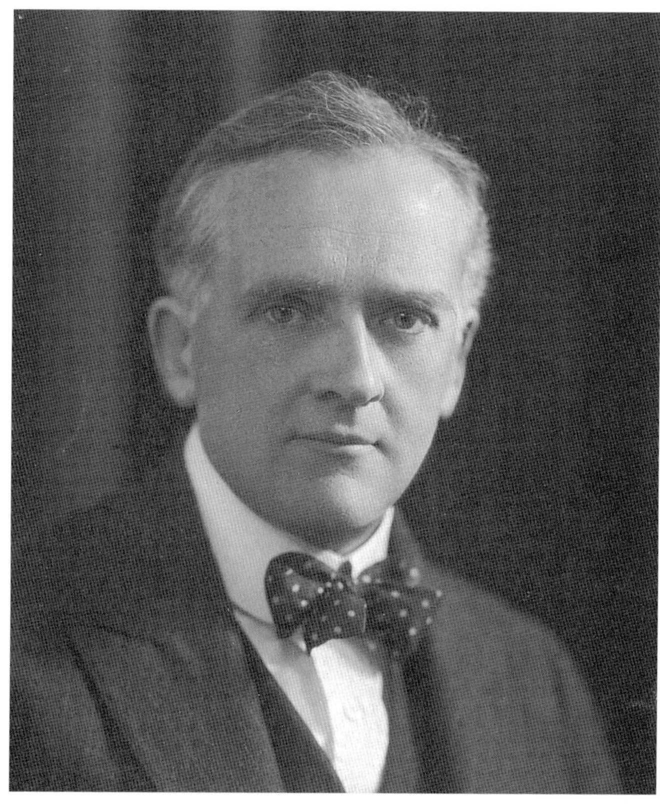

Gilbert Bayes in his thirties.

evening classes at the City & Guilds School liberated him and enabled him to escape office drudgery and become a full-time painter. Although he never achieved great fame, he had a distinguished career as painter, teacher and writer – he was head of Westminster School of Art from 1918 to 1934 and later Director of Painting at Lancaster – but he is best remembered today for his association with Sickert and his participation in the first Camden Town Group Exhibitions. Despite being a painter himself, Alfred Bayes seems to have wished his children to adopt more financially secure professions. His second son, Gilbert, was also sent to work in the City, in his case with a firm of tie merchants, before, once again, the City & Guilds and later the Royal Academy Schools came to his rescue. Jessie, in her turn, was rescued from the Prudential Assurance Company only because Gilbert paid for her to take evening classes at the Central School of Arts and Crafts. In *The Bayes Saga* Jessie recalls Gilbert – 'Bertie' as the family knew him then – bringing home scraps of material from the tie merchant's to make clothes for dolls 'he had a craftsman's fingers and in his spare time fashioned exquisite trifles – toys for me, beautiful little cut-out

Gilbert Bayes

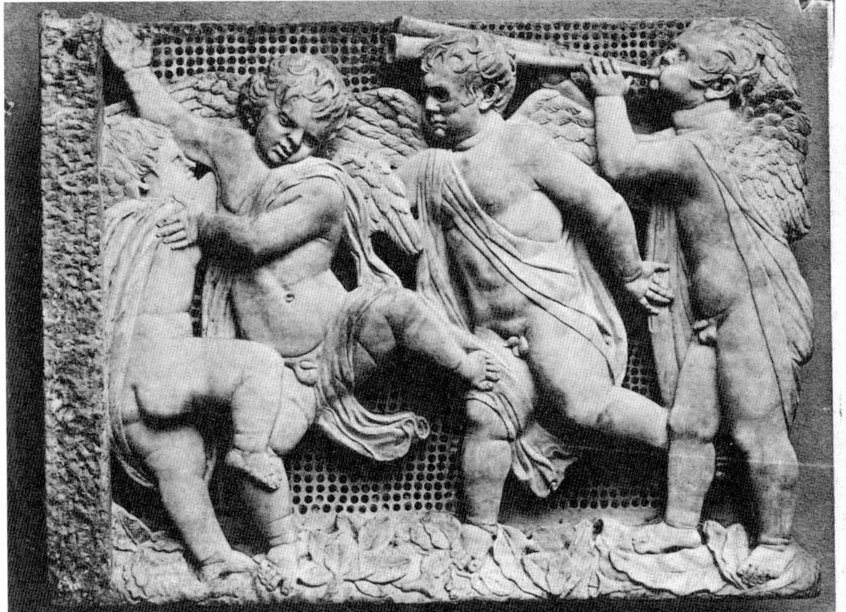

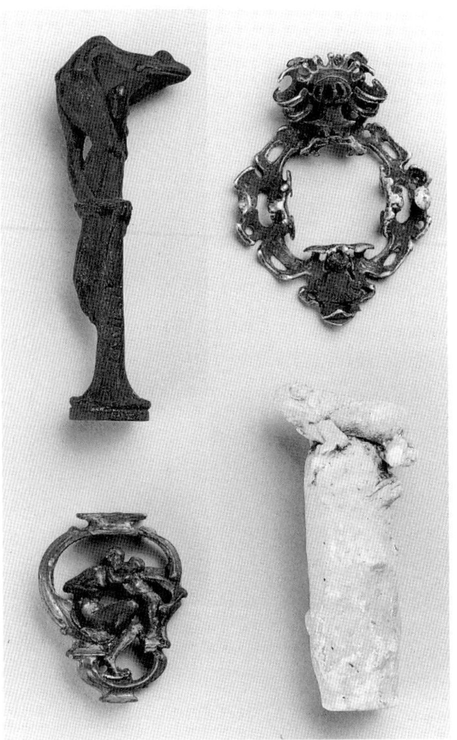

Postcard sources from the Bayes' album:
Above, Donatello, below left, Michelangelo, below right, Frémiet.
Top right, Frémiet bronze frog seal with unfinished plaster version by Bayes, with two early
examples of Arts and Crafts metalwork by Bayes.

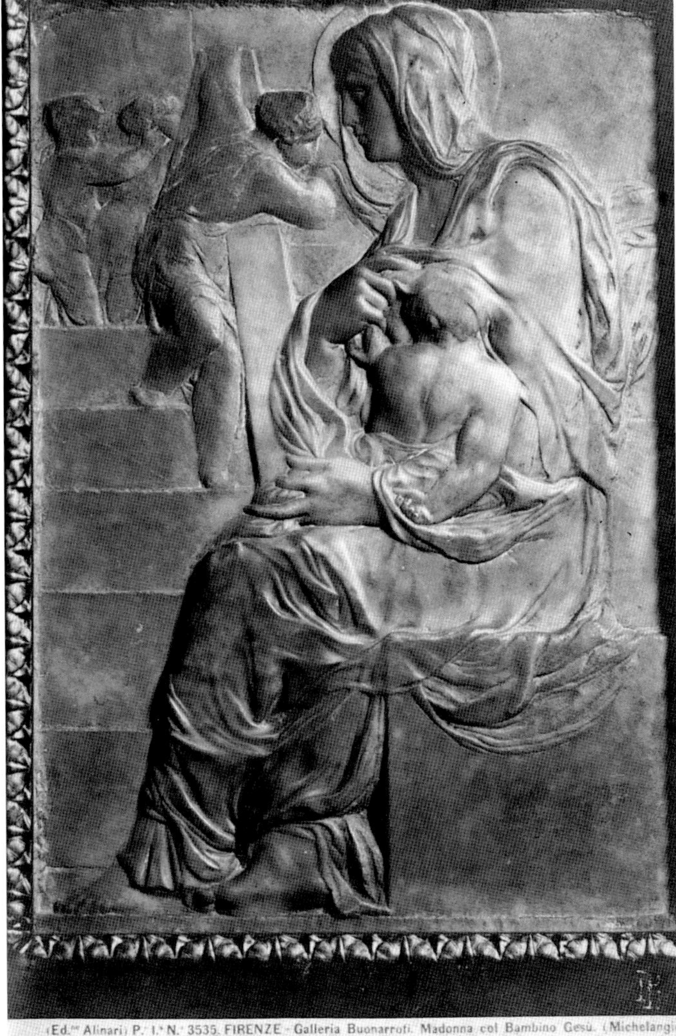

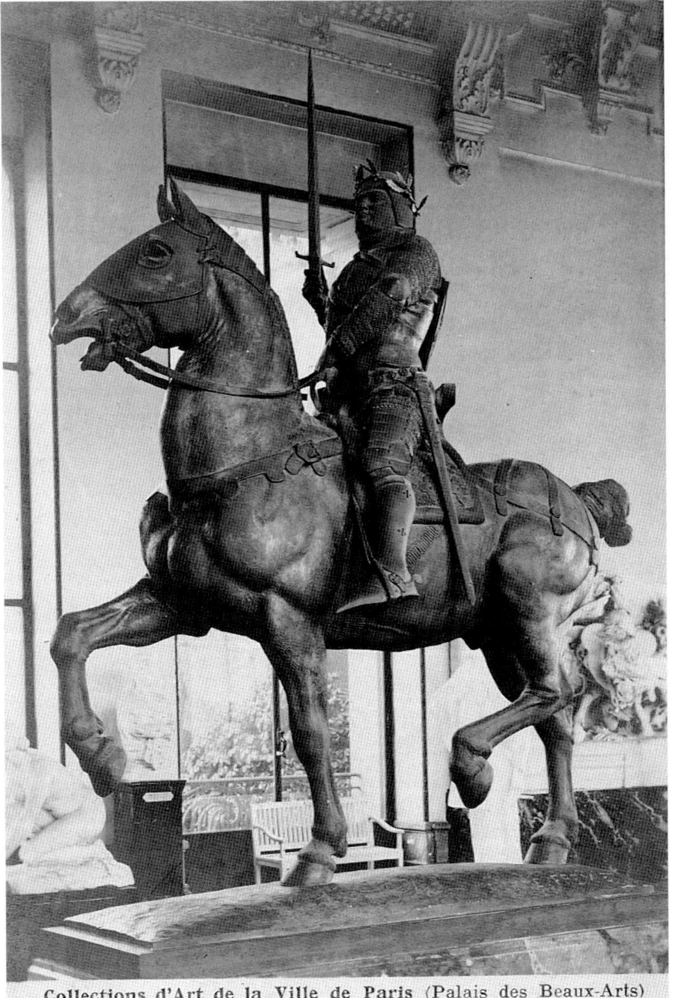

figures of romance; for me too, villages, castles and theatres (but of course he loved playing with them too). His theatres were wonderful, and we invited the family and friends to puppet shows in them, with lighting effects from coloured matches. Generally I did the script. It was a few sticks of cobbler's wax that started him as a sculptor. He began to model, and exhibited a small high-relief of galloping horses at the Academy when he was seventeen'. Although this memoir was written many years later, Jessie's pride in her brother's achievements is palpable and in 1889, at the age of seventeen, Gilbert exhibited two wax models in the manner of Randloph Caldecott at the Royal Academy, *The Fortunes of War* and a *Lancashire Mill-horse*. These were his first exhibits in what was to be an unbroken line of fifty-five years, yet he was never made even an associate of that august institution. C.R. Ashbee, who referred to Bayes' 'Jolly art friezes', may have put his finger on the reason for his exclusion when, in writing of his admiration for the figures of *Peace* and *War*, he said 'I have seen figures of his in Australia – outside the Sydney Museum – that sit well in the saddle. We have always to remember that there is a colonial mood. It is not cheap exactly, but it is less sophisticated than Chelsea, St John's Wood, Piccadilly or Queen's Square; Bayes caught that mood.'

At this stage Gilbert was still virtually self-taught. He had already exhibited with the Arts and Crafts Exhibition Society, prior to his debut at the Royal Academy, but he did not start attending evening classes at the City & Guilds School in Finsbury for another two years. During the five years he was there, 1891-1896, he studied modelling from life, but he also learnt other craft-skills, which were to stand him in good stead. One of his teachers, Finn Brophy, who was later to put Bayes' name forward for membership of the Art Workers' Guild, was a designer with a penchant for enamelling; he exhibited two or three pieces at the Royal Academy during the 1890s. Brophy had originally been introduced to the Guild by Alexander Fisher, the leading exponent in the art of enamelling at this period. The fact that throughout his career Bayes regularly used enamel to enrich many of his bronze figures can be traced back directly to Brophy's training. The City & Guilds also ran courses in drawing, plaster and sgraffito work, cabinet-making, gold and silversmithing and casting. At the end of his five years Gilbert won a County Council Scholarship, entering the Royal Academy Schools in 1896, where he was taught by three of the finest sculptors in the country: Thomas Brock, who had been Lord Leighton's assistant, Harry Bates and George Frampton.

George Frampton was probably the single most influential figure in Bayes' life and the pair remained friends until Frampton's death in 1928. Frampton had trained for a short time in an architect's office before working for a firm of architectural carvers, and his lifelong interest in the relationship between architecture and sculpture is clearly reflected in his many successful collaborations including that with T.E. Collcutt on Lloyd's Registry of Shipping in Fenchurch Street, London, and with J.W. Simpson at Kelvingrove, Glasgow. Like his new pupil, Frampton was interested in polychromy in sculpture, and incorporated other materials into his bronzes, most sensationally his turn-of-the-century figure of *Lamia* (Royal Academy Collection, London), in which the flesh is of ivory, while the head dress and bodice are inset with opals. Frampton was also intensely interested in Arthurian legend and art nouveau symbolism and undoubtedly fuelled Bayes' enthusiasm for mediaeval knights and the heroic figures from Norse sagas. One of Frampton's most complete Arthurian cycles is the set of nine silver-gilt relief door panels for Astor House, Westminster, dating from 1895-96, and it was probably in deference to these that Bayes made the door-panels that he exhibited at the 1896 Royal Academy Summer Exhibition and at the Paris International Exhibition, four years later.

Bayes' years at the Academy Schools were marked by considerable success. In 1897 he won the Armitage Prize for composition; in 1898 a Silver Medal for life modelling, and in 1899 he won the Gold Medal, the Landseer Scholarship and a £200 travelling scholarship, on the proceeds of which he spent three months in Italy and nine months in France. With the Great International Exhibition, it was an exciting and stimulating time to be in Paris. Jessie, in the memoir describes a delirious weekend visit by Emmeline and herself to see both their brother and the exhibition: 'It was magical; never before or since was there such an exhibition. All the centre of Paris with its river and its bridges formed the setting, but new facades had converted the ordinary streets into mediaeval France or cities beyond the seas. I can still savour the green tea I drank in an enchanted Chinese garden under a vast elephant temple, served by exquisite Chinese girls, whilst camels and elephants drifted about amicably, and lovely rickshaw boys plied for hire.'

Apart from exposing him to French sculpture, his months in Paris were important to Bayes for another reason. His growing friendship with the Canadian singer Margaret Huston, and his too frequent mentions of her in his letters, prompted Gertrude Smith, a fellow-student from Bayes' London days to 'scurry off' to Paris, where she and Gilbert became engaged. Jessie describes Margaret Huston as 'quite irresistible – a big warm, generous creature, like a ship in full sail. To be embraced by her was like being

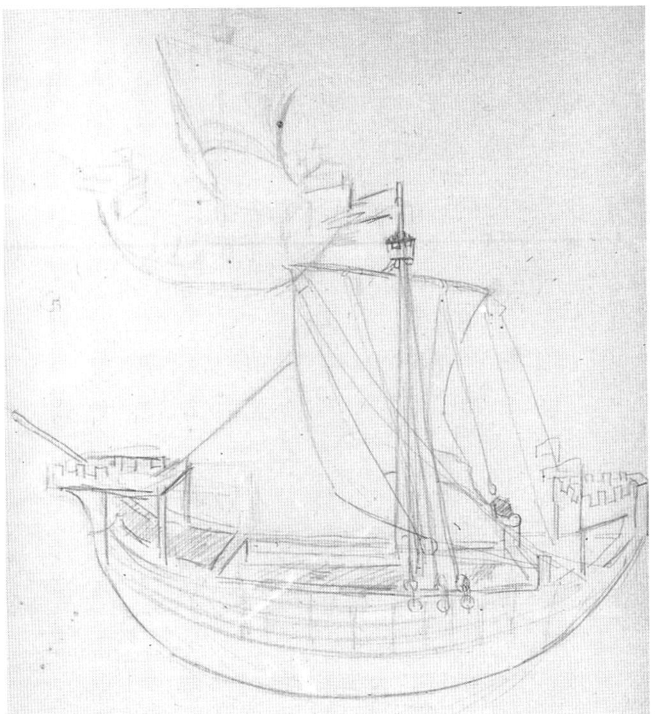

Sketch by Bayes, perhaps for the Selfridge's ship.

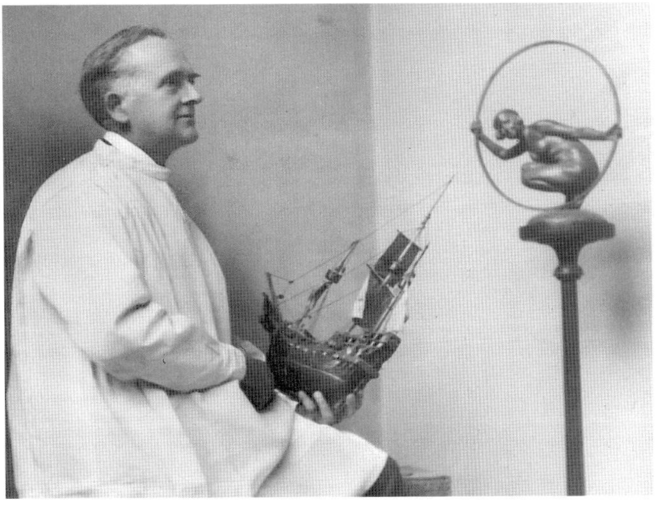

Studio portrait of Bayes by Beatrice Cundy, c.1929 with Greek Dancer and the Selfridge's ship.

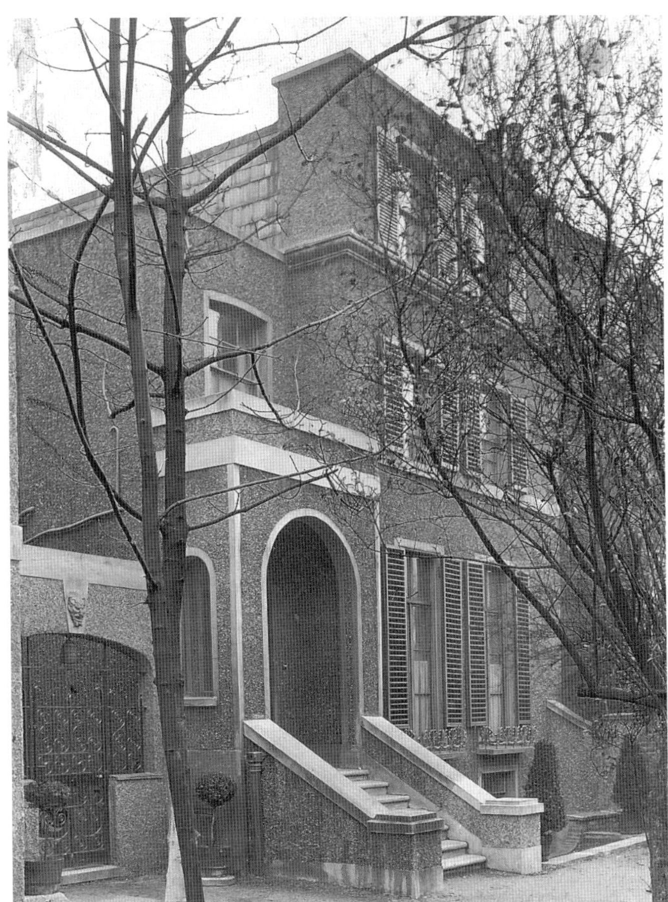

4 Greville Place, St John's Wood, London, Bayes' home from 1930.

enveloped by a tidal wave.' And she records that 'Gilbert, at that time like a pocket Galahad, was lost in them, for her embraces were freely given long before it became the fashion to begin friendships or love affairs in the middle!' His elder sister, Emmeline, always said that this precipitated Gilbert and Gertrude's engagement. The friendship with Margaret, however, endured. Margaret is supposed to have been intent on marrying money, which she did and, with her first husband, Bill Carrington, she established herself as a popular and discriminating hostess in New York and Santa Barbara, and commissioned work from both Gilbert and Jessie. After Carrington's death she married the poet Robert Edmond Jones who, in turn, became a friend of the Bayes' family.

When Gilbert returned to England from Paris he took a studio at 42 Linden Gardens in West London, but continued to live at home in Fellows Road. His parents had not prospered during these years owing to the collapse of The Liberator, a building society in which Alfred had invested all his savings. Luckily, however, back in the 1880s, Alfred, along with James Aumonier's father, had bought the land in Fellows Road, and between them they had built the pair of semi-detached houses. After the financial reverse, Jessie records, the maid-of-all-works was sacked, the big studio was let, Emmeline started a dress-making business and Jessie herself went to work for the Prudential at a salary of £40 per annum, and so they got by. The extra income from having Gilbert back in Fellows Road must have been welcome, but in 1906 he and Gertrude got married and set up home at 40 Boundary Road, St John's Wood. Their first child, Jean, was born there two years later and their son, Geoffrey, in 1912.

In 1911, Gilbert was commissioned to design the new Great Seal for King George V. This was an important sign of official recognition but, with a growing family, he still felt it prudent to augment his income by teaching at Camberwell School of Art. With the outbreak of war he volunteered for service but was initially classed as medically unfit; later when

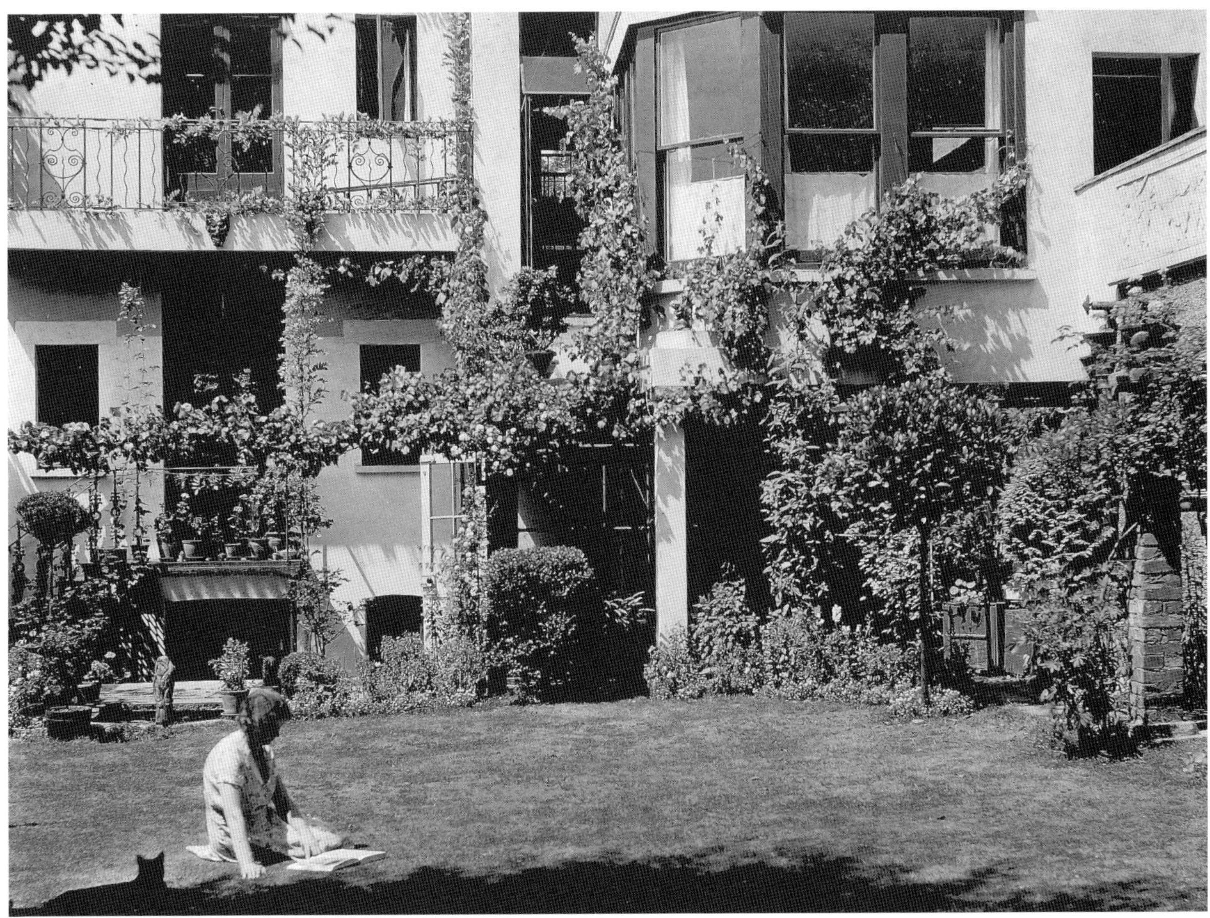

The garden at Greville Place, c.1932.

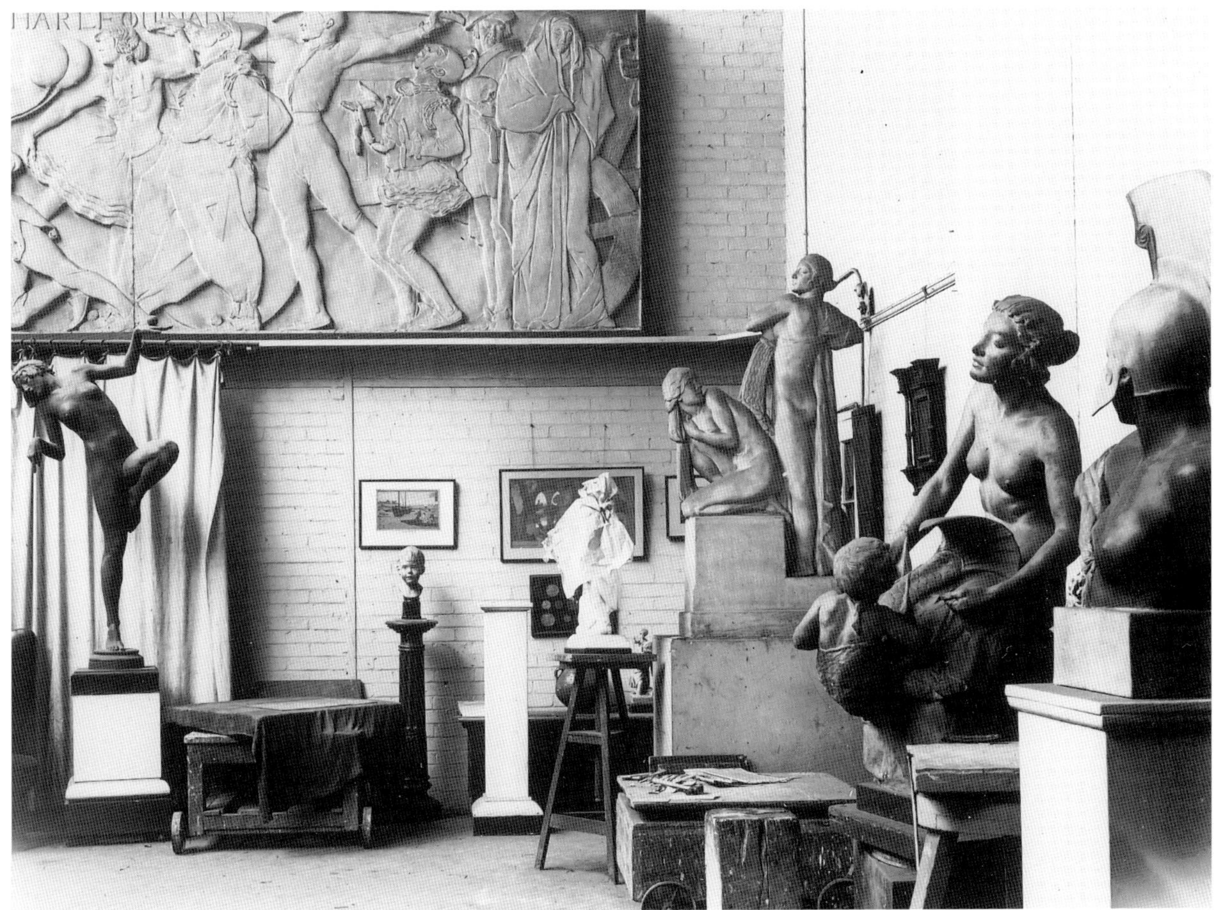

The studio at 4 Greville Place in the early 1950s.

he was called up, he was exempted from military service because of the importance of the Australian War Memorials, upon which he was already engaged. His first quarter-size model for *Peace* was exhibited at the Royal Academy in 1917 and *War* the following year. Eric Gill had similarly been exempted from military service on the grounds that the *Stations of the Cross* he was carving for Westminster Cathedral was of national importance. Lloyd George's wartime government, in which Lord Beaverbrook served, was particularly conscious of the propaganda uses of art and, although this was promoted primarily through the Official War Artists' scheme, certain other projects were given official approval.

The Australian War Memorial commission was a great boost to Gilbert's professional standing and, although he continued to teach a little – now at the Sir John Cass School – his career was fully established. Much of the rest of his life is best told through his work and through his involvement with the Art Workers' Guild, which provided both friendships and professional contacts. One of these many Guild contacts was the sculptor John Angel, whom Gilbert met again years later when, in 1929, he went to America in the company of Reginald Blomfield, Sir John Squire and Gustav Holst at the invitation of the New York Academy of Arts and Letters. Angel was working on sculptures for the Cathedral of St John the Divine and, as he was not planning to return to England, Gilbert asked him if he would like to sell his house in Maida Vale. Gilbert and Gertrude already knew 4 Greville Place, which in an earlier guise, had served King George III as a hunting lodge. It was a handsome, detached house, set back from the road, with a substantial garden, and they bought it from him for £3,000. The garden had space for building two large studios – his and hers – designed by Gervais Bailey, one of Gilbert's many architect friends. Apart from work, the studios were perfect for entertaining, especially for the annual 'at homes' at the end of March, when friends and fellow-artists came to view Gilbert's Academy exhibits. The house had two substantial rooms on the ground floor, with French windows onto a veranda, from which steps led down into the garden. Gilbert designed this with brick piers, pergolas and ponds, inlaid with mosaic, as a foil to show off his garden sculpture. *The Great God Pan* presided in one corner, and the North and South panels from *The Fountain of the Months* were fixed to the garden wall after they came back from the Royal Academy. Their surface was protected from the weather by a roofing of green Doulton pantiles. Other plasters were also incorporated: *Wisdom*, one of the panels conceived for the Commercial Bank of Scotland formed the end wall of the conservatory.

Official and professional honours accrued during these inter-war years. He served as Master of the Art Workers' Guild in 1925; he won a Bronze Medal at the Paris Salon in 1929 and a Gold Medal in 1939; he was awarded the Royal Society of British Sculptors' Medal for the frieze on the Saville Theatre in 1931 and two years later was awarded the Freedom of the City of London; he became a Liveryman of the Worshipful Company of Glaziers, and an Honorary member of the Societé des Artistes Français. During the years of the Second World War he served as President of the Royal Society of British Sculptors, and Vice-President of the Incorporated Association of Architects and Surveyors. All were well-earned tributes to a long and distinguished career, but he outlived his time. The war, with all its deprivations, took its toll and sapped both his and Gertrude's reserves of energy. He was out of sympathy with the new and increasingly dominant artistic trends and, although he was not as intemperate as Sir Alfred Munnings, his disillusionment shows clearly in his notes for a lecture in 1944 to the Ealing Art Club, of which he was president: 'If you like a bust that has both eyes on one side of its face, and a surface that looks like one of the rockeries that fish swim through in aquariums, which the sculptor says represents the soul of the sitter – well that is your affair and his...'

The declaration of peace in 1945 did not provide the same opportunities for sculptors as had occurred in 1918, not even for the younger generation, and the post-war years were not particularly happy ones for Gilbert. Gertrude was effectively bed-ridden for the last seven years of her life and required his constant attention. This, together with a lack of commissions, inevitably drained his natural sense of optimism, and after Gertrude died in April 1952 his health steadily deteriorated and he died fifteen months later on 10th July, 1953.

BAYES AND THE ARTS AND CRAFTS MOVEMENT

Paul Atterbury

In the last decades of the nineteenth century, the status of sculpture in Britain was radically reviewed. The influence of France in general, and Jules Aimé Dalou in particular during his period of teaching at South Kensington in the 1870s, swung younger sculptors away from conventional classicism towards informality and realism. At the same time, there was a new interest in Assyrian sculpture and other so called 'primitive' sources. This period was also marked by a developing enthusiasm for the applied arts, encouraged by the Arts and Crafts movement, and sculptors were looking with fresh eyes at new materials, techniques and types of subject. Among the writers and critics of the day a recurring theme was the need for artists to bridge the widening gap between the fine and the applied arts, a gulf seen by many as both arbitrary and artificial. As a young student, Gilbert Bayes was at the heart of this debate, and he made his views clear at various points in his career. Looking back on his life in a lecture delivered to the Ealing Art Club on 6th August 1944 he said 'In the early days I think there was no difference made between the crafts and what today we call the fine arts. An artist was the master of his craft or guild and no nonsense was talked about it and there were no exhibitions. At what point, certainly comparatively recently, the term Fine Art came into being and the crafts were divorced from it and became the Cinderella of the arts, I don't know, but this was certainly hastened by the advent of the seasonal exhibition'. Another lecture to the same club the following year took this further: 'It is up to the artist to serve the community and deserve well of it - not to make feeble things that won't function. It is also part of their task to make themselves understood by those that have to live with their work... I am not at all sure that we are not training too many people to paint vague pictures rather than make fine craftsmen in a wider sense. Let us remember that art is not just pictures for exhibition, or sculpture conscientious nudes. Many who today frame their works and claim them as high art would be better if they thought for other materials – designs for textiles, theatre drop curtains, wall papers, ceramics and the like.'

At the start of his career, Bayes' inclinations, like his contemporaries such as George Frampton, Eric Gill and Richard Garbe, certainly encompassed the applied arts. In the 1890s and 1900s, a period when he was prolific and successful, he produced large numbers of low relief plaques and panels, in wax, plaster, electrotyped and beaten metal and other materials, some of which were designed to be set into furniture and woodwork. The oak cabinet which he exhibited in 1901 indicates the way in which these panels could be incorporated into woodwork. Even more relevant was the steady stream of practical objects dating from this period. The sequence starts with the wax model for a doorknocker, exhibited in 1889, and then continues with hand and standing mirrors, door plates and door furniture, a letterbox, bell and switch covers, a cabinet, a chess set, caskets, presentation cups, jewellery, fireplace panels and the first medals. He worked in wax, plaster, wood, copper, bronze, silver, enamel and other materials and most of these early works were exhibited. Indeed, despite his rather dismissive remarks about exhibitions quoted above, Bayes was always a keen exhibitor, making the most of this primary way for sculptors to gain commissions and sales. This was, after all, the period of such vital organisations as the Art Workers' Guild and the Arts and Crafts Exhibition Society. Bayes' applied work was also well received by contemporary critics, for example Walter Shaw Sparrow writing in *The Studio* in 1902 or Rudolf Dircks in *The Art Journal* in 1908. However, the most relevant article was 'The Recent Work of Gilbert Bayes', written by Charles Marriott and published in *The Studio* in 1917. This begins 'The decline of art began with the advent of the professional artist as distinct from the craftsman – painter, carver, glazier or whatever he might be; and it is to men like Mr Gilbert Bayes that we must look for its revival. He has the two chief qualifications for the purpose: a keen sense and trained understanding of materials, and an imaginative grasp of all the circumstances and conditions for which the work is intended... It does not follow that all future art must be 'applied' art, but if art is to play its proper part in the work of reconstruction there will have to be a much closer connection between it and the material circumstances of life as it is lived... Mr Bayes will help it on because he belongs to the comparatively small class of artists who have never lost sight of the dependence...When you go into his studio you are struck by the variety of materials and the wide range in scale, from the miniature to the colossal...When all the qualities of his work are considered – his

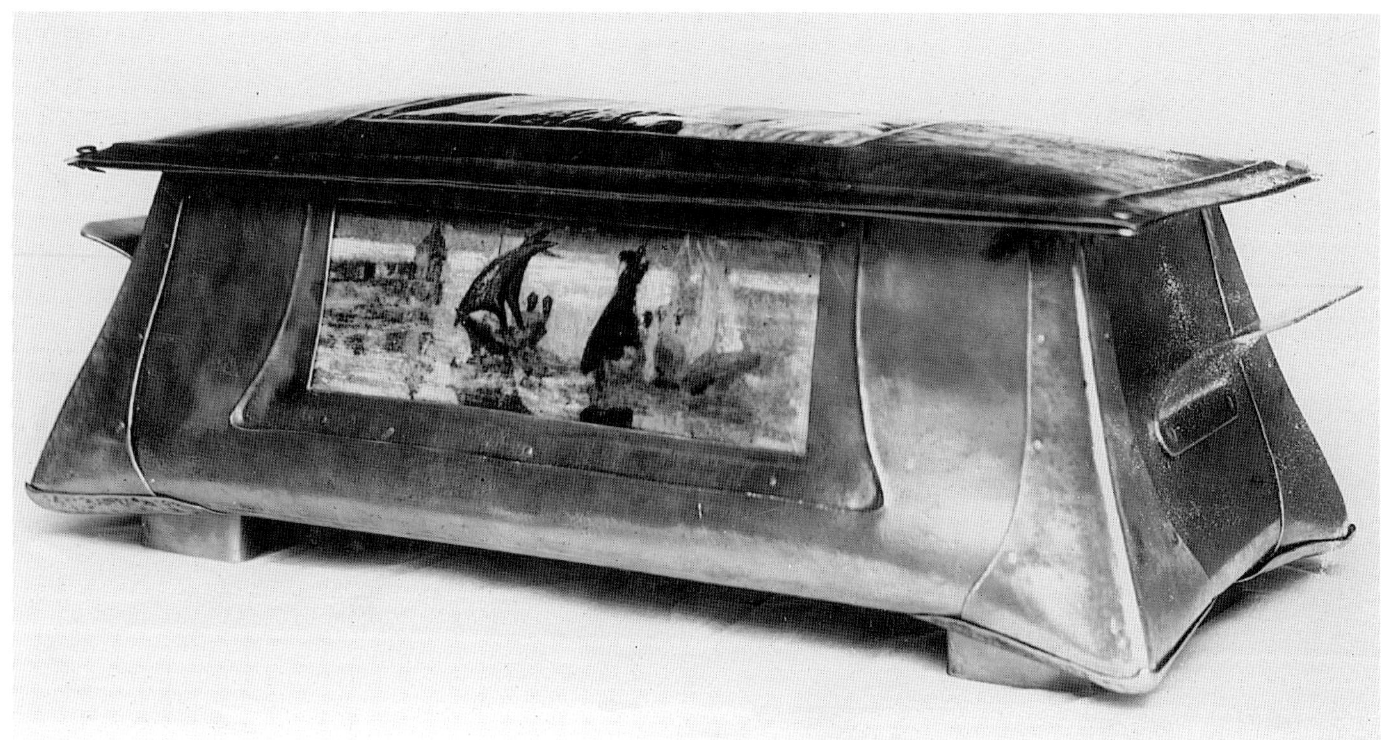

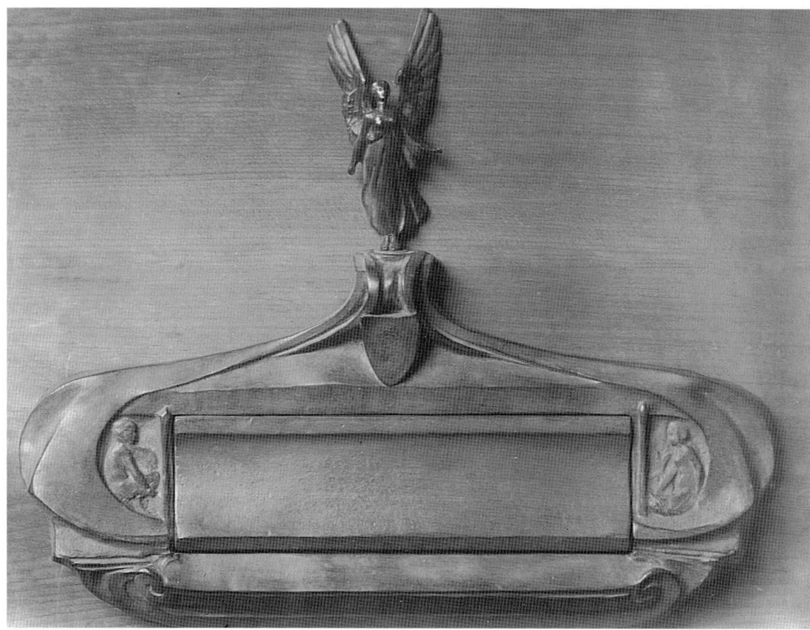

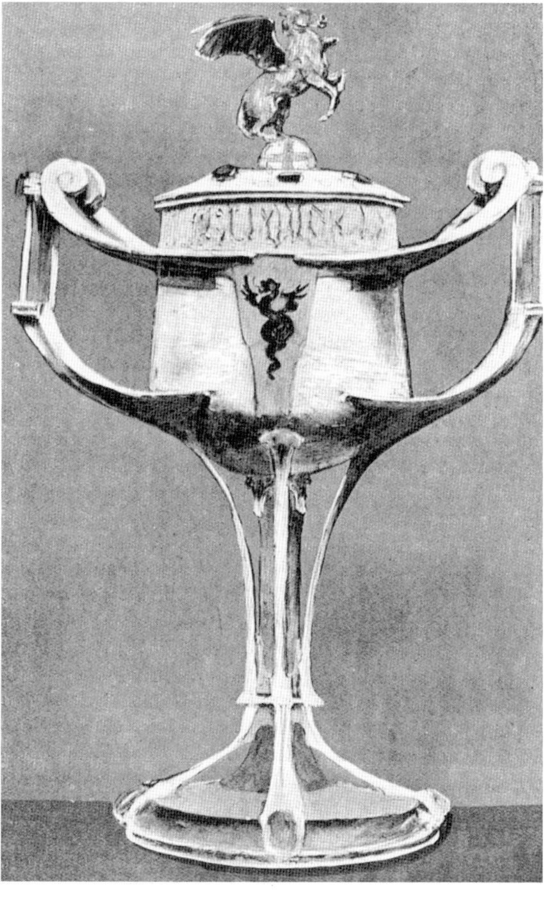

imagination and taste as a designer, and his tact and skill as a craftsman, one comes back to his unusually keen sense of artistic organisation, of the nice adaptation of means to end, of the place of the artist in the community in respect of both material and social conditions.'

The habits and attitudes that Bayes developed as a young man never really changed and he continued to work as an applied artist up to the Second World War. His output remained extraordinarily diverse, and he never lost his essential enthusiasm for materials. Between 1915 and 1945 he designed and produced lecterns, clocks, rood screens and rood figures, presentational, smoking and funerary caskets, carved and painted wooden screens and panels, stained glass, a processional cross, a standing crucifix, a candlestick, a silver tablecentre, even an inn sign and a range of panels and objects associated with architectural and garden commissions. His sources were as diverse as his subjects and his materials. He clearly drew inspiration from the work of his contemporaries and there are links with work by friends such as George Frampton, Phoebe Stabler, William Goscombe John and William Reid Dick. He travelled extensively in Europe and assembled an enormous collection of postcards of places and works of art that he mounted into albums. These, and his scrapbooks of cuttings from newspapers and magazines, were the source of many ideas.

It is worth exploring some of the applied art in greater detail. Particularly interesting is the group of religious commissions. Bayes believed that the sculptor had always had an important role to play in the church and gave lectures on this area of activity, emphasising the historical importance of a rich variety of materials, and particularly the use of colour: 'Colour properly used has a very strong appeal to people and is often more easily understood by them than form, yet in the past the church recognised that when the two, form and colour, were properly blended a greater result was obtained... many marbles, stones and woods, metals cast or wrought, ivory and enamel and many other materials await the touch of the sculptor's hand to wake them into life in the service of the Church and through her of mankind.'

One of the earliest examples of religious work is the large stone figure of *St Hugh*, carved by Bayes for St Hugh's Catholic Church, Lincoln, and installed in 1907 in memory of Francis Jonathan Clarke. While based clearly on mediaeval precedents, the figure has at the same time the naturalism of its time. A much later *Madonna and Child*, a large plaster of 1935 for an unknown location, is, by contrast, a far more conventional image. However, the first major religious commissions came to Bayes early in the First World War, the rood screen for St Mary's Church, Primrose Hill, London and the Irving lectern for the Royal Savoy Chapel, London. The rood, with its figures and angel corbels, was made in memory of the printer and lithographer, Thomas R. Way. Completed in 1914, and reflecting Bayes' commitment to Arts and Crafts ideals, it was designed for a church built in 1873 which already had a Bodley reredos, some 1890s stained glass by Kempe and a small Comper window. Colour, structural practicality and relevant decoration made this a memorable work, a far more total statement than his second rood commission which came in 1922. In this case, Bayes produced figures for a rood designed by his architect friend Sir John Burnet for St James' Church, Inverleith Row, Edinburgh. The

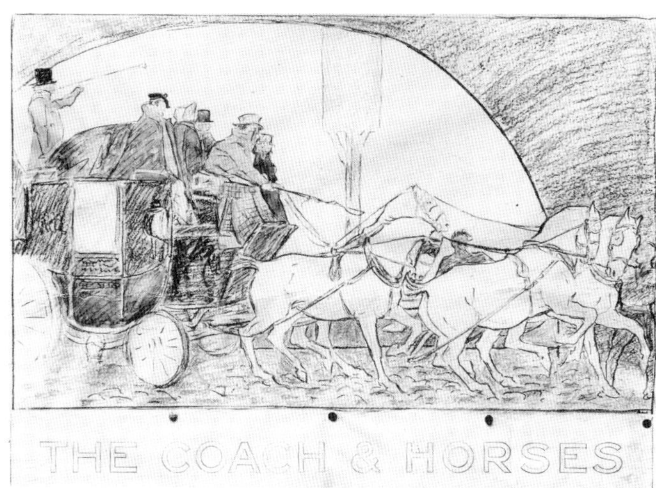

Sketch design for a pub sign, 1930s.

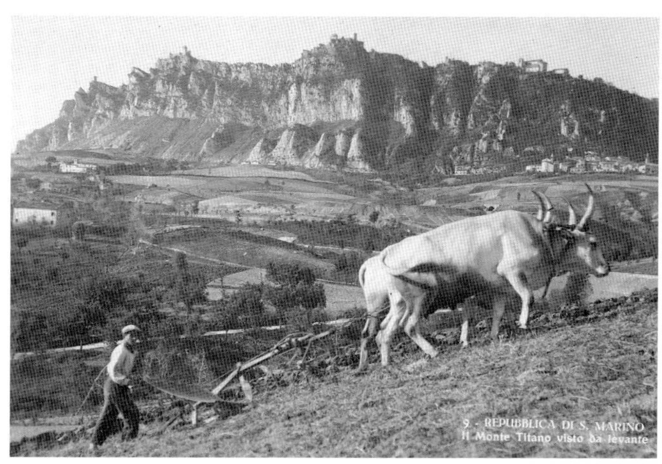

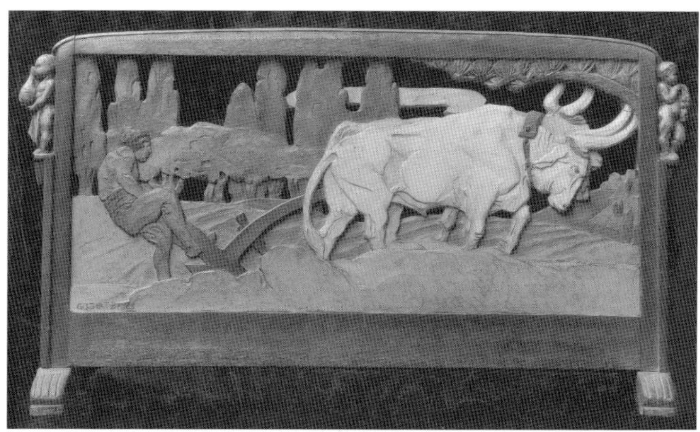

Postcard sources from the Bayes albums 1924:
Above, possible inspiration for the Oxen of Siena panel.
Below, fourteenth-century French censer, possible inspiration for the Lawrence funerary casket, 1929.

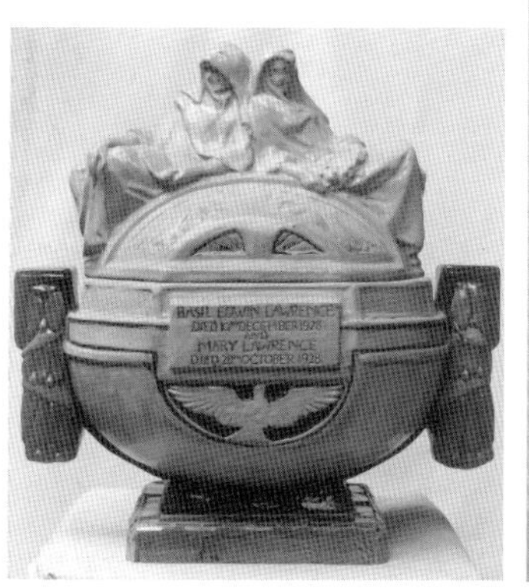

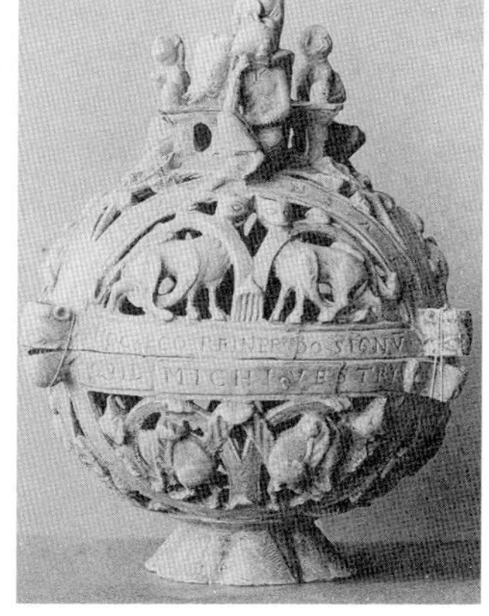

lectern, in enamel and bronze, a personal memorial to Laurence Irving, the great actor's son, and his wife Mabel, who had drowned when the *Empress of Ireland* was sunk in 1914, is a striking object, well received at the time. Writing in *The Studio* in 1917, Charles Marriott said: 'The lectern... deserves particular attention because it gives us an opportunity to see how Mr Bayes meets a question of practical utility. The idea of support could hardly be expressed with greater economy, and yet there is a certain generosity in the branching above as if to suggest the moral gravity of the book supported. The sources of light are made important, every turn of the structure is properly emphasised and the decoration is relevant... the symbolism, moreover, has just enough reference to the manner of death of the persons commemorated. This work, too, bears on the important question of colour in sculpture...' It is a measure of Bayes' own opinion of the rood and the lectern as potential sources for future commissions that he included them in the War Memorials Exhibition at the Victoria & Albert Museum in 1919.

Also in the group of religious work is the processional cross made in 1926 for St Mark's Church, Hamilton Terrace, London, a powerful modern interpretation in silver, bronze and enamel of a traditional form. Shown in the Festival of English Church Art in 1930, this stands well in the group of contemporary liturgical forms associated with silversmiths such as Harold Stabler and John Paul Cooper. On a grander scale, but more conventional in form, is the calvary made for St Saviour's Catholic Church in Ealing as a memorial to Father Augustine Charles Buckell, the first vicar of the parish who had died in 1936. Dedicated by the Bishop of Kensington on 5 June 1937, the calvary cost £524, a sum raised by the parishioners. The church was severely damaged by bombing and not rebuilt, but the calvary, for which Bayes made both small scale and full-size plaster maquettes, survived.

Bayes' diversity is underlined by his designs for stained glass windows. The first commission, for Aldeburgh Church, Suffolk, was completed in 1928. This is the memorial window for Samuel Garrett, 1850-1922, a prominent member of a local family based in the town since 1841. Garrett's profession of corn merchant is reflected in the design of the window, along with the ship that is the symbol of Aldeburgh and a lighthouse. The design is colourful and competent rather than exciting, but has elements in it that are typically Bayesian, for example the drawing of the angel figures. Bayes was helped by Leonard Walker, a leading stained glass expert, and it was probably Walker that led him to become a member of the Worshipful Company of Glaziers in

1933, and subsequently to be described as 'citizen and glazier' when he was given the Freedom of the City of London. The Garrett window was destroyed during the Second World War, and so it has to be judged today from photographs, and from surviving sketches by Bayes. The only other stained glass commission known today is the memorial window to Captain Glyn Rhys-Williams of Miskin Manor, Wales, killed in North Africa on 9th April 1943, aged twenty-one. This is a strong if conventional design featuring St George and St Michael.

In the secular field, Bayes was more adventurous, and more diverse. Typical was his work for Selfridge's which in the applied art area included floor panels, coronation decorations and the *Queen of Time* clock, a complex and colourful structure in a variety of materials. Rather simpler was another Bayes clock, cast in bronze in 1920 as a result of a commission from a Mr Horne. The angel finial, attendant figures and face surrounds all echo other work by Bayes and show his great ability in reworking and representing his design ideas. When the clock was sold at auction in 1983, it was accompanied by a letter from Bayes discussing the choice of movement. Apparently, he was able to offer a pendulum striking movement for £6 -£6.10s, a lever movement for £4.10s, or an English lever movement with a new face for £9.10s.

More unusual, and perhaps harking back to the Arts and Crafts styles of the pre-First World War era are the carved and pierced wooden panels of the early 1920s. Mounted as self-supporting screens, perhaps for use in front of a fire, these are highly stylised and decorative objects that underline Bayes' great enthusiasm for colour. Their style and form was drawn from a complex variety of sources, including Italian, and particularly Sicilian, painted woodwork and images from the postcard collection. Postcards also seem to have played a part in helping Bayes with the design of a funerary casket, made in Doulton's coloured stoneware for the Lawrence family in 1928.

Throughout his working life Bayes designed and made caskets of all kinds. The early ones, of which no examples are known, seem close in style to the silver presentation cups and have an Art Nouveau fluidity that echoes both contemporary work for Liberty and the hand hammered copper wares of Birmingham. There is a significant use of enamel panels and decoration, showing Bayes' skill in this area and his close links with the Arts and Crafts design ethos. In the 1920s there is a new style of casket, architectural, grandiose, complex in both form and use of materials and exotic, perhaps reflecting the background and tastes of some of his clients. The best is probably the smoking cabinet made in 1925 for Sir Dorabji Tata and still owned today by his descendants in India.

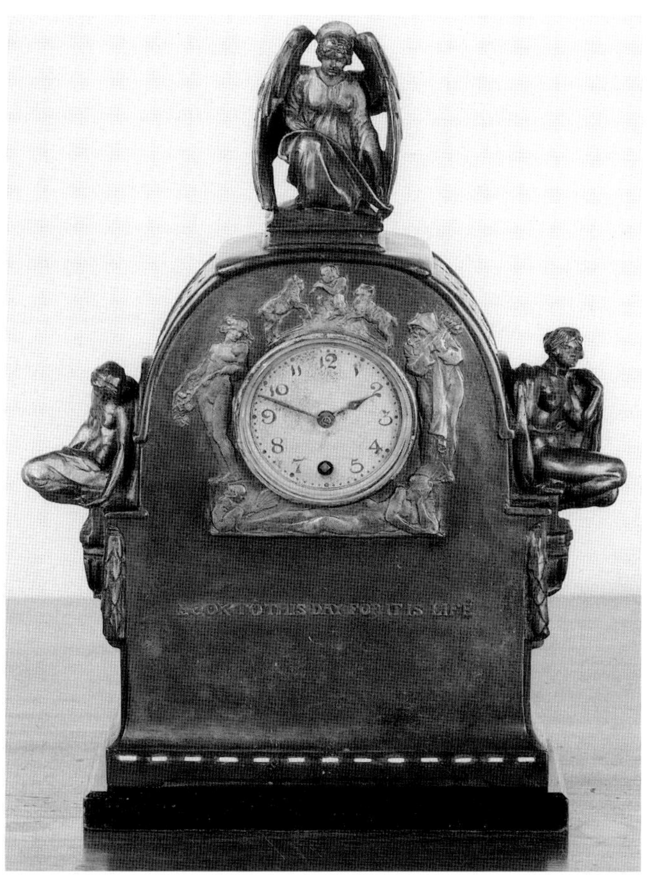

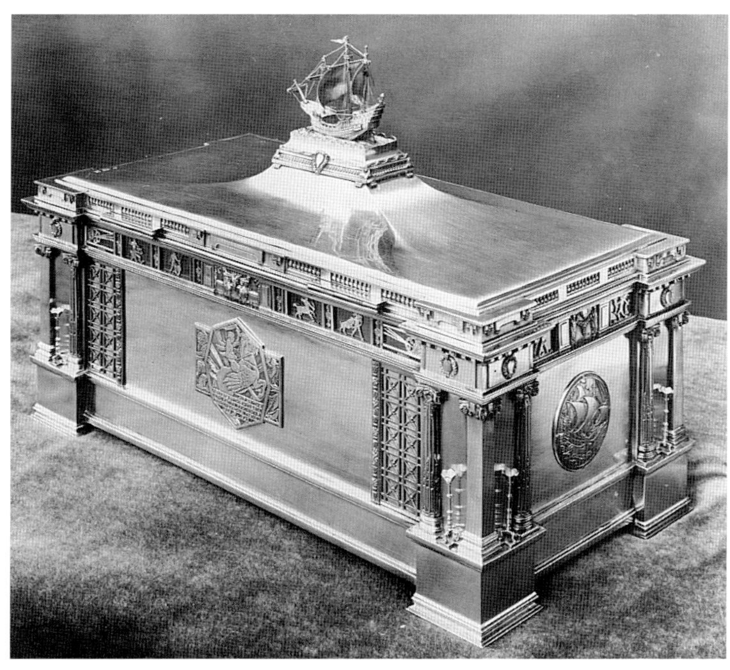

Left, bronze clock case made for Mr Horne in 1920.

Above, silver casket made for Gordon Selfridge in the 1930s and featuring motifs from the Bayes Selfridge's sculptures (Selfridge's Archives).

Below, smoking cabinet made for Sir Dorabji Tata in Bombay in 1925.

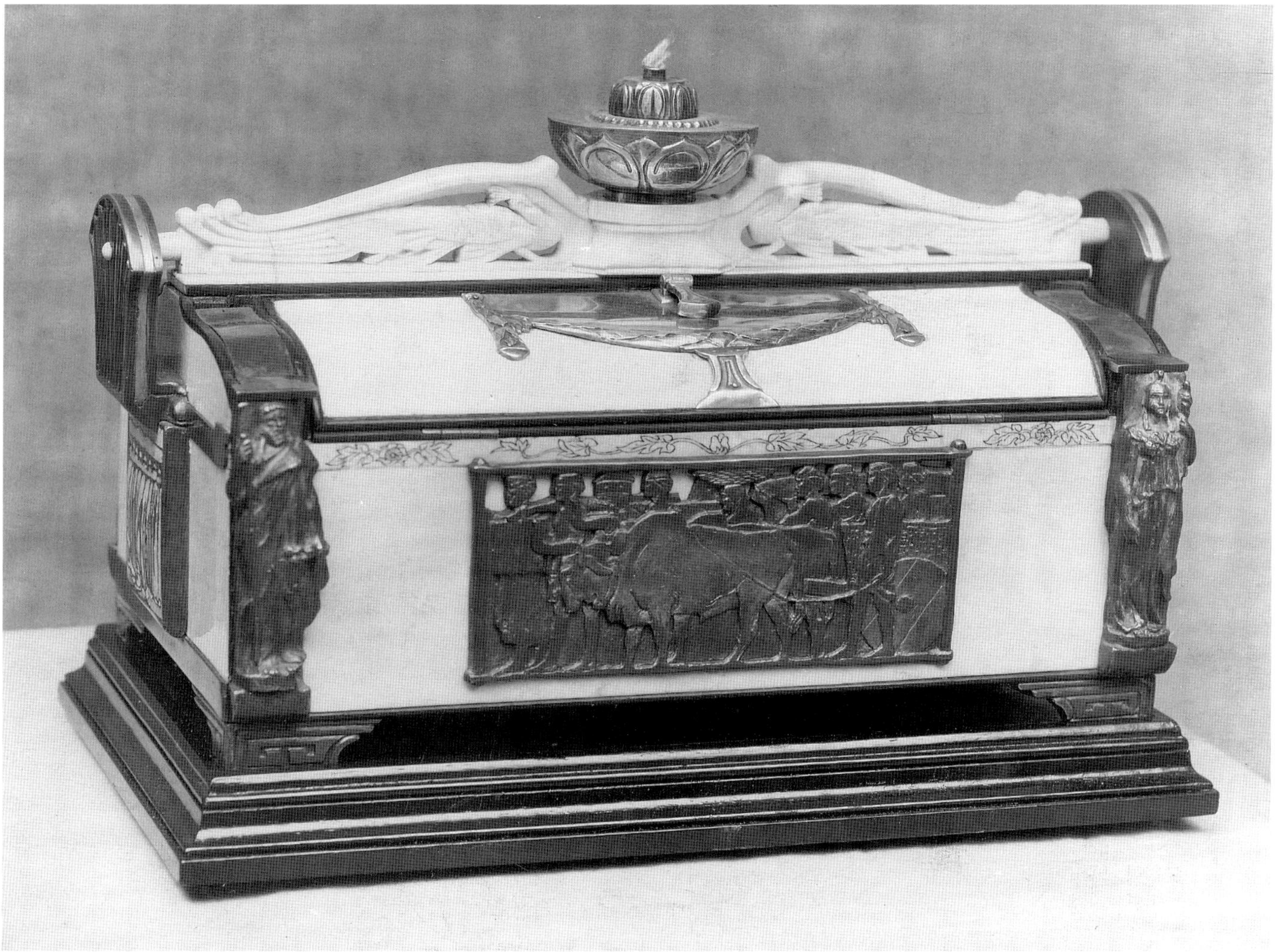

Rich in its use of materials, and in its low relief bronze panels, its bronze attendant figures, its ivory fittings and its enamel panels, the cabinet captures the spirit of the 1920s. It also shows Bayes' consummate abilities as a decorative artist. Later caskets are more predictable, lacking the bravura and stylistic richness of the smoking cabinets. An exception is the silver casket made for Selfridge's in the 1930s, a grand object full of stylish Art Deco detailing. Unfortunately, Bayes does not seem to have designed this in its entirety, even though it incorporates a number of his Selfridge motifs, including a floor panel and the ship finial from the *Queen of Time* clock.

On a more practical level are objects associated with the table. The most successful is the candlestick made for Allied Newspapers in 1935, a fine example of low relief modelling combined with the soft finish and green glaze of the Doulton stoneware. The design is dramatic, showing Gutenberg hard at work on his printing press. Like the colourful washing post finials for the St Pancras Housing Association flats, the candlestick shows how good Bayes could be at designing what was, in effect, a popular mass-produced object. More rarified, and presumably expensive, was the silver Invicta table centre. With his passion for horses, Bayes must have enjoyed designing an object in which the horse motif was paramount, and in which mythology and symbolism could be so directly combined. Invicta, the rearing horse symbol of both Kent, and the formerly Kent-based engineering company, Aveling Barford, was turned by Bayes not just into a striking table centre but also into a mascot to be attached to a range of steam rollers and other heavy vehicles.

In his later years Bayes produced little applied or decorative art, mainly because the commissions were no longer there. As his lectures showed, his commitment to the applied arts, or rather to the building of bridges to link the fine and the applied arts, was undiminished. Ironically, he spent his last years increasingly out of step with a world in which the gulf between the fine and the applied arts was becoming ever more permanent. In the end, Bayes was one of the last survivors of a tradition of applied and practical sculpture, one of the last of a generation who believed that sculpture could be a figure, a frieze, an architectural detail, a medal, a casket, a silver cup, a candlestick, a processional cross, a necklace, a door handle, a lectern or a stained glass window.

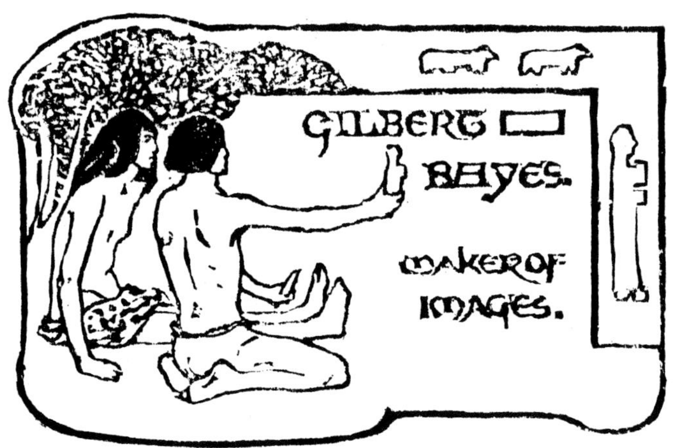

Design for a woodcut trade card c.1900.

BAYES AND THE ART WORKERS' GUILD
Peyton Skipwith

The Art Workers' Guild, to which Gilbert Bayes was elected in November 1896, was to play an important part in his professional and social life for well over half a century. At the time of his election, the Guild had been in existence for just twelve years, having evolved from a series of meetings initiated by a group of young architects in Norman Shaw's office. Gerald Horsely, W.R. Lethaby, Ernest Newton, Mervyn Macartney and Edward Prior wished to create a forum where they could meet other artists and craftsmen in congenial surroundings, for the exchange of ideas and the exploration of topics of mutual interest. In the months prior to the foundation of the Guild, this group of five called themselves the 'St George's Art Society', as they met under the shadow of St George's Church, Bloomsbury. The gist of their deliberations was summed up by H.J.L. Masse in *The Art Workers' Guild 1884-1934*: 'Art and Architecture were drifting asunder. Was it possible to do anything to bring them together again? Close connection had been historically necessary to both. Was this now to be accepted as mere ancient history? To all seeming the Societies which had the right to foster the unity of the Arts, had come to emphasise their distinctions. On one hand was the Royal Academy, chartered for Architecture, Painting and Sculpture alike, but now giving its favour entirely to oil-painting, allowing to Architects a membership of five out of a total of seventy, and it would seem selecting these more often on the basis of culture or professional success, than in view of the merit of their art. On the other there was the Institute of British Architects, whose theory of architecture had driven from its doors most of those architects whose art was acknowledged; which had forbidden to Artists a personal interest in their handicrafts, and had opened its doors so widely to business that Surveyors had become the largest element of its body. Still the unity of Art, and the place of architecture therein, supplied the principle on which the most thorough artists worked. There were many such who were neither the oil-painters of the Academy nor the Surveyors of the Institute, but craftsmen in Architecture, Painting, Sculpture, and the kindred Arts, and on the basis of a principle they could be brought together. Such an Association would be the body of the Art of the time, and would hand on its traditions to another age.' The structure that they devised for the Guild, with an elected Master, two Honorary Secretaries, and a membership of between two hundred and fifty and three hundred, drawn from a wide range of disciplines, has endured to this day.

Henry Wilson, an early member, in his inaugural address at the commencement of his Mastership on 12th January, 1917, asked the rhetorical question 'What is the Guild?' and went on to provide his own answer: 'For us it is a spiritual oasis in the wilderness of modern life, a haven and heaven. For me, I know no more consoling atmosphere, few more recreative, regenerative influences than those found in the Guild.' The creation of this oasis was almost entirely due to the impulses and vision of its founders and early members, who wished to move towards the realisation of the Morrisean vision of the reunification of the fine and decorative arts. In December 1886 J.D. Sedding, the second Master, in whose architectural office Wilson trained, had outlined his aspirations for the Guild thus: 'There are two ways of affecting the work we have set ourselves to do – firstly by sympathetic social intercourse, secondly by combining with this intercourse some united effort of practical work. The Art Workers' Guild means to try both ways. Our success in the first line emboldens enterprise in the second; to have established friendly relations between long estranged brethren is to have done much, but there is more to be done yet. Let us bear in mind that the Art Workers' Guild is not a club for cronies. A mere club does not to my mind represent a force that communicates an electric shock to the thick hide of the Art Philistine of the present day.'

The names of those elected in the early years of the Guild reads like a roll-call of the great and the good of the Arts and Crafts movement: W.A.S. Benson, Heywood Sumner, John Belcher, Walter Crane, C.F.A. Voysey, Selwyn Image, Harrison Townsend, A.H. Macmurdo and William Morris himself. Morris had initially been sceptical about the Guild's chances of survival and had, uncharacteristically, stood aside, but he was elected in 1888 and became master four years later. After the architects, the second largest group was the sculptors; in the early years Onslow Ford, Hamo Thornycroft, W.S. Frith, Harry Bates, George Frampton, F.W. Pomeroy, Reynolds Stephens and Alfred Gilbert were all elected and played active roles within the Guild, Pomeroy and Frampton both becoming Masters. The 1880s and 1890s were to see the realisation of some of the most important arts and

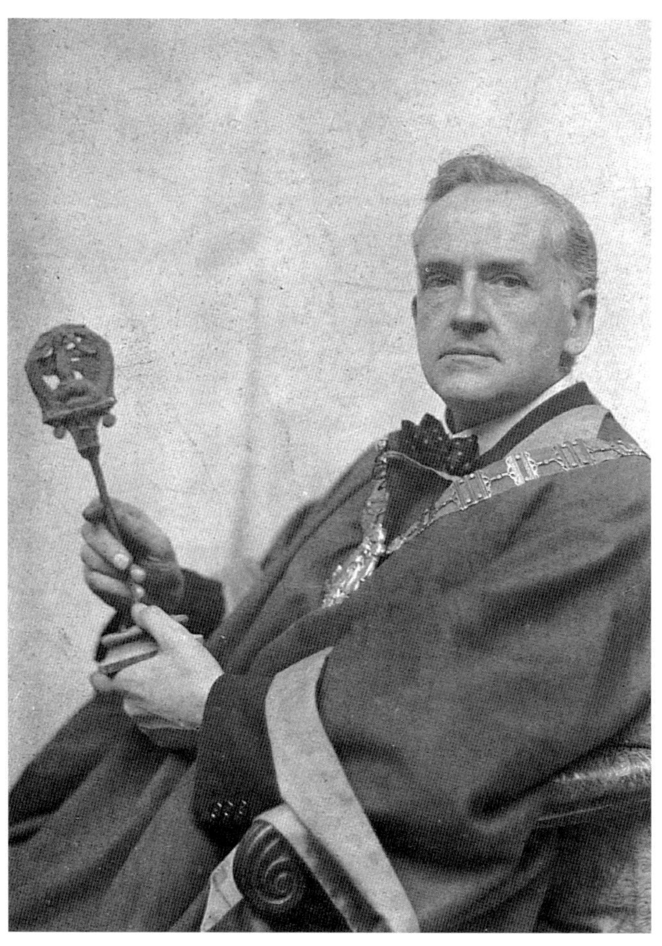

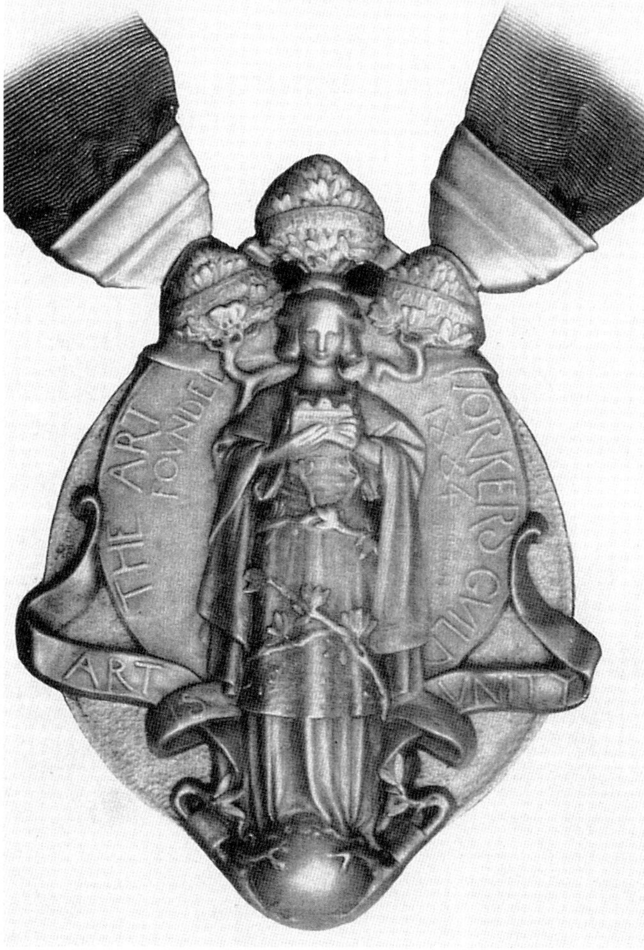

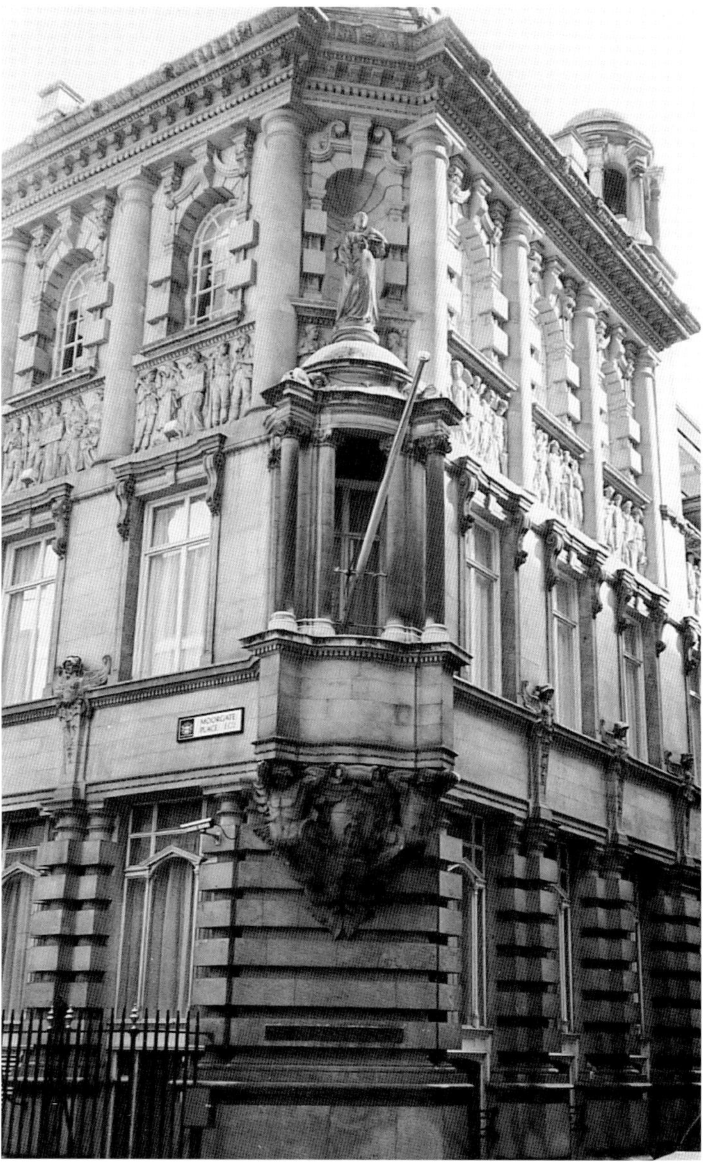

Above left, Bayes in the robes of Master of the Art Workers' Guild, 1925.
Above right, Belcher's Institute of Chartered Accountants, 1888-1893,
with sculpture by Hamo Thornycroft and Harry Bates.
Below left, Master's badge of office, designed by George Frampton.
Below right, ticket designed by Walter Crane for Beauty's Awakening
Masque, 1899.

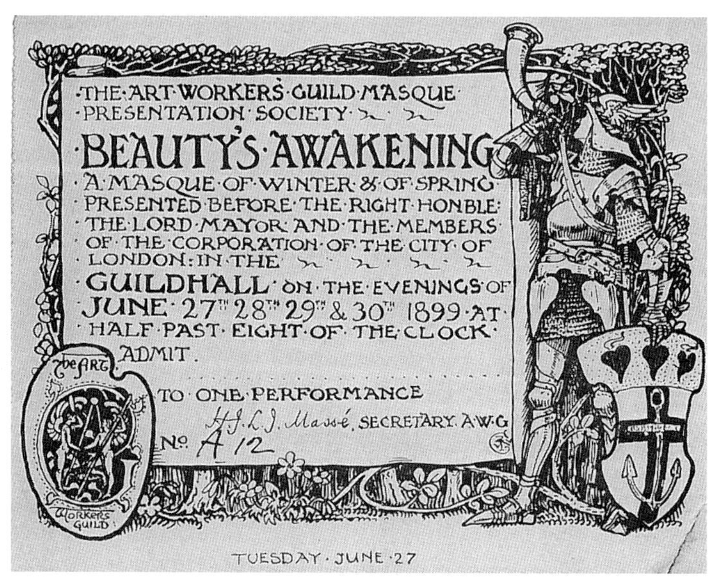

crafts buildings, including J.W. Simpson's Kelvingrove Art Gallery, Glasgow, and Sedding's Holy Trinity, Sloane Street, Chelsea, which were prime examples of the Guildean ethic of collaboration between architect and sculptor. Probably the most important of these, and one of the earliest, was Belcher's Institute of Chartered Accountants Building, 1888-1893, with its great wrap-around frieze by Hamo Thornycroft and console and winged terms by Harry Bates. Thornycroft's frieze depicting ordinary people in modern dress certainly shocked, but it also breathed new life into a tired classical form, and it can be regarded as a direct precursor of the friezes Bayes was to execute for T.P. Bennett during the 1930s. The other building in the City of equal importance as a jewel-box of sculpture is T.E. Collcutt's slightly later Lloyd's Registry of Shipping, 1898-1901; here it was George Frampton and Frank Lynn Jenkins who supplied the sculptural decoration. Surprisingly, Collcutt, unlike Simpson, Sedding and Belcher, was never a member of the Guild, although he clearly shared the aspirations summed up by its motto 'Art is Unity.'

It was into the company of these men that Gilbert Bayes was elected, having been proposed by George Frampton, with whom he was studying at the Royal Academy Schools, and seconded by A.F. Brophy, his former teacher at the City & Guilds School. Bayes found the atmosphere of the Guild congenial; not only did he like the serious side of the Friday evening lectures, when Brothers read papers and discussed topics of mutual concern, but he also enjoyed the more light-hearted moments when Guildsmen turned their minds to pleasure. Two years after Bayes had joined, there was discussion about the idea of reviving the form of the mediaeval masque. This was achieved, and in June 1899 the Guild presented *Beauty's Awakening* at the Guildhall. The masque was written by C.R. Ashbee, Walter Crane, Harrison Townsend and other Guildsmen, and part of it dealt with the contentious subject of civic apathy, corruption, incompetence and bribery; despite this, it was enthusiastically received not only by the public but also at the performance reserved for the Lord Mayor and his guests. Bayes is not listed in the beautifully produced book *Beauty's Awakening*, published by *The Studio*, but he became an enthusiastic performer at the later Shrovetide Revels which, in the aftermath of the masque, became an important feature of the Guild calendar. His name appears in many of the extant programmes and broadsheets, and he was frequently singled out for praise, either for his performances or for the scenery he devised. In these annual Revels the Guildsmen indulged their taste for bad puns, and were happy to poke fun at themselves. The last of the Revels in the hall at Clifford's Inn, which had been

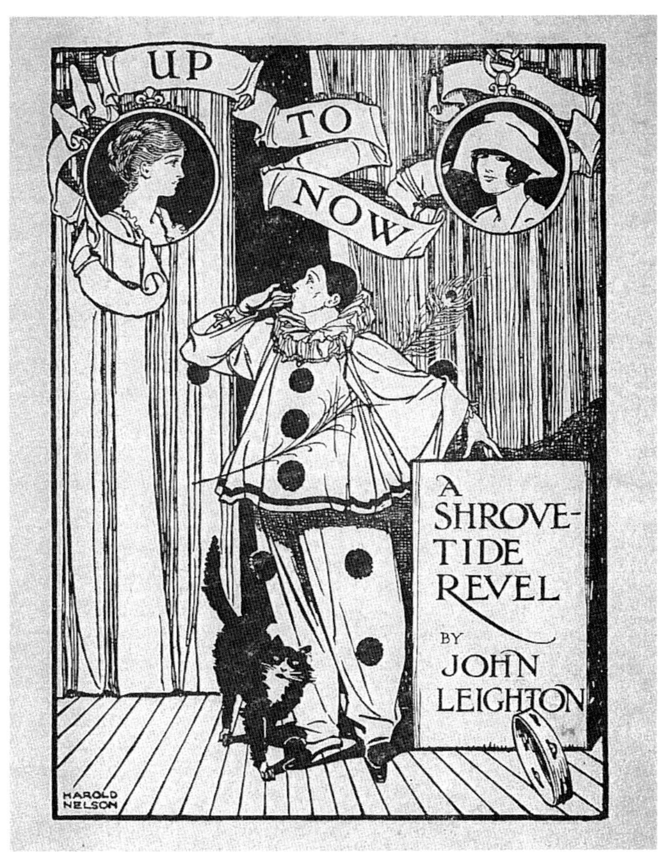

Cover for the booklet for the 1922 Revels, in which Bayes played the role of Arabella Parkinson.

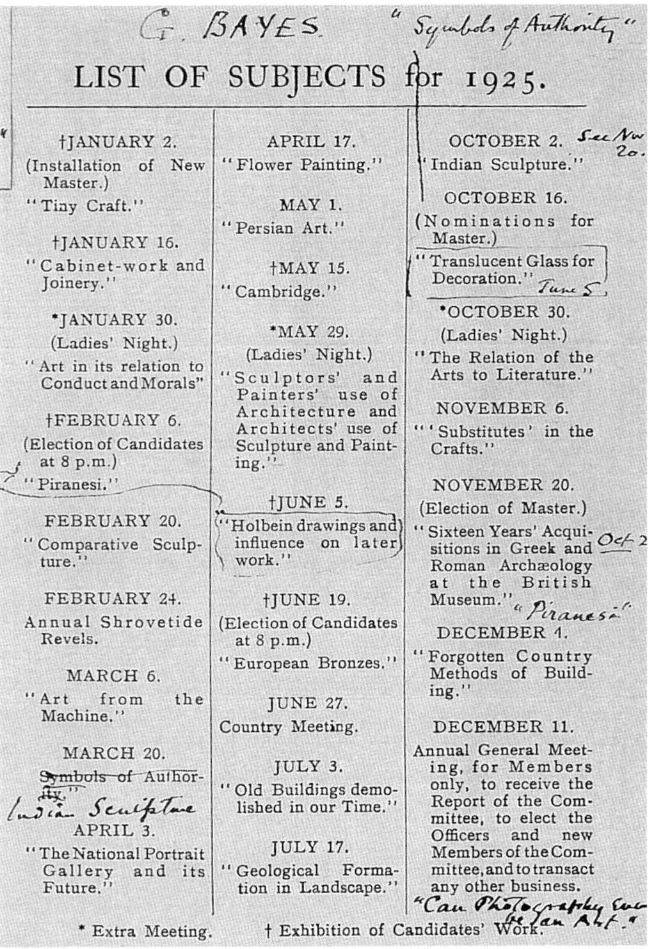

G. BAYES.   "Symbols of Authority"

LIST OF SUBJECTS for 1925.

†JANUARY 2. (Installation of New Master.) "Tiny Craft."	APRIL 17. "Flower Painting."	OCTOBER 2. "Indian Sculpture."
†JANUARY 16. "Cabinet-work and Joinery."	MAY 1. "Persian Art."	OCTOBER 16. (Nominations for Master.) "Translucent Glass for Decoration."
*JANUARY 30. (Ladies' Night.) "Art in its relation to Conduct and Morals"	†MAY 15. "Cambridge."	*OCTOBER 30. (Ladies' Night.) "The Relation of the Arts to Literature."
†FEBRUARY 6. (Election of Candidates at 8 p.m.) "Piranesi."	*MAY 29. (Ladies' Night.) "Sculptors' and Painters' use of Architecture and Architects' use of Sculpture and Painting."	NOVEMBER 6. "'Substitutes' in the Crafts."
FEBRUARY 20. "Comparative Sculpture."	†JUNE 5. "Holbein drawings and influence on later work."	NOVEMBER 20. (Election of Master.) "Sixteen Years' Acquisitions in Greek and Roman Archæology at the British Museum."
FEBRUARY 24. Annual Shrovetide Revels.	†JUNE 19. (Election of Candidates at 8 p.m.) "European Bronzes."	DECEMBER 4. "Forgotten Country Methods of Building."
MARCH 6. "Art from the Machine."	JUNE 27. Country Meeting.	DECEMBER 11. Annual General Meeting, for Members only, to receive the Report of the Committee, to elect the Officers and new Members of the Committee, and to transact any other business.
MARCH 20. Symbols of Authority."	JULY 3. "Old Buildings demolished in our Time."	
APRIL 3. "The National Portrait Gallery and its Future."	JULY 17. "Geological Formation in Landscape."	

* Extra Meeting.   † Exhibition of Candidates' Work.

Lecture programme for Bayes' year as Master, 1925.

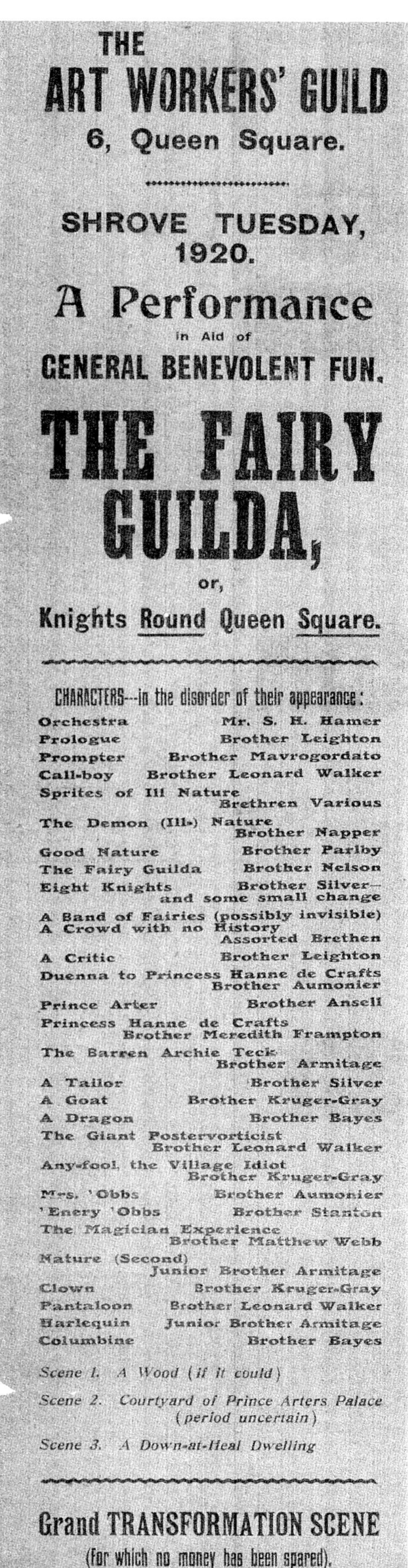

Broadsheet advertisement for the 1922 Revels.

the home of the Guild since its foundation, were held on Shrove Tuesday, 1914, and were entitled 'Rip van Winkle.' In it, emphasis was given to 'changes that have taken place in the Art World in the course of twenty years... Mr Gilbert Bayes deserved especial praise for his cheery embodiment of a Jester, the Master of the Revels, in spite of the serious inconvenience of a broken arm.' From 1914 onwards, all Guild activities centred on its new premises at 6 Queen Square, with its purpose-built hall, designed by F.W. Troup, which was ideal both for ordinary meetings and Revels. In 1924, the chosen theme for the Revels was 'The Future of the Past', with the 'denizens of the Elysian Fields' visiting the Wembley Exhibition in which, of course, Bayes and many other Guildsmen had participated. The 1925 Annual Report records that 'Imitations of Guild speakers, homemade properties, costumes, songs and scenery caused interest and amusement...' Again, in the fiftieth anniversary Revels in 1934, still showing the Guild's penchant for puns, we find him doing a spirited impersonation of the famous cricketer 'A.W.G. (Grace)', with a score of 'fifty not out.' The most bizarre minute, however, also from 1934, does not concern the Revels, but refers to the ordinary meeting on 23rd March; it was a Ladies' Night and the topic of the lecture was 'The Art of Walt Disney'. 'This meeting was held at a private cinema in Bush House, Aldwych, WC2, when Mr Rob Lawson read a paper and showed lantern-slides of the method of producing the films. After this several of Mr Walt Disney's coloured films were shown, to the enjoyment and amusement of the audience. The discussion was opened by Mr Arthur Wimperis, followed by Mr John L. Hodgson, Bros. D.S. MacColl, G. Spencer Watson RA and Past-Master Gilbert Bayes. The appreciative thanks of the Guild were expressed to the lecturer, Mr Lawson, by past-Master Sir Edwin L. Lutyens, RA and his suggestion to make Mr Walt Disney an honorary member of the Guild was received with acclamation.'

In addition to the Revels, Bayes took part in the serious life of the Guild and spoke often on aspects of his craft and on other subjects that interested him. In the records he is listed as reading a paper on Flaxman, and another accompanied by a demonstration on 'Plaster Modelling'. In March 1907 he and H.R. Hope-Pinker read papers on 'The Armature in Sculpture', with Bayes demonstrating the construction of various armatures. Again, in 1928 Bayes and Mr Fiorini, the foundry-man, went into the complexities and skills of 'Bronze Casting', which was followed by a discussion with Richard Goulden, Ernest Gillick and John Paul Cooper. Over the years Bayes either gave papers or contributed to discussions on a wide variety of subjects ranging from 'Horse-trappings' to 'Railway

Stations' but the ones we would particularly like to have a record of are those most closely related to his own profession: 'Ferro Concrete and Cement Casting' with Maxwell Ayrton; 'Mestrovic and the Modern Spirit' with Allan Wyon; 'Brancusi and Abstractionist Sculpture' with Percival Tudor-Hart and Frank Dobson; 'Modern Architectural Sculpture' with W. Aumonier; 'Sculpture Carved and Modelled' with Eric Gill; 'Glazed pottery and Stoneware' with Cyril Carter and Nicholson Babb; 'Sculpture on Buildings' with Charles Wheeler; 'American Sculpture' with Alec Miller; 'Colour in Sculpture' with Harold Brownsword; 'The Work of Alfred Stevens' with Ernest Gillick. Unfortunately, however, the minutes of these meetings record little more than the topic, the principal speaker, and the names of those who contributed to the discussion.

William Aumonier's 1930 lecture coincided with the publication of his great compendium *Modern Architectural Sculpture*. In his foreword he apologised in advance for the fact that 'if the Ultra-Modernists seem to predominate it is not by intention, but only because this style is very much to the fore.' Despite this warning, in a survey that sweeps across the world, he concentrated almost exclusively on the 'Conservative' rather than the 'Ultra' Modernists, hailing Carl Miles as the greatest of them, lauding Bourdelle's reliefs for the Theatre des Champs Elysée, Lee Lawrie's great Assyrian panels for the Nebraska State Capitol, Professor Obsieger's sculpture at the Woodworkers' School in Vienna and, of course, the work of Mestrovic. To represent Britain, apart from reproducing Henry Moore's 1929 brown Hornton stone *Reclining Figure* (Leeds City Art Gallery), and Epstein's *Night* and *Day* from 55 Broadway, he concentrates primarily on the work of his fellow-Guildsmen. In addition to reproducing Bayes' *Italian Wine Cart* and panels from the Concrete Utilities Building and the Saville Theatre, he illustrates work by John Angel, Percy Bentham, Reid Dick, Alan Durst, Richard Garbe, Eric Gill, Gilbert Ledward and Herbert Paliser. A true celebration of those Guild values – at once forward looking, but deeply conscious of history and the importance of craftsmanship – that Bayes so pithily sums up in *Modelling for Sculpture*: 'At none of the best periods of sculpture have art and slovenliness been synonymous.'

Many years before in 1896, at the first Annual General Meeting that Bayes would have attended, T.G. Jackson, in his valedictory address, described the Guild as a 'free artistic club, where one is always sure of finding a brother artist who can tell us exactly what we want to know – a debating ground for the interchange, correction, or confirmation of ideas...' Bayes entered fully into the spirit of the Guild and, as is clear even from these sparse records, he was generous with his knowledge as well as his time. He contributed bronze busts of W.R. Lethaby and F.W. Troup to the hall to mark their Masterships, whilst his own portrait as master was painted by Meredith Frampton, the son of his old friend and patron George Frampton. He made many friends within the Guild and according to his daughter, Jean, the Ladies' Nights and Revels were high-spots in the family's social calendar.

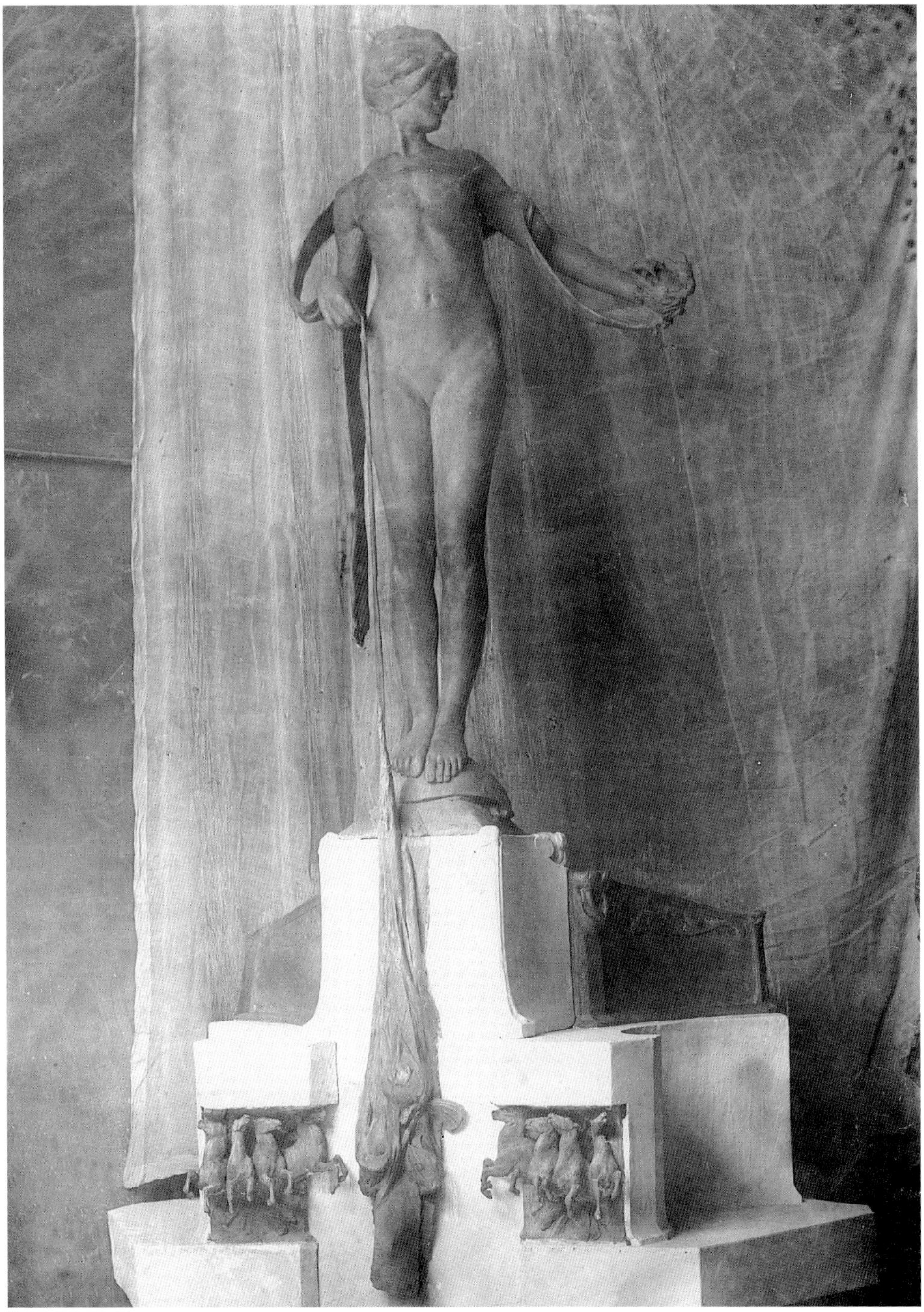

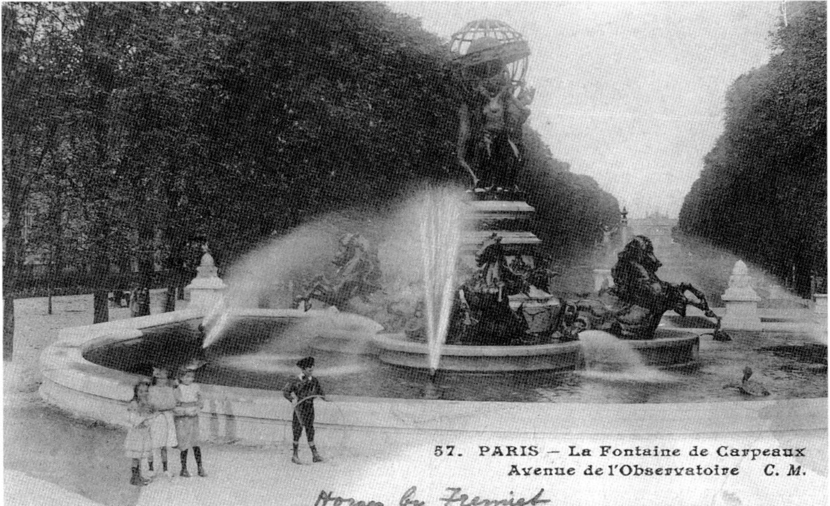

Above, The Fountain of the Zodiac Belt in plaster, 1902.

Left, postcard from Bayes' albums showing Carpeaux's fountain in Paris with a note by Bayes that the horses are by Frémiet.

SCULPTURE AND THE GARDEN
Louise Irvine

Bayes loved his garden at Greville Place. When the light faded, he would sit on the veranda outside his studio and listen to the water splashing from his *Water Baby* fountain or, on a sunny afternoon, he might swing in his hammock reading detective novels or writing letters. In a letter written in 1945 to the Ealing Art Club concerning 'gardens of the future' he talks about 'lying in a hammock with white petals from the big pear tree overhead falling like summer snow and with the birds enjoying a bath in a petal covered pool a few feet away'. This was the mosaic pool that he created around his Doulton stoneware fountain figure, the *Blue Robed Bambino*, which was awarded a Gold Medal at the Paris Exhibition of 1925. Above it hung a pendant with pierced decoration in green Doulton ware and behind on the wall was a polychrome stoneware panel depicting Diana, the huntress. Nearby sat *The Lilymaid* figure, and another corner of the garden was dominated by his *Great Pan*. There were also tributes to the Greek god of nature in the front garden where *The Lure of the Pipes of Pan* emerged from the bushes, and a leering mask of Pan greeted visitors to his studio. Other Doulton ware masks of children incorporated in roundels decorated the facade of his studio together with a panel of child musicians, and this garden idyll was completed with colourful models of animals, including two frogs, a squirrel and a blackbird.

The Doulton ware garden ornaments provided vivid colour all year round, which was ideal for Bayes, who did not particularly enjoy planting flowers or weeding. He designed his garden with terraced lawns, trees and shrubs, describing them in sculptural terms in his letter to the Ealing Art Club: 'the tone and colour of their foliage, the different types of growth, the scale of their leaves and the possibility of making one a foil to the other'. He also makes a plea for 'more fountains and pools and more imagination in the treatment of water'.

The water theme recurs many times in Bayes' lectures and essays. His travels in France and Italy had introduced him to some delightful fountains in public squares and private gardens and he thought the British should follow the example of their European neighbours. Although the cooling and refreshing qualities of fountains were not so necessary in the northern climate, Bayes argued that there was still a need for more water features in British parks and gardens. In a lecture to the Royal Horticultural Society in 1928 he maintained: 'It is a fact that the love of moving water is ingrained in most of us. It is one of the delights and wonders of childhood, and it lasts on throughout life, whether it be the swirl of the sea, the great waterfall or the quiet rivers of nature, or whether it is the spray from the man-made fountain falling in diamonds from the sun, or whether it is a small artificial pool. To all of us it comes as a charm, taking our thoughts away from the cares of the day by its gaiety or quieting our unrest with its still reflections.'

Bayes' lecture was illustrated with slides of some of his favourite fountains, including the bronze boar in the Mercato Vecchio in Florence and the fountain by Carpeaux and Frémiet in the Luxembourg Gardens in Paris. During his lifetime, Emmanuel Frémiet, 1824-1910, enjoyed a considerable reputation as a sculptor of monumental figures and small animal bronzes, particularly equestrian subjects, which were often of a romantic nature. As a teacher, he was an important influence on several young sculptors visiting Paris, including Bayes, who spent nine months in the French capital as part of his travelling scholarship from the Royal Academy in 1900.

When Bayes returned from France, he submitted his *Fountain of the Zodiac Belt* to the Academy as a testimony to his studies abroad. As well as his French heroes, he was obviously influenced by Alfred Drury's *Circe* which was shown at the Paris Exhibition of 1900. A graceful nude is the major feature of both compositions but Bayes has managed to include his beloved horses, prancing incongruously on the base. The critic of the *Art Journal* in 1908 was very impressed with this work and commented: 'This composition, charming and effective as a whole, leaves one with some regret that the authorities who have the control of the decorative features in our parks and public places do not more frequently commission such pleasant art as Mr Bayes.' It was ten years, however, before Bayes was asked to work on any more fountain designs.

In one early commission, he did not design the whole fountain but was asked to provide a bronze figure of St John to be placed on an existing fountain basin in the courtyard of the Merchant Taylors' Hall in the City of London. The former name of this fraternity was The Guild and Fraternity of St John the Baptist of London, and St John has remained the

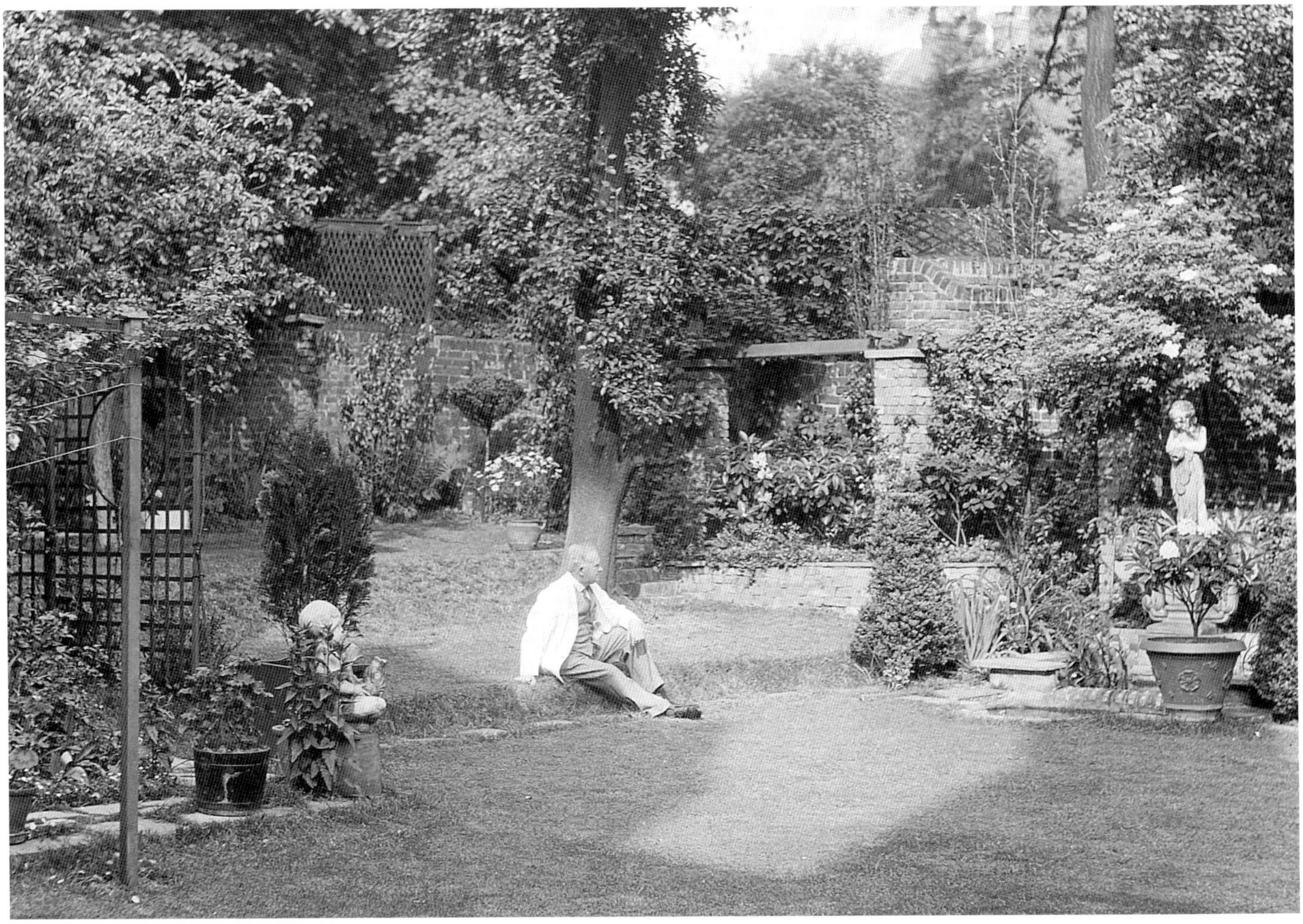

Bayes in the garden at Greville Place, with the Blue Robed Bambino fountain, 1930s.

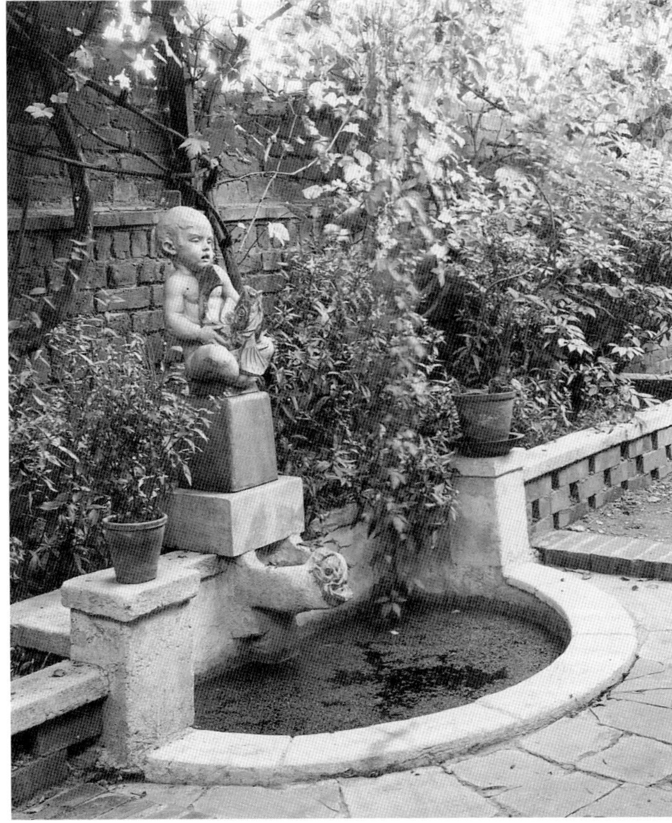

Water Baby fountain in Bayes' first garden at Boundary Road, London, late 1920s.

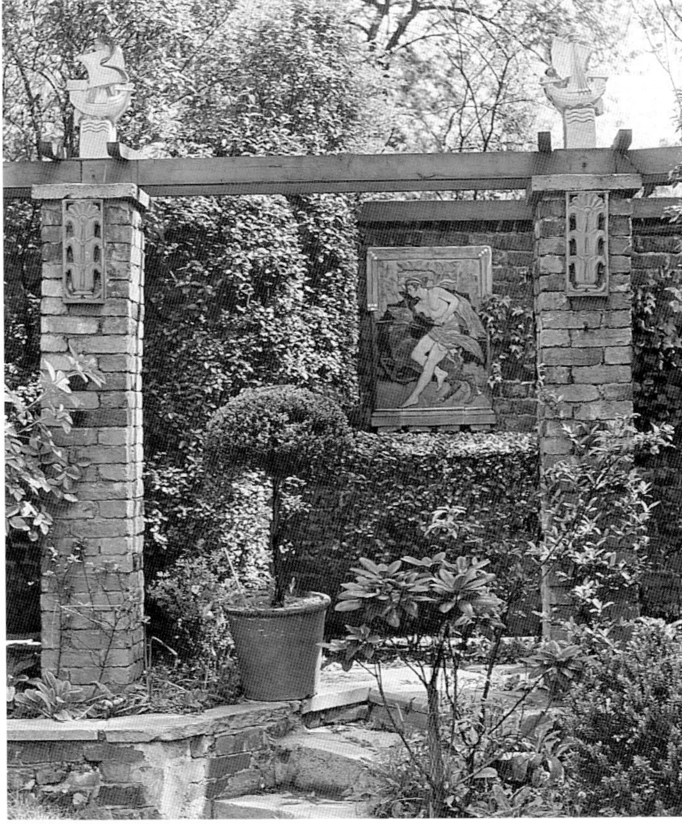

Garden at Greville Place with Diana panel and ship finials, late 1930s.

company's patron saint. Bayes produced a delightful study of the young saint holding a lamb, which he exhibited at the Royal Academy in 1914. The Merchant Taylors' garden was re-designed in 1985, but the fountain is still there.

Another early fountain is on public view at the Domain Gardens in Auckland, New Zealand. Bayes' impressive *Fountain of the Valkyries* was first exhibited at the Royal Academy in 1912 and subsequently shown at Wembley in 1924 and the Royal Horticultural Society in 1928 where it was purchased by R.S. Hellaby and presented to the city of Auckland. A stone base supports the gargoyle water spouts in bronze and on top of these is a marble block, vigorously carved in low relief with Valkyries galloping through the clouds. A bronze equestrian figure of Brynhilde, in full armour, crowns the design. This group was later re-worked as an independent statuette in 1920.

Bayes received several commissions for memorial sculptures to be placed in public spaces, including parks, graveyards and town squares, although he always maintained that 'he would rather do a piece of work for people to live with and enjoy than one to be used after their death'. At St James' Churchyard at Warter in Yorkshire, two allegorical figures mark the graves of C.H. Wilson and G.V. Wilson who died in 1907 and 1908 respectively, and some years later he modelled a symbolic figure to commemorate his wife's nephew for Radlett Cemetery in Hertfordshire. The First World War increased the demand for memorial work and, instead of decorative garden ornaments, Bayes was now required to work on statues symbolising the trauma of war and the huge loss of life. His evocative figure of *Destiny* in Portland Stone was exhibited at the Royal Academy in 1916 and later formed the centrepiece of the Ramsgate War Memorial. He also produced fountains and symbolic figures for The Grove at Hythe and the Garden of Remembrance at Todmorden in Yorkshire, where his family originated. Bayes felt guilty about prospering from such human tragedy and, according to his sister Jessie, he was later able to salve his conscience by contributing garden sculptures for the new 'Homes for Heroes', in particular the London estates pioneered by Father Basil Jellicoe for the St Pancras House Improvement Society.

Until the early 1920s, Bayes had worked only in conventional materials such as bronze, stone and marble, adding colour with enamel or mosaic as required. However, in 1923, he began experimenting with a colourful ceramic body, known as polychrome stoneware, which was made at the Royal Doulton pottery in Lambeth. He was drawn to the material, not just because of the wide range of colours available, but

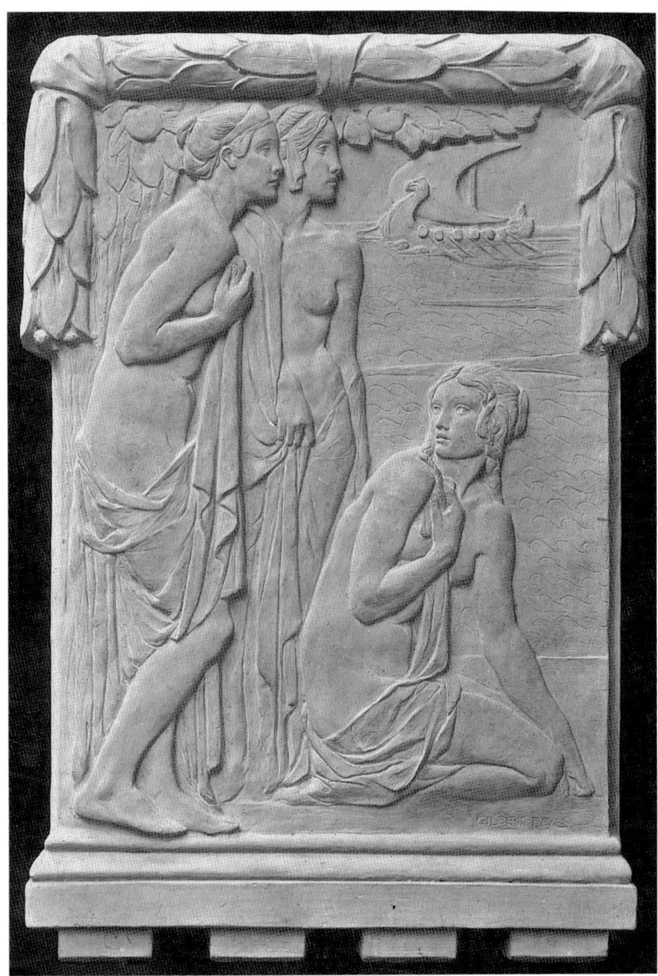

Plaster model for the Hesperides panel, 1928.

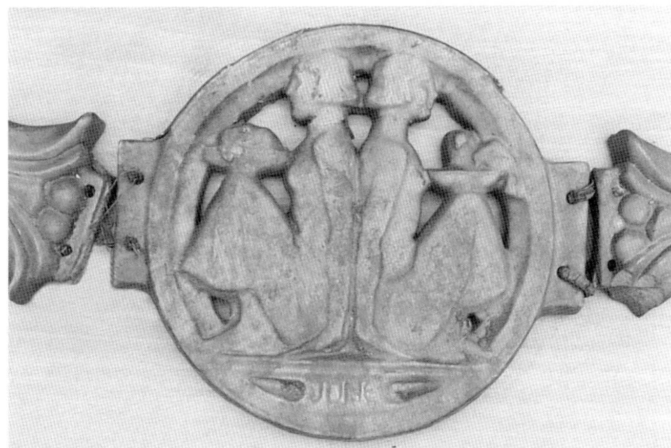

June, a Doulton stoneware garden pendant, 1920s.

also because of its durability. It was resistant to frost and corrosion and so was ideal for garden settings. His first notable essay in polychrome stoneware was the *Blue Robed Bambino* fountain, which he exhibited several times following its success at the Paris Exhibition of 1925. One version of this fountain was kept in his own garden while another, standing on a tall pedestal with relief panels of a galleon and a steamer, was made for the International Labour Offices in Geneva. The base is inscribed with a verse

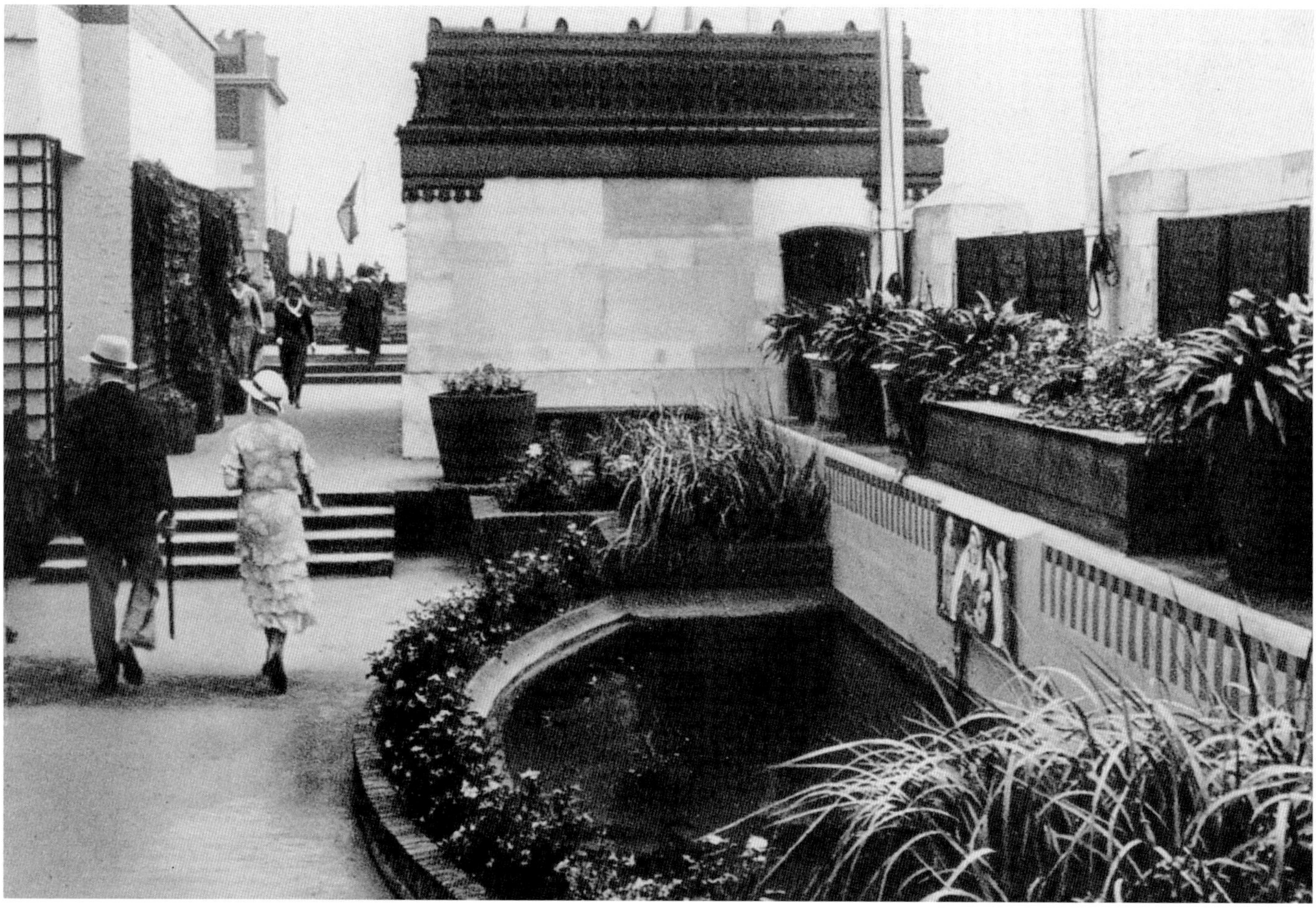

Bayes' Madonna and Child panel by the rose garden pool in Selfridge's roof garden, 'The hanging gardens of London', 1929.

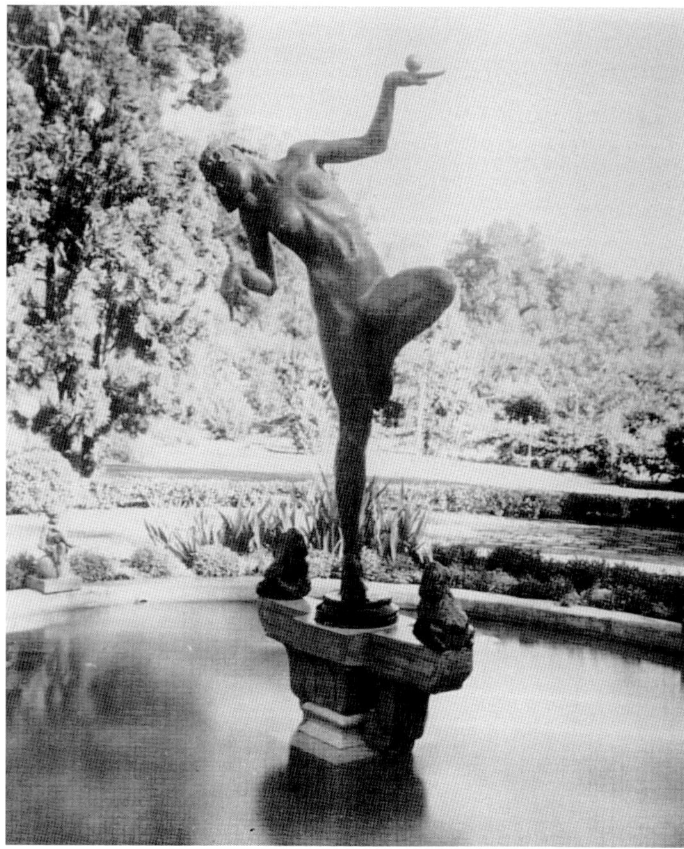

Frog Princess garden sculpture at Montecito, Santa Barbara, 1931.

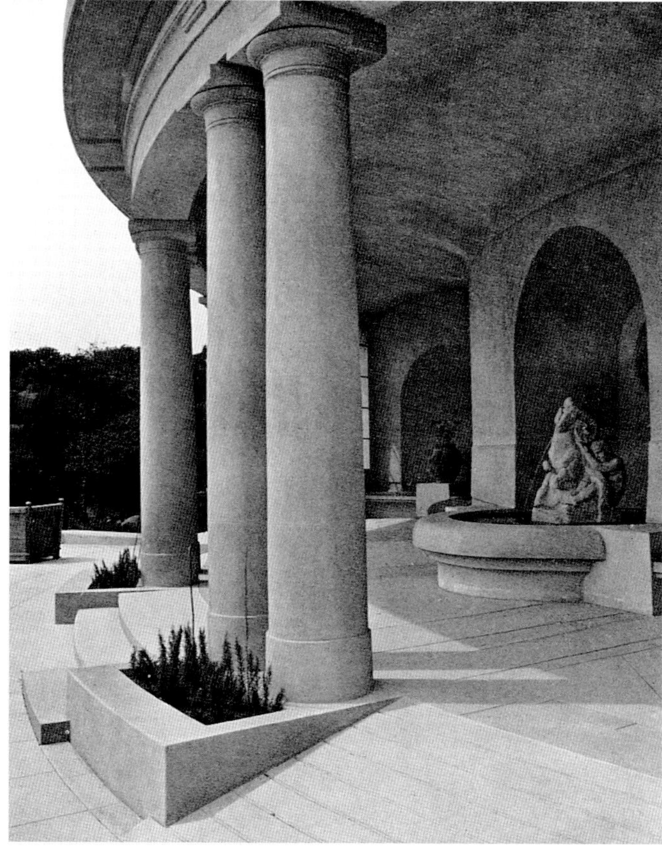

The Pavilion in the Winterstoke Gardens in Ramsgate, Kent, designed by J. Burnet, with Ram fountain by Bayes, c.1927.

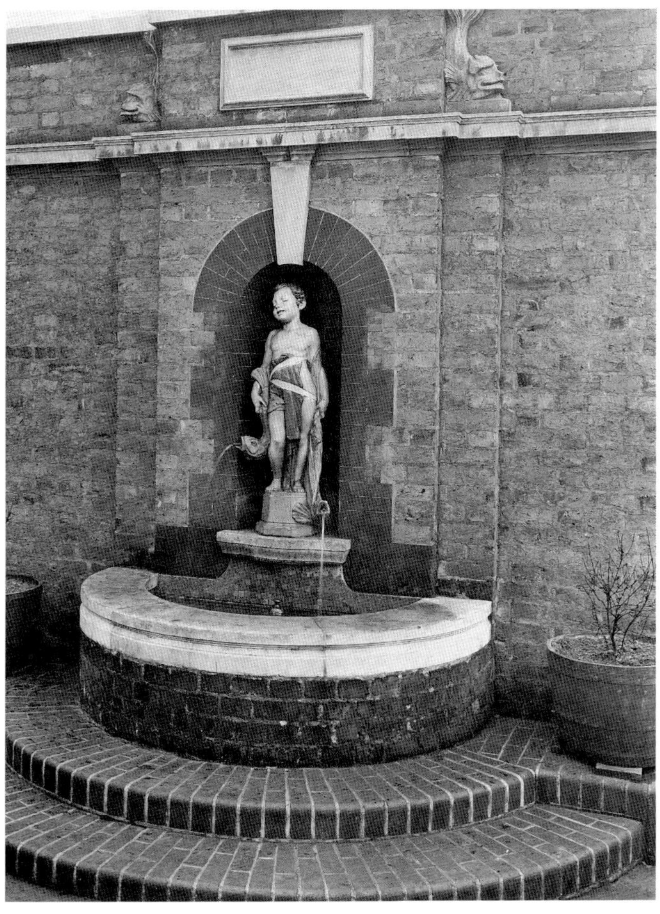

Fisherman fountain, Sidney Street estate, St Pancras Housing Association, late 1930s.

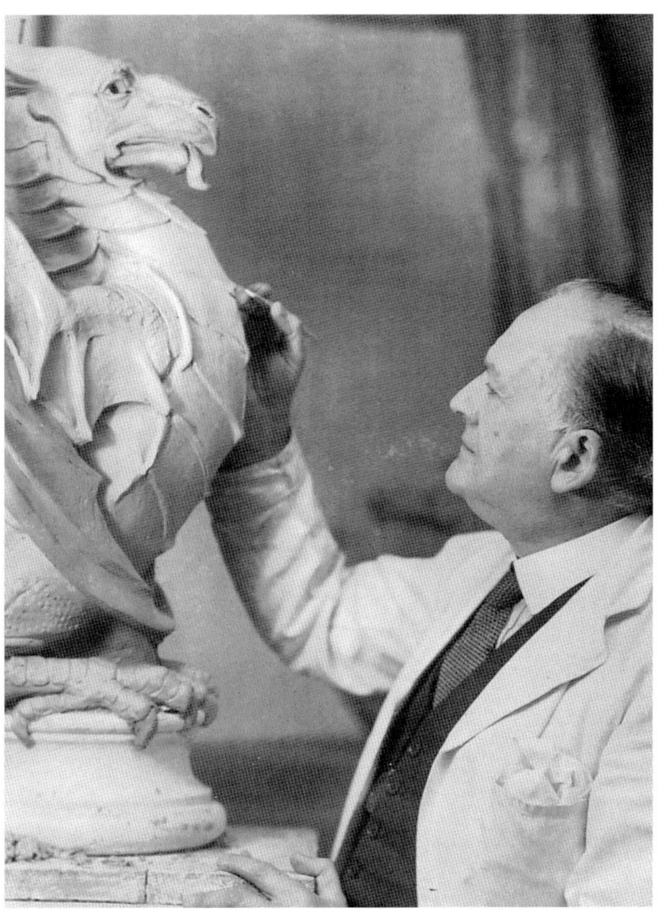

Bayes modelling the Dragon finial for the St Pancras Housing Association flats, 1937.

of his own composition 'O stream of life run you slow or fast all streams come to the sea at last'. He also designed another setting for this fountain against a wall with two Doulton ware monkeys standing sentinel and two roundels of children on the wall. Known also as *Trevor* and *The Lilymaid*, these roundels were later used on the front of his studio at Greville Place and he exhibited them at the Royal Horticultural Society in 1928.

The exhibition at Horticultural Hall was held in conjunction with the Royal Society of British Sculptors, and Bayes assisted William Reynolds-Stephens and William Reid Dick with all the arrangements at the Hall. The aim of the show was to display sculpture in a suitable garden setting, unlike the galleries at the Royal Academy, where rows of statues were crammed into a limited space. Sculptors were concerned that visitors to Burlington House could not visualise their work in an appropriate environment and that sales therefore suffered. By displaying their art to a wider audience in this practical way, the exhibitors at the Royal Horticultural Society hoped to encourage the sale of contemporary sculpture rather than hackneyed copies of the antique to ornament gardens. Thirty-five sculptors participated in this show, among the better-

known being William Goscombe John, C.S. Jagger and Richard Garbe. The majority of works were in lead, bronze or stone, so Bayes and his friend Phoebe Stabler were unusual with their ceramic contributions. Bayes' wife, Gertrude, also took part in the event with a Portland stone statue of a girl fishing, which later found a home in the family garden.

The following year, 1929, Selfridge's completed their famous roof garden on top of their Oxford Street store and Bayes was invited to submit some suitable garden ornaments. A Doulton ware relief of the *Madonna and Child* was chosen to decorate one of the ornamental pools and this was in place by 1930 when Selfridge's organised an open-air display of sculpture by the London Group. Consequently Bayes' traditional Della Robbia-style panel was displayed alongside more radical work by artists such as Henry Moore, Barbara Hepworth and Jacob Epstein. Bayes was not a fan of the new primitive style of sculpture but his more conservative approach did not extend to his materials.

During the 1930s there was growing interest in the new artificial stones for garden sculptures as these offered similar advantages to ceramic in terms of durability and affordability. Bayes had experimented with concrete as a medium for sculpture in the early

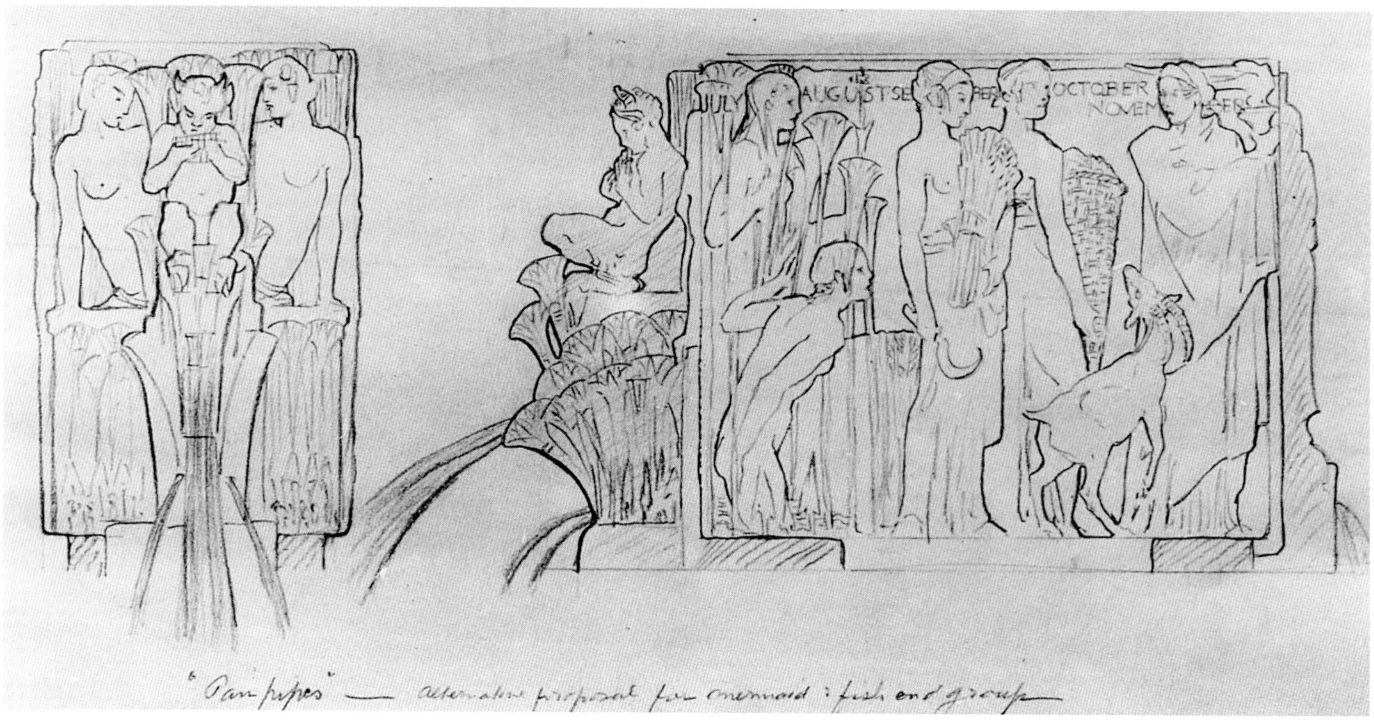

'Pan pipes' — alternative proposal for mermaid & fish end group

Sketch drawing by Bayes for The Fountain of the Months, 1937.

1920s and produced several panels in the material for the Wembley Exhibition of 1924, including one showing its advantages for garden work. The material evolved during the 1920s with the use of different aggregates until a variety of colours and textures could be produced, making it closer in appearance to stone. Bayes used the new concrete mixtures for a fountain at Winterstoke ornamental gardens in Ramsgate, designed by Sir John Burnet, as well as for a set of garden panels, including *The Hesperides* and *The Judgement of Paris*, which he displayed in his own garden. He also reproduced these panels in coloured Doulton ware for a private garden in the West End of London. A few years later, he created two garden statues in artificial stone, *The Lure of the Pipes of Pan*, in 1932 and *The Water's Caress*, in 1934. His method was to cast the statue and then, while it was still 'green', to carve the surface and expose the carefully selected aggregate. The weather resisting properties of the material were proven by the cast of the *Pipes of Pan* that he kept in his own garden. Bayes described the unusual treatment of this subject as a 'two sided pierced relief' as it is only six inches deep. *The Water's Caress* is similar in style and not much deeper at nine inches.

Bayes was always eager to try out new materials and techniques but he could also find new challenges and methods in traditional media. His *Unfolding of Spring* of 1923, was carved in the hardest marble that he had ever cut and was suggested to him by watching the unfolding of pear blossom on a tree outside his studio which linked in his mind to the budding of youth to womanhood. His towering *Great Pan* was originally designed in 1929 for a garden in Greenwich, USA, and the stone was gilded and inlaid with thin lines of blue mosaic to highlight the god's features and lead the eye upwards. *The Frog Princess* fountain was another American commission from 1929, in this case for his old friend the singer Margaret Huston Jones, who lived in California and was a voice coach for actors such as Lilian Gish and John Barrymore. She wanted something gay and light, with a touch of colour, for her garden at Montecito near Santa Barbara, and Bayes selected the story of the princess who dropped her golden ball into a pond and scorned the frog that found it. The dancing figure is in bronze with a gilded ball balanced on the back of her hand and she stood originally on a colourful Doulton stoneware base with bright blue stoneware frogs spouting water at her. She was later loaned to the Santa Barbara Botanic Garden and graced the meadow pond from 1952 until 1979, when she was sold to a private collector and entered the London art market. Another version of *The Frog Princess* with four spouting frogs was made for a garden in Chobham, Surrey, and was acquired for the Devonian Gardens in Calgary, Canada, in 1977. Bayes exhibited *The Frog Princess* several times during the 1930s, including at the Royal Academy in 1931 and the Paris Salon in 1939, where he won a Gold Medal.

During the 1930s, Bayes was working on an exciting community art project for the St Pancras House Improvement Society. As part of a slum clearance scheme in Somerstown, just north of Euston Station, the architect Ian Hamilton designed a garden estate at Sidney Street and, despite the obvious financial constraints, he was able to include many advanced ideas to improve the quality of life in the area. A nursery school was provided on the roof of the flats, as well as play areas for the older children and drying grounds for laundry. Space was also reserved for flower gardens and window boxes to bring a splash of colour into the new community, but Bayes was asked to contribute colour of a more permanent nature in the form of Doulton stoneware sculptures to decorate the buildings and courtyards.

Bayes had always believed that art should be accessible to the people and so he chose subject matter that would be entertaining and easily understood by the new residents. His relief modelled lunettes depicting Hans Anderson's fairy tales were set above French windows throughout the scheme and figurative finials were used on top of all the washing line posts. Nursery rhymes provided the inspiration for many of these little ceramic sculptures, for example 'Four and twenty tailors went to catch a snail' in the drying ground of St Francis' flats and in the courtyard of St Christopher's flats 'Four and twenty blackbirds baked in a pie.' At St Anthony's flats, it was the life of the saint for whom the court was named that suggested the theme of preaching to the fish. Nearby at St Michael's flats, an assortment of grotesque devils perched on top of the posts with the saint in the centre warding them off with his sword. The finials were made at the Doulton Pottery between 1931 and 1938 and Bayes showed several of them at exhibitions, priced between six and eight guineas. A few were sold as ornaments for private gardens during this period.

Novel Doulton ware embellishments were also used at other St Pancras Housing projects, including the Athlone Estate in Kentish Town, where there were duck finials, and the York Rise Estate near Highgate Hill where there were finials of heraldic dragons, roses and thistles. Unfortunately the finials have all been removed but the St Pancras Housing Association hopes to raise funds to replace some of them. Still surviving is the roof-top nursery garden that was decorated with a number of Doulton ware ornaments modelled by Bayes, including *The Fisherman* and *The Water Baby* fountains, a figure of a *Mermaid* and a set of four roundels depicting *Drama, Romance, Adventure* and *Terpsichore*.

As well as all his Doulton work for the St Pancras projects, Bayes also designed some ambitious fountain groups for other media which he exhibited at the Royal Academy during the 1930s. His *Sea Urchin*, was shown in 1934 and, although originally intended for bronze, did not get beyond the plaster stage. Three years later, he showed two plaster panels for his impressive *Fountain of the Months*, which was later produced in artificial stone for a London garden. Sadly this major work was a victim of the Blitz but fortunately two of the original plaster panels survived under an awning in Bayes' own garden. Here they could be admired by guests at the annual garden party that Bayes instigated when he was elected President of the Royal Society of British Sculptors in 1939. No more garden commissions came his way after the Second World War, but his interest in the subject never waned and his work has continued to bring pleasure in private and public settings, just as he intended.

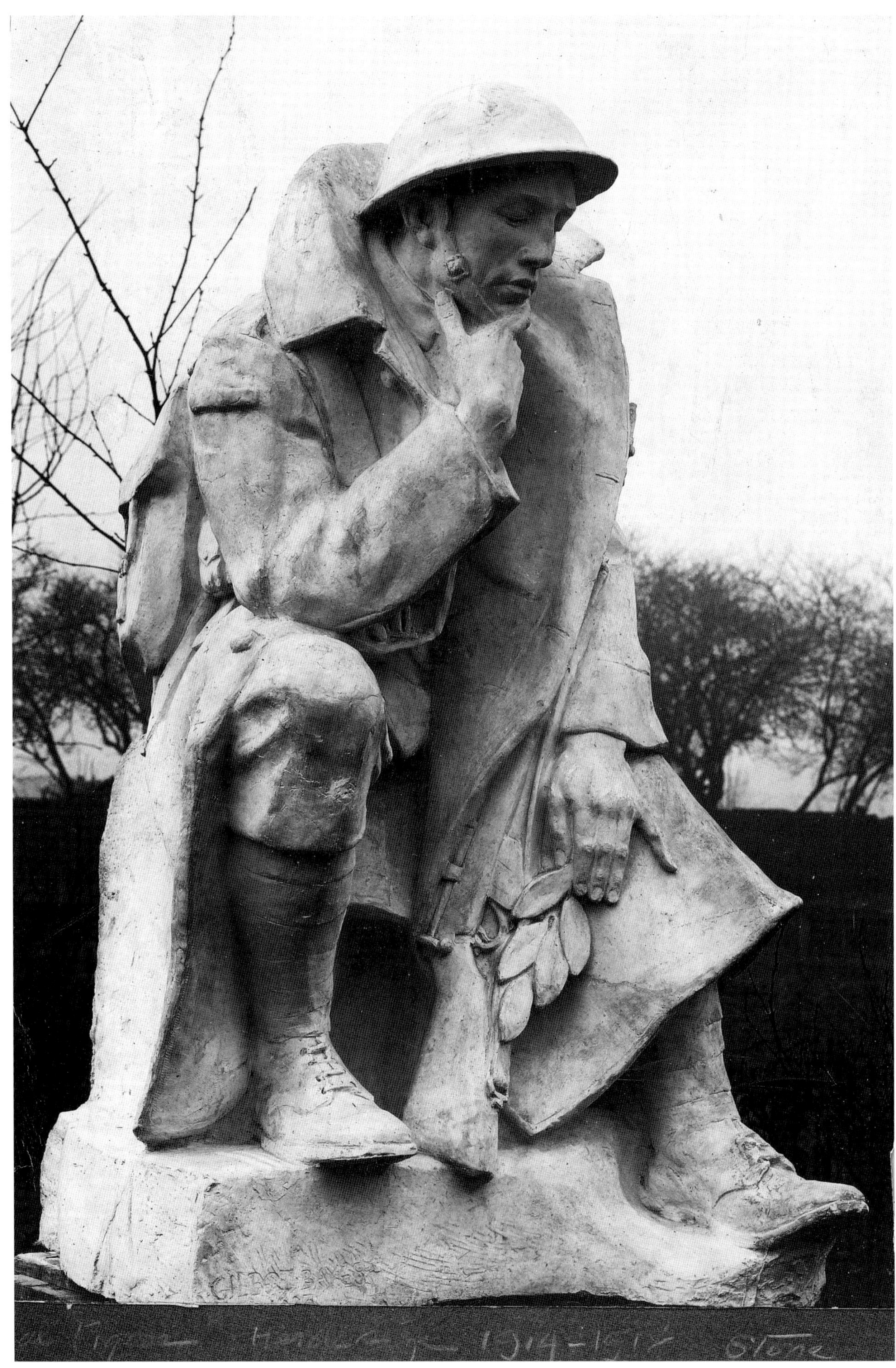

Plaster by Bayes for the Pensive Soldier figure for an unknown war memorial.

WAR MEMORIALS
Paul Atterbury

In the immediate aftermath of the First World War there was great public concern about the need to commemorate, both nationally and locally, the conflict and those who had lost their lives. In cities, towns and villages throughout Britain and the Empire committees were established to raise funds and determine the nature of their particular war memorial. The need for such memorials had been greatly increased by the government's decision to bury soldiers close to where they had fallen, a decision made in the face of enormous pressure from the public to bring the dead home. The result of this debate was the setting up of the Imperial War Graves Commission with the task of establishing formal military cemeteries in all areas of conflict, and creating monuments to the missing that would list the names of the hundreds of thousands with no known grave. The listing of names was also the driving force behind the war memorial movement, which gathered huge impetus during the 1920s. The years that followed the ending of the war were marked by the unveiling of thousands of memorials, ranging from simple crosses and obelisks to major sculptural conceptions. Exhibitions were held at the Royal Academy and the Victoria & Albert Museum, and in other regional centres, to guide local committees in their choice of sculptors, manufacturers, materials and styles, and subject matter.

In many ways the war memorial movement represented the greatest example of national patronage of sculpture since the Renaissance, bringing work to almost every sculptor, letter cutter and monumental mason in Britain. Indeed, a number of sculptors had the foresight to anticipate this likely demand well before the conflict was over. In 1917, for example, there was a debate in *The Times* about the suitability, or otherwise, of both sculptors and styles of sculpture for war memorials, with a number of well known figures, such as Sir George Frampton, taking part. This debate spread into the pages of general interest, art and trade journals. In the 17th August 1917 issue of *The Builder* a writer noted: '...if we want great sculpture it may be necessary and wise to wait for a great sculptor, for we can wait for our memorials though our soldiers cannot wait for munitions of war.'

The debate was also carried on by various organisations concerned with architecture and the arts, a number of which produced booklets or articles offering advice. Typical is the Civic Arts Association's booklet, *On War Memorials*, written by the critic A. Clutton-Brock: 'We must, in this matter of war memorials, give up thinking of art as a mystery practised and understood by a few, since now we wish it to speak for all of us and to say what we all understand... we must set the artist to make what we like as well as he can, not to produce something artistic... We are all anxious to have good war memorials, even if we do not trouble ourselves much about art in general; and this anxiety, if it causes us to give time and pains to this one matter, may make us see the value and meaning of art in general.' Widespread and commonly expressed were concerns about taste. In a review of the exhibition of 400 war memorials held at the Royal Academy over the winter of 1919, *Country Life's* critic commented: '...for the first time the task of designing these memorials has been taken out of the hands of tradesmen and put into the keeping of artists... without such guidance a great deal of money, easily acquired when the heart of the nation is torn, may be put to ignoble uses...' There was also a sense of the need to draw inspiration from the past, and in the War Memorials Exhibition at the Victoria & Albert Museum in 1919 the Director stated in his introduction that along with designs and models for memorials by living artists there were also 'objects, designs and photographs chosen from the Museum collections which may be regarded as offering suitable suggestions.' This exhibition included work by well over 200 sculptors, artists, designers, letter cutters, silversmiths, potters, embroiderers and calligraphers, with many major names represented: Nicholson Babb, Herbert Baker, Anning Bell, Frank Brangwyn, Walter Crane, Nelson Dawson, Eric Gill, Gilbert Ledward, Gerald Moira, Omar Ramsden, Charles Sims, Harold Stabler, Hamo Thornycroft, Albert Toft, C.F.A. Voysey and, of course, Gilbert Bayes, with five exhibits.

Already a well established sculptor with noted abilities in a variety of styles and media, Bayes was in a good position to respond to the opportunities offered by the war memorial movement. Indeed, he seems to have been particularly quick off the mark, for all his exhibits at the Victoria & Albert Museum were related to actual commissions. The first, catalogue 813, was a photograph of a rood beam and figures from St Mary's Church, Primrose Hill, London. A personal rather than a war memorial, this had been installed in the church in 1914, and so its presence in the

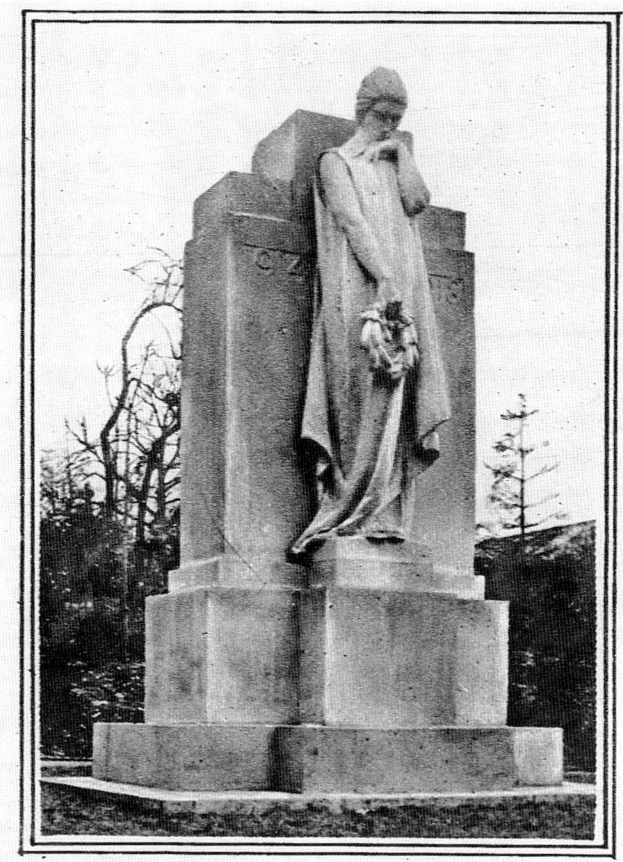

UNVEILED BY THE EARL OF CAVAN: THE BUSHEY
WAR MEMORIAL.

The War Memorial at Bushey, designed by Mr. Reid Dick, A.R.A.,
was unveiled on Sunday, March 12, by General the Earl of Cavan,
who recently succeeded Field-Marshal Sir Henry Wilson as Chief
of the Imperial General Staff.—[*Photograph by Illustrations.*]

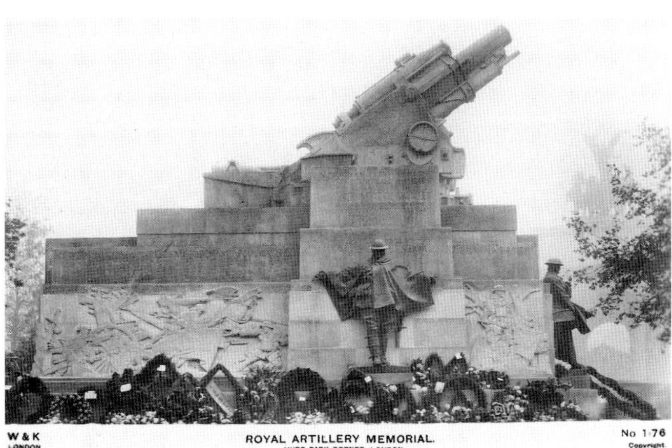

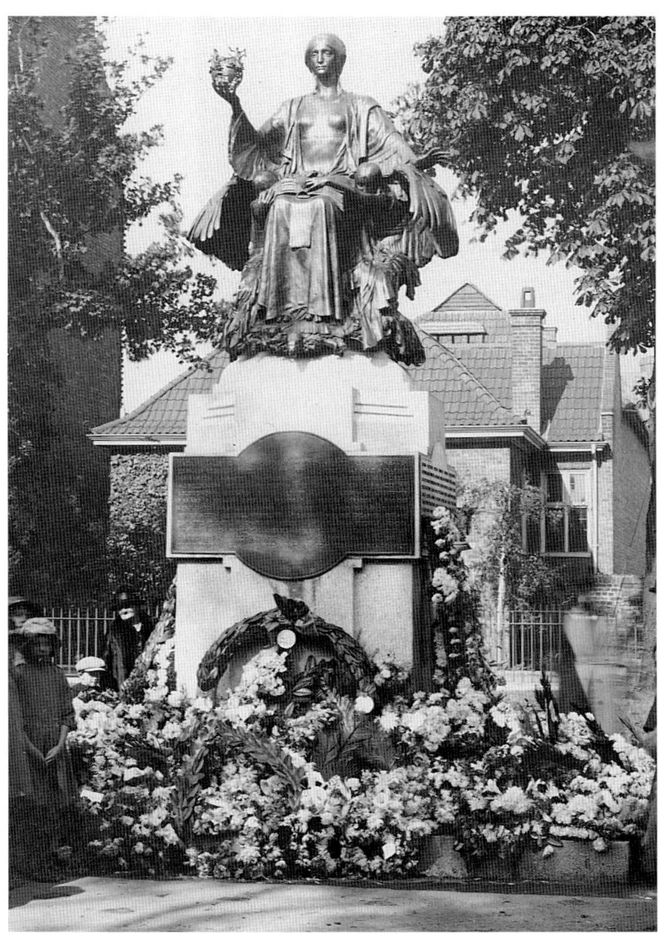

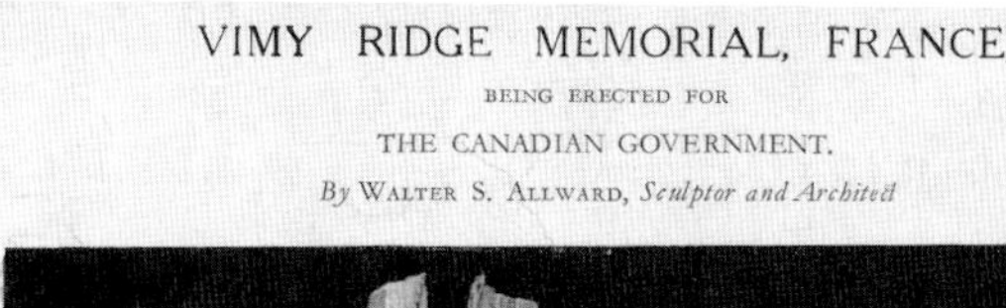

VIMY RIDGE MEMORIAL, FRANCE,

BEING ERECTED FOR

THE CANADIAN GOVERNMENT.

By WALTER S. ALLWARD, *Sculptor and Architect*

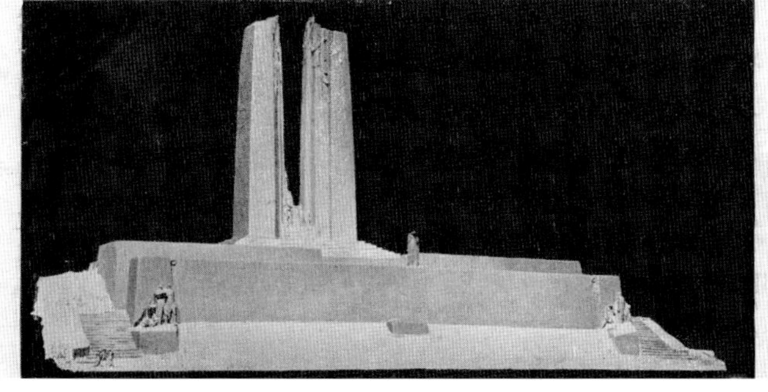

*War memorials from Bayes' scrap books: top left, Bushey Memorial
by William Reid Dick; top right, Bridgwater Memorial by John Angel;
bottom left, the Artillery Memorial by C.S. Jagger; bottom right, the
Vimy Ridge Memorial by Walter Allward.*

exhibition was simply an attempt by Bayes to advertise
his abilities and seek further similar work. In a similar
category was the next exhibit, catalogue 818A, a
design for a lectern for the Royal Savoy Chapel, in
memory of Mr and Mrs Irving. The Irvings had died in
1914 when the liner carrying them was sunk, but the
lectern, again already in existence in 1919, was a
personal rather than a war memorial.

Far more relevant was catalogue 878, a plaster copy
of a relief erected at Aldeburgh, Suffolk, and shown

subsequently at the Royal Academy exhibition. A
marble version of this powerful panel, showing a dead
or dying soldier awaiting resurrection and flanked by
classical attendants, had been erected in Aldeburgh
Church in 1918, an unusually early date for such a
general war memorial. Bayes made no allowance for
lists of names and so these were added as separate
metal panels. The theme is unusual, for memorials
depicting death in battle are rare in Britain. In this
case, the death is sanitised, with the uniformed figure

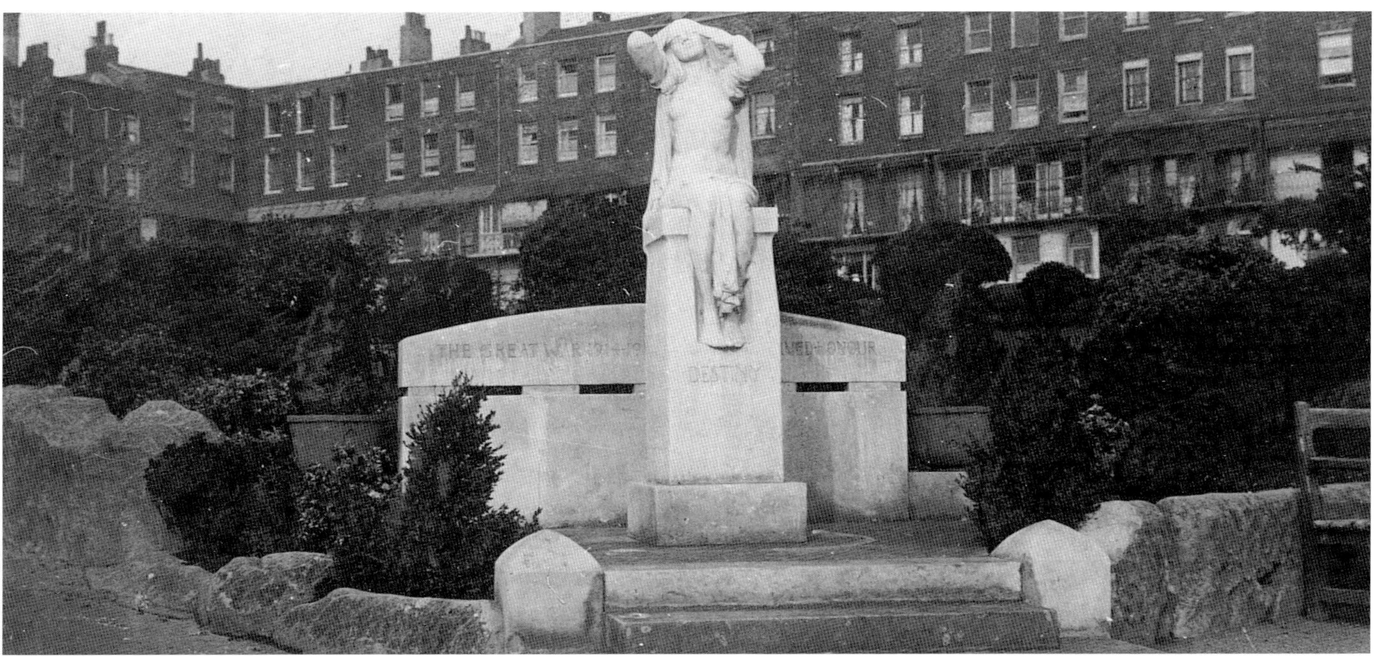

Destiny, the Ramsgate War Memorial in its original setting, 1920.

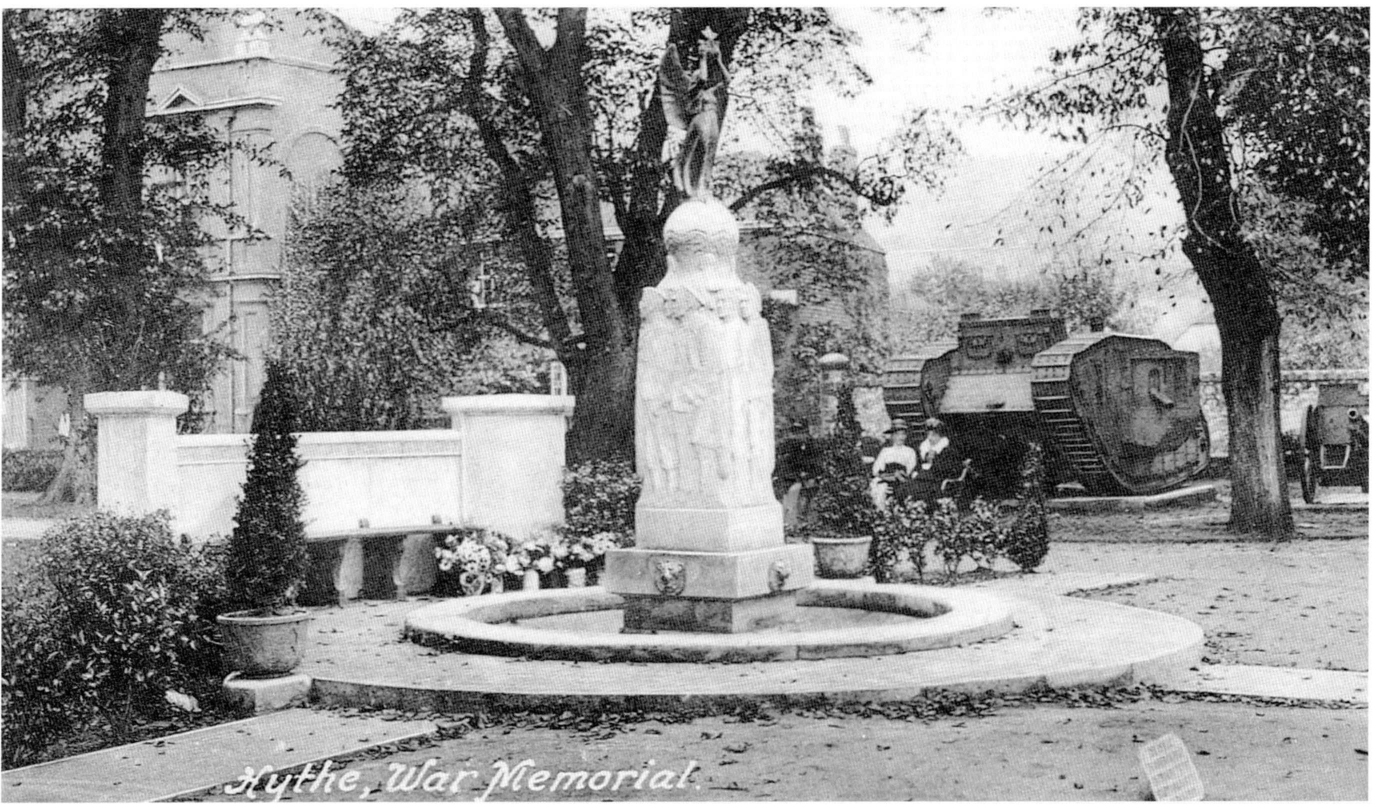

Postcard showing the Hythe War Memorial as erected in 1921, complete with tank.

recumbent in a rural riverside landscape, his head surrounded by a halo of gilded sunbeams suggesting resurrection and the whole flanked by two classically draped female attendants carrying symbols of bread and wine. A parallel can be drawn with some of Ferdinand Blundstone's memorials, for example the Prudential Assurance group formerly in Holborn, London, where the dead or dying soldier is supported by angels. The master of this genre was, of course, C.S. Jagger, both in his relief panels, as for example at

Louverval in northern France, and in particular on the Royal Artillery Memorial at Hyde Park Corner, London. Jagger's greatcoat-covered recumbent figure is uncompromising as a statement about death in battle, and it is interesting that Bayes copied this figure fairly closely in the memorial/sacrifice panel in the modern life series of friezes for the BBC. In his collection of ephemera and source material, Bayes had images of memorials by Jagger, William Reid Dick, John Angel and others, along with a cutting showing

Walter Allward's Vimy Ridge Memorial. Reid Dick and Angel were, of course, among his close friends.

More typical of Bayes was catalogue 966, a plaster memorial figure entitled ANATKH, or *Destiny*. This figure was subsequently used as the focal point of the war memorial in Ramsgate, Kent, unveiled in December 1920. Unfortunately, there is no way of knowing whether Bayes received this commission as a result of the War Memorials Exhibition. The memorial was presented to the town by Councillor Dame Janet Stancomb-Wills who apparently selected Bayes as '...one of the younger school of mystical British sculptors... who had the artist's vision, and was able to give us in statues of enduring grace the meaning of the great destiny of the past.' (*East Kent Times*, 22 December 1920). Bayes was present at the unveiling, and spoke briefly to explain that the figure of destiny was depicted with her face unveiled but her eyes closed, not mislead by the present but seeing beyond into the greater vision of the future. Abstract symbolism of this kind is not a common war memorial theme, and apparently the citizens of Ramsgate still regard the figure as much as an optimistic marker for peace as a conventional war memorial. In 1924 George Frampton sent Bayes a postcard of the Ramsgate Memorial, and wrote on the back: 'Destiny is simply perfect. Our united heartfelt congratulations.'

Bayes' final exhibit, catalogue 982, was a large plaster of an equestrian statue representing *War*. This was also shown at the Royal Academy exhibition. It was one of a pair of large figures symbolic of peace and war whose commissioning predated the exhibition by some years. In 1915 Bayes had submitted to the Art Gallery of New South Wales a pair of 18-inch bronzed plaster figures, entitled *Offerings of Peace* and *Offerings of War*. In 1916 he was commissioned to make much larger bronze versions to be mounted outside the Museum's main facade. Bayes was already known to the Museum, as one of a group of modern European sculptors whose work had consciously been collected, and his figures in bronze and marble were well represented. In addition, his massive low relief bronze panel, depicting the King and Queen of Assyria, had been selected by George Frampton in 1903 as part of the sculptural programme on the outside of the building and placed in position in February 1907. The completion of the equestrian figures was delayed by the war and they were not finally cast in England until 1923, and then installed in 1926. By that time, they had become, de facto, a kind of grand, generalised war memorial. However, their style, and their symbolism, ties them to a much earlier period in Bayes' career, when his sources were still the classicism of the Elgin marbles and the flat reliefs of Assyria. It was this commission above all else that established Bayes as a

modern sculptor with a growing reputation, and so the presence of one of the statues in the exhibitions must have been a forceful reminder of Bayes' suitability as a war memorial artist.

Bayes was clearly seeking war memorial commissions and a number of pieces may have been made and exhibited with this in mind. Typical are the plaster panel entitled *The Guns*, made in 1919 though harking back to the low relief panels of the pre-war period, and the group known as *Comrades* or *1914-19*, shown at Goupil and the Royal Academy. In any case, directly or indirectly, Bayes was to benefit from the publicity generated by the war memorials exhibitions, and he received a number of commissions in their immediate aftermath.

The first of these was for the memorial for Broadstone, Dorset, the maquette of which was shown in the Royal Academy war memorials exhibition. Here a distinctive style emerges. The memorial is in the form of a stylised classical female figure representing grief or mourning, mounted on a tall, tapering obelisk. On the sides of the square base are two low relief panels of soldiers, notably informal and hinting once again at Jagger. They look ahead to the series of low relief architectural panels and compositions that were to characterise Bayes' large scale architectural work in the later 1920s and the 1930s.

Next came two stylistically related memorials, for Hythe in Kent and Todmorden in Yorkshire. The Hythe Memorial was unveiled in July 1921 by Earl Beauchamp, the Warden of the Cinque Ports, having cost about £1,000. Erected in a pleasant garden setting, the memorial stood as a square stone column rising from a circular pond, and surmounted by a stone ball supporting a bronze angel. Carved on the faces of the column in a notably modernist, informal and almost primitive style was a continuous frieze of soldiers, sailors, airmen and other uniformed figures. For some years a First World War tank was also displayed in the gardens near the memorial, a not unusual conjunction during the 1920s. Since then, the memorial has had a rather chequered career, and what remains today has little to do with Bayes. The central column is a replica, poorly carved in the early 1980s in Italian marble, following serious wear to the original, which is now outside the British Legion Headquarters. The ball is a re-creation, following the destruction of the war memorial by vandals in 1996, while the bronze angel has been stolen twice and was eventually replaced by another artist's work.

The Todmorden Memorial, a more complex but stylistically similar conception, was unveiled in October 1921 by Major Barker, MP for the Sowerby Division. The architect was Norman Thorp and it was constructed by local builders at a cost of £13,500. A grand and formal garden composition, the memorial takes the form of a large screen wall carrying panels of names. At its centre the wall rises to form a curved background to a tall stone fountain set in a rectangular pond. Two smaller stone guardian figures, carrying the Lamp of Memory and the Shield of Honour, stand in front, some distance away. Bayes was responsible for the guardian figures and the fountain. This, like Hythe, takes the form of a tall squared block carved with a continuous frieze of figures, surmounted by a ball. In this case the frieze figures are classically inspired, and standing on the ball is a large stone figure of St George, resting on his sword. The formal garden setting at Todmorden seems to have been important in establishing a compositional style that Bayes used in other garden schemes during the 1920s. As his mother came from Todmorden, there may perhaps have been some family link behind the commission.

The National War Memorial in St John's, Newfoundland is the final large scale sculptural memorial by Bayes that relates to the First World War. Commissioned in 1920 and unveiled by Field Marshall Earl Haig on 1st July, 1924, the eighth anniversary of the start of the Battle of the Somme in which the Newfoundlanders played a major role, and paid a heavy cost, the memorial takes the form of a large granite pedestal supporting a bronze female

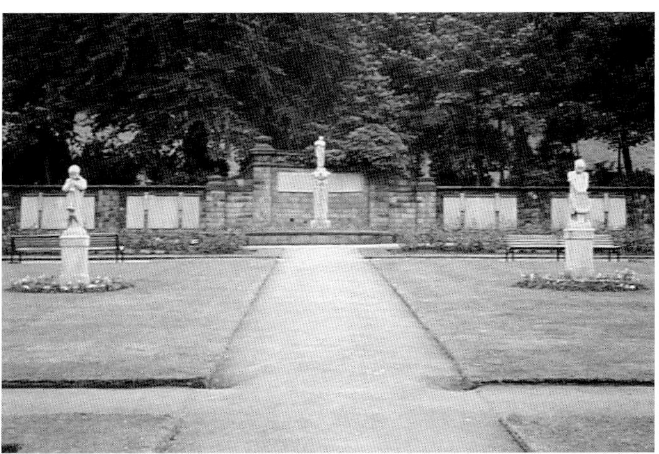

The Todmorden War Memorial in its garden setting.

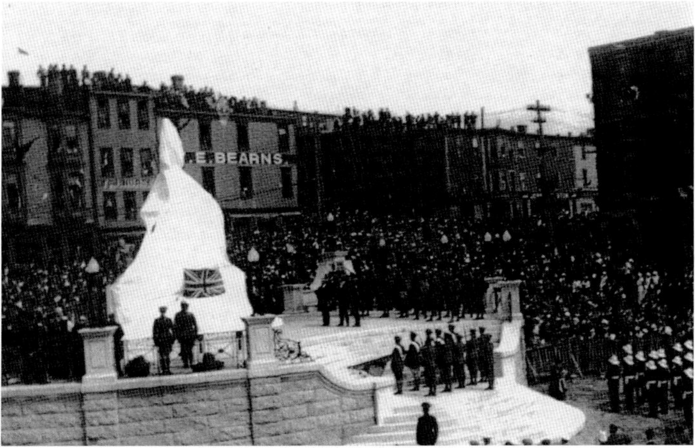

The unveiling of the Newfoundland National War Memorial in 1924.

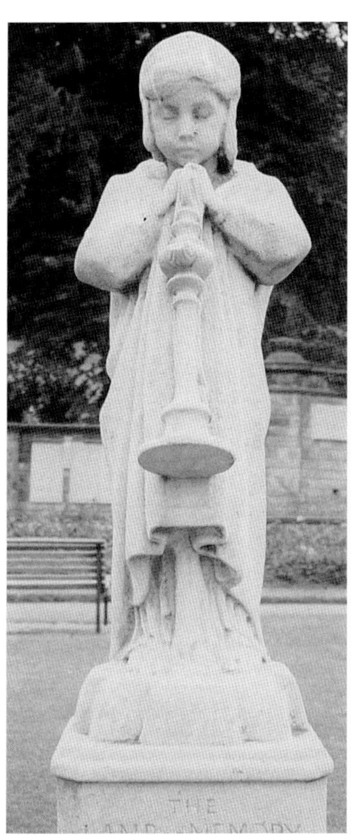

The Lamp of Memory, one of the guardian figures at Todmorden.

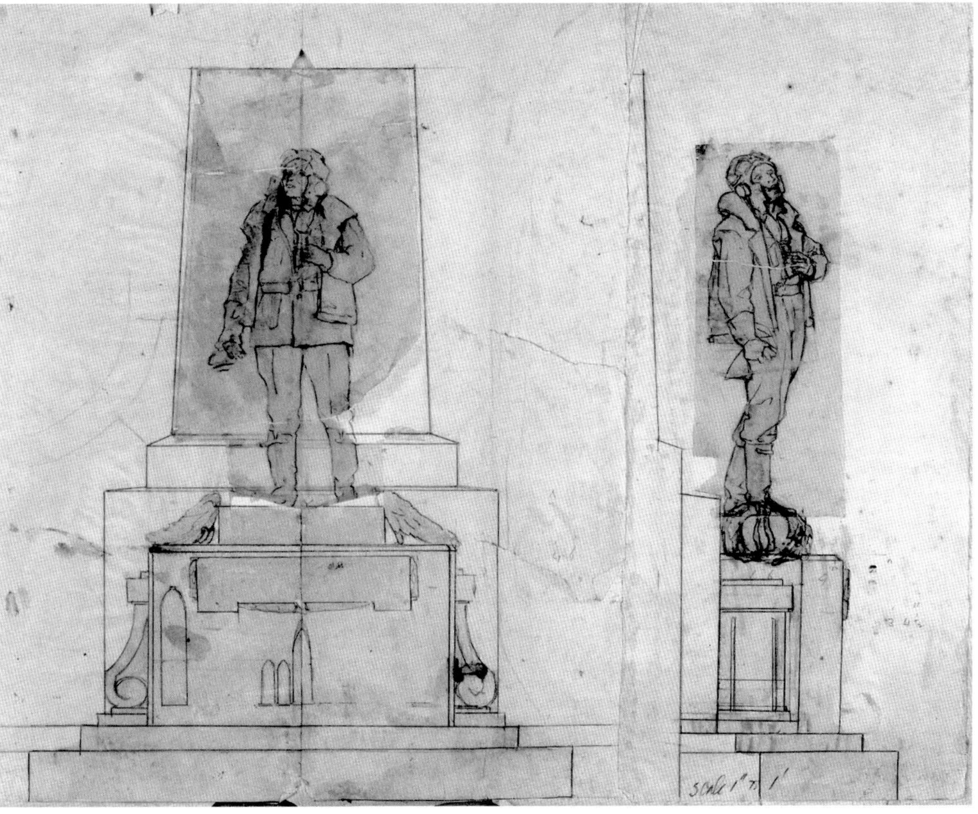

Drawing for the airman figure, planned as an addition to the Newfoundland Memorial after the Second World War, but not carried out.

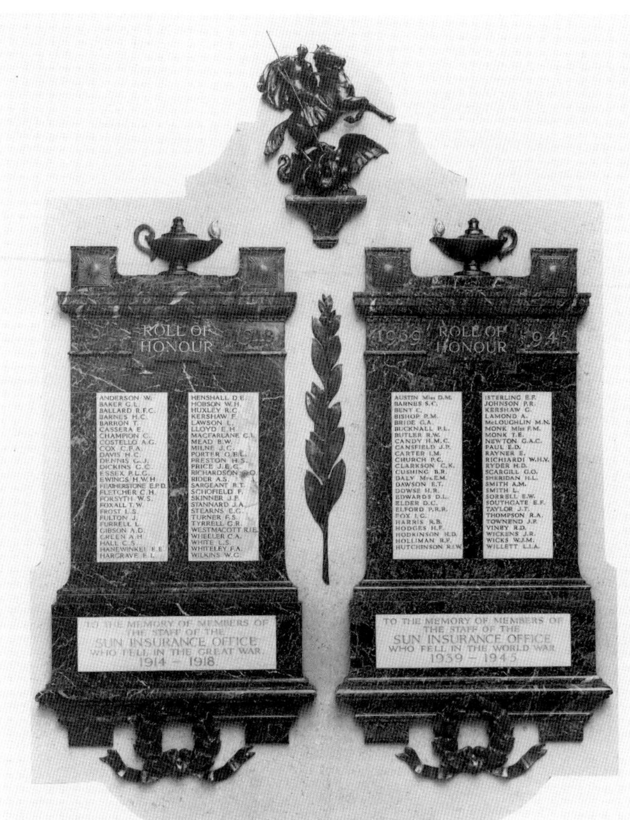

Memorial panels for the Sun Insurance office, c.1950.

figure carrying a torch and representing the Spirit of Newfoundland, and flanked at a lower level by a bronze soldier of the Royal Newfoundland Regiment and a bronze sailor of the Royal Naval Reserve. In front are two standing bronze figures representing the Newfoundland Mercantile Marine and the Forestry Corps. Bayes and Ferdinand Blundstone worked together on this memorial and, a month after the unveiling, a friend sent Bayes a postcard of it, saying: 'You and Blundstone should be very proud of your memorial if you could see it now.'

After the Second World War Bayes was commissioned to design an airman figure to be added to the memorial. Drawings and a maquette were prepared, along with costings, including casting in bronze by the Singer foundry but by 1951 the project had been abandoned.

In addition to these free-standing memorials, Bayes was also busy during the early 1920s designing and making a series of memorial panels and tablets. The most significant was the elaborate scheme for the Law Society, a series of marble slabs listing the names of the solicitors and articled clerks killed in the war flanking a fireplace and incorporating two classically

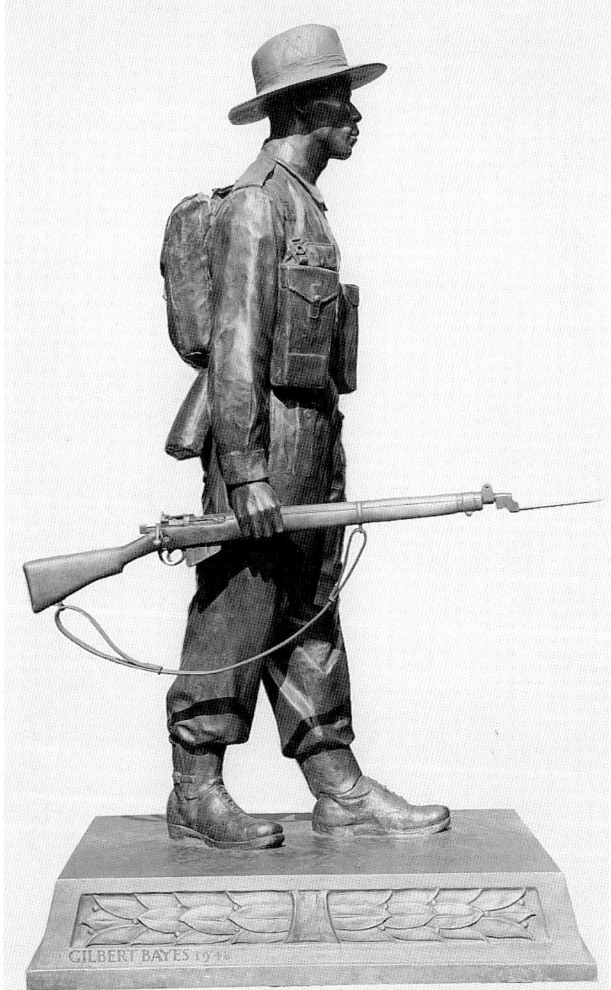

Bronze soldier figure for the Goldcoast Forces Memorial, 1946.

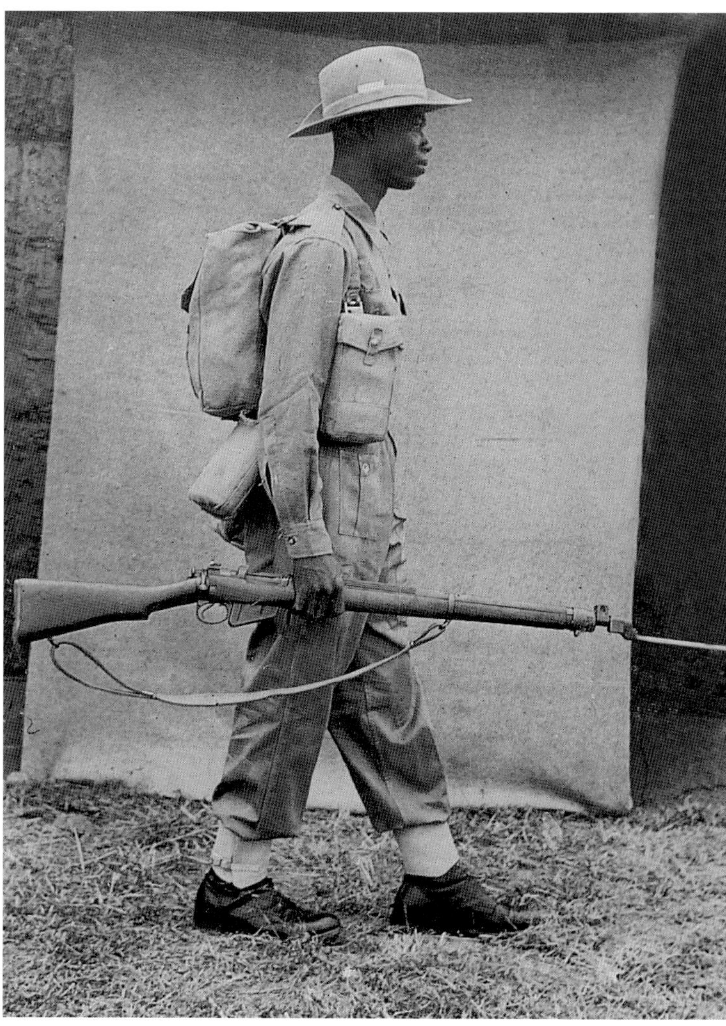

Life model for the bronze soldier figure.

inspired low relief panels by Bayes, entitled *Their Glory Shall Not Be Blotted Out* and *They Died That We Might Live*. This was unveiled in March 1921 by the Lord Chancellor. Unusually, Bayes was called back after the Second World War by the Law Society who, not content with the normal process of simply adding more names, wanted a quite separate memorial to the dead of that conflict. For this commission, Bayes created a standing bronze classical figure holding a spear and enriched with gilding, which he called *The Vigil*. Dedicated by the Archbishop of Canterbury in August 1949, the memorial is impressive, though clearly archaic in style and relating to the series of Guardian figures of the late 1920s and 1930s.

In December 1920 the Earl of Athlone unveiled the war memorial tablet in the Royal Savoy Chapel, listing those killed in the war associated with the chapel and the Royal Victorian Order. Bayes was, of course, already represented in the chapel by the Irving memorial lectern. The warm coloured alabaster panels are set in bronze flanking a standing figure of St George, in bronze and enamel. Above is a bronze lunette with a low relief frieze of marching men, with the lamps of sacrifice and freedom to right and left. This memorial was illustrated in *The Studio* in 1921.

Not dissimilar, and close in date is the memorial tablet in St Leonard's Church, Hythe. Here, the alabaster panels of names are set into a bronze frame and surmounted by a bronze group of soldiers and horses above the enamelled arms of Hythe. The group, in this case dated 1920, is a version of one that Bayes called *Comrades*. A related, but smaller and simpler group, entitled *1914-1919*, was shown at the Goupil Gallery in 1921. It has to be assumed that, like the Royal Savoy Chapel, one Hythe commission led to the other.

St George is a theme commonly used by many war memorial sculptors, and Bayes was no exception. The standing St George figure used on the Royal Savoy Chapel tablet was also made separately as a free-standing bronze, but it is not known on other memorials. On a much larger scale, and quite close to a Frampton St George, was a standing version of the saint, fully armoured, and driving his spear through the dragon's neck. This powerful piece seems to have been Bayes' only contribution to the war cemeteries constructed under the aegis of the Imperial War Graves Commission, and was made to be set above the gateway leading into chapel for the Memorial to the Missing of the Egyptian Expeditionary Force in Jerusalem. The whole composition, including the domed chapel and the cemetery, has echoes of Lutyens, the War Graves Commission's Principal Architect, but was actually designed by Sir John Burnet, a source of much work for Bayes. The memorial was unveiled on 7th May, 1927 by Field

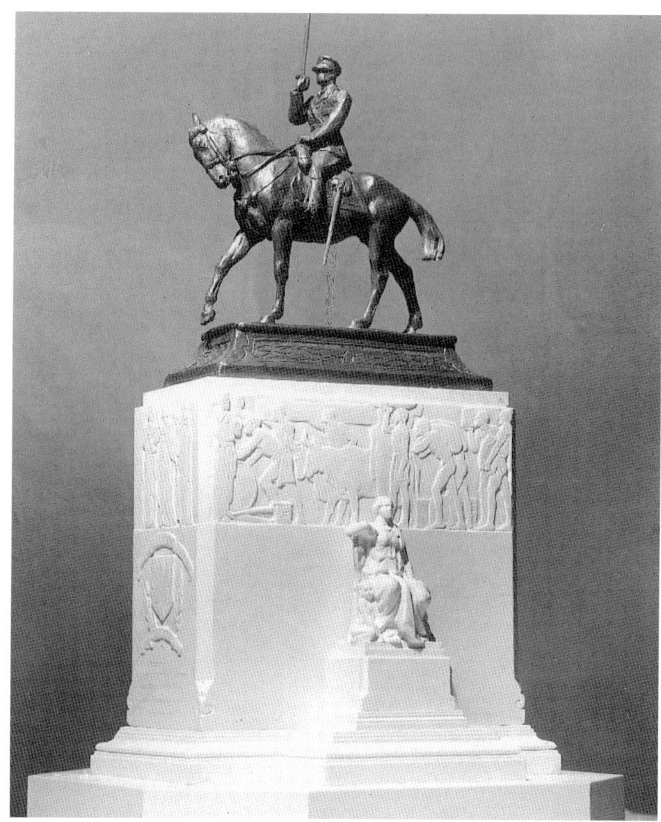

Maquette for an unknown memorial, 1930s.

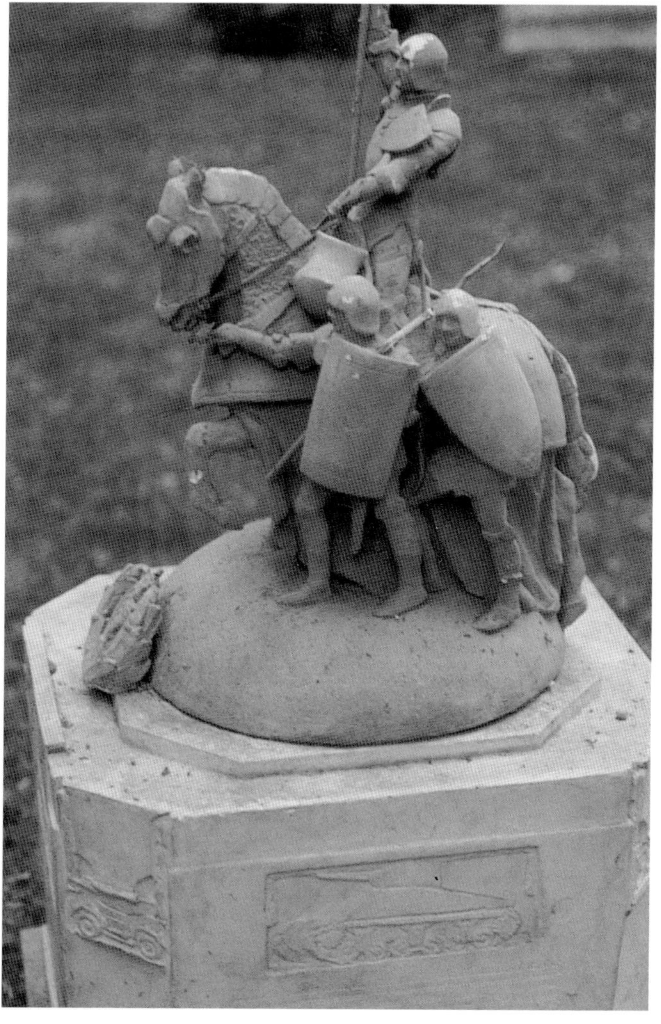

Maquette for an armoured corps memorial, c.1947.

Marshall Viscount Allenby. Another, rather more passive St George figure, mounted in a more conventional manner, is the main feature of an unusual memorial, the lych gate for St Basil's Church, Bassaleg, near Newport, Gwent. This commemorates the dead of Dyffryn, Craig and Rogerstone and was completed in 1926.

Bayes' last memorial commission relating to the First World War was unveiled on 1st October, 1933, in All Saints Church, Langham Place, London. This, a stone tablet flanked by two relief panels in gilded bronze representing David and Jonathan, is the memorial to the 12th Service Battalion of the Royal Fusiliers. Damaged by bombing in 1940, the memorial was removed and broken up in the 1970s. However, the David and Jonathan panels survived and are now in a private collection.

There remains one unresolved mystery from this period, the large figure of a seated pensive soldier that Bayes produced in 1923. It is clear from photographs and family records that this was made first as a full-size plaster and then in stone. It must, therefore have been a war memorial commission but the location or setting is unknown today. There is no record of the figure or any memorial incorporating it at the National Inventory of War Memorials and so either it has been destroyed or it was for an overseas location. Perhaps, for reasons that will also remain uncertain, the commission was cancelled. In its restful realism, it is unlike any other Bayes war memorial figure. Indeed, in style it is close to the seated soldier on the Exeter war memorial by John Angel, a fellow brother of the Art Workers' Guild, and a good friend of Bayes.

The memorials that followed the Second World War were far more limited in both style and quantity. In most cases panels of additional names were added to existing memorials, and so the sculptural bonanza of the 1920s was not repeated. Despite this, Bayes was not without some memorial work. Some commissions were for personal memorials, for example the stained glass window for Captain Glyn Rhys-Williams, who was killed in North Africa in April 1943, or the bronze memorial panel for Major Jack Elliott MC. However, there were at least three major commissions. The first was from Imperial Chemical Industries for whose Billingham factory Bayes designed a stone obelisk mounted with bronze panels of names. This was commissioned in 1947 and unveiled by Lord McGowan in 1949. Bayes also designed a bronze memorial panel for Imperial Chemical Industries Scottish dyes works. The second was more significant, a commission in 1946 from the Crown Agents for the Colonies for a war memorial to commemorate the contribution made by Gold Coast forces. Bayes designed this as a life-size marching figure of a Gold Coast soldier mounted on a stone plinth set with bronze panels. For his model, Bayes used a soldier in full uniform, complete with rifle and other equipment, echoing almost the method of working used much earlier by Gilbert Ledward for his Guards memorial. Working in this manner from life, Bayes produced a full-size plaster, from which the bronze was cast. The final composition, which was unveiled in 1950, is predictably archaic in style and harks back to First World War memorials.

The third, for the Sun Insurance Office, is a rather archaic and conventional pair of stone wall panels inset with lists of names, and decorated with wreaths and eternal lamps in bronze. This very formal composition is surmounted by the only Bayesian detail, a mounted figure of St George slaying the dragon.

Echoes of the First World War also dominate the other memorials that date from this period, three schemes that were never completed. The first, *Flight Wings*, is a naked male figure mounted on a globe and reaching towards the sky, perhaps releasing a bird. As a composition it is effete and anachronistic. More impressive are two equestrian figures mounted on grand plinths, about which little is known. One, featuring a typically Bayesian St George figure set on a plinth decorated with low relief panels of tanks and armoured vehicles, and thus perhaps a scheme for a Royal Armoured Corps memorial, exists only as a plaster maquette in the Bayes Trust collection. The other, which probably belongs to an earlier period, is a splendid soldier figure with raised sword, in the manner of the Haig memorials. This is known only from photographs of the maquette.

In his output and stylistic diversity, Bayes made a significant contribution to the war memorial movement. His commissions, from 1916 to 1950, spanned both World Wars. Inevitably, some of his memorials are predictable and repetitive but the best ones, Aldeburgh, Hythe, Todmorden, Ramsgate, were in their original form major contributions to the genre. Through his working methods, his extensive use of exhibitions, his contacts with friends like George Frampton and John Burnet and his use of modern yet familiar forms and styles, Bayes reveals the ways in which sculptors of his time gained war memorial commissions, and just how valuable those commissions were for him and his contemporaries.

SCULPTURE AND ARCHITECTURE
Louise Irvine

'What is the function of sculpture today? Is it to give added interest and beauty to our surroundings, to our streets, or is it to give passers-by a headache wondering why and wondering what it all means?' Bayes posed this question in a lecture to the Incorporated Association of Architects and Surveyors in 1935 and proceeded to present a case for sculpture that is accessible to the man in the street without sacrificing art or integrity. He rejected the fashion for Primitivism between the wars and argued that work 'more suitable to the African kraal' had no place in British cities: sculpture should be intelligible and interesting to the intended audience. It was an issue that he felt strongly about throughout his career and he always considered his public when working on architectural commissions. Of course 'sculptors must be ready to assimilate the style of a building and bow to its claims' and he maintained 'the only style not worth trying is the incomprehensible!' Armed with this philosophy, he was ready to tackle all the commissions that came his way in a career which spanned half a century.

Bayes received his first architectural commission after entering a competition in 1903 to design a bronze relief panel for the facade of the New South Wales Art Gallery. Subjects typical of Assyrian or Egyptian art were required and his design, depicting Assur-Natsir-Pal, King of Assyria, at the opening of a new building, was selected by the assessors, Alfred East and George Frampton. The panel took its place in 1907 beside an earlier Greek subject by Percival Ball and the winning Egyptian design by Countess Feodora Gleichan. Funds for the proposed series of art history panels ran out, but there was one later addition in 1931, a Roman subject by William Reid Dick. In this early essay, Bayes has not fully resolved his handling of the monumental relief and is still digesting the influences of his models, the severe Assyrian and the freer, more realistic Greek friezes that he studied at the British Museum.

This architectural relief was unusual in his early career, but he was gradually making a name for himself as a sculptor of monumental statues. He was one of the young sculptors chosen to contribute figures of famous artists and architects for the facade of the Victoria & Albert Museum in 1905. The decorative scheme of thirty-four statues was devised by Aston Webb and the sculptors were required to submit quarter-size models and, if successful, full-size models within two months. These were hoisted into position on the building and,

once approved, the stone carving had to be completed within three months. A fee of £150 was offered for two statues, and Bayes produced portraits of Sir Charles Barry and Sir William Chambers in Portland stone for the Cromwell Road facade. It was perhaps at this early stage in his career that Bayes decided that laborious stone carving was not for him. He much preferred modelling in clay and usually engaged craftsmen to carve from his plaster casts before he added the finishing touches.

The decoration of another national museum was the subject of a limited competition in 1914. Smith and Brewer, the architects of the National Museum of Wales, sought the advice of Sir William Goscombe John on the sculptural decoration of their new building in Cardiff and he recommended a monumental and symbolic approach rather than a pictorial treatment. Sixteen figurative groups representing History, Art, Science and Industry were envisaged, and models were invited from selected sculptors. Bayes was successful with his submission of 'The Bronze Age', along with Richard Garbe and T.S. Clapperton, and he was invited to design a companion group. However, the titles of the sculptures were changed and he was asked to produce instead 'The Prehistoric Period' and 'The Classic Period' for the main facade, which he visualised as statuesque groups of three figures. Work on the sculptures continued apace despite the outbreak of the First World War, full-size plasters were ready in 1916, and the carving was completed by 1917.

Fortunately Bayes was exempted from war service because of his work on another museum commission, the heroic equestrian groups of *War* and *Peace* for the entrance of the New South Wales art gallery in Sydney, Australia. Bayes' plaster models were approved by the museum trustees in 1916 and a fee of £3,000 was proposed. The contract specified delivery in two years and Bayes completed the plaster model of *War* in 1918, showing it at the Academy that year. However, the bronze founders were engaged in munitions work, which caused delays, and prices had risen dramatically. It was 1924 before the bronze of *Peace* arrived in Australia. The local press made much of the occasion describing how eight live horses had pulled one bronze horse from the wharf to the art gallery.

Although the statues of *War* and *Peace* were situated at the other end of the world, they established Bayes' reputation as a major sculptor of monumental

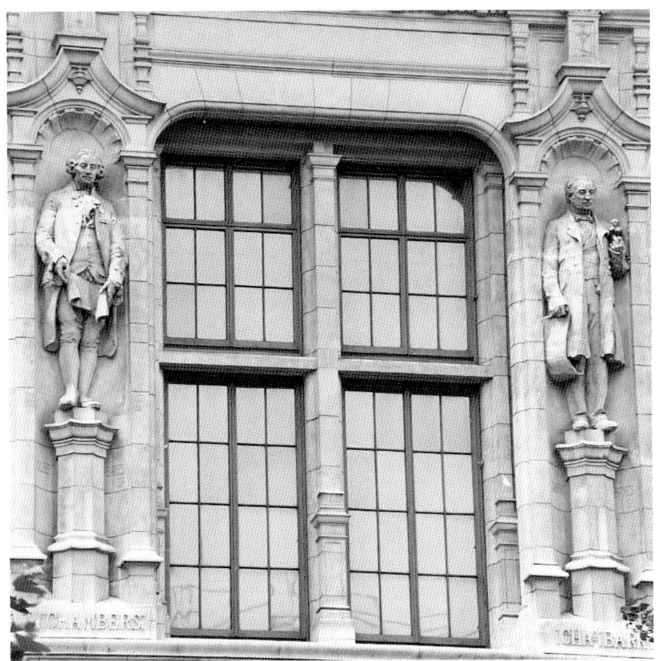

Chambers and Barry on the facade of the Victoria & Albert Museum, 1905.

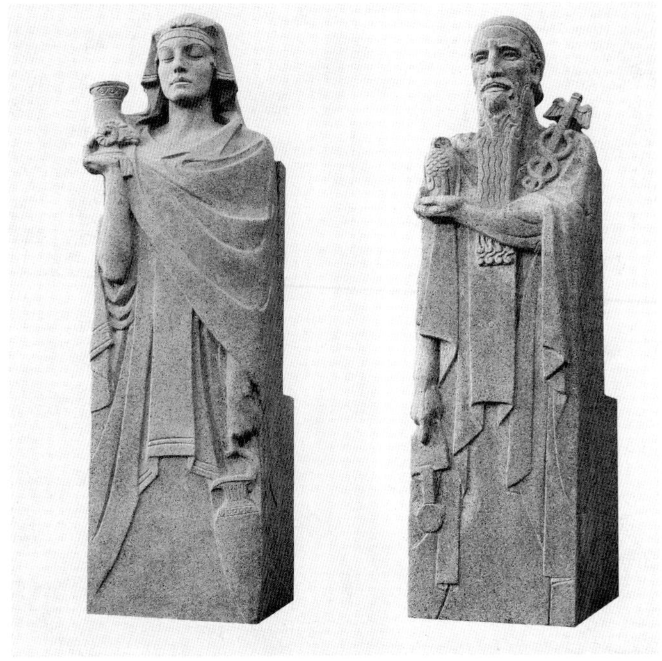

Hebe and Aesculapius, cast and carved concrete terminal figures for the Royal Masonic Hospital, 1933.

and architectural works. Sir George Frampton wrote to the art gallery director congratulating him on his choice of artist and many commissions followed in the UK and overseas. Sir John Burnet, who was chosen to design all the cemeteries for the Imperial War Graves Commission in Egypt and Gallipoli, asked Bayes to design a bronze niche figure of St George for the memorial chapel in Jerusalem and this was erected in 1927. This was not the first time Burnet had worked with Bayes as he had designed the Institute of Chemistry, the setting for Bayes' stone statue of Joseph Priestley in 1914. A few years later, they worked together again on the rood screen erected in memory of the Reverend Charles Jenkins at St James' Church in Edinburgh. Perhaps their most important collaboration, however, was on the extensions for Selfridge's department store in Oxford Street.

After completion of the first stage of Selfridge's building, Sir John Burnet and his partner Thomas Tait worked in association with the American firm Graham, Anderson, Probst and White to design the western extensions. Part of the proposed scheme was a massive tower, 300-feet tall, to crown Selfridge's emporium and Bayes was commissioned to produce heroic statues of the *Four Winds* for the top. Building work began on the tower and Bayes completed full-size plaster models before the project was halted in 1924 when planning permission was denied. Selfridge's were not to be allowed to exceed the eighty feet height restriction then in force to prevent any building competing with the dome of St Paul's cathedral. Fortunately, Bayes was paid for his work and went on to his next project for Selfridge's, the provision of a monumental clock for the main doorway. Elevations of 1926 show the outline of the monumental time piece, which was approved by Selfridge's house

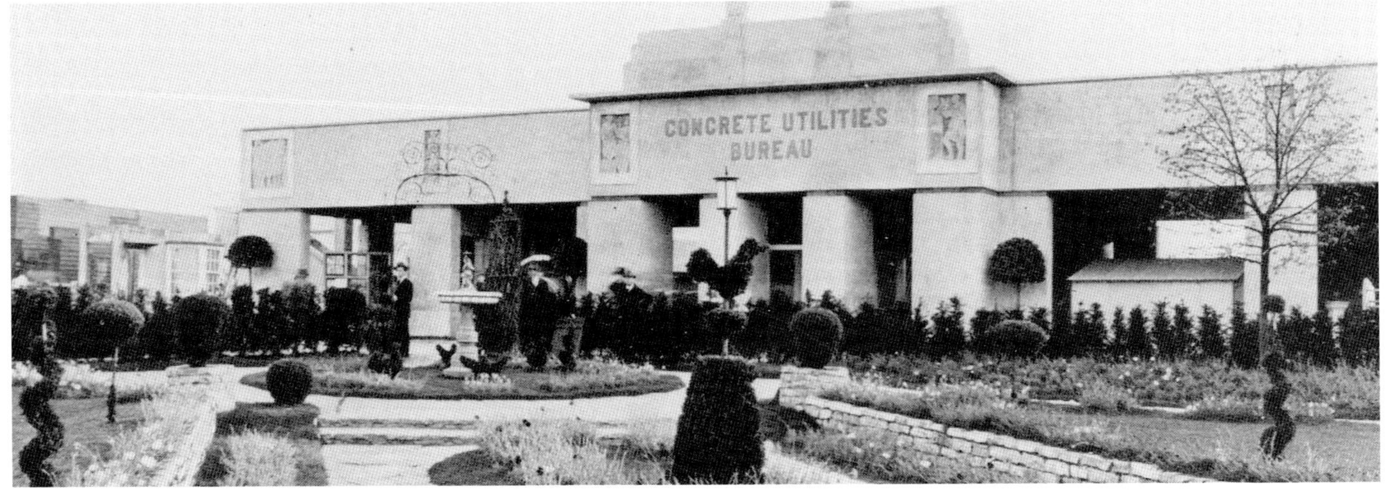

Concrete Utilities Bureau building at the Wembley Exhibition, 1924, showing the Bayes concrete making panels in situ.

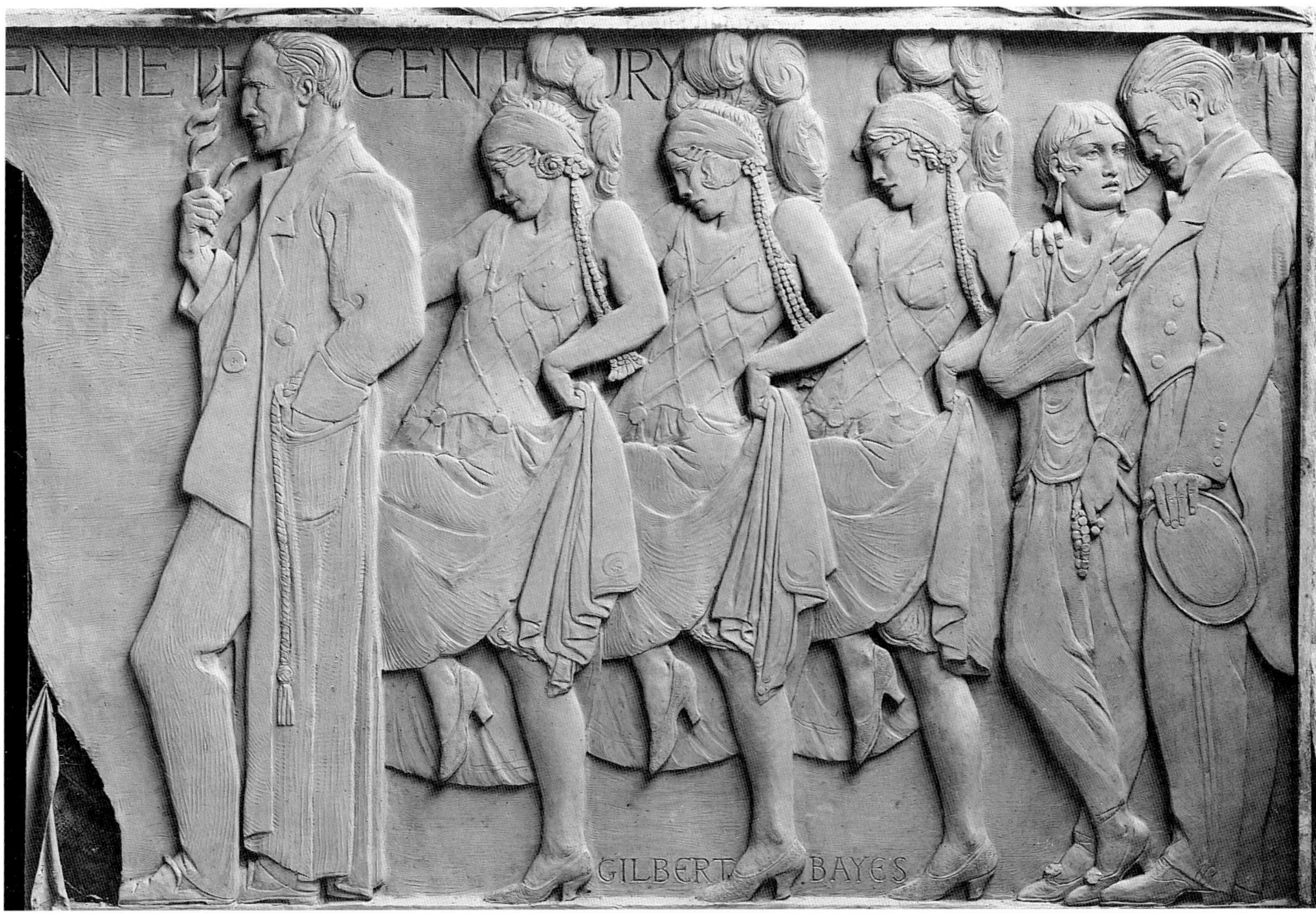

Full-size plaster for the twentieth-century section of the Saville Theatre frieze, 1930.

architect, Alfred D. Millar, in 1930. The main figure, which stands eleven feet high on the prow of a ship, symbolises the 'Sea of Eternity' but was soon dubbed 'The Queen of Time'. In one hand she holds the figure of Progress and in the other an olive branch; she is accompanied by two nymphs holding waxing and waning moons that represent the tidal ebb and flow. The bronze, cast by Burton's, was embellished with gold and inlaid with blue stoneware supplied by Doulton's of Lambeth and was finally installed in 1931. Contemporary postcards proclaim it as 'One of the sights of London' and 'London's newest meeting place – under the clock at Selfridge's.'

Bayes also contributed several other sculptural adornments for the new part of the store, including bronze and mosaic floor roundels of trading vessels for the lift entrances and a bronze panel of Pegasus laid in the floor of the main entrance in honour of Gordon Selfridge, the store's founder. Selfridge was a great admirer of Bayes' work and displayed a cast of *The Guardian of the Seas* from 1927 in his private office. When it came to finding appropriate sculpture for the roof garden in 1929, Bayes was invited to submit suggestions and a Doulton ware relief of the *Madonna and Child* was chosen. He also worked on the temporary sculptural decorations produced for

Selfridge's to mark the Coronation in 1937 and, under the direction of Sir William Reid Dick, he created a colossal figure of *Peace* to crown the main facade. Finally, when Gordon Selfridge was forced to retire in 1939, Bayes designed a memorial relief and portrait which was accompanied by an illuminated address produced by his sister, Jessie.

Bayes continued to enjoy a fruitful working relationship with Sir John Burnet and Thomas Tait during the 1920s and 1930s, and they were regular visitors to his home. He worked on some of their most prestigious buildings, including Lloyds Bank in Lombard Street, which won the RIBA London Architectural Medal in 1932. Bayes produced an impressive bronze and mosaic floor roundel, similar to the type used at Selfridge's, for the main banking hall and it was featured in the building press of the period. Two years later Sir John Burnet and partners won the RIBA Medal again, this time for the Royal Masonic Hospital in Ravenscourt Park, with Bayes as their collaborating sculptor. For this building he produced two massive terminal figures of Aesculapius, the god of medicine, and Hebe, the goddess of youth, who could ward off old age by means of nectar and ambrosia. The figures are highly stylised, almost severe in conception, and were cast in concrete using a granite

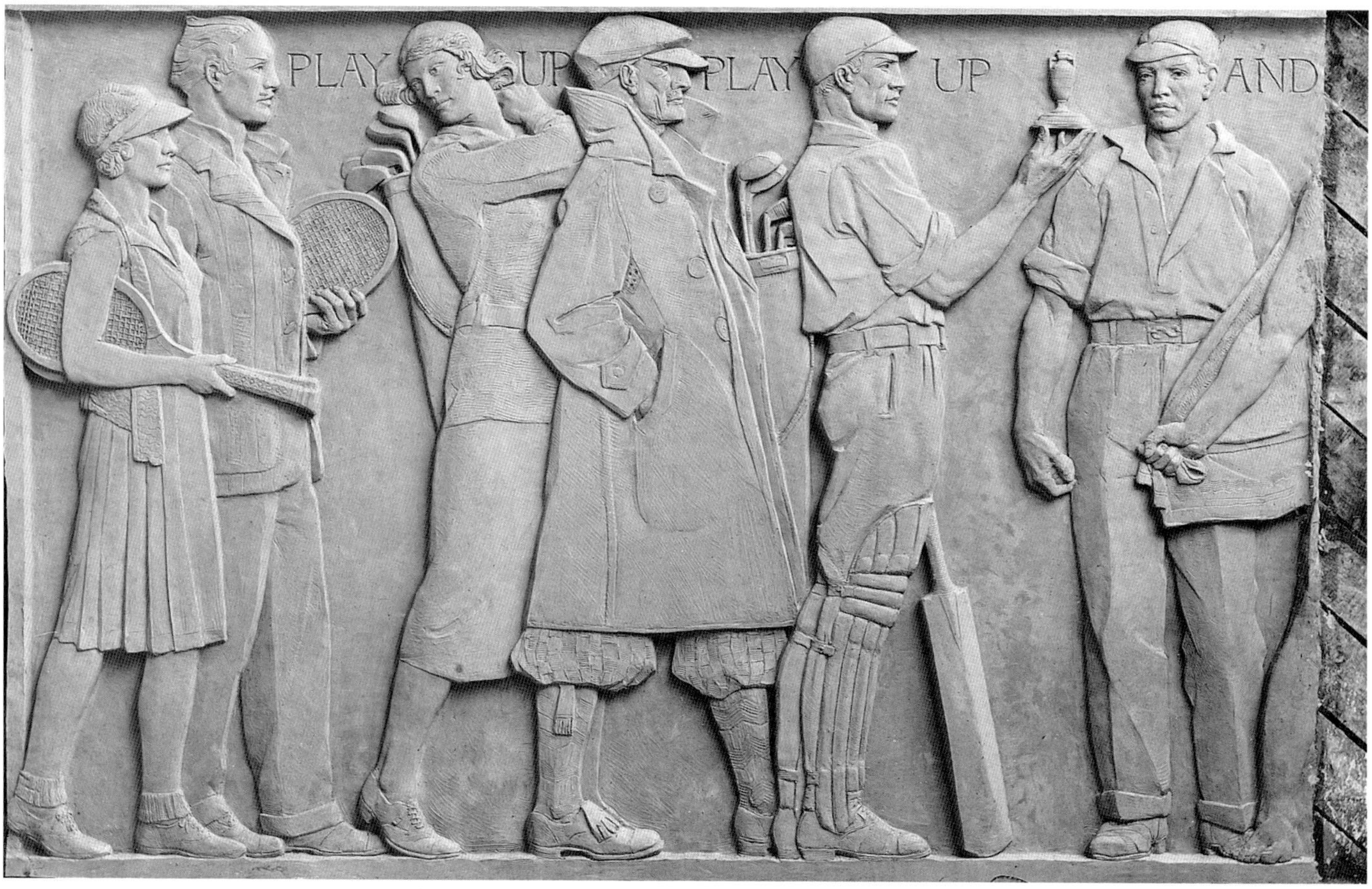

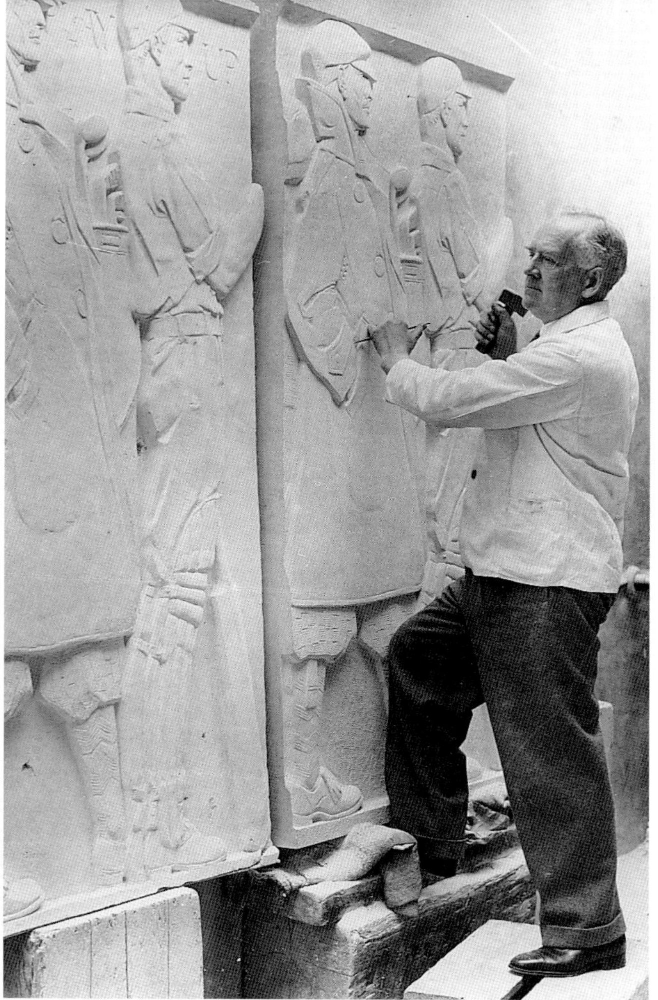

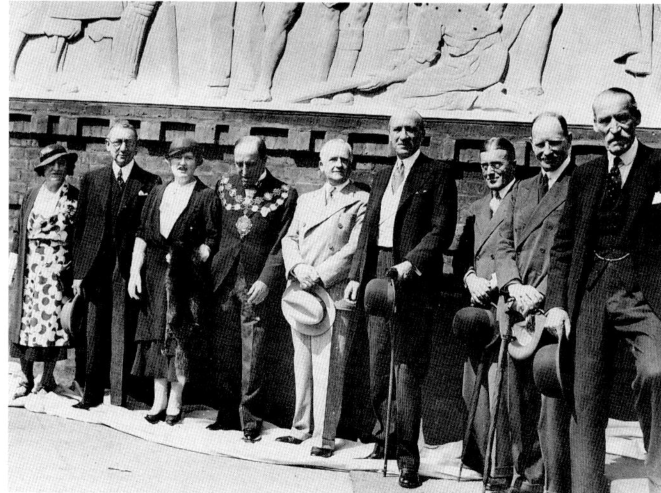

Top, section of the full-size plaster for the Lord's panel; left, Bayes at work on the Portland stone version of the panel; above, after the unveiling in September 1934, group includes Lord Cromer, President of the MCC, Alderman John Fettes, Mayor of Marylebone and David Issacs, the donor of the panel. Bayes is in the centre.

aggregate. Bayes then carved them when they came from the mould to reveal the texture of the material.

By this period, Bayes already had considerable experience with concrete. During the 1920s, he had been one of the first sculptors in the country to experiment with the new building material and some of his first essays in the medium were used on the Pavilion of Concrete Utilities Bureau designed by Clough Williams Ellis at Wembley in 1924. His low

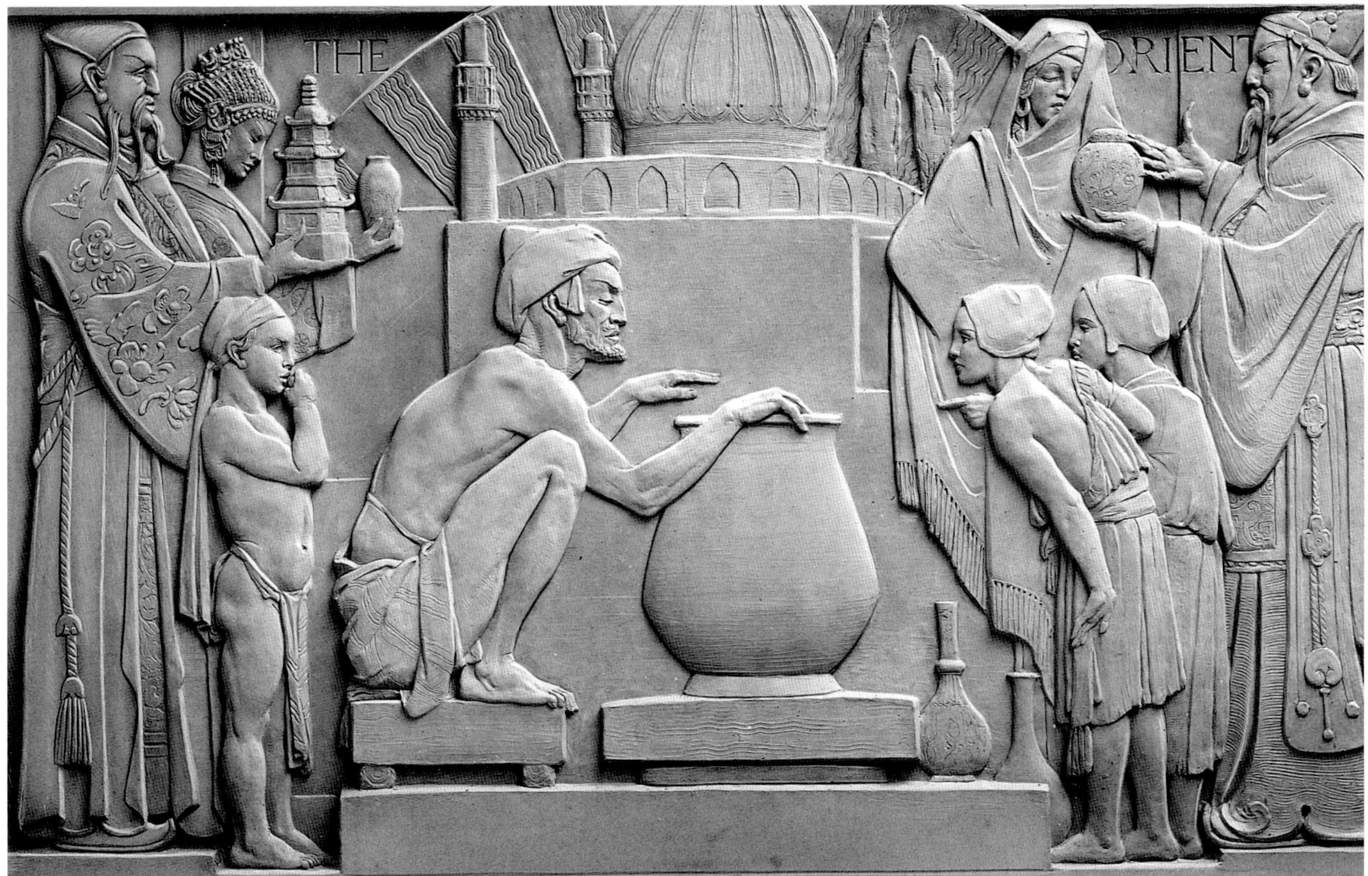

Full-size plaster for a section of the Pottery Through the Ages frieze for Doulton House, 1939.

relief panels depict various stages in the concrete-making process from filling the moulds to the humorous image suggesting its sculptural potential. The new material dictated a more stylised treatment with increasing simplification of forms within a bold design. In the accompanying exhibition booklet, Bayes predicted that concrete would supplant stone for the decoration of the outside of buildings in cases where cost was crucial. Not only was it cheaper and easier to produce, it was also lighter in weight and more durable than most stone. He therefore recommended more study into surface texture and colour variation.

Another of Bayes' friends and collaborators, the architect Thomas Penberthy Bennett, was an early pioneer in the use of concrete and in 1927 he wrote one of the first books on the subject *Architectural Design in Concrete* which features Bayes' sculpture for Burnet's ornamental gardens in Ramsgate. Bennett was also a keen protagonist for the use of sculpture in architecture and in an earlier book, *The Relation of Sculpture to Architecture* from 1916 he stressed the importance of establishing a good working relationship with a suitable sculptor at an early age, ideally while still at art school. He also insisted that the sculptor be intimately involved at the beginning of a building project and not be asked to add a decoration or two at the end. Bennett had a very good understanding of the sculptor's art and for many years

reviewed the sculpture at the Royal Academy for *The Builder* magazine. He thought very highly of Bayes' work and said of him in 1924: 'The value of Mr Bayes' work is enhanced when it is placed in an architectural setting because he has a wonderful facility for catching the spirit of his surroundings and for modelling work which achieves complete harmony. It therefore comes about that he can work with architects of widely different aims; he can catch the spirit of buildings with different intentions and will add to their beauty and interest in every case.'

Bayes and Bennett worked together in 1924 on the conversion of the Earl of Bessborough's Adam-style residence in Cavendish Square into a showroom for Brinsmead and Sons, the piano manufacturers. Ever willing to experiment, Bayes' produced low relief panels in cement that were then painted to resemble neo-classical stucco work. The theme Music, Art and Science was suggested by statuesque muses in clinging drapes and a frieze of cherubs playing musical instruments. The figures were originally painted cream against a red background, a colour scheme that harmonised with other decorations on the premises. Although the panels remain in good condition, they are now totally painted in cream so the Adam look has been lost.

This commission reflects one of Bayes' major concerns – the role of colour in sculpture and,

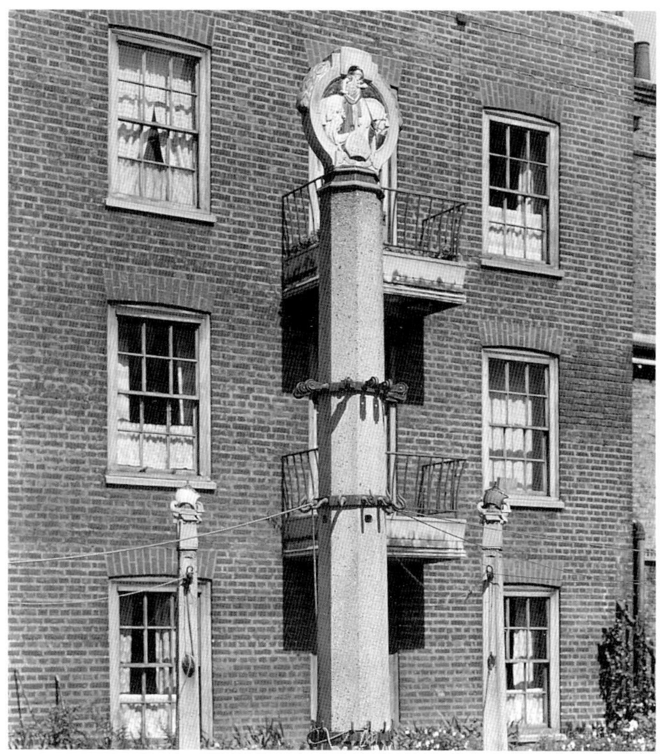

St Martin finial, with Ship washing posts, St Martin's flats, St Pancras Housing Association, 1937.

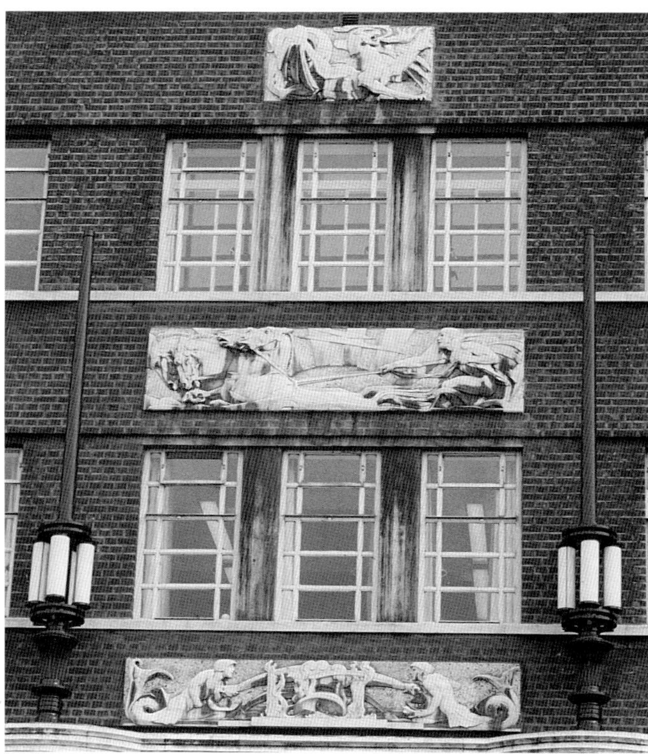

Dragon, Helios in his Chariot and Mermaids Firefighting panels on the facade of the London Fire Brigade headquarters, 1936.

indirectly, architecture. His views are best summed up in his own words: 'In the past there is no doubt that colour was used in many, if not all, the great periods of art and it may be used again since colour is a quality more easily understood and appreciated than form. But if it is to be used successfully, it must not be used realistically but must be used for the beauty of colour and the form under it must receive special consideration. If the realistic use of colour were the highest form of sculpture then the art of the wax-work image maker would be the most inspiring of the arts, and we all know this is not the case.'

It was this interest that initiated a singularly long and successful association with the ceramic manufacturers Doulton and Company. At the end of the nineteenth century, this pottery had perfected polychrome stoneware, a highly colourful material like its precedent from Florence, Della Robbia ware, but more durable and able to withstand the rigours of a northern climate. Bayes was the first artist to take a serious interest in this new medium and it was owing to him that it was so successfully exploited in the inter-war years. One of the sculptor's first experiments with Doulton was a plaque depicting two cherubs playing musical instruments, identical to one of the groups on the Brinsmead frieze and probably taken from the same mould. The ceramic plaque, however, is vividly painted in bright blue and flesh tones, completely transforming the decorative effect.

The first architect to take advantage of Bayes' designs in Doulton ware was C. Cowles Voysey, son of

Charles Voysey. He commissioned two early schemes and for the first, a nursery school in Bow, Bayes produced a panel depicting the *Madonna and Child*, which was set above the entrance doorway in 1924. He also carved and painted a wooden sign board for the school but this no longer survives. Bayes showed the *Madonna and Child* panel at a couple of exhibitions in the mid-1920s and it was later used in Selfridge's roof garden and on the Westminster Diocesan Archives building in London. For the second Voysey building, the White Rock Pavilion in Hastings, Bayes designed a series of colourful Doulton ware roundels representing Drama, Romance, Adventure and Terpsichore, set into a stucco finish. The same panels were later used at St Christopher's Nursery School on the Sidney Street Estate owned by the St Pancras Housing Association. Throughout the 1930s, Bayes produced a number of Doulton ware sculptures to decorate the estates being built by Ian Hamilton for the St Pancras Housing Association and these are also discussed in the chapter on gardens. Although they were low-budget schemes, money was found for sculptural adornments and Bayes' lunette panels of fairy tales are set like jewels in the brick walls, emphasising the value of concentrated ornament in a plain wall space. He also contributed a large square clock, vigorously modelled in low relief with chubby children representing the four seasons. The experience gleaned on the St Pancras commission served Bayes well for his major work in Doulton ware, the fifty feet long frieze of *Pottery through the Ages* for the company's new headquarters on the Lambeth

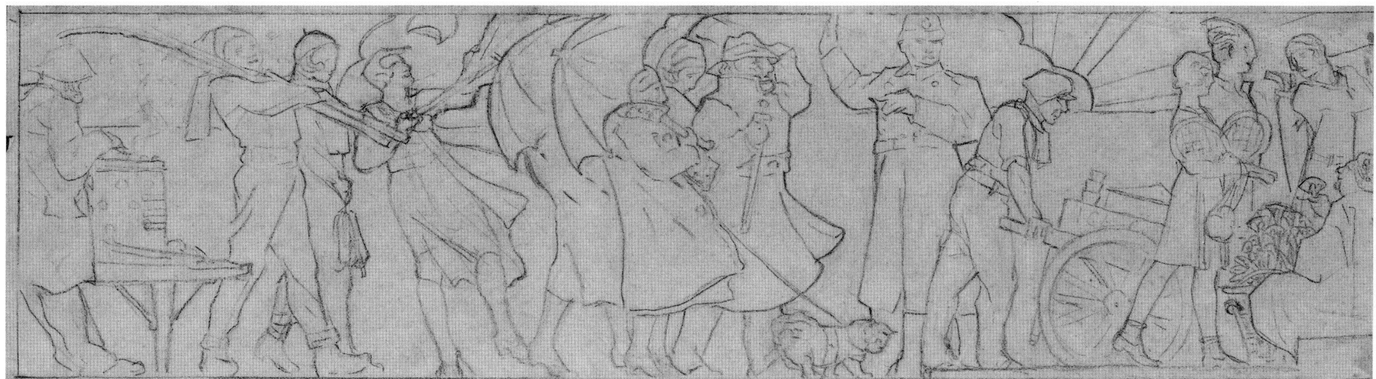

Above, drawing by Bayes for a scheme for an architectural panel, 1930s. Below, drawing by Bayes for an architectural panel, In the Days When the Arts Were Loved, late 1930s.

Embankment. The building was designed by T.P. Bennett in 1939 and was entirely clad in Doulton's architectural ceramics. The frieze was modelled in Bayes' distinctive low relief style and the treatment is reminiscent of his occasional excursions into stained glass design in both the intensity of colour and the division of the blocks. The Doulton House frieze was dismantled in 1979 when the building was demolished, but it was restored and re-erected in the Victoria & Albert Museum in 1988. A smaller side panel, depicting Dutch Potters arriving in Lambeth, was presented to the Ironbridge Gorge Museum in return for their help in salvaging this important Bayes commission.

Large-scale friezes in very low relief became Bayes speciality between the wars and he successfully combined a wide range of historical styles with a contemporary look. His surviving scrap books and post card albums show that he sought inspiration in works as diverse as the Parthenon frieze and the Renaissance bas-reliefs of Michelangelo and the Della Robbia family. A more austere Assyrian-style relief was his choice for the Masonic Temple in Birmingham, which he executed in 1926-27. Bayes was an active Freemason and it is likely that several commissions came his way through these circles. The subject of the frieze is the building of King Solomon's temple, regarded as an important event by Freemasons, and Bayes depicts the story in an appropriate archaic style. The frieze is carved in Portland stone and consists of two sections, each thirty-two feet long, positioned high on the facade of the building. In *The Artist* magazine of 1934, Bayes describes the rush to complete this job. About one third of the frieze was modelled and cast in plaster and the rest was drawn full-size and traced directly on to the stone. Several men were involved in cutting away the stone to the depth indicated in the modelled section and Bayes finished the carving. So close was the timing that, as he descended the ladder on the last day of carving, men were waiting below to strike the scaffold. Bayes showed a model of the Masonic Temple frieze at the

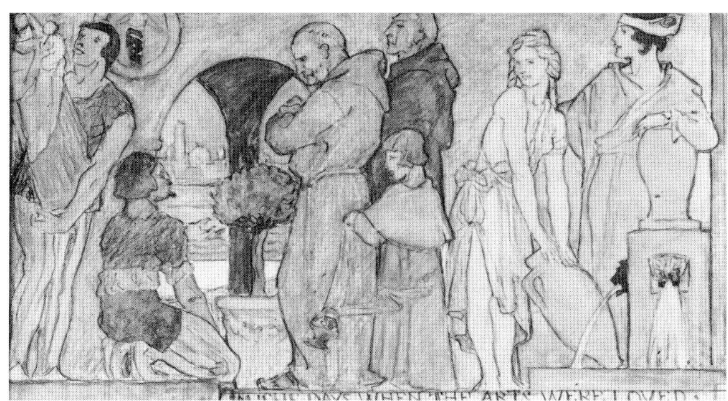

Royal Academy in 1928, where it was favourably reviewed by T.P. Bennett.

A few years later, when Bennett came to design the Saville Theatre in Shaftesbury Avenue, Bayes was the obvious choice to tell the story of *Drama through the Ages* on the facade. A continuous stream of characters, portraying different eras of theatrical history, progress around the exterior of the building in the manner of a Roman triumphal procession. The frieze is 120-feet long and six feet tall with seventy life-size figures and animals but the maximum projection of the relief is only one-and-a-half inches. It is made of artificial stone and Bayes produced around ten feet a week, with the help of his assistant Frank Ransome. His working method involved producing a lantern slide of his small scale drawing which he would project and trace full-size onto a huge sheet of paper. Then he would begin modelling his slab of clay which would later be cast in plaster.

According to Jean Bayes, Bennett would drop in to see her father every Sunday after playing golf to see how the plaster model was progressing. Not surprisingly, with such an intimate involvement, Bennett's praise of the frieze was glowing when models were shown at the Royal Academy in 1930. He writes in *The Builder* of that year: 'The breadth of treatment is very well suited to the position that the frieze will occupy. The horses are excellent examples of Mr Gilbert Bayes' well-known handling and the figures of the bacchanalian dancers are particularly beautiful examples of the nude'. The frieze was undoubtedly

Bayes' *tour de force* and won for him the coveted RBS Silver Medal in 1931.

The resulting publicity brought Bayes another important commission, to provide a series of tinted bas-reliefs for the interior of the new BBC concert hall designed by G. Val Myer. Six panels depicting classic subjects were completed for the western wall in 1932 and six more with modern themes for the eastern wall in 1934. The classic panels are inspired by Greek mythology, the poetry of Keats and Shakespeare's plays, and incorporate a number of Bayes' favourite images. The winged horse Pegasus, for instance, appears in the two Selfridge's memorials and in a panel for Cleland House at Millbank by T.P. Bennett. In addition, the two nymphs peeping out from behind the bull rushes in the *Music* panel was re-worked to become the garden statue *The Lure of the Pipes of Pan*. The six modern panels show characters in contemporary dress and the *Sacrifice* scene, featuring a dead soldier, is particularly poignant and echoes his war memorial for Aldeburgh Church. In contrast, his *Games* panel, showing sportsmen and women in 1930s clothes, is in the same jaunty mood as his large Portland stone relief on the wall of Lords Cricket Ground *Play Up! Play Up and Play the Game*. This was unveiled in 1934 and now has considerable charm as a period piece. Bayes justified his occasional use of topical subject matter because it appealed to the general public and therefore should not be ignored.

The demand for architectural reliefs continued to keep Bayes very busy throughout the 1930s. Six large square panels were produced for the Commercial Bank of Scotland in 1935-36 and samples were shown at the Royal Academy. Then there was the series of relief sculptures for the river frontage of London Fire Brigade's new headquarters on the Albert Embankment, as well as the memorial panels for the interior. Bayes attended the official opening of this building by King George VI and Queen Elizabeth in 1937 and was flattered when the Queen remarked 'I see you've brought your horses here again.'

As war loomed in Europe, Bayes was working on a series of heraldic reliefs to decorate the British pavilion at the New York World's Fair in 1939. The designs were executed under the direction of the Portcullis Pursuivant of Arms, Anthony Wagner, and Bayes worked with Cecil Thomas and Gerald Cobb on this extensive scheme. The large plaster panels were brilliantly coloured and gilded as can be seen in Wagner's book *Historic Heraldry of Britain* which is illustrated with many of the exhibition panels.

A coat of arms was also one of the sculptural panels required for the new assembly hall at Belfast University, which Bayes began working on in 1940.

The building was designed by a local architect John MacGeagh in consultation with Edward Maufe, a great friend of Bayes, and together they devised the sculptural scheme. War interrupted the building work, which was suspended until 1946, and Bayes eventually completed the commission in 1948. The complete project consisted of a bronze bust of Sir William Whitla, the distinguished physician whose bequest provided the funds for the building, together with low relief plaster panels of *Music* and *Drama* and keystones representing the humanities and sciences. Bayes was assisted in the stone carving by Morris Harding, and he added the finishing touches in his usual way. Records reveal that the total fee was £770.

Bayes last architectural commission in 1951 was also for a university building, Withersdane Hall at Wye College, formerly the agricultural school of London University. Appropriately, he modelled a relief panel symbolising Harvest but all did not go smoothly with his clients, who criticised the anatomy of the calf in the sketch model. Fortunately Bayes' classic style was to their taste and the panel was cast by the Empire Stone Company and erected in 1952.

In the last years of his career, Bayes felt increasingly out of sympathy with contemporary architecture and sculpture. The main criterion of judgement that he applied to his work was that it should be likeable – in other words, it should have human interest, beauty of form and be attractive, so that it creates a feeling of pleasure or satisfaction in the onlooker. He lamented the fact that the modern movement seemed disinclined to consider the public and felt that the new avant garde work positively alienated sculptors from society. He expounded these beliefs throughout his life in his occasional articles and in his lectures to the RIBA, the Architectural Club and the Incorporated Association of Architects and Surveyors, where he served as Vice President from 1939-44. Bayes was not alone in expressing this point of view; some of his colleagues at the Royal Society of British Sculptors were even more vehement in their derision, having undertaken to stand by representational form and to eschew 'significant' and abstract form.

However, there was little call for representational sculpture in the more austere buildings of the post-war era. In any event, Bayes was in his seventies and was unlikely to receive strenuous architectural commissions. Shortly before he died in 1953, he destroyed most of his drawings and papers, but fortunately many photographs of his work survived. With these, and the reports in the contemporary building press, it has been possible to create an overview of his architectural work that shows him to be a remarkably versatile, productive and popular sculptor throughout an extraordinarily long career.

PORTRAIT SCULPTURE
Michael Barker

Gilbert Bayes executed his first portrait sculpture nearly a century ago: a marble bust of Sir Richard Moon, Chairman of the London and North Western Railway. Made in 1899, the year of Moon's death and the year that Bayes won the Gold Medal and travelling scholarships at the Royal Academy Schools, the sculpture is a conventional bust, but depicts Moon in an unflattering light: his brooding, bearded visage gazes down, his eyes averted from the onlooker. It was succeeded over the long years of Bayes' career by numerous memorials of the great and the good some of them now long forgotten.

A precocious exhibitor – his first showing was at the Royal Academy at the age of seventeen – Bayes was one of the younger generation of artists who developed the New Sculpture. Before the turn of the century, his output, influenced by his mentor Sir George Frampton, largely consisted of small decorative pieces in the Arts and Crafts tradition, usually reliefs and often featuring animals, especially horses, of which he was particularly fond. After 1900, as his reputation grew, commissions became more numerous, not least to commemorate men and women who had achieved distinction in their lives. As a professional sculptor, Bayes was clearly prepared to complete his commissions expeditiously, and as a member of the Athenaeum, a Freemason and a

Brother of the Art Workers' Guild, he was well placed to establish good contacts with the people who mattered.

In 1902 Bayes was asked by colleagues of Dr David Yellowlees at Gartnavel Hospital, Glasgow, to execute a bronze, set in marble, to be erected in its chapel to mark Yellowlees' retirement the previous year. Another Scottish commission in the following year, from Glasgow University, was to commemorate the philosopher and Hellenist, Robert Adamson, who had died in 1902. Adamson was Professor of Logic and Rhetoric at Glasgow, and had previously been a professor at Owens College, Manchester, where he supported the admission of women students, and at Aberdeen. Bayes' portrait of the fifty-year old don with pince-nez and walrus moustache, looking old for his years, is a bronze relief with typical Arts and Crafts lettering and foliage. The dates inscribed are those of his professorship. Also in 1903 came a commission from English students of electricity to honour the memory of the Italian scientist who invented the electric battery, Count Alessandro Volta, 1745-1827. The 'discoverer of the Voltaic pile' was showered with medals and titles, and had been summoned to show his discoveries to Napoleon. This curious bronze relief, shaped like a shield with a heraldic lion but with no portrait, is dominated by the rather eccentric lettering

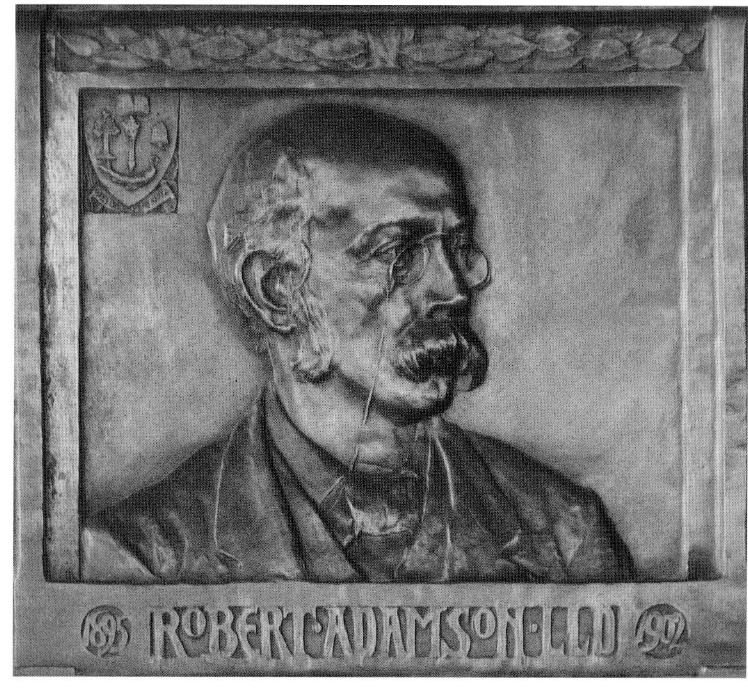

Robert Adamson, 1903.

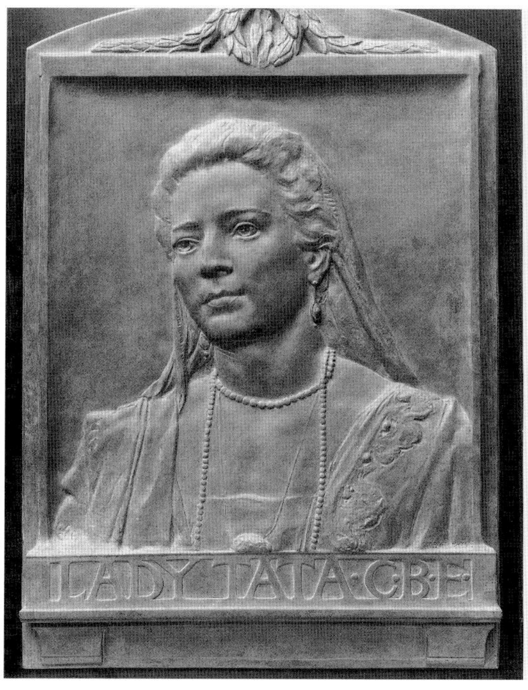

Lady Tata Memorial, 1911.

of the inscription. Lettering was not Bayes' strong point and in later years he was often assisted by his daughter Jean, who had trained in this field.

The distinguished philosopher Professor Henry Sidgwick, 1838-1900, was the subject of a much more elaborate relief of 1905. Sidgwick, a fellow of Trinity College, Cambridge, and something of a pioneer of feminism, started lectures for women at Cambridge in 1870 and founded Newnham College. (He was to marry its principal, Eleanor Balfour, 1845-1936, sister of Arthur Balfour, the Cambridge philosopher who became Prime Minister and 1st Earl Balfour). Bayes' treatment here is architectural: an Arts and Crafts bronze aedicule, surmounted by small female nude figures, encloses a silver relief panel, a lively portrait of Sidgwick shown in his gown, with, top right, a coat of arms.

On 26th June 1909, Bayes' father died. Alfred Walter Bayes, artist father of three artist children, Gilbert, Walter and Jessie, was a genre painter and etcher who had exhibited at the leading London venues, including the Royal Academy. In 1907 Gilbert Bayes executed his bust, unsentimentally, as a severe unsmiling man holding his palette and brushes. In 1909 the leading French actor, Benoit Constant Coquelin died, and Bayes was commissioned by a group of English actors to make a memorial for presentation to the Comédie-Française, the most venerable institution in the French theatre. Dating back to the days of Moliére, the theatre building itself, which adjoins the Palais-Royal near the Louvre, was built in 1787 by Victor Louis but, following a fire in 1900, had recently been rebuilt. Bayes was in eminent company: the foyer has busts by Rodin, Carpeaux, David d'Angers and Houdon. Benoit-Constant Coquelin, born in 1841, was the elder of two famous actor brothers, sons of a baker of Boulogne-sur-Mer in the Pas-de-Calais (where, opposite the theatre, is a statue of both of them by Auguste Maillard). The younger brother made an offer to Rodin – it was not accepted – to pose for one of the figures of *The Burghers of Calais*. Bayes' memorial was not a particularly happy solution. Eschewing his Arts and Crafts background, he provided, in black patinated bronze, a four foot high Greek Ionic temple as an aedicule to frame an allegorical relief of a classically robed female figure holding a wand and a wreath and flanked by masks representing Comedy and Tragedy. The whole composition seems archaic for 1909; it has now been removed and consigned to store far from Paris.

A far more satisfying result came with the two commissions for memorials erected in 1910 in the churchyard of St James, Warter in Yorkshire. The one is to Lord Nunburnholme, 1833-1907, of Warter Priory, commissioned by his wife, née Florence Wellesley and a great niece of the Iron Duke, the other to Gerald Valerian Wilson of Shillinglee Park, Surrey (burnt out during the Second World War), commissioned by his mother after his death in 1908.

Charles Henry Wilson, a Hull shipowner, JP, local Liberal MP and ardent freetrader, was created First Baron Nunburnholme in 1905. His peerage was short-lived, however, for he died two years later. His younger brother Arthur, 1836-1909, a partner in the family ship owning firm (which had the largest private fleet in the world at the time) and a generous benefactor to Hull, was host in 1890 at Tranby Croft, his home in Hull, to Edward VII, then Prince of Wales, when a guest was accused of cheating at baccarat; the libel suit resulting from this scandal caused great acrimony in those circles and the obloquy heaped upon Wilson probably hastened his death. It was also at Tranby Croft that the young Winston Churchill, a close friend of Muriel Wilson, a daughter of the house, practised pronouncing 's' properly by repeating the lines: 'the Spanish ships I cannot see, for they are not in sight'. Churchill was later a guest at the other Wilson family home, Warter Priory, very much a Liberal stronghold where, in company with several Liberal peers at a shooting party, he reported 'pheasants in thousands'. As Bayes did not move in upper class circles, one assumed the commissions came through Frampton, who executed three elaborate Wilson family monuments in marble, inside Warter Church, to Lord Nunburnholme, 1907, his unmarried son Gerald Valerian Wilson, 1908, and Mrs Wilson, 1905. The latter is a curious solecism since the wife of the Hon. Guy Wilson, one of Nunburnholme's seven children, was Lady Isabel Innes-Ker, a daughter of the 7th Duke of Roxburghshire and therefore Lady Isabel Wilson. She died at the age of twenty-six. Bayes, an admirer of Alfred Gilbert and one of the very small group at Gilbert's cremation in 1934, created life-size allegorical female figures, one with wings, for each of the two bronze memorials in the churchyard. The attendant cherub figures have unfortunately now disappeared. Set on stone plinths, the pieces were described by Nikolaus Pevsner as 'Gilbertian with a dash of Père Lachaise'.

Lord Nunburnholme's second daughter, Enid, married Edwyn Francis Scudamore-Stanhope, the 10th Earl of Chesterfield. They lived at 41 Grosvenor Square, London (previously her father's address), and at Beningborough in Yorkshire. The Earl was Master of the Horse and Lord Steward of the Royal Household. On his death in 1933 he was buried at Holme Lacey, Herefordshire, home of the Scudamores since the sixteenth century. Gilbert Bayes' highly detailed bronze memorial to the Earl of 1934, placed in the churchyard, is a mediaeval knight, standing erect, his right hand on the pommel of a great sword,

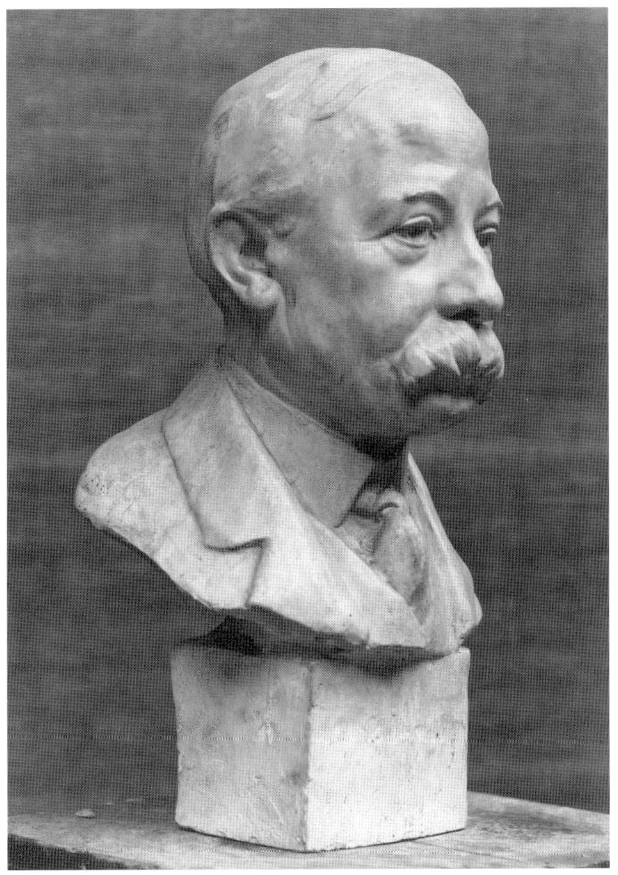

W.R. Lethaby, 1923.

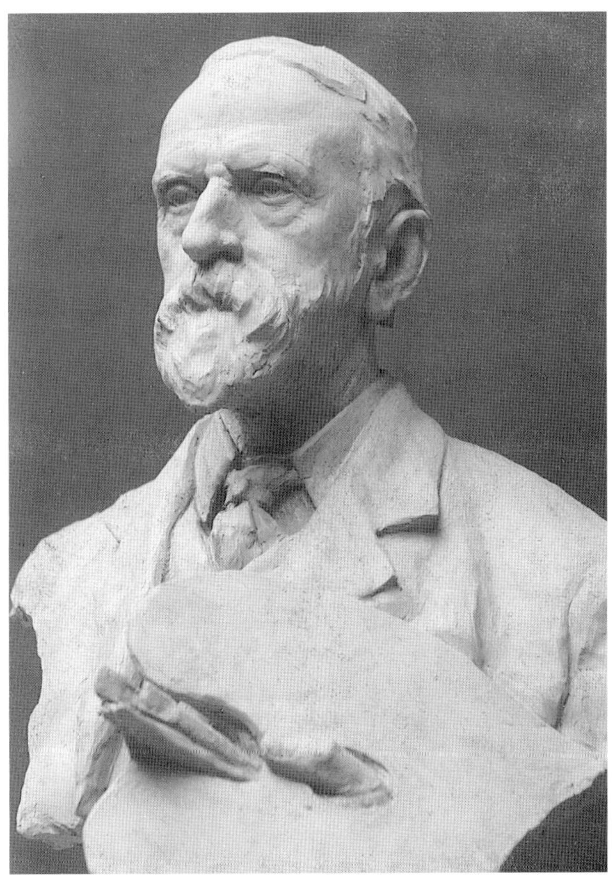

Alfred W. Bayes, 1907.

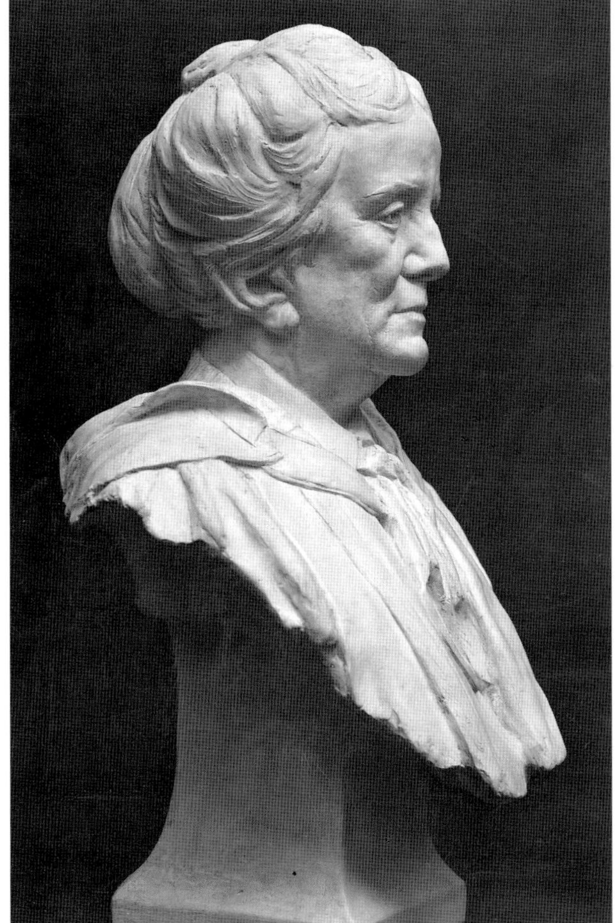

Dame Ethel Smyth, 1938.

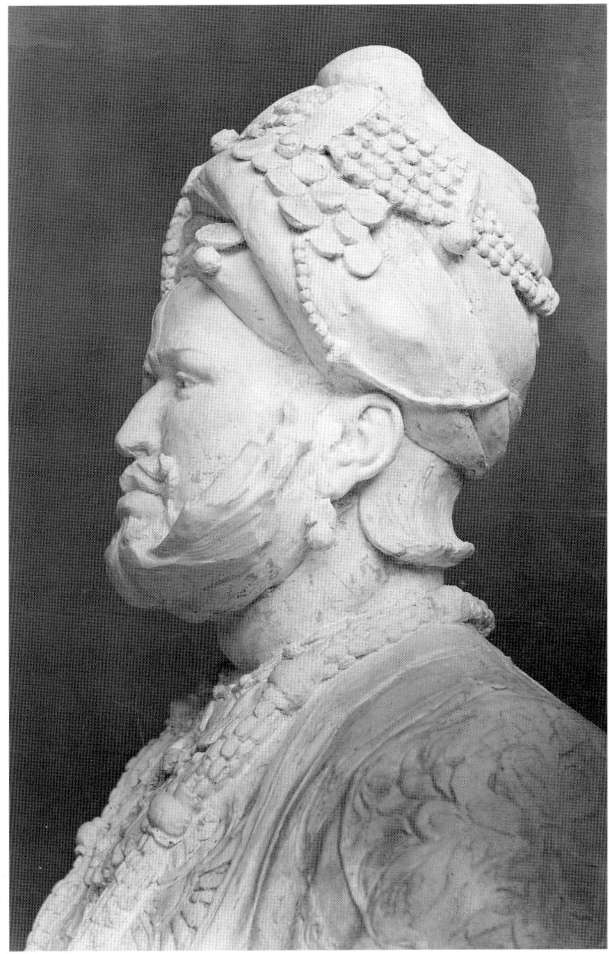

Detail of the Maharajah of Bikaner Memorial, 1913.

his left clutching a shield with the family quarterings, and a hound at his feet. In the same year Bayes produced a bronze equestrian statue of John Churchill, the 1st Duke of Marlborough, 1650-1722, son of an earlier Sir Winston Churchill, impoverished West Country Royalist. John Churchill's youthful affair with his voluptuous cousin, Barbara Villiers, Duchess of Cleveland, the manipulative mistress of Charles II, led to the acquisition of funds that provided the foundation of his considerable fortune and the launching of an extraordinary military and political career. (A.L. Rowse's *The Churchills* offers a fascinating account.) It included imprisonment in the Tower of London and exile, but culminated in his crushing victory over the French at Blenheim in 1704, a dukedom and a palace to rival Versailles.

The Indian merchant prince, Sir Ratanji Jamsetji Tata, born in 1871, knighted in 1916, was a member of the powerful Parsee family from Bombay who, through their cordial relationship with Imperial Britain – they built ships for the Royal Navy – pioneered heavy industry in India in the nineteenth century and built the vast Taj Mahal Hotel in 1903 on the waterfront in Bombay, still one of the world's great hotels. It was designed by an English architect, Chambers. Sir Ratan, as he is usually known, came to live in England in

1906. He settled at York House, Twickenham, a seventeenth-century mansion by the Thames that had formerly been occupied by the exiled family of the Comte de Paris, Pretender to the French throne. Bayes' bronze relief of Lady Tata (who had been awarded the CBE) shows her in western dress and is very simply framed with just a small wreath at the head.

Another Indian commission came in 1913, this time for one of the great Desert Kings, rulers since the fifteenth century of the much fought over domain of Bikaner in Rajputana. In fact the Maharajah of Bikaner's immense palace, Lallgarh, had been built only recently, at a time when Bikaner was emerging as one of the British rulers' favourite examples of a 'Native State'. Lallgarh, built outside the city walls, was designed by a British army officer, Sir Samuel Swinton Jacob, and was built on the profits of railways and coal-mines. Ganga Singh, who came to the throne in 1887 and assumed full ruling powers in 1898 when only eighteen years old, created the flamboyant Bikaner Camel Corps and fought with the British Army in China. He formed close links with the royal family, attending the coronations of Edward VII, George V and George VI. As honorary aide-de-camp to the Prince of Wales, he welcomed the future George V to his palace in 1905 for the famous Bikaner sand-grouse shoot. He served in the Great War and was one of the two Indian representatives at the 1919 Peace Conference, signing the Treaty of Versailles for his country. The much decorated maharajah, who devoted his busy life to public service, died in 1943.

It would appear that Bayes' commission was for Ganga Singh's father, the previous maharajah, Ratan Singh, who died in 1913. It is on a splendid scale: an over-life-size white marble statue of the magnificently robed Indian Prince who, having provided 200 camels to the British in 1842 to assist them in the Afghan war, started the relationship that brought Bikaner favour and political importance.

The Beaux-Arts trained Scottish architect, John Burnet, best known for the Edward VII Galleries of the British Museum completed in 1914, for which he gained his knighthood, commissioned Bayes, a fellow Brother of the Art Workers' Guild, to provide a sculpture for the main entrance to the Institute of Chemistry at 30 Russell Square, Bloomsbury. In the broken pediment of this rather conventional building by Burnet of 1914 (neo-Georgian in deference to the neighbourhood) Bayes sculpted a stone seated and reading figure of Joseph Priestley, 1733-1804, the scientist who identified oxygen. The original inscription has since been re-carved to read 'The Royal Institute of Chemistry'. Priestley was a controversial man in his time, with something of an international perspective. A Presbyterian minister,

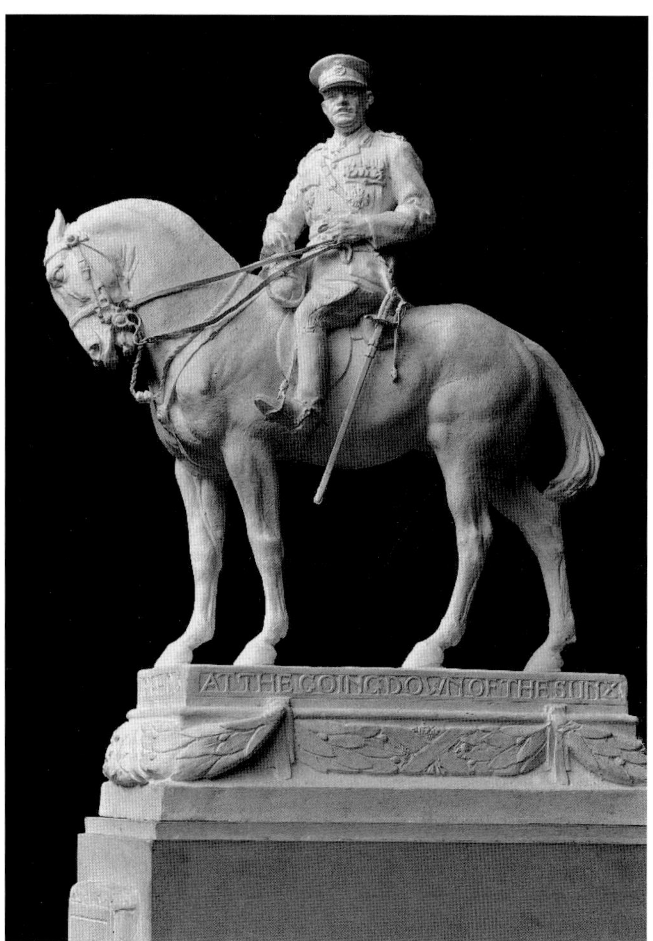

Haig Memorial, first version, 1933.

radical and Fellow of the Royal Society, he was also member of the St Petersburg Academy and the French Academy of Sciences, and had met Benjamin Franklin. His house was sacked in 1791 as a result of his support for the French Revolution and he emigrated three years later to America where he died.

At the end of the Great War, Bayes was commissioned by the Machine Gun training centre to provide a presentation bronze of Earl Brownlow, squire of Belton House, Lincolnshire. The Machine Gun Corps was raised at Belton and during the war its park became a small tented town with railway tracks and training grounds. Adelbert Wellington Brownlow Cust, owner of 58,000 acres, was the third and last Earl Brownlow. Known as 'Addy', he was a tall, handsome and charismatic figure who, with his beautiful wife Lady Adelaide, moved on the fringes of the Souls, the group of high-minded aristocratic aesthetes whose name is said to have been given at a Brownlow dinner party. Patron, collector and a trustee of the Tate, Addy spent much of his life in politics, serving in three Conservative administrations. The childless couple divided their time between their London house in Carlton House Terrace, the vast neo-gothic Ashridge park in Hertfordshire (which in those days had only two bathrooms) and the Brownlow family seat, Belton House, which, uncharacteristically for the period, they restored to its Caroline appearance. Addy had been painted by G.F. Watts and sculpted by Boehm in 1871 in a conventional pose standing by his horse, Queen Bess. For Bayes' Machine Corps memorial, the standing figure is shown in uniform, set on a base, archaically in Art Nouveau style, that depicts a machine-gun team, a crest and the inscription 'As a memento of many kindnesses'. It remains at Belton.

In the following year, Bayes executed two memorials to men eminent in the City and who both lived in Surrey. Sir Edward Hopkinson Holden, a Mancunian born in 1848, a barrister and Liberal MP, created a Baronet in 1909, became the Chairman of the London City and Midland Bank. With the style of this memorial, Bayes is still harking back. The bluff figure of Holden, arms folded, is set in an arched niche surmounted by his coat of arms and flanked by two small symbolic, cloaked females. Holden's near contemporary, Sir Walpole Lloyd Greenwell, born in 1847, died in 1919 leaving a widow, four sons and seven daughters. A Lieutenant of the City of London, JP and High Sheriff of Surrey, Greenwell had addresses in County Durham and Portman Square but since it features on his memorial his main residence seems to have been Marden Park, near Woldingham, Surrey, a house in a secluded valley, described by Pevsner as a ferocious Victorian (Tudor) house of 1880. An alabaster panel, with the inscription and low relief

figures of angels surrounding an oval bronze portrait of Greenwell, is set in a bronze frame with his coat of arms. Apart from the female angel's 1920s hairstyle, the memorial has the appearance of having been modelled twenty years earlier.

One of the founders, in 1884, of the Art Workers' Guild – formed 'to reverse the drifting apart of the arts' – of which Bayes was an active member and Master in 1925, was William Richard Lethaby, architect, designer and reformer, a key figure of the Arts and Crafts Movement and his church, All Saints at Brockhampton, one of its greatest monuments. Although his actual built output was limited, Lethaby's inspiration to a whole generation of architects, his writings and his influence as an educationalist, he helped found the Central School of Arts and Crafts, was widespread. Lethaby was Master of the Guild in 1911 (he designed the Master's chair) but Bayes did not execute his portraits until 1923 – a bronze relief plaque in the RIBA and a bust in the Art Workers' Guild.

The Master of the Guild in 1923 was F.W. Troup, whose smiling bronze bust was executed by Bayes that year and which he used to illustrate *Modelling for Sculpture*, his book for the beginner. Francis William Troup, born in Aberdeen in 1874, was a proficient but not particularly outstanding architect with a practice

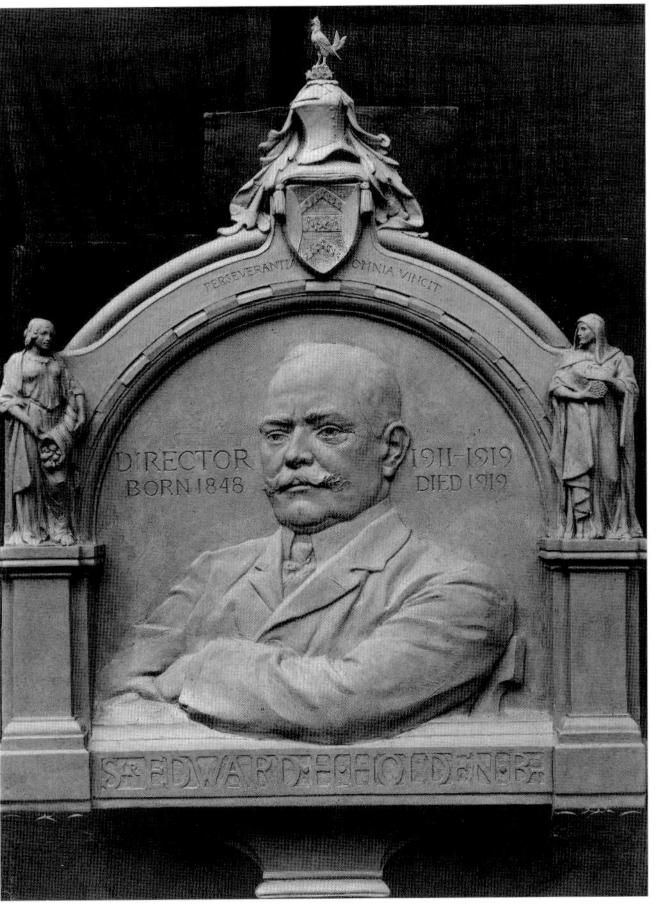

Sir Edward Holden, 1919.

in London and a particular interest in ornamental leadwork in building. Described by Goodhart-Rendel as 'Art and Crafts *in excelsis*, an extreme Lethabite', Troup designed the Guild's Hall in Queen Square which, though war-damaged in 1914 soon after its construction, is still used by the Guild today. Troup died in 1941.

A much decorated soldier of the Great War, Lt Col Percy Robert Laurie, CBE, DSO, Croix de Guerre, mentioned in dispatches six times, left the Royal Scots Greys to join the mounted Branch of the Metropolitan Police. Bayes modelled a small equestrian statue of Laurie in his role as its chief. Later as Brigadier, Lord Lieutenant of the City of London and knighted (in 1933), the hunting, shooting and polo-playing Laurie became Provost Marshal of the United Kingdom in 1942. He died in 1962 at the age of eighty-two.

Another Great War hero sculpted by Bayes, but this time a national figure, was Field Marshal Douglas Haig. Bayes modelled two versions of an equestrian statue whose title 'At the going down of the sun', was taken from Laurence Binyon's famous poem *For the Fallen*, written in response to British losses in Flanders and now the official expression of mourning for the Great War dead. Each shows Haig mounted on his horse, *Miss Ypres*, but the man is in different dress and the horse in differing stances. The statues are set on tall classical plinths, each with a frieze depicting the cavalry, a panel destined for an inscription, and a trio of wreaths at the base. Paul Landowski created a similar statue for Montreuil-sur-Mer in Northern France but the pose more relaxed and the horse slim-necked and modern compared with Bayes' which seems to derive from the antique.

Haig, the 29th Laird of Berneyside, Roxburghshire, was born in 1861. Gazetted to the 7th Hussars in 1885, he served in the Sudan and South Africa under Major-General French and under Kitchener in India before becoming an important figure in the Great War. His leadership at the Battle of Mons, the first Battle of Ypres and the attack on Neuve Chapelle, which marked a new epoch in the war, led him to succeed French as commander-in-chief. He was a courageous, inspirational general, and his victory gave him an earldom, the viscountcy of Dawick, £100,000 voted by Parliament, and public gratitude – albeit with carping at the number of men lost in the field. Despite his differences with Lloyd George, the premier acknowledged in his war memoirs: 'there was no conspicuous officer in the Army who seemed to be better qualified for the Highest Command than Haig ... for so overwhelming a position as the command of a force five times as great as the largest army every commanded by Napoleon ...' Haig, the cavalry officer who wrote *Cavalry Studies* in 1907 and rose to the top

at a time when tanks superseded horses, died in 1928. It is surprising that is was not until 1937, nineteen years after the war and seven years after the erection of the equestrian statue of Foch facing Victoria Station that a public statue to Haig was unveiled. Alfred Hardiman's very stylised statue, erected in Whitehall in 1937, opposite the Banqueting Hall, caused quite a furore. Haig is hatless, despite wearing uniform, and the cavalry opined that no horse could synchronise its legs as this one did.

Horse and rider are also the central feature of a presentation plaque to the great shopkeeper Gordon Selfridge, commissioned by his staff in 1930, the twenty-first birthday of his store. Selfridge's proved to be a fruitful client of Bayes during the 1930s. Harry Gordon Selfridge, born in Wisconsin in 1858, a bank clerk at fourteen and a partner of Marshall, Field of Chicago in 1890, retired in 1904 with a fortune of £300,000. Bored with travelling and growing orchids, he came to London in 1906 to spy out the opportunities. He wasted no time: his gigantic department store in Oxford Street opened just three years later and London had never seen anything like it. His emporium of splendid Edwardian vulgarity was designed by Robert Atkinson in collaboration with Daniel Burnham of Chicago but apparently the mammoth columns came from a sketch presented to Selfridge by Francis Swales. Employing 5,000 staff over some fifteen acres of floor space, this was a store designed to compete with both its long-established rivals, such as Harrods, and newcomers. The bronze presentation plaque set in the floor at the store is an octagon twisted on a rectangle with symbolic motifs but let down by its lettering. Bayes also designed the *Queen of Time* clock on the facade the following year, and Coronation decorations in 1937, both subjects discussed elsewhere. In 1939, not long after being naturalized, Gordon Selfridge, heavily in debt to the company because of personal overspending, tactfully retired – or was so persuaded – with the honorary title of president. Bayes produced a splendid bronze plaque to celebrate 'A great merchant', as the inscription has it. The image of Selfridge, based on Orpen's portrait, shows him in profile holding some plans. Below is one of Bayes' characteristic low relief friezes of figures, predictably with a horse at its centre. Selfridge died at his home on Putney Heath in 1947.

Another department store provided Bayes with a commission, but this time to commemorate its architect, Maurice Webb. Bentalls, the well-known store in the county town of Surrey, still in the charge of the family, had its origins as a haberdashery, founded in 1867 by Frank Bentall from East Anglia. His eldest son, Leonard Bentall transformed the town centre of Kingston in the 1930s by building a huge

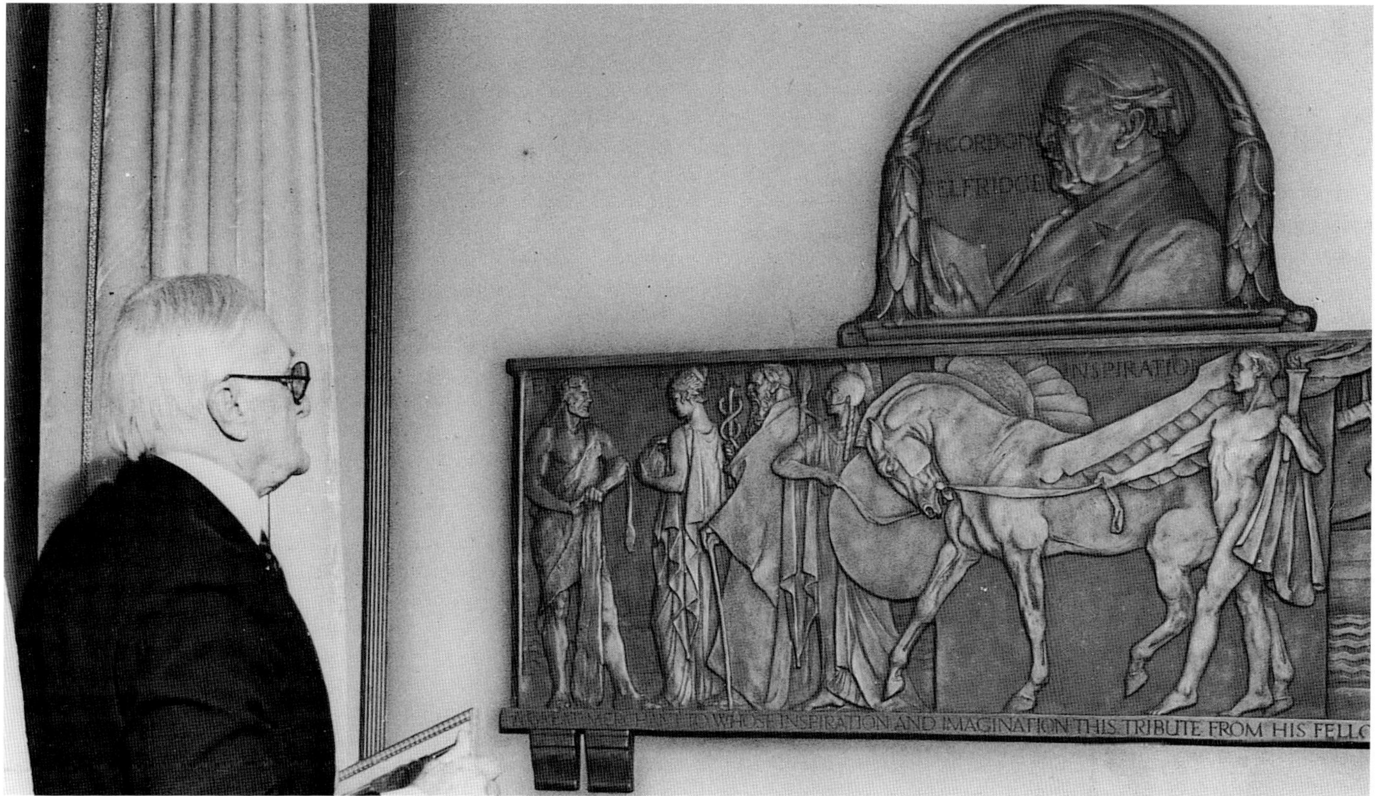

Above, Gordon Selfridge at the unveiling of the Selfridge panel, 1940. Below, design by Bayes for the Selfridge panel. Right, illuminated scroll by Jessie Bayes, presented to Gordon Selfridge at the unveiling of the panel (Selfridge's Archives).

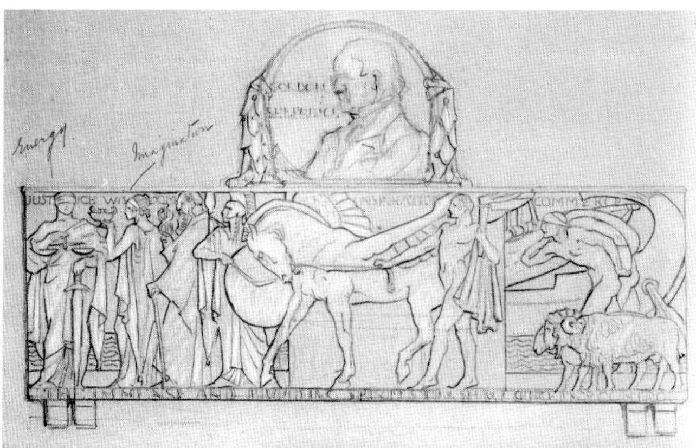

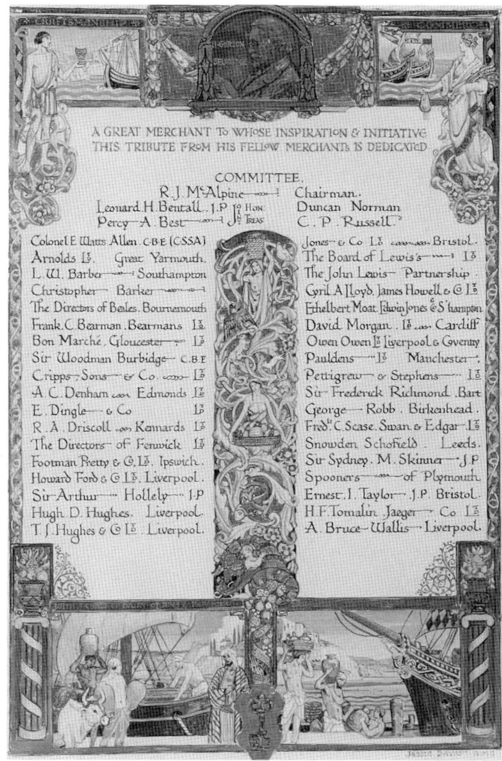

department store in the so-called Hampton Court Wrenaissance style, accompanied by a large garage and depository. The store opened in 1935 with the adornment of reliefs and the Bentall coat of arms on the facade by Eric Gill. All these buildings were designed by Maurice Webb, the eldest son and partner of Sir Aston Webb which in its heyday was the largest architectural practice in Britain and, after Sir Aston's death in 1930 also its principal. Born in 1880, Maurice fought in the Great War, gaining the DSO and MC. President of the Architectural Association and Vice President of the RIBA, he died in 1939. Leonard Bentall paid due tribute by commissioning Bayes to execute a large memorial, which was set into an archway at the store. In the late 1980s the store was rebuilt behind Webb's facade and Bayes' memorial has been removed to store.

Ralph Knott is not a well-known architect, but his County Hall in London is one of the most successful and proud public buildings of the Imperial era and has been described as the crowning monument of the golden age of local government. Against all the great guns, Knott won the competition in 1908 when still an assistant architect in the office of Sir Aston Webb, who was one of the assessors which caused controversy and led to the rules being changed. Born in 1879, Knott died young, in 1929, before his magnum opus was completed. Bayes did the model for the bronze lions' heads on the Embankment wall of County Hall for Knott, and after his death produced a bronze commemorative portrait plaque of him, shown in profile, which was set up at the former Members' entrance at County Hall.

One of Bayes' most diverting sitters, although he was not much interested in music, was the formidable Dame Ethel Smyth, the leading female composer of her time. A fearful snob and a lesbian, though she once loved a man, Harry Brewster, a rich and scholarly American, she fell in love with Virginia Woolf in 1930 and two years later, Lady Ottoline Morrell. By then Dame Ethel was increasingly deaf and composing little music, devoting her energies to writing an entertaining series of racy memoirs. But Ethel Smyth was the first woman to compose in the largest musical forms, opera, oratorio and concerto. Born in 1858 at Sidcup, the daughter of General Smyth who fought in the Indian Mutiny, she decided on a career in music at the age of twelve, much against her father's wishes. The rebellious young woman finally got her way and spent her formative years in Germany as a pupil of Brahms and a student at the Leipzig Conservatory. Her *Mass in D* was performed at the Albert Hall in 1893 but her most successful work was an opera, 1916, *The Wreckers*. A militant Suffragette, when marching in 1912, she composed *The March of the Women* which became the anthem for the movement. During a spell in Holloway Prison she was remembered for conducting with a toothbrush from the window of her cell. Despite this she was made Dame in 1922. That old gossip Jacques-Emile Blanche recalled a party in the drawing room at 30 Old Burlington Street, home of Ethel's sister Mary Hunter. Thomas Beecham conducted one of Ethel's compositions and the audience included a bevy of 'professional beauties, Lady Helen Vincent, the Duchesses of Portland, Sutherland, Rutland, and her daughters, Lady Marjorie, Lady Lettie, Lady Diana, and the Countess of Warwick – Rodin's idols – and Sargent'. Mrs Hunter was an ambitious hostess who brought together high society, artists and writers, George Moore, Henry James, Helleu, Sickert. She bought an important Elizabethan house, Hill Hall, near Epping in 1923 for weekend house parties, pulling it apart and creating what Blanche called a 'baroque museum... with furniture of every imaginable style and oddities which she picked up on her travels in Spain, Italy and Normandy'. She told Ethel, 'I consider it my sacred duty to spend every penny I can of Charlie's money'. Her husband, Charles Hunter, owned a coal mine in Durham and she duly impoverished the poor fellow.

Dame Ethel was a vigorous eighty-year-old woman when she sat for her bust. Judging by contemporary photographs, it is a striking likeness and Bayes has done admirable justice to this spirited, eccentric Englishwoman. She died in 1944 at her home in Woking.

With the outbreak of the Second World War Bayes' commissions inevitably decreased. A young Welsh Guards army officer, Captain Glyn David Rhys-Williams, son of Sir Rhys Rhys-Williams, the first baronet and an MP, of Miskin, Glamorganshire, was presented by friends with a statuette of him in uniform by Bayes for his twenty-first birthday, 1st November 1942. Only a few months later he was killed in action in North Africa, mentioned in dispatches. A sad commission came in the wake of the celebration, and Bayes prepared a design for a stained glass window in memory of the young soldier, to be placed in Miskin Church and followed by other memorials of the Rhys-Williams family.

In the dark days of the war in 1943, Bayes created a light-hearted portrait of his daughter, Jean, jokingly entitled the 'Sultana' of Champough.' Jean washed her hair and wrapped her head in a towel and her father transformed her into a young Indian princess.

After the Second World War Bayes, now an elderly sculptor whose prodigious output spanned several momentous decades of modern history, might be thought to have been due a quiet retirement, but the commissions continued right up to his death in 1953. A sculptor named Leonard Merrifield was given the commission in 1939 for a statue of Herbert Asquith, created 1st Earl of Oxford and Asquith in 1925, the barrister who became Liberal Prime Minister 1908-1916. Merrifield died before finishing it, and Bayes took over the job, completing it in 1948. The statue can now be found in the Commons Lobby of the Houses of Parliament, in a modern Gothic setting.

Bayes' last major memorial, commissioned by Co-operative societies and completed after his death by W.C.H. King, was to Robert Owen at Newtown, Montgomeryshire. Owen, the pioneer Welsh social reformer, 1771-1858, founded the New Lanark model community and promoted many communistic ideas well before Marx. He instituted the world's first day nursery, created evening classes and initiated a Co-operative movement.

Aristocrats and philosophers, dons and war heroes, city men and merchant adventurers, Indian kings and mercantile princes, worthy professional men and energetic radicals or other mortals who deserved poignant memorials, Gilbert Bayes took them all in his stride in his long career and gave of his best.

BAYES IN THE 1920s AND THE 1930s
Peyton Skipwith

The 1920s was one of the most turbulent and stimulating decades in the whole history of sculptural development in Britain. The years up to the outbreak of the First World War were dominated by the major figures, born in the 1850s and 1860s, of what Sir Edmund Gosse had christened the New Sculpture Movement: Alfred Gilbert George Frampton, Hamo Thornycroft, Derwent Wood, F.W. Pomeroy and others – although by 1910 younger sculptors such as Bayes, Eric Gill and Jacob Epstein were beginning to make their mark. Then in 1914 the practice of sculpture, like that of architecture, virtually ceased, with a few rare exceptions. Eric Gill, for instance, was excused military service because his work at Westminster Cathedral was deemed of national importance. Able-bodied sculptors volunteered for the armed forces, their elders lost essential studio assistants, and the supply of bronze was diverted to the war effort. This hiatus lasted, in effect, until 1919 when, prompted by the patriotic demand for war memorials, there was suddenly the most frenetic outpouring of sculptural energy that the country had ever witnessed. However, it was not just this new and urgent demand for memorials that made the ensuing decade so frantic; it was the unique circumstances created by the advent of a period of unprecedented activity following immediately upon a prolonged famine. Thus, during the 1920s, four generations of sculptors were in effect competing to establish, or to re-establish, their reputations and take the moral and aesthetic high ground.

Many of the pre-war sculptors from the New Sculpture generation were still alive and eager to rebuild their interrupted careers, Alfred Gilbert, Hamo Thornycroft, George Frampton and Derwent Wood among them. The same was true of sculptors such as Bayes, Gill and Epstein, born in the seventies and eighties of the previous century. Then there was the generation of young Turks such as Gilbert Ledward, Charles Sargeant Jagger and Harold Brownsword, now in their early thirties, who after prolonged training had been unable to start their professional careers because of the outbreak of war. As if this was not sufficient, a number of the students now entering art schools, like the young Henry Moore, were not the callow youths of former times, but battle-hardened young men, with little time or respect for their elders who had led the country into one of the bloodiest wars of all time. These students, men and women, were angry and in a hurry, they wished to sweep away the old order and, to paraphrase the title of Paul Nash's great First War Painting, wanted to make a 'new world'. Something of these tensions can be seen at London's Hyde Park Corner with the dichotomy between Derwent Wood's Machine Gunners' Memorial and Jagger's Artillery Memorial. The former is an epicene, if classical, naked youth holding a down-pointed sword, in the continuing sculptural tradition that had already extended from Michaelangelo's *David* to Leighton's *Sluggard*, whilst the latter has uncompromisingly naturalistic figures of Tommies straight from the trenches, including one lying dead, covered by his cape and with his helmet placed reverently upon his chest, set against a monumental stone howitzer.

In the natural course of evolution, sculptors of the Bayes, Gill, Reid Dick, Epstein generation would, during the years following 1910, have fully established their right to be regarded as the outstanding figures of their time, but now everything was thrown back into the melting pot. For a very few years, before the Modern Movement became dominant, there appeared to be a reasonably even pitch, and this competition between the generations brought out the best in many sculptors. Alfred Gilbert's *Queen Alexandra Memorial* from 1932, his first public monument in London since *Eros*, 1890-93, quickly became one of the best-loved art nouveau sculptures in the capital, while Frampton's slightly earlier *Edith Cavell* of 1920, which showed an awareness of the changing aesthetic, became one of the most abused. Epstein built upon the reputation he had established before the war as the sculptor the public most loved to hate and *Rima*, his memorial to W.H. Hudson, became a prime focus for anti-semitic attacks. Gill and Epstein both contributed to Charles Holden's London Underground headquarters building of 1928 at St James's Park, one of the icon buildings of the period and the first to feature sculpture by Henry Moore, and Gill followed this up with his great carvings on Broadcasting House in 1932. Bayes thrived in this vitally creative atmosphere and produced many of his finest works during these inter-war years. In his great equestrian figures, *War* and *Peace*, commissioned to flank the entrance to the Art Gallery of New South Wales, he built on his earlier interest in Norse legends and sagas, but now he was able to create enduring and timeless symbols, stripped of their literary allusions. However, it was in his architectural work and in the

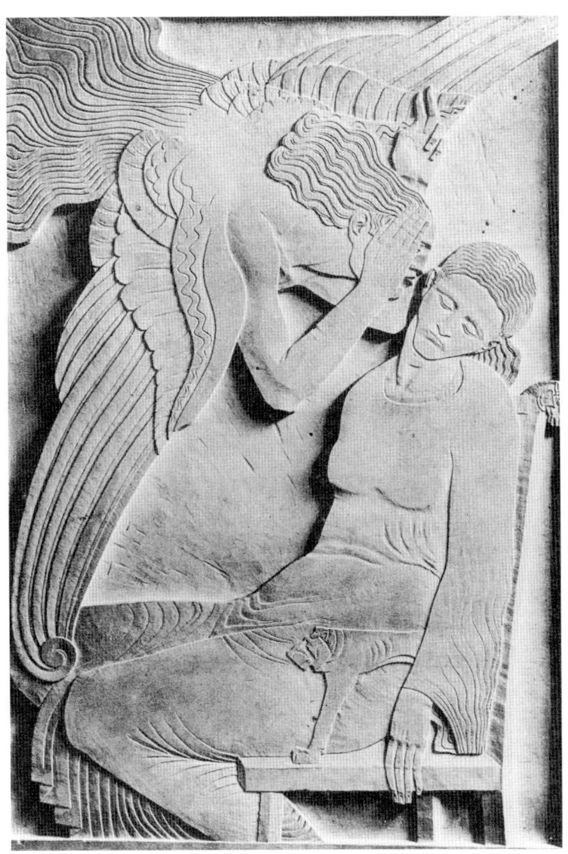

Annunciation panel by Mestrovic, c.1912.

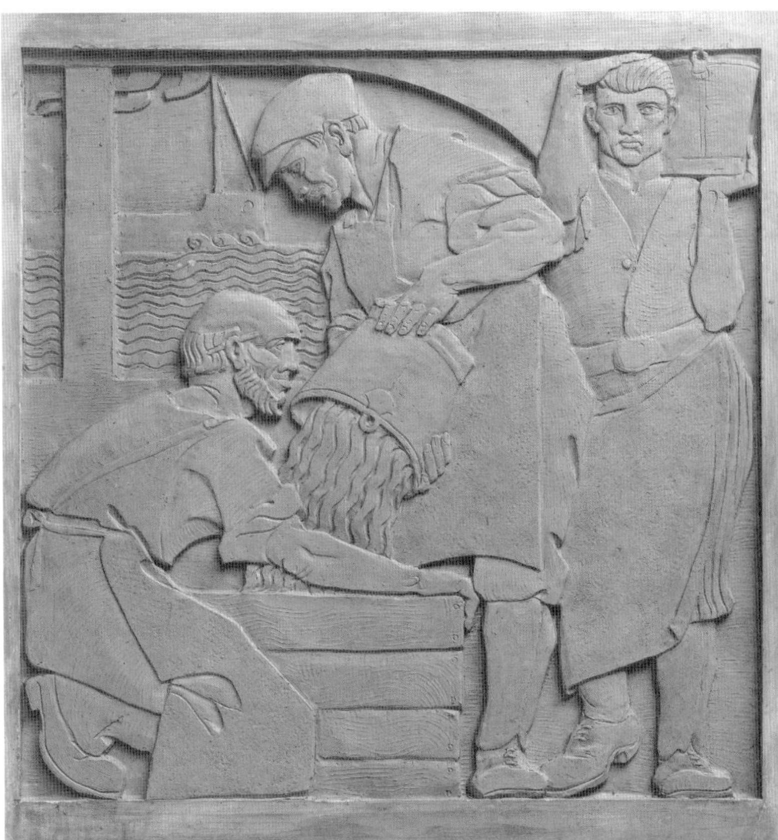

Filling moulds, for the Concrete Utilities Bureau, 1924.

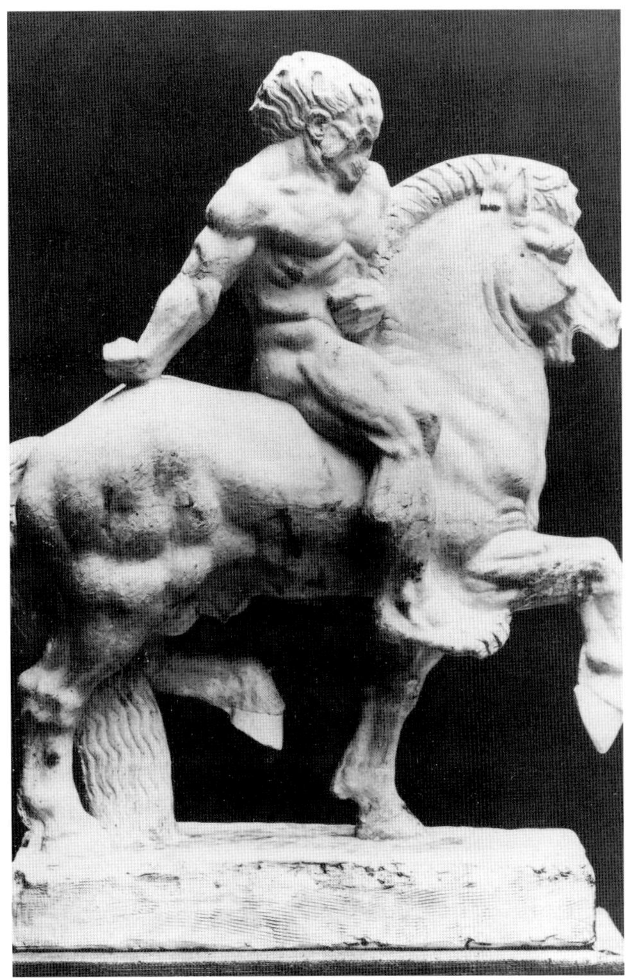

Mestrovic, study for Marko, c.1910.

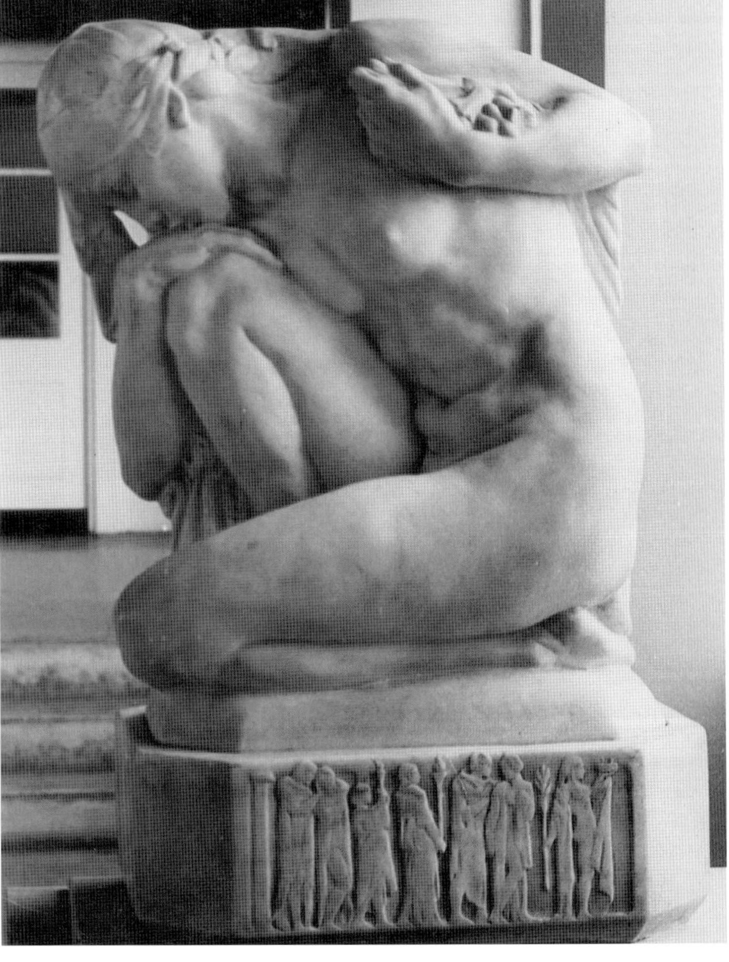

The Unfolding of Spring, 1923.

development of double-sided reliefs such as *The Lure of the Pipes* and *Water's Caress* that he made his most distinctive contribution.

This new-found freedom probably resulted from Bayes' growing familiarity with the work of the great Serbian sculptor, Ivan Mestrovic, which first impinged on North European sensibilities at the 1911 Rome International Exhibition. Bayes exhibited *Sigurd* and the *Greek Dancer* at this exhibition and may well have visited Rome and seen the Serb's work at first hand. However, even if he did not, he could not have failed to register the impact that it made on other artists, including John Lavery, who wrote in an introduction to a monograph on Mestrovic edited by M. Curcin: 'I well remember the day, in Rome, when I saw his work for the first time... The day was hot and I was very tired. When I came to the Serbian Pavilion, devoted almost entirely to the work of Mestrovic, all the tiredness disappeared and I felt in the presence of a great spirit – a terrible spirit! The Serbian hero, Marko Kraljevic, was there on horseback.' James Bone, in his article in the same monograph, informs us that 'Marko is the Serbian Siegfried, with the stature of a giant and the soul of a child, who, mounted on his white horse, slays monsters, delivers maidens, and drinks deep of the wine of life and joy.' Given this shared preoccupation with heroic, historic and mythological characters, even if Bayes failed to get to Rome, he certainly did not miss the major exhibition of Mestrovic's work at the Victoria & Albert Museum in 1915. His admiration for the Serbian artist's work is born out by the fact that among his surviving archive is a postcard album marked 'Mestrovic', which also includes a newspaper clipping about The Fine Art Society's 1924 Mestrovic exhibition. Bone, in addition to acknowledging the power of individual pieces, put his finger firmly on its most important ingredient when he stated that 'What was most disturbing was its freedom from realism and from the Renaissance tradition...' In the post-war world of the twenties, when the more extreme iconoclasts of the Modern Movement were preparing to jettison not only every last vestige of the 'Renaissance tradition' but tradition in general, the revelation of Mestrovic's work, with its insights into an alternative tradition, was like a strong draught of oxygen.

Bayes, who was already seeking to move on from his New Sculpture beginnings was, by instinct and training, a modeller. He was dismissive of the arguments propounded by Gill and others in favour of direct carving and of their holier-than-thou attitude, claiming a unique virtue because no hand but the craftsman's had touched the stone. He saw no point in wasting his own time and energy when skilled masons could be employed at a shilling an hour to do all the basic work. Whether working in relief or in the round,

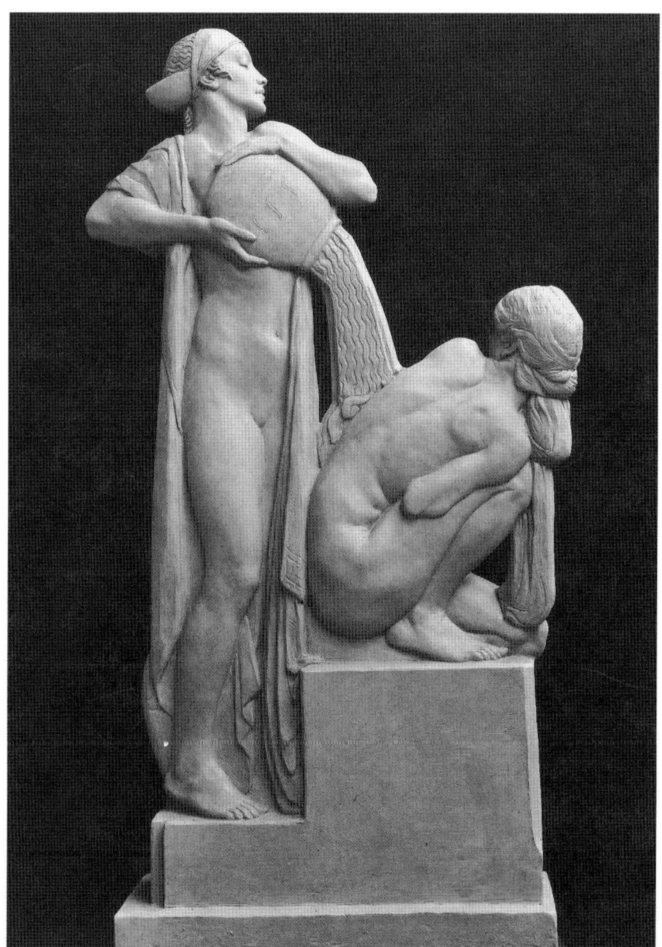

The Water's Caress, 1934.

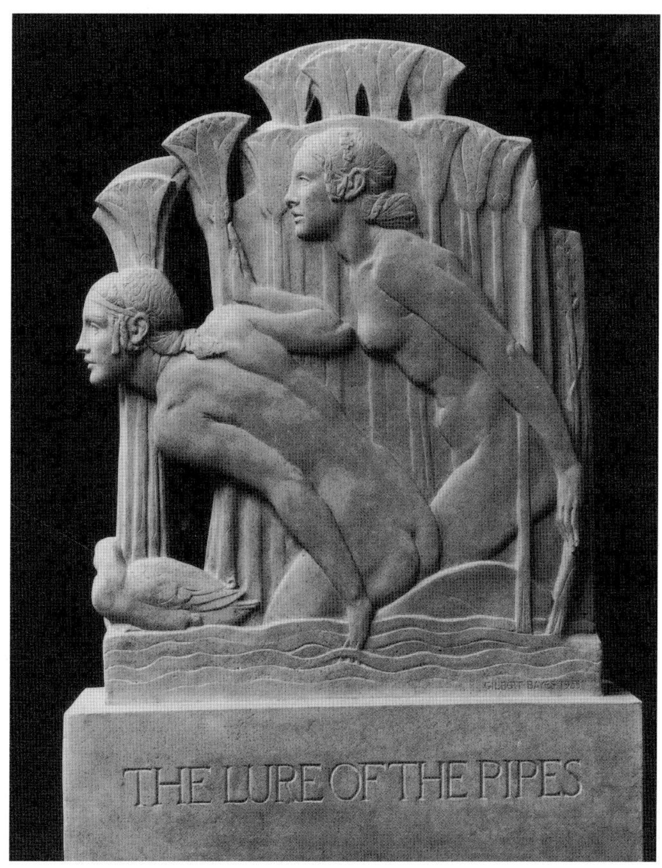

The Lure of the Pipes of Pan, 1932.

he liked to model in clay and then have his model cast in plaster, and it was from this model that the carving was done. He set out his attitude quite clearly in the Foreword to *Modelling for Sculpture*: 'It has been said by some that sculpture is carving and that it should be nothing but direct carving, that is, direct onto the stone or marble without a preliminary model in wax or clay. In warmer climates, where marble is natural to the soil, and in earlier times, when the style of work was primitive and simple in outlook, something might be said for this view, but today in England, when ideas are changing so constantly, we should be seriously handicapping ourselves if we did not make use of all media that come to hand, many of them so much more suitable climatically to this country than marble. Again, the making of preliminary models is almost a necessity with us with so many styles in vogue and where the outlook tends to become increasingly complicated owing to the more realistic viewpoint of people in general.' He then goes on to divide modelling into 'work in the round' and 'work in relief'; the latter he subdivides again into 'alto-relievo' and 'basso-relievo' – high and low relief.

Relief modelling, with its potential for use in the form of architectural friezes, was near to his heart, and he rejoiced in its richness and variety. Later in *Modelling for Sculpture* he details the historic precedents: 'the incised, so often used by the Egyptians, the bold though severe Assyrian, the freer Greek ranging from the early archaic through the metope friezes, the wingless Victory, the Renaissance work including the subtle reliefs of Desiderio da Settignano, Donatello, and the school of their time, and the bolder work of the Della Robbias, so suitable for glazed ware, in which it was so frequently carried out. Add to these the lessons to be learnt from the deep pierced reliefs of China and Japan and the deep incised work of India, Java and Ceylon and you have a store to meet almost any requirement.'

Although he does not say so, the media more suitable to the British climate, to which he refers in this foreword are, almost certainly, the burgeoning variety of artificial stones – variations on types of concrete – which were playing an increasingly important part in post-war building construction, and hence in architectural sculpture. T.P. Bennett, who was to become both a friend and patron, in his book *Architectural Design in Concrete*, comments on the prevalence of pre-cast blocks, usually described as artificial stone, and notes: 'Concrete blocks of this description have important points of construction which are capable of considerable use in designing, thus mouldings can be produced with practically no increase in cost over that of plain work, suggesting that considerable richness may be a characteristic of the material, while in the hands of a skillful sculptor

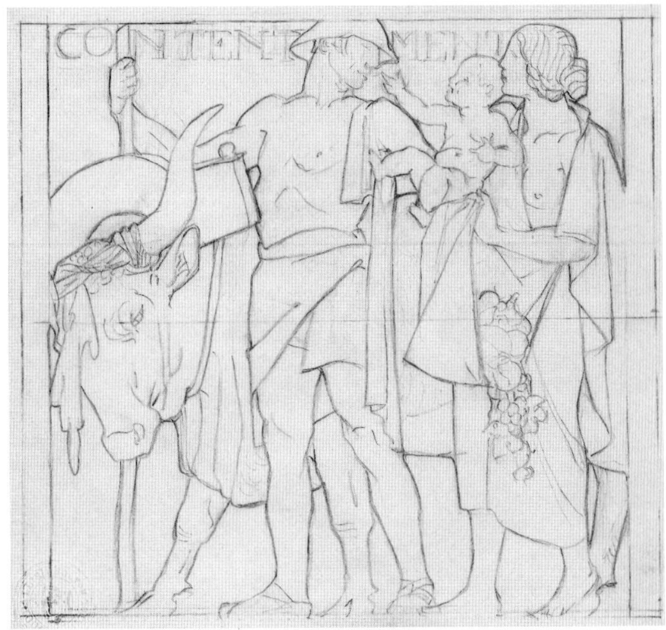

Drawing by Bayes for a Royal Bank of Scotland panel, 1935.

the concrete can be carved before it is set, so that the finest and richest modelling may be introduced into it with one-tenth of the effort which is necessary to produce the same effect in stone. One or two modern artists in England have indicated the extreme value of work of this kind, notable amongst them being Mr Gilbert Bayes, Mrs Phoebe Stabler and Mr Doyle Jones.' Bennett's book was published in 1927, and it was probably Bayes' reliefs for Clough Williams Ellis' Concrete Utilities building at the Wembley Exhibition that he particularly had in mind.

Whilst Bayes clearly responded to these new materials, and was able to exploit their potential, his working method remained consistent. He worked in clay, which he then had cast in plaster. If the model was for a sculpture in the round intended to be carried out in marble, such as *The Unfolding of Spring*, a mason would then do the bulk of the work translating the clay model into marble and, in the case of *The Unfolding of Spring*, leaving Bayes with about three weeks work completing the finished figure. He did exactly the same for his bronzes, whether small table-top pieces such as *Diana*, or life-size figures like *The Guardian of the Seas*, but in these cases, after any necessary refinement of the plaster, it went off to the foundry for casting. Equally with the figures or reliefs in artificial stone or ceramic, the clay model was cast and recast as necessary, and he would often have an additional set of plasters cast for exhibition purposes. During the 1920s and 30s he showed a number of these plaster relief panels at the Royal Academy, including portions of the friezes for the Masonic Temple, Birmingham in 1928, the Saville Theatre in 1930 and 1931, the Commercial Bank of Scotland in 1935 and 1936, and Doulton House in 1939, as well as

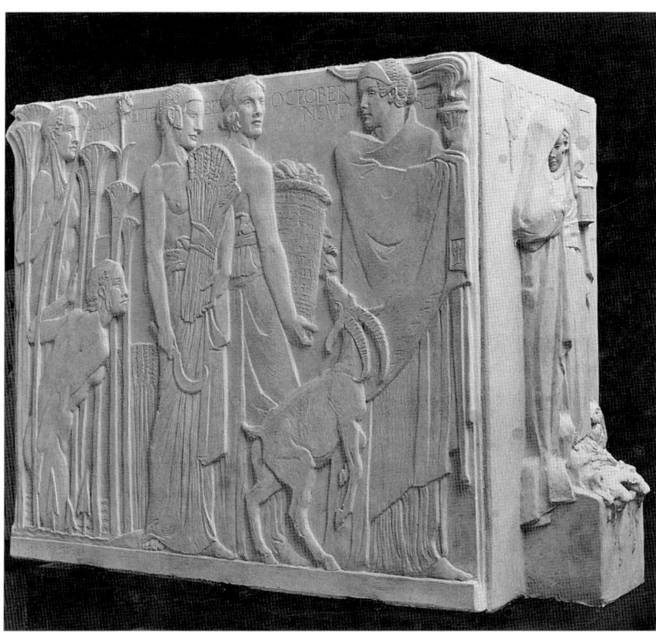

The complete Fountain of the Months in plaster, 1937.

those for the splendid *Fountain of the Months* of 1937. Although he preferred to carry out as much of the work as possible in the initial clay, Bayes could work on these sculptures at every stage. There is clear evidence of chiselling and refining on the extant plasters and, in the case of the plaster for the Doulton frieze it has been coloured in addition to any other work. Equally, with the artificial stone pieces he could work on the final casting before the concrete was completely set. There is a clear distinction in the groups of works he exhibited between those finished, free-standing, sculptures in marble or bronze that were for sale, and the plasters, virtuoso displays of work in progress, which were clearly intended to attract further commissions.

One small group of work in artificial stone as well as in bronze stands out, not only because of its quality, but also for its distinctiveness. It is never possible to claim any particular use of the sculptural language as being unique to one person, but Bayes developed and refined the double-sided relief in such a way that these pieces have an individual quality that makes them immediately identifiable as his work: *England, The Guardian of the Seas, The Segrave Trophy, The Lure of the Pipes of Pan* and *The Water's Caress*. They rank alongside the architectural friezes as the finest productions of the second half of his career. Eric Gill, whose polemical approach to craftsmanship so irritated Bayes, also produced a few double-sided reliefs, such as the magical, biscuit-thin, *The Bath* of 1920, but these were small-scale works, whereas Bayes in *The Water's Caress* in Empire Stone and the bronze of *The Guardian of the Seas* was creating works six and eight feet high, pitched more to the architectural client than the private collector. *The Guardian of the*

Seas found a permanent home in the Royal Automobile Club and its imagery, already explored in the smaller-scale statuette, *England*, led on directly to the *Segrave Trophy*, also housed at the Club. *The Water's Caress*, despite its stylishness, failed to find a buyer, but Bayes was more successful with the somewhat smaller, but equally stylish, double-sided relief, *The Lure of the Pipes of Pan*, one cast of which went to Birmingham City Art Gallery. In *The Guardian of the Seas* and its related images, Bayes combined the qualities of relief modelling with the pointed sleekness of a ship's prow, giving a sense of energy and forward thrust to an otherwise static, and statuesque, figure, particularly appropriate for its adaptation for the *Segrave Trophy*.

Excited as he may have been by the potential of new materials and his close affinity to the 1920s Conservative Modernist aesthetic prefigured by the work of Ivan Mestrovic, Bayes, along with many of his contemporaries was alienated by the intolerance of the younger generation who were committed to the blinkered, if Utopian, ideals of the Modern Movement. One protagonist of the Modern Movement, the Australian, John Power, described tolerance as 'the worst of the deadly sins', and this attitude, regrettably, created a counter-intolerance. The open antagonism between the two camps, and the growing feeling that tradition was dead, combined with the horrors and deprivations of yet another world war, led to Bayes' complete disillusionment with the world in general and sculpture in particular. Despite having exhibited at the Royal Academy every year, without exception, from 1889 to 1944, during the final years of his life he exhibited only two works, a medal for the Order of St John of Jerusalem and a head of his grandson Martin. During these last years his depression, exacerbated by his wife's illness, and the general gloom resulting from rationing and high taxation, caused Bayes to destroy a great deal of his work. Plasters were smashed, drawings were torn up and note-books burnt in a final sad act of retreat from a world with which he no longer felt in sympathy.

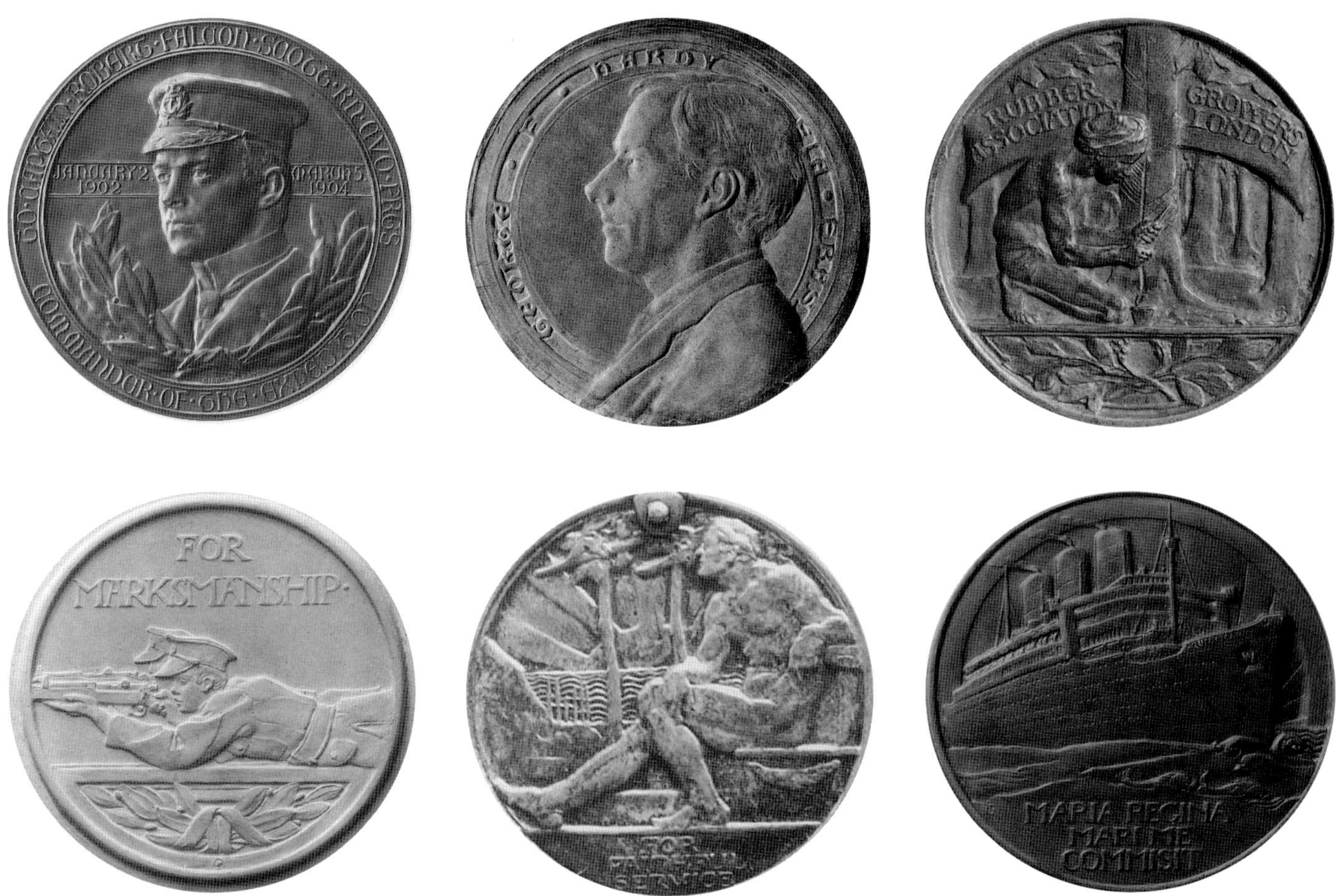

*Top row, left to right, Scott Antarctic Medal, 1904, Sir George Hardy Medallion, 1909, Rubber Growers Medal, 1910;
bottom row, left to right, Country Life Marksmanship Medal, 1912, Imperial Service Medal, 1919, Queen Mary Medal, 1935.*

BAYES AND THE MEDAL
Philip Attwood

Gilbert Bayes exhibited one or more (usually more) sculptures at the Royal Academy virtually every year for over half a century between 1889 and 1944. His medals are worth considering, not only for their aesthetic appeal in what is usually regarded as a lean period in British medallic art, but also for the light they throw on the complex web of relationships which existed between medallists, the Royal Mint, the various government departments, the medal trade, and private patrons in the early years of this century.

Bayes, 1872-1953, trained first at the City and Guilds College at Finsbury in the early 1890s, and then from 1896 at the Royal Academy Schools where his prizes included a travelling scholarship which took him to Rome and, more importantly, Paris. His earliest works were small-scale low-reliefs and decorative objects in bronze which he exhibited at the Royal Academy and the Arts and Crafts Exhibition Society, and in which the influence of Alfred Gilbert and George Frampton is apparent. An example of an early sculpture in the round is the *Sigurd* exhibited at the Royal Academy in 1910. Here the use of enamel to provide colour on the horse's caparison derives from the example of Gilbert; the application of colour to sculpture was to be developed further by Bayes in the 1920s and 1930s in his experiments with Doulton's polychrome stoneware. Two points about this piece are relevant to Bayes' medals. Firstly, there is the inscription around the base, quoting from William Morris' *Sigurd*. Bayes had incorporated lettering into some of his earliest reliefs, and this practice of juxtaposing word and image made involvement in medallic work a natural progression for the artist. Secondly, there are the boldly modelled forms of the piece which already show a move away from the decorative fussiness of much 'New Sculpture' and which was to culminate in, for example, the group of cast concrete panels executed for the Concrete Utilities Bureau at the Wembley exhibition of 1924. Susan Beattie has noted the 'almost futurist handling of planes' in the *Sigurd,* and we shall observe similar traits in the medals, for Bayes was always concerned with what he called 'the bigger sculptural effects.'

Bayes' first medal was the Orchardson Medal, a presentation medal commissioned by the St John's Wood Art School. Charles Orchardson was one of the School's principals and his father, the celebrated Scottish painter William Quiller Orchardson, was a visitor. Bayes was a resident of St John's Wood and active in the artistic life of the area, and it is most likely that the commission fell to him in this way. He was already known for his work in relief, and many of the sculptors admired by the young Bayes – Gilbert, Frampton, Goscombe John, Reynolds Stephens – had progressed from bronze reliefs to medal work. Being cast and rectangular, the Orchardson Medal is closer to his early reliefs than to the medals that follow, and belongs in spirit with the cast medal revival of the 1880s and 1890s. But the future development of his medallic work is suggested by the skilful way the artist has divided up the surface area into a balanced arrangement of sculpted areas and voids, and also – and not so happily – by the lettering. Bayes never relished modelling the inscriptions so common in his work, and in later years would often delegate them to an assistant. As a young artist, this course of action was not open to him, and the result is the weak and uneven letters that we see here.

The artist's second medallic commission was from the Royal Geographical Society for a medal to be presented to Captain Scott and his colleagues on their return from the Antarctic expedition of 1902-04. That Bayes was given the commission was thanks to the Deputy Master of the Royal Mint, Sir William Ellison-Macartney. After de Saulles' death in 1903, the post of Engraver to the Royal Mint had been abolished, with the intention of 'obtaining greater freedom in procuring designs.' Evidently, Bayes was amongst those sculptors whose talents Ellison-Macartney wished to draw upon, for the president of the Royal Geographical Society, Sir Clements Markham, recorded that it was as a result of a visit from the Deputy Master on 26th June 1904, that Bayes was chosen as medallist for the proposed medal.

By August, Bayes had produced the plaster models of obverse and reverse. Markham made a number of suggestions which were adopted by the artist, but the general composition of both sides including, on the reverse, the large central figure and the penguins and seals below, was devised by Bayes. The sun-ray motif, behind the *Discovery* and Mount Erebus, is one of those decorative devices which recur in Bayes' work. The Gothic lettering is of a type used elsewhere by Bayes, but here it has been tidied up by Allan Wyon who was responsible for the production of the dies. Wyon's quotation for the engraving of the dies and striking of the medals was accepted by the Society's secretary J.S. Keltie in a letter dated 19th October. As the distribution ceremony was to take place in the Royal Albert Hall on 7th November, Wyon was asked to supply dummy medals in wax or plaster; the medals themselves – one in gold for Scott and thirty-seven in silver for the crew – were ready the following January.

The Society was evidently pleased with the results, for, when Ernest Shackleton returned from his Antarctic expedition in 1909, it again approached Bayes for a medal. The obverse of the Shackleton Medal is similar in design to that of Scott's, with the dates of the expedition placed symmetrically in the field; and, as on the Scott, the reverse bears a view, this time over the Beardmore glacier with a sledge drawn by ponies in the foreground. The principal difference between this and the Scott Medal is in the lettering, which resembles more that of the Orchardson Medal. Its unevenness would suggest that this time Wyon was not involved, and that this was so is confirmed by the Royal Geographical Society records, which show that his exclusion was the result of some shrewd businesslike activity on the part of Bayes. When he was approached by the Secretary of the Royal Geographical Society on the subject of the medal, the artist replied that he would be 'pleased to carry out the designs for the medal to Lt Shackleton on the same terms as the medal to Captain Scott, viz. 60 guineas for the plaster casts of the obverse and reverse', but added: 'Should you wish me also to carry out the reduction and striking I shall have pleasure in giving you an estimate for this also.'

Upon receiving Keltie's request for an estimate, Bayes replied that the reducing process and the two steel dies would cost £24.10s. Wyon's quote at £52.10s was more than double that of Bayes, and accordingly Keltie wrote once more to the sculptor asking him to confirm that his price included both dies. When assured that this was so, Bayes was given the commission, although Keltie stressed in two letters – of 26th and 30th April 1909 – that a condition of the agreement was to be that the work was to be in no way inferior to that of Messrs Wyon. From this point the Society dealt only with Bayes, who, as well as designing the medal, arranged for the striking (of one in gold, sixteen in silver and six in bronze), the engraving of the recipients' names, and even the provision of the cases.

It is evident that Bayes undercut the Wyons by appointing a different firm of medallists. This firm is identified by a catalogue entry in the American Numismatic Society's International Medallic Exhibition of 1911, where the medal is given as having been engraved by J.H. Pinches. Pinches evidently did not think it necessary to sharpen up the lettering, and the crispness that Wyon's engraving gave to the inscriptions on the Scott Medal is here

absent. It should be noted, however, that given the likelihood that both firms were using reducing machines, the large discrepancy in price between the two is difficult to understand.

The correspondence concerning the commission shows clearly Bayes' willingness to accept suggestions from his patrons. Along with photographs of Shackleton and of the Antarctic landscape, he received from Keltie a proposal for the reverse: 'a sort of rough ice plain in the foreground, with an indication of a range of mountains or mountain plateau in the background, with two or three men about.' Bayes sent in sketches, to which Keltie responded: 'They are both very effective, but I think you give too much exclusive prominence to the ponies and the men should be quite tiny, leaving the mountains rising to a sort of plateaux in the distance.' The finished medal shows that Bayes responded positively to the suggestion, recognising the potential of the small scale of the men and animals for creating a vivid impression of the vastness of the polar region.

The Royal Geographical Society commissions earned for Bayes something of a reputation as a medallist, and other organisations began to turn to him for their medals. In 1907, the National Rose Society instituted a Gold Medal in memory of its founder and recently deceased president, Dean Samuel Reynolds Hole, and Bayes was asked to design it. The dies were ready in 1908, and the first presentation was made in 1909. Another commission came from the Rubber Growers' Association, formed in 1907 and still in existence, nowadays under the name of the Tropical Growers' Association. The annual reports of the association show that the medal, which is struck in gold and presented for services to the rubber industry, was first distributed in 1911. Bayes' obverse design was used in the Association's publicity material for some years; on the reverse, the artist has made a novel and pleasing composition out of the traditional wreath and panel on which the recipient's name is engraved.

A further commission resulted in a medal for *Country Life* magazine. In 1912, the magazine – with the support of Lord Roberts – set up an annual rifle competition for schools. The winning teams were to be awarded a trophy and three miniature rifles; initially the individual members of those teams received silver pencil cases in the shape of Lee-Enfield rifles, but in the following years these were superseded by a medal designed by Bayes and issued in silver and bronze. The slightly shaky lettering, the boldly modelled planes of the figures, the exergue filled with laurel, and the novel panel design on the reverse, are all similar to the Rubber Growers' Medal. The year of distribution is engraved on the reverse and the winner and his school on the edge. The medal has now been presented continuously for over seventy years.

Another privately commissioned medal of about the same time was produced for the Brentford Gas Company. It features on the reverse a brave attempt to render a gas works artistic. The circular Roman temple on the obverse is perhaps intended to suggest a classical prototype for the modern gasometer. The figure holding a statuette and the burning tripod are features we shall meet again in Bayes' work.

Besides these private medals, Bayes also received official commissions. In July 1909, as the result of a request by the Association of Chief Constables, Edward VII issued a royal warrant instituting the King's Police Medal, to be awarded for acts of courage on the parts of members of police forces and fire brigades in Britain and throughout the Empire. The obverse was to feature one of de Saulles' portraits of the King. For the reverse, the customary limited competition was set on foot, and, in October 1909, designs were invited from Bayes, Spicer-Simson, Ernest Gillick, David MacGill, Sydney March and the Bromsgrove Guild. At the insistence of the Home Secretary, Herbert Gladstone, the designs were to be simple and of an allegorical rather than an illustrative nature, and the India Office advised that, as colonial forces were also eligible for the medal, nude figures and religious symbols (such as the Cross) should be avoided.

MacGill and the Bromsgrove Guild declined to compete and March's sketches were judged unacceptable; the other three – Bayes, Spicer-Simson and Gillick – were asked to supply designs in relief, and in November these were taken from the Mint to the Home Office for Gladstone to examine. The Home Secretary was satisfied with none of the designs, but thought that those of Bayes or Spicer-Simson might be suitable if certain changes were made. Of Bayes' model, R.F. Reynard, Gladstone's under-secretary, wrote to Ellison Macartney: 'The design showing the figure of a watchman standing and holding a large sword might, he (Gladstone) thinks, be easily altered. The head is too far sunk in the body and the bulky left shoulder might be lowered so as to display more of the face. The left hand might rest on the large shield bearing the inscription 'To guard my people' and the details of the warders on the City wall might be omitted as they seem of too military a character.'

An increasingly heated correspondence arose. Ellison-Macartney replied that the Home Secretary's suggested alterations amounted to a request for a new design, in which case the artist would have to be paid afresh. When Reynard hinted that 'Mr Gladstone would not object to some small additional expense being incurred', the Deputy Master responded curtly: 'the question of additional expenditure if required is a matter wholly for the Treasury and this Department.' And when Reynard wrote that Gladstone requested details to be altered only so that the medal would suggest 'civil guardianship' rather than 'military defence', Ellison-Macartney requested an illustration of how this distinction could be achieved, adding: 'I cannot say that I know of any medal 'emblematic of Protection from danger' which conveys the idea of civil guardianship by an allegorical or emblematic design. In fact I cannot imagine how civil protection from danger can be symbolically indicated.' To this, Reynard sent a conciliatory reply with a reduced number of alterations, but Ellison-Macartney remained adamant that the design would be accepted as it stood or not at all, adding archly: 'I should have liked to have given him (that is, Bayes) a hint as to the manner in which the Secretary of State thinks 'civil guardianship' could be 'emblematically' expressed, but I observe you are silent on this point.' It is clear that Ellison-Macartney resented Gladstone's interference in the artistic aspect of the commission, and was determined not to ask the artist to modify what appeared to him to be a perfectly satisfactory medal. At this point, Reynard, also losing patience with his superior, wrote in an unofficial letter to Ellison-Macartney, 'I *personally* like some of the designs you sent.'

In December, Ellison-Macartney discussed the problem with Bayes, and it was agreed that he should provide new designs. These were ready in January 1910, and although some of the features to which Gladstone had objected, such as the warders on the city-walls, were retained, the Home Secretary announced that he was satisfied with one of the two new designs. He did, however, show it to 'some lady friends of his', who suggested that the figure's head should be larger and that it should not project above the inner rim. Reynard was charged with communicating this to Ellison-Macartney, but in his letter could not resist adding a personal observation that these suggestions might spoil the artistic effect. Ellison-Macartney agreed, replying that the size of the head could be slightly altered in the plaster cast, but that the design could not be changed in any other way. At this point Gladstone brought up again one of his original points (that the left shoulder was too high), and added that the platform on which the figure stood should also be lowered. On 24th January, Ellison-Macartney wrote a determined letter to the Home Office, in which he stated that he had discussed the matter fully with the artist and that, with the exception of the head, nothing could be altered. He explained that lowering the head and the platform would destroy the medal's effect, and that the left shoulder was higher as a result of the placing of the weight of the figure on the right leg: and he ended by pointing out that the medal was the artist's considered work, and should be accepted or rejected as it was.

At this point, Gladstone capitulated, and the design was submitted to the King the following month. Bayes received an extra twenty guineas for the additional work. The civil aspect of the medal is expressed, both by the townscape in the background and by the night-watchman's lantern in the foreground; the city-walls also suggest civic protection besides aiding the composition by raising the background into the centre of the medal. If the design was accepted only grudgingly by Gladstone, it found other admirers, and when twenty-three years later at the wish of George V the medal was to be replaced by two separate police medals, one for long service and one for gallantry, Bayes' design was retained with new legends fitted in the exergue. Ellison-Macartney also was pleased with the medal, and on the accession of George V later that year it was to Bayes that he turned for designs for the Great Seal.

To help him with his work on the Seal, the artist was provided with two recent publications: Allan Wyon's *The Great Seals of England* of 1887 and Walter de Grey Birch's *Seals* of 1907. Both books illustrate and praise the fourteenth-century Bretigny seal of Edward III, with Wyon writing: 'This remarkably beautiful seal marks the culminating point of excellence in design and execution in the series of Gothic Great Seals of England.' It was on this seal that Bayes based his obverse: the central facing figure, the Gothic throne and ornate canopy, the shields to either side, the figures in the outer niches – all are elements that appear in the mediaeval design. The Counterseal, on the other hand, is completely original, for virtually all previous counterseals had shown the monarch on horse-back. The decision to show the new King on the deck of a *Dreadnought* was taken at a meeting between George V and Ellison-Macartney on 5th June 1910. Although this was a radical departure from precedent, the principle of the Great Seal, that the ruler is shown in peacetime on one side and at war on the other, was retained, but with a battleship replacing the horse as the instrument of war. Bayes' first designs were accepted after a few minor modifications. However, the merits of the Seal were called into question very soon after its delivery to the Chancellor's office in February 1912, and again Ellison-Macartney found himself having to defend Bayes.

The criticisms both artistic and technical, were answered by Ellison-Macartney in a report made out in November 1912. On the artistic question, he wrote of the Great Seal: 'I assert that with one exception – the first seal of Queen Victoria – it is far superior to any of its predecessors in the last three hundred years.' Turning

to the Counterseal, he prefaced his remarks with the statement that 'a modern battleship is not a thing of beauty', but went on to state that in his view 'the artist has coped very successfully with the great difficulties of this scheme.' As regards the technical criticism, as these had only come from England, and not from Scotland or Ireland where the seal was also used, Ellison-Macartney suggested that training for the English operator might be the answer. But his reasoning failed to stem demands from the Lord Chancellor's office for a new seal. Bayes' sculptural style did not provide the crisp definition considered necessary for a seal matrix, and the general view that the designs were aesthetically deficient added to the dissatisfaction. In the following year the pressure became such that Ellison-Macartney had to give way, and the opinions of a wide range of figures in the art world were sought as to who should be asked to design a replacement. In the end, Gill, Lanteri and Bowcher were chosen, and one of Gill's designs was unofficially accepted, but the outbreak of war put a stop to the plan, and it was revived only in 1927 when a change in the King's title made a new seal necessary. The problems of a finding a suitable design then occupied the Royal Mint Advisory Committee for nearly three years, until eventually a design by Percy Metcalfe was accepted.

Another official commission came to Bayes while he was still working on the Great Seal, when it was decided to seek a replacement for Kathleen Scott's design for the reverse of the Edward Extension Medal, awarded for acts of bravery in the work-place. Although Scott's design had been in use for only two years, it had been widely criticised for its uneven modelling and clumsy perspective. In January 1911 Sir Frederick Ponsonby, the Keeper of the Privy Purse, was approached unofficially by R.F. Reynard, the Home Office under-secretary whose praise of Bayes' Police Medal we have already noted, about the possibility of the King agreeing to a new design by Bayes. Ponsonby forwarded the letter to Clive Wigram, the King's assistant private secretary, with the comment: 'I know that his Majesty does not admire the present design but as to whether he would approve of a new design being submitted to him I am hardly in a position to judge.' On 19th January, Wigram informed Reynard that the King would approve the scheme, and an official request was made in a letter from the Home Office to Lord Knollys the following month. 'Bayes... is a capable artist and has done very good work', the letter said, and cited the Police Medal as an example.

In April, the artist submitted three designs, one of which was described as a 'figure of Courage flourishing a sprig of laurel and wearing a civic crown – in the background a town, possibly including some factories and workshops.' The description suggests the design of the finished medal, and it was this design that Winston Churchill, who had succeeded Gladstone as Home Secretary, recommended for the King's acceptance. However, the King, whilst agreeing it was the best of the three, would not approve it, and the Home Office was asked to obtain more designs from the artist. This was done, but it was not until December that year that royal approval was given. The design has the crowned figure of Courage, the laurel branch and the industrial landscape of the earlier rejected design. It also has a number of features characteristic of the artist: the unsure lettering, the laurel exergue, and the bead and reel border.

A final official commission came to Bayes after the First World War, when in 1919 for reasons of economy it was decided to change the Imperial Service Medal from a star to a circular medal. Mackennal's portrait was to be used for the obverse, and a design for the reverse was requested from J.W. Cawston, then Deputy Master of the Royal Mint. The design put forward, seemingly, the work of a Royal Mint artist and consisting of a small Royal cypher and the words *For Faithful Service,* was rejected forthwith by the King. The impasse was overcome after Reynard, still at the Home Office, suggested in a telephone call to the Royal Mint that Bayes should be entrusted with the design. He explained later, 'I only mentioned his name because I know of no other good medal designer in England.' Bayes duly submitted drawings, followed by a model, and for once the process went smoothly. The medal that resulted is of a bold design. The figure shown resting after labour is robustly modelled, whilst the hillside, sea, setting sun and vines form themselves into almost abstract patterns.

The arrival of Robert Johnson at the Royal Mint in 1922 effectively put a stop to this sort of commission, for Johnson was committed to the principle that sculptors do not make good medallists. His avowed aim was to build up a body of artists who would specialise in medal design, and who could also be called upon to design coinage for Britain and abroad, and for this reason he encouraged the commissioning of medals from younger men. Bayes, who, when Johnson arrived at the Mint, was fifty years old and a successful sculptor, was not then the kind of artist sought by the new Deputy Master for medallic work. Moreover, during his time at the Mint he came to know Bayes principally through the artist's Great Seal, for which he struggled to find a replacement for some years, and through Bayes' opposition to the Mint's private medal work and the activities of the Royal Mint's Advisory Committee, the two aspects of the Mint's work that Johnson was keenest to encourage.

But if public commissions for medals now dried up, private commissions continued to come in, largely as a result of personal friendships. Two medals for the Institute of Actuaries resulted from Bayes' friendship with a number of eminent actuaries including Sir George Hardy. Bayes had previously executed a cast portrait medal of Hardy and on the latter's death in October 1914 the council of the Institute of Actuaries, knowing that Bayes was then engaged on a bust of its past president, offered to pay for its completion and purchase the finished work. This was unveiled at Staple Inn Hall in January 1916.

The first of the two commissions was for the Gold Medal in honour of George James Lidstone, to be presented jointly by the Institute of which Lidstone had been a member for many years, and the Faculty of Actuaries in Scotland of which he was a past President. At a meeting of the council of the Institute in May 1929, it was resolved to make some formal recognition of Lidstone's contribution to actuarial science, the form of which was to be decided by the presidents of the two societies. By October it had been resolved to commission a medal from Bayes, the sculptor of the Hardy bust and a personal friend also of Lidstone. The speed with which the commission was completed was assisted by the absence of prolonged debate on the iconography of the medal: a portrait of the recipient on the obverse, and the seals of the two societies, given equal prominence, on the reverse.

When, in 1937, another eminent actuary, Sir William Palin Elderton, was to be honoured, Bayes was again approached. The decision of the Faculty of Actuaries in Scotland once more to participate in the presentation and share the cost, announced by the President of the Institute at a council meeting in February 1937, made the reverse of the Lidstone Medal equally appropriate for Elderton. Alterations to the date on the reverse and the obverse legend and a new portrait were all that was required. Although Elderton was a member of the Institute's council, knowledge of the scheme was successfully kept from him until it became necessary for him to sit for the artist. The presentation was held at Staple Inn Hall in November 1937.

Another commission of the inter-war years came in 1924 from the Worshipful Company of Musicians, again as a result of a personal friendship, in this case with the musician, painter and sculptor, Sigismund Goetze. The medal was endowed by Walter Wilson Cobbett, a generous benefactor of the Musicians' Company who in 1928 was to become its master. It was to be presented annually to a distinguished musician for services to chamber music. Tradition in the Musicians' Company has it that the medal was originally struck by the Royal Mint, until production was handed over to Pinches. Certainly Pinches struck the medal in later years, and, as there is no record of the medal in the Mint archives, and as it is not listed amongst the dies transferred from the Wyon firm to Pinches in the 1930s, it would seem more likely that this was another of those medals that Bayes himself took to Pinches to have struck. Again, the reverse bears an unusually shaped panel, in this case bearing the Company's emblem, the swan.

In the following year, Bayes received a commission for a medal from the Royal Society of British Sculptors. The medal, a silver medal to be awarded annually for the best work by a British sculptor exhibited in London during the previous twelve months, was endowed by Sir Otto Beit. The procedure for choosing a medal design was discussed at two meetings of the Society's council in May 1925. It was decided that members should be invited to submit examples of their medallic work for inspection; each member of council would then vote for three artists at their meeting in July 1925. Bayes (who received nine votes), Charles Doman (eight) and Allan Gairdner Wyon (seven) were asked to supply designs, from which Bayes' entry was unanimously selected four months later. Again, Bayes went to Pinches for production of the medal, which was completed by March 1926. The first was awarded to William McMillan for his *Syrinx* exhibited at the Royal Academy summer show of 1925. The figure of British sculpture on the obverse of the medal, holding a statuette in one hand and a trident in the other, we shall meet again in a different guise in Bayes' work. The tripod on the reverse is accompanied by an assortment of sculptors' tools.

Also in 1925, the London and North Eastern Railway Company decided on a medal to commemorate the railway centenary. The circumstances by which Bayes was chosen are unknown, but the railway's records throw light on the medal's design and amply document its distribution. A major feature of the railway's elaborate celebrations of July 1925 was a procession of locomotives along the original Stockton-Darlington line before an invited audience which included the Duke and Duchess of York. The climax of the procession was two trains drawn by the engines shown on the medal, Stephenson's *Locomotion No.1* and a modern locomotive of the *Pacific* class. These two engines were also juxtaposed in the logo of the International Railway Congress that was held in Britain to coincide with the celebrations.

The medal was advertised in the souvenir programme of the celebrations and on the back of the menu for the luncheon given in Darlington for the delegates to the conference, and was also reproduced in *The Railway Gazette* and *The Railway Magazine*. It was available at an exhibition illustrating the history of railway travel held in the Faverdale wagon works near Darlington, and, after the exhibition closed, could be obtained from King's Cross or direct from the manufacturers, Pinches. It was struck in bronze in two sizes: 3 inches (available for 10 shillings) and $1^3/4$ inches (5 shillings), the proceeds going to the Railway Benevolent Institution. Given the importance of the two locomotives in the celebrations, their inclusion on the medal was almost certainly demanded by the company, whereas the figure of Vulcan, which acts as the focus of the reverse composition, is more likely to be the artist's invention. The obverse, bearing portraits of Edward Pease, chairman of the Stockton & Darlington Railway, and George Stephenson and the coats of arms of the two towns, has no such unifying factor, and the different elements – also included in all likelihood at the request of the company – are not so satisfactorily resolved. It comes as no surprise to discover that Robert Johnson appears to have considered the design deficient.

It is evident, however, that the LNER board was satisfied, for when, during the Second World War, the railway decided on a medal to be awarded to its employees for acts of bravery it was to Bayes that it turned. The proposal for the medal was approved by the board in November 1940, and models were submitted and passed in May the following year. The obverse bears the company's coat of arms, whilst on the reverse there is again the laurel wreath, the panel and the rising sun. The most novel feature of this medal is the greatly improved lettering. This is not the work of Bayes, but was delegated by the artist to his daughter who had trained at the Royal College of Art under the celebrated practitioner of that art, Edward Johnston. The influence of Johnston's teaching can be detected in the elegant, evenly spaced letters of the medal which are both easy to read and pleasing to the eye.

From the 1930s, much of Bayes' lettering was executed by his daughter, who also did casting for her father. Another assistant was Frank Ransom, a medallist in his own right who had worked on the London County Council school attendance medals and been employed by George Frampton until his death in 1929, before going to work for Bayes. Although Bayes wrote in his book on modelling: 'The student should make the study of good lettering a part of his training', he himself was principally interested in modelling, and preferred to leave what he saw as technicalities such as lettering and casting to others. Increasing commitments – his work for Doulton's, commissions for monumental sculpture, membership of council and subsequent presidency of the Royal Society of British Sculptors, and so on – made this especially desirable.

An example of his larger workload is a series of

linked commissions from the Royal Automobile Club. The Segrave Trophy, named after Sir Henry Segrave, the holder of the world landspeed record from 1927 until it was taken by Sir Malcolm Campbell in 1931, was instituted by the Club in 1930, and is awarded annually to British subjects who give outstanding demonstrations of the possibilities of transport by land, sea or water. Bayes' portrait medal of Segrave forms part of the plaque also designed by the artist and given to each recipient. It also appears on the front of the base of the trophy itself, whilst the reverse (which bears a tripod similar to those of the Brentford Gas and RBS medals) appears on the back of the base. The trophy, which remains at the Club's headquarters in Pall Mall, is again by Bayes and is a complex work in bronze with gold inlay and gilding. The figure, with her curious stylized helmet and outstretched hand holding a trident (the top part of which is now broken off) is another example of Bayes' recycling of a design. We have already noted its appearance in the RBS Medal. A version was exhibited at the Royal Academy in 1926 under a title taken from Kipling: *England my Mother, Warder of Waters, Builder of Cities, Maker of Men*. A bronze statuette of the same name was exhibited the following year, and in 1928 the sculptor showed a bronze statue entitled *The Guardian of the Seas*, also at the Royal Academy. This last version would appear to be the eight foot tall figure now facing the swimming pool in the RAC's clubhouse. This is dated 1927, and was presented to the Club by the 6th Earl Howe. It is now entitled *Speed*, a name bearing little relation to the pose of the figure but with an obvious application to the RAC . But whether the figure on the Segrave Trophy be intended for Speed or England, it is equally appropriate, as the Club's intention was also patriotic. Its hope, as reported in its *Jubilee Book* of 1947, was that the award would 'stimulate others... to uphold British prestige before the world by demonstrating how the spirit of courage, initiative and skill... can assist progress in mechanical development.'

In June 1935 Bayes suggested to Robert Johnson that a medal should be produced to commemorate the maiden voyage of the *Queen Mary*. The Deputy Master responded enthusiastically, and requested from the artist a sketch of one side of the proposed medal. This he sent to Cunard with an accompanying letter, in which he strongly recommended the scheme, intimating that, if Cunard did not wish to take it up, the Royal Mint might well go ahead and issue a medal itself. The Cunard board agreed to commission the medal, but were not happy with the sketch which showed the *Queen Mary* and below a medallion containing Columbus' *Santa Maria*. Percy Bates, chairman of the shipping line, wrote to Johnson: 'As

regards the design submitted by Mr Bayes, I rather think this needs some changes. Columbus' Santa Maria came to a sticky end on San Domingo and never came home to Europe, I rather incline to the Cunard company's first ship the Britannia. Will you take the matter up with Mr Bayes or would you prefer to put him in touch with me in Liverpool? I don't think we need to go beyond him, at all events at present, but I am ready to be guided by you as to this.'

During the correspondence which followed, the possibility of employing an alternative medallist was at no point raised, despite the antipathy to sculptors-turned-medallists we have already noted in Johnson. In the end the second ship was dropped, enabling the scale of the liner to be increased, and, by turning the ship slightly, the artist succeeded in suggesting even greater size. Whilst retaining the inner rim, the legend above the ship was also removed, and a Latin legend introduced below in its stead. The phrasing of this legend was the subject of much discussion, to which Rudyard Kipling and several eminent classicists contributed.

But it was the other side of the medal that caused the most problems. It was originally hoped that Queen Mary might allow her portrait to appear on the obverse, but this idea had to be abandoned when Ponsonby, now created Lord Syonsby, made known the royal wish that effigies of the King and Queen should appear only on those medals actually conferred by them. As a result, it was decided that the view of the ship should form the obverse of the medal, but the problem of what to show on the reverse was more difficult to resolve. Suggestions were numerous. Kipling wrote to Bates in July 1935, suggesting that, if nothing else could be decided upon, 'why not chuck all design on the reverse and have an exquisitely lettered, beautifully spaced description, giving her tonnage, length, breadth and building yard.' He enclosed designs, which were forwarded to the artist. Another idea, that the ship should be shown under construction in the dry dock, was rejected on the grounds that the appearance of the ship on both sides of the medal would be repetitive and dull. A suggestion that the coastlines of Britain and America could be shown with the path of the first voyage indicated between was rejected on account of the problem posed by the different scale of the two countries.

Finally, the artist decided upon a reverse based upon one of Johnson's proposals. The Deputy Master had written to Bayes in July suggesting an 'impressionistic view of New York on one side and Southampton on the other: sky-scrapers, and old walls of Southampton or the old Gate in the High Street, with space between representing the sea. The two flags could then be included, or lion and eagle...'

Bayes had adapted this idea to something like the final design by October, when Bayes wrote to Johnson: 'We have had before us an alternative design for one side of the medal embodying a view of the sky-line of New York as seen through the old arch at Southampton. My colleagues all liked this suggestion...' The design went before the Royal Mint Advisory Committee meeting of 31st October, and was approved in general, but with the recommendation that some changes be made in the arrangement of the shields. The final design, with shields bearing the arms of New York and Southampton to each side and another in the centre with the shipping line's coat of arms, was settled in November, and by the 18th of that month Bayes had completed the plaster models. By the end of the following January, the first thousand medals had been struck by the Royal Mint. Five gold medals were produced, two for presentation to King Edward VIII and Queen Mary, two for Mr and Mrs Roosevelt, and one for Percy Bates as a gift from the board of Cunard. Of 3,000 bronze examples some were presented to the workmen of John Brown's shipyard; the remainder went on sale on the ship and at Cunard offices for one pound or five dollars each.

Bayes' final medal was commissioned in 1948 by the Chapter-General of the Order of St John and was the second of the revived series of portrait medals of the Grand Priors of England. The Duke of Gloucester had acceded to the post in 1939, but the medal proposal was delayed by the outbreak of war and by the Duke's governor-generalship of Australia, from which he did not return until 1947. On the reverse is St John's Gate at Clerkenwell with the shield of the Grand Prior above. The minutes of the Chapter-General show that the reverse subject was suggested by Bayes, as was the division of the legend between obverse and reverse.

Bayes' medallic career brings into focus the very different policies of successive Deputy Masters of the Royal Mint in the first few decades of this century, from Ellison Macartney's attempts to bring medallic art to the attention of the country's ablest sculptors, through the years of weak leadership when Reynard at the Home Office put more effort into obtaining good medal designs than the Deputy Master, to Robert Johnson's attempts to exclude sculptors from official medal making. It says much for Johnson's discernment that he abandoned this principle in the face of Bayes' proposal for the Queen Mary Medal.

Bayes' private commissions came in more regularly from the 1900s through to the late 1940s. The success of these medals can be judged by the number of organisations (the Royal Geographical Society, the Institute of Actuaries and the London & North Eastern Railway Company) that came back to him for a second design, and also through the continued use of medals, such as the *Country Life*, Cobbett, Dean Hole and RBS medals, to the present day.

At a time when avant garde sculptors were carving directly into stone and turning their back on the medal, the more conservative Bayes was flexible enough to include medals amongst his varied output. The quality of their design and modelling ensures for Bayes a foremost position amongst British medallists for the first half of the twentieth century.

This article is a revision of a paper first published in *The Numismatic Chronicle* Vol 152 (London 1992) and now reprinted by kind permission of the Royal Numismatic Society.

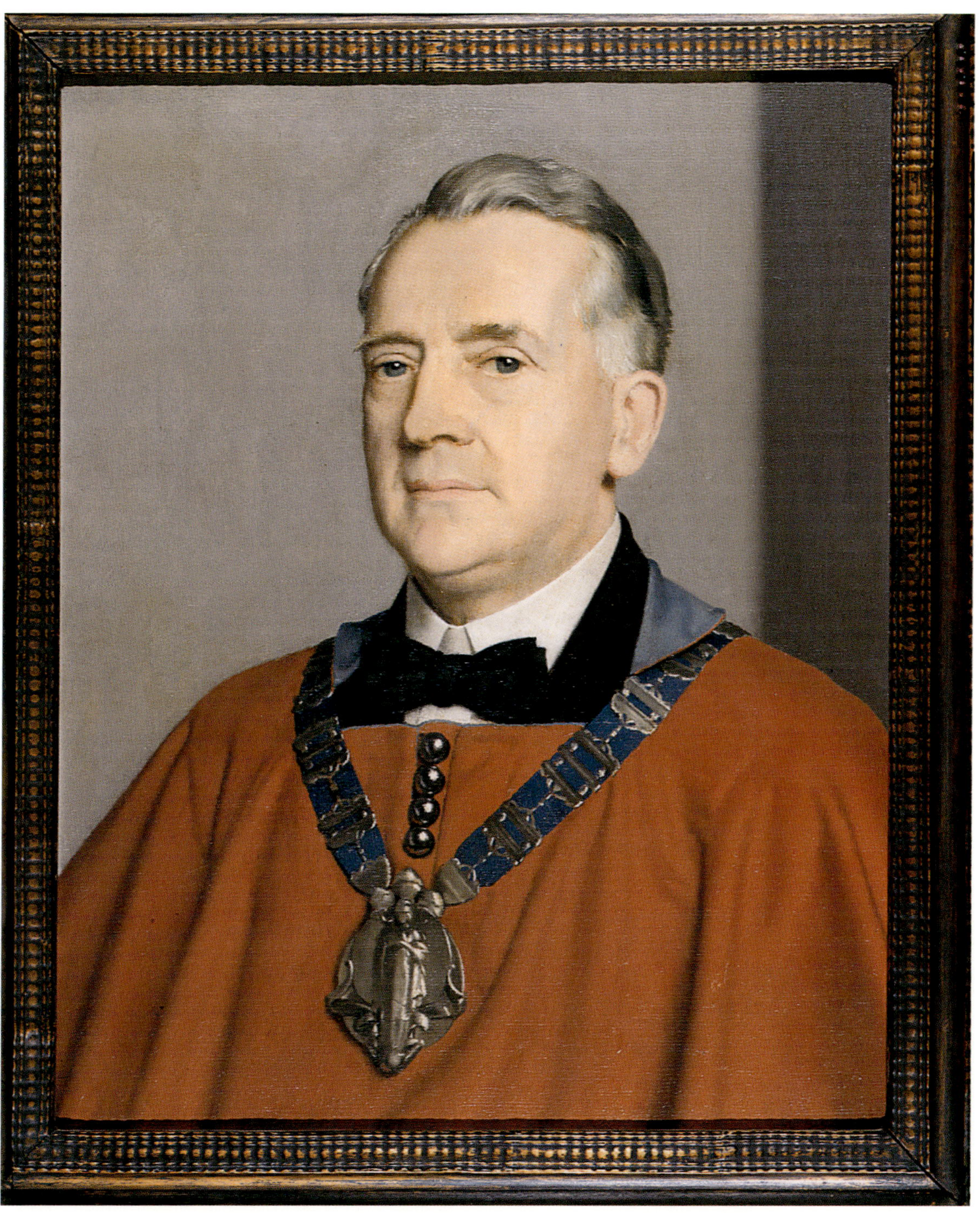

Bayes as Master of the Art Workers' Guild, painted by Meredith Frampton (Art Workers' Guild).

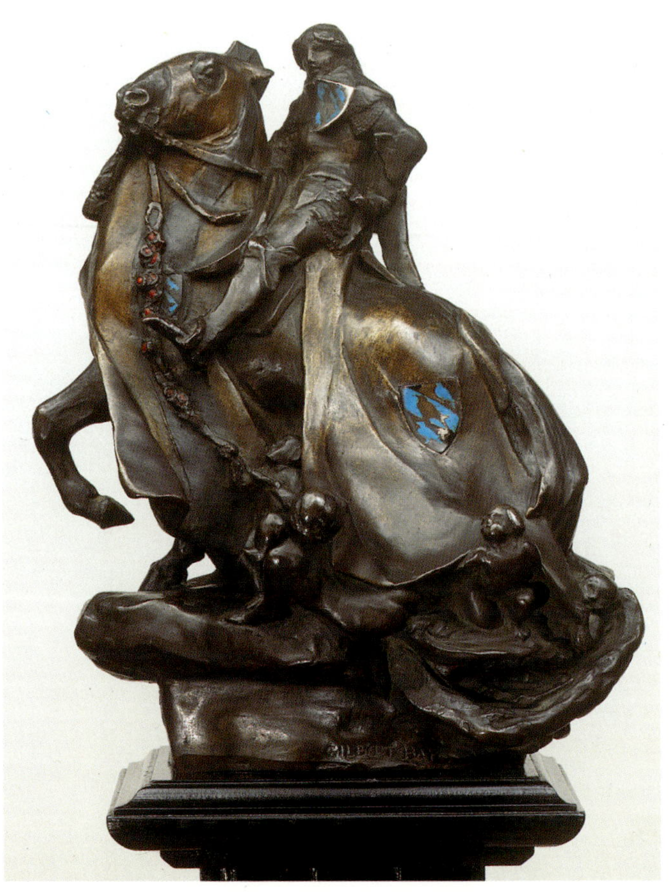

The Underworld, bronze with enamel, 1913.

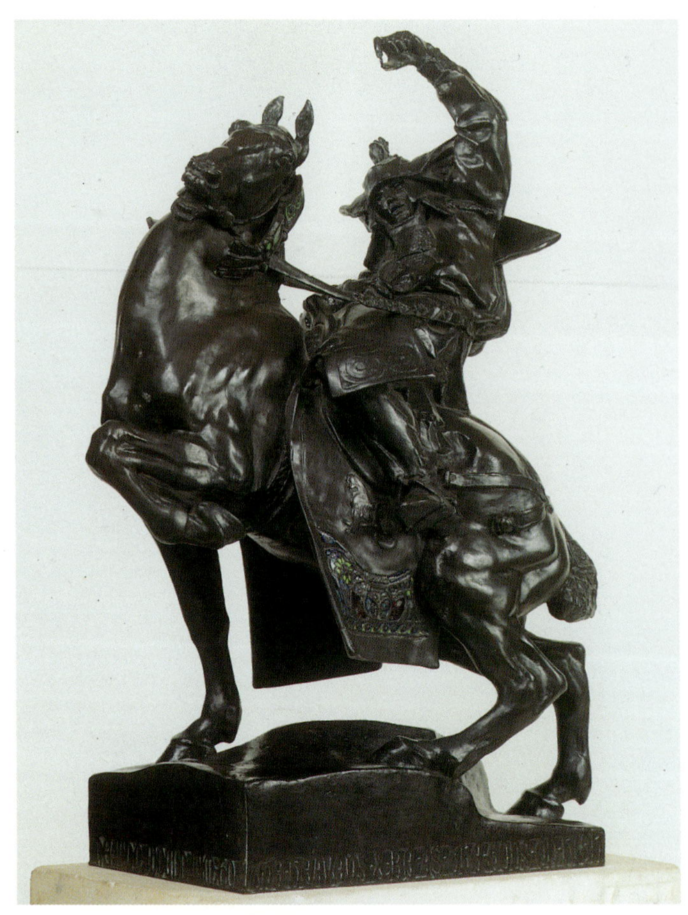

Sigurd with Ring, bronze, 1909.

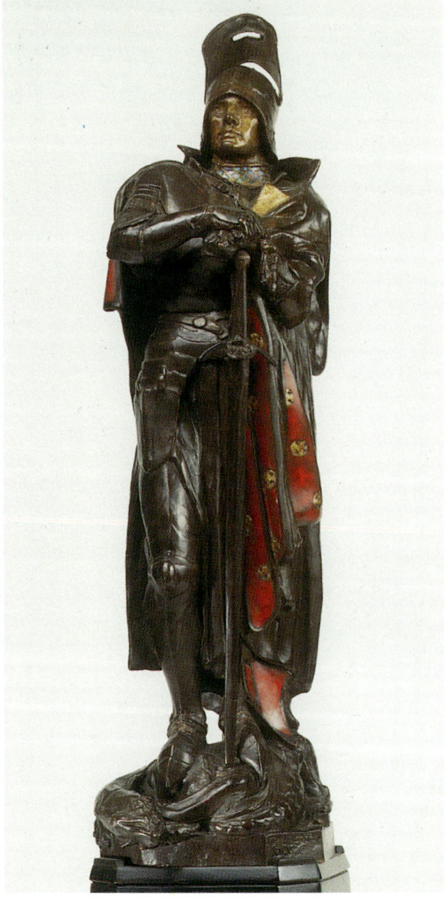

The Guardian or St George, bronze with enamel and mother of pearl, 1920.

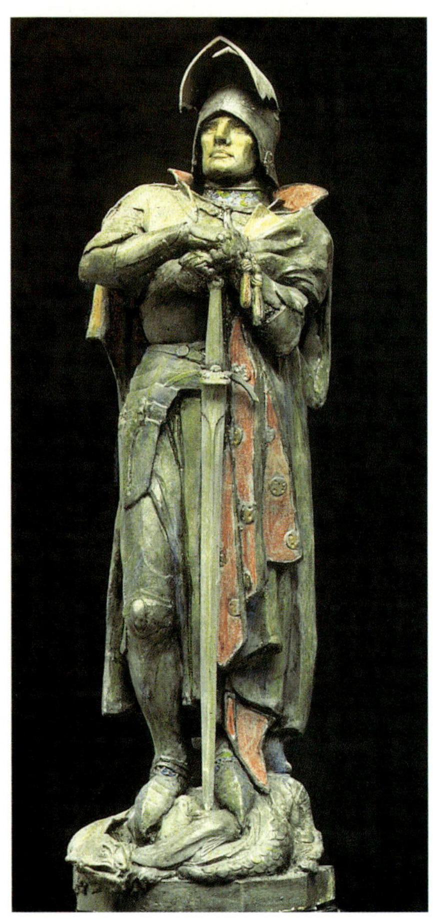

Plaster for The Guardian or St George, hand-coloured by Bayes, 1920.

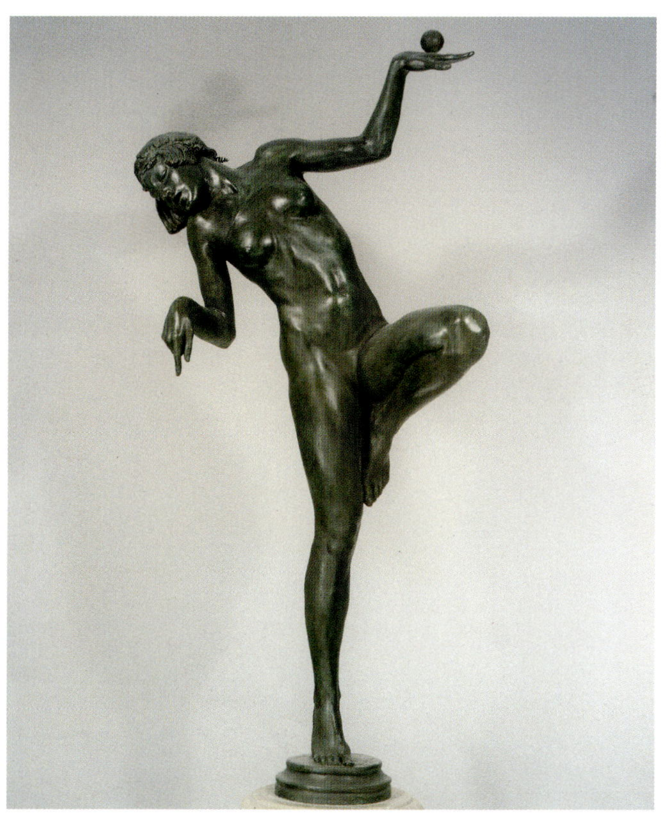

The Frog Princess, garden figure, bronze, 1929.

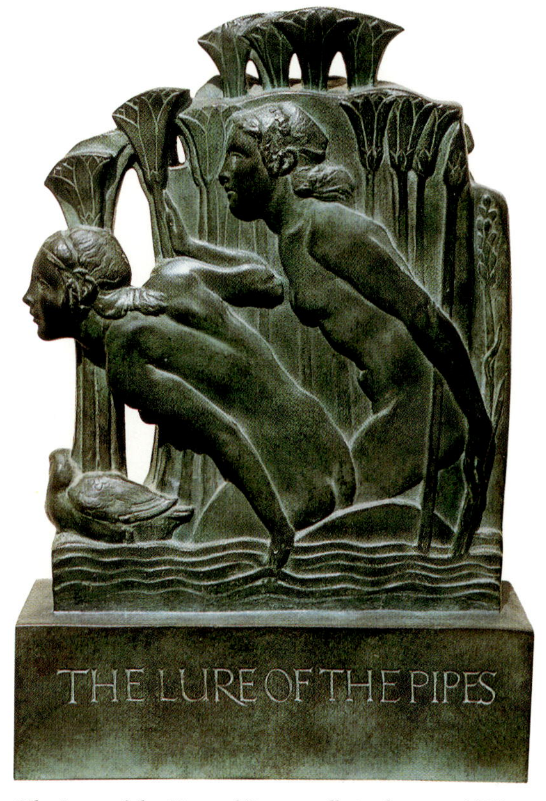

The Lure of the Pipes of Pan, small size bronze, 1933.

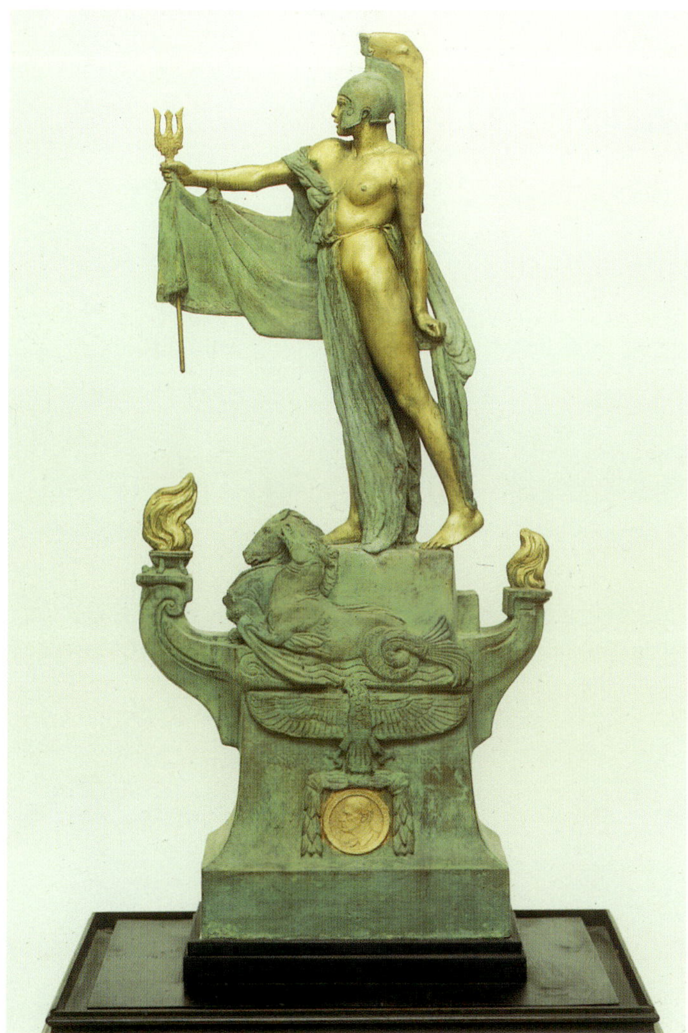

Plaster for the Seagrave Trophy.

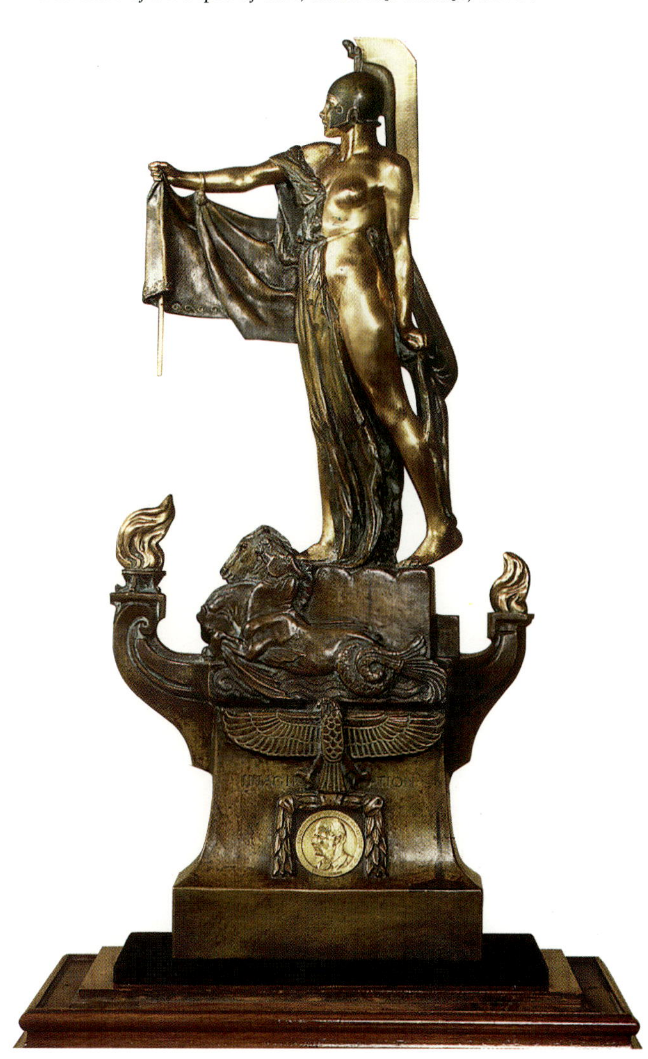

The Segrave Trophy, bronze and gold, 1930 (Royal Automobile Club).

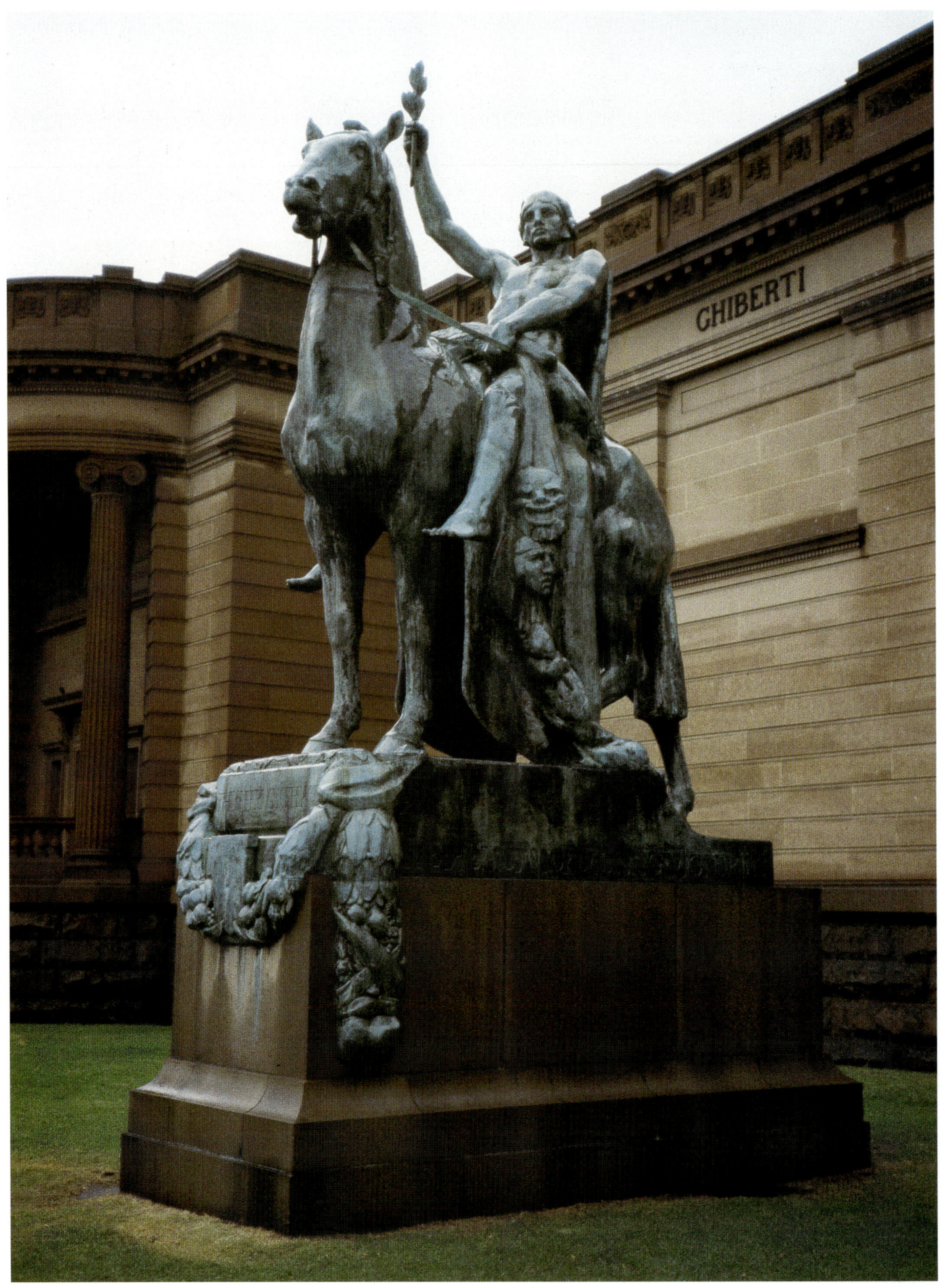

Offerings of Peace, monumental bronze, erected Art Gallery of New South Wales, Australia, 1926.

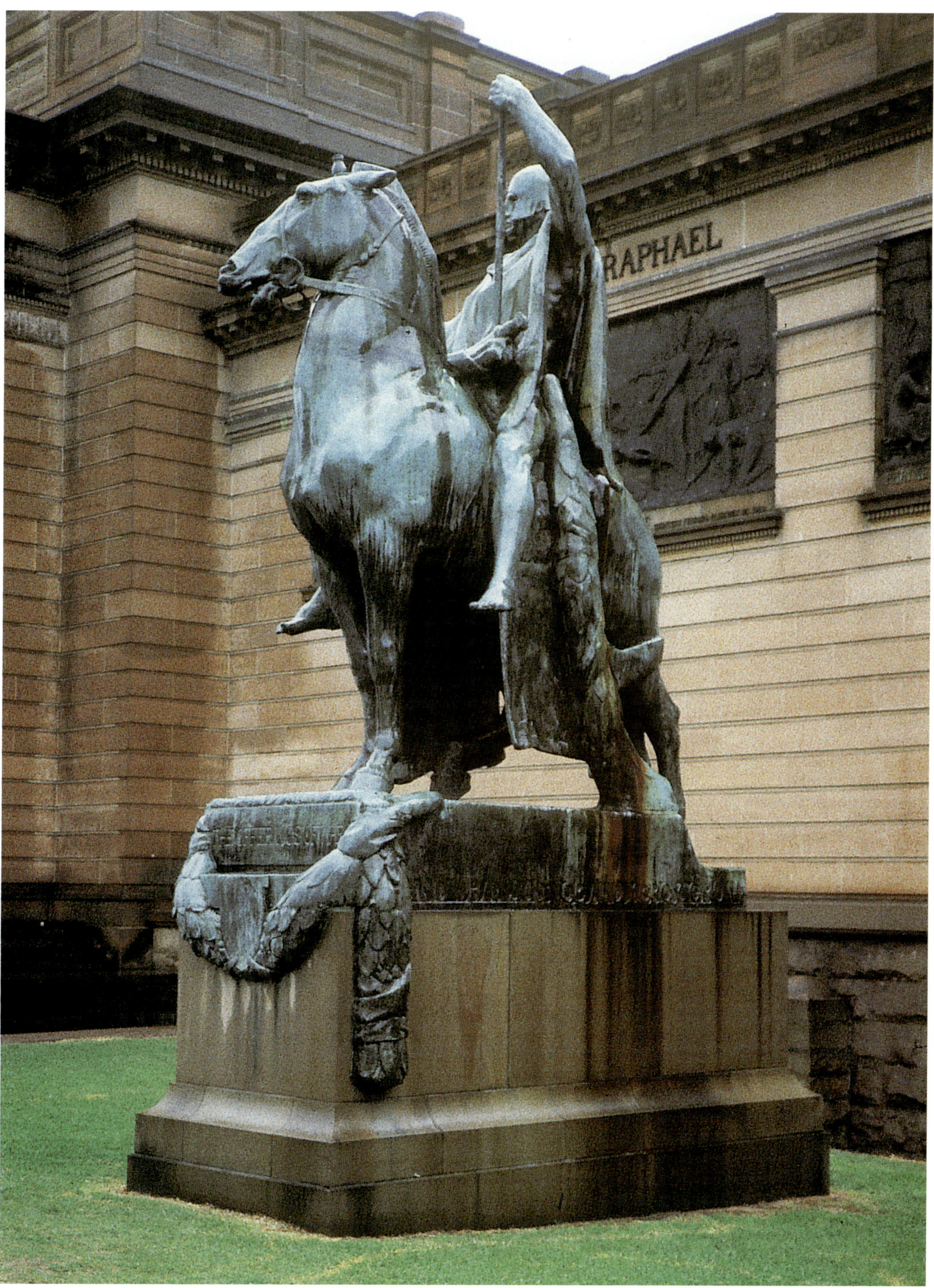

Offerings of War, monumental bronze, erected Art Gallery of New South Wales, Australia, 1926.

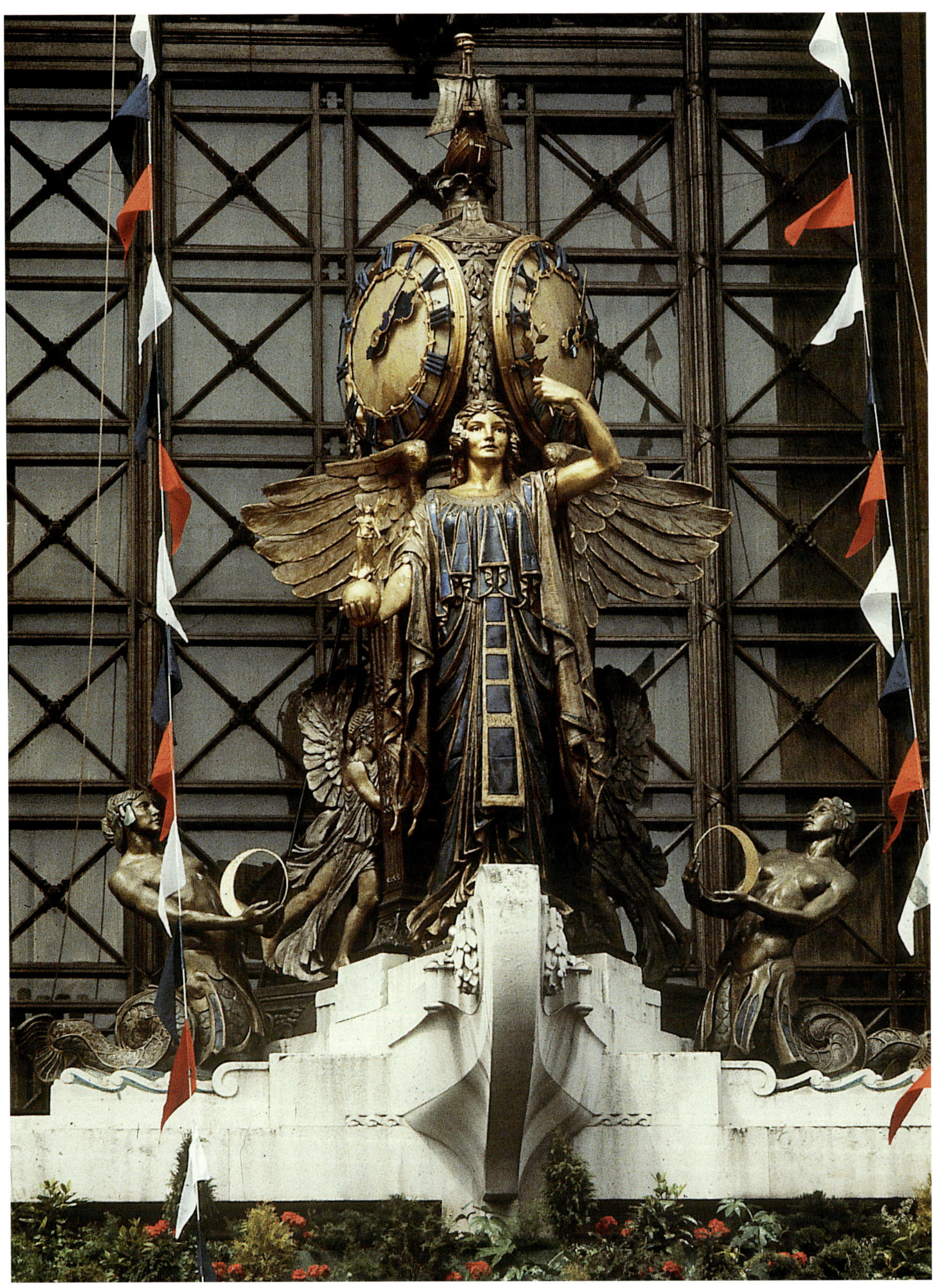

The Queen of Time clock, Selfridge's, London, 1930.

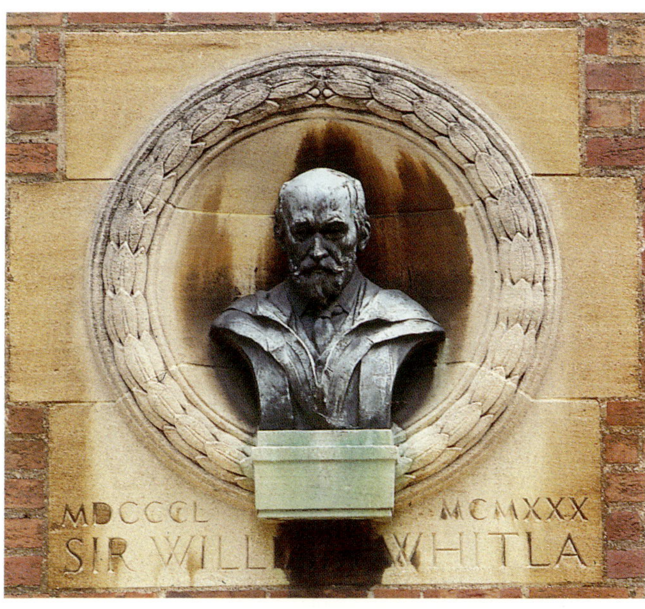

Sir William Whitla portrait, Queen's University, Belfast, 1948.

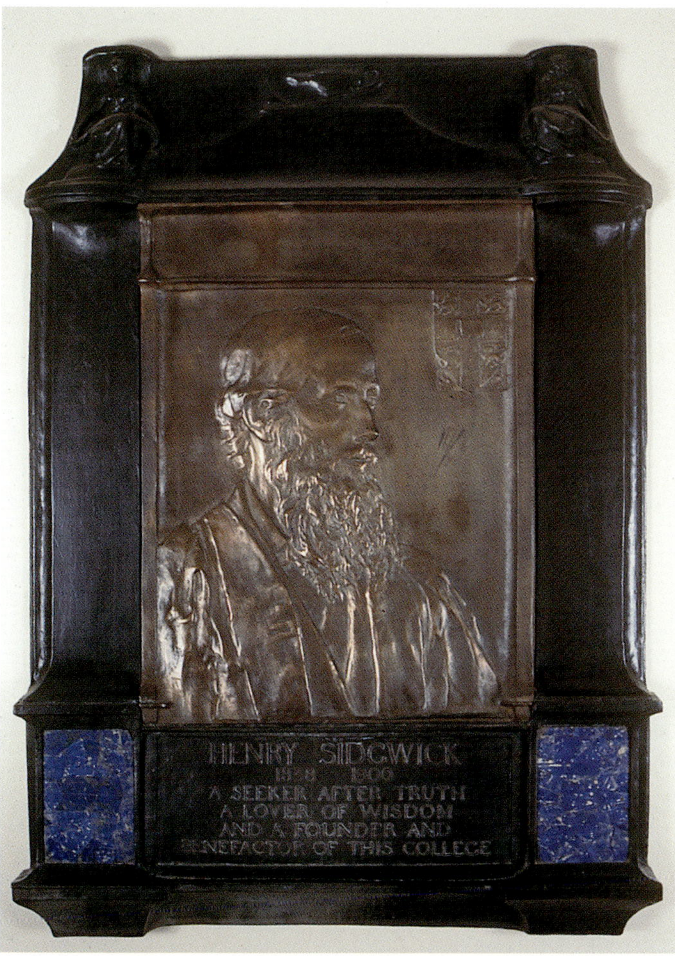

Henry Sidgwick panel, 1905 (The Principal and Fellows of Newnham College, Cambridge).

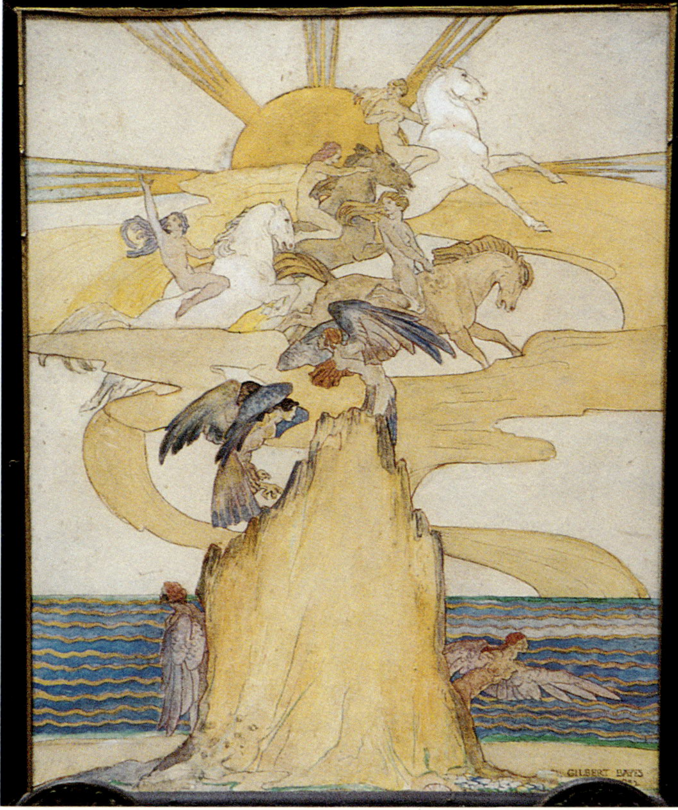

Watercolour by Bayes, 1936, for his scheme for the gesso panel for the RMS Queen Mary.

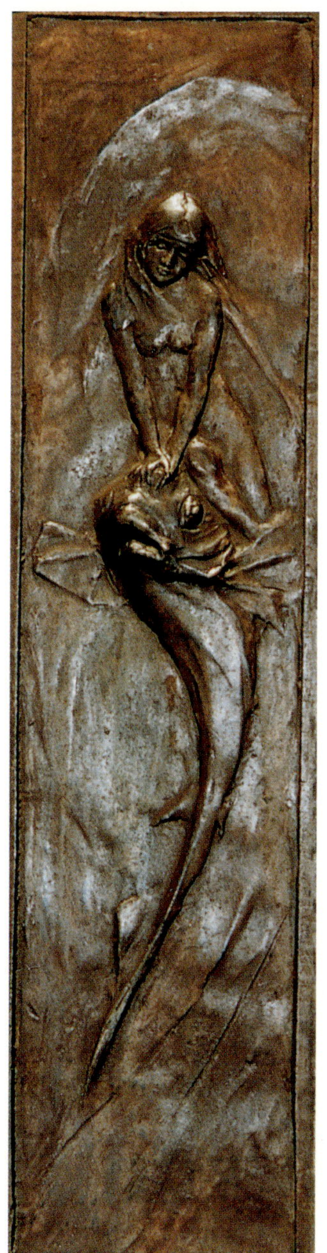

A Sea Frolic, bronze relief, 1893.

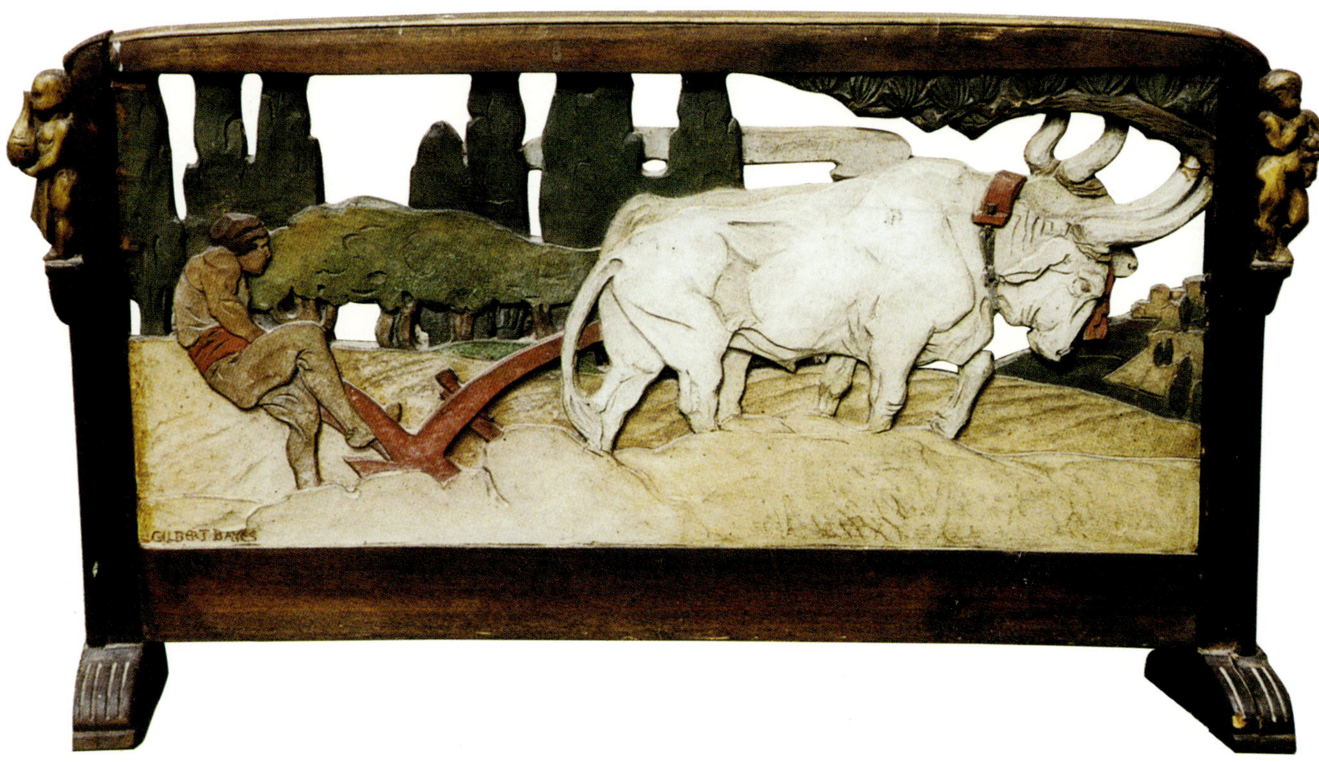

The Oxen of Siena, carved and painted wood panel, 1924.

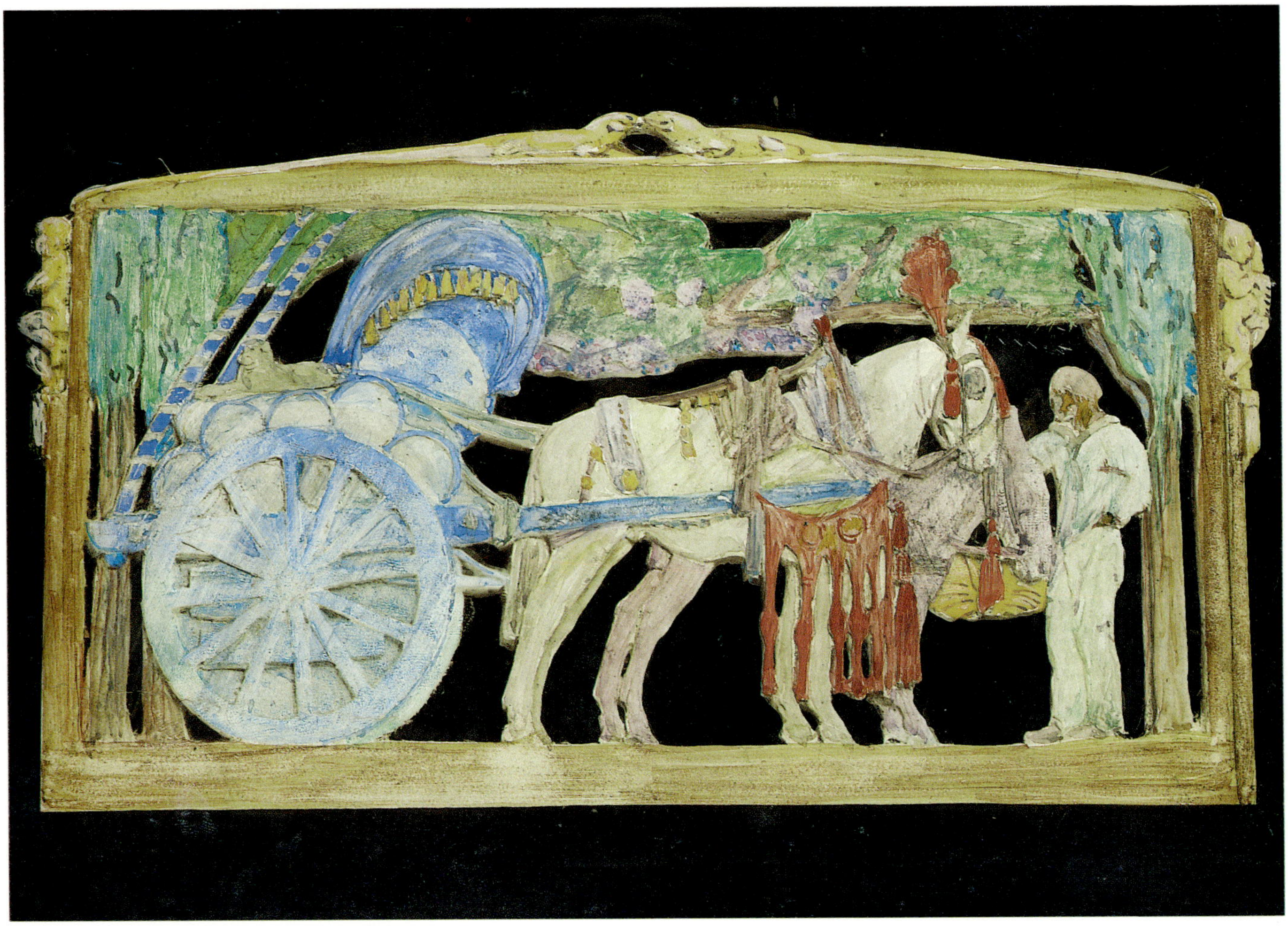

Photograph of The Roman Wine Cart, 1924, hand-coloured by Bayes.

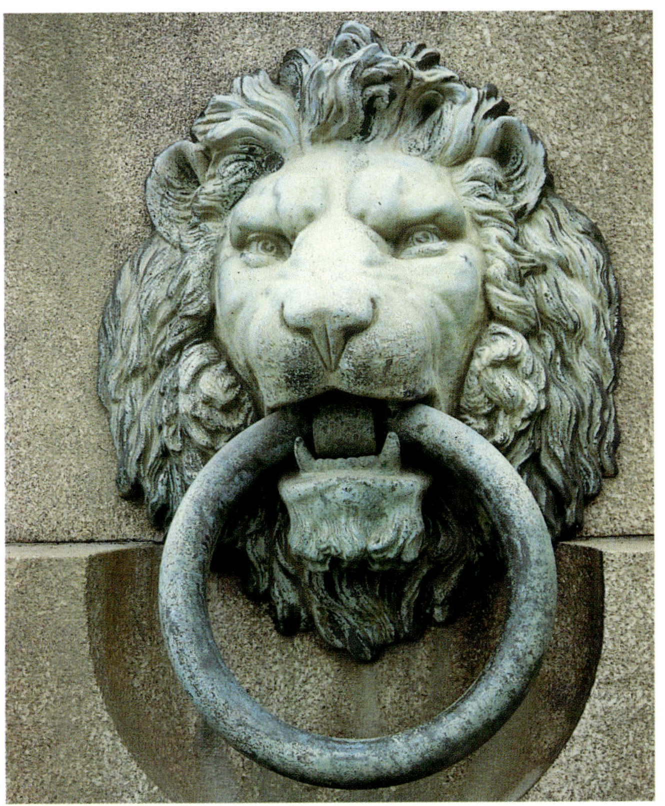

Lion chain support for the Albert Embankment, London, 1910.

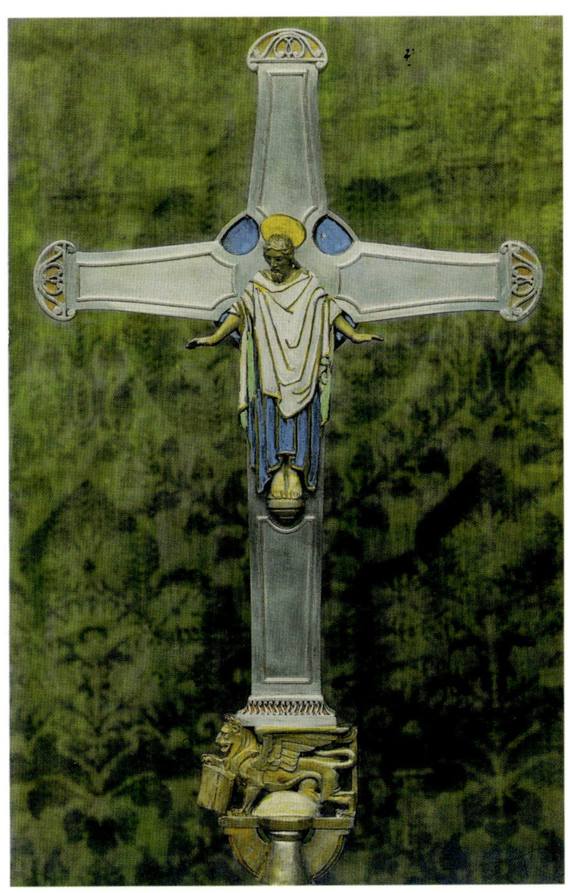

Photograph hand-coloured by Bayes of the St Mark's processional cross, 1926.

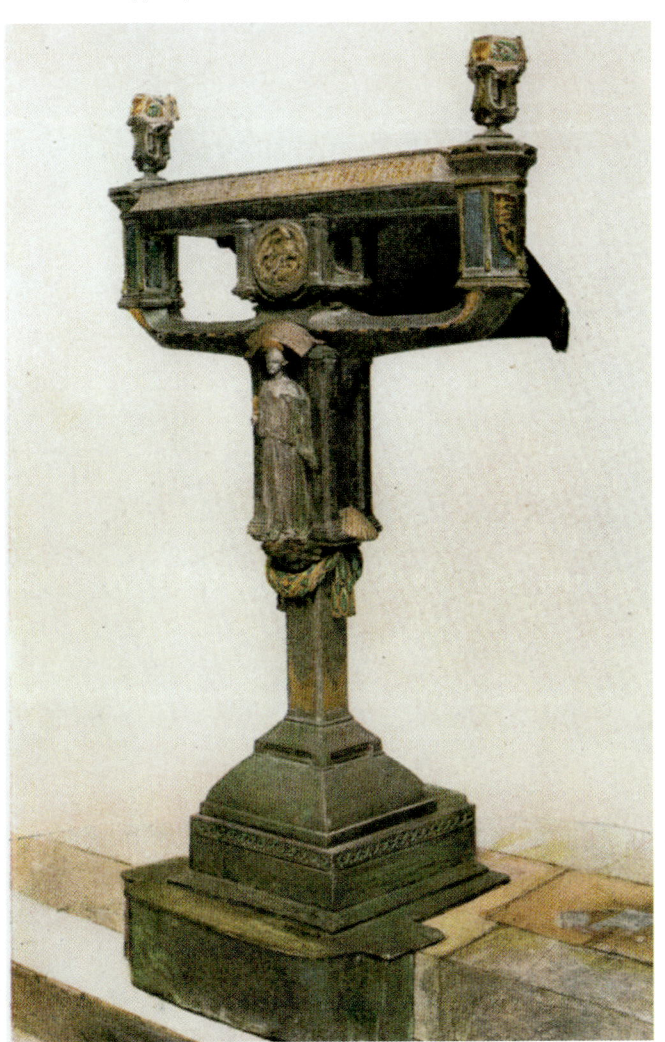

The Laurence and Mabel Irving memorial lectern, 1915.

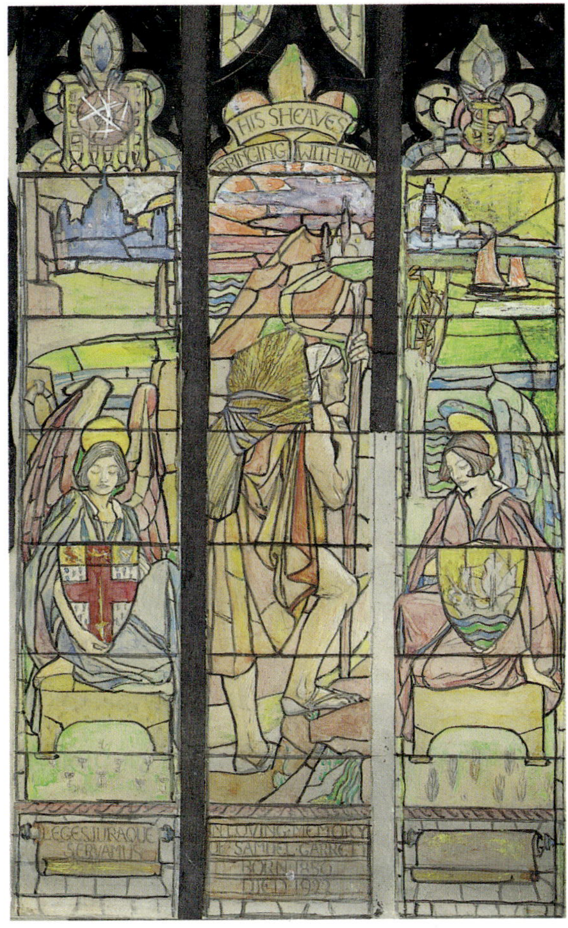

Watercolour design for the Samuel Garrett window, 1927.

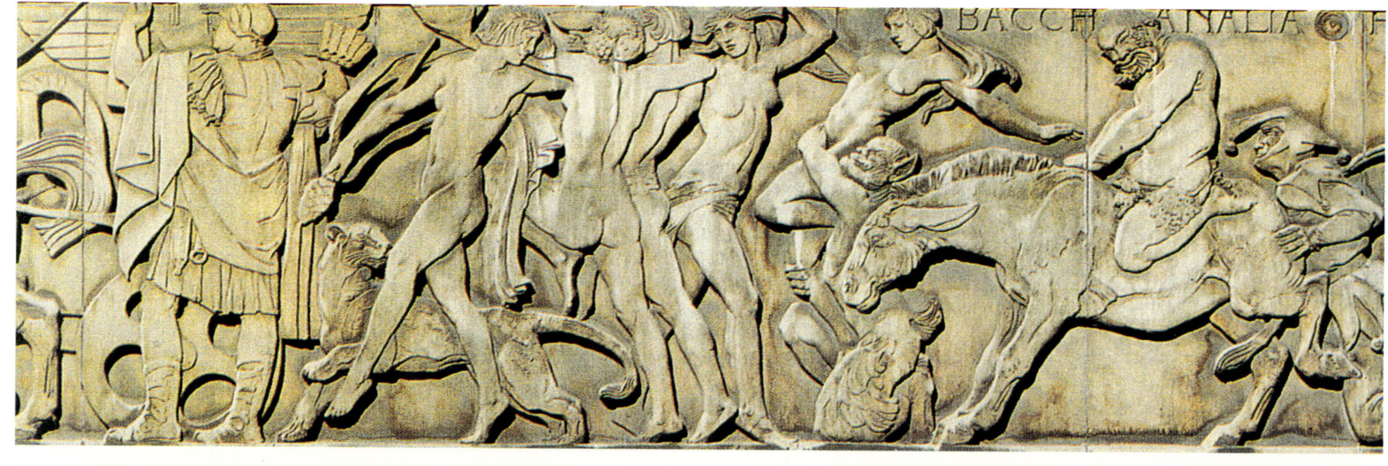

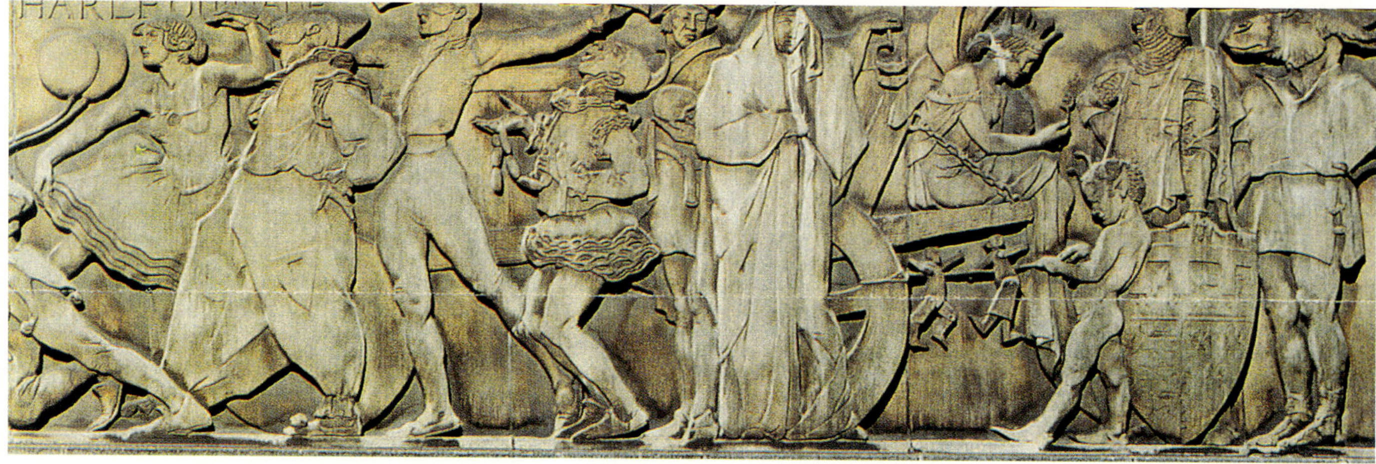

Sections of the Drama Through the Ages
frieze, former Saville Theatre, 1930.

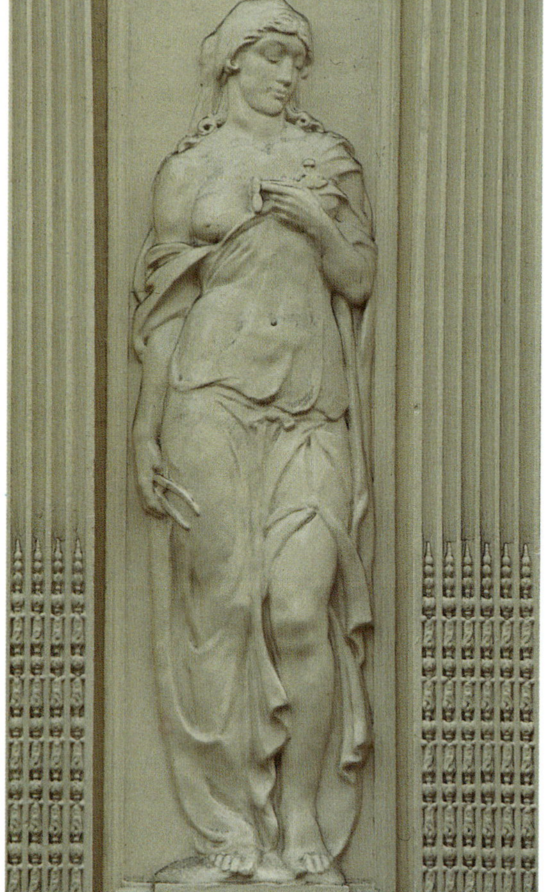

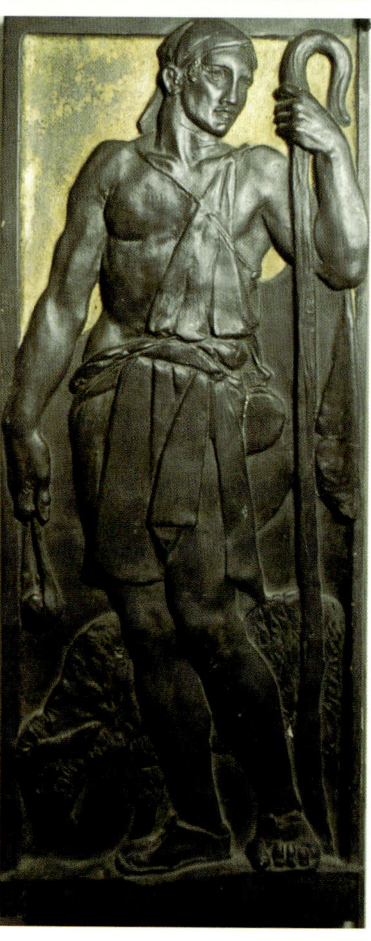

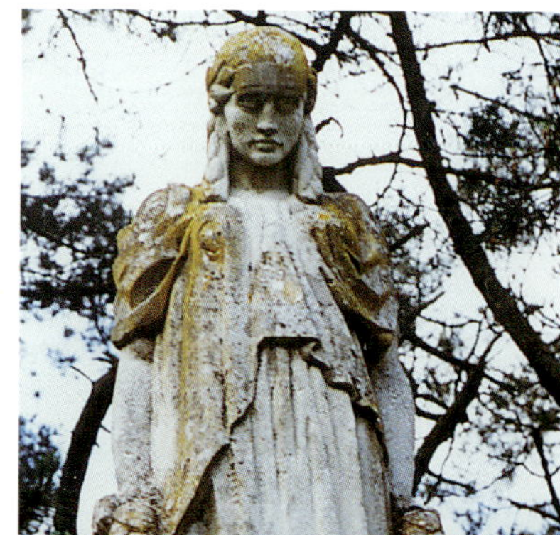

*Figure representing Music, Cavendish Square, London,
1924.*

*Jonathan, bronze panel from the Royal
Fusiliers Memorial, 1933.*

Broadstone War Memorial, 1918, detail.

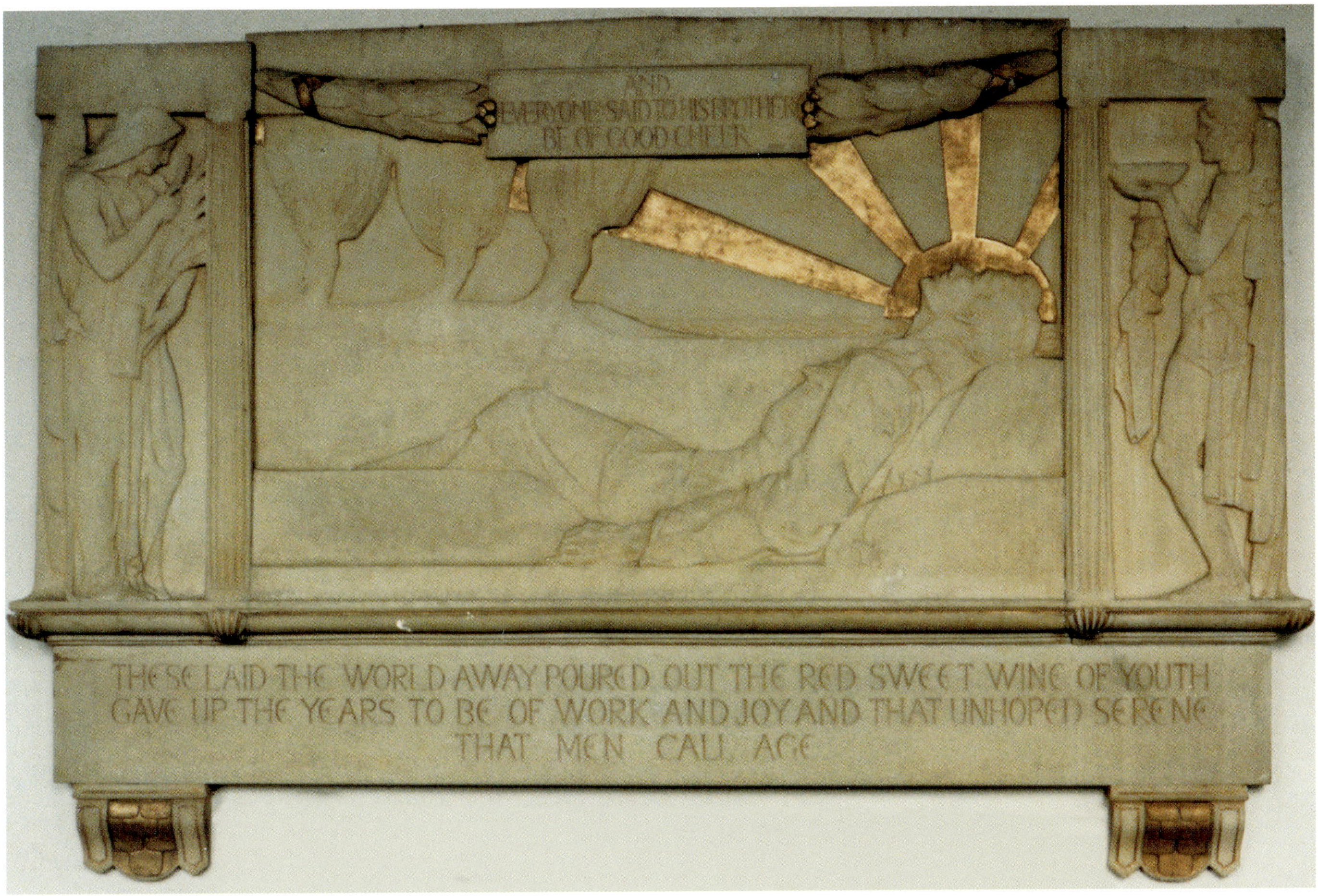

Dying Soldier panel in stone, Aldeburgh War Memorial, 1918.

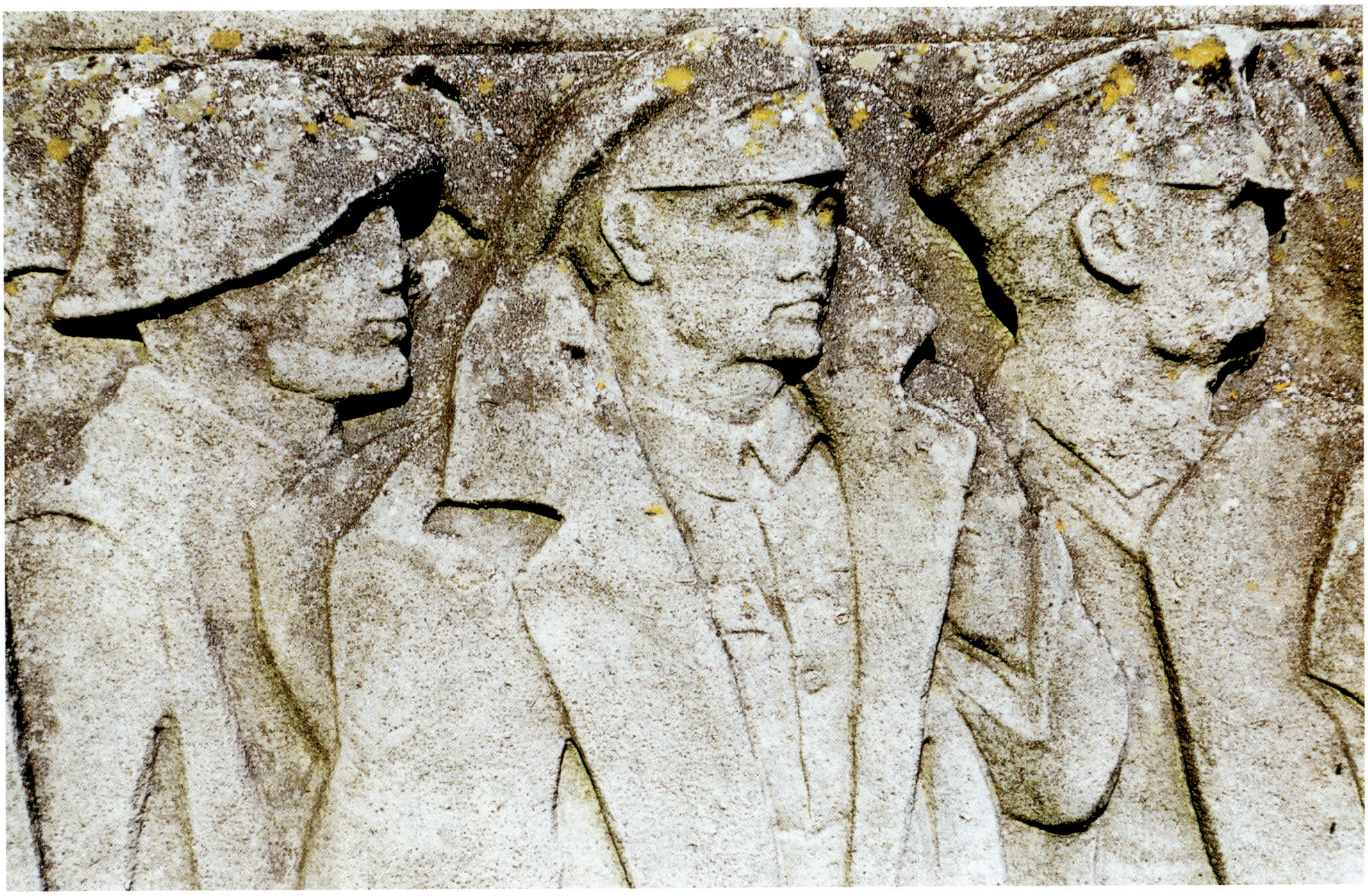

Soldiers panel from the Broadstone War Memorial, 1918.

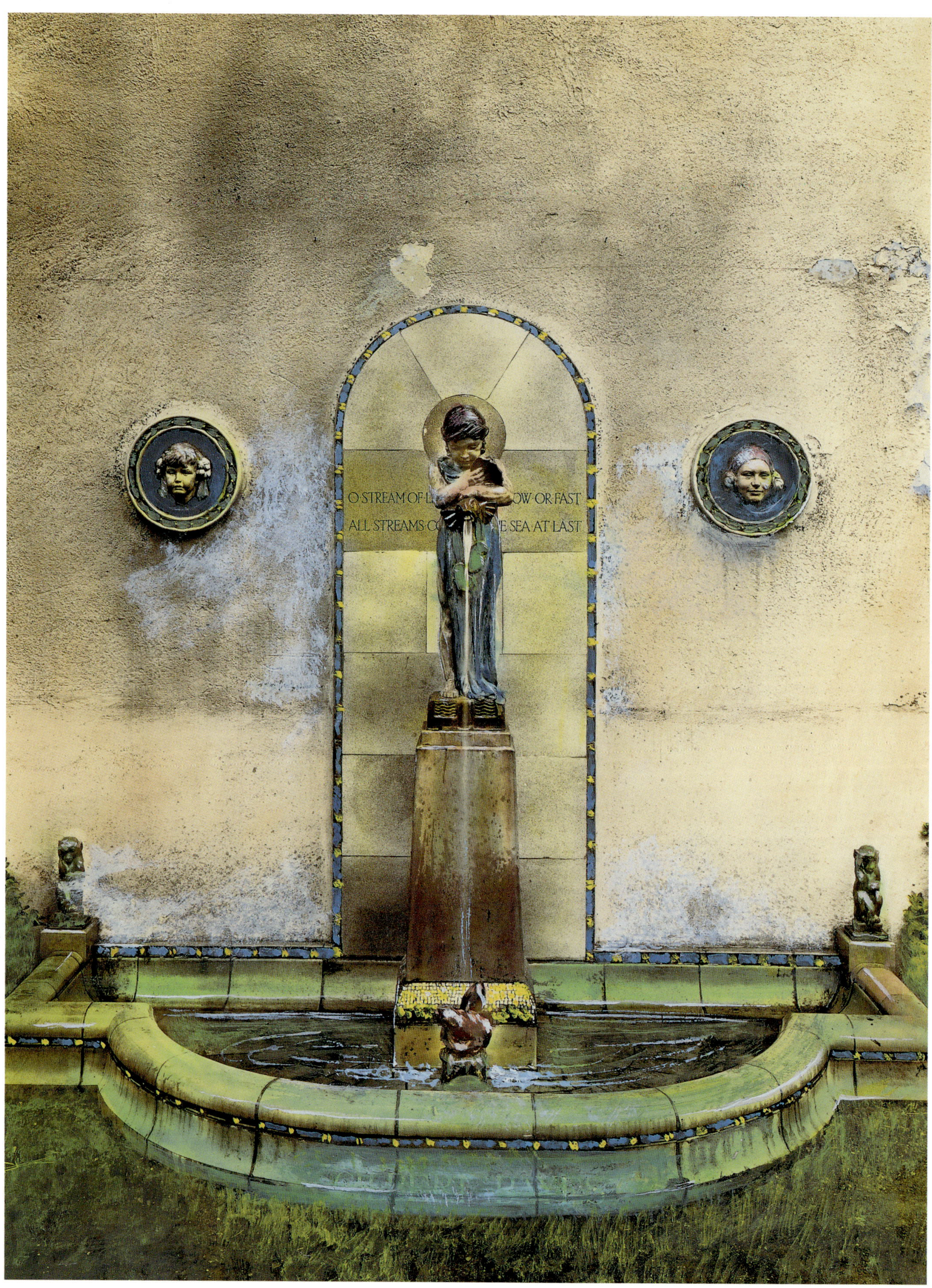

Hand-coloured concept by Bayes for a garden scheme, featuring the Boy with Fish, or Blue Robed Bambino fountain, c.1928.

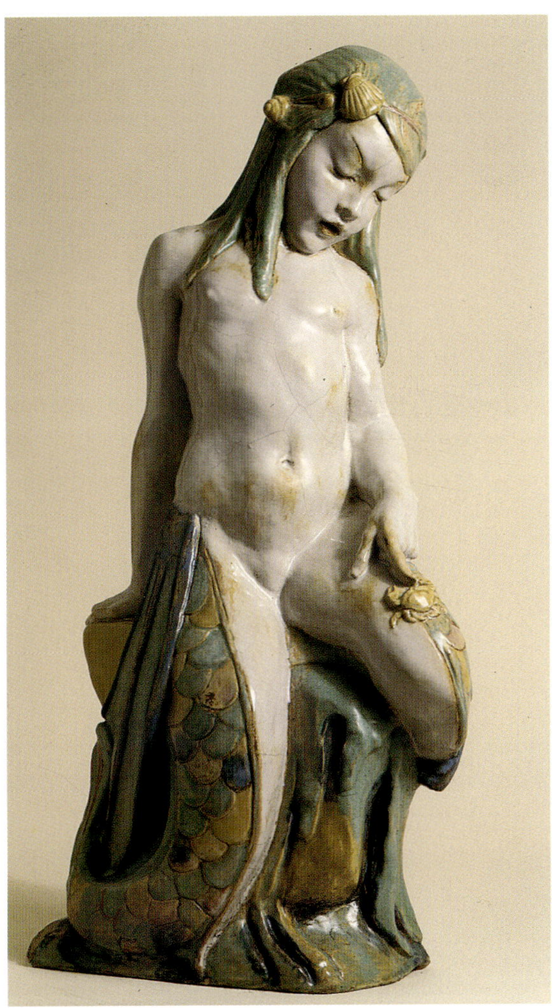

The Mermaid, Doulton stoneware, 1934.

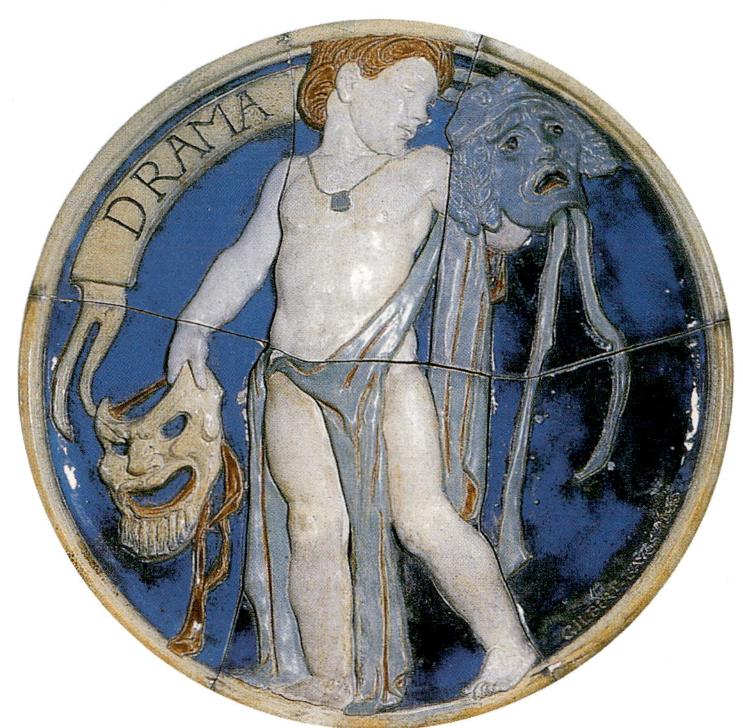

Drama roundel, Doulton stoneware, 1926.

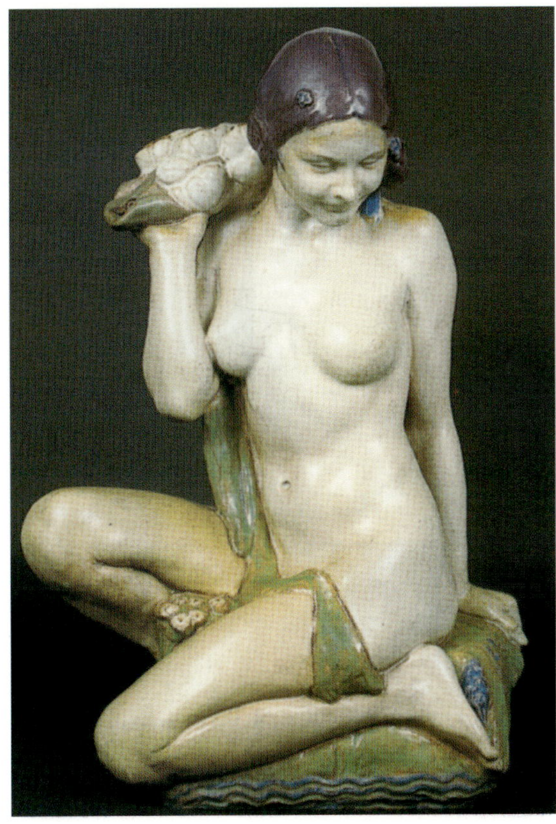

Lilymaid garden statue, Doulton stoneware, 1924.

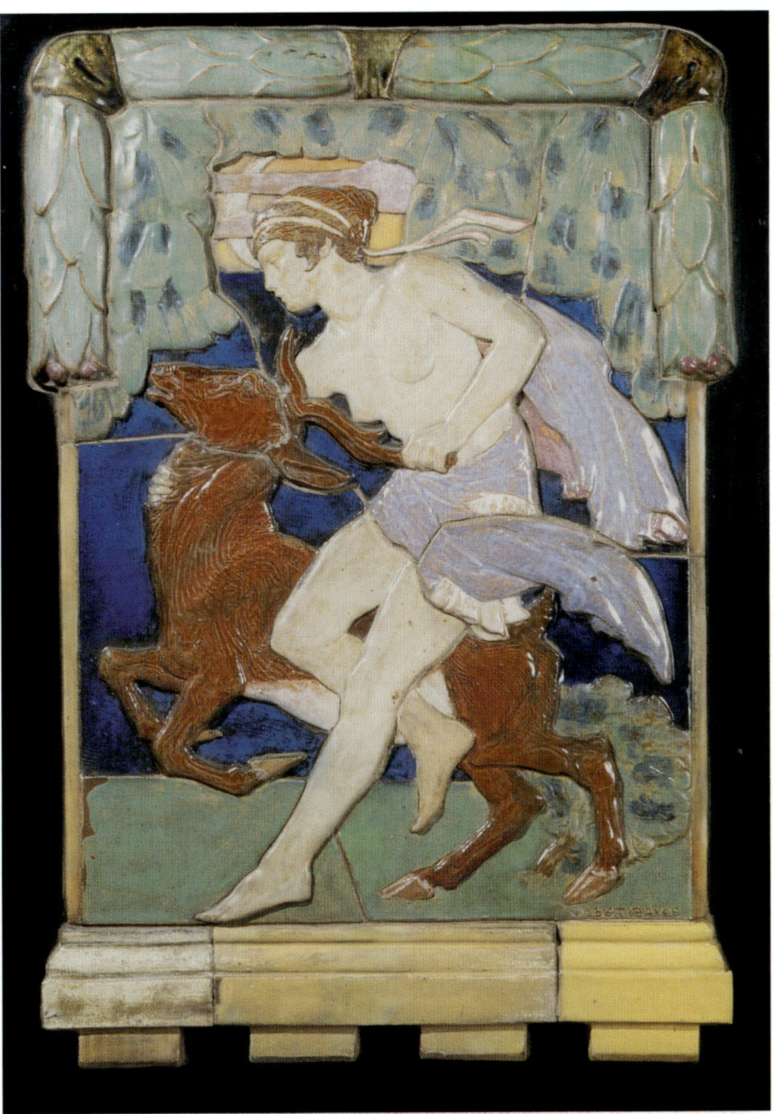

Diana garden panel, Doulton stoneware, 1928.

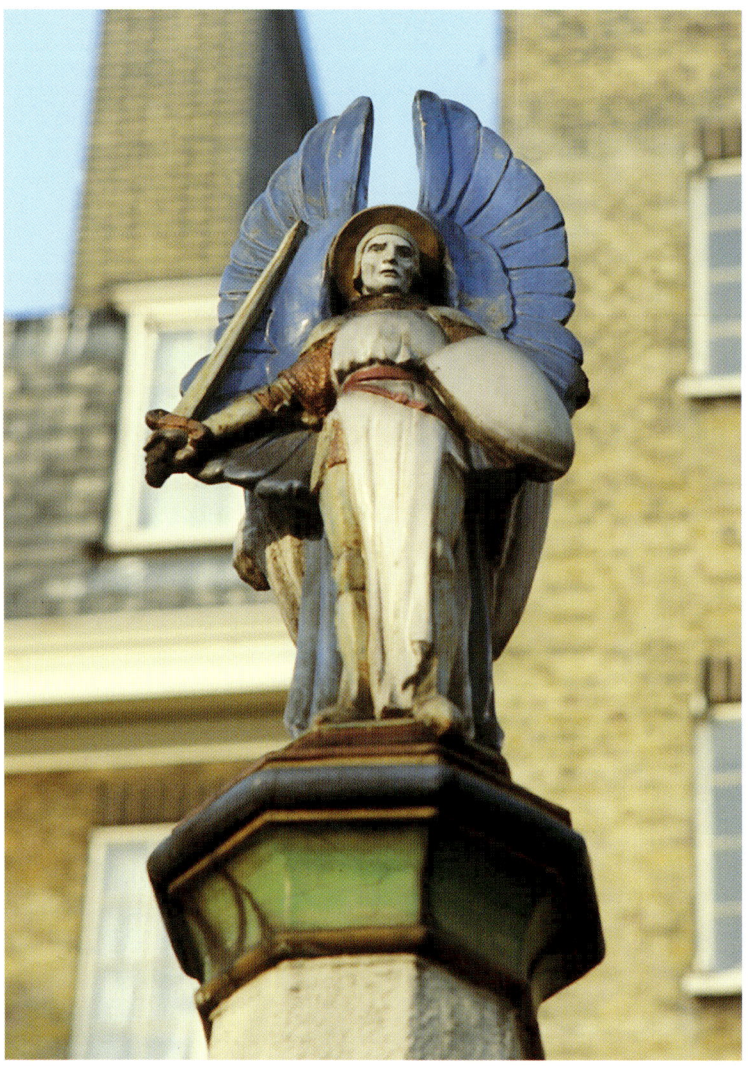

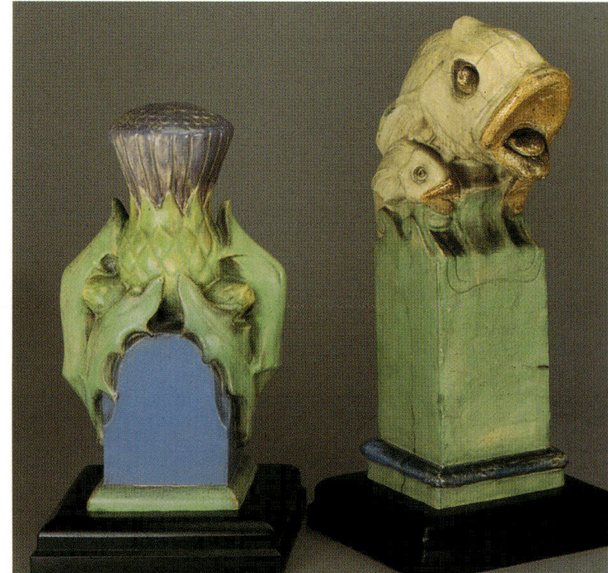

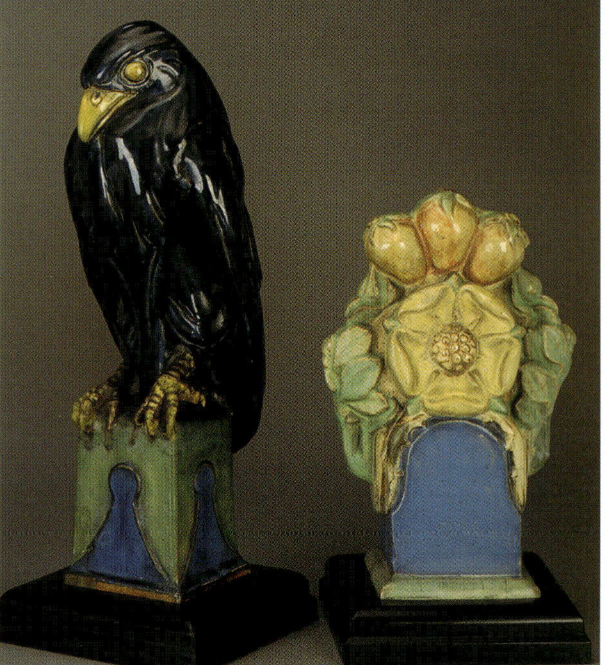

St Pancras Housing Association flats, finials and window lunettes in Doulton stoneware, 1937. Above and right: washing post finials, St Michael, Thistle, Fish, Blackbird and Rose; below: window lunettes, left, The Princess and the Swineherd, right, The Soldier and the Princesss.

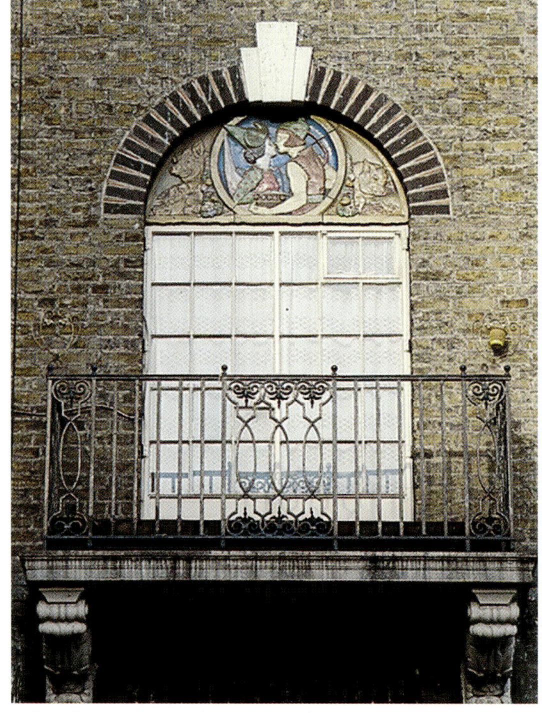

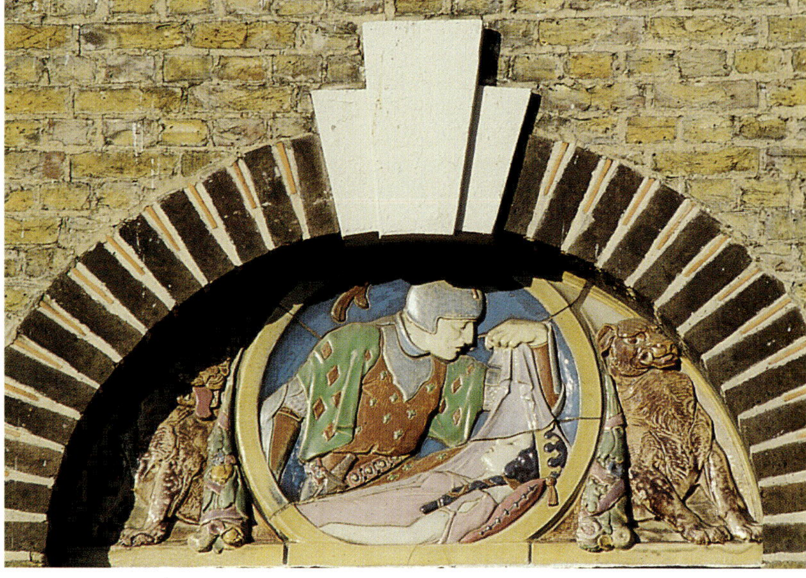

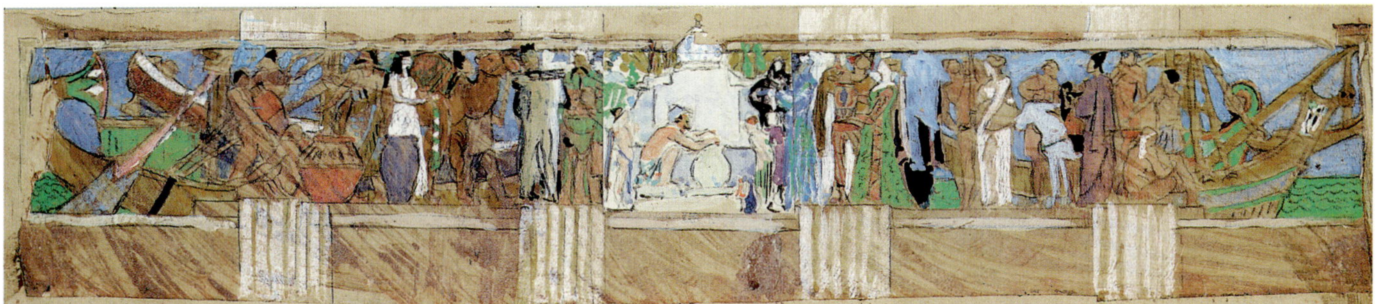

Sketch by Bayes for the Pottery Through the Ages frieze for Doulton House, 1939.

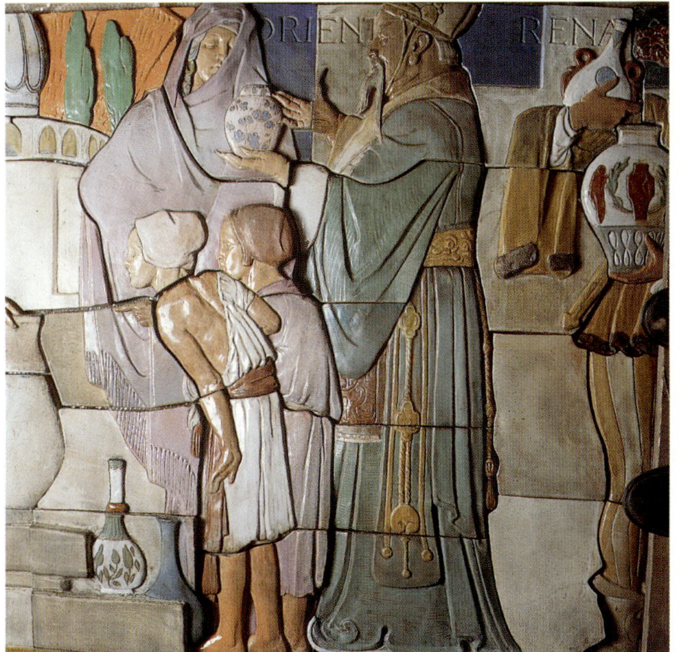

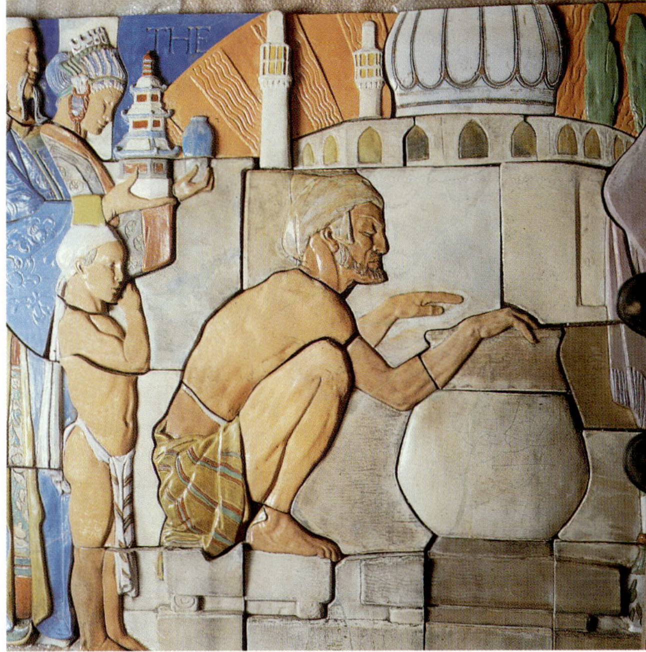

Left and right, details of the Pottery Through the Ages frieze made in Doulton stoneware for Doulton House, Lambeth, 1939. Now in the Victoria & Albert Museum, London.

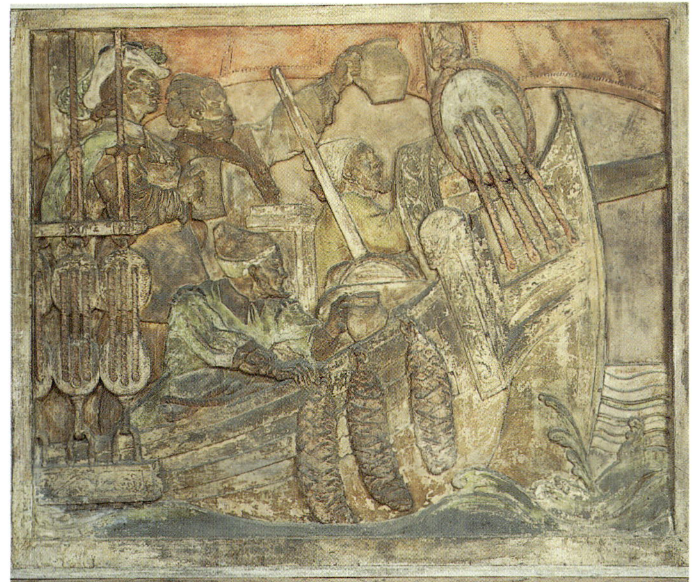

Hand-coloured plaster for the Dutch Potters panel for Doulton House, 1939.

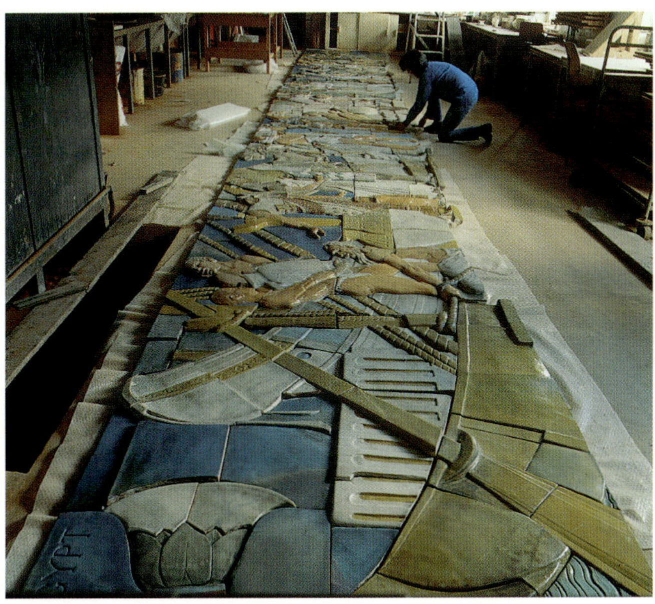

The Pottery Through the Ages frieze during conservation at Ironbridge Gorge Museum, Shropshire.

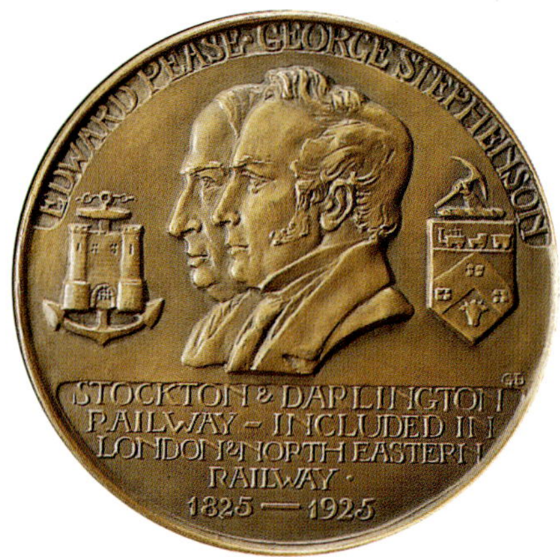
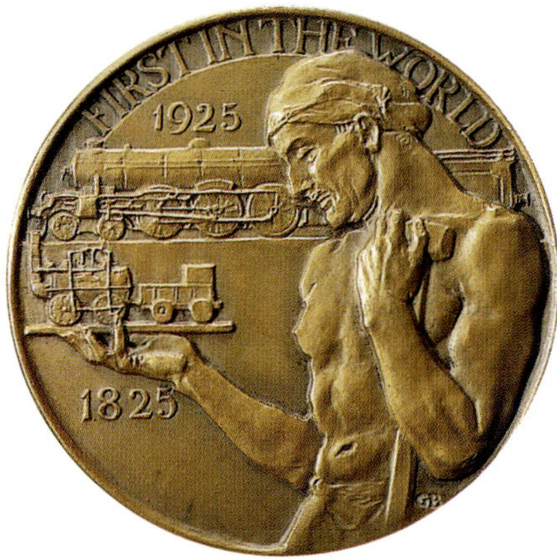

Railway Centenary Medal, 1925.

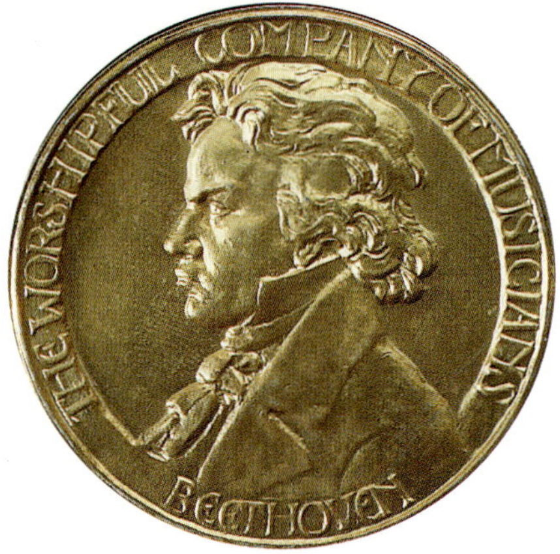
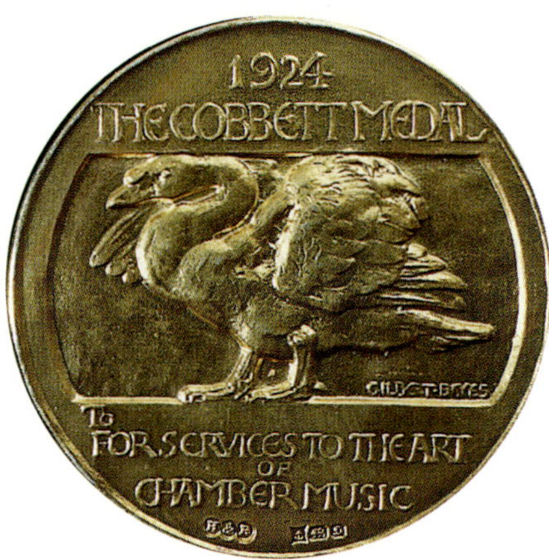

Worshipful Company of Musicians Cobbett Medal, 1924.

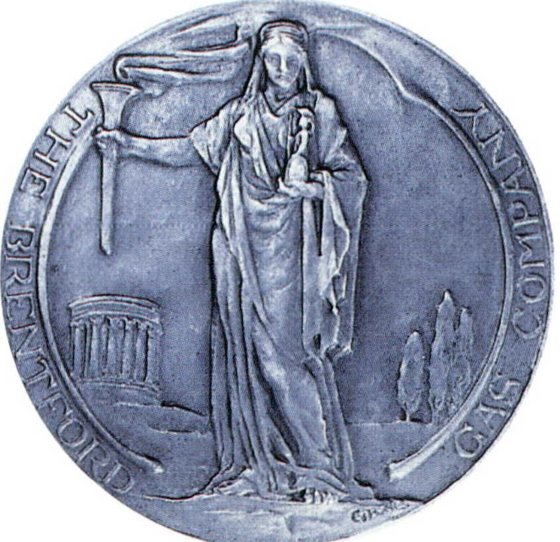
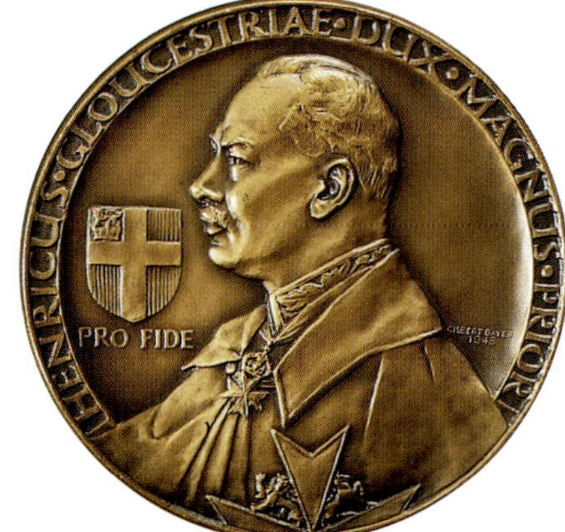

Brentford Gas Company Medal, 1912.

Order of St John Duke of Gloucester Medal, 1948.

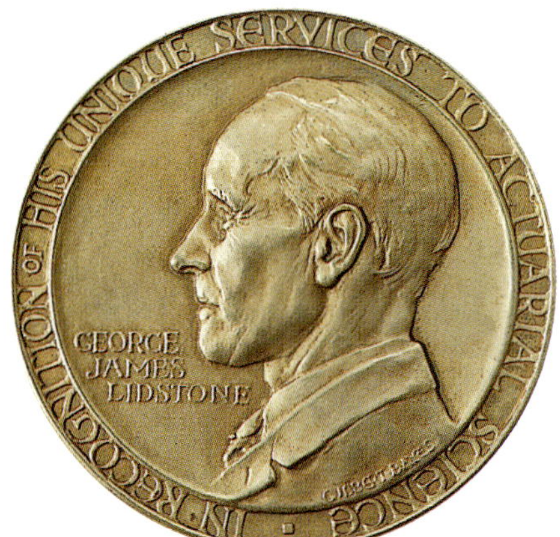
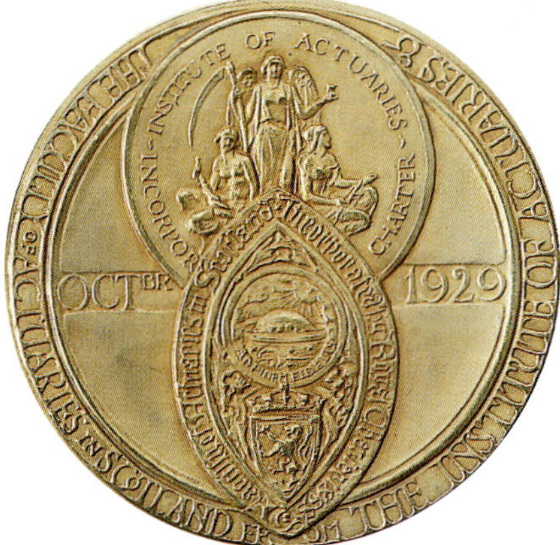

Institute of Actuaries Lidstone Medal, 1929.

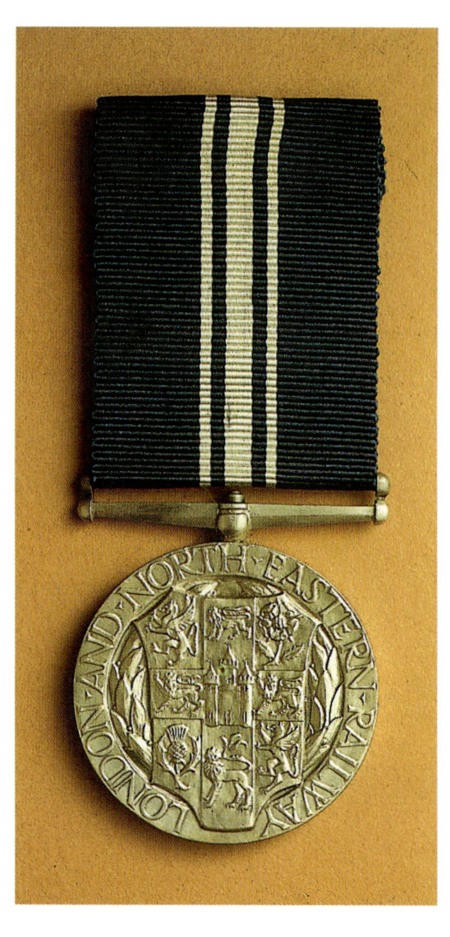

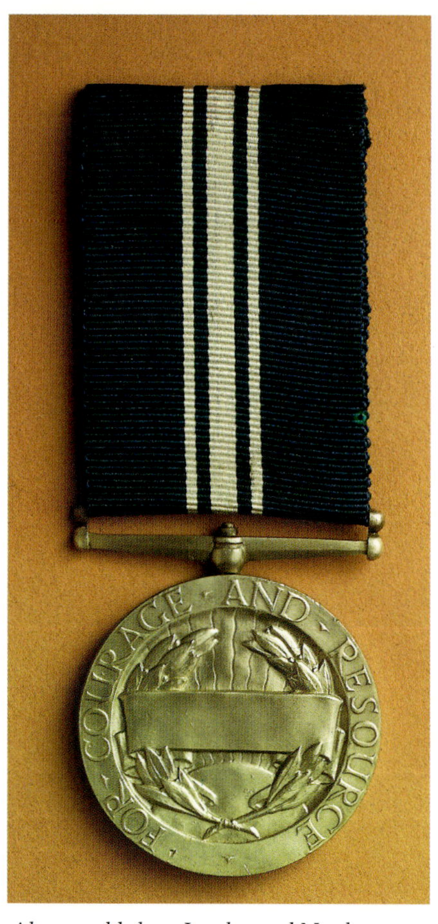

Above and below, London and North Eastern Railway Medal for bravery, 1943 (Imperial War Museum, London).

CATALOGUE RAISONNE
Louise Irvine

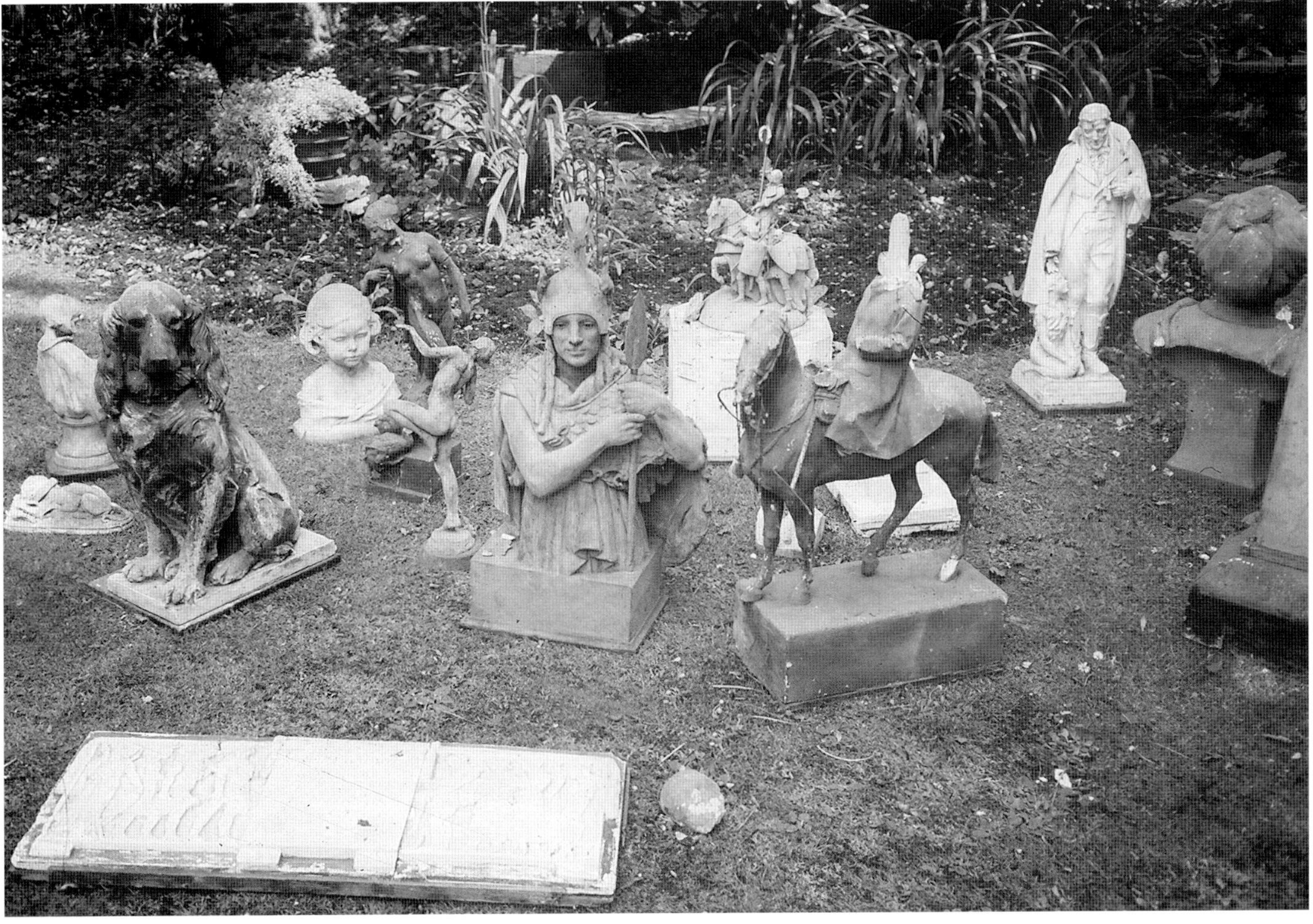

Group of plasters by Bayes, formerly stored in the garden shed at his house, 4 Greville Place, London.

KEY TO CATALOGUE

This catalogue is arranged in chronological order. There is also an alphabetical index on page 191. The year is based on dated examples or the first recorded exhibition or publication reference. The medium and size are given when known. The exhibition listings have been derived from brief details in Bayes' exhibition notebook and contemporary exhibition catalogues. A key to the known venues is given below. There is a more detailed list of art galleries and other venues where Bayes exhibited on page 189. The locations of architectural works are included when known as well as details of pieces in public or private collections. Published references to Bayes' work are given in the literature section and illustrations are recorded when known as 'illus'.

Aberdeen	– Aberdeen Artists Society
Anglo-Japanese	– Anglo-Japanese Exhibition, London, 1910
Arts and Crafts	– Arts and Crafts Exhibition Society, London
Beaux Art	– Beaux Art Gallery, London
Birmingham	– Royal Society of Artists
Bolt Court	– National Competitions and Scholarships Exhibition, 1896
Bournemouth	– Russell Cotes Gallery
Bristol	– Royal West of England Academy
Christchurch, NZ	– New Zealand International Exhibition of Arts and Industries, 1906-07
City and Guilds	– City and Guilds Technical College, Finsbury, London
Dunedin, NZ	– New Zealand and South Seas International Exhibition, 1924-26
Ealing	– Ealing Arts Club, London
Fine Art Society	– The Fine Art Society, London
Franco-British	– Franco-British Exhibition, London, 1908
Ghent	– Exposition Universelle et Industrielle, 1913; Arts and Crafts Exhibition, 1913
Glasgow	– Royal Glasgow Institute of Fine Arts
Glasgow 1938	– British Empire Exhibition, Glasgow, 1938
Goupil	– Goupil Gallery, London
Graphic Arts	– Society of Graphic Arts, London
Horticultural Society	– Royal Horticultural Society, London
Institute	– Royal Institute of Painters in Watercolours
International Medallic	– American Numismatic Society Exhibitions, New York, 1910
Leicester Galleries	– Leicester Galleries, London
Liverpool	– Walker Art Gallery Autumn Exhibitions
LCC	– London County Council Exhibitions
New York 1939	– New York World's Fair, 1939
Newcastle	– North East Coast Exhibition
Paris 1900	– Paris Exposition Universelle, 1900
Paris Arts and Crafts	– Paris Arts and Crafts Exhibition, 1914
Paris 1925	– Exposition International des Arts Decoratifs et Industriels Modernes, 1925
Paris 1927	– British Artists Exhibition, Paris, 1927
Paris Salon	– Paris Salon
Pastel Society	– Pastel Society, London
Portrait Painters	– Royal Society of British Portrait Painters
Rawlson Townsend	– Rawlson Townsend, Dover Street, London
Ridley	– Ridley Arts Club, London
Rome	– International Fine Arts Exhibition, 1911
Royal Academy	– Royal Academy of Arts, Burlington House, London
Royal Scottish Academy	– Royal Scottish Academy of Arts
St Louis	– World's Fair, St Louis, USA, 1904
Sir John Cass	– Sir John Cass Arts and Crafts Society
Southport	– Atkinson Art Gallery Spring Exhibition
Sussex Artists	– Sussex Artists, Brighton, Hove and Lewes
Toronto	– Canadian National Exhibition, Toronto
Wembley	– British Empire Exhibition, London, 1924
Whitechapel	– Exhibition of Contemporary British Art, Whitechapel Art Gallery, London
White City	– White City Exhibition Centre, London
Wolverhampton	– Wolverhampton Art Gallery and Museum Autumn Exhibition

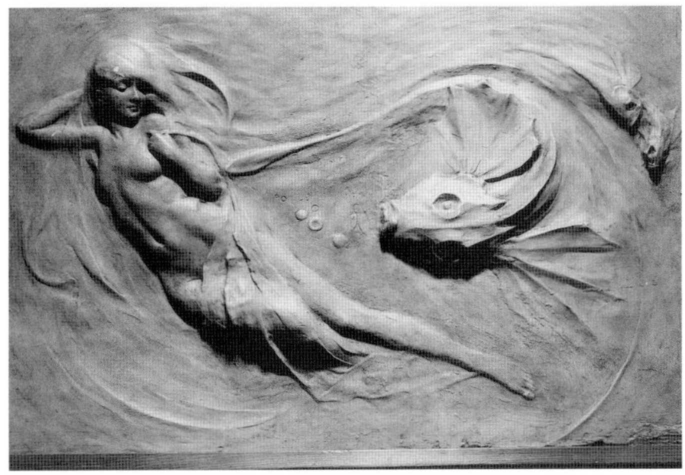

The Sea Maid's Frolic

The Pet of the Ring

1888

Artillery Horses
Medium: Wax
Exhibitions: Arts and Crafts 1888

1889

The Fortunes of War
Medium: Wax group
Exhibitions Royal Academy 1889

Doorknocker
Medium: Wax model
Exhibitions: Arts and Crafts 1889

A Lancashire Milk Horse
Medium: Wax model
Exhibitions: Royal Academy 1889

Tam o' Shanter
Medium: Wax
Exhibitions: Arts and Crafts 1889
Model for the sternboard for the sloop,
The Grey Mare.

1890

The Sea Maid's Frolic
Medium: Plaster relief
Size: H 15³/₄ ins W 23ins
(40 x 58.5cms)
Exhibitions: Arts and Crafts 1890
Inscribed 'His Gift to AR from GB'.

Pets
Medium: Plaster reliefs
Exhibitions: Arts and Crafts 1890

The Pet of the Ring
Medium: Wax relief
Exhibitions: Royal Academy 1890
Literature: *A Biographical Dictionary of
Wax Modellers*, E.J. Pyke,
pl.17, illus.

St George
Medium: Wax model
Exhibitions: Royal Society of British
Artists 1890 (4gns)

Two in Hand
Medium: Wax model
Exhibitions: Royal Society of British
Artists (3gns)

1891

Houp La
Medium: Relief
Exhibitions: Royal Academy 1891

The Forge
Medium: Relief
Exhibitions: Royal Academy 1891

An Arab Fantasia
Medium: Relief
Exhibitions: Royal Academy 1891

The Last Load
Medium: Relief
Exhibitions: Royal Academy 1891

1892

Carting Sand, France
Medium: Relief
Exhibitions: Royal Academy 1892

A Farmer Went Trotting upon his Grey Mare
Medium: Wax group
Exhibitions: Royal Academy 1892

Young Horses, Barnet Fair
Medium: Wax group
Exhibitions: Royal Academy 1892

A Favourite Watering Place
Medium: Plaster relief
Exhibitions: Royal Academy 1892
Locations: Bayes Trust

The Goal
Medium: Electrotype frieze
Size: H 5¹/₂ ins W 25¹/₂ins
(14 x 65.5cms)
Exhibitions: Royal Academy 1892; Arts
and Crafts 1893; International
Medallic, New York 1910.
Locations: Sotheby's 26.3.80 (sold);
Christie's 28.1.86 (sold).
Literature: *The Magazine of Art* 1895 p66,
illus; *The Art Journal* 1908 Jul
p199.
For illustration see next page.

Encore
Exhibitions: Royal Society of British
Artists 1892 (10gns)

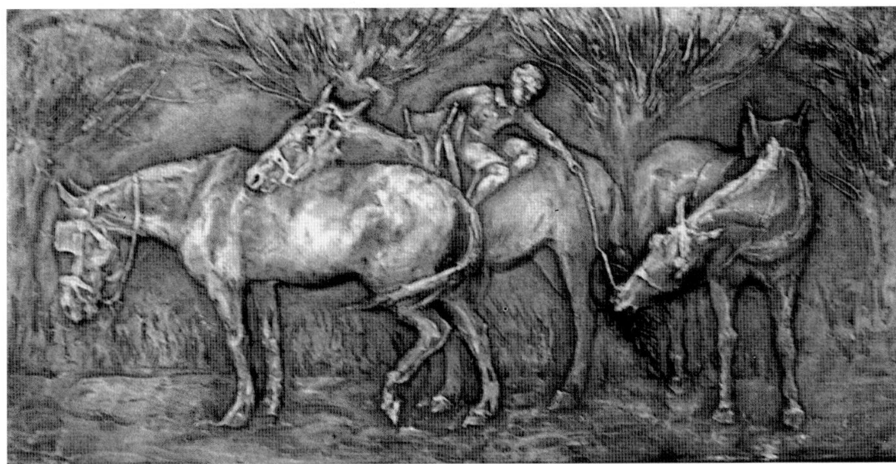

A Favourite Watering Place

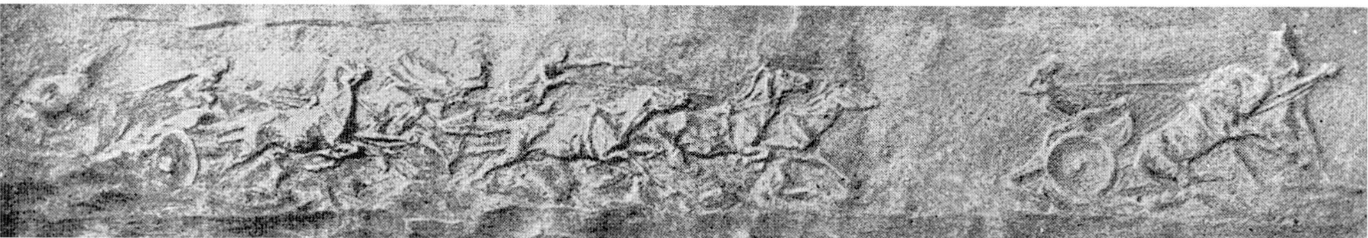

The Goal

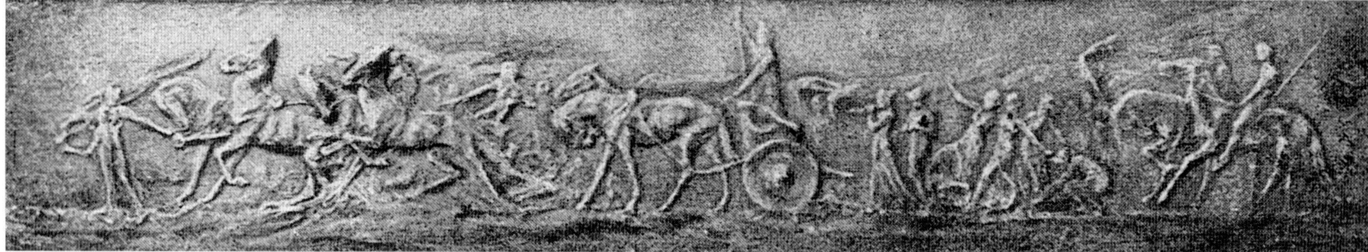

The Triumph

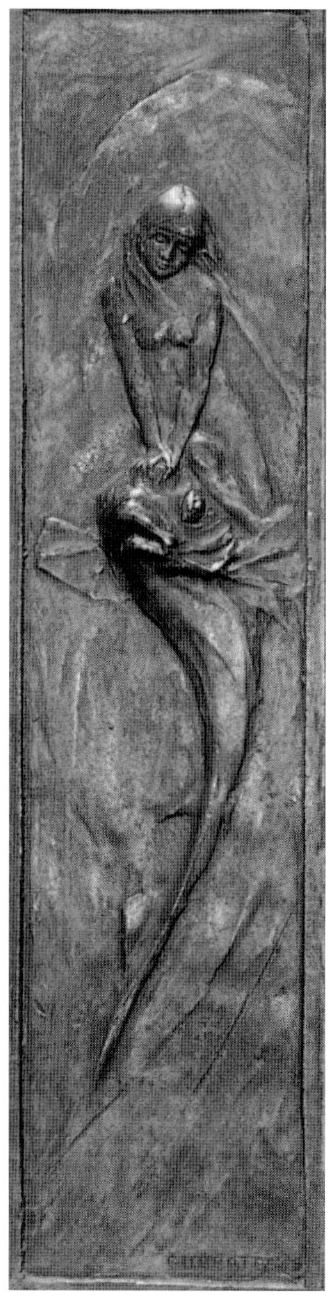

A Sea Frolic

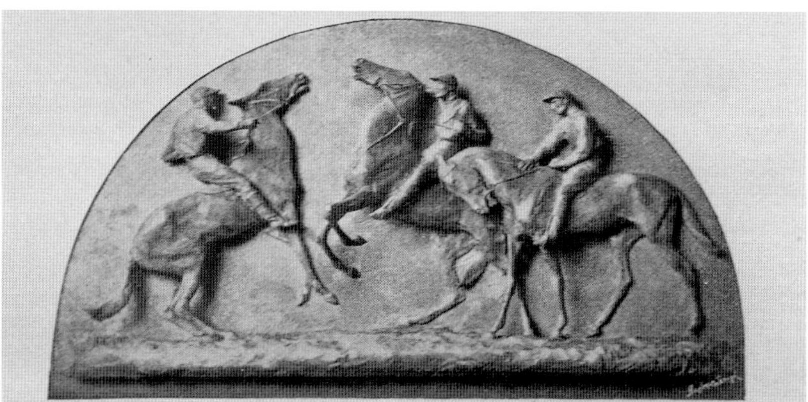

Probable Starters

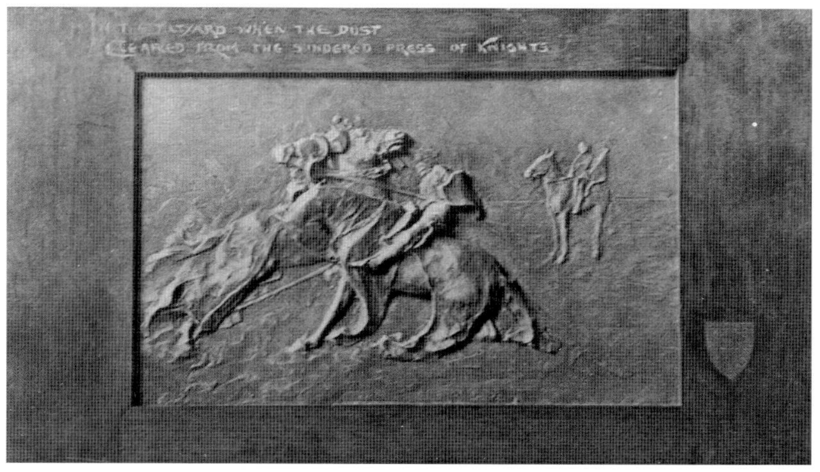

In the Tilt Yard

1893

A Sea Frolic
Medium: Bronze relief
Size: H 12ins W 3ins (30 x 7.5cms)
Exhibitions: Royal Academy 1893
Locations: Private collection

Showing his Points
Medium: Wax
Exhibitions: Royal Academy 1893

The End of the Furrow
Medium: Relief
Exhibitions: Royal Academy 1893

Probable Starters
Medium: Wax
Size: H 14 in W 23ins (35.5 x 58.5cms)
Exhibitions: Royal Academy 1893
Literature: *Royal Academy Pictures 1893*
             p205, illus; *British Sculpture and*
             Sculptors of Today, M.H.
             Spielman 1901 p144.

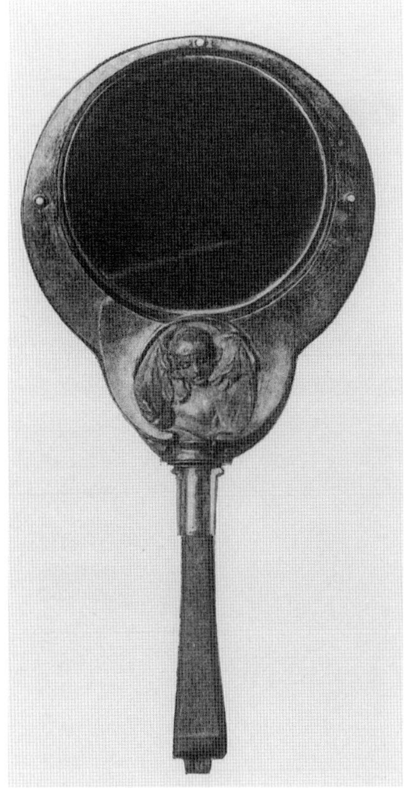

Hand Mirror

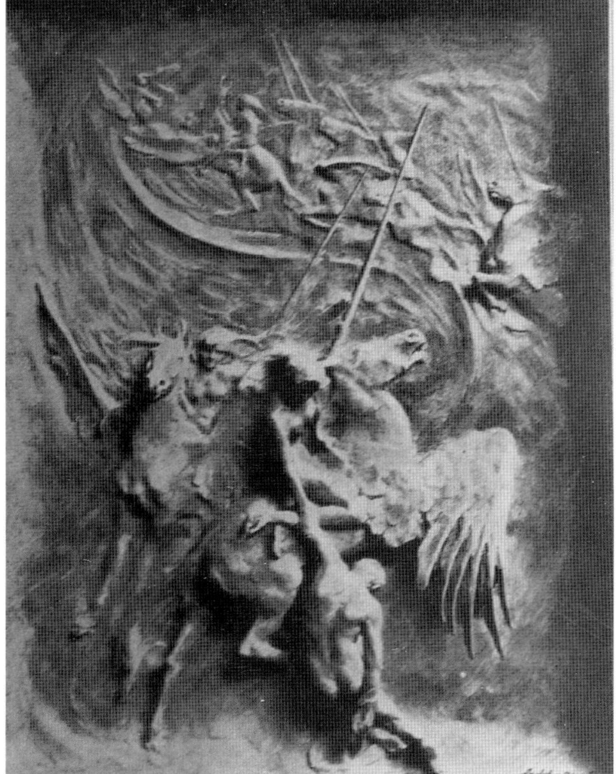

The Ride of the Valkyries

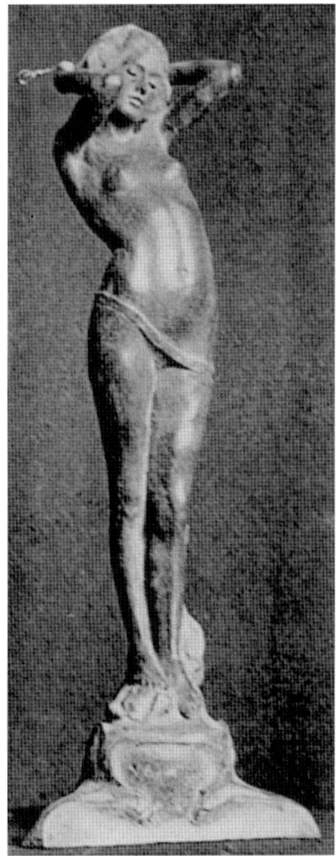

Vanity

The Triumph

Medium: Metal relief
Exhibitions: Arts and Crafts 1893;
Glasgow 1905 (£6).
Literature: *Royal Academy Pictures* 1894
p104, illus; *The Magazine of
Art* 1895 p34, illus; *British
Sculpture and Sculptors of
Today*, M.H. Spielman 1901
p144.

1894

The Ride of the Valkyries

Medium: Relief
Size: H 24ins (61cms)
Exhibitions: Royal Academy 1894
Literature: *Royal Academy Pictures*, 1894
p104, illus; *British Sculpture
and Sculptors of Today*, M.H.
Spielman 1901 p144.

1895

In the Tilt Yard

Medium: Bronze relief
Size: H 17ins W 29ins
(43 x 73.5cms)
Exhibitions: Royal Academy 1895
Literature: *Royal Academy Pictures* 1895,
p23, illus; *British Sculpture and
Sculptors of Today*, M.H.
Spielman 1901 p144.

1896

The Banners of the Faithful

Medium: Metal relief
Size: H 10ins W 27ins
(25.5 x 68.5cms)
Exhibitions: Royal Academy 1896;
Birmingham 1898 (10gns).
Literature: *Royal Academy Pictures* 1896
p53, illus; *British Sculpture and
Sculptors of Today*, M.H.
Spielman 1901 p144.

Hand Mirror

Medium: Copper, silver and turquoise
Exhibitions: Arts and Crafts 1896;
Woodbury Gallery 1904.

Night

Medium: Metal panel
Exhibitions: Arts and Crafts 1896;
Birmingham 1899 (3gns).

The Raiders

Exhibitions: Birmingham 1896

Vanity

Medium: Bronze statuette
Exhibitions: Bolt Court, London 1896;
Birmingham 1897, (15gns).
Literature: *The Magazine of Art* 1896
p294, illus; *British Sculpture
and Sculptors of Today*, M.H.
Spielman 1901 p144, illus.

The Four Winter Months Entering the Arena

Exhibitions: Royal Academy 1896;
Birmingham 1897 (12gns);
Paris 1900.
These were a set of door panels and a fire-place panel.

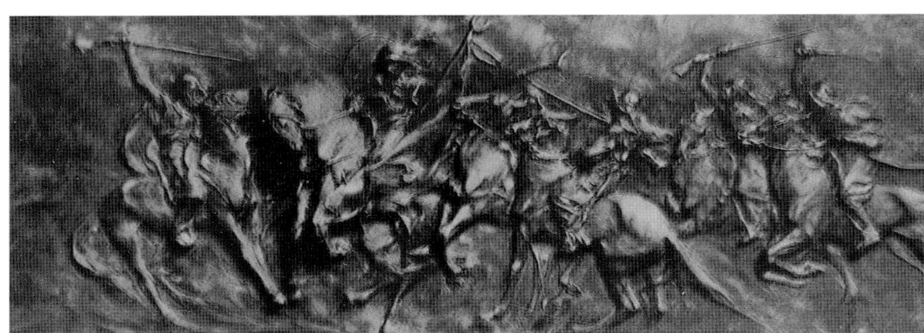

The Banners of the Faithful

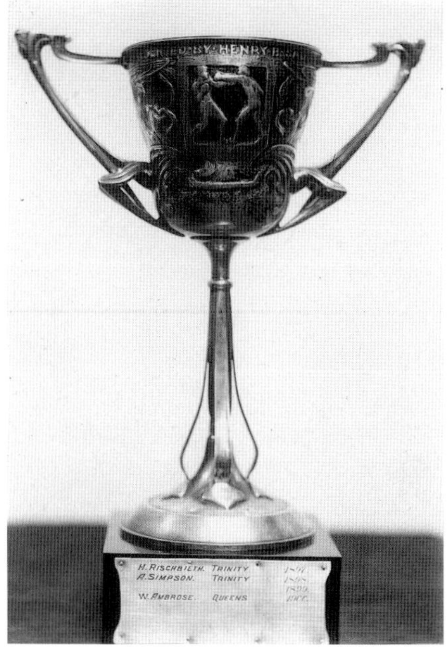

Presentation Cup for Boxing

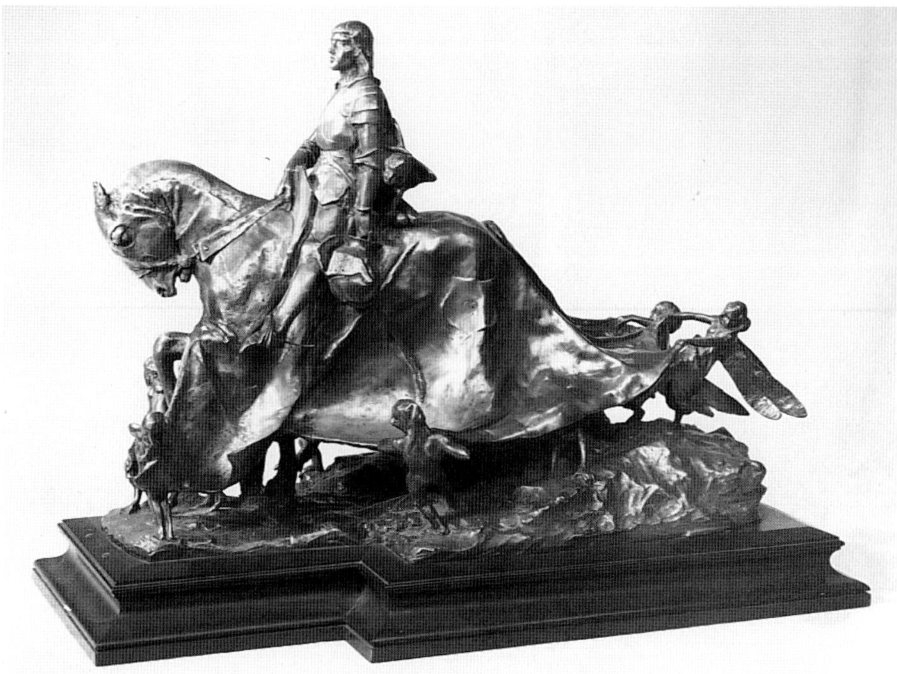

A Knight Errant

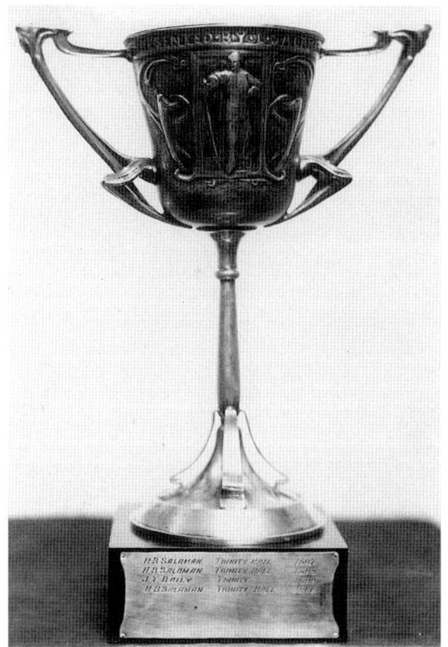

Presentation Cup for Fencing

1897

Presentation Cup for Boxing
Medium: Silver
Presented by Henry B. Salaman, Trinity
Hall, Cambridge.

Presentation Cup for Fencing
Medium: Silver and enamel
Presented by L. Salaman, Trinity Hall,
Cambridge.

1898

The Valkyries
Medium: Relief
Exhibitions: Royal Academy 1898;
             Birmingham, 1898.

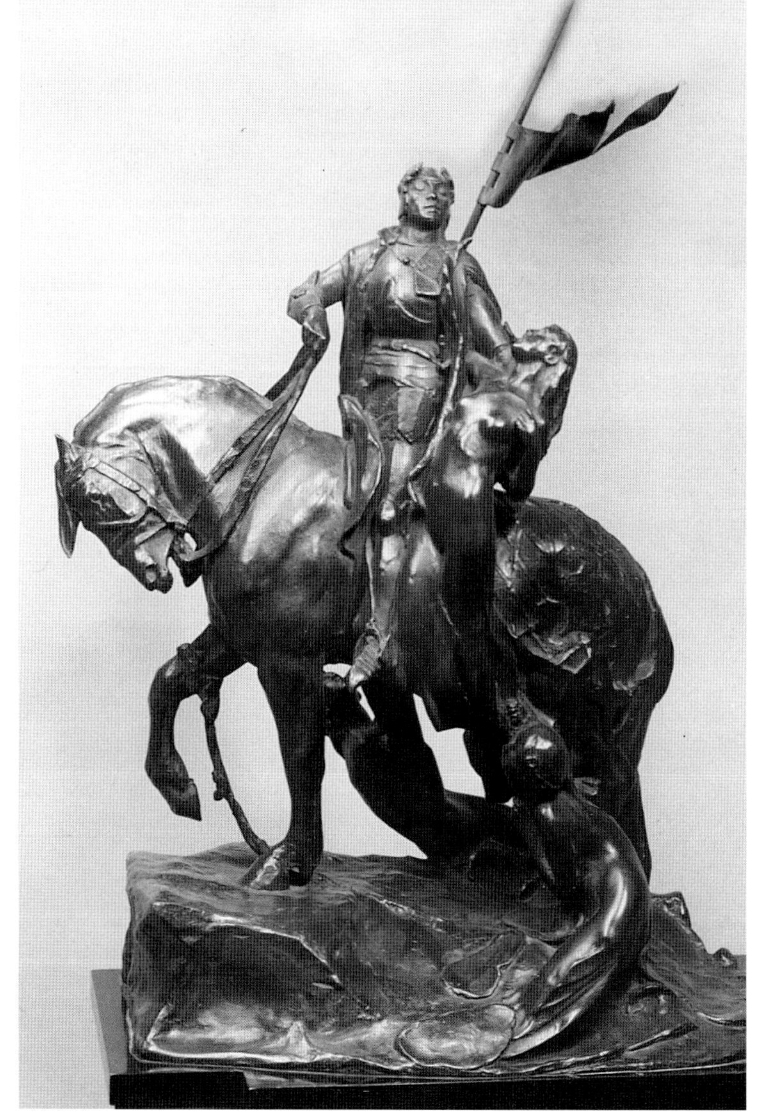

The Sirens of the Ford

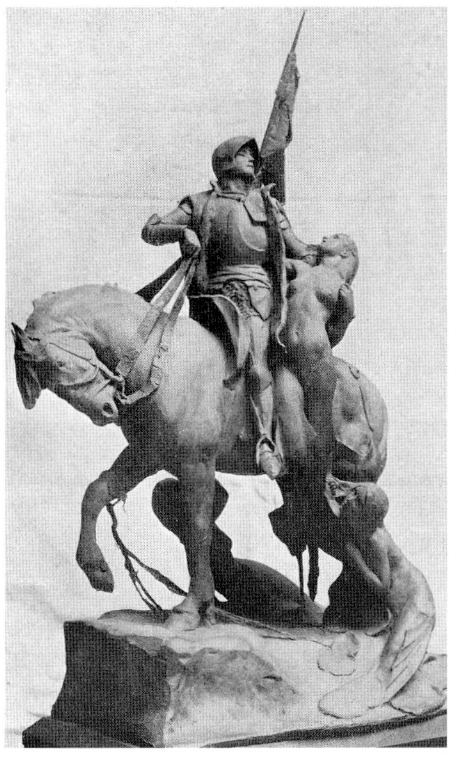

Plaster for The Sirens of the Ford

A Knight Errant

Medium:	Silver on ebonised base
Size:	H 25ins (63.5cms)
Exhibitions:	Royal Academy 1898 (plaster)
Locations:	St John's College, Oxford; private collection (formerly Handley Read Collection).
Literature:	*Royal Academy Pictures* 1898 p145, illus; *The Studio* 1902 Vol 25 p109, illus; *The Art Journal* 1908 Jul p194, illus.

1899

Sir Richard Moon, 1815-1899

Medium:	Marble bust
Locations:	Sotheby's 13.6.84, lot 239, (sold)

Sir Richard Moon was Chairman of the London and North Western Railway.

Maritime Chess Set

Medium:	Plaster
Exhibitions:	Arts and Crafts 1899
Literature:	*The Studio* 1899 Vol 18 p269, illus.

The Sirens of the Ford

Medium:	Bronze group
Size:	H 25¹/₂ins (65cms)
Exhibitions:	Royal Academy 1899; Glasgow 1901 (bronze £100); Fine Art Society 1902 (plaster); Leicester Galleries 1918 (sold); Ridley 1919; Fine Art Society 1968 (formerly Handley Read Collection).
Locations:	Harris Museum, Preston purchased 1920 (100gns)
Literature:	*Royal Academy Pictures* 1899 p158, illus; *British Sculpture and Sculptors of Today*, M.H. Spielman 1901, illus; *The Studio* 1900 Vol 20 p185, illus.

Sea Horses

Medium:	Bronzed plaster relief
Exhibitions:	Arts and Crafts 1899
Literature:	*Architectural Review* 1899 Vol 6 p209, illus; *The Studio* 1899 Vol 18 p265; *The Studio* 1902 Vol 25 p107, illus.

In *The Studio*, the writer stated: 'For decoration of a chimney piece in a white room'.

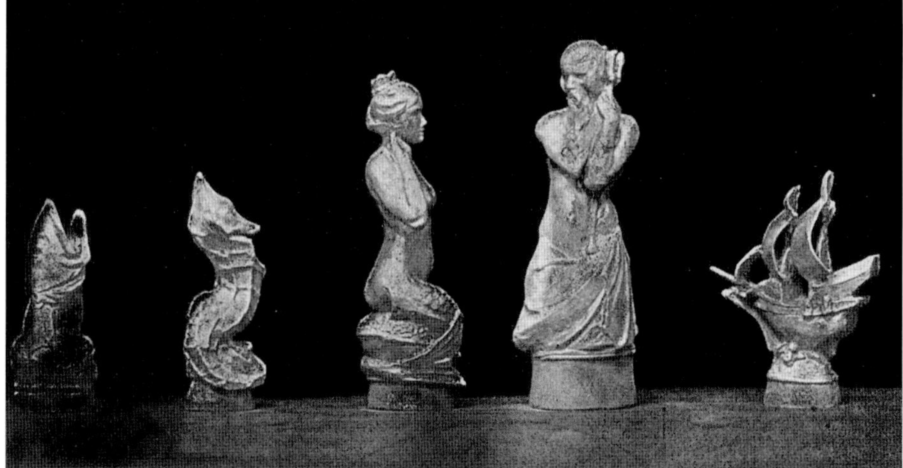

Maritime Chess Set

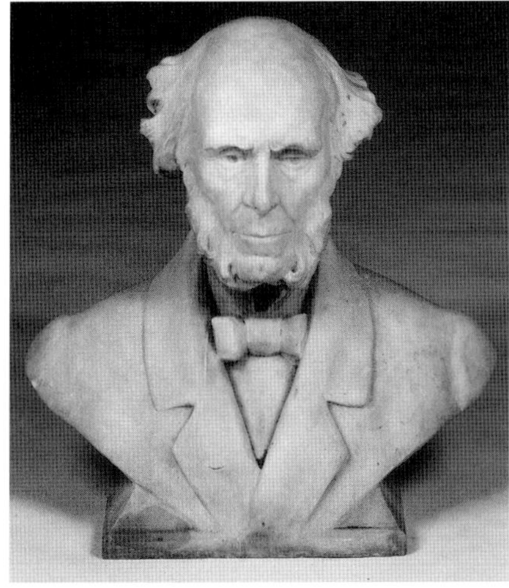

Sir Richard Moon

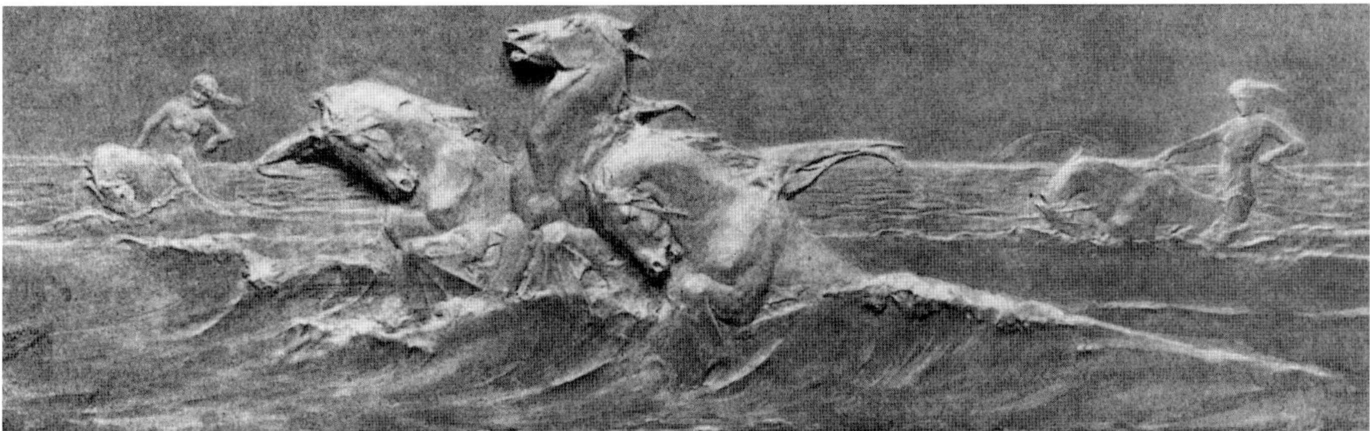

Sea Horses

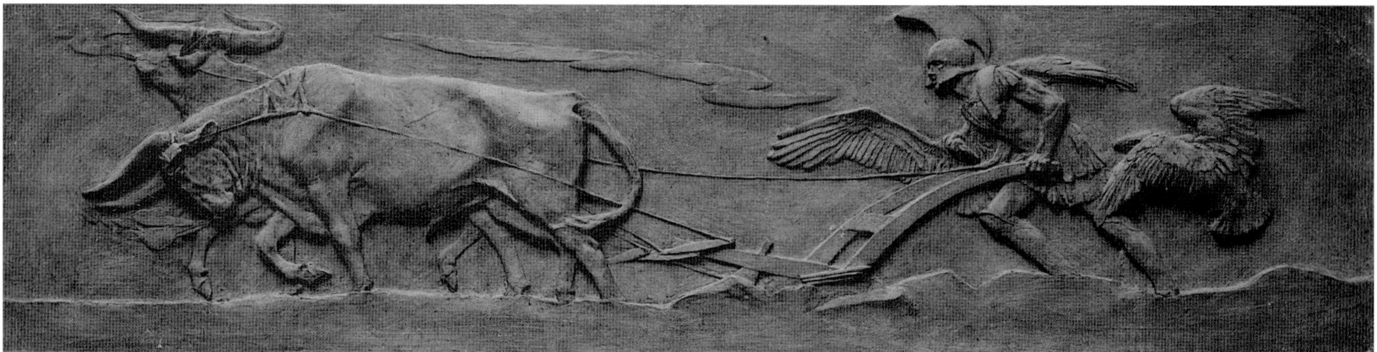

Jason Ploughing the Acre of Mars

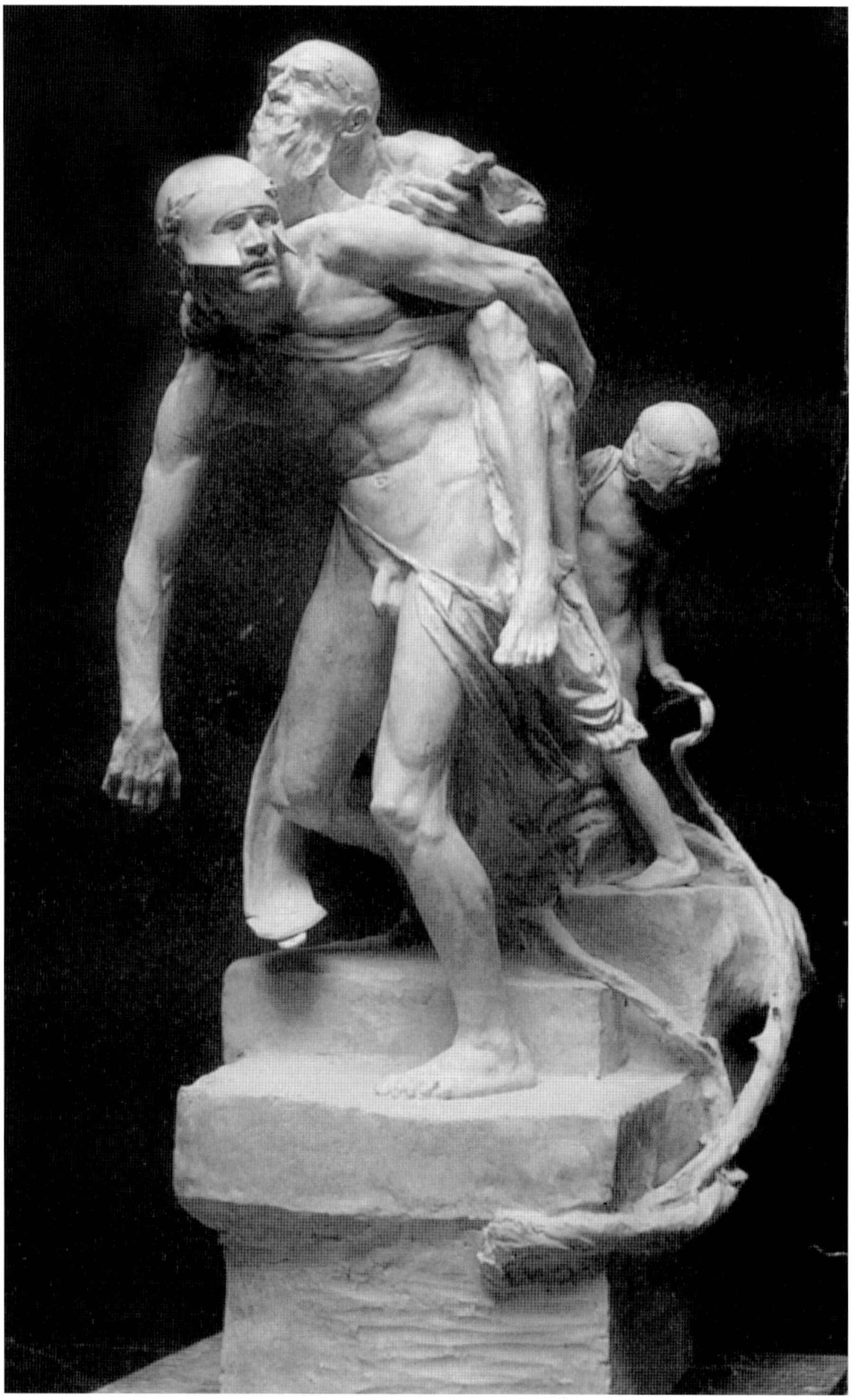

Aeneas Fleeing from Troy
Medium: Plaster group
Exhibitions: Royal Academy 1900
Literature: The Studio 1899 Vol 18
               p287, illus; *British Sculpture
               and Sculptors of Today*, M.H.
               Spielman 1901 p144, illus.

Under the Sea
Exhibitions: Birmingham 1899 (3gns)

1900

Jason Ploughing the Acre of Mars
Medium: Metal relief
Size: H 17ins W 60ins
             (43 x 153cms)
Exhibitions: Royal Academy 1900; Paris
             1900; Christchurch, New
             Zealand 1906/7; Anglo-
             Japanese 1910; Ghent Arts
             and Crafts 1913 (£50); Paris
             Arts and Crafts 1914.
Literature: The Studio 1902 Vol 25 p104,
             illus; *The Art Journal* 1908
             July p193, illus.
Locations: Robert McDougal Art Gallery,
             Christchurch, New Zealand
             purchased by Canterbury
             Society of Art 1906.

Cabinet
Medium: Oak with metal reliefs
Exhibitions: Arts and Crafts 1901;
             Birmingham 1901 (£21).
Locations: Bayes Trust
Literature: The Studio 1901 Vol 23 p128,
             illus.

The Dragon Slayer
Medium: Plaster for bronze
Size: H 31ins (79cms)
Exhibitions: Royal Academy1900;
             Birmingham 1900 (£100); St
             Louis 1904; Portrait Painters
             1905; Glasgow 1909 (100gns).
Literature: *Royal Academy Pictures* 1900
             p158, illus; *British Sculpture
             and Sculptors of Today*, M.H.
             Spielman 1901 p144.

While studying in Paris, Bayes was
influenced by the work of the sculptor,
Frémiet. There are many parallels at this
time, for example, the two St George
figures.

Aeneas Fleeing from Troy

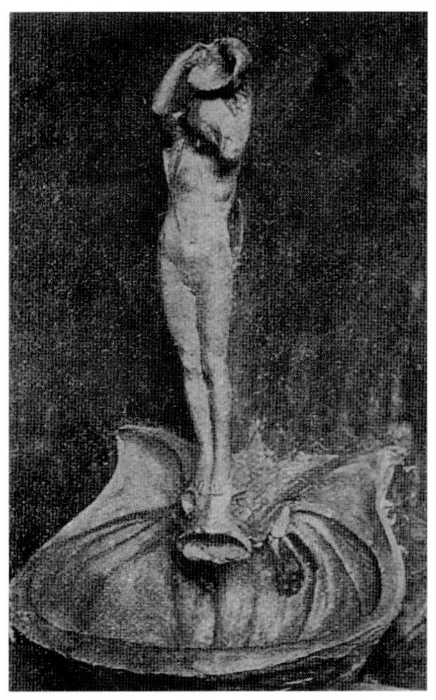

Fountain Figure

Medium: Plaster
Exhibitions: City and Guilds 1900;
Portrait Painters 1905.
Literature: *The Art Journal* 1900 p90,
illus.

Under the Moon

Exhibitions: Birmingham 1901, 1910
(10gns); Glasgow 1903 (£13),
1911; Fine Art Society,
Ghent Fine Arts, 1913; Leeds
1916.

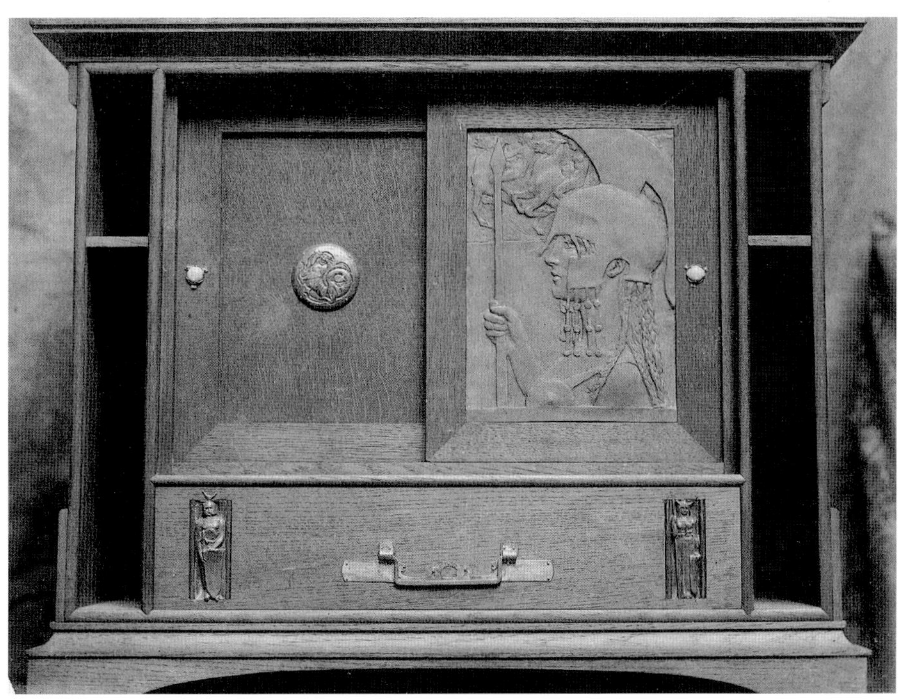

Cabinet

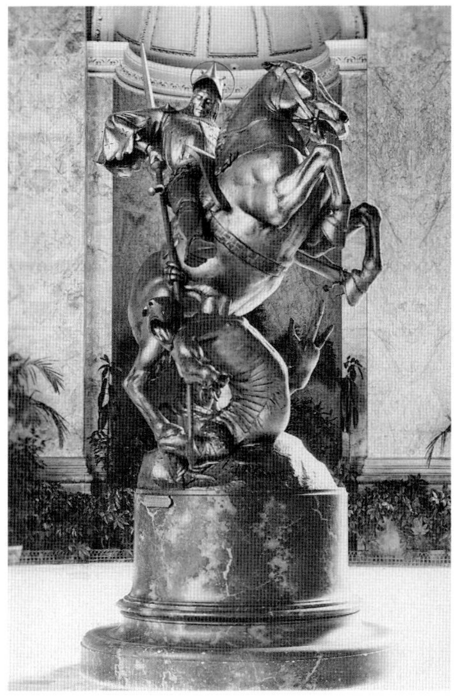

Postcard from one of Bayes' albums showing Frémiet's sculpture of St George Slaying the Dragon in the Palais de Beaux Arts, Paris.

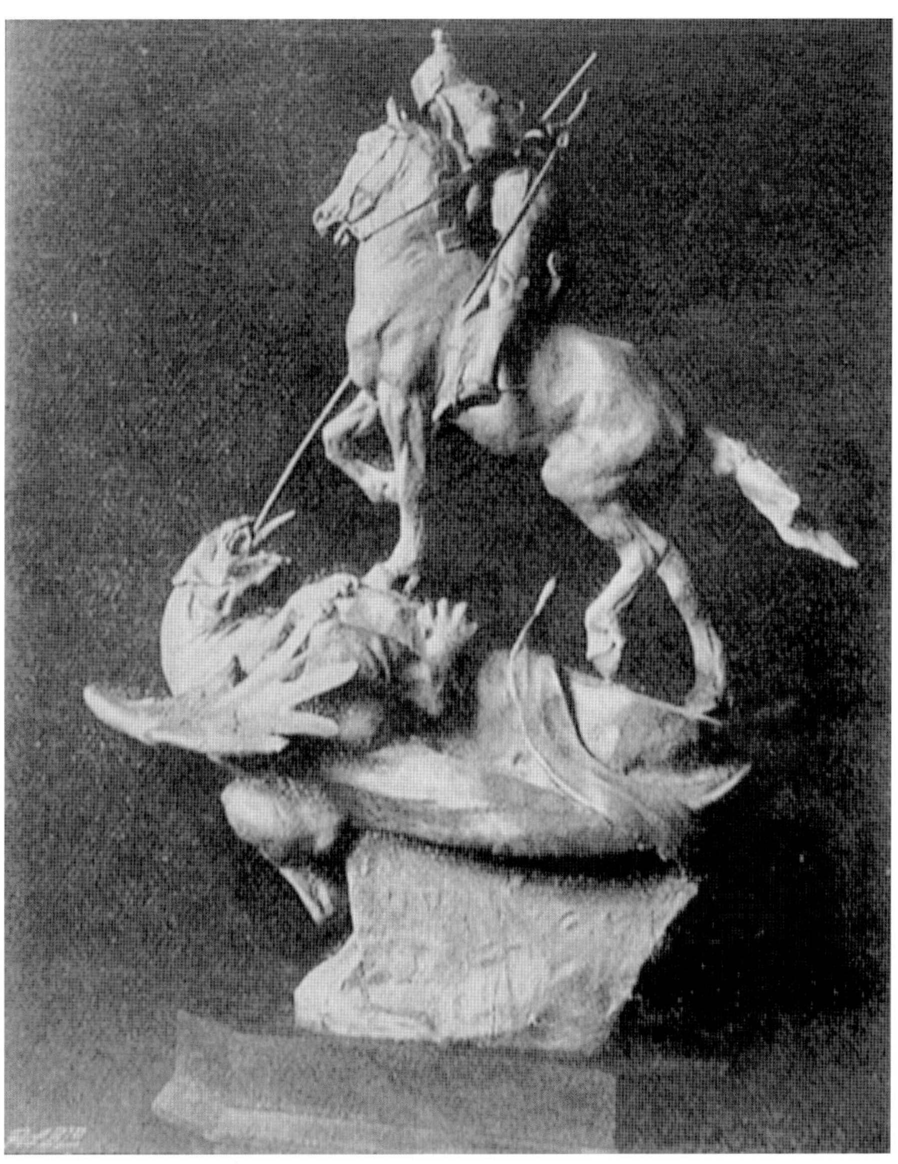

The Dragon Slayer

Gilbert Bayes

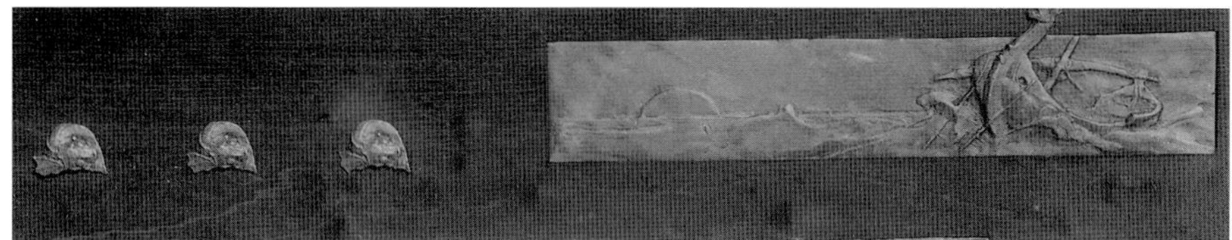

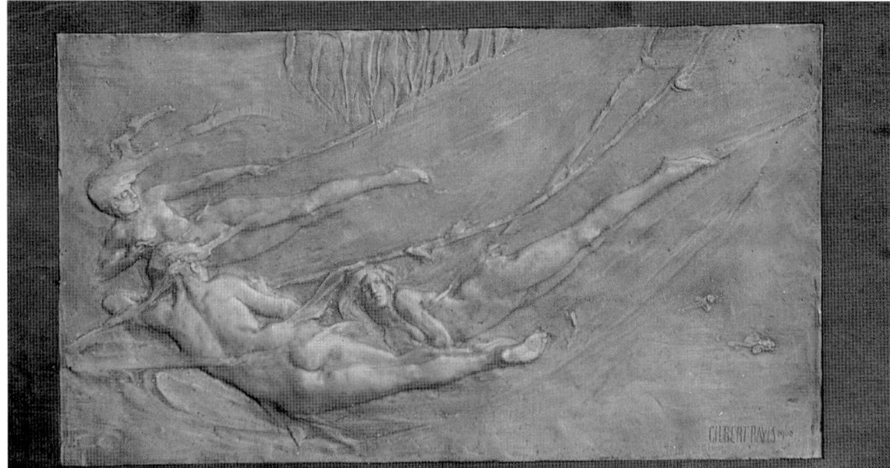

The Derelict

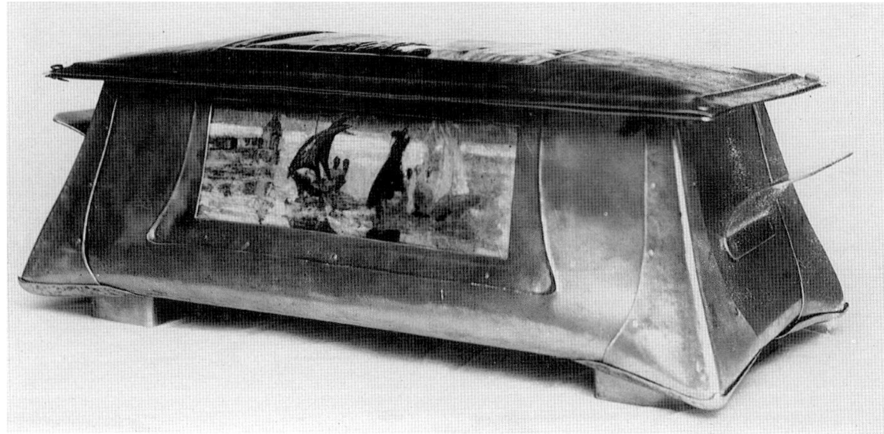

Casket

The Derelict
Medium: Metal reliefs for furniture
Exhibitions: Royal Academy 1902;
         Birmingham 1902 (15gns);
         Sir John Cass 1909;
         International Medallic, New
         York 1910.
Literature: *The Studio* 1902 Vol 25 p102,
         illus.

Casket
Medium: Copper and enamel

The Sketch Club Panel
Medium: Plaster
Exhibitions: City and Guilds 1900
Literature: *The Art Journal* 1900 p90,
         illus.

1901

Presentation Cup 'Moon Sprites'
Medium: Silver with jewels.

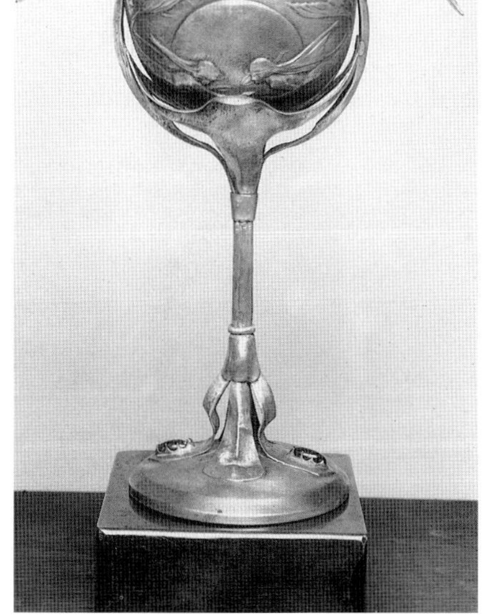

Presentation Cup 'Moon Sprites'

Sea Nymph on Crest of Wave
Medium: Plaster
Size: H 12ins W 8¼ins (30 x 21cms)
Exhibitions: City and Guilds, 1900
Locations: Private collection
Literature: *The Art Journal* 1900 p90, illus.

Racing Cup
Medium: Sketch design for silver cup
Literature: *The Studio* 1901 Vol 22 p275,
         illus.

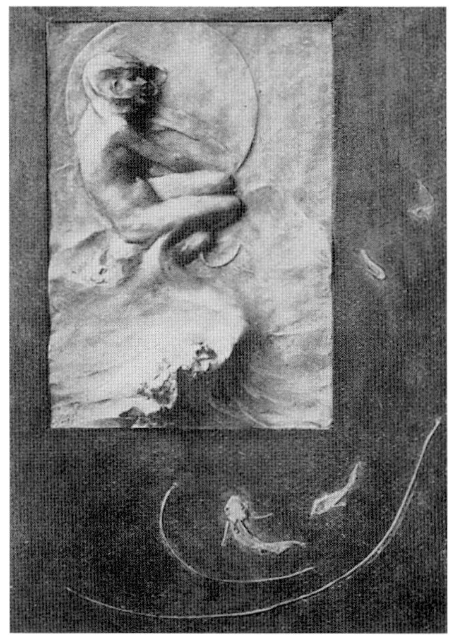

Sea Nymph on Crest of Wave

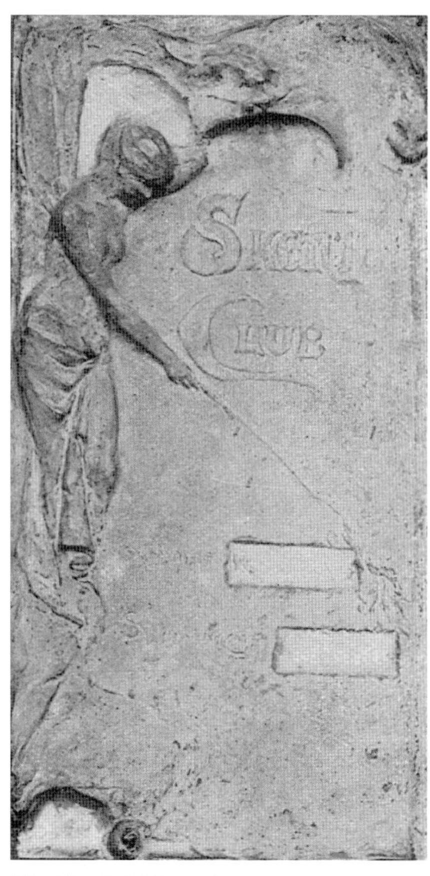

The Sketch Club panel

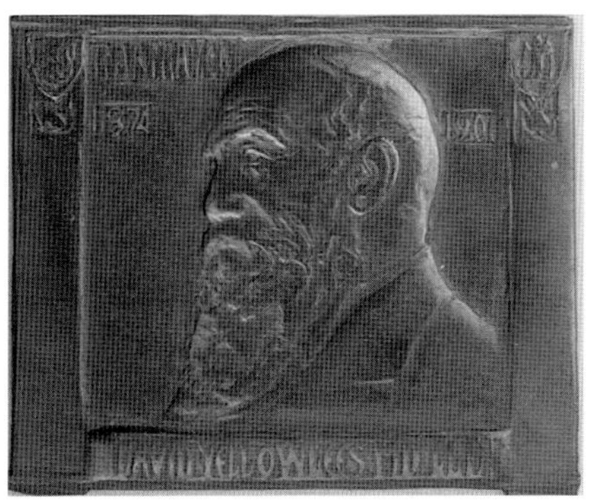

Dr David Yellowlees plaque

1902

A Knight on his War Horse

Medium: Plaster maquette and bronze
                statuette
Exhibitions: Royal Academy 1902;
                Glasgow 1903 (plaster £84).
Literature: *Royal Academy Pictures* 1902
                p19, illus; *The Studio* 1902 Vol
                25 p104, illus; *Modern
                Tendencies in Sculpture*, Lorado
                Taft 1921 p76, illus.

Dr David Yellowlees MD LLD

Medium: Bronze plaque
Size: H 1²/₃ins W 2ins (4 x 5cms)
Exhibitions: Portrait Painters 1905
Locations: Bayes Trust
Dr Yellowlees was Physician
Superintendent at Gartnavel Hospital,
Glasgow from 1874 to 1901.

Dr David Yellowlees MD LLD

Medium: Bronze panel set in marble
Size: H 30ins W 40ins (77 x 102cms)
Exhibitions: Royal Academy 1903
Locations: Hospital Chapel, Gartnavel
                Hospital, Glasgow

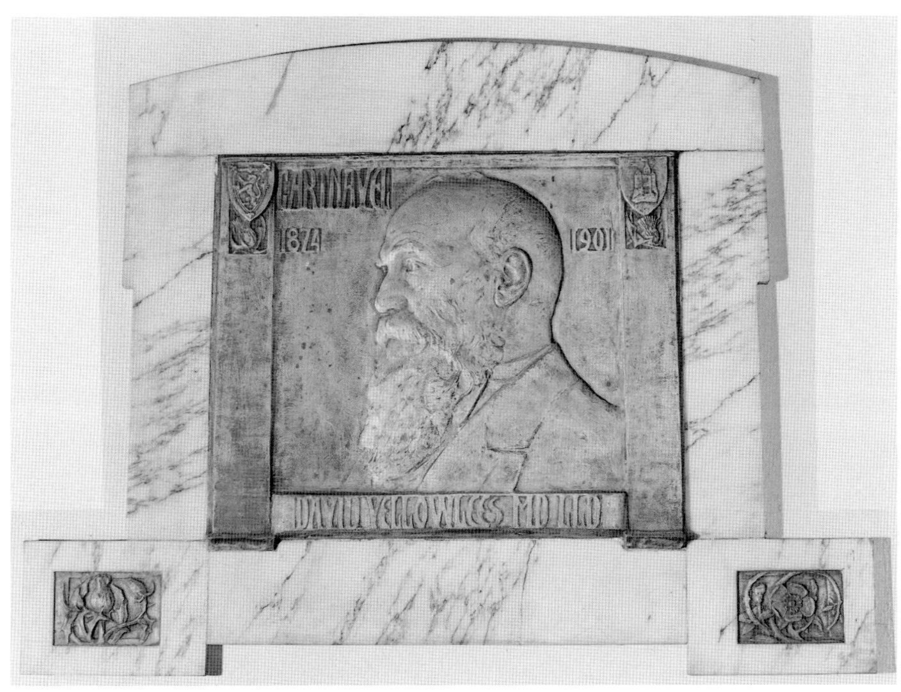

Dr David Yellowlees panel

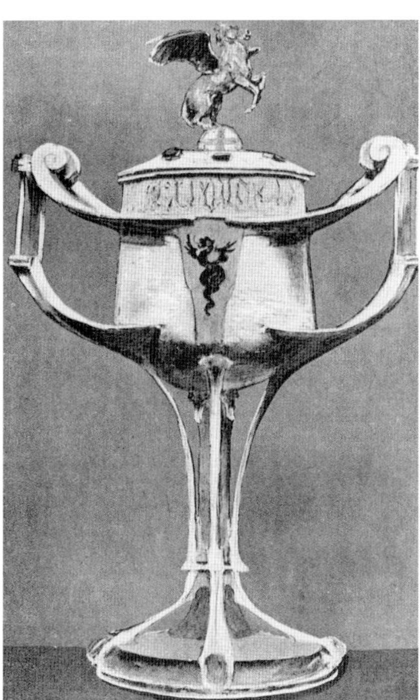

Racing Cup

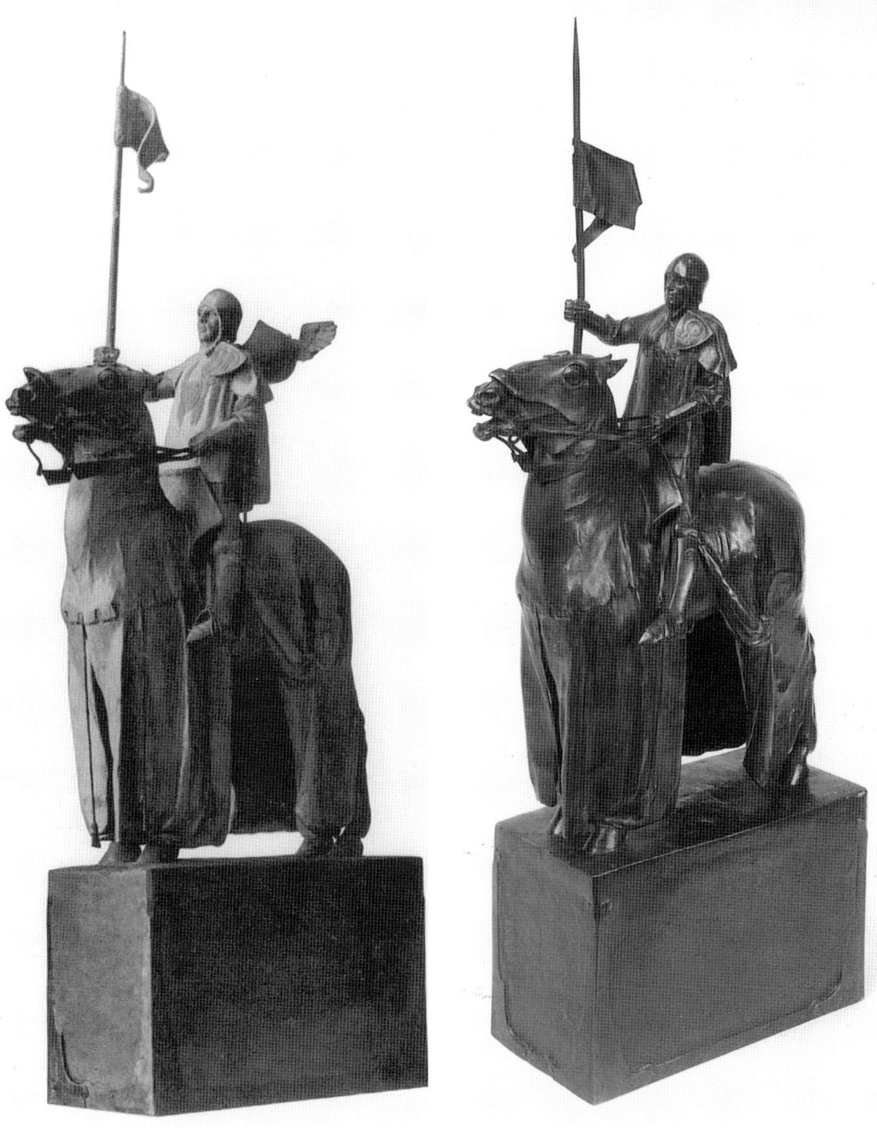

Plaster for Knight on his War Horse   *A Knight on his War Horse*

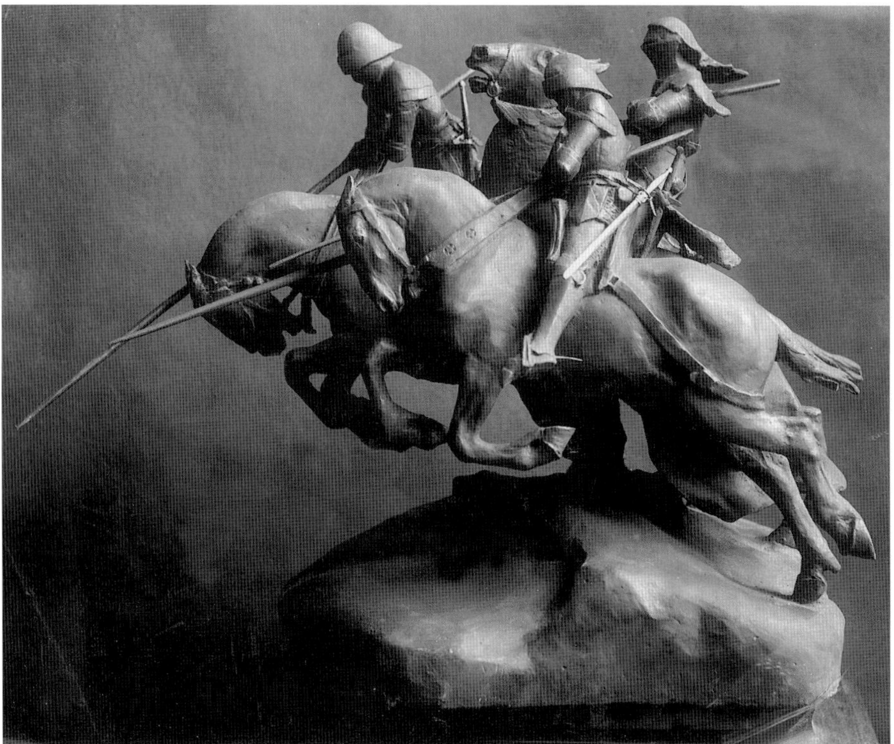

At the Top of the Hill

At the Top of the Hill
Medium: Bronze
Exhibitions: Birmingham 1902 (£105)
Literature: *The Studio* 1902 Vol 25 p108,
illus; *The Magazine of Art* 1902
p417, illus; *The Art Journal*
1908 Jul p197, illus.
This was one of the works that Bayes
submitted after his travelling scholarship.

The Fountain of the Zodiac Belt
Medium: Plaster figure on pedestal with
panels
Exhibitions: Royal Academy Schools
Exhibition 1902; Royal
Academy 1903; Portrait
Painters 1905.
Literature: *The Studio* 1902 Vol 25 p108,
illus; *Royal Academy Pictures*
1902 p105, illus; *The Magazine
of Art* 1902 p417, illus; *The Art
Journal* 1908 Jul p197, illus.
This was one of the works that Bayes
submitted after his travelling scholarship.

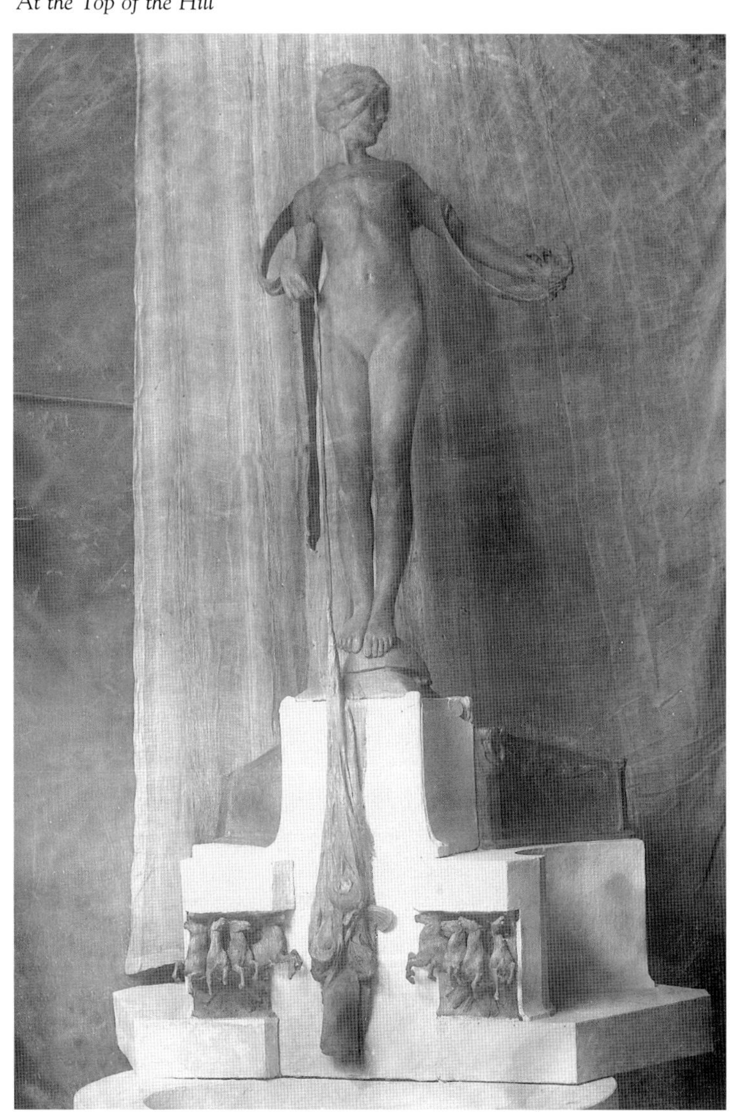

The Fountain of the Zodiac Belt

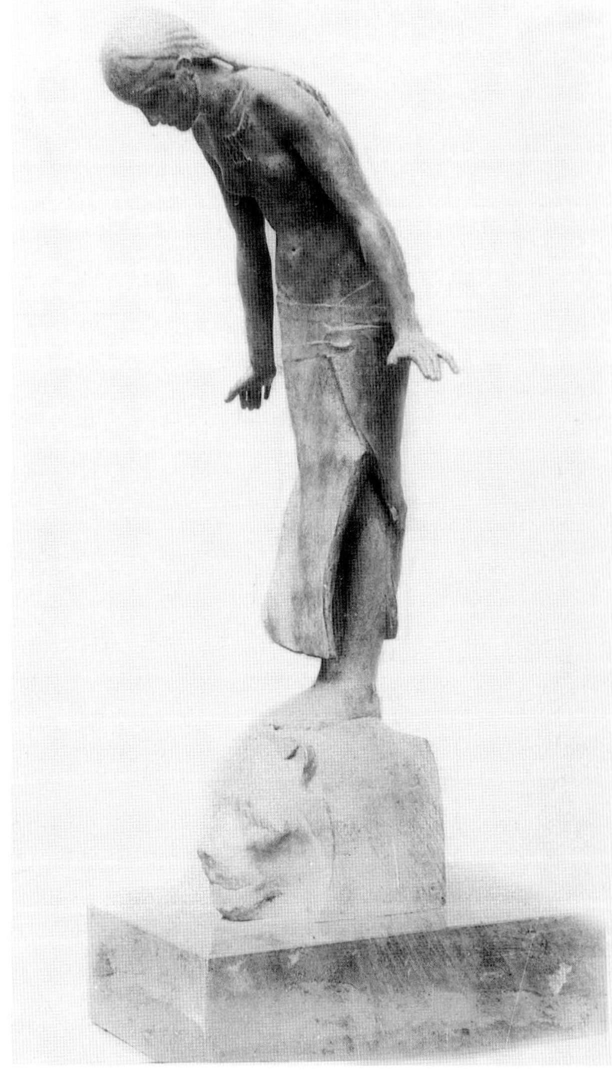

The Invocation

Pegasus

Medium: Plaster for bronze
Exhibitions: Royal Academy 1903; Portrait Painters 1905; Anglo-Japanese 1910; White City 1911.
Literature: *The Studio* 1902 Vol 25 p109, illus; *The Art Journal* 1908 Jul p199.

The Invocation

Medium: Bronze statuette on plinth
Exhibitions: Fine Art Society 1902 (plaster £40); Birmingham 1903; Glasgow, Portrait Painters 1905; Royal Academy, Wolverhampton 1912; Ridley, Edinburgh 1913; Leicester Galleries 1914; Sculpture Society 1915 (sold).
Literature: *The Studio* 1902 Vol 25 p278, illus.

Langham Collar

Medium: Metal on fabric
Literature: *The Studio* 1902 Vol 25 p110, illus.

1903

Switch and Bell Push Cover

Medium: Made by George Wragge Ltd
Exhibitions: Arts and Crafts 1903

Alessandro Volta Memorial

Medium: Bronze panel
Locations: Fondazione Francesco Somaini, Como, Italy

Robert Adamson Memorial

Medium: Bronze relief
Size: H 23½ins W 21ins (59 x 54cms)
Exhibitions: Royal Academy 1904; Portrait Painters 1905.
Locations: Logic Classroom, Glasgow University
Literature: *The Art Journal* 1908 Jul p199; *The Studio Year Book* 1909 p40.
Robert Adamson, who died in 1902, was Professor of Logic at Glasgow University.

Door Fittings

Medium: Bronze made by George Wragge Ltd
Exhibitions: Arts and Crafts 1903
Literature: *The Studio* 1903 Vol 28 p184, illus.
Gertrude Smith, who later became Bayes' wife, did some enamelling on these fittings.

Egyptian Head

Medium: Copper pendant
Exhibitions: Glasgow 1903 (£4); Ridley 1909 (1½ gns).

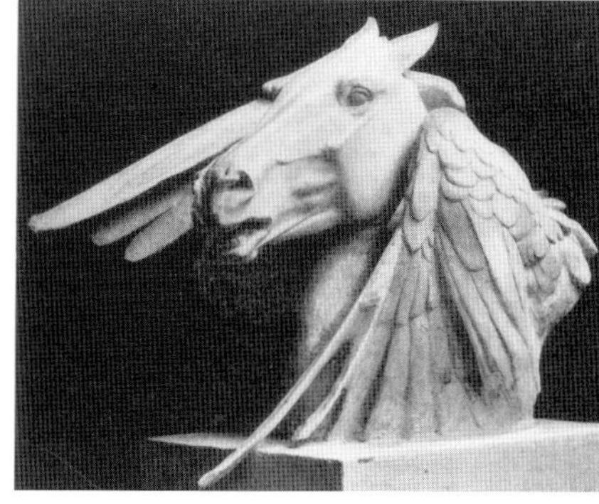

Pegasus

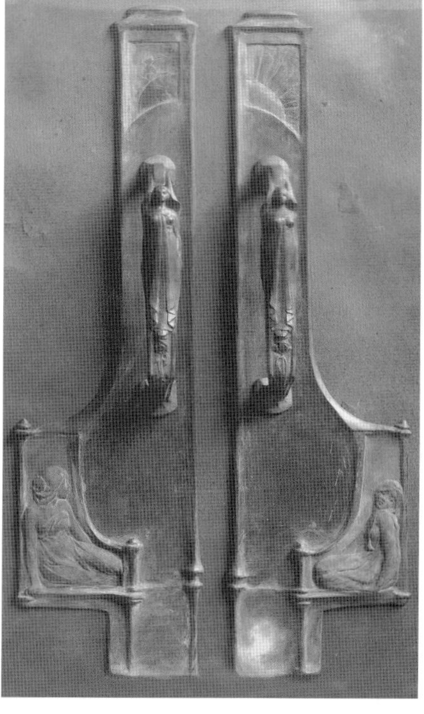

Door fittings

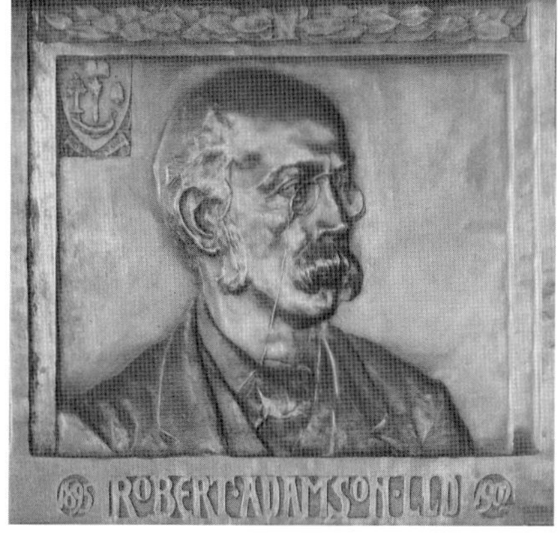

Robert Adamson Memorial

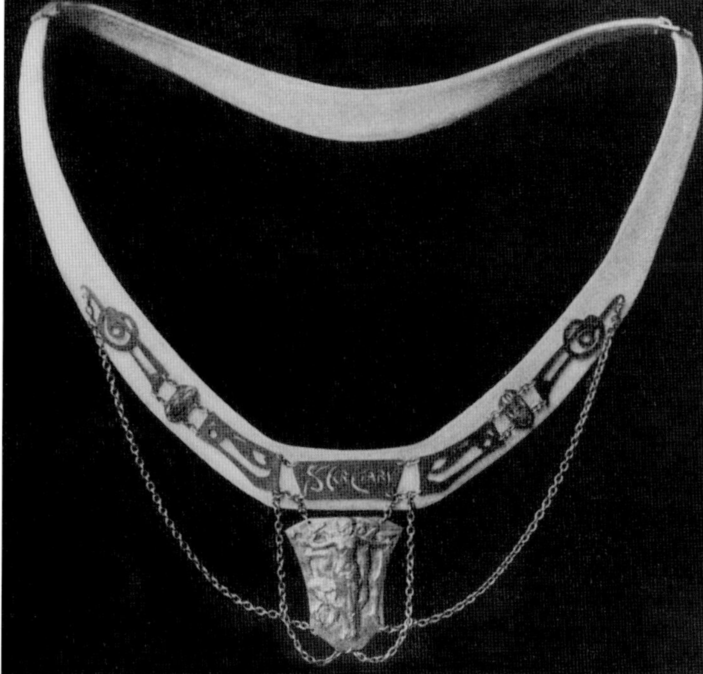

Langham Collar

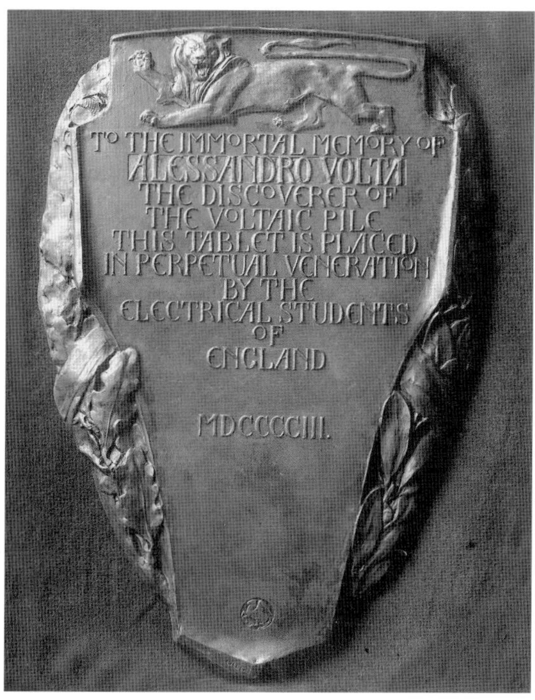

Alessandro Volta Memorial

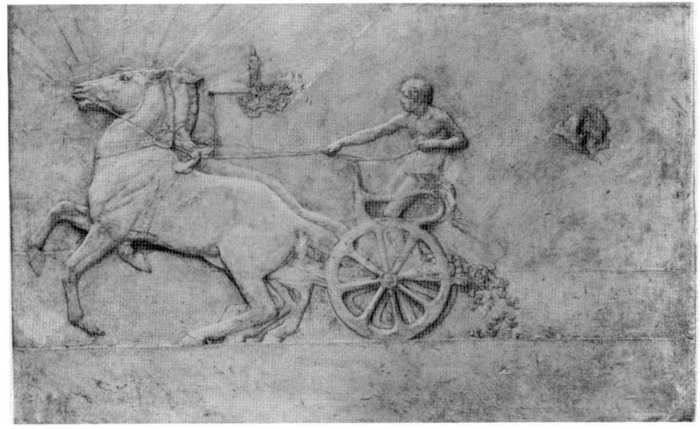

The Coming of Spring

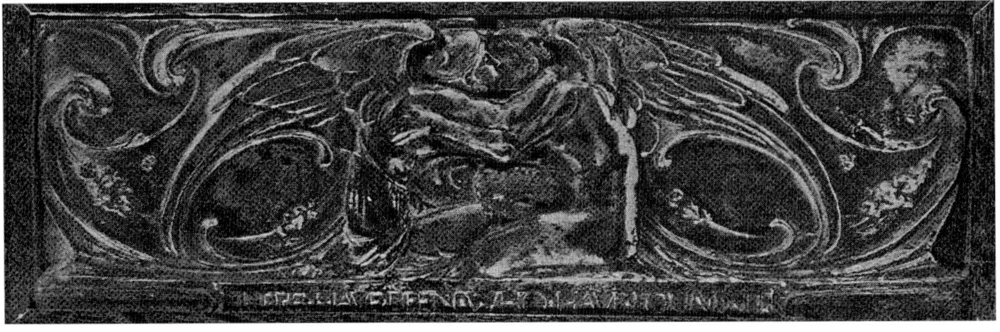

Orchardson Medal

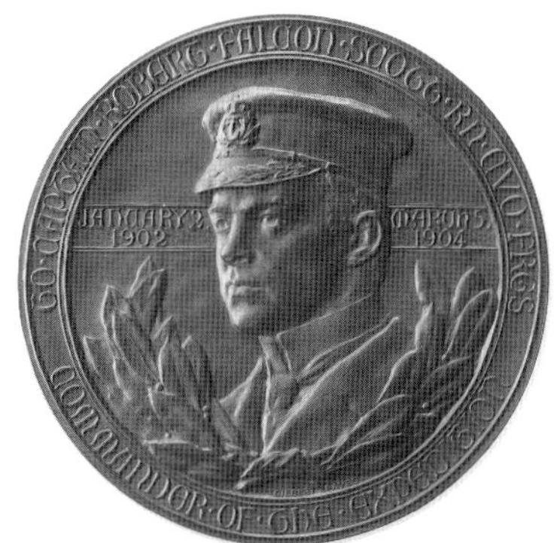

'There Have Been Who Have Found It'

1904

Orchardson Medal

Medium:	Silver metal
Size:	H 2½ins W 4ins (6.5 x 10cms)
Locations:	Presented by Charles Orchardson, Principal of St John's Wood Art School and awarded to students; 1904 medal won by Esther M. Shelton; 1905 medal won by Dorothy Webster Hawkins; Bayes Trust.
Literature:	*The Art Journal* 1904 p69, illus; *The Studio* 1907 Vol 40 p64; *The Numismatic Chronicle* 1992 pl 17, illus.

Antarctic Medal presented to Captain Robert Falcon Scott

Medium:	Gold, silver and bronze
Size:	D 3ins (7.5cms)
Exhibitions:	Portrait Painters 1905; International Medallic New York 1910.
Locations:	Royal Geographical Society
Literature:	*The Art Journal* 1908 Jul p195, illus; *The Numismatic Chronicle* 1992 pl 18, illus.

A Gold Medal was presented to Captain Scott, thirty-seven Silver and six Bronze Medals were also made.

The Coming of Spring

Medium:	Marble relief
Size:	H 60ins W 84ins (152.5 x 213.5cms)
Exhibitions:	Royal Academy 1904; Portrait Painters 1905; White City 1911 (450gns).
Literature:	*Royal Academy Pictures* 1904 p122, illus; *The Art Journal* 1908 Jul p193, illus.

'There Have Been Who Have Found It'

Medium:	Electrotype relief
Size:	H 6½ W 19½ins (16.5 x 50cms)
Locations:	Sotheby's, Belgravia 7.11.73 (sold)

Given by Gilbert Bayes to Ethel Lester as a wedding present in 1904. Miss Lester was a friend of Gertrude Smith who became Bayes' wife.

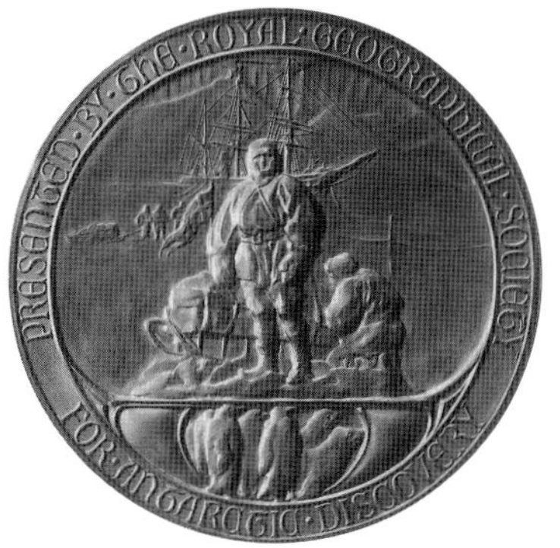

Antarctic Medal presented to Captain Robert Falcon Scott

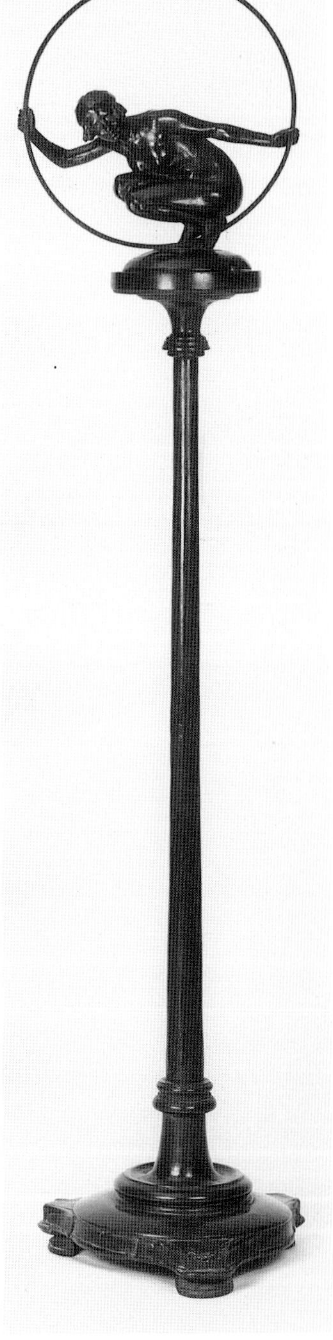

Greek Dancer

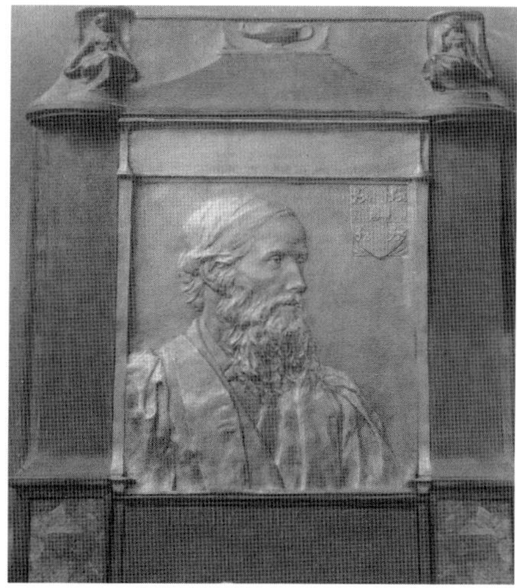

Professor Henry Sidgwick panel

1905

Greek Dancer on Stand

Medium: Bronze statuette on stand
Size: H 14¹/₂ins, 65ins including stand (37cms, 166cms)
Exhibitions: Royal Academy, Portrait Painters 1905; Christchurch, New Zealand 1906-07; Anglo-Japanese (25gns), Venice (sold 25gns), Ridley, Goupil 1910; Rome, Institute 1911 (£26); Brighton, Toronto 1912; Fine Art Society 1913 and 1920, Glasgow 1913; Paris Arts and Crafts 1914; Aberdeen 1921 (£31.10s); Liverpool 1923 (£52.10s).
Locations: Ferens Art Gallery, Hull; Lady Lever Gallery, Port Sunlight; Sotheby's 21.6.91 (sold); private collection.
Literature: *Royal Academy Pictures* 1905 p110, illus., (plaster); *The Art Journal* 1908 Jul p197, illus; *The Builder* 1921 Feb p179, illus; *Modern Tendencies in Sculpture*, Lorado Taft 1921 p79.
This sculpture was exhibited at least twenty times between 1905 and 1930.

Professor Henry Sidgwick 1838-1900

Medium: Silver, bronze and lapis lazuli
Exhibitions: Royal Academy 1905; Portrait Painters 1905.
Locations: Newnham College, Cambridge
Literature: *The Art Journal* 1908 Jul p199; *The Studio Year Book* 1909 p40.
Professor Sidgwick was the founder and benefactor of Newnham College, Cambridge.

The Mushroom Sprite

Medium: Silvered bronze statuette
Size: H 12¹/₂ins (32cms)
Exhibitions: Christchurch, New Zealand 1906-07
Locations: Christie's New York 19.5.87 (sold)
Literature: *New Zealand International Exhibition 1906-7* catalogue p209, illus.

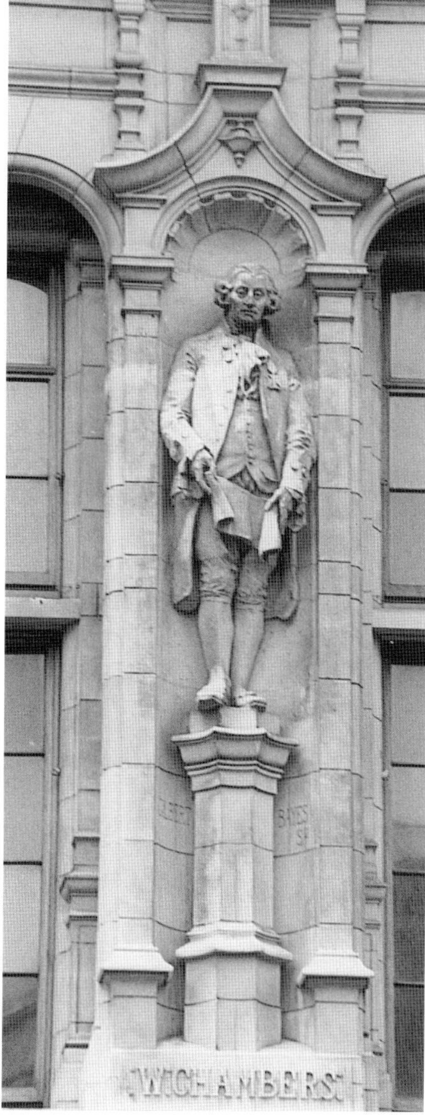

Sir William Chambers

Sir William Chambers and Sir Charles Barry

Medium: Portland Stone
Size: H 7ft 6ins (2.3m)
Locations: In the sequence of great artists and architects, the facade of the Victoria & Albert Museum, commissioned and completed in 1905.
Literature: *The Studio Year Book* 1909 p40

Presentation Plaque

Medium: Silver
Exhibitions: Portrait Painters 1905
Presented to William Goscombe John by the Institute of Journalists.

The Angel of Walter of Birbach

Exhibitions: Portrait Painters 1905

Fate

Exhibitions: Portrait Painters 1905
Literature: *The Art Journal* 1908 Jul p197
This figure, a winged nude playing with two puppets, was made as a companion statue to the *Greek Dancer*.

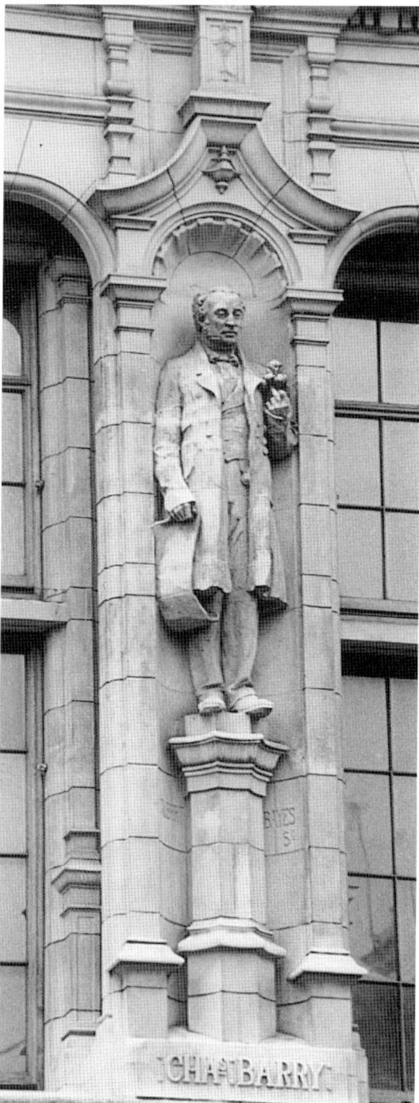

Sir Charles Barry

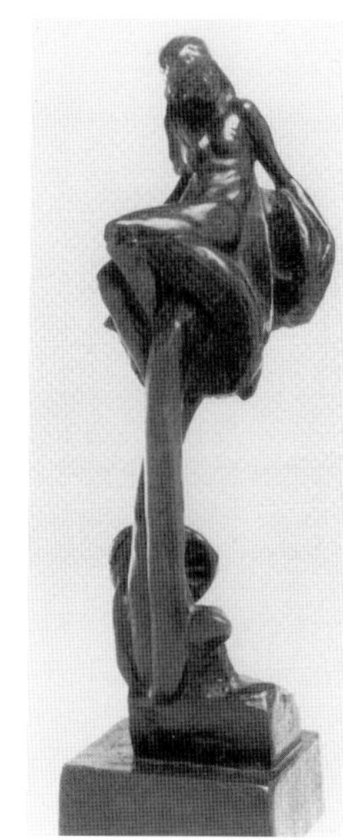

The Mushroom Sprite

Gilbert Bayes

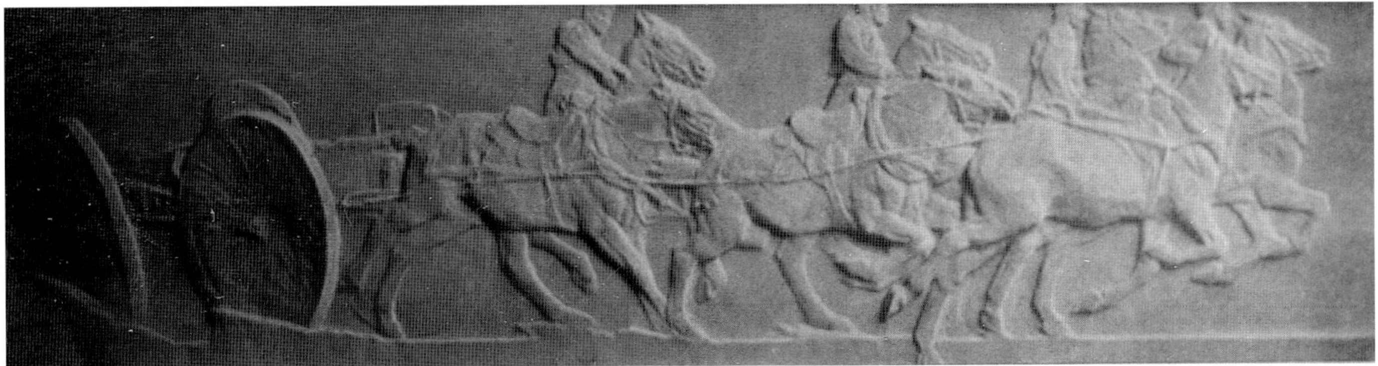

The Gallopers

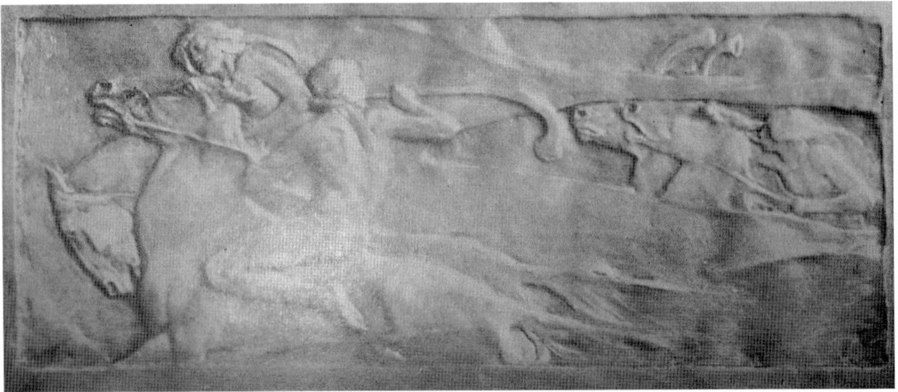

The Storm Ride

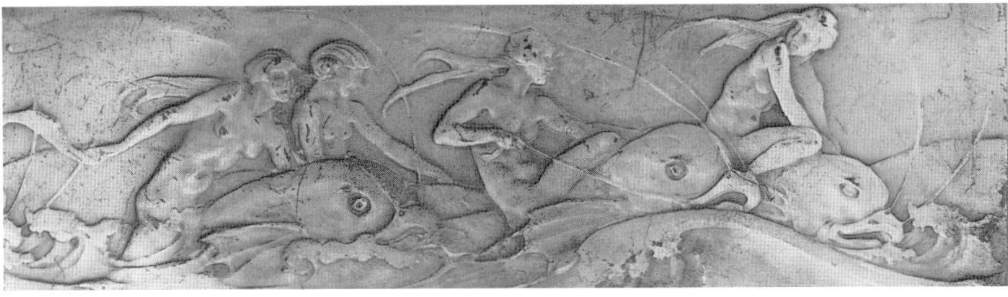

Water Nymphs

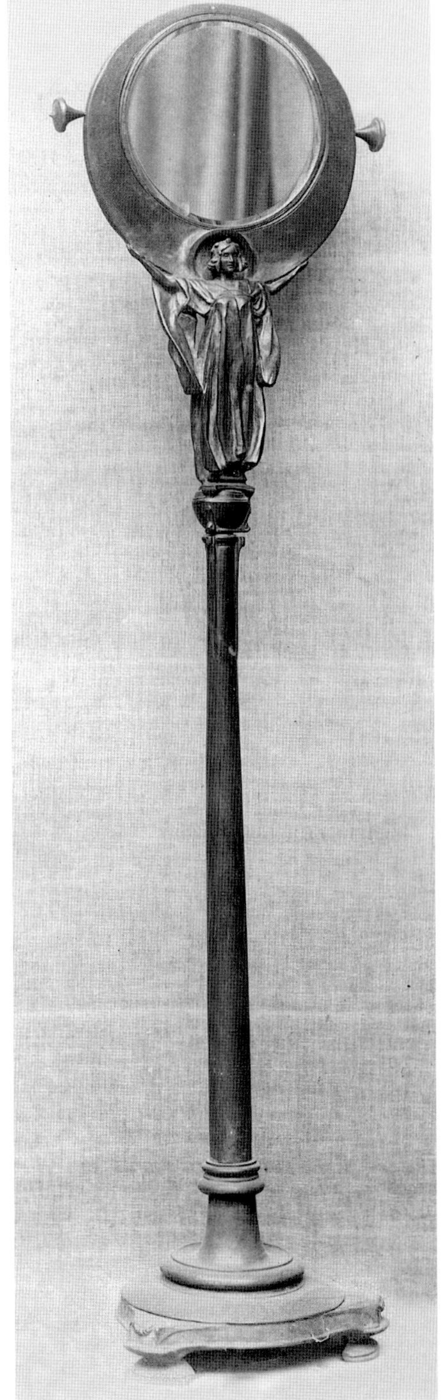

Standing Mirror

The Gallopers

Medium: Bronze relief
Size: H 18ins W 66ins
      (45.5 x 167.5cms)
Exhibitions: Royal Academy 1905; Portrait
      Painters 1905.
Literature: *Royal Academy Pictures* 1905,
      p148, illus.

The Storm Ride

Medium: Metal relief
Exhibitions: New Gallery 1904; Glasgow
      1905 (£10); Portrait Painters
      1905; Ipswich 1909 (10gns);
      Goupil 1909; International
      Medallic, New York 1910;
      Toronto 1912.
Literature: *Sculptures from Academy
      Architecture,* A. Koch 1908
      illus.

The Guns

Medium: Plaster relief
Exhibitions: Portrait Painters 1905;
      International Medallic, New
      York, 1910.

1906

Water Nymphs

Medium: Silvered copper relief
Size: H 2¼ins W 6½ins (5.5 x 16.5cms)
Exhibitions: Christchurch, New Zealand
      1906-07; Glasgow 1908 (£10).
Locations: Bayes Trust
Literature: This design was later enlarged
      and made in Doulton
      stoneware.

Standing Mirror

Medium: Bronze
Exhibitions: Arts and Crafts 1906
      (£31.10s); Goupil 1908
      (£31.10s); Glasgow 1909
      (30gns); Birmingham 1910;
      Southport 1912.

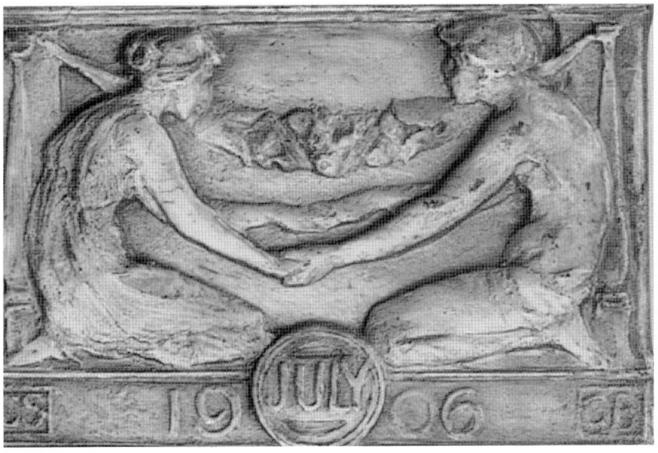

Marriage plaque for Gilbert Bayes and Gertrude Smith

Marriage Plaque for Gilbert Bayes and Gertrude Smith

Medium: Silver
Size: H 1⅝ins W 2¼ins (4 x 5.5cms)
Locations: Bayes Trust
This is close in style to the Ethel Lester marriage panel of 1904. It is possible that Gertrude Smith modelled this with her husband.

For the Right

Medium: Bronze and ivory statue on plinth
Size: H 6ft with stand (1.83m)
Exhibitions: Royal Academy 1906; Glasgow 1908; Goupil 1910 (150gns); White City 1911 (200gns).
Literature: *Royal Academy Pictures* 1906 p49. illus; *The Art Journal* 1908 Jul p196, illus.

A Royal Horse Artilleryman

Medium: Plaster equestrian statue
Literature: *The Art Journal* 1908 Jul p196, illus.

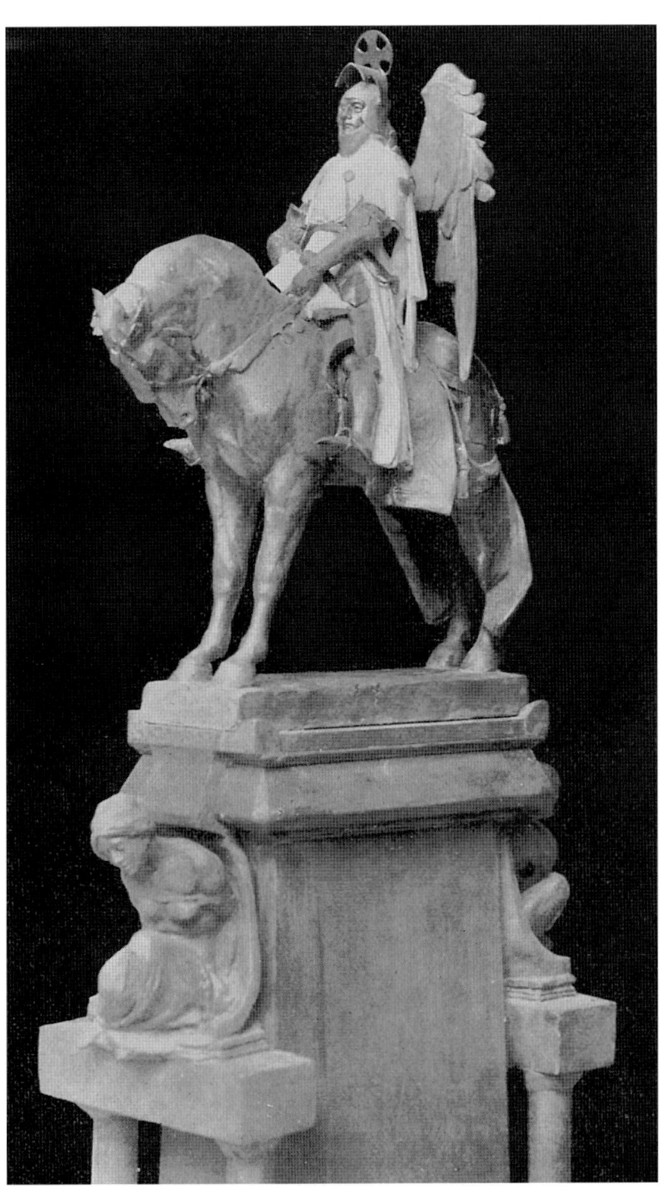

For the Right

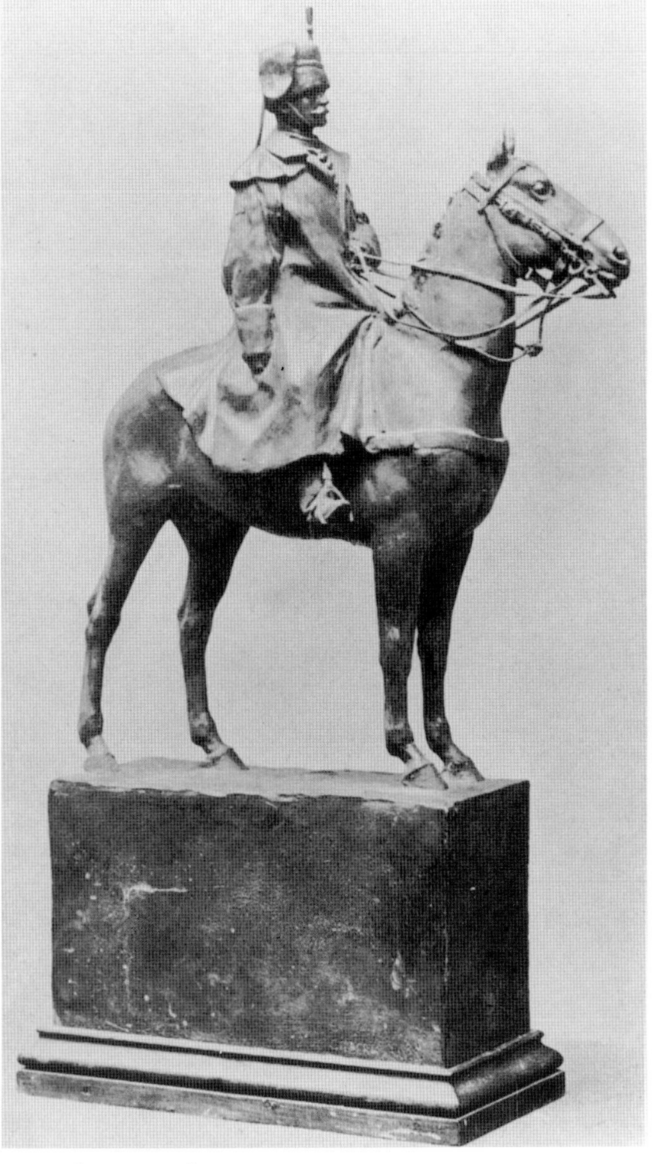

A Royal Horse Artilleryman

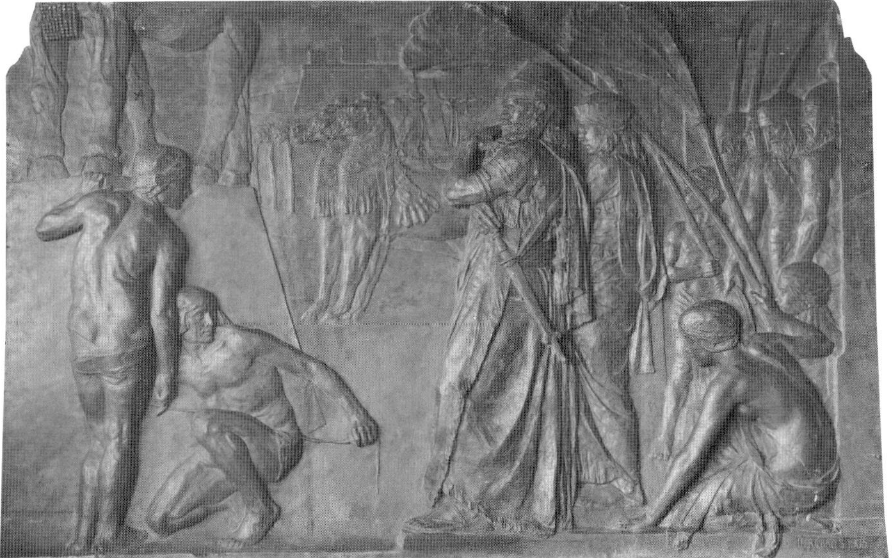

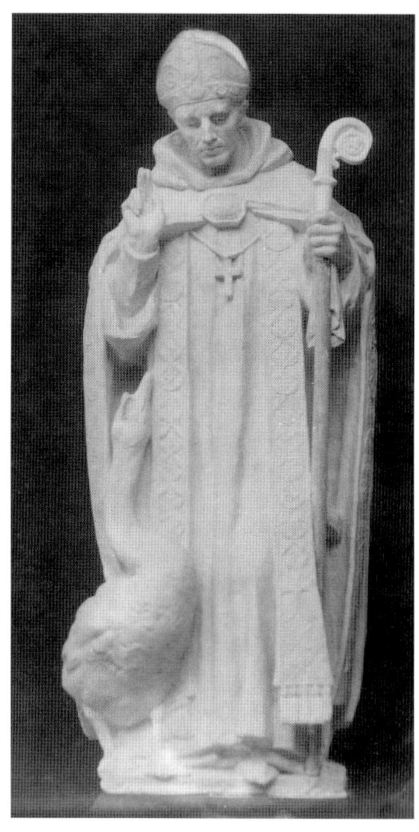

Plaster for St Hugh

Assur-Natsir-Pal, King of Assyria

Medium: Bronze relief cast by A.B. Burton
Size: H 8ft x W 12ft (2.4 x 3.6m)
Locations: Art Gallery of New South Wales. Commissioned in 1903 after a competition entry
selected by Arthur East and George Frampton, and erected in 1907.
Literature: *The Art Journal* 1906 Feb p31, illus; *The Art Journal* 1908 Jul p197; *The Studio* 1905 Vol
36 p86, illus; *The Studio Year Book* 1909 p40; *Decorative Arts Society Journal* 1980, illus.

This subject is particularly apposite as Bayes was, like so many of his generation, greatly
influenced by Assyrian war relief sculpture in the British Museum. This panel depicts the
Assyrian King and Queen watching the building of the Palace of Ninevah.

St Hugh

Medium: Plaster model for stone figure
Size: H 4ft (1.2m)
Locations: Niche above the entrance to St Hugh's Catholic Church,
Broadgate, Lincoln, donated in 1907 in memory of Francis
Jonathan Clark (d 1888).
Literature: *The Art Journal* 1908 Jul p199, illus; *The Studio Year Book*
1909 p240.

1907

The Wings of the Wind

Medium: Bronze statuette on plinth
Size: H 6¹/₂ins, 11ins including plinth (16.5cms, 28cms)
Exhibitions: Royal Academy 1907; Goupil 1909 and 1910 (8gns);
Southport 1911; Toronto 1912; Fine Art Society 1913
(13gns) and 1918; Glasgow 1920 (sold); Ridley 1923 (sold);
Rio 1930 (sold).
Locations: National Museum of Wales, Cardiff; Peter Nahum, London,
(another sold for £7,500); Christie's 19.10.95 (sold £2,600);
Bonhams 9.5.96 (sold £1,600).
Literature: *The Art Journal* 1908 July p197

This sculpture was exhibited around twenty times between 1907 and 1948.

Amor Victor

Medium: Plaster relief
Size: H 9ft (2.75m)
Exhibitions: Royal Academy 1907; Franco-British Exhibition 1908; Ghent
Arts and Crafts 1913 (£100).
Literature: *Royal Academy Pictures* 1907 p147, illus; *The Art Journal* 1908 July
p198, illus; *Franco-British Exhibition Catalogue* 1908 p247, illus; *The
Studio Year Book* 1909 p39, illus; *Sculpture and the Sculptors Art*,
H.H. Stansfield 1918 p128.

Moon Sprite

Medium: Silvered statuette
Exhibitions: Sir John Cass 1907; Ipswich 1909 (10gns); Glasgow 1911
(£10); Ghent 1913.

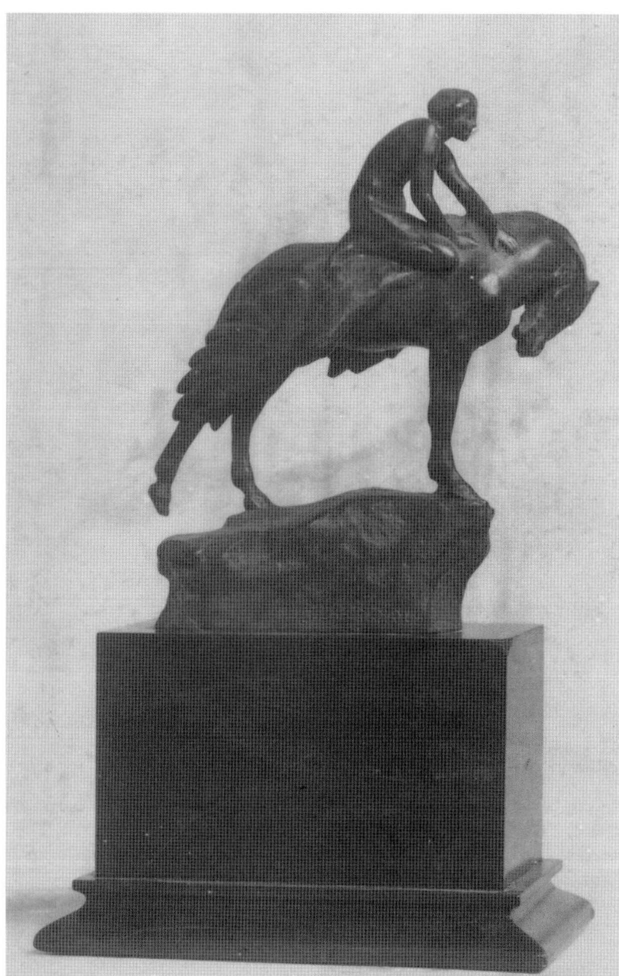

The Wings of the Wind

Artemis
Medium: Bronze and enamel group
Size: H 13ins (33cms)
Exhibitions: Goupil 1907 (£63); Royal Academy 1911;
Southport, Glasgow 1913 (£200); White City
1914; Liverpool 1915 and 1920 (sold £157.10s);
Glasgow 1916 and 1919 (150gns); Bristol
1916; Fine Art Society 1918; Institute 1919.
Locations: Walker Art Gallery, Liverpool purchased
1921 (110gns)
Literature: *The Art Journal* 1908 Jul p197; *Royal Academy
Pictures* 1911, p61, illus; *The Studio Year Book*
1914 p79, illus; *The Studio* 1917 Vol 72 p106,
illus; *The Studio* 1921 Vol 81 p70; *The Builder*
1920 Dec p712.

The Top Spinner
Medium: Bronze statuette
Exhibitions: Sir John Cass 1907; Whitechapel 1910;
Goupil 1910 and 1913 (8gns); Ridley 1911;
Toronto 1912; Fine Art Society 1912.
Literature: *The Art Journal* 1908 Jul p197

Alfred W. Bayes, 1832-1909
Medium: Plaster maquette for bronze bust
Exhibitions: Portrait Painters 1907; Glasgow 1909; Goupil
1910; Royal Academy 1913; Ridley 1913
(plaster); Pastel Society 1933.
Painter and etcher, father of Gilbert.

1908

Knight Roland
Medium: Plaster statuette
Exhibitions: Franco-British 1908; Sir John Cass 1909.
Literature: *The Art Journal* 1908 Jul p196. This model
was inspired by Morris' *Father John's War
Song*: 'Father John, you have got you a son,
Seven feet high when his helm is on.'

Laissez Aller
Medium: Relief
Literature: *The Art Journal* 1908 Jul p199

The Mule Cart of Siena
Literature: *The Art Journal* 1908 Jul p199

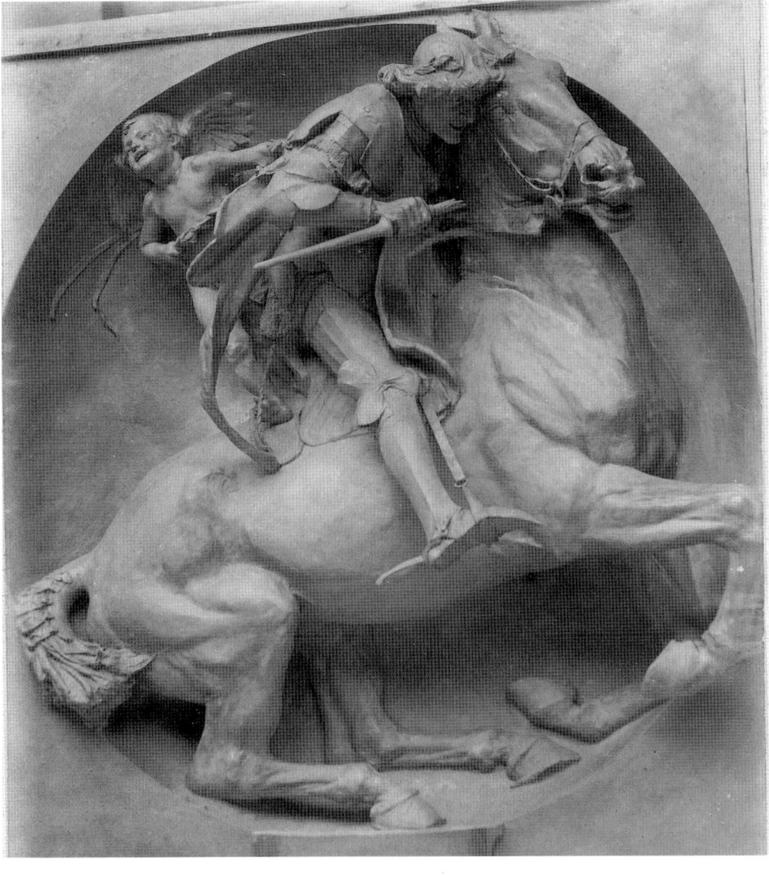

Amor Victor

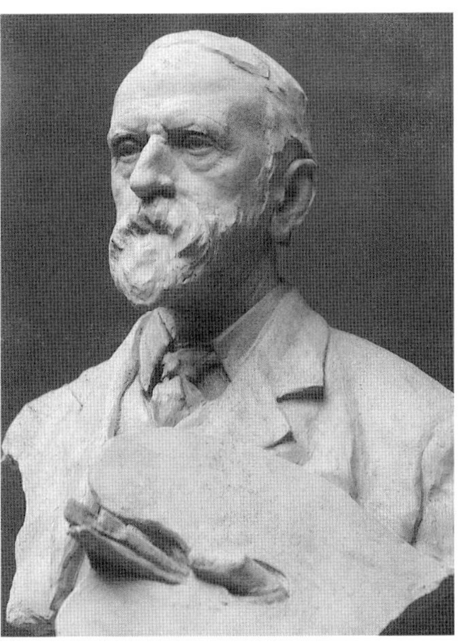

Alfred W. Bayes

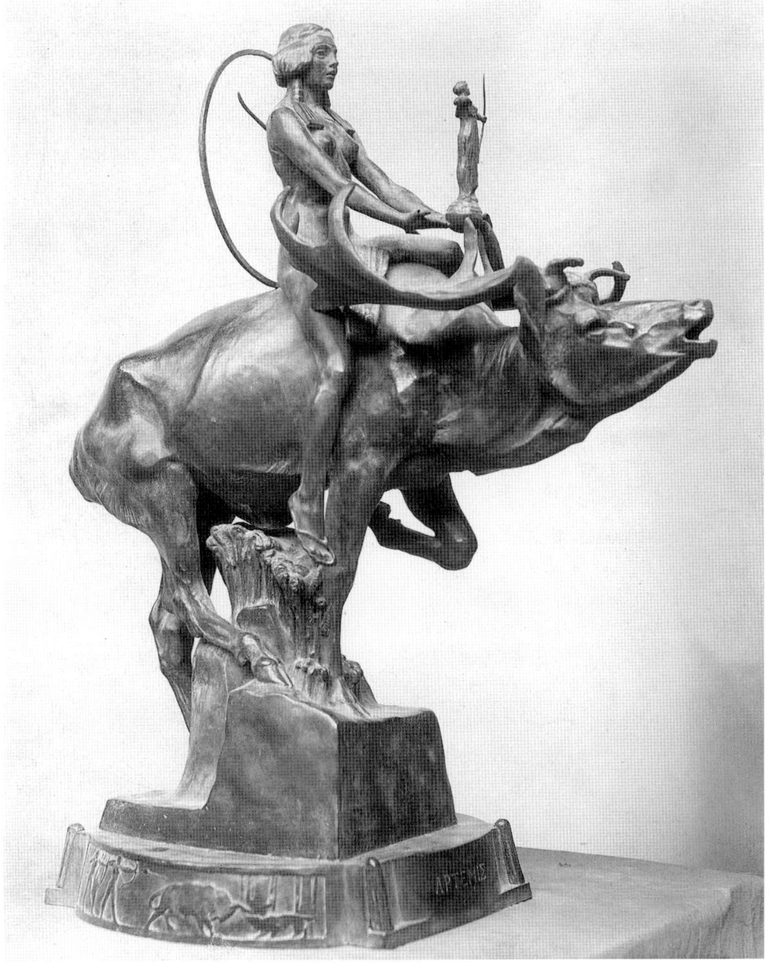

Artemis

Gilbert Bayes

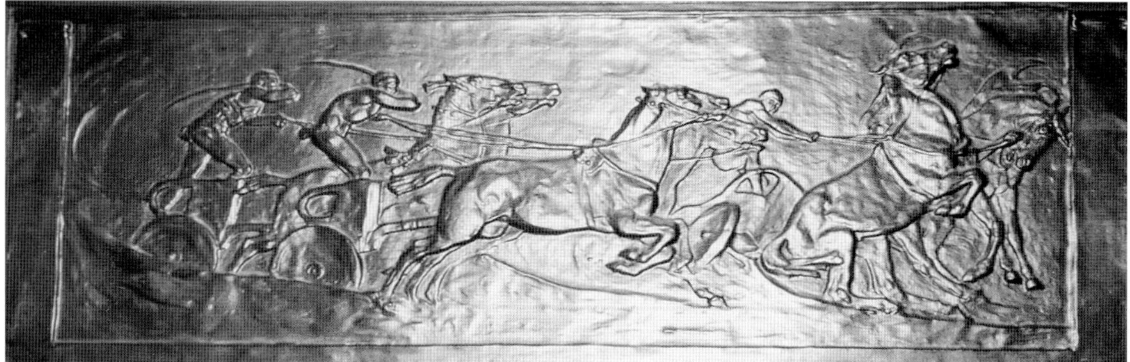

The Race

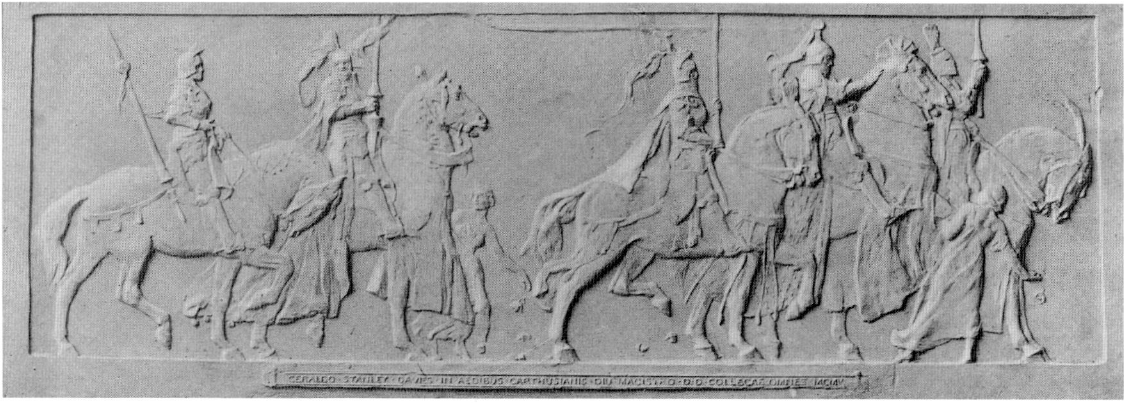

The Road to the Tournay

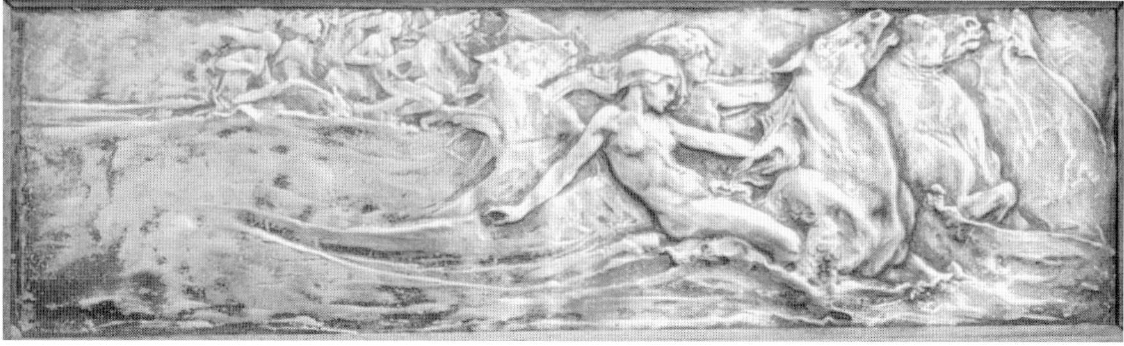

White Horses

White Horses
Medium: Electrotype bronze relief
Size: H 6ins W 19½ins (15 x 49cms)
Exhibitions: Franco-British, 1908; Goupil 1909;
   International Medallic, New York,
   1910; Brighton, 1912; Toronto, 1912.
Locations: Private collection

National Rose Society Medal
Medium: Gold
Exhibitions: International Medallic, New York,
   1910
Literature: *The Numismatic Chronicle* 1992 pl 18,
   illus.
The medal depicts Dean Samuel Reynolds Hole,
the founder of the National Rose Society.

The Race
Medium: Electrotype relief
Exhibitions: Ridley 1909
Locations: Private collection

The Road to the Tournay
Medium: Plaster panel
Literature: *The Art Journal* 1908 Jul
   p194, illus.

The War Chariot
Medium: Relief
Exhibitions: Royal Academy 1909
It is possible that this is another
name for *The Goal*.

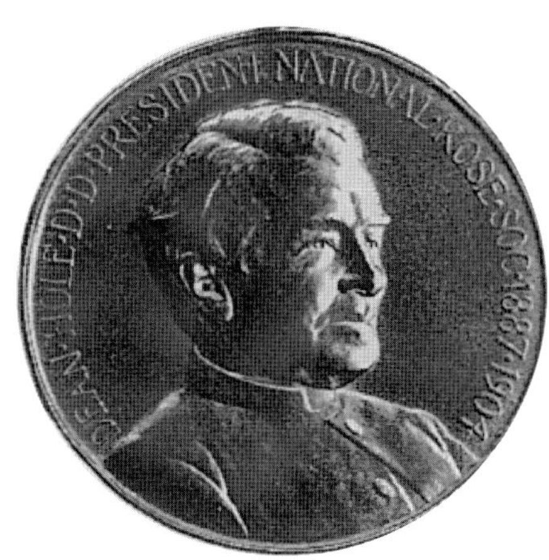

National Rose Society Medal

The Scales of Time

Medium: Plaster maquette and bronze on stand
Size: H 17½ins (44.5cms)
Exhibitions: Royal Academy 1908; Goupil 1908 (£10gns); Sir John Cass 1909.
Locations: Art Gallery of New South Wales purchased 1914 for 10gns (scales missing); Sotheby's 18.12.85 (dated 1908 – unsold at £1,400); Sotheby's 15.3.91 (dated 1908 – sold); Christie's 28.4.94 (dated 1908, no scales – sold); Christie's 7.11.97 (£1,400).
Literature: *The Art Journal* 1909, Jan, p30

Tazza

Medium: Silver gilt
Exhibitions: Ridley 1909

The Crown of War

Medium: Equestrian statuette
Size: H 39ins (99cms)
Exhibitions: Royal Academy 1908; Ridley 1909; Southport 1910.
Literature: *Royal Academy Pictures* 1908, p113, illus.

1909

Antarctic Medal Awarded to Ernest Shackleton

Medium: Gold, silver and bronze
Size: D 2¾ins (7cms)
Exhibitions: International Medallic, New York 1910.
Locations: Royal Geographic Society; British Museum
Literature: *The Builder* 1924 Vol 126 p409; *The Numismatic Chronicle* 1992 pl 19, illus.

A Gold Medal was presented to Shackleton. Sixteen Silver Medals were also awarded and six Bronze Medals were made.

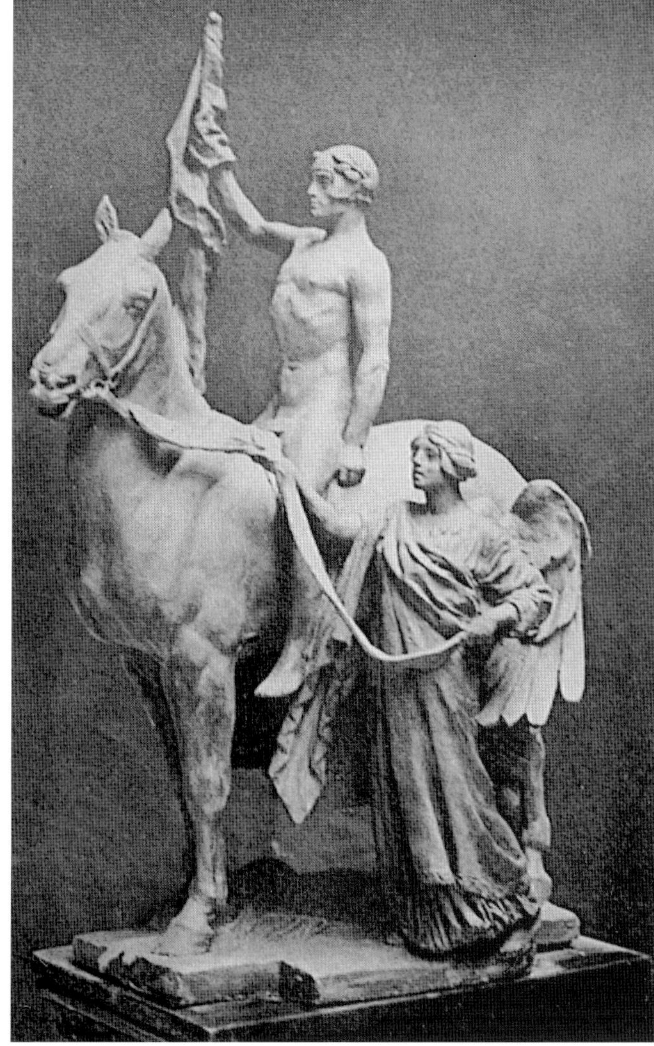

The Crown of War

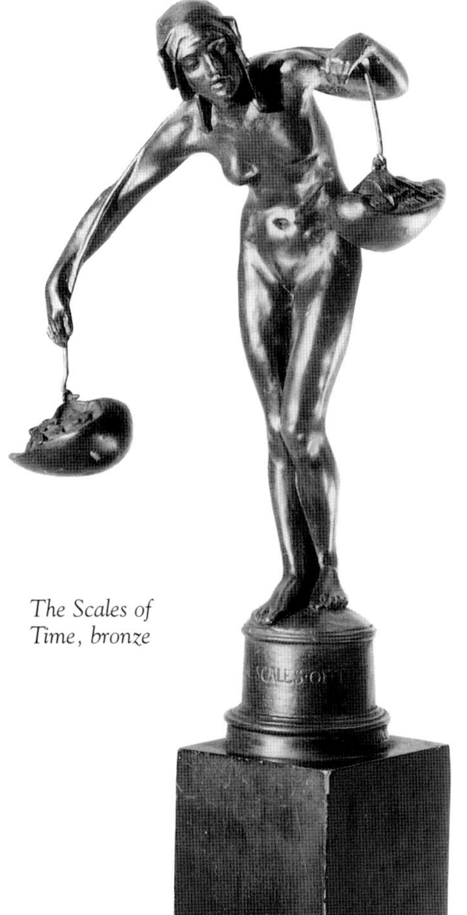

The Scales of Time, bronze

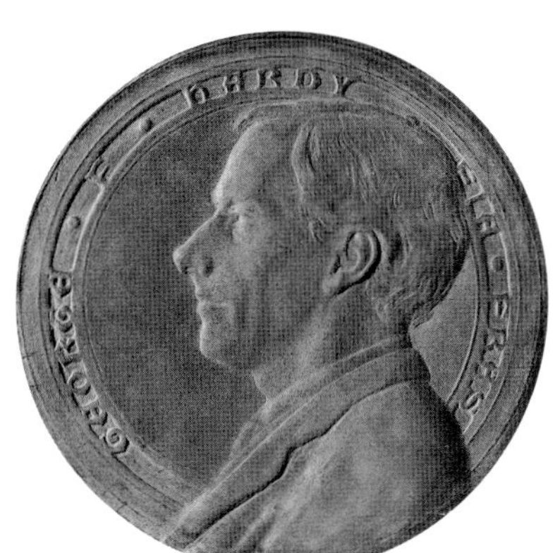
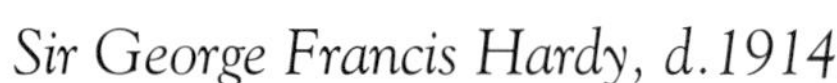

Sir George Francis Hardy

Sir George Francis Hardy, d.1914

Medium: Electrotype medallion
Size: 5¼ins (13.5cms)
Exhibitions: Portrait Painters 1909; Ridley 1924.
Locations: Bayes Trust
Literature: *The Numismatic Chronicle* 1992 pl 21, illus.

Sir George Hardy was President of the Institute of Actuaries.

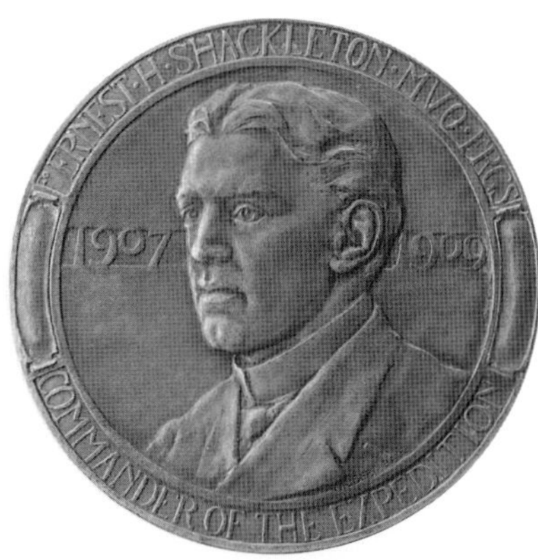
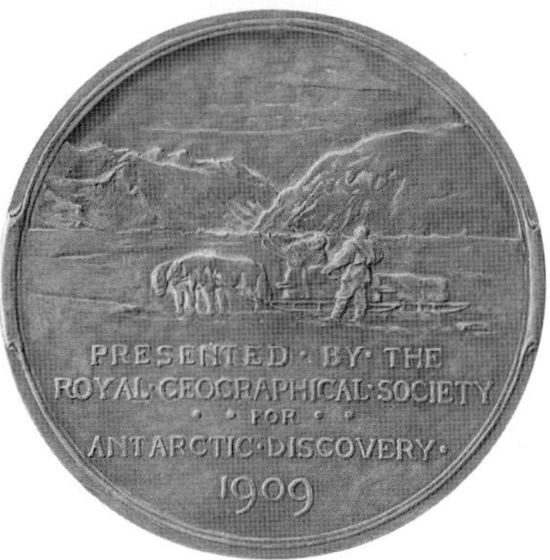

Antarctic Medal

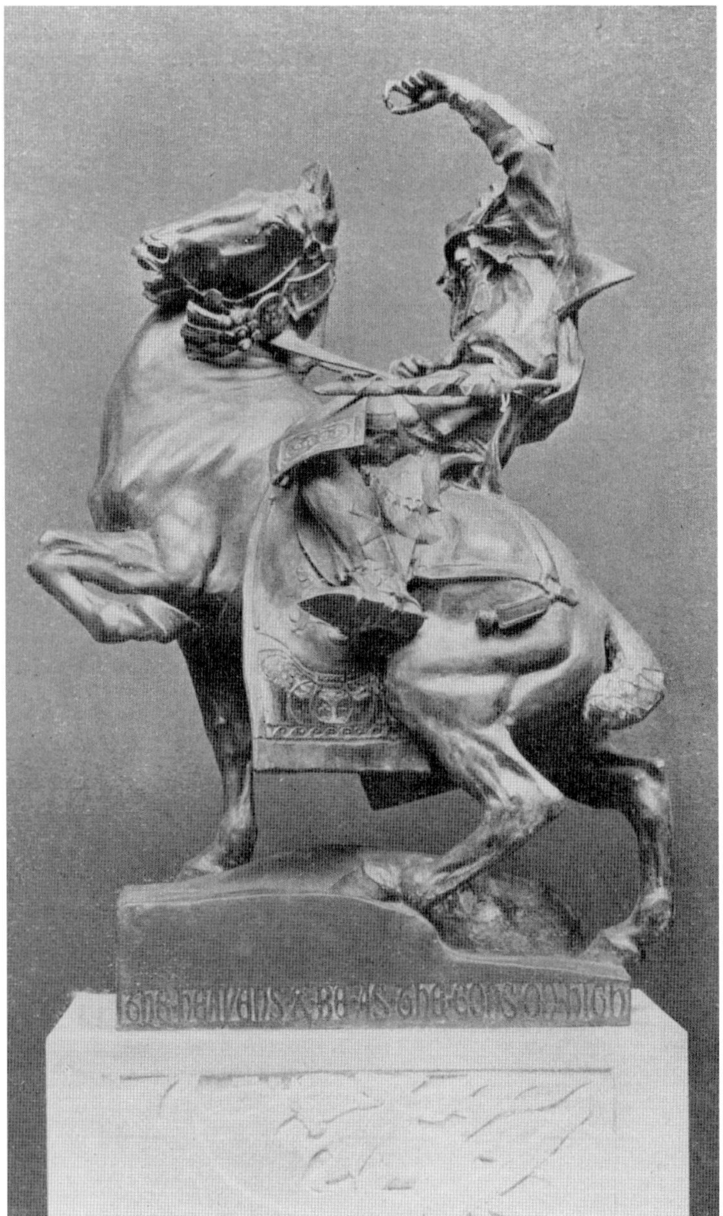

Sigurd with Ring

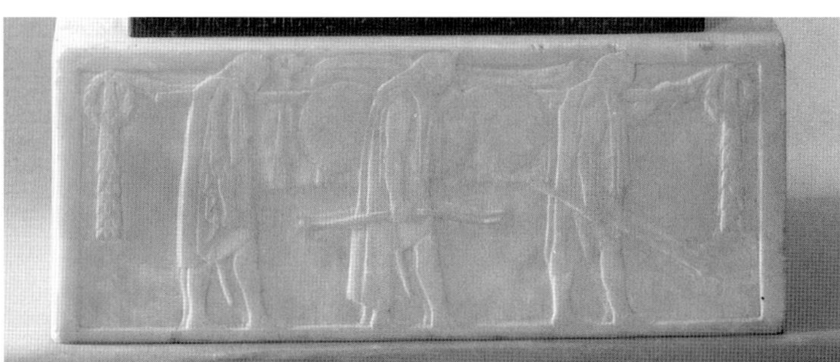

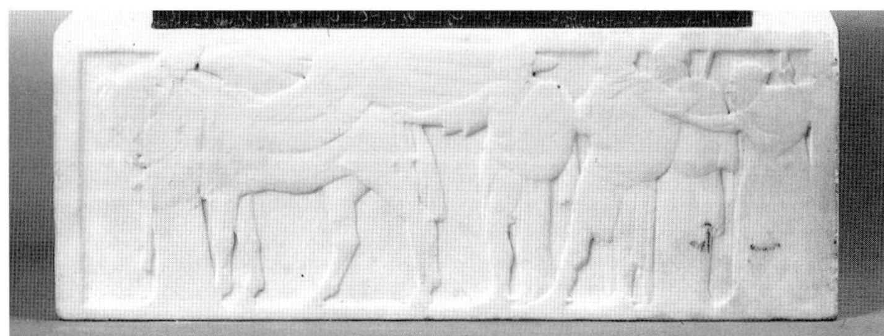

Marble base variants for Sigurd

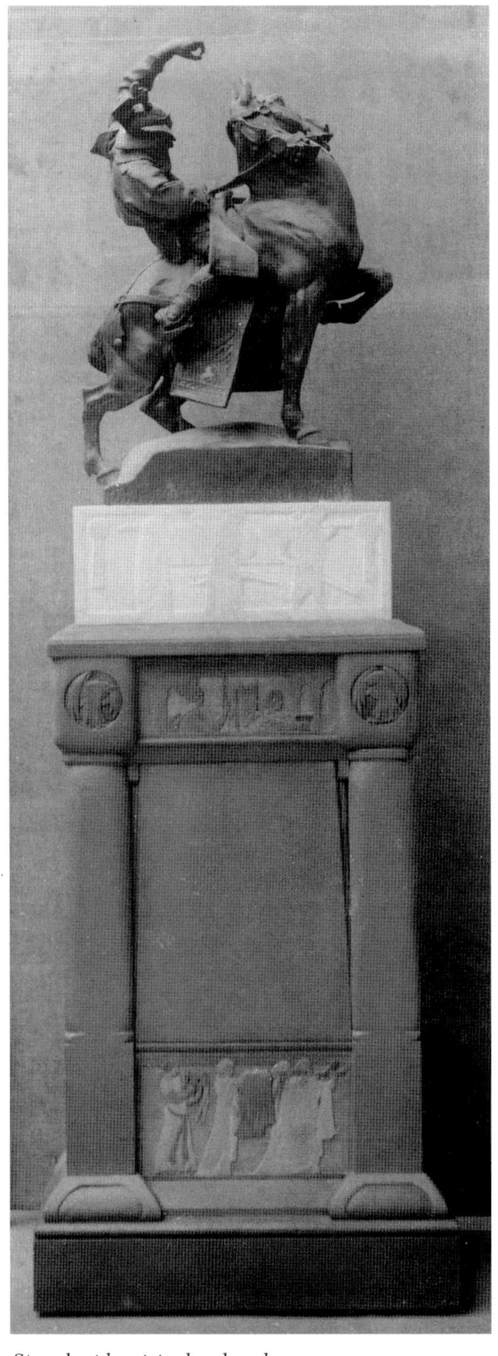

Sigurd with original pedestal

Sigurd with Ring

Medium: Bronze with marble base on stand
Size: H 27¹/₂ins (70cms)
Exhibitions: Royal Academy, Ridley 1909; Rome 1911; Glasgow 1912; Ghent Fine Arts 1913; Southport, Bristol 1914; Liverpool 1915 and 1920 (sold); Royal Scottish Academy 1917; Institute, Glasgow 1918 (£157.10s); Bristol 1919.
Locations: Bayes Trust; Walker Art Gallery, Liverpool purchased 1920 (£120); Armstrong Davies Gallery, Sussex 1985 (formerly Sir George Frampton Collection); Sotheby's 12.4.85 (sold £58,000 – later destroyed in fire); Fine Art Society.
Literature: *The Art Journal* 1909 Jan p171; *Royal Academy Pictures* 1909 p113, illus; *International Fine Arts Exhibition Catalogue* 1911 p442, illus; *The Builder* Jan 1921 p22, illus; *The Artist* 1935, illus; *Sculpture and the Sculptors Art*, H.H. Stansfield 1918 p139.

Three different marble bases are known.

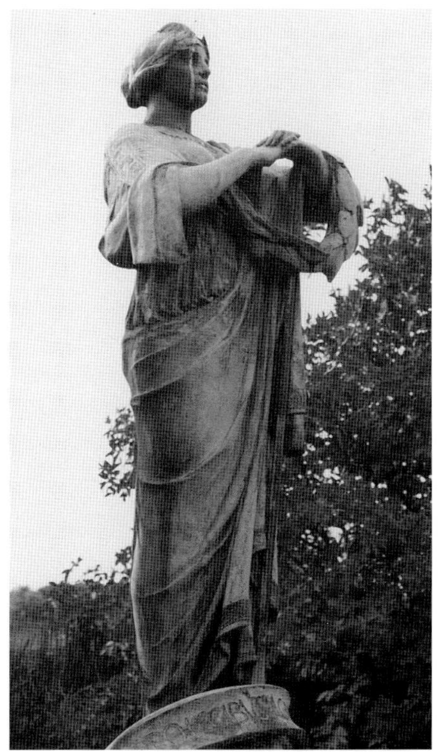
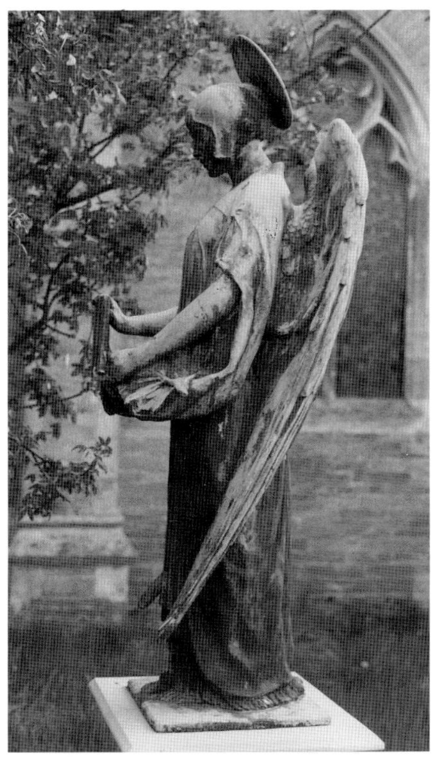
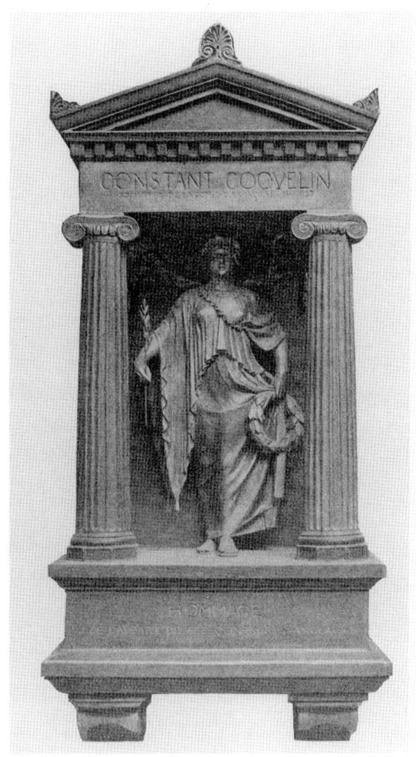

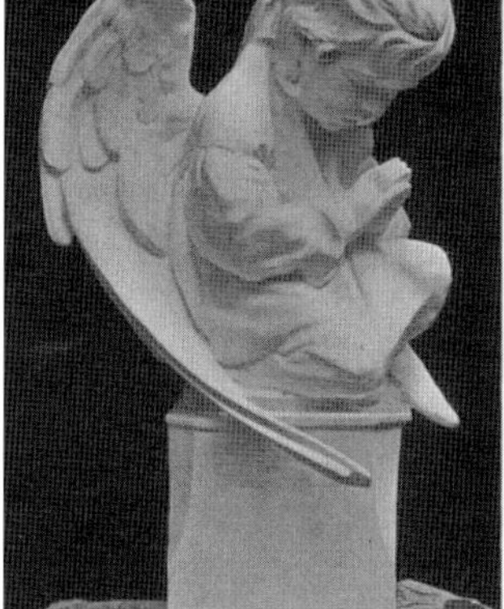
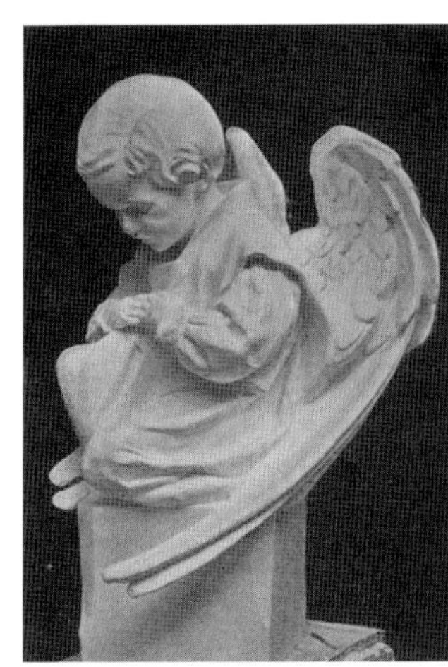

Plasters of the original attendant angel figures

Constant Coquelin Memorial

Medium: Bronze
Size: H 49¹/₂ins (126cms)
Exhibitions: Royal Academy 1910;
Glasgow 1911.
Locations: Comédie Française, Paris,
presented by English actors
(now in store).
Literature: The Studio 1915 Vol 66 p186,
illus.
Constant Coquelin, 1841-1909, was a
noted French actor.

Lord Nunburnholme Memorials

Medium: Bronze figures
Size: 5ft (152.5cms)
Exhibitions: Royal Academy 1910 (angels
shown); Arts and Crafts,
Ridley 1910; Glasgow 1911;
Ghent Fine Arts 1913;
Aberdeen 1921.
Locations: St James Churchyard, Warter,
Yorkshire.
Literature: The Studio 1909 Vol 48 p301,
illus., (attendant angels only);
Royal Academy Pictures 1910
p105, illus.
The two allegorical figures which remain
in the churchyard commemorate Gerald
Valerian Wilson, 1885-1908 and Charles
Henry Wilson, 1833-1907. The original
attendant figures have now gone.

Birds of Venus

Exhibitions: Southport 1912; Fine Art
Society 1912; Glasgow 1916.

Sir W. Moore

Medium: Bronze
Locations: Made for Bombay
Literature: The Studio Year Book 1909 p40

Knight on Horseback

Medium: Seal
Exhibitions: Ridley 1909 (1gn).

Reverie

Medium: Bronze
Size: 8ins (18cms)
Exhibitions: Sir John Cass 1909; Arts and
Crafts, Goupil, Ridley 1910
(8gns – two sold); Southport
1911; Toronto 1912; Goupil
1913 (sold); Fine Art Society
1912, 1918 and 1920; Leicester
Galleries, Glasgow 1918 (£15 –
two sold).
Locations: Sotheby's Billinghurst 21.1.97
(sold £1,650); Sladmore Gallery,
London.

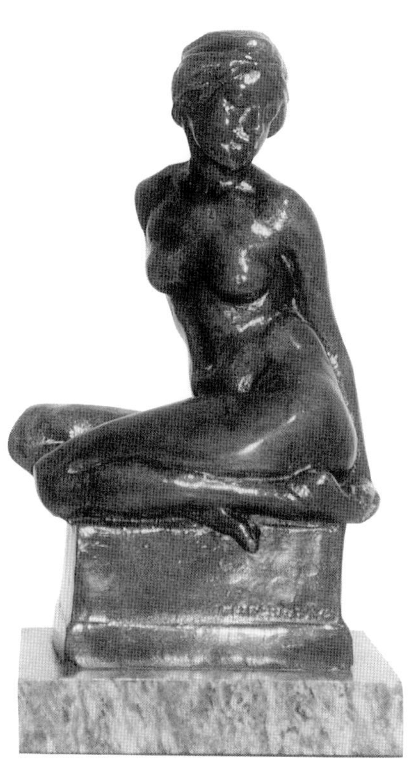

Reverie (Sotheby's)

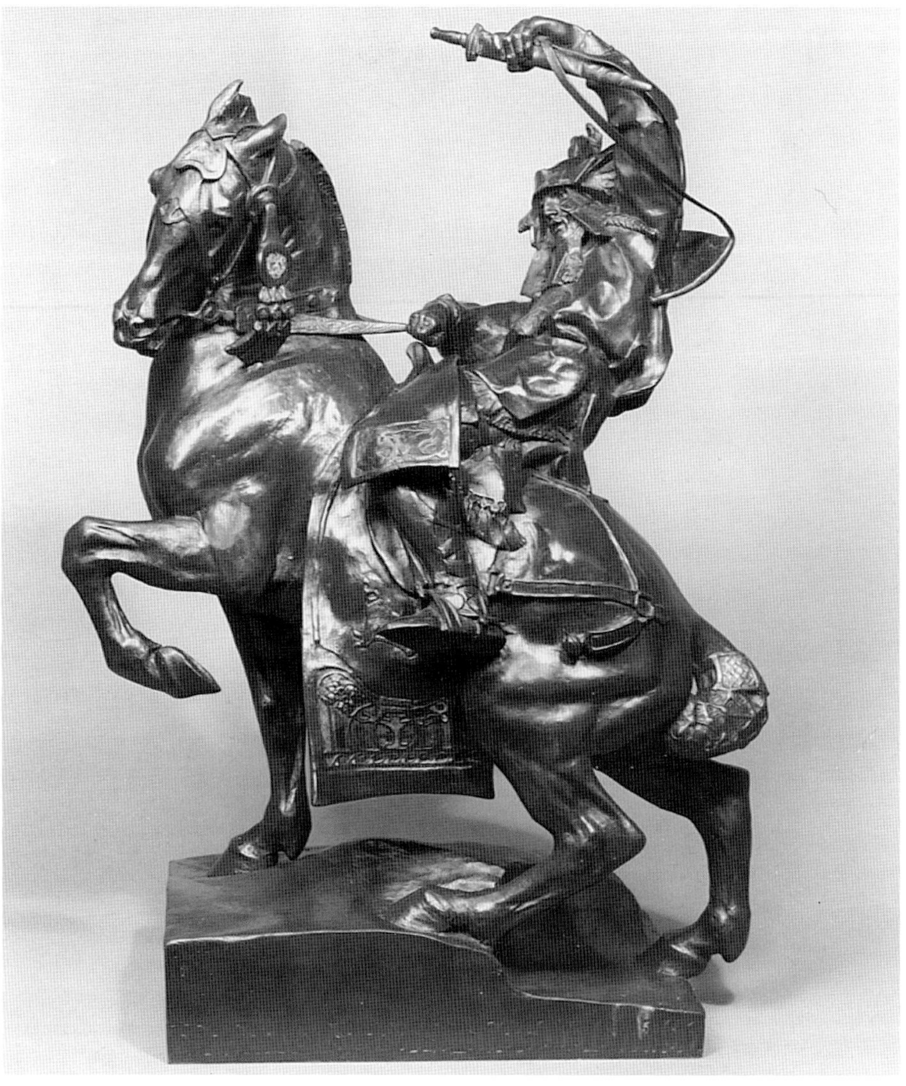

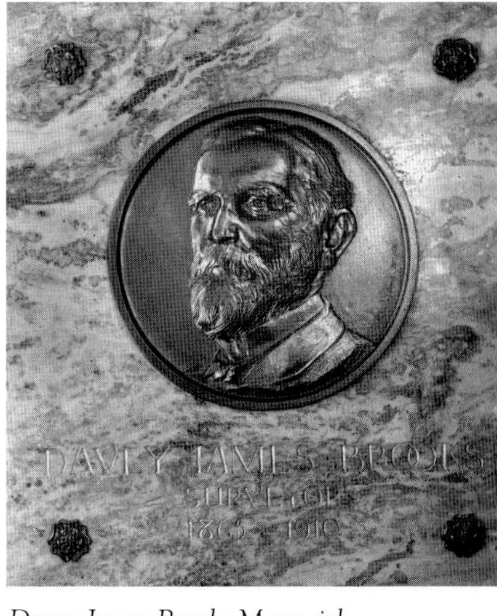

Davey James Brooks Memorial

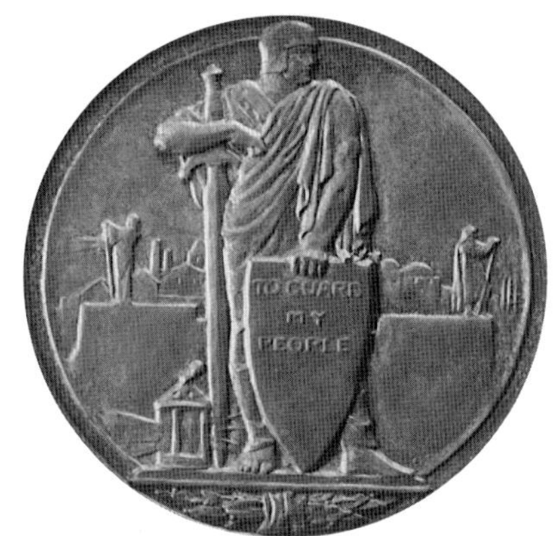

Edward VII King's Police Medal

1910

Sigurd with Gram Sword

Medium:	Bronze figure on plinth
Size:	H 35ins W 37ins (89 x 94cms)
Exhibitions:	Royal Academy 1910; RA Bicentennial 1968.
Locations:	Tate Gallery, Chantrey Bequest purchased 1910; Ashmolean Museum. Bequeathed in 1927 by Rev W.E. Brocklebank who bought it in 1910 for £150. Bayes designed a wooden pedestal for £50.
Literature:	Priced at £105 in *The Year's Art*

Rubber Growers Association Medal

Medium:	Gold and bronze
Locations:	British Museum
Literature:	*The Numismatic Chronicle* 1992 pl 19, illus.

This medal was first distributed in 1911 to members of the Rubber Growers Association, now the Tropical Growers Association.

Davey James Brooks Memorial, 1863-1910

Medium:	Bronze panel

Mr Brooks was a surveyor.

Edward VII King's Police Medal

Medium:	Silver
Exhibitions:	Sir John Cass 1913
Locations:	British Museum
Literature:	*The Builder* 1924 Vol 126 p409; *The Numismatic Chronicle* 1992 pl 21, illus.

This medal was awarded for acts of courage to policeman and firemen in the British Empire. It replaced two separate models, one for long service and one for gallantry. In 1933 the Bayes designs were updated with new legends.

Janet Laudelis McEwan

Exhibitions:	International Medallic, New York, 1910

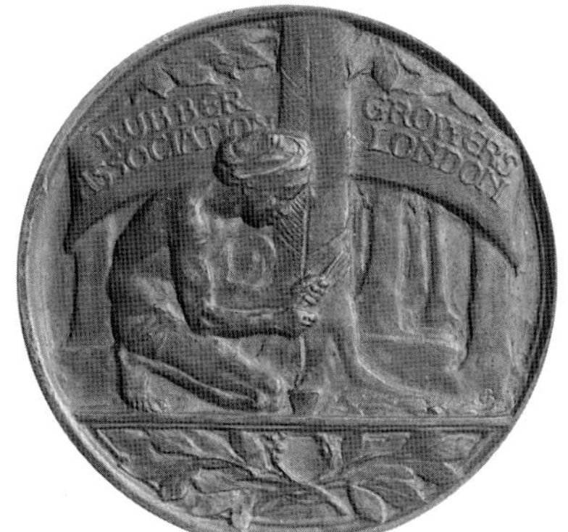

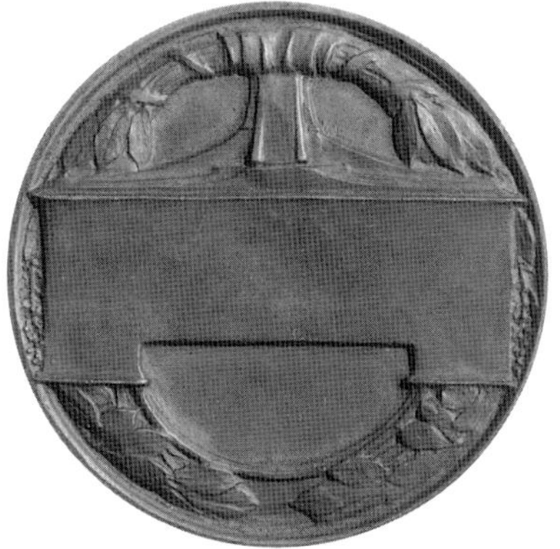

Rubber Growers Association Medal

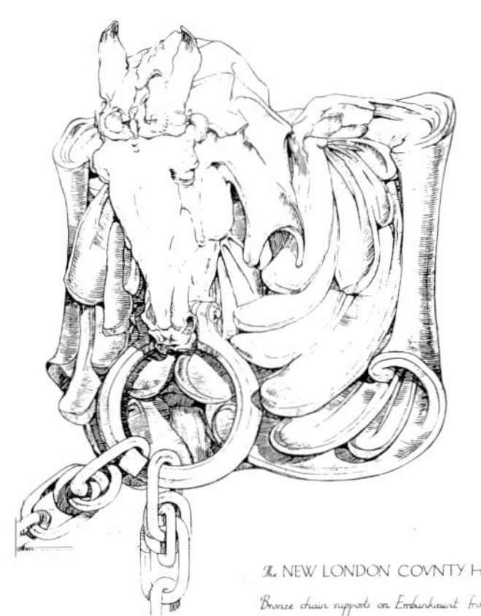

*Drawing of horse head support by
J.R. Leathart, from The Builder, 8th Sept 1911*

Lion and Horse Head Chain Supports

Medium: Bronze cast by Singer's
Locations: Albert Embankment, London.
              Commissioned by Ralph Knott
              for the new London County
              Hall.
Literature: The Builder 1911 Sep p274, illus.

1911

Lady Tata Memorial

Medium: Bronze in marble setting
Exhibitions: Royal Academy Memorial
              Exhibition 1917
Locations: Bangalore, price 150gns
Lady Tata was the wife of Sir Ratan Tata.

Great Seal of George V

Medium: Plaster designs for metal
Exhibitions: Model at Royal Academy 1911;
              Glasgow 1912; Ghent Arts and
              Crafts 1913; Southport 1914.
Locations: Delivered to Chancellor's Office
              1912
Literature: The Builder 1924 Vol 126 p409;
              The Numismatic Chronicle 1992,
              illus.

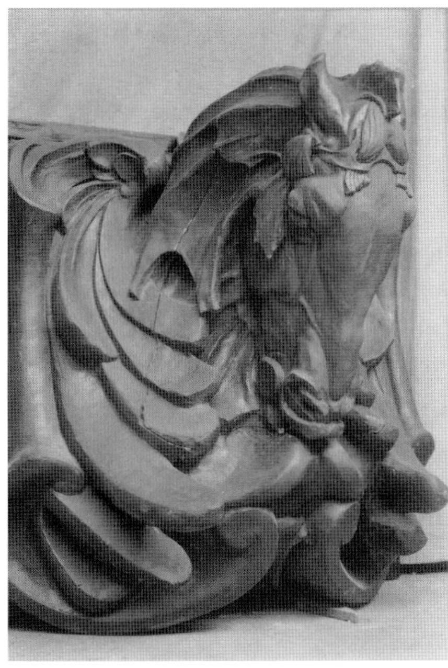

Plaster of Horse Head support

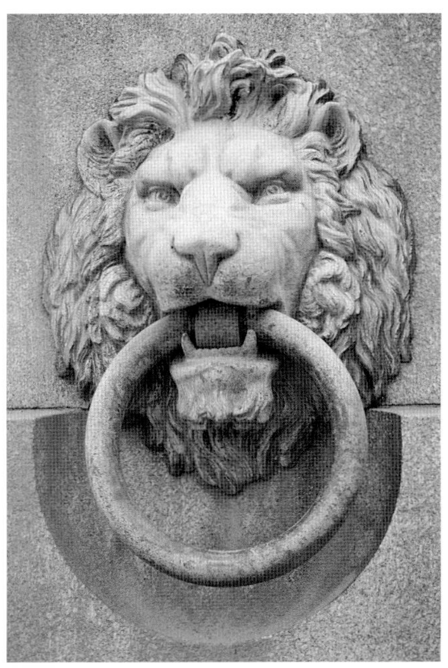

Lion in situ

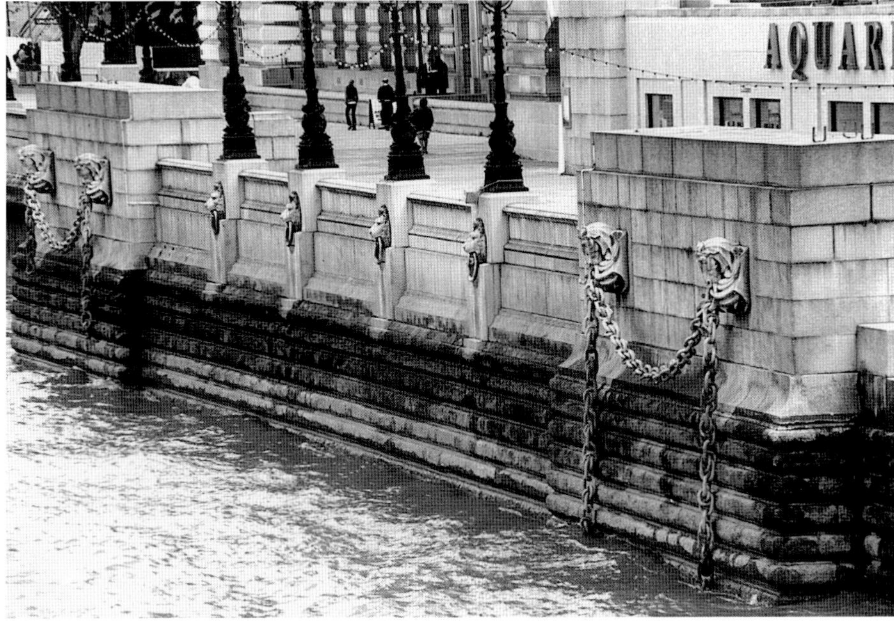

The chain supports in situ

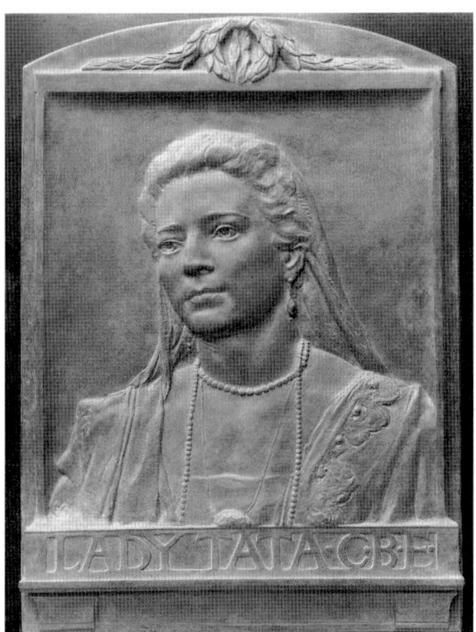

Lady Tata Memorial

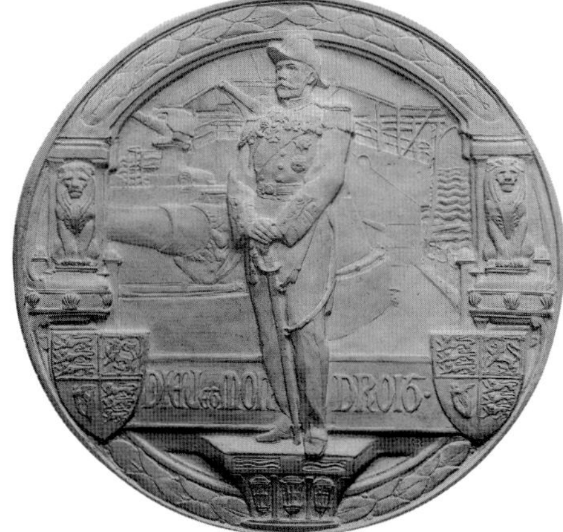

Great Seal of George V

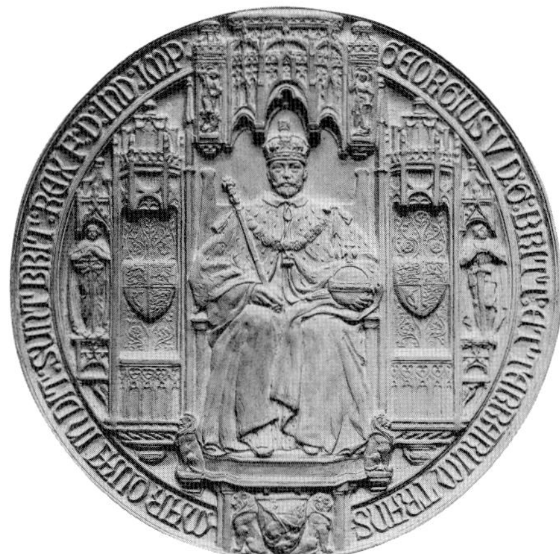

Midsummer Night's Dream

Medium: Bronze statuette
Exhibitions: Ridley 1911
Literature: This might be another name
for *Mushroom Sprite*

Bust of Child

Medium: Marble
Exhibitions: Ridley 1911 (plaster);
Southport 1912 (marble) 50gns.

The Angel of the Off Shore Wind

Medium: Bronze statuette
Exhibitions: Goupil 1911(£21); Royal
Academy, Brighton, Toronto
1912; Bristol 1913; Fine Art
Society 1913, 1918 and 1920;
Rawlson Townsend 1914;
Glasgow 1915 (£16); Royal
Academy Memorial
Exhibition 1916; Ridley 1924
(30gns).

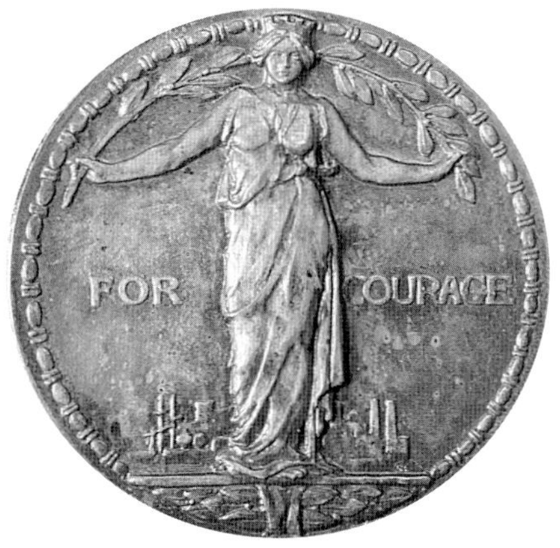

Edward Extension Medal

Medium: Silver
Locations: British Museum
Literature: *The Numismatic Chronicle*
pl 21, illus.
Awarded for bravery in the workplace.

1912

The Fountain of the Valkyries

Medium: Bronze, marble and mosaic
Size: H 7ft (2.1m)
Exhibitions: Royal Academy 1912;
Liverpool 1912 (£400);
Ghent 1913 (£400); Paris
1914 (£400); Wembley 1924;
Horticultural Society 1928.
Locations: The Domain, Auckland, New
Zealand, presented by R.S.
Hellaby in 1930.
Literature: *Royal Academy Pictures*, 1912,
p57, illus; *Walker Art Gallery*

Fountain of the Valkyries

Catalogue 1912, pl LXIII; *The
Studio Year Book* 1914 p79,
illus; *The Studio Year Book*
1914 p79; *The Studio* 1917 Vol
72 p100.
The statuette of Brynhilde was adapted
from this fountain.

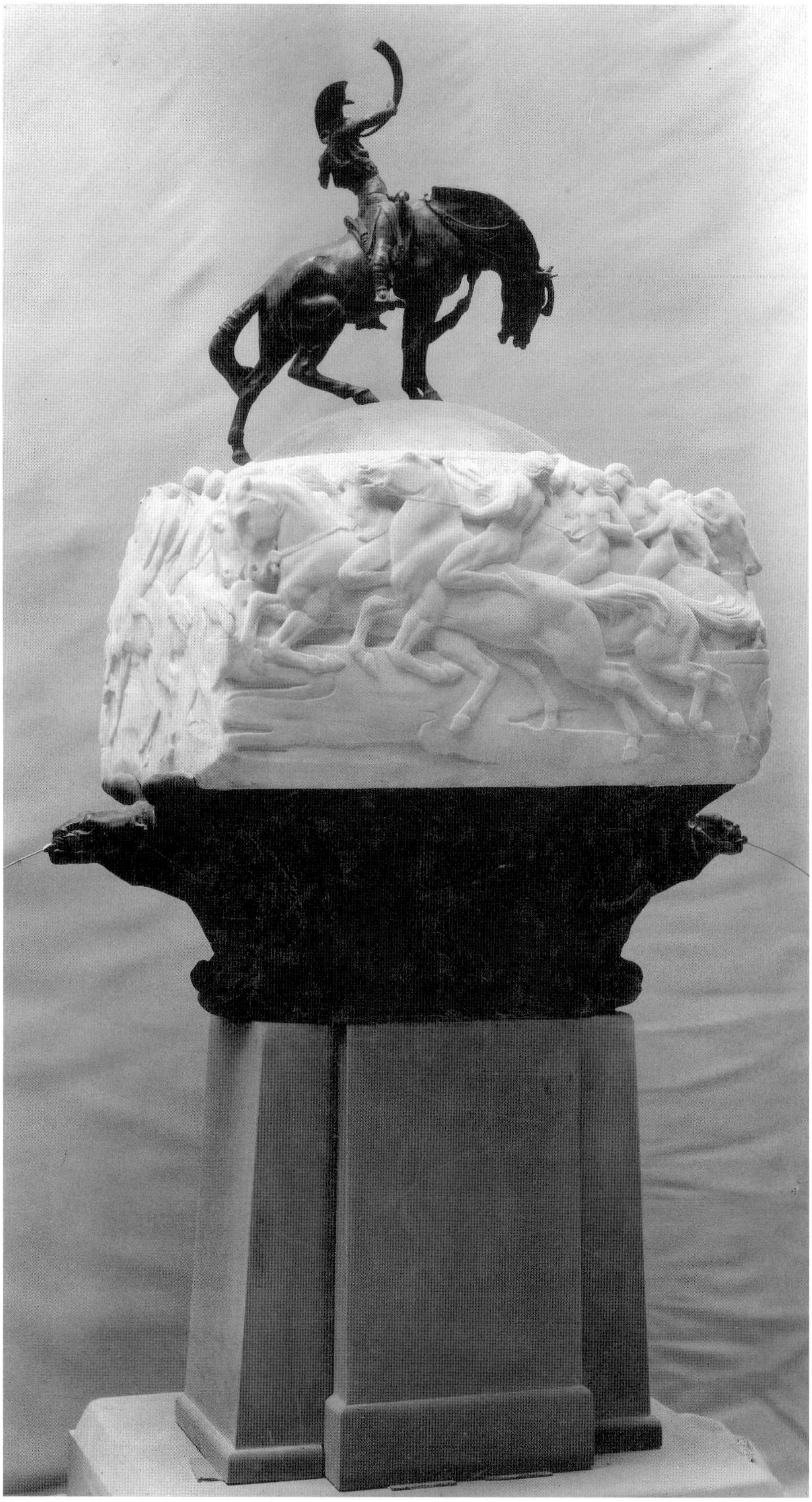

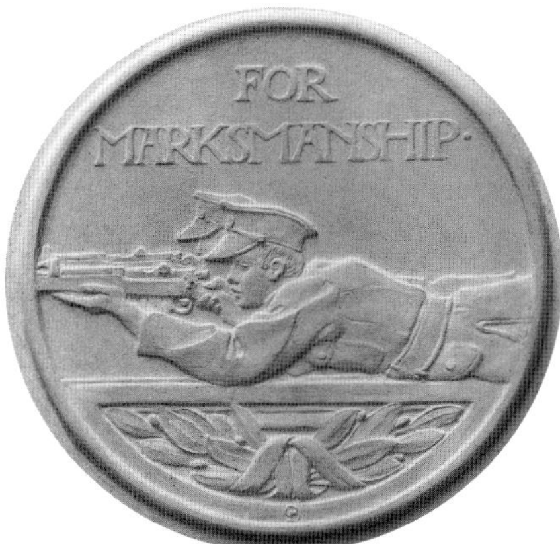

Plaster model for the Country Life Medal

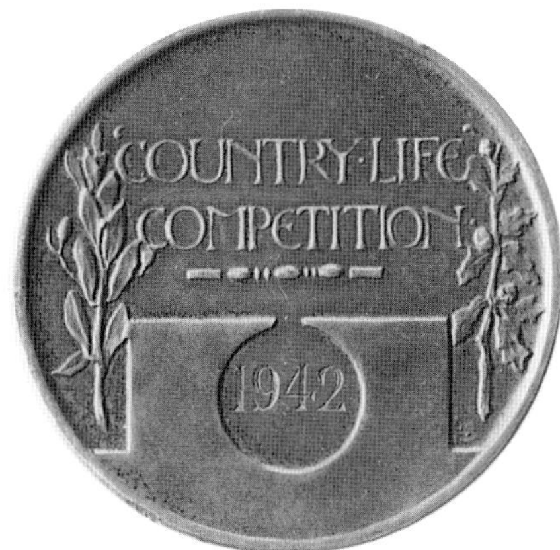

Country Life Medal, verso

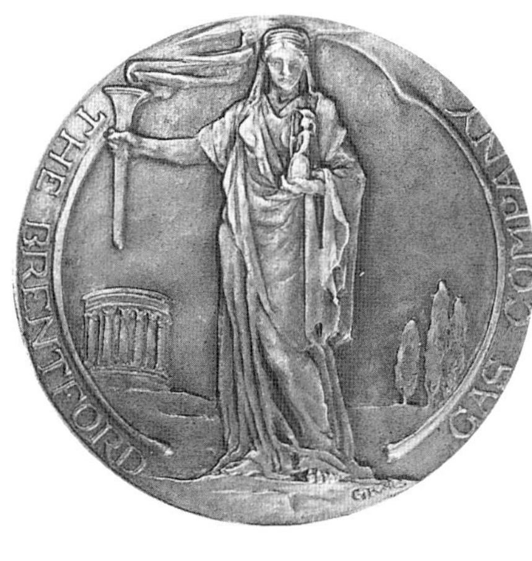

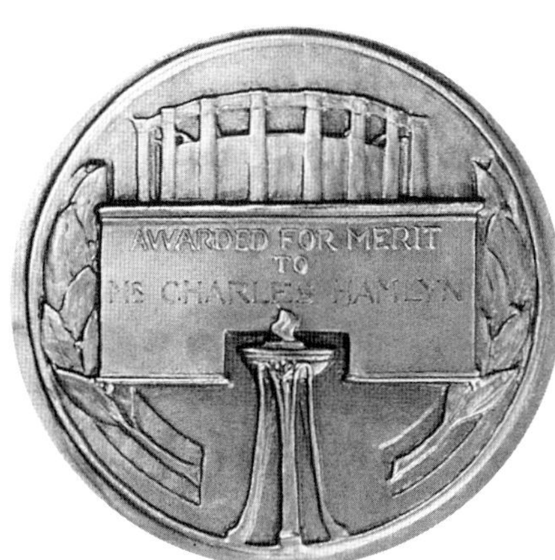

Brentford Gas Medal

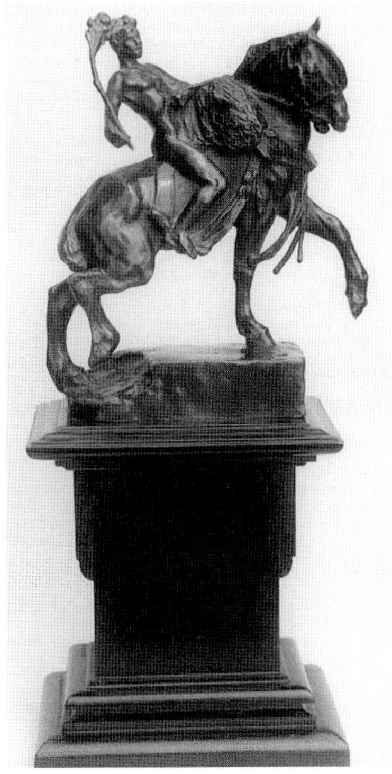

Youth

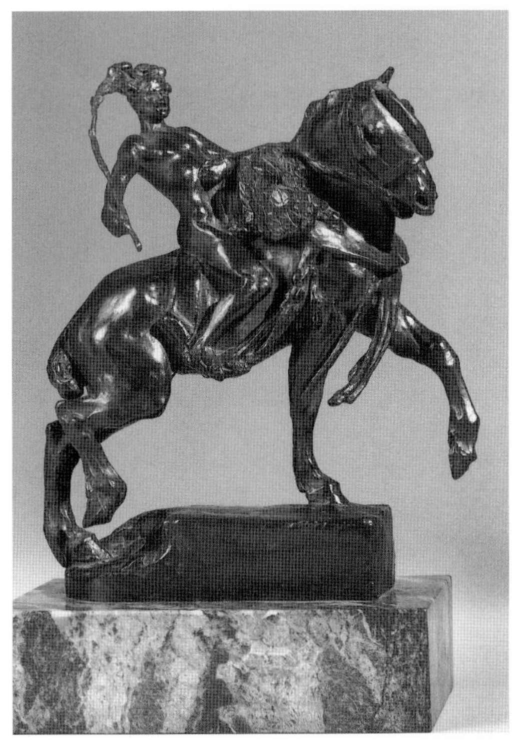

Variant of Youth in bronze

Country Life Marksmanship Medal

Medium: Silver and bronze
Locations: British Museum
Literature: *Country Life* 1912, illus; *The Numismatic Chronicle* 1992 pl 20, illus. This medal has been presented continuously for over seventy years.

Brentford Gas Company Medal

Medium: Bronze made by Pinches
Literature: *The Numismatic Chronicle* 1992 pl 20, illus.

1913

Baldwin's Newel Post

Exhibitions: Ridley 1913 (plaster); Sir John Cass 1913.
Literature: This could be the figure of *Youth*. See below.

Monkey Newel Post

Exhibitions: Sir John Cass 1913; Paris Arts and Crafts (£5).

Youth

Medium: Bronze
Size: 9ins (23cms)
Exhibitions: Goupil 1913; Rawlson Townsend (sold), Glasgow 1914 (£10); Fine Art Society 1918.
Locations: This is probably a version of the bronze (dated 1913) shown at Joanna Barnes Gallery in 1995.

This sculpture once formed part of a newel post in F.W. Pomeroy's sister's house.

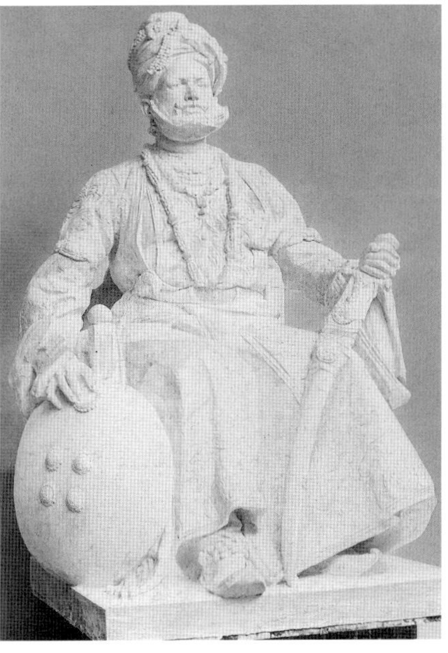

Maharajah of Bikaner Memorial

Maharajah of Bikaner Memorial

Medium: Plaster maquette for marble
Size: Over life-size
Exhibitions: Sir John Cass 1913; Royal Academy 1914.
Literature: *The Studio* 1917 Vol 72 p100, illus; *Sculpture and the Sculptors Art*, H.H. Stansfield 1918 p150, illus.

The Years at the Spring

Exhibitions: Toronto 1913; Goupil 1913 (sold), 1916, 1918; Glasgow, Bristol 1914; Fine Art Society 1920.

Also known as *The World's at the Spring*.

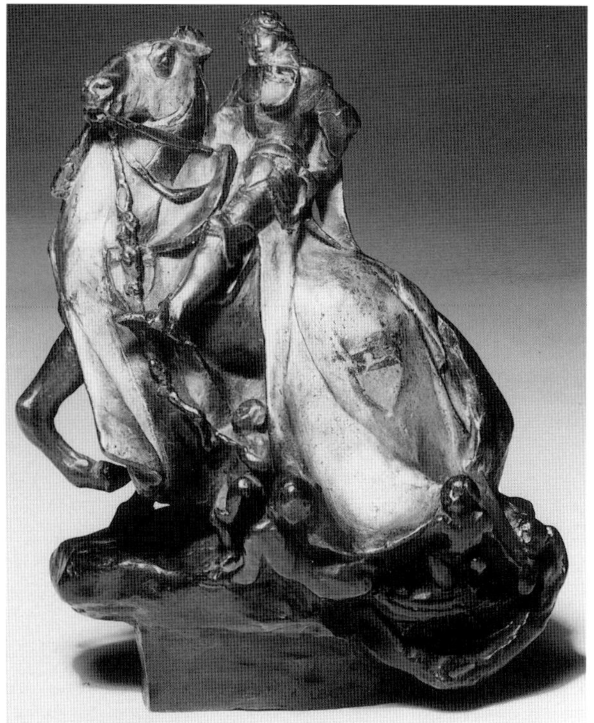

The Underworld

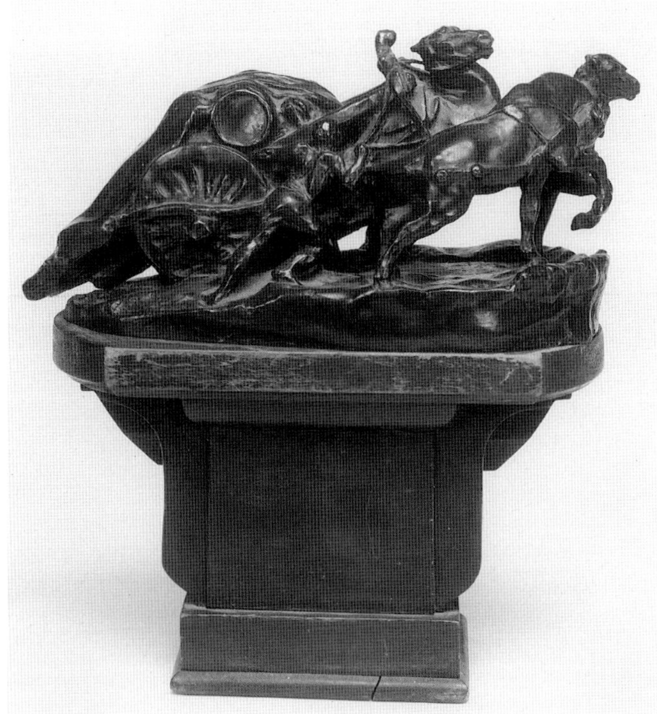

The Wine Wagon

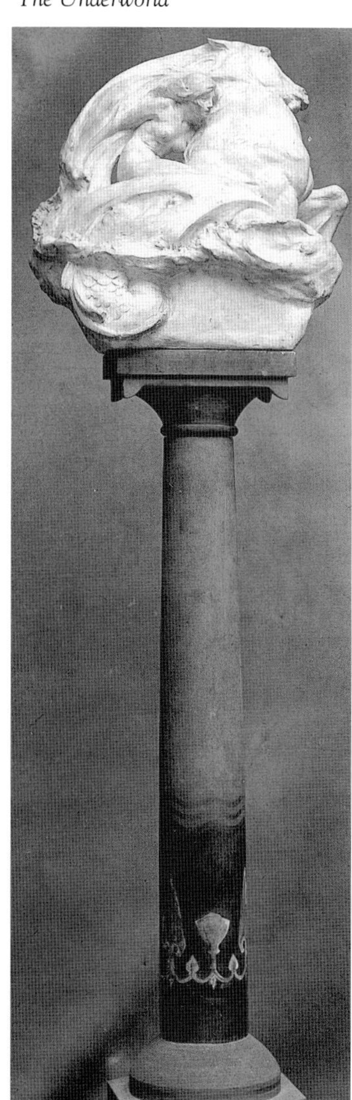

The Sea King's Daughter

The Sea King's Daughter on Stand

Medium: Marble on red stone column
Size: H 19¹⁄₂ins (49.5cms)
Exhibitions: Royal Academy 1913; Liverpool 1913
    (£157), and 1920; Arts and Crafts Paris
    1914 (sold) also Rome and Ghent; Fine
    Art Society 1918; Glasgow 1919 (50gns);
    Royal Scottish Academy 1925, 1939;
    Whitechapel 1929; Aberdeen 1935.
Locations: Art Gallery of New South Wales,
    Australia, purchased 1915
Literature: *The Year's Art* 1915, illus; *The Studio* 1917
    Vol 72 p102, illus; *The Builder* 1919 May
    p482, illus.

The Wine Wagon

Medium: Bronze group
Size: 10³⁄₄ins (27cms)
Exhibitions: Goupil 1913; Ridley 1914; Bristol 1917
    (15gns); Glasgow 1916, 1918; Fine Art
    Society 1920; Institute 1931 (18gns).
Locations: Christie's 30.4.85; Sotheby's 18.12.85
    (dated 1913 – sold for £900); Bayes Trust.
Also known as *The Italian* or *Naples Wine Cart*.

The Underworld

Medium: Bronze statuette
Size: H 9ins (23cms)
Exhibitions: Rawlson Townsend, Ridley 1914; Royal
    Academy 1915 (sold); Leicester Galleries,
    Glasgow 1916 (£16); Royal Scottish
    Academy 1917; Fine Art Society, Bristol
    1918, 1924 (£26); Institute, Liverpool
    1920; Aberdeen 1921; Cooper Hewitt
    Museum, New York 1979.
Locations: Bayes Trust, dated 1913; private collection;
    St Cross College, Oxford – silver version
    (formerly Fine Art Society); Scottish
    National Gallery of Modern Art,
    bequeathed by Sir D.Y. Cameron 1945.
Inspired by Kipling's poem, *The Last Rhyme of True Thomas.*

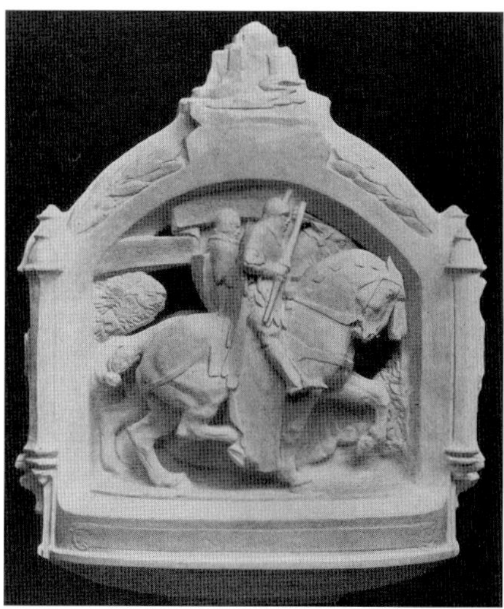

Romance

Romance

Medium: Marble relief on plinth
Size: H 6ft 6ins (1.98m)
Exhibitions: Royal Academy 1913 and 1914;
    Edinburgh 1914; Bristol 1915
    and 1920 (250gns); Liverpool
    1914, 1922 (£210); Royal
    Scottish Academy 1924.
Locations: Bayes Trust
Literature: *The Studio* 1913 Vol 59 p306, illus;
    The Studio 1917 p108, illus; *Royal
    Academy Pictures* 1913, p49, illus.
Inscribed 'Gather the Harvest of Worth. All departeth save Fame.'

Newel Post

Medium: Oak
Exhibitions: Sir John Cass 1913; Arts and
    Crafts 1916.
Locations: Formerly at the Poultry Court,
    Painswick, Gloucestershire

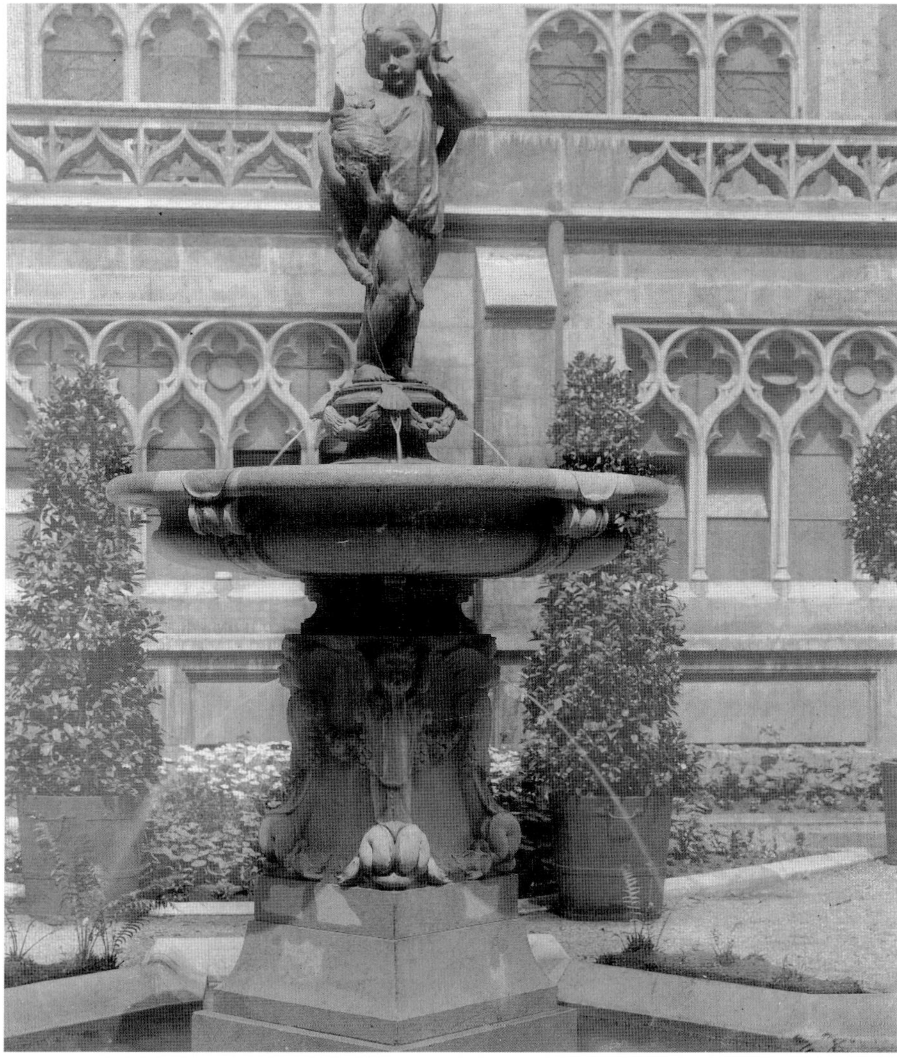

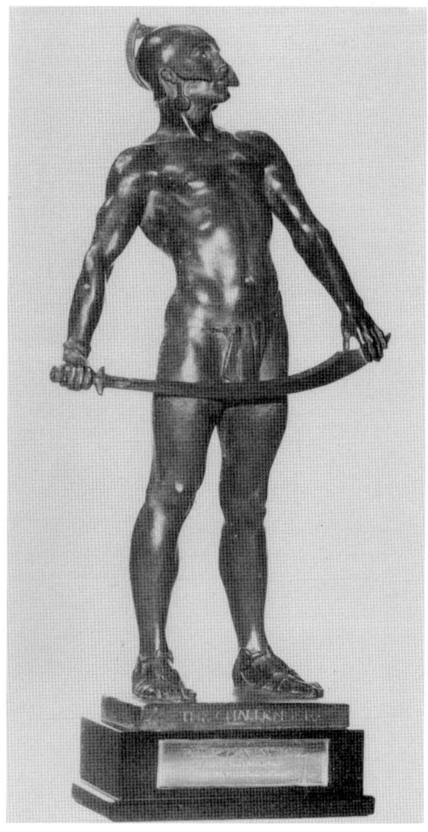

The Challenger (Sotheby's)

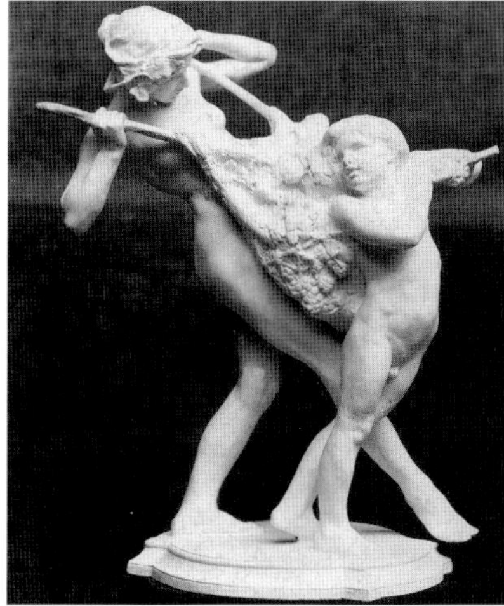

Plaster for the Wealth of the Earth

The Wealth of the Earth

Medium: Plaster maquette for bronze
Size: H 16ins (40.5cms)
Exhibitions: Ridley 1914; Royal
             Academy, Glasgow 1915
             (£52); Leeds 1916; Institute
             1917 (£52.10s); Leicester
             Galleries 1918; Fine Art
             Society, Bristol 1920 (sold);
             Liverpool 1921 (£63); Venice

1922; Goupil 1924; Dunedin, New
Zealand 1925; Royal Scottish
Academy 1935.
Locations: An example dated 1913 sold
             Sotheby's, Sussex, 22.4.97, £3,600
Literature: *The Studio* 1917 Vol 72 p112, illus.
This bronze sculpture was exhibited twenty
times between 1914 and 1938.

1914

The Challenger
Medium: Bronze
Size: H 22¼ins (56.5cms)
Locations: Sotheby's 5.11.80, plinth inscribed
             to Phillip Ernest Hill 1914, (sold
             £700)

Joseph Priestley, 1733-1804
Medium: Stone
Exhibitions: Royal Academy 1916 (model)
Locations: Above the doorway to the Institute
             of Chemistry, University of London,
             30 Russell Square. Erected 1914.
             Architects, Sir John Burnet and
             Partners.
Literature: *The Artist* Sep 1934 p13, illus.

Fountain of St John the Baptist
Medium: Bronze and stone
Size: Figure H 4ft 6ins (1.37m)

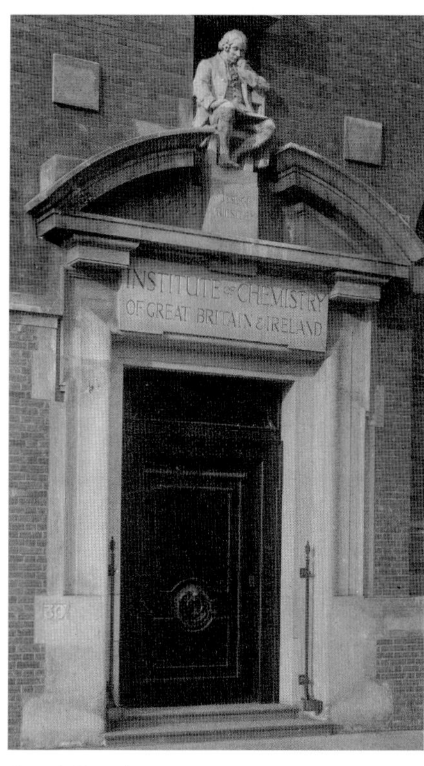

Joseph Priestley

Exhibitions: Royal Academy 1914
Locations: Merchant Taylor's Hall
             Courtyard, London
Literature: *Royal Academy Pictures* 1914
             p147 illus; *The Studio* 1917 Vol
             72 p107 illus; *Journal of the
             Royal Horticultural Society* LIV
             1929 fig108.

Gilbert Bayes

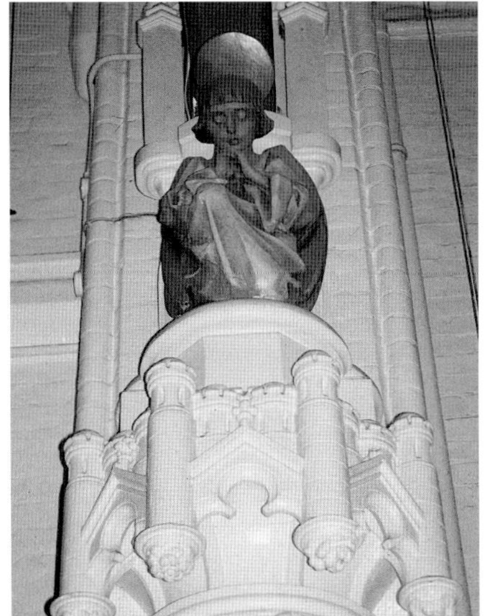

One of the screen's angel corbels

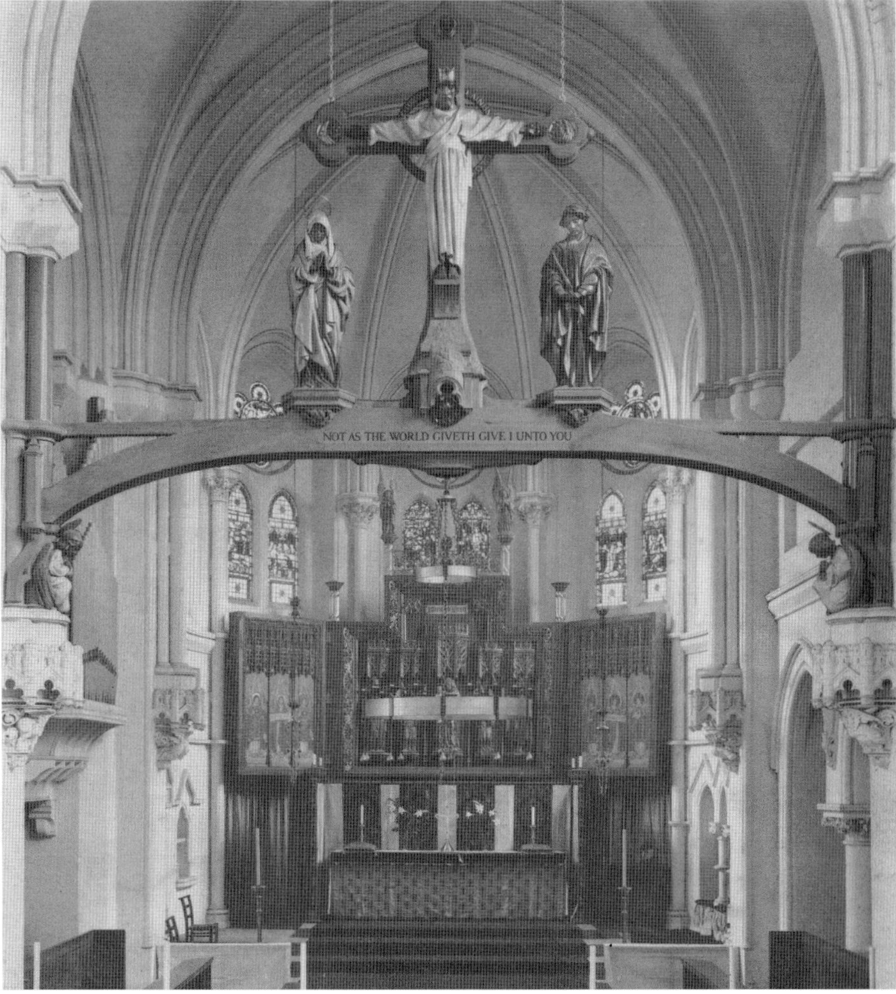

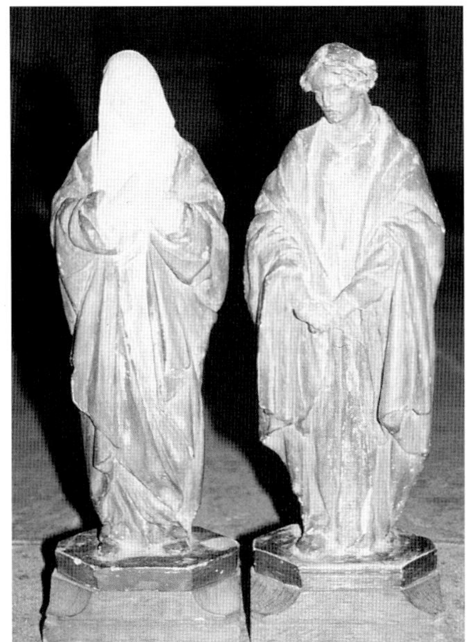

Original plaster models for the screen figures

Rood Screen

Medium: Wood carved and painted
Exhibitions: Victoria & Albert War Memorials 1919
Locations: St Mary's, King Henry's Road, London
Literature: *The Studio* 1916 Vol 68 p239, illus; *The Builder* 1919
         Aug p115, illus.
The rood screen, in memory of the lithographer and printer
Thomas R. Way (1861-1913), is inscribed 'Not as the world
giveth I give unto you.' Completed in 1914, this screen was
altered by Bayes thirty years later.

Prehistoric and Classic Periods

Medium: Plaster models for stone
Locations: South front, National Museum of Wales, Cardiff.
         Architects, Smith and Brewer.
Literature: *The Builder* 1924 Mar p409
Bayes was responsible for two of the sixteen sculptural groups in
this scheme devised by Sir W. Goscombe John, RA. The first six
were executed in 1914-16 by Bayes, Richard Garbe and Thomas
J. Clapperton. These groups were initially known as *Stone Age*
and *Bronze Age*.

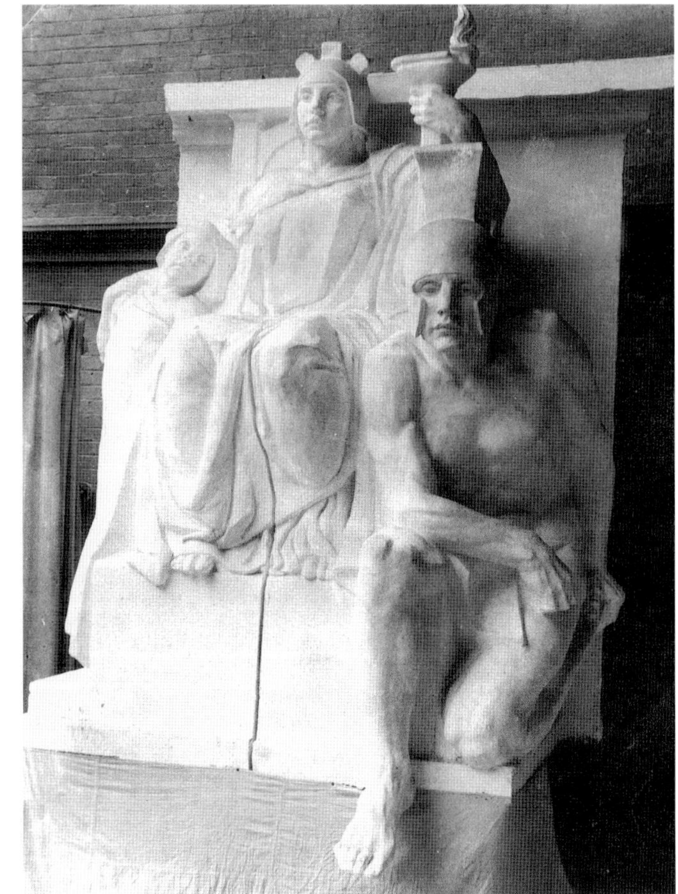

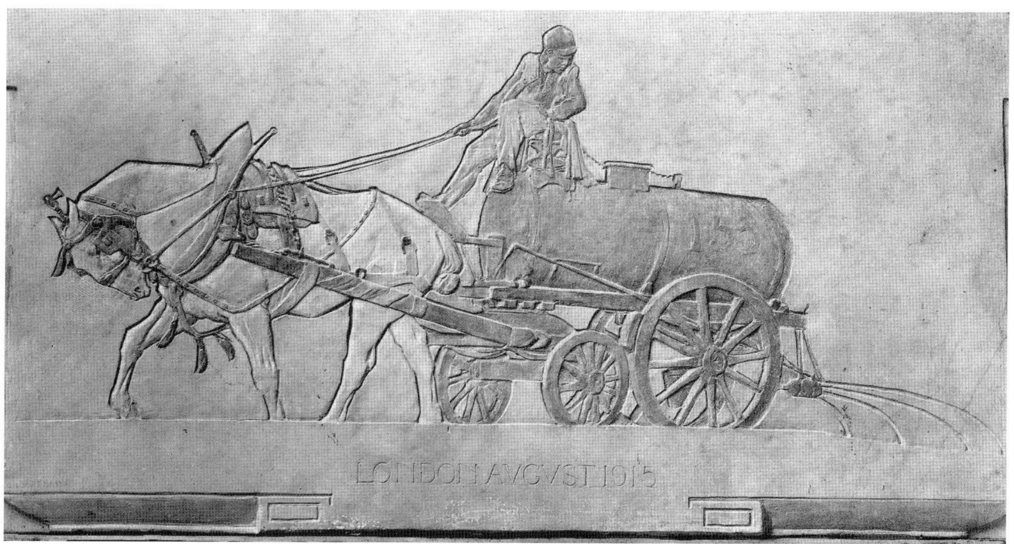

The Water Cart

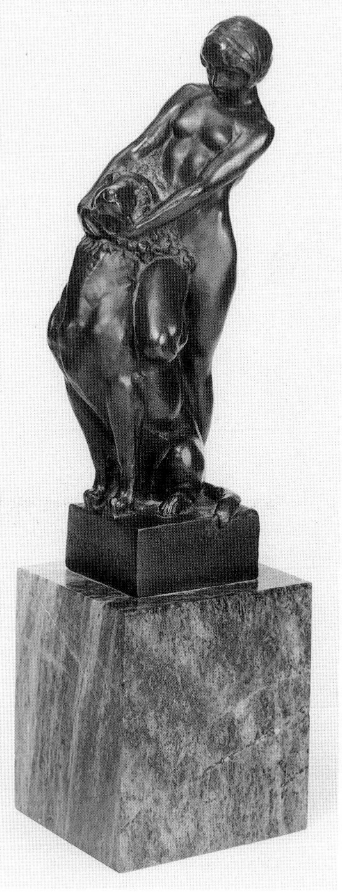

A Young Diana

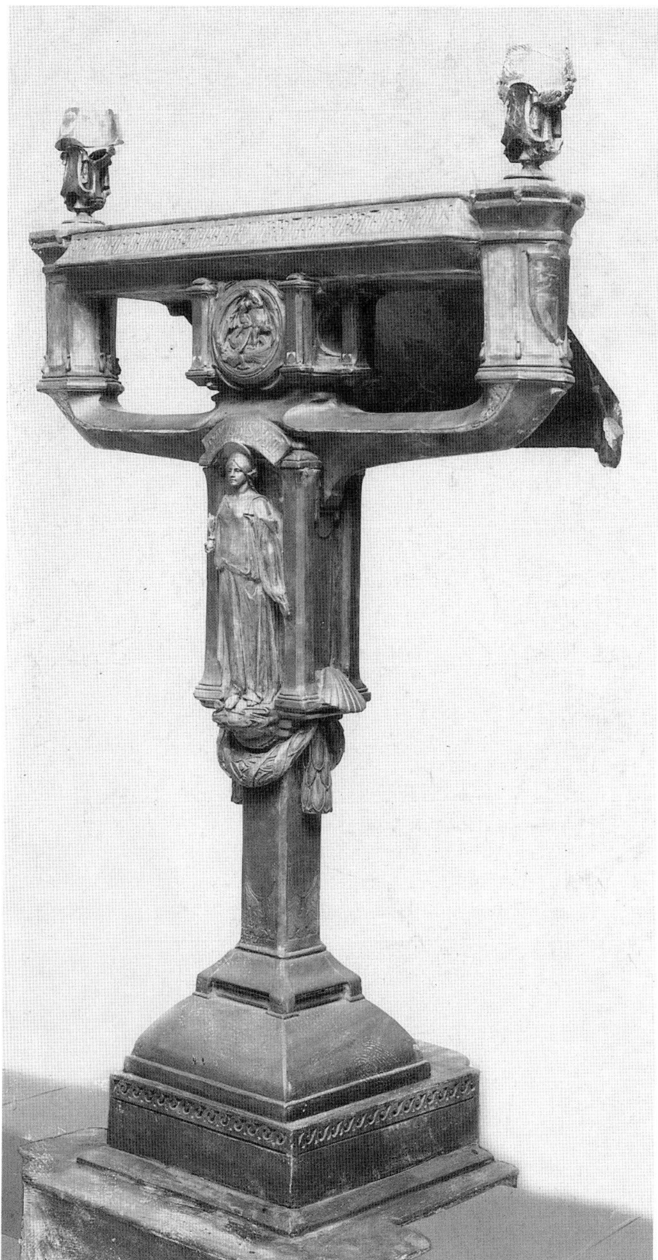

Laurence and Mabel Irving memorial lectern

1915

A Young Diana

Medium: Bronze with marble plinth
Size: H 11ins (28cms) plus plinth
Exhibitions: Edinburgh 1914 (sold 10gns); Leicester Galleries, Glasgow, Leeds 1916; Bristol 1917; Ridley 1918; Fine Art Society 1918 and 1920; Russell Gallery, Bradford 1919 (sold); Royal Academy, Bristol 1920; Goupil 1924; Manchester 1928; Rio 1930; Institute 1933 (18gns).
Locations: Bayes Trust, dated 1915, no plinth; private collection dated 1915; Sotheby's 12.4.85, (dated 1915 – sold for £1,800); Agnews 1986 (dated 1915 – sold for £2,750); Sotheby's 15.3.91 (dated 1915); Sotheby's 6.6.97 (dated 1915).

The Water Cart

Medium: Hopton Wood stone
Size: H 23ins W 46ins (58.5 x 117cms)
Exhibitions: Arts and Crafts 1916 (coloured plaster); Royal Academy 1919 (Hopton Wood stone); Glasgow 1920.
Locations: Bayes Trust
Literature: *The Studio* 1917 Vol 72 p111, illus; *The Builder* 1917 Sep p179, illus; *Architectural Review* 1926 Jul p124, illus.

This panel was originally coloured.

Lectern, Truth and St George

Medium: Bronze, enamel and mosaic
Exhibitions: Victoria & Albert War Memorials 1919
Locations: Royal Savoy Chapel, Savoy Hill, London
Literature: *The Studio* 1917 Vol 72 p108, illus; *Festival of English Church Art* 1930 p76, illus; *The Artist* 1934 Nov p78, illus.

The lectern was created in memory of Laurence and Mabel Irving who died on the Empress of Ireland in 1914. The son of Henry Irving, the famous actor manager, Laurence was also an actor.

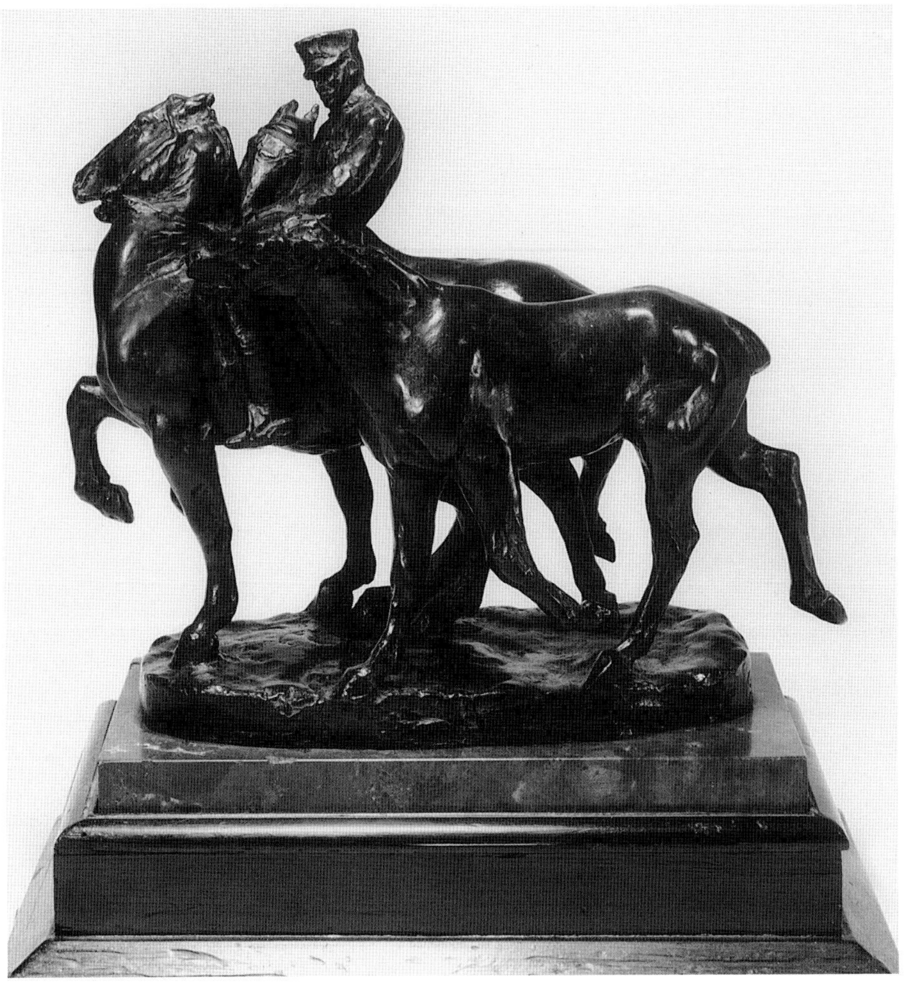

The Remounts (Sotheby's)

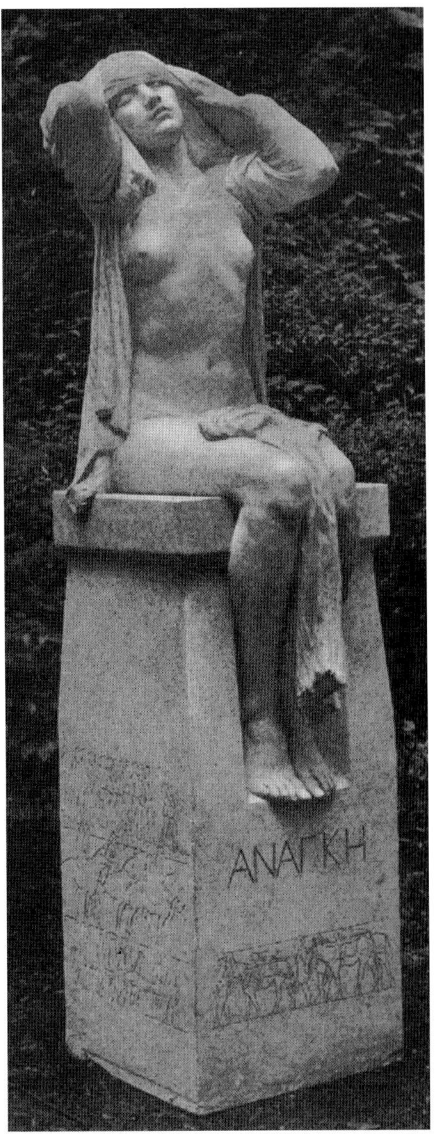

Anatkh (Destiny)

The Remounts

Medium: Bronze with marble plinth
Size: H 9ins (23cms) plus plinth
Exhibitions: Glasgow, Leeds 1916; Royal
               Academy 1917; Fine Art
               Society 1918; Ridley 1921;
               Whitechapel, Manchester
               1929.
Locations: Art Gallery of New South
               Wales, Australia dated 1915
               purchased 1919 for £16;
               Sotheby's 12.4.85 (dated 1915
               – sold for £2,400); Agnews
               1986 (sold for £3,250).

1916

Anatkh (Destiny)

Medium: Plaster statue
Exhibitions: Royal Academy 1916;
               Victoria & Albert War
               Memorials 1919.
Literature: *The Studio* 1917 vol 72 p113,
               illus; *The Artist* Dec 1934 p127,
               illus.

A version of this figure was later
incorporated into the Ramsgate War
Memorial. It was also made as a bronze
statuette.

On Sundays

Exhibitions: Leicester Galleries, Arts and
               Crafts 1916; Ridley, Glasgow
               1917 (£42); Fine Art Society
               1918.

Wreath and Crown

Medium: Bronze
Exhibitions: Goupil 1916

Keystones and Pier Caps for the Hall of Heroes, Royal Academy, Burlington House

Exhibitions: Arts and Crafts 1916

The subjects of the pier caps were Castor
and Pollux, and the keystones, Hercules,
Theseus, Perseus and Jason. The Hall of
Heroes was a temporary structure
designed by H. Wilson and F.W. Troup.

St George Doorknocker

Medium: Bronze
Size: H 12ins (30.5cms)
Exhibitions: Arts and Crafts 1916 (12 gns)
Locations: Bayes Trust

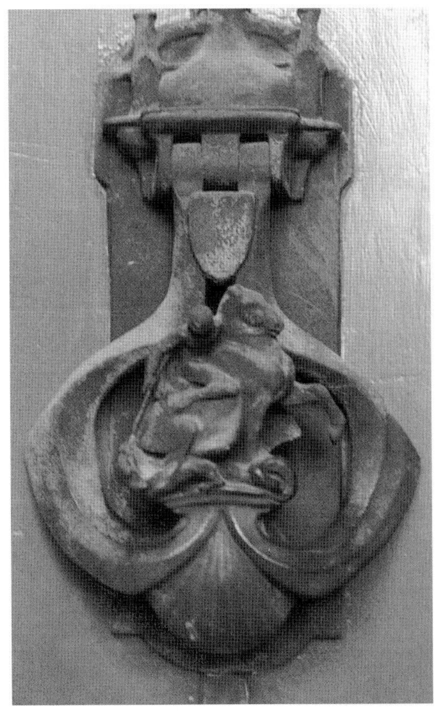

St George doorknocker

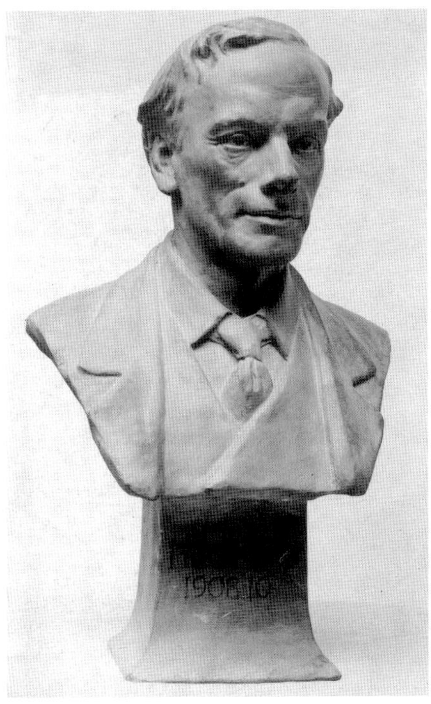

Sir George Francis Hardy, d.1914

Medium: Plaster maquette for bronze
Locations: Institute of Actuaries, Staple
Inn Hall, unveiled 1916
Sir George Hardy was President of the
Society of Actuaries.

1917

The Dying Soldier

Medium: Plaster maquette for stone
Size: H 39¹/₂ins W 79ins (1 x 2m)
Exhibitions: Royal Academy 1917; Ridley
1917; Victoria & Albert War
Memorials 1919.
Locations: St Peter and St Paul, Aldeburgh,
Suffolk inscribed: 'And everyone
said to his brother be of good
cheer' Isaiah XLI6. 'These laid
the world away, poured out the
sweet wine of youth, gave up the
years to be of work and joy and
that unhoped serene that men
call age'.
Literature: *The Studio* 1917 Vol 72 p111,
illus; *The Builder* 1919 Aug
p114, illus.
A gilded stone version was carved as a war
memorial for Aldeburgh, Suffolk.

1918

Earl Brownlow ADC

Medium: Bronze
Exhibitions: Royal Academy 1918
Locations: Belton House, Lincolnshire
Presentation bronze given by Machine
Gun Training Centre to Earl Brownlow
ADC 'As a memento of many kindnesses'.

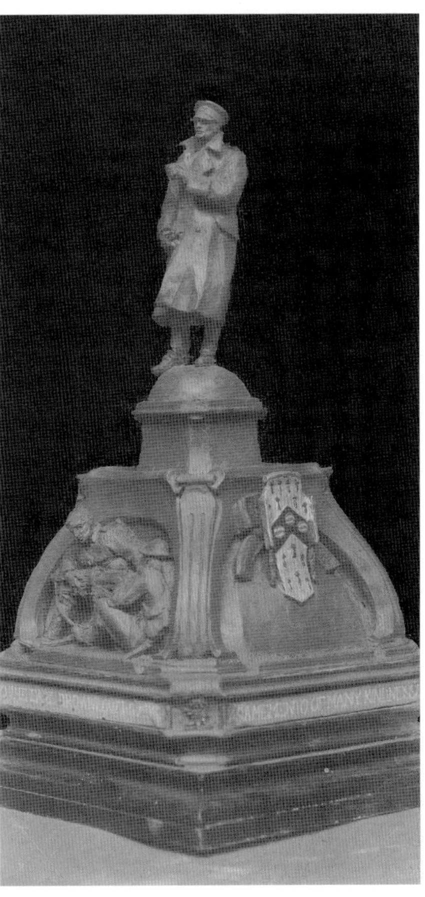

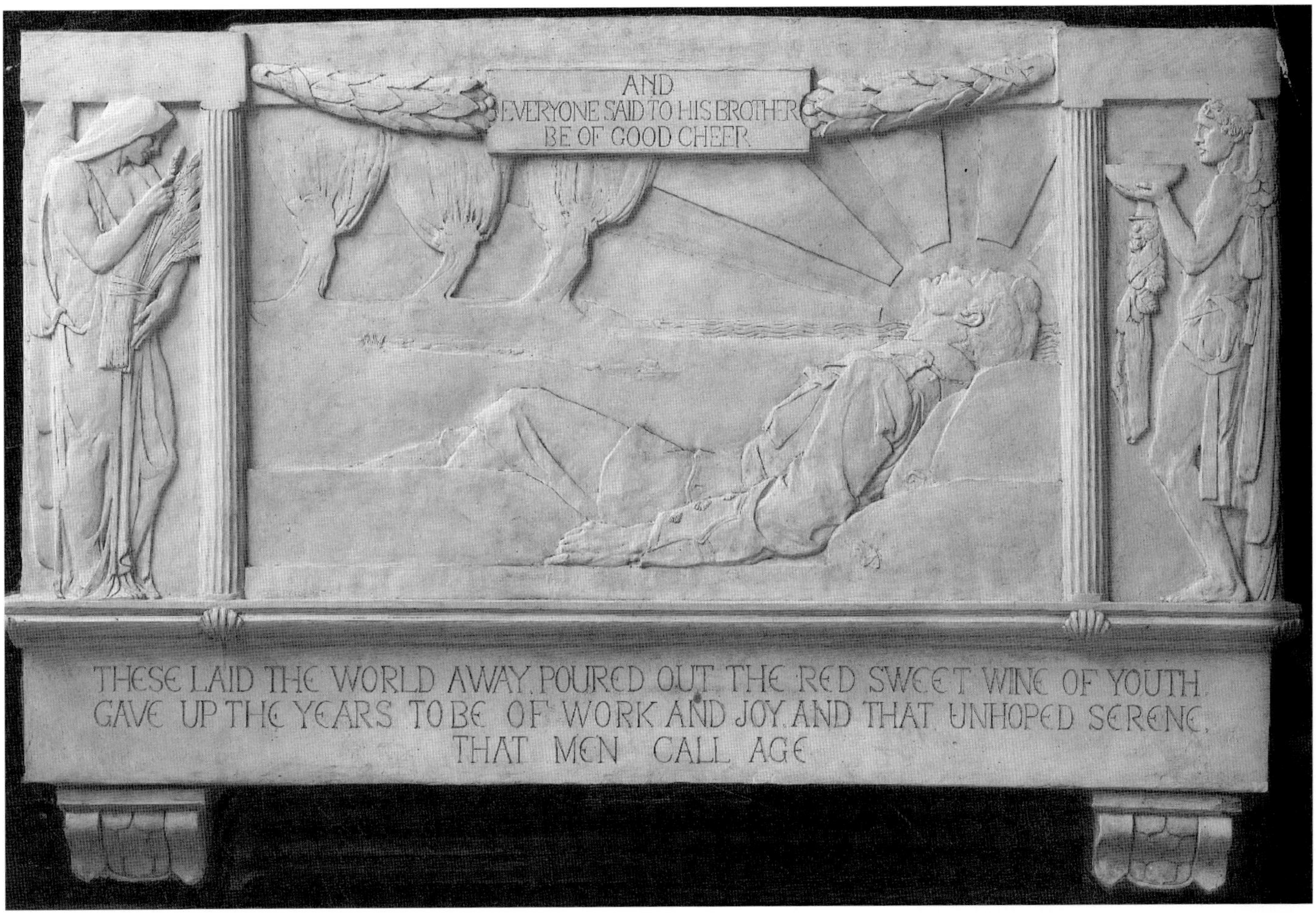

The Dying Soldier, plaster

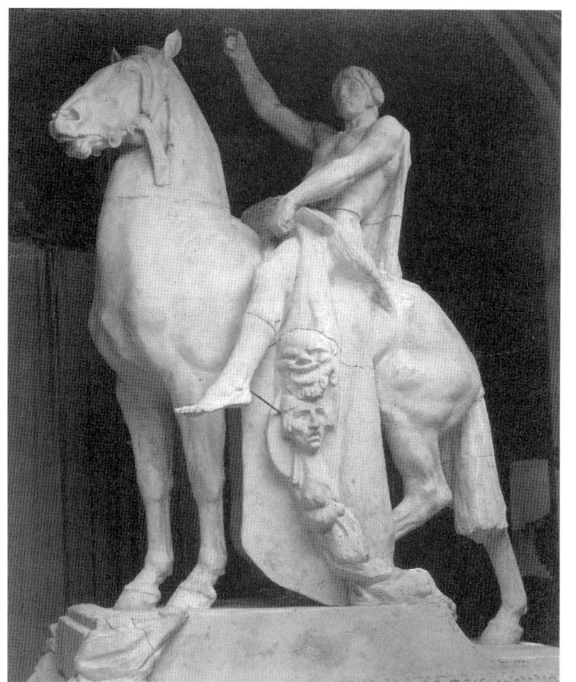 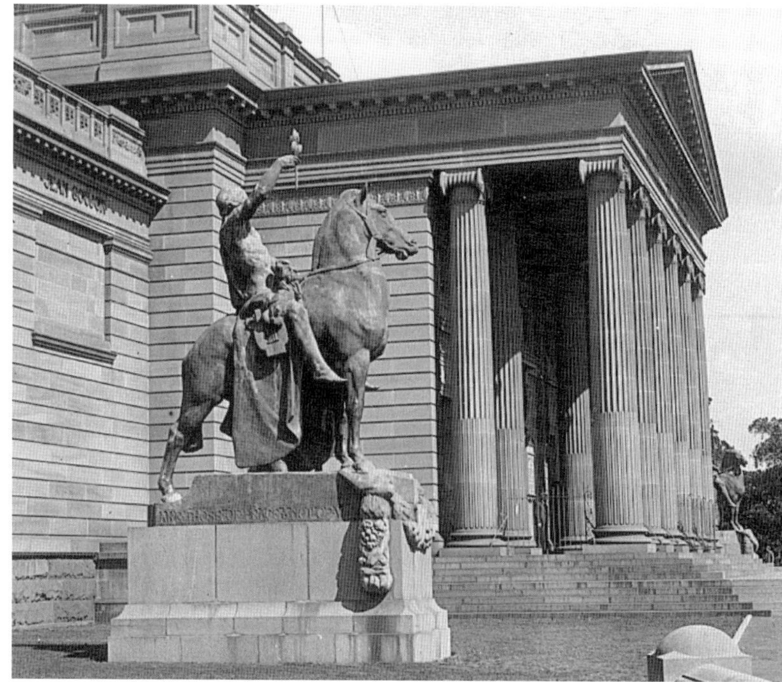

Offerings of Peace, the plaster model and the full-size bronze in Sydney, Australia

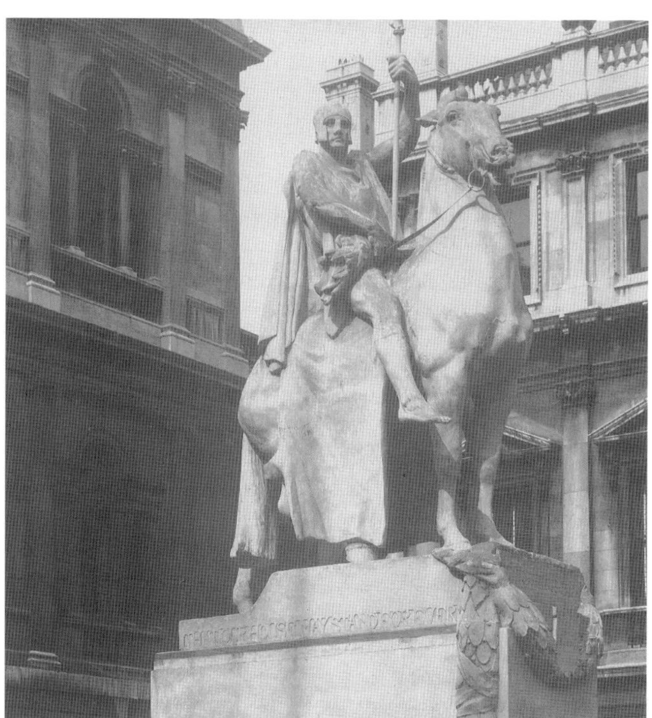 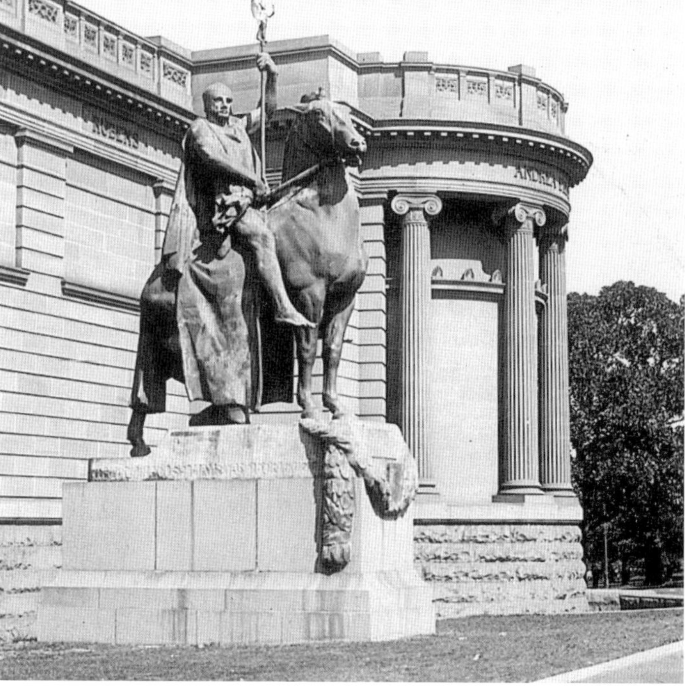

Offerings of War, the full-size plaster at the Royal Academy in 1918 and the bronze in Sydney

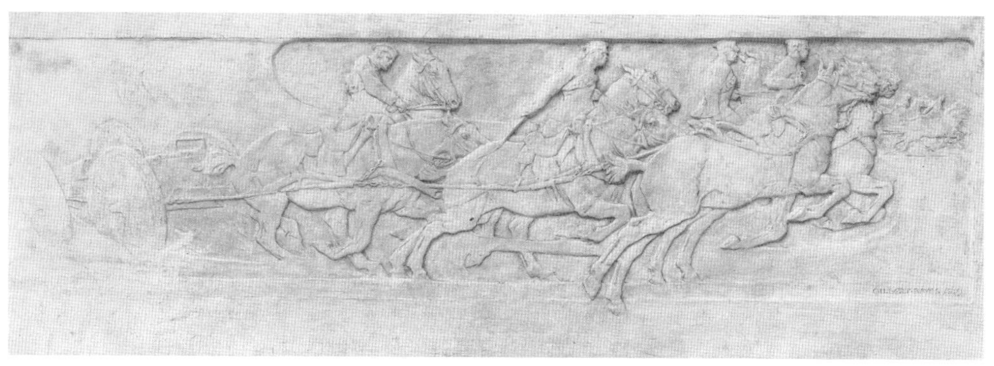

The Guns

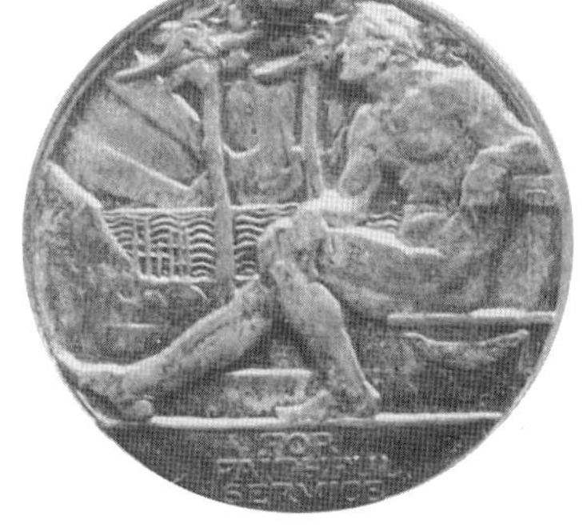

Imperial Service Medal

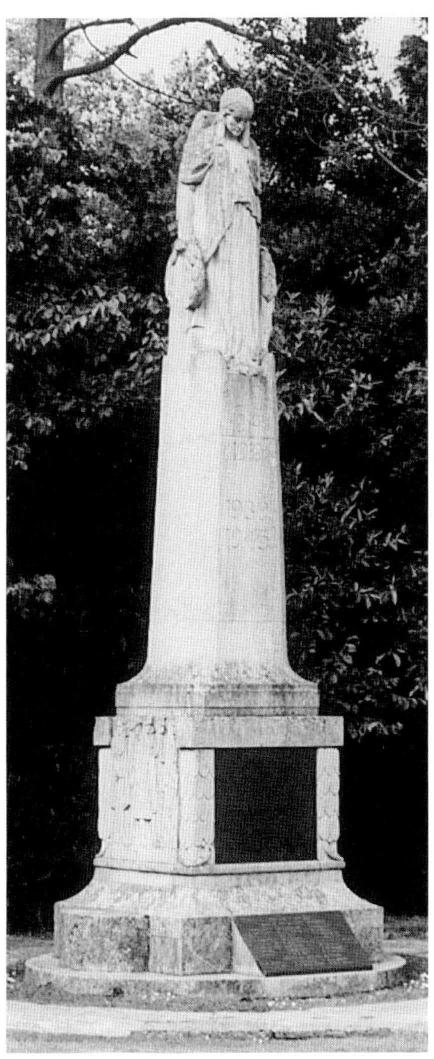

The Broadstone Memorial today.

Offerings of Peace and Offerings of War

Medium:	Bronze cast by A.B. Burton
Exhibitions:	Royal Academy 1917, *Offerings of Peace* quarter-scale model; Royal Academy 1918, *Offerings of War*; Victoria & Albert War Memorials 1919.
Locations:	Art Gallery of New South Wales, Sydney, Australia. Plaster maquettes were purchased by the gallery and the commission for the bronzes followed in 1916. The full-size plaster statues were completed in 1919. Bronzes were cast by 1923 and erected in 1926.
Literature:	*The Builder* 1918 Jun p398 (War), illus; *The Builder* 1924 Mar p412 (Peace), illus; *Sculpture Today*, 1921 pl24, *The Studio* 1925 vol 89 p201, illus ., (Peace); Kineton Parkes, illus; *Modelling for Sculpture*, Gilbert Bayes 1930, illus.

Bayes was exempted from war service because of this commission.

The Chequer Board

Medium:	Statue
Exhibitions:	Royal Academy, Bristol 1918; Ridley 1919.

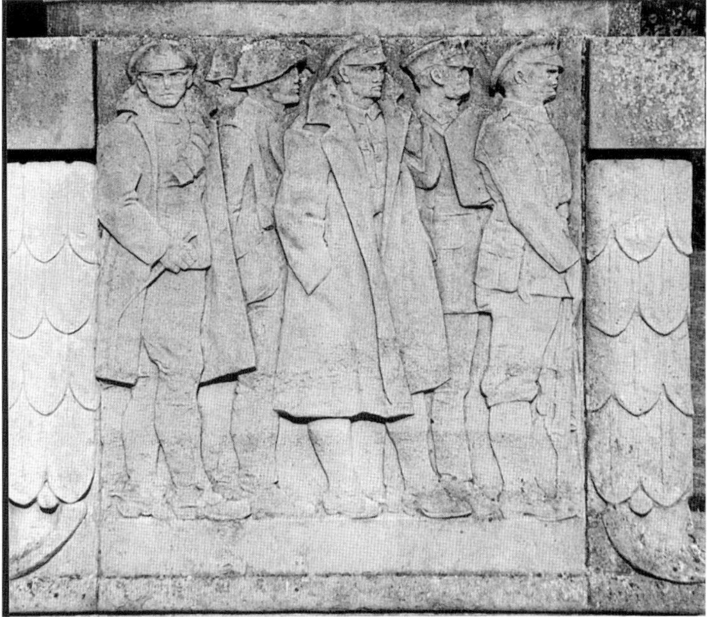

Anatkh (Destiny)

Medium:	Bronze statuette
Size:	23ins (59cms)
Exhibitions:	Fine Art Society 1918; Royal Academy 1919; Bristol 1919 (sold); Wembley 1924.
Literature:	*The Builder* 1919 May p482, illus.

This bronze was based on a large size figure, later used in Ramsgate War Memorial.

1919

Imperial Service Medal

Medium:	Silver
Locations:	British Museum
Literature:	*The Numismatic Chronicle* 1992 pl 21, illus.

Mackennal did the obverse portrait of the King for this medal.

The Unknown

Exhibitions:	Ridley 1919

This may be part of a war memorial listed elsewhere.

Sir Edward Holden, 1848-1919

Medium:	Plaster maquette for bronze relief

Holden was chairman of the London, City and Midland Bank.

The Guns

Medium:	Plaster relief

The Guns is a reworking of an earlier panel, *The Gallopers* of 1905.

Broadstone War Memorial

Medium:	Stone
Size:	H 30ft (9m)
Exhibitions:	Royal Academy Memorials 1919 (maquette); Imperial War Museum 1925 (maquette).
Locations:	The Memorial Park, Broadstone, Dorset
Literature:	*Sculpture of Today*, Kineton Parkes 1921

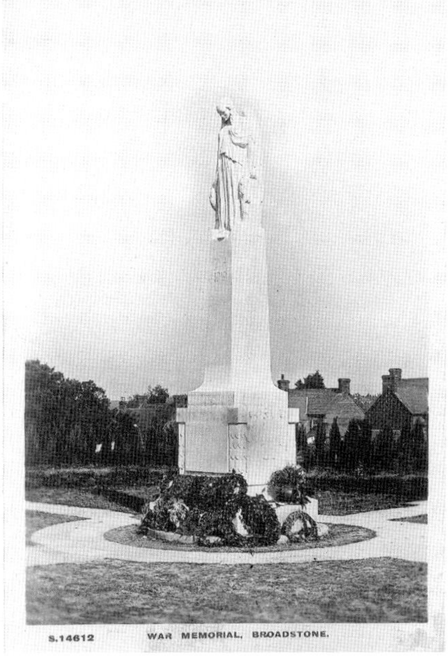

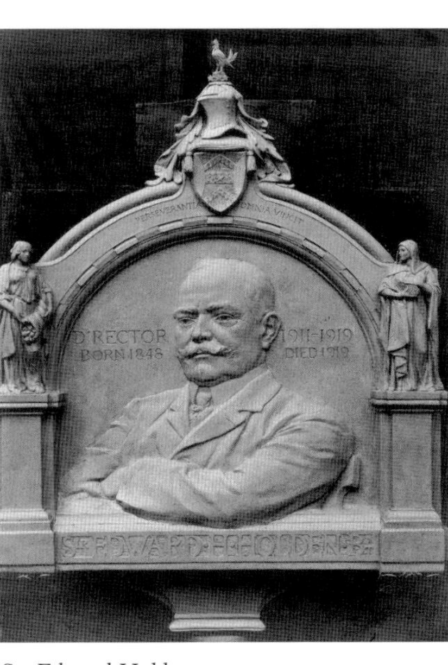

Sir Edward Holden

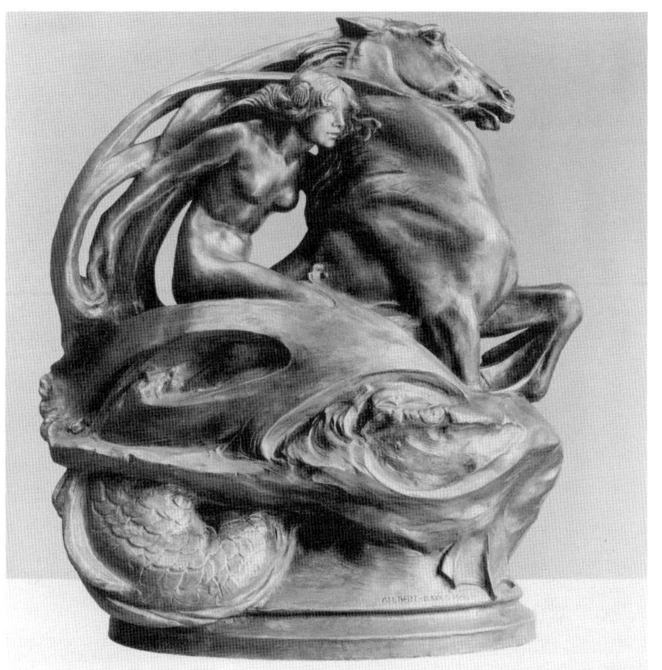

The Sea King's Daughter, bronze (Phillips)

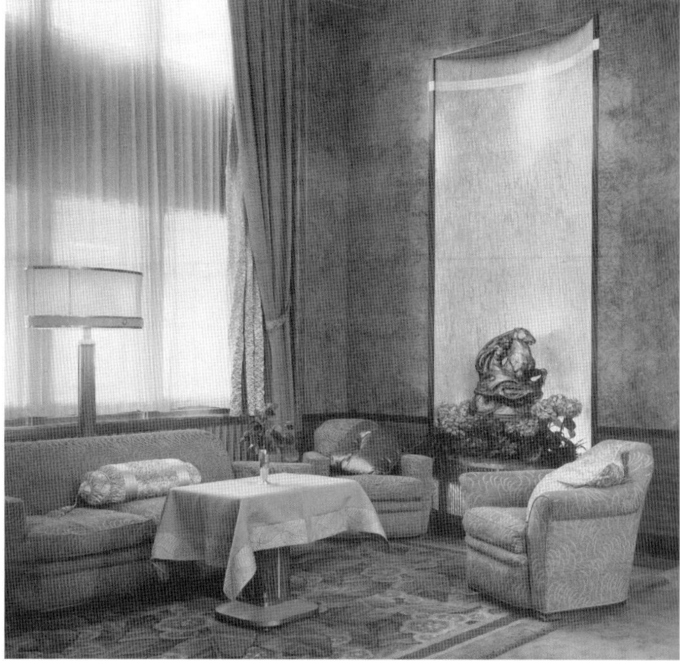

The later cast of the Sea King's Daughter in the RMS Queen Mary

The Sea King's Daughter

Medium: Bronze group
Size: H 19ins (48cms)
Exhibitions: Royal Academy 1919; Fine Art
Society 1920; Ridley 1921;
British Trade 1922, 1923;
Lincoln 1927; Manchester
1928; Toronto 1928; Royal
Scottish Academy 1929; Rio de
Janeiro 1930; Institute 1932
(£63); Edinburgh 1939.
Locations: Bayes Trust – plaster model; RMS
Queen Mary, later cast 1936.
Literature: *The Illustrated London News*
1936 May p902, illus.
This figure was also produced in marble.

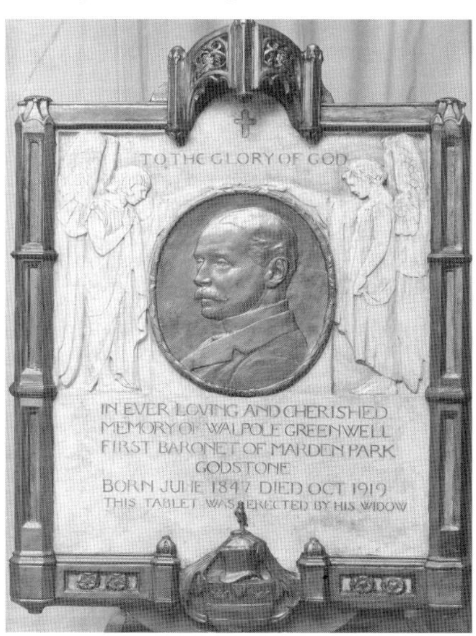

Walpole Greenwell, 1847-1919
Medium: Alabaster and bronze panel
Locations: St Nicholas Church, Godstone
This memorial cost 300 gns. Walpole
Greenwell was 1st Baronet of Marden
Park, Surrey.

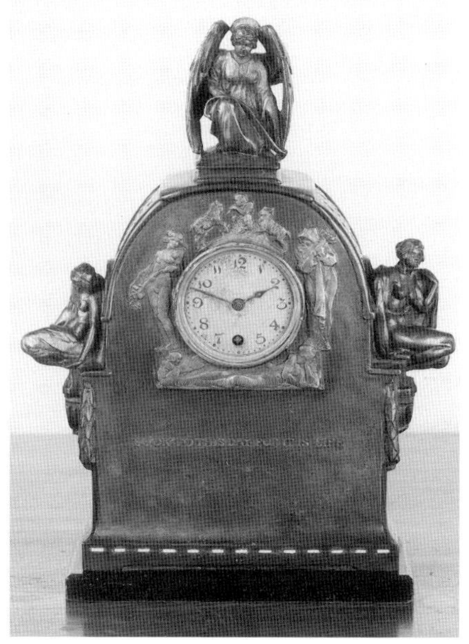

1920

Clock
Medium: Bronze
Size: H 17³/₄ins W 13¹/₄ins
(46 x 33.5cms)
Exhibitions: *Sculpture Between the Wars*, Fine
Art Society 1986
Locations: Mr Horne, the original owner,
sold the clock at Phillips in 1983
together with a letter from
Gilbert Bayes (dated 8.4.20.)
about the choice of clock move-
ments. The clock was then
acquired by the Fine Art Society
and sold to a private collector.
Literature: *Sculpture in Britain Between the
Wars*, B. Read & P. Skipwith,
1986 p31, illus.
The angel on top of the lock was also made
separately in bronze.

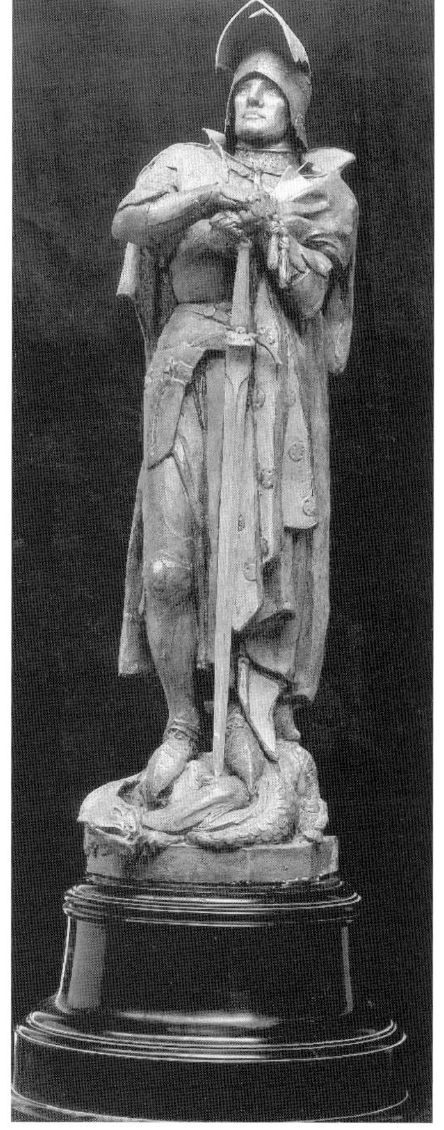

The Guardian, plaster

The Guardian, or St George

Medium: Bronze, enamel and mother of pearl
Size: H 24ins (61cms)
Exhibitions: Royal Academy 1921; Liverpool 1921 (£126), 1923; Institute 1923 (£132.6s); Royal Scottish Academy 1924; Dunedin, New Zealand 1926-27; *Gibson to Gilbert*, Fine Art Society 1992; *Reverie, Myth, Sensuality*, Stoke on Trent 1992; *Colour in Sculpture*, Leeds 1996.
Locations: Dunedin Art Gallery (dated 1920) acquired 1926; Sotheby's 14.11.79 (sold £2,500); Fine Art Society.
Literature: The Builder 1921 Jul p3, illus.
This figure was originally designed for the Royal Savoy Chapel War Memorial, and then made as a free-standing bronze figure.

Royal Savoy Chapel War Memorial

Medium: Alabaster, bronze and mosaic
Size: W 6ft (1.83m)
Locations: Royal Chapel of Savoy, Savoy Hill, London
Literature: The Studio 1921 Vol 81 p70, illus; The Builder 1920 Dec p720, illus.
This memorial was unveiled by the Earl of Athlone in December 1920.

Ramsgate War Memorial

Medium: Portland stone
Locations: Albion Gardens, Ramsgate
This war memorial was adapted from Anatkh (Destiny). It was presented by Dame Janet Stancomb Wills and unveiled on the 17th December 1920. The base is inscribed with representatives of all those who helped in the Great War.

Law Society War Memorial Panels

Medium: Marble reliefs
Exhibitions: Royal Academy 1920
Locations: Reading Room Law Society's Hall, London. Architect Vernon Compton. 'Their glory shall not be blotted out'. 'They died that we may live'. Original inscription 'Not today only but the future thanks thee'. Illuminated roll of honour by Jessie Bayes.
Literature: The Builder 1920 May p597, illus.

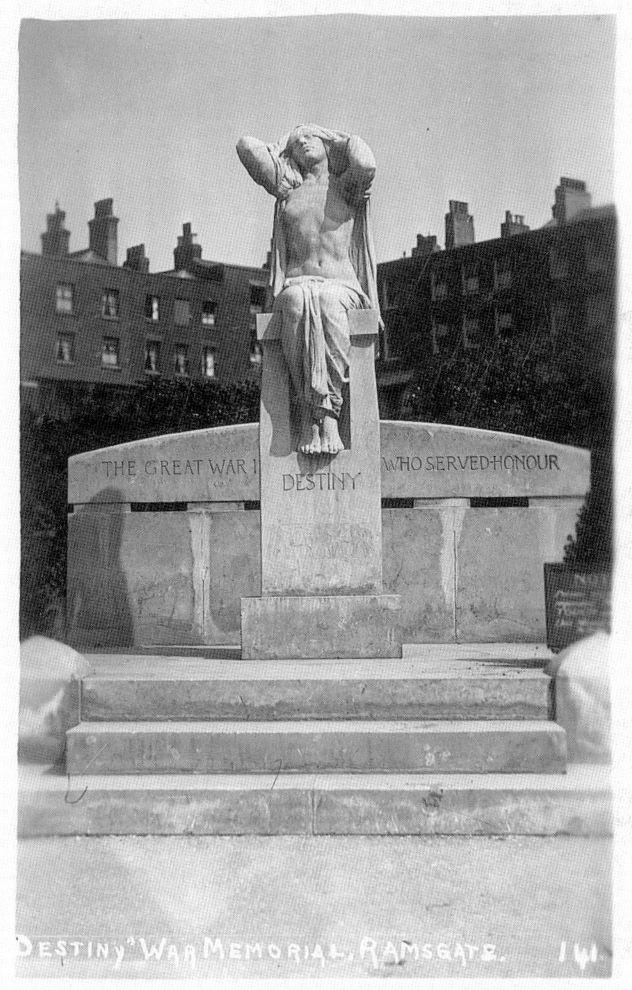

Postcard showing Ramsgate War Memorial

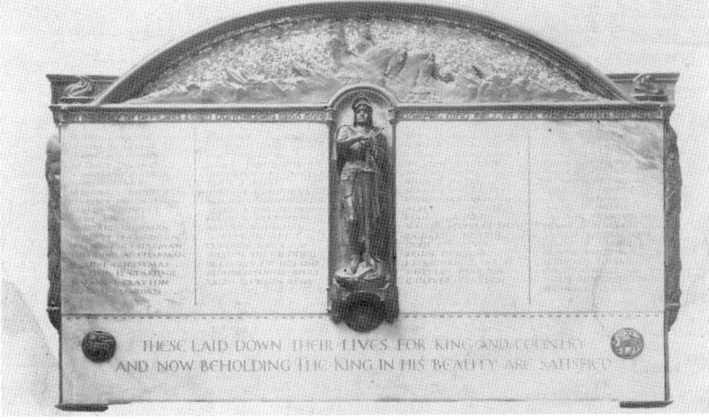

The Royal Savoy Chapel War Memorial

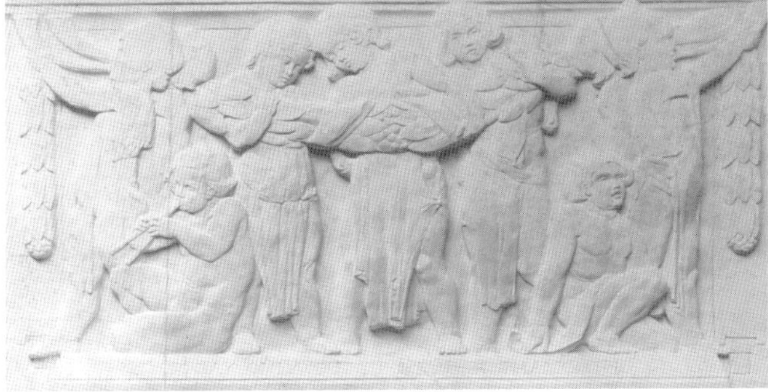

Panel, Law Society War Memorial

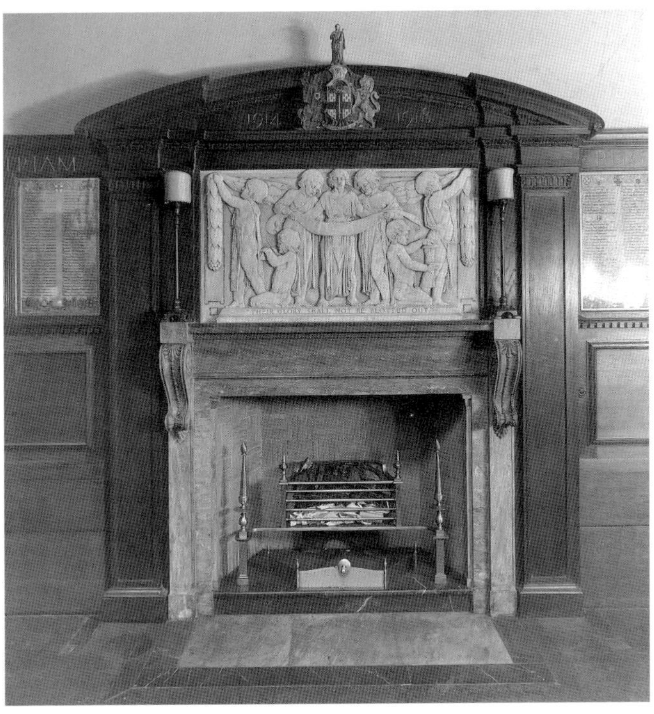

Law Society War Memorial

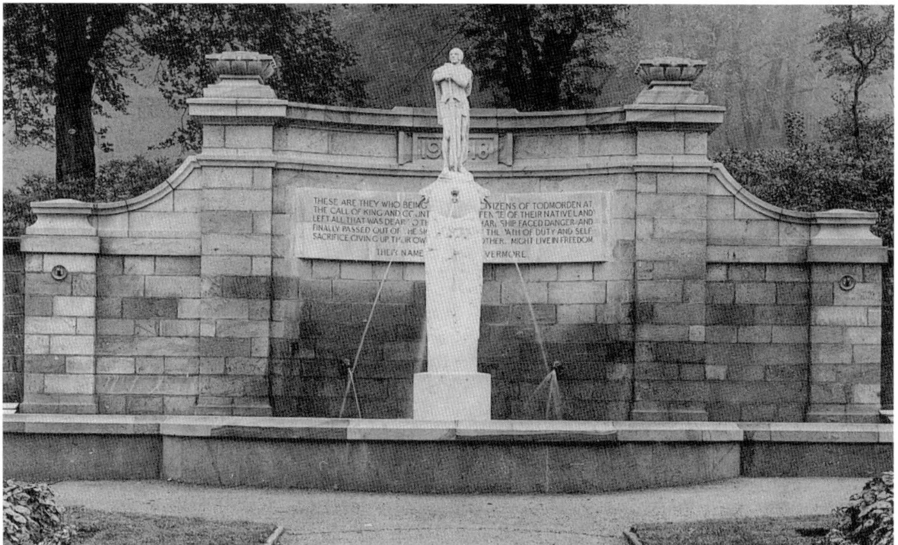

Todmorden War Memorial

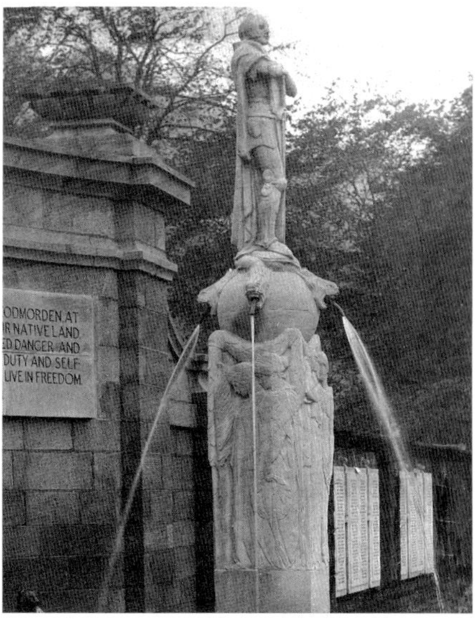

Todmorden War Memorial

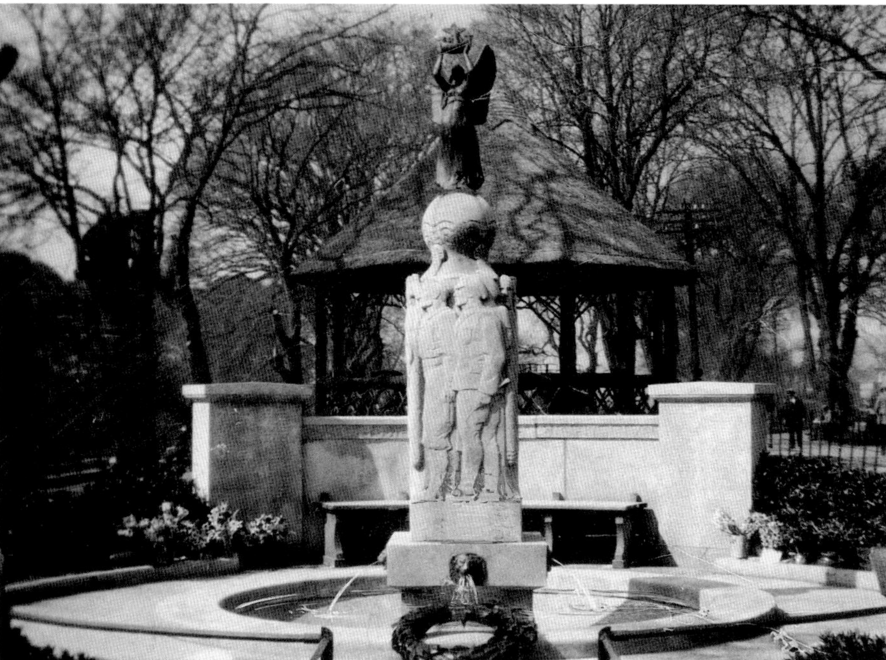

Hythe War Memorial when first completed

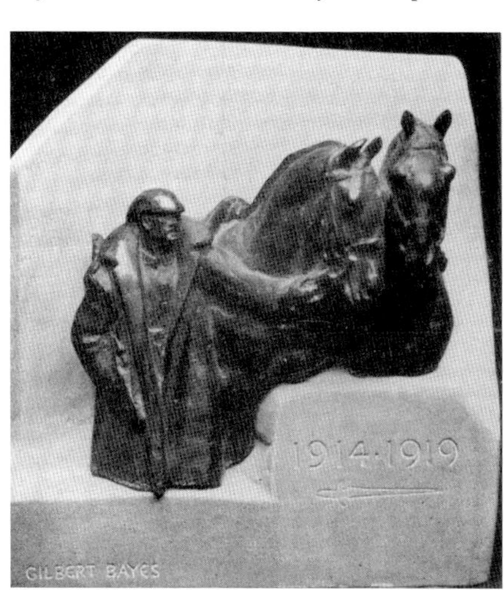

1921

Comrades
Medium: Bronze group on stone mount
Exhibitions: Royal Academy, Bristol, Goupil
             1921; Institute, Liverpool 1922
             (£47.5s); Ridley 1924; Glasgow
             1925 (£21); Manchester 1926;
             Graphic Art 1934 (25gns).
Literature: *The Studio* 1922 Vol 83 p44, illus.
A more developed version of this group was
used on the top of the war memorial in St
Leonard's Church, Hythe.

Todmorden War Memorial
Medium: Stone
Exhibitions: Royal Academy 1921 (*The
             Lamp of Memory*); Ridley 1921
             (*The Shield of Honour*).
Locations: Garden of Remembrance,
             Todmorden, Yorkshire

Architect, Norman Thorp
ARIBA.
Literature: *The Builder* 1921 May p642
             (Lamp), illus; *The Builder* 1924
             Mar p407 (Lamp) and p408
             (Shield), illus; *Todmorden
             Advertiser* 14 Oct 1921; *The
             Artist* Dec 1934 p125, illus; *War
             Memorials*, Arnold Whittick
             1946 p87, illus.
The memorial, a St George figure on a
fountain pedestal in an architectural setting
with attendant figures, recently stolen, was
unveiled in 1921 by Major Barker, MP for
Sowerby, Yorkshire.

Hythe War Memorial
Medium: Bronze and marble
Size: Angel H 36ins (91.5cms)
Exhibitions: Goupil 1921
Locations: Prospect Road, The Grove,
             Hythe
The stone base was replaced c.1978 and the
angel, Victory, was stolen and replaced by
another sculpture in 1994. The original base
still stands outside the Legion of Honour
HQ. The memorial was unveiled by Earl
Beauchamp KG, Lord Warden of the
Cinque Ports.

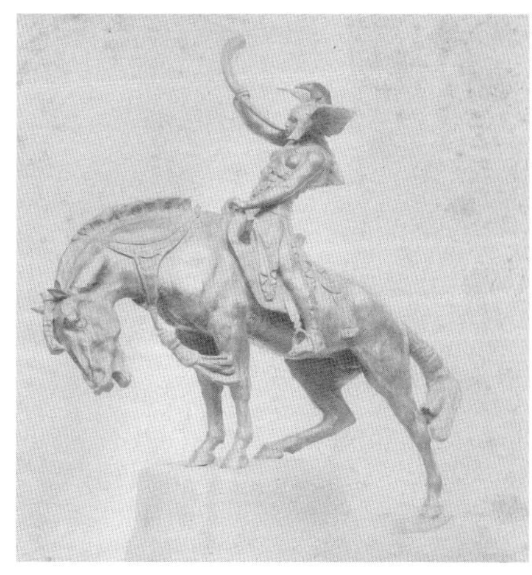

Brynhilde

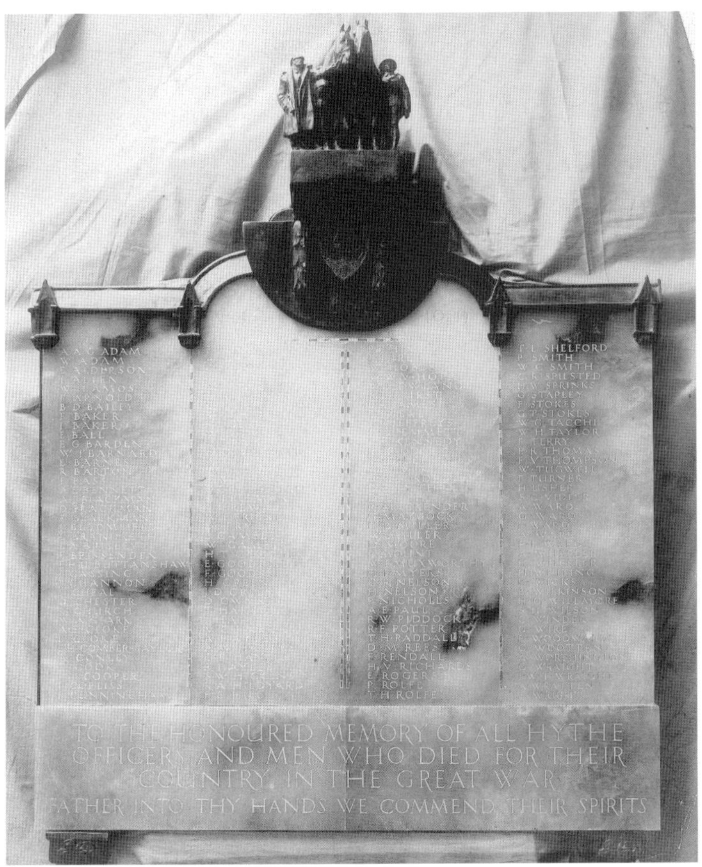

St Leonard's Church War Memorial, Hythe

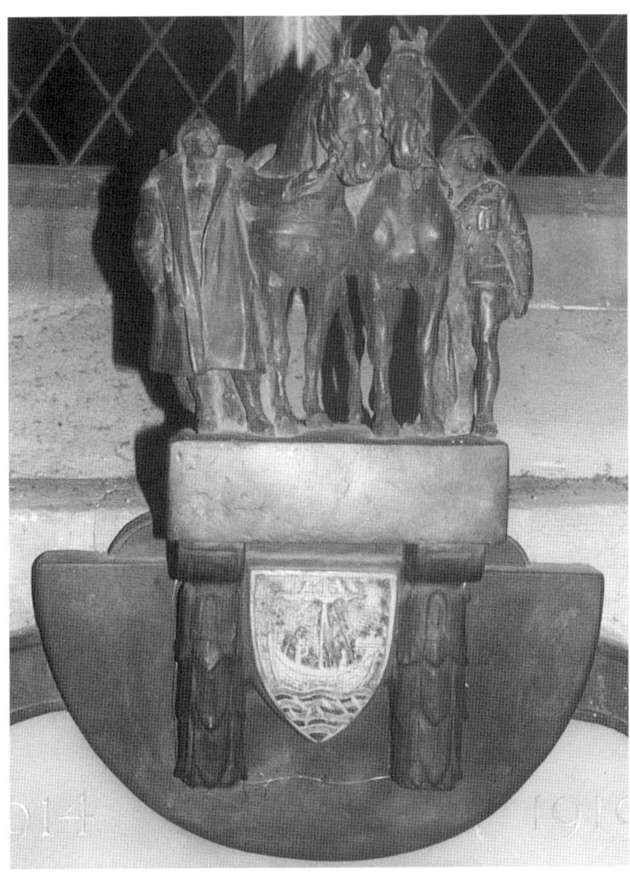

Comrades group on St Leonard's Church War Memorial

Brynhilde

Medium: Plaster maquette for bronze figure
Size: H 30ins (76cms)
Exhibitions: Institute, Glasgow (100gns); British Trade, Ridley
1923; Goupil 1924; Bradford 1927; Toronto 1927;
Liverpool 1928 (£78.15s); Royal Scottish Academy
1928; Manchester 1929; Bristol 1930; Graphic Art
1931 (£84); Southport 1939.
Literature: *The Builder* 1920 Dec p713, illus.
This figure is similar to the one on top of the *Fountain of the Valkyries*.

War Memorial

Medium: Alabaster and bronze
Size: H 41ins W 45^1/$_2$ins (104 x 115.5cms)
Locations: St Leonard's Church, Hythe
The memorial, dated 1920, was unveiled by the Lord Bishop of
Dover on 26th January, 1921.

1922

Bacchante

Medium: Bronze statuette
Size: H 28^3/$_4$ins (73cms)
Exhibitions: Royal Academy, Bristol, Glasgow 1922 (£63); Ridley
and British Trade 1923; Institute, Liverpool 1924,
1929; Toronto 1928 (75gns); Royal Scottish
Academy 1929; Pastel Society 1935 (£63).
Locations: Art Gallery of New South Wales purchased 1926 for
£57; Bonhams 9.12.88 (sold).

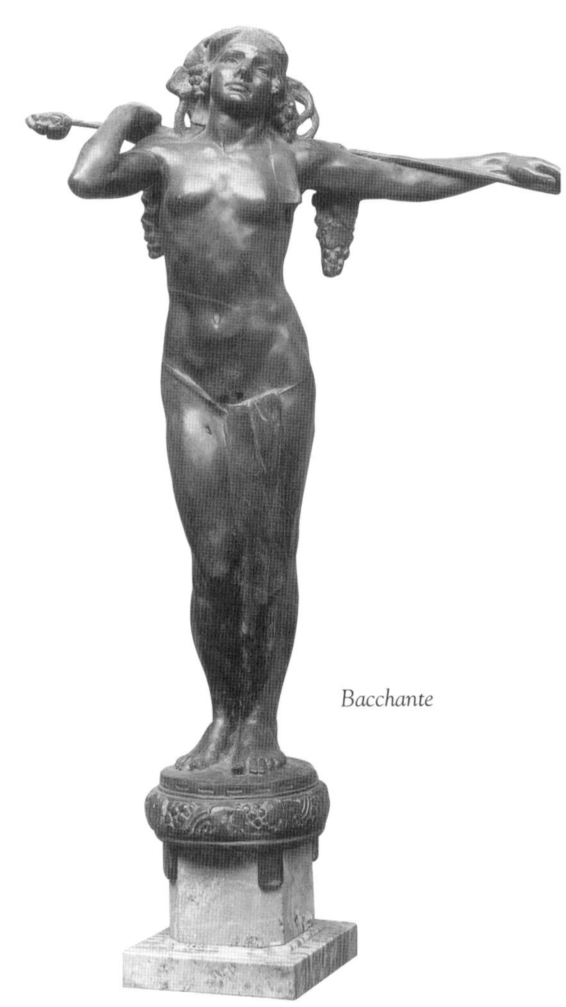

Bacchante

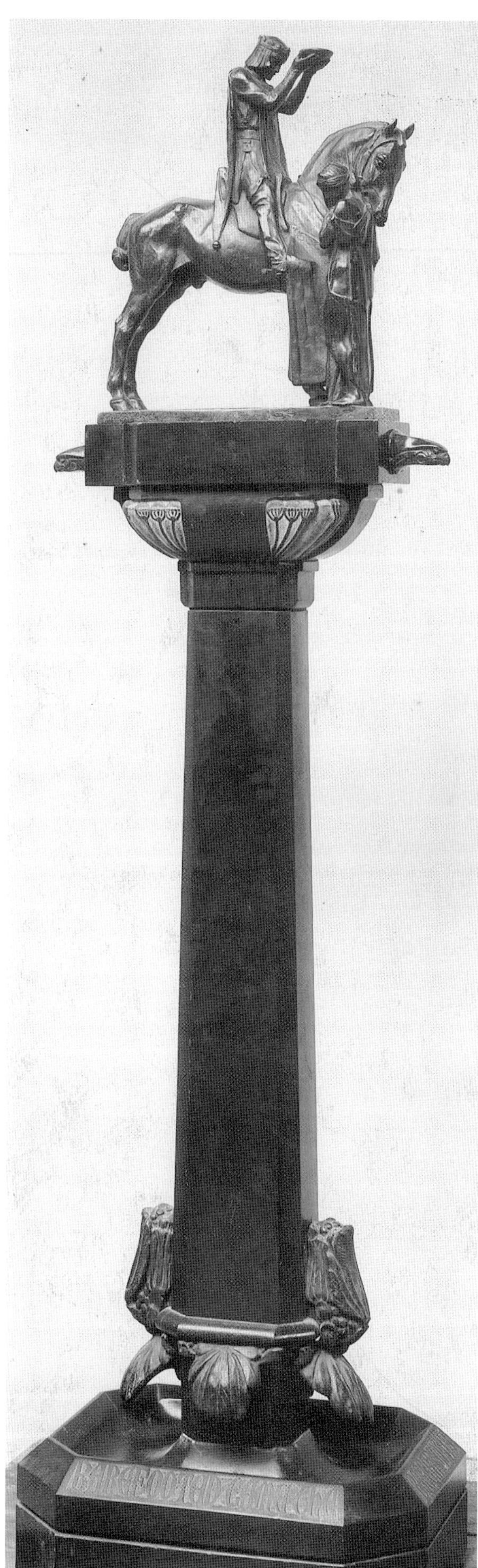

King Cophetua and the Beggar Maid on stand

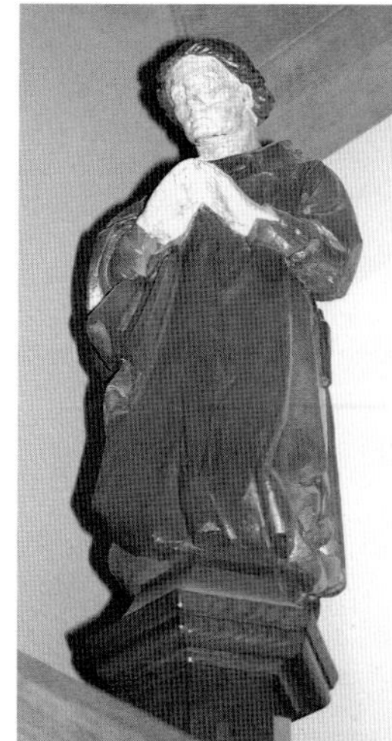

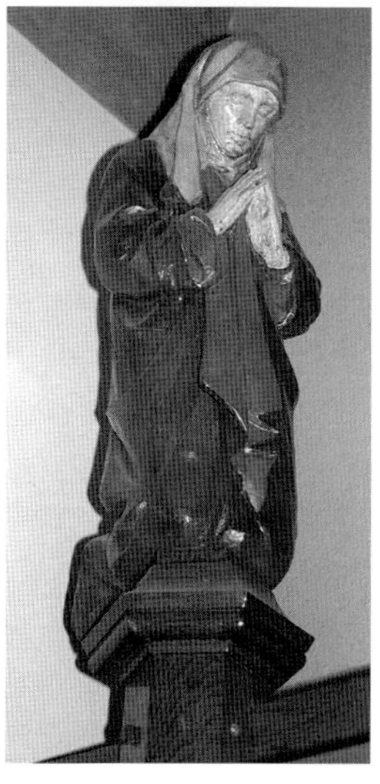

Rood Screen figures by Bayes

King Cophetua and the Beggar Maid on Stand

Medium: Bronze group
Size: H 22ins, 66ins with stand
                   (56.5cms, 168cms)
Exhibitions: Royal Academy, Liverpool 1922;
                   Bristol 1923; Wembley 1924; Paris
                   Arts and Crafts 1925; British Artists,
                   Paris 1927; Venice 1928; Institute,
                   Liverpool 1930 (£105).
Locations: Bayes Trust
This sculpture, inspired by Tennyson's line,
'Barefooted came the beggar maid, Before the
King Cophetua', was exhibited seventeen times
between 1922 and 1952.

Sea Maid

Exhibitions: Goupil, Liverpool 1922; Glasgow
                   1925 (£21); Manchester 1926
                   (20gns); Sussex Artists 1949.
Literature: This is probably another name for
                   the *Sea King's Daughter*.

James Oliver Salter

Medium: Plaster relief for bronze

Rood Screen

Medium: Carved and coloured oak
Locations: St James Church, Inverleith Row,
                   Edinburgh. The figures are now
                   re-sited in the entrance vestibule.
The rood screen was designed by Sir John
Burnet and the figures were by Bayes. The cost
was £600. It was erected in memory of the
Reverend Charles Jenkins, Rector of St James
1892-1917.

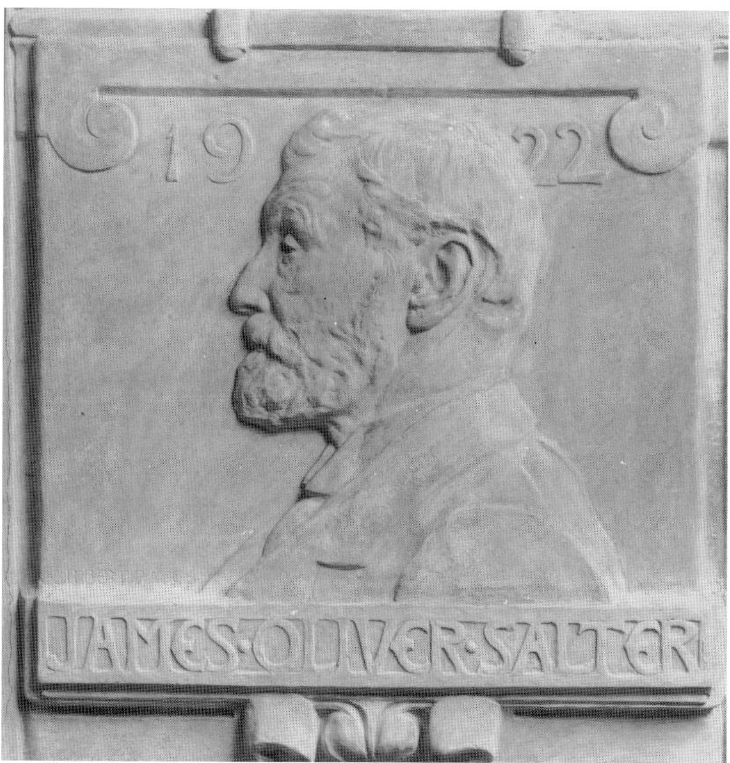

James Oliver Salter

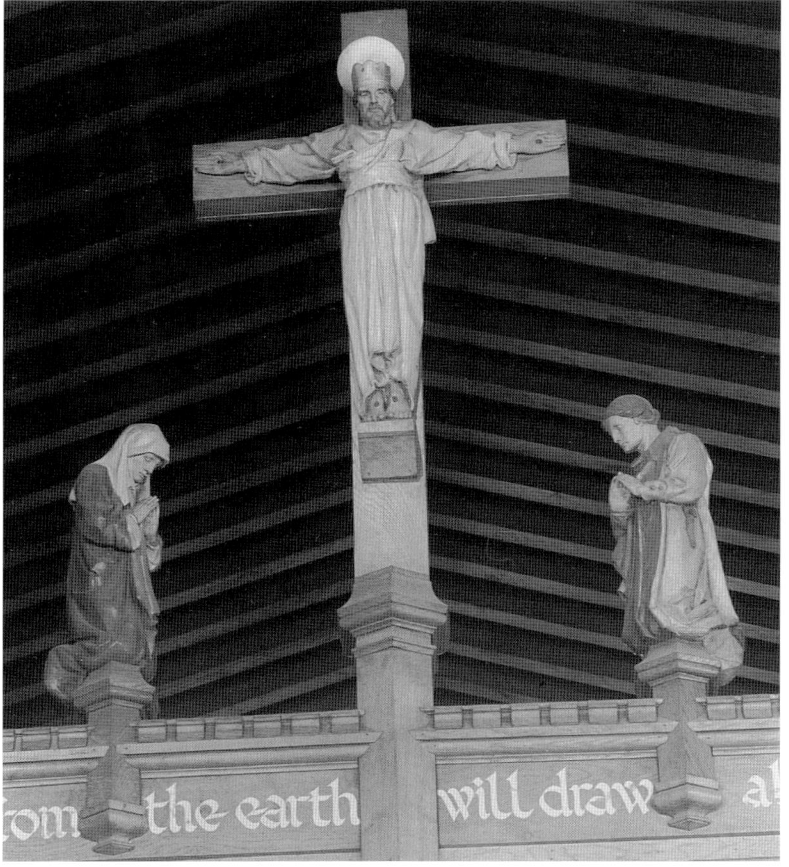
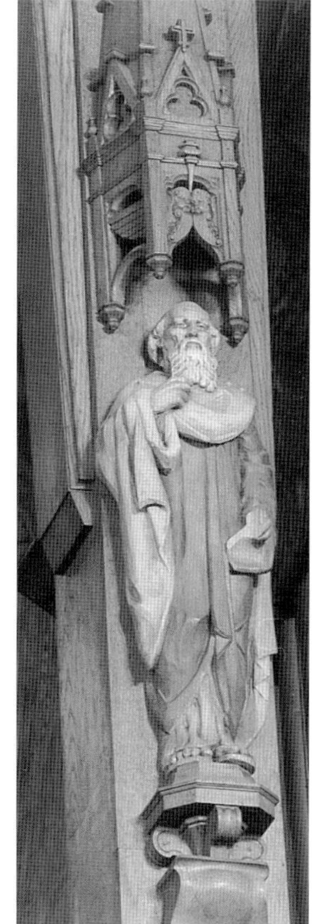
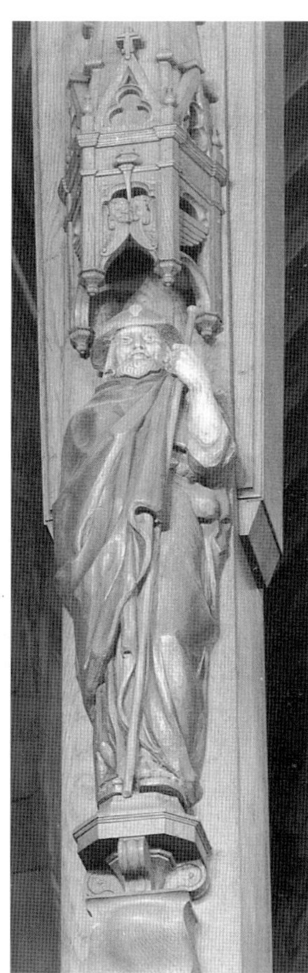

Rood screen and figures, St James' Church, Edinburgh (Conway Library, Courtauld Institute of Art)

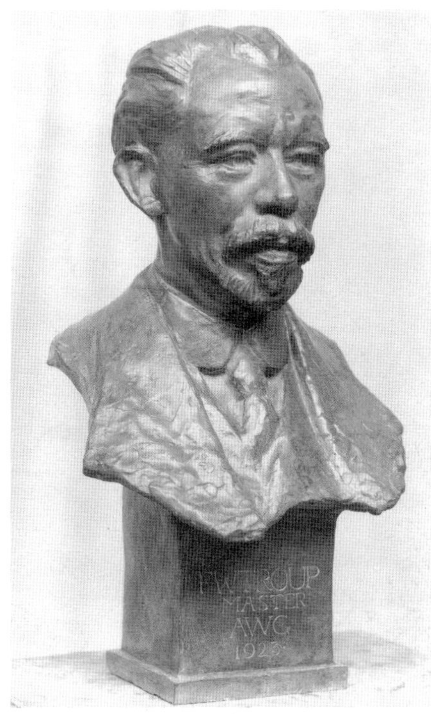

F.W. Troup

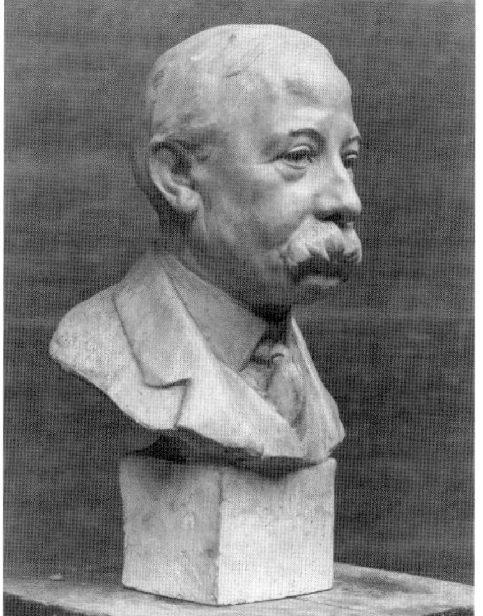

W.R. Lethaby

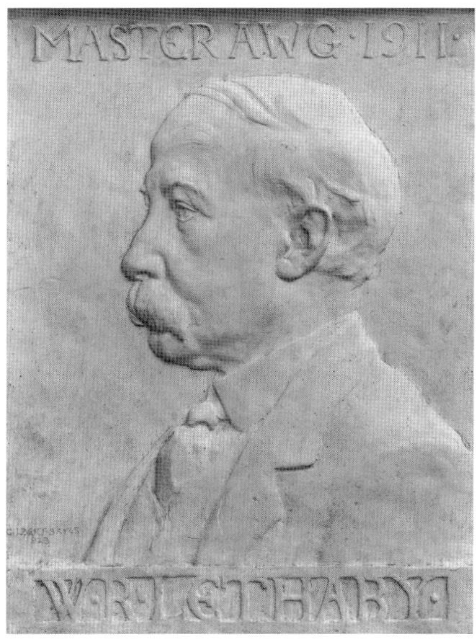

W.R. Lethaby

1923

F.W. Troup

Medium: Plaster for bronze bust
Size: H 26ins (66cms)
Exhibitions: Royal Academy 1925
Locations: Art Workers' Guild 1923, Queen Square, London
Architect and Master of the Art Workers' Guild, 1923.

W.R. Lethaby, 1857-1931

Medium: Bronze bust
Size: H 16ins (41cms)
Exhibitions: Royal Academy 1923
Locations: Art Workers' Guild, Queen Square, London
Master of the Art Workers' Guild, 1911.

W.R. Lethaby

Medium: Bronzed plaster relief
Size: H 22ins W 16ins (56 x 40.5cms)
Exhibitions: Royal Academy 1924
Locations: Royal Institute of British Architects, Portland Place, London
Literature: *The Builder* 1924 Mar p408, illus; *RIBA Journal* 1935.

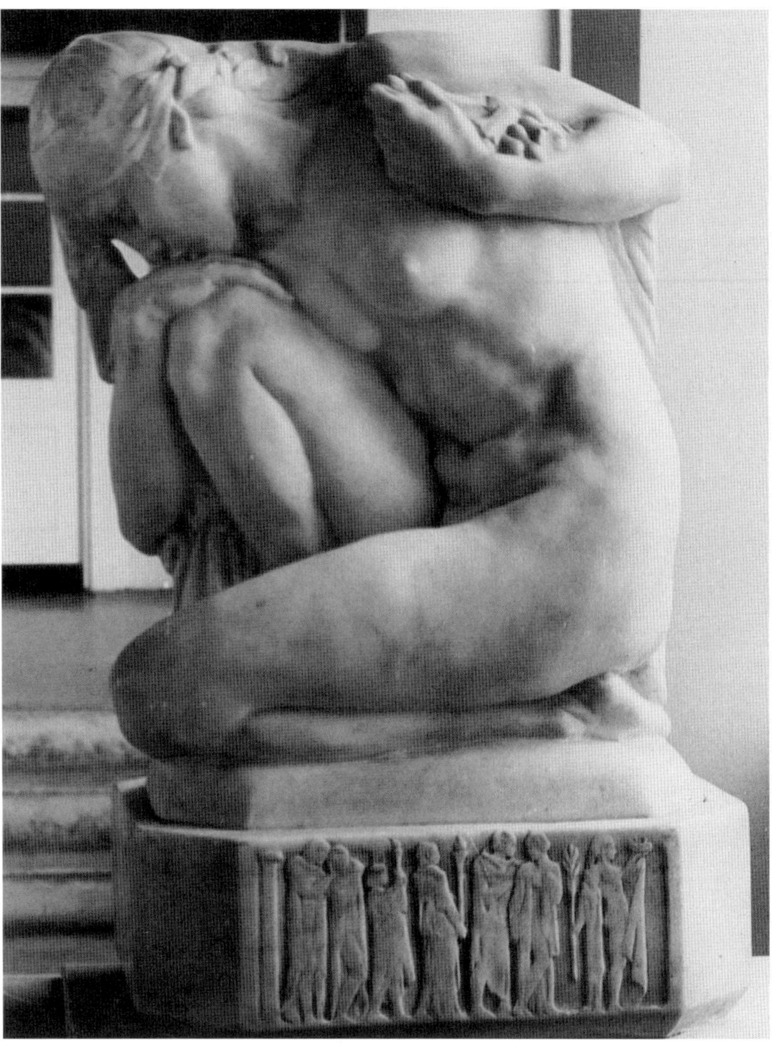

The Unfolding of Spring

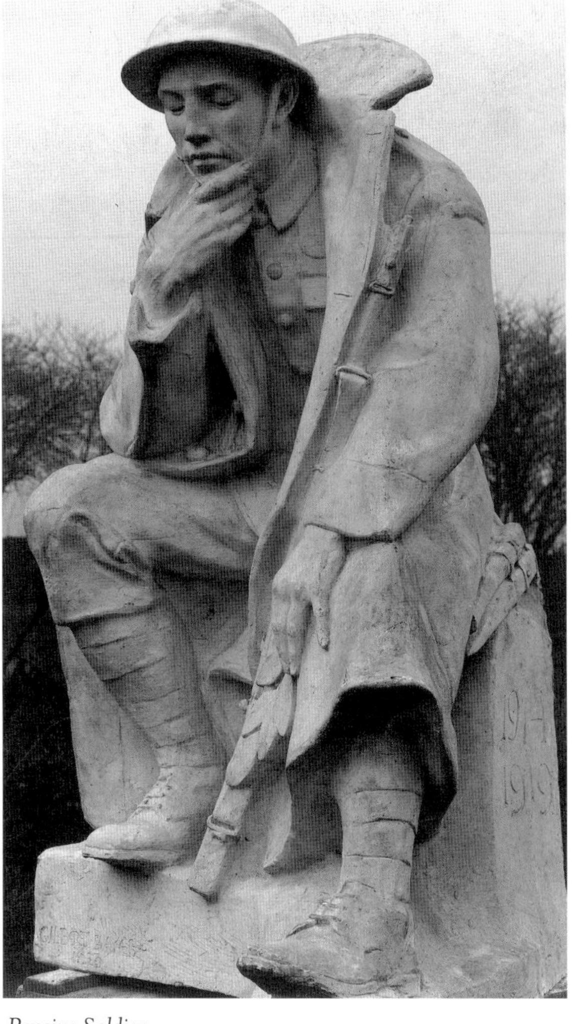

Pensive Soldier

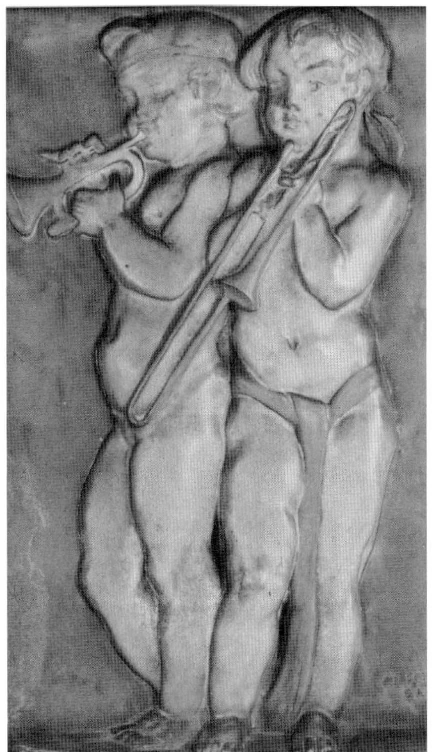

Child Musicians

Child Musicians

Medium: Doulton stoneware
Size: H 25ins (63.5cms)
Locations: Bayes Trust; Sotheby's
Belgravia 7.11.73 (sold).
This panel is similar to the orchestra
panel on the Brinsmead building,
London.

The Unfolding of Spring

Medium: Marble statue
Size: H 39ins (99cms)
Exhibitions: Royal Academy 1923;
Liverpool 1924 (£630); Royal
Scottish Academy 1927
(500gns); Waring and Gillow
Galleries 1931.
Locations: Manchester City Art Gallery
on loan from The Bayes Trust
Literature: *Royal Academy Pictures* 1923
p111, illus; *The Builder* 1923
May p807, illus; *The Builder*
1924 Mar p409; *Modelling for
Sculpture*, Gilbert Bayes 1930,
illus; *The Artist* 1935 Feb
p193, illus.

Pensive Soldier

Medium: Plaster model for stone

Locations: This seated soldier was carved
in stone and placed in
position against a wall with
inscription. Location unknown.
Literature: *The Artist* 1934 Dec p125, illus.

The Roman Wine Cart

Medium: Carved and coloured wood
Size: H 19ins W 30ins (48 x 76.5cms)
Exhibitions: Royal Academy 1923
(plaster); Liverpool 1925
(£26.5s).
Locations: Bayes Trust
Literature: *The Builder* 1924 Mar p411,
illus; *The Studio* 1923, vol 85
p102, illus.

Signboard for Nursery School

Medium: Carved and painted wood
Locations: Eagling Road School, Bow,
London (destroyed)
Literature: *The Architect's Journal* 1930
Apr p582-3

1924

Girl in a Hammock

Medium: Carved and coloured wood
Literature: *The Builder* 1924 Mar p409

The Moon and the Lotus Pond

Medium: Bronze statue
Size: H 28ins (71cms)
Exhibitions: Royal Academy 1924; Venice,
Ridley, Institute 1928 (£105);
Toronto 1929, 1935; Bristol
1930; Aberdeen 1931.

The World We Live In

Medium: Life-size statue
Exhibitions: Royal Academy, Glasgow 1924
(£472)
Literature: *The Builder* May 1924 p827,
illus; *Royal Academy Pictures*
1924 p123, illus.

Madonna and Child

Medium: Doulton stoneware panel
Size: H 20ins W 50ins (51 x 127cms)
Exhibitions: Liverpool (1924) (£63); Arts
and Crafts 1926.
Locations: Nursery School, Eagling Road,
London E3. Architect C.
Cowles Voysey; another formerly
Sidney Street Estate, St Pancras,
another formerly in Selfridge's
roof garden; part of panel on
Westminster Diocesan Archives,
Abingdon Road, London.
Literature: *The Builder* 1924 Mar p409,
illus; *The Architectural Review*
1926 Mar p189, illus; *The
Architect's Journal* 1930 Apr
p582, illus.

Oxen of Siena or The Plough

Medium: Carved, coloured and gilded
wood
Size: H 18ins W 30ins
(46 x 76.5cms)
Exhibitions: Bristol 1924; Glasgow 1926 (£26).
Locations: Bayes Trust
Literature: *The Builder* 1924 Mar p410,
illus; *The Studio* 1925 Vol 89
p198, illus.

Figure of Child Memorial

Medium: Marble
Locations: Radlett Cemetery, Hertfordshire
(now removed)

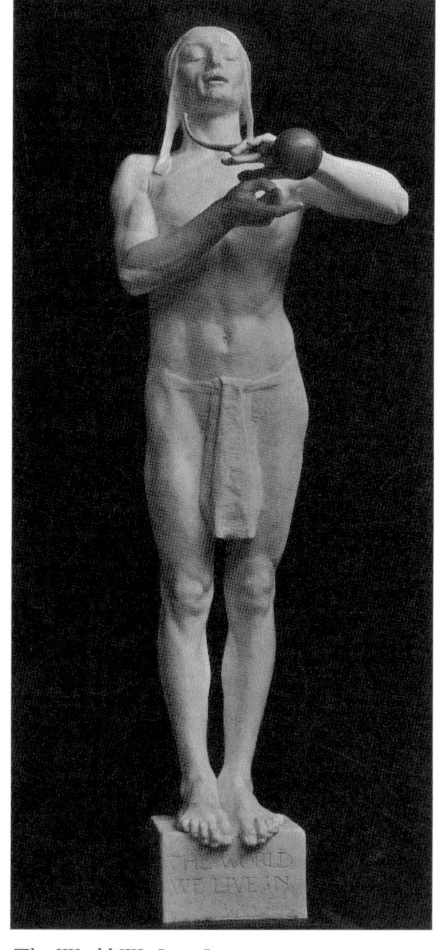

The World We Live In

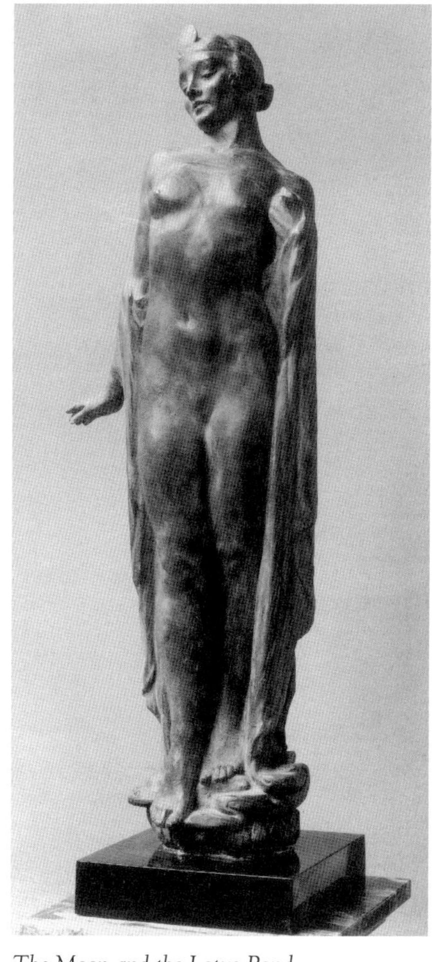

The Moon and the Lotus Pond

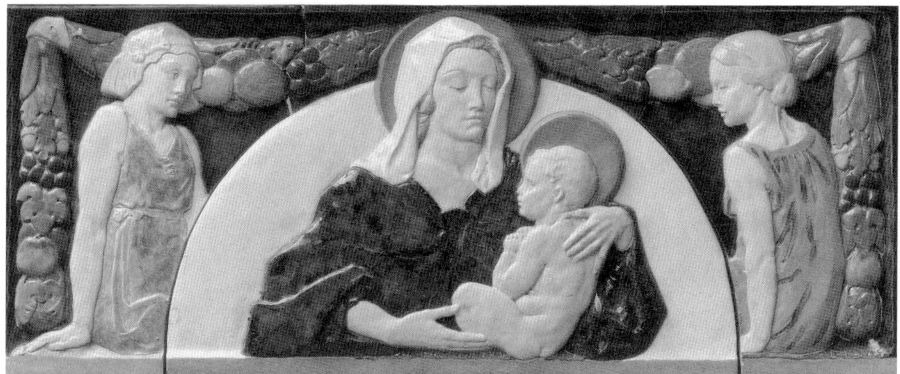

Madonna and Child

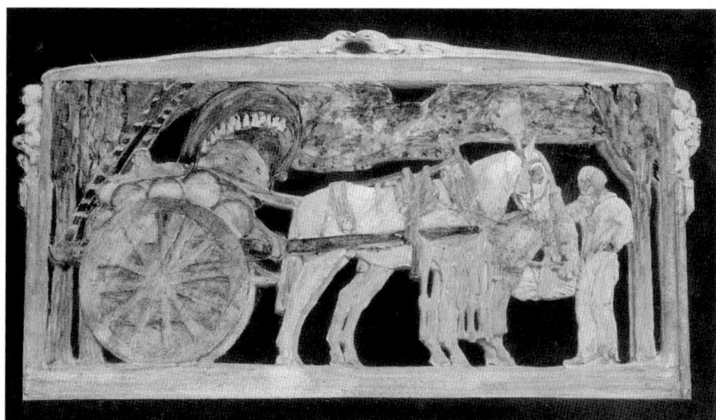

The Roman Wine Cart

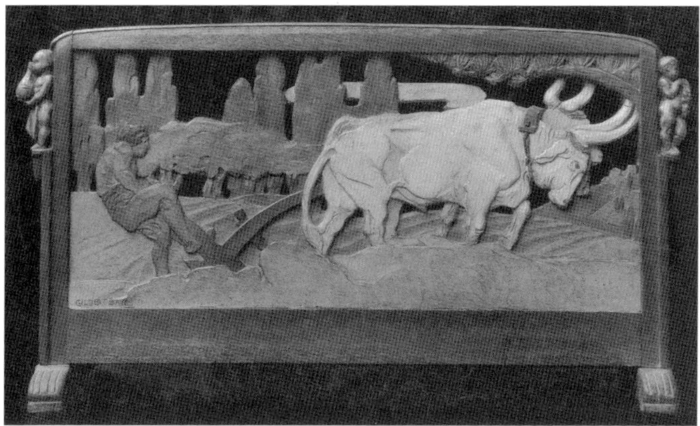

Oxen of Siena

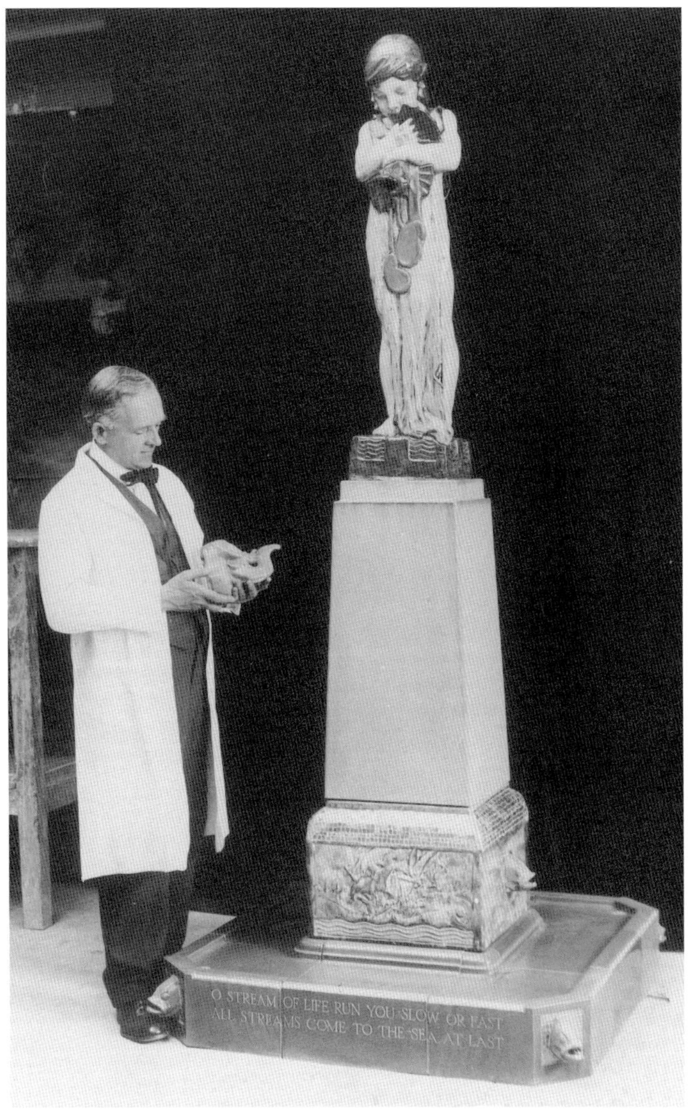

Child with Fish

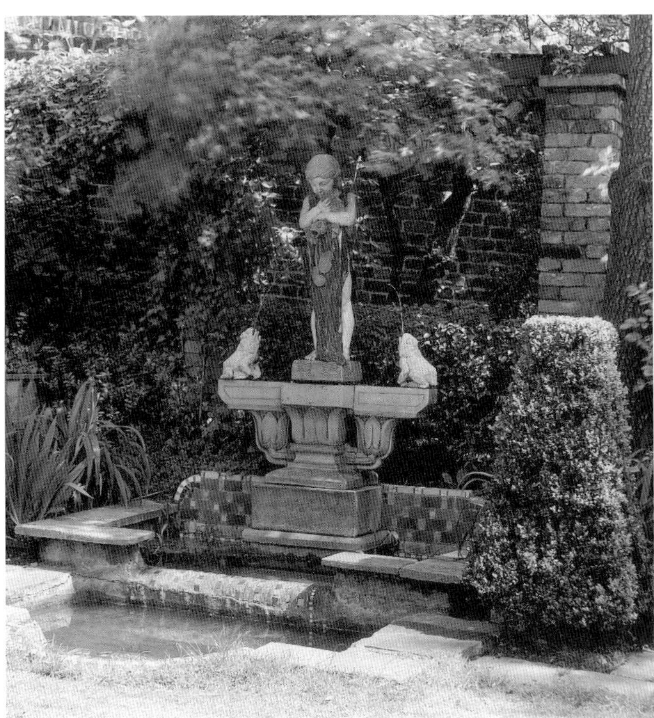

Child with Fish as a garden fountain in Greville Place, London

Child with Fish, or The Blue Robed Bambino

Medium: Doulton stoneware fountain

Size: H 62ins (157cms)

Exhibitions: British Pavilion Paris Exhibition 1925 (Gold Medal) with squirrel; Arts and Crafts 1926 (£69 5s); Royal Scottish Academy 1927 (65gns); Horsham 1928 (sold); Institute 1930 (£78.15s); Bullfrog at Beaux Arts 1930; Royal Academy Arts and Industries 1935.

Locations: Bayes Trust. A similar fountain figure was made for the International Labour Offices, Geneva, presented by the Sailor's and Fireman's Union of Great Britain (H 78ins, 195cms with tall pedestal).

Literature: *The Studio* 1925 Vol 89 p198, illus; *The Builder* 1924 Mar p409, illus; *The Architectural Review* 1926 Mar p189, illus; *Journal of the Royal Horticultural Society* LIV 1929 fig107: *The Artist* 1935 Jan p159, illus; *The Connoisseur* 1979 Aug p252, illus; *War Memorials*, Arnold Whittick 1946 p87, illus.

This figure was used as a garden fountain with bullfrog, monkey or squirrel attendants.

Concrete Making Processes and Britannia

Medium: Concrete reliefs

Exhibitions: British Empire, Wembley 1924. The concrete processes depicted are: labourers carrying concrete; filling moulds; garden work; sculpture.

Locations: Pavilion of Concrete Utilities Bureau (temporary exhibit now destroyed but panels were subsequently installed by Williams Ellis at Portmeirion). Architect Clough Williams Ellis. Some panels in private collection.

Literature: *The Builder* 1925 Jan p40, 45, 51, illus; *The Studio Year Book* 1925 p158; *Modelling for Sculpture*, Gilbert Bayes 1930, illus; *Decorative Arts Society Journal* 1980 p9, illus.

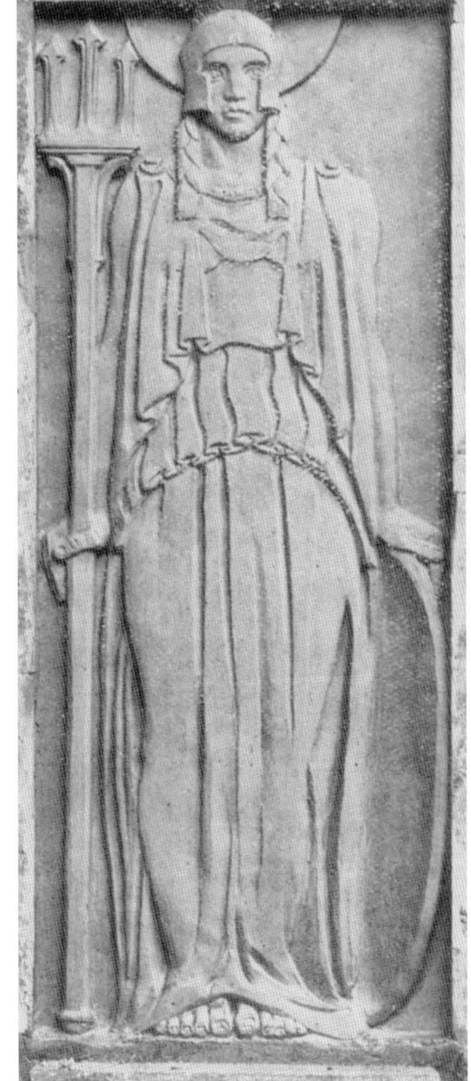

Britannia

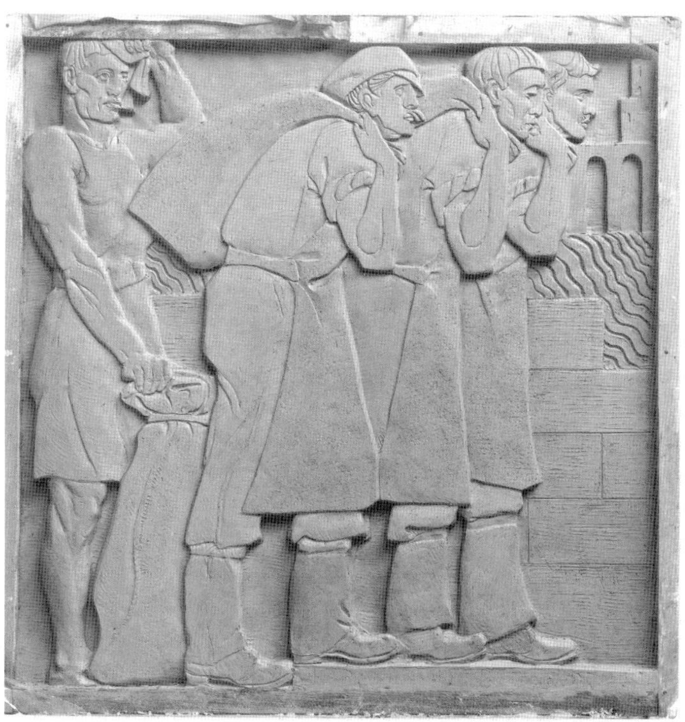

Labourers carrying concrete

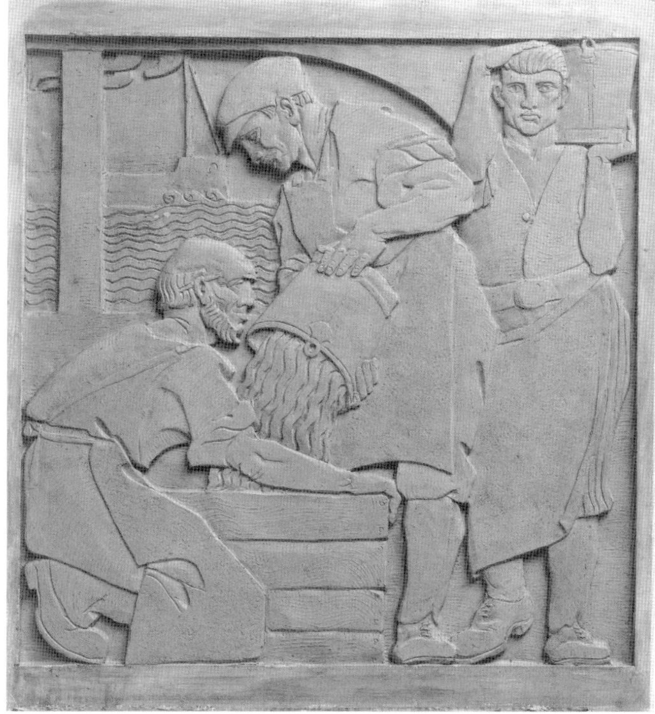

Filling moulds

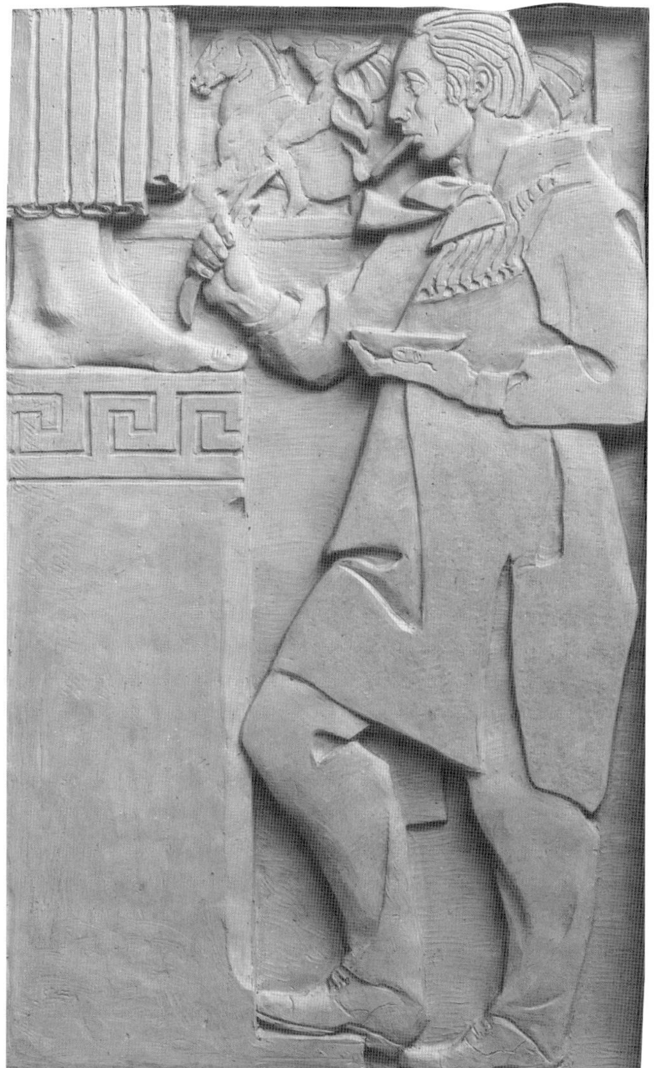

Sculpture

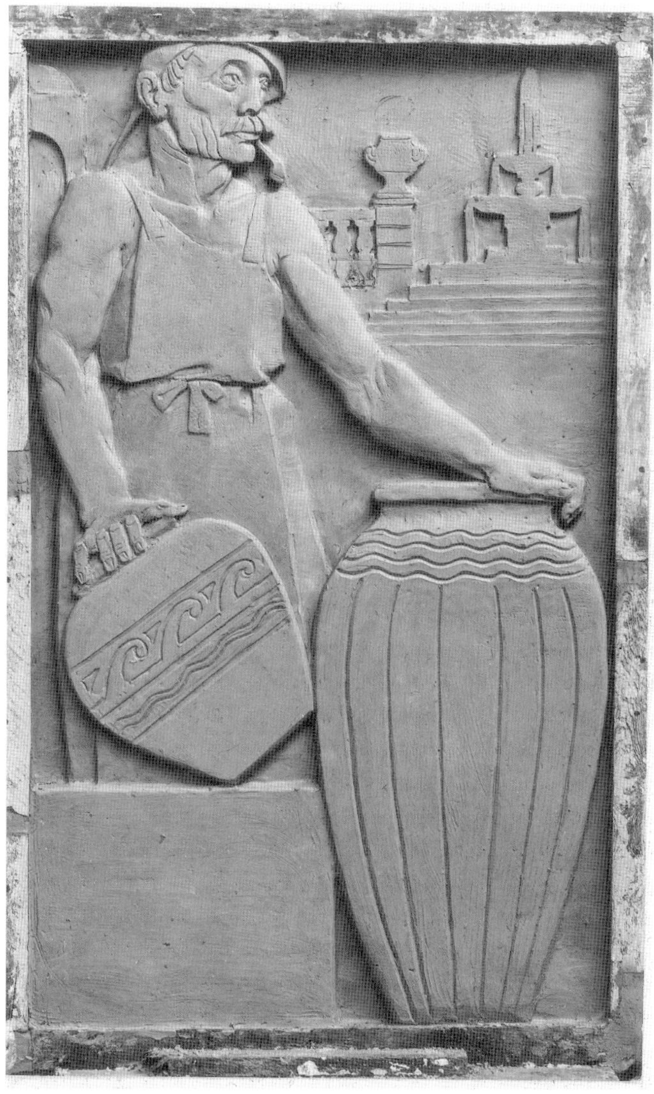

Garden work

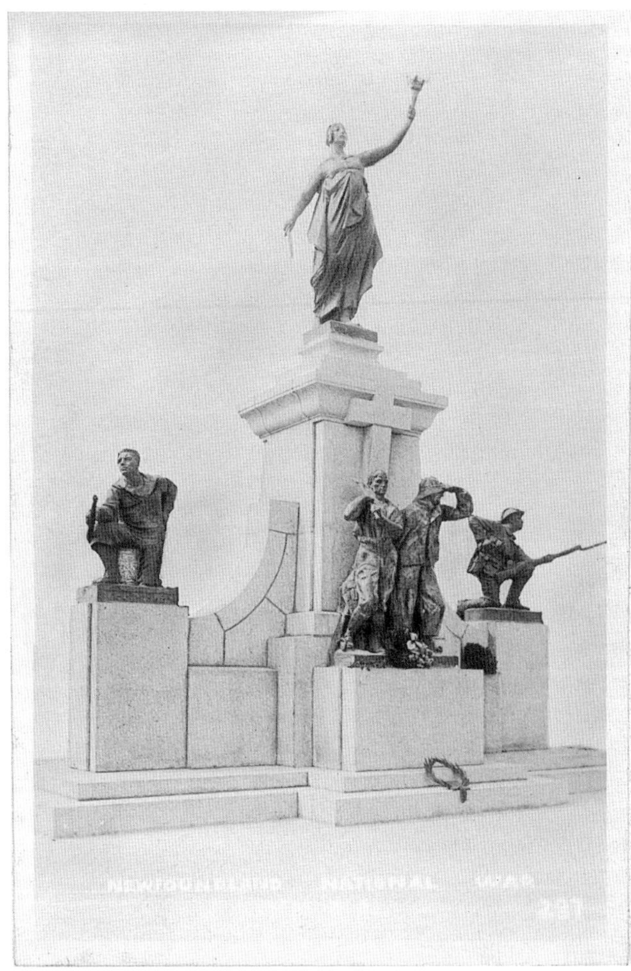

Postcard of Newfoundland National War Memorial

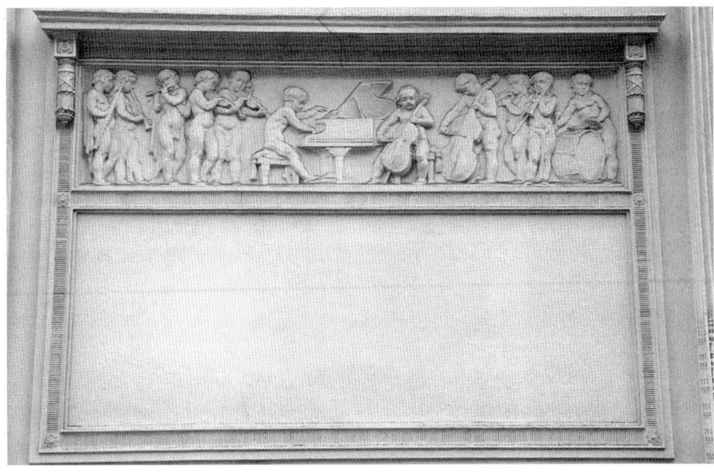

Children's Orchestra panel, formerly Brinsmead's, 17 Cavendish Square, London

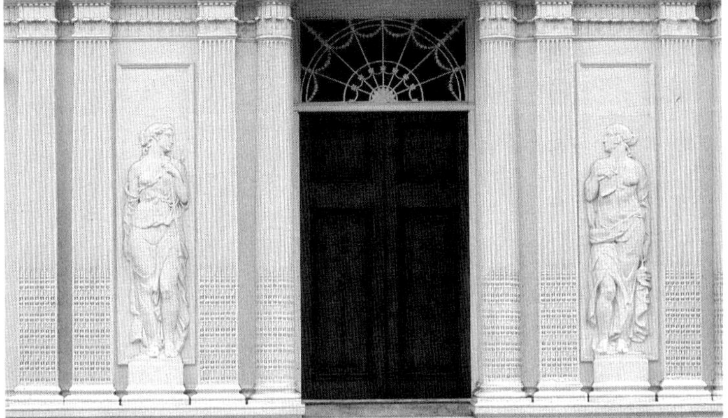

Figures symbolising Music and Art, formerly Brinsmead's, 17 Cavendish Square, London

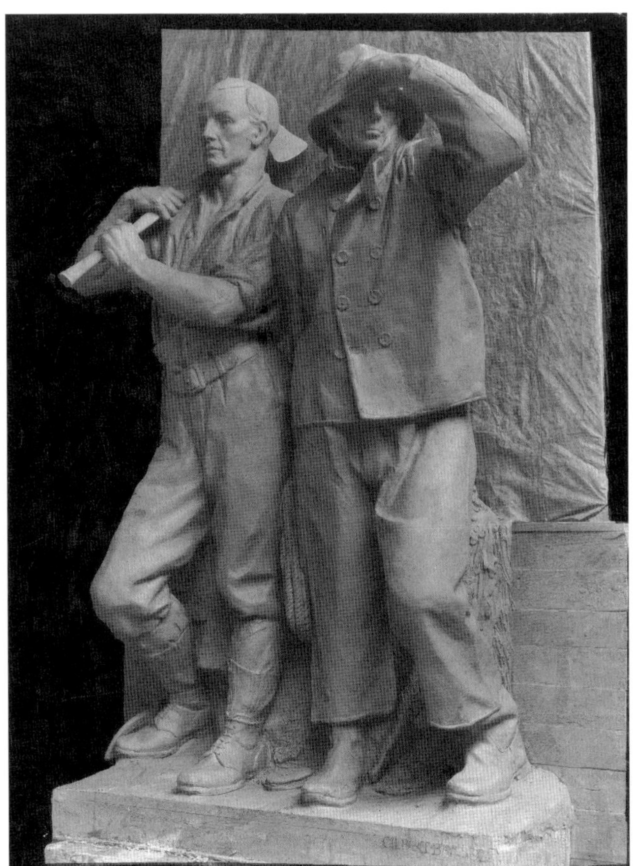

Plaster model of the Mercantile Marine and Forestry Corps group

Newfoundland National War Memorial

Medium: Granite and bronze
Locations: St John's, Newfoundland, Canada, sited at former
              Haymarket Hill from Duckworth Street to Water Street
              Commissioned 1920 and unveiled by Field Marshal Earl
              Haig on the 1st July 1924.

The memorial shows the Spirit of Newfoundland holding the torch
flanked by a soldier of the Royal Newfoundland Regiment, a sailor of
the Royal Naval Reserve and in the centre, representatives of the
Newfoundland Mercantile Marine and the Forestry Corps. Bayes
worked on this memorial with Ferdinand Blundstone. After the
Second World War Bayes designed an airman figure to be added, but
this was never carried out.

Children's Orchestra and Symbolic Figures of Science, Music and Art

Medium: Coloured cement reliefs
Locations: John Brinsmead, 17 Cavendish Square, London,
              formerly the residence of the Earl of Bessborough and
              converted to a piano showroom in 1924. The architects of
              the conversion were Bennett and Hossack.
Literature: *The Builder* 1924 Mar p412, 415 and 417, illus; *The
              Architect* 1924 Mar p222, illus.

The Philosopher

Medium: Doulton stoneware
Exhibitions: Goupil 1924 (£8); Glasgow 1925 (sold £8); Royal Scottish
              Academy (8gns); Leeds, Manchester 1926 (sold 8gns);
              Institute 1927 (sold), 1928; Toronto, Whitechapel 1929;
              Newcastle, United Society of Artists 1932; Pastel Society
              1934 (5gns); Bournemouth 1947 (sold).

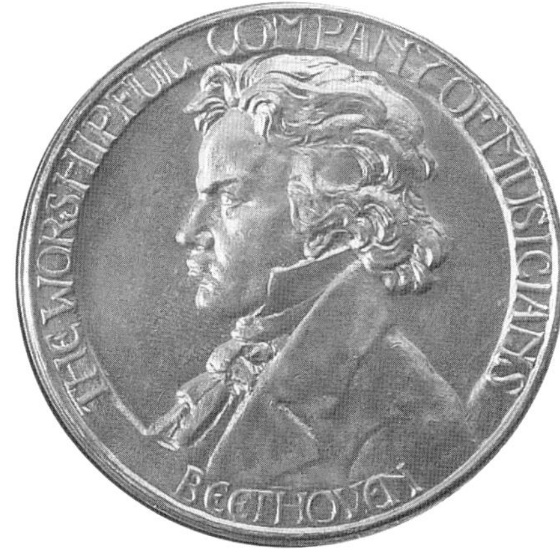

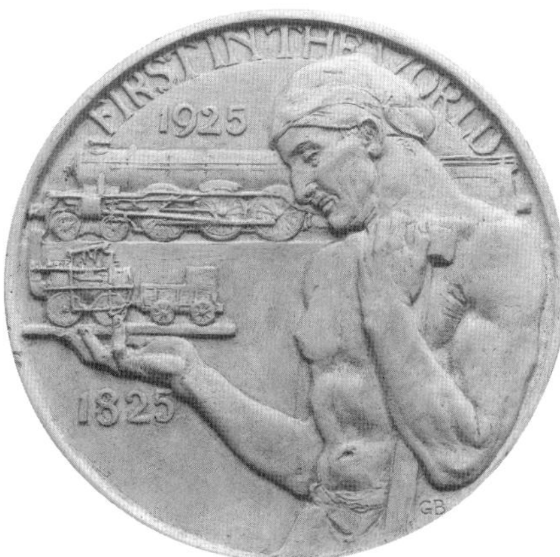

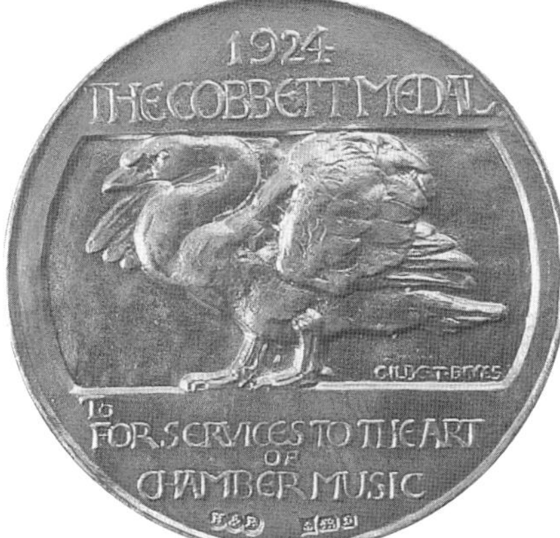

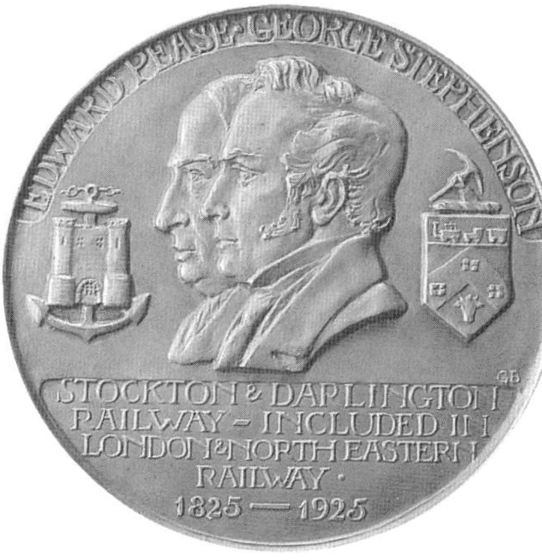

Cobbett Medal

*Railway Medal for Stockton
and Darlington Centenary*

Cobbett Medal

Medium: Silver, gold and silver gilt
cast by Pinches
Size: D 1³/₄ins (4.5cms)
Exhibitions: Arts and Crafts 1926; Royal
Academy 1943.
Locations: Bayes Trust
The medal is awarded for services to the
art of chamber music. This commission
came through Bayes' friendship with
Sigismund Goetze. The medal was
endowed by Walter Wilson Cobbett and
commissioned by the Worshipful
Company of Musicians.

1925

Railway Medal for Stockton and Darlington Centenary

Medium: Bronze, two sizes, cast by
Pinches
Size: D 3ins or 1³/₄ins
(7.5 or 4.5cms)
Exhibitions: Arts and Crafts 1926
Locations: Bayes Trust; British
Museum; private collections.
Literature: *The Studio* 1926 Vol 91 p43,
illus; *Modelling for Sculpture*,
Gilbert Bayes 1930, illus;
The Numismatic Chronicle
1992 pl 22, illus.

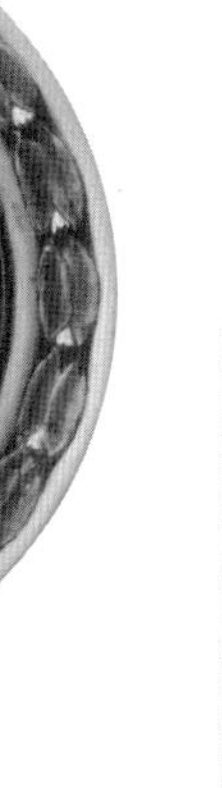

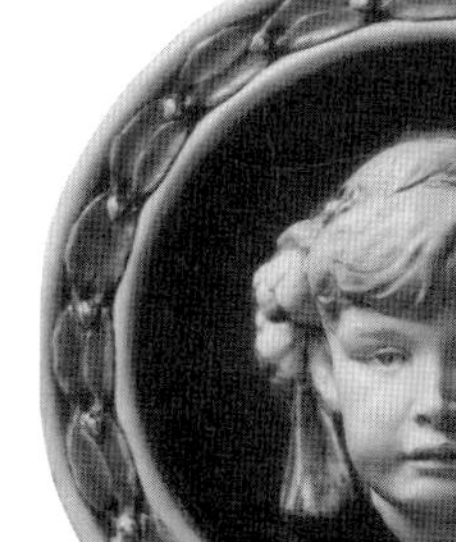

Trevor

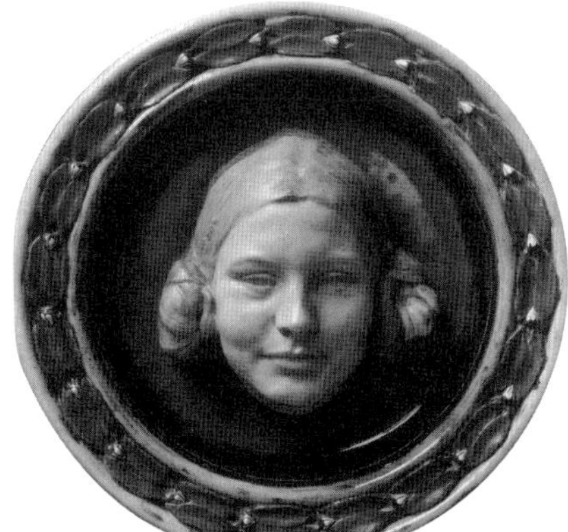

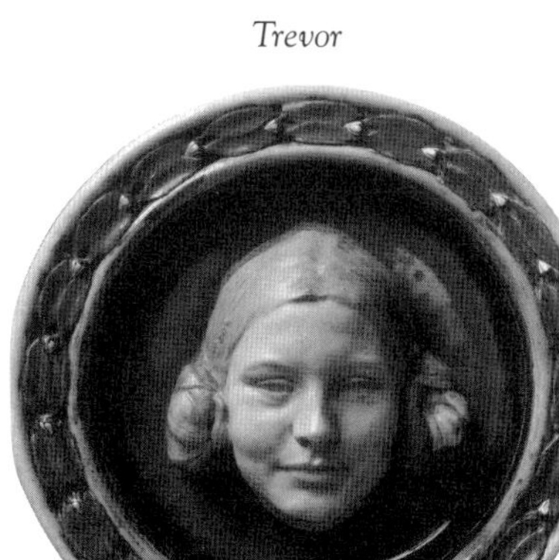

The Lilymaid

Trevor or Youth

Medium: Doulton stoneware roundel
Size: D 17ins (43cms)
Exhibitions: Liverpool 1926 (18gns);
Horticultural Society 1928
(18gns).
Locations: Bayes Trust
Commissioned by the child's grandfather,
Mr Jones.

The Lilymaid or Spirit of Water

Medium: Doulton stoneware roundel
Size: D 17ins (43cms)
Exhibitions: Liverpool 1926 (18gns);
Ridley 1927; Horticultural
Society 1928 (18gns).
Locations: Art Gallery of New South
Wales, purchased 1926; Bayes
Trust.
Literature: *Modelling for Sculpture*, Gilbert
Bayes 1930, illus.
The model is the same as for the *Lilymaid*
figure and the *Spirit of Streams* fountain.

Mask of Woman

Medium: Doulton stoneware
Size: H 11ins without stand
(28cms)
Exhibitions: Goupil 1925, 1926 (25gns);
Royal Academy 1927; Ridley
1927 (21gns); Liverpool 1927
(£26.5s); Institute 1928
(£21); Pastel Society 1935
(15gns).
Locations: Bayes Trust
Literature: *The Builder* 1927 Jun p962,
illus; *Modelling for Sculpture*,
Gilbert Bayes 1930, illus.

The Recorder

Medium: Bronze statuette
Exhibitions: Toronto 1925 (8gns)

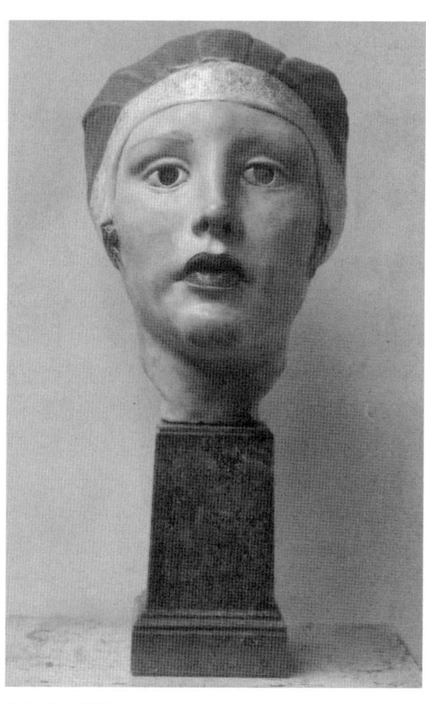

Mask of Woman

Gilbert Bayes

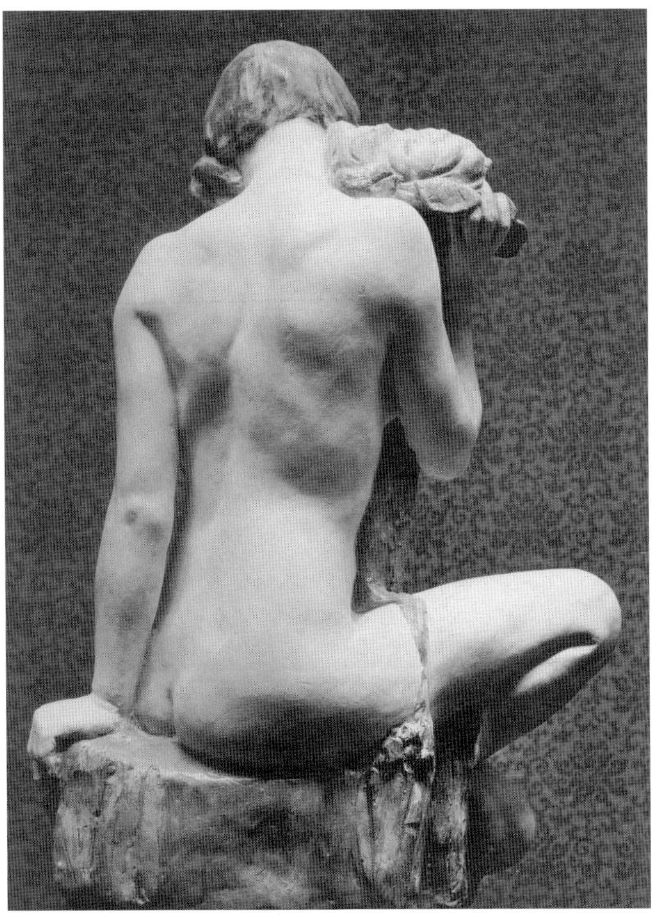

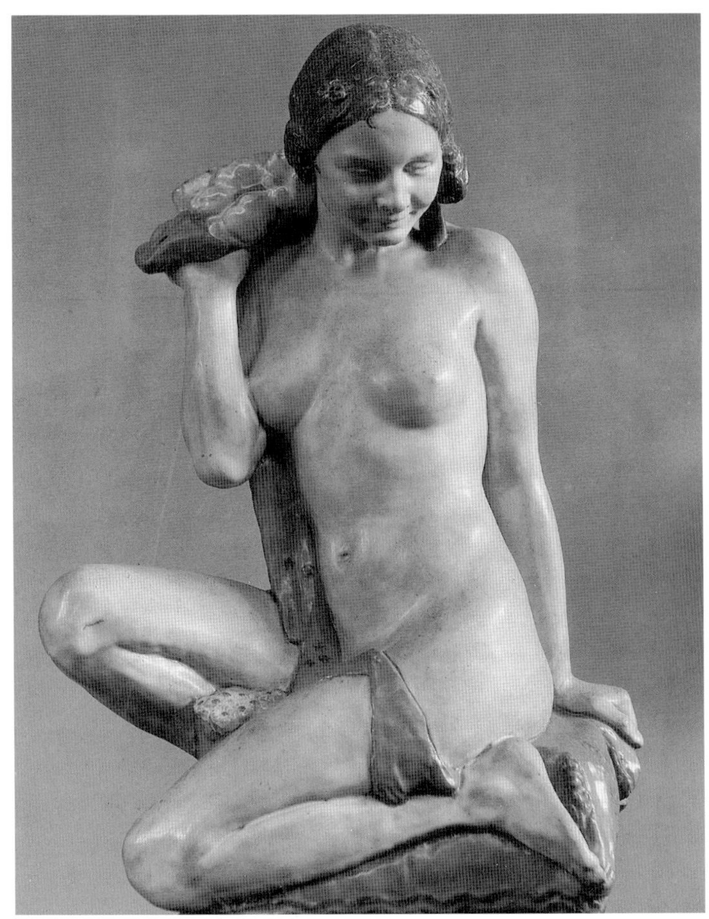

Lilymaid garden statue, back view

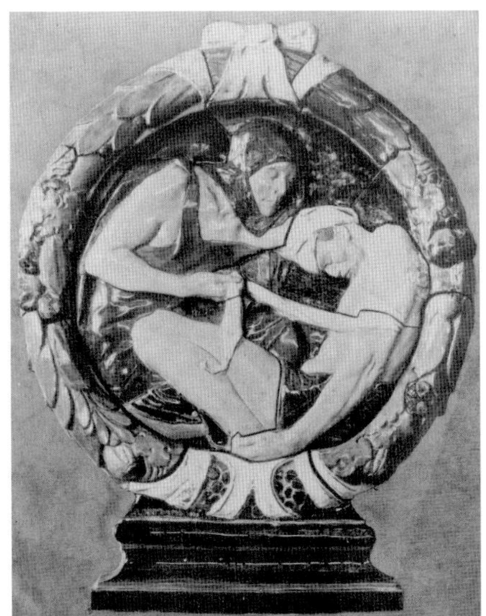

The Good Samaritan

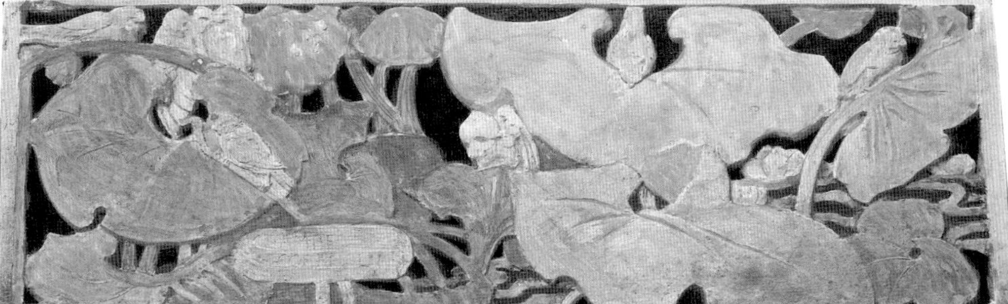

Waterlilies

The Lilymaid Garden Statue

Medium: Doulton stoneware
Size: H 26ins (66cms)
Exhibitions: Bristol 1926; Liverpool 1927,
                1929 (£52.10s); Institute 1927
                (£52.10s); Royal Academy 1929;
                Waring and Gillow Galleries
                1931.
Locations: Christie's 30.9.85 (sold £8,500);
                Bayes Trust.
Literature: *The Builder* 1925 Dec p799, illus;
                The Builder 1931 May p573.

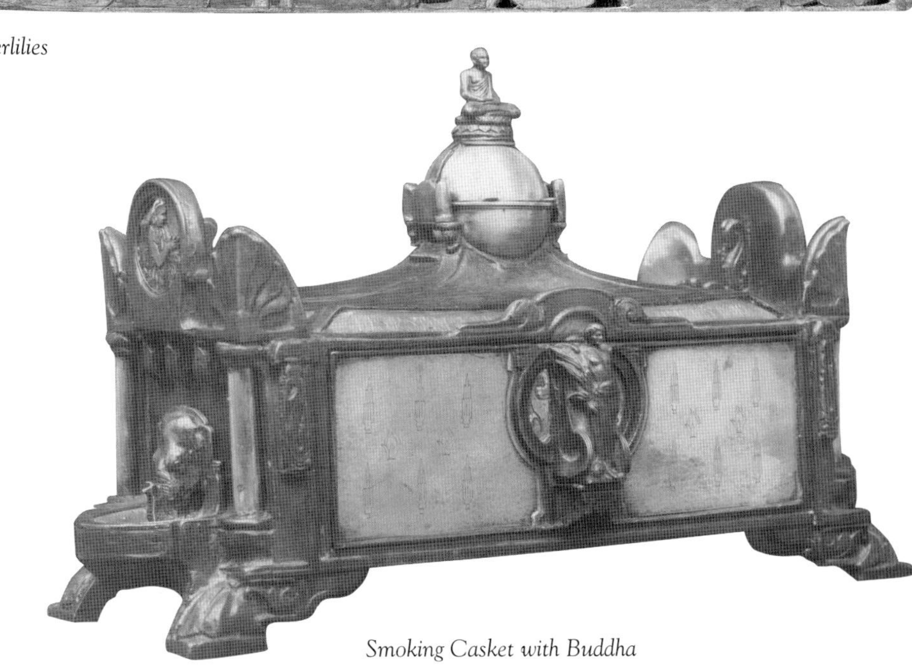

Smoking Casket with Buddha

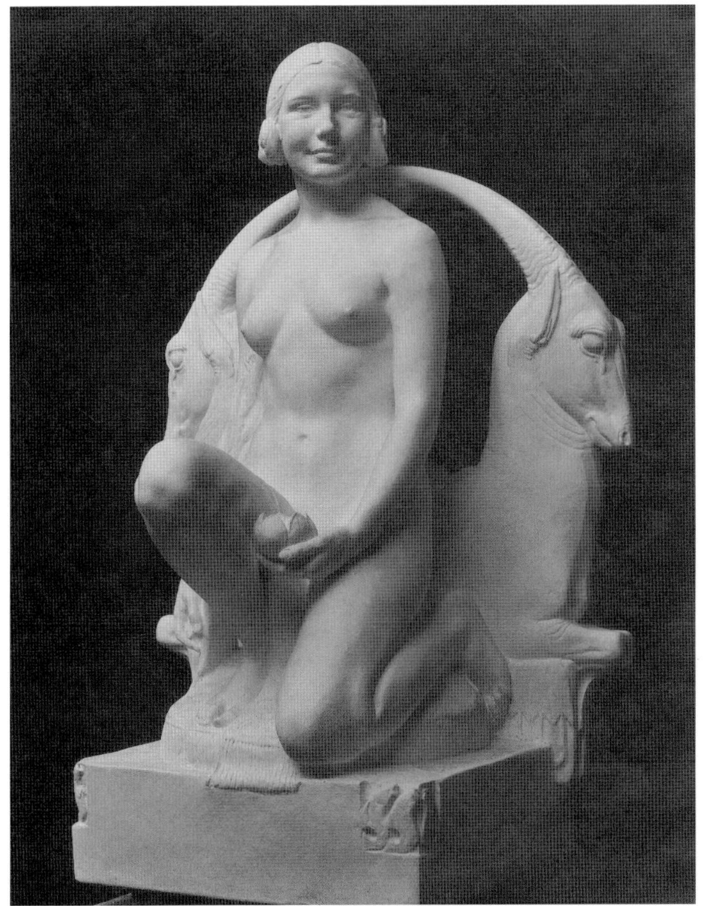

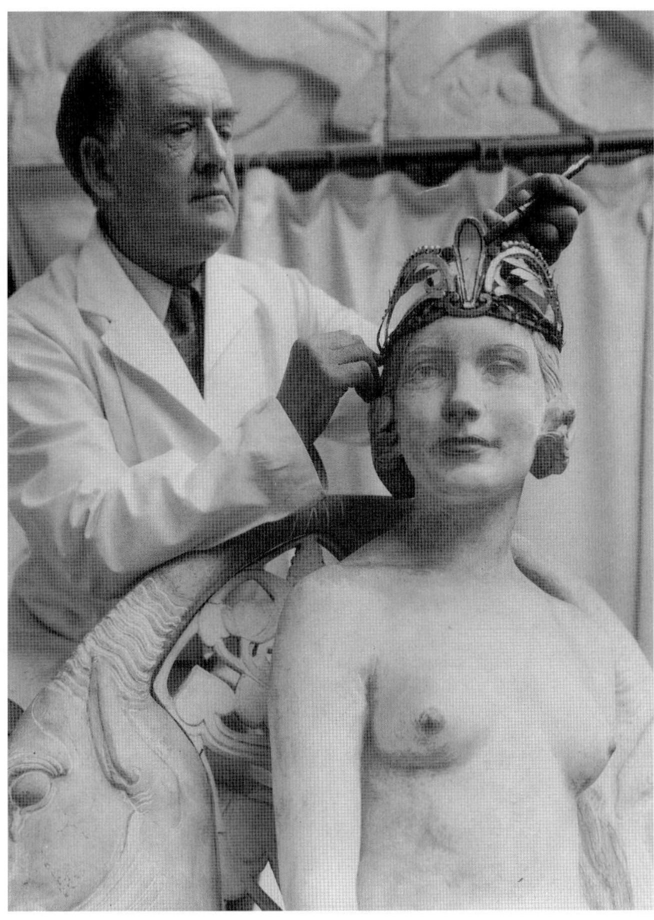

Bayes with a crown for the Spirit of the Streams

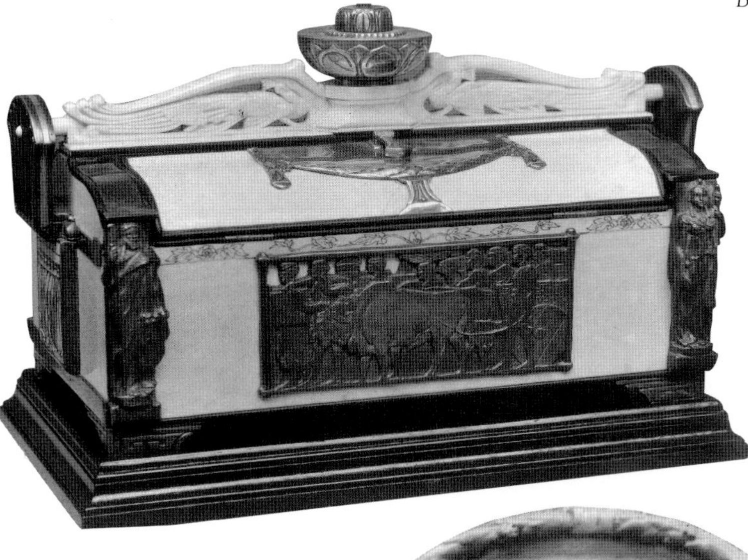

Fish Relief

Waterlilies
Medium: Carved and coloured wood

The Good Samaritan
Medium: Doulton stoneware
Literature: *The Builder* 1924 Mar p409

Fish Relief (Two versions)
Medium: Doulton stoneware roundels
Size: D 13¹/₂ins (34cms)
Locations: Private collection; Bayes Trust.

The Spirit of the Streams
Medium: Life-size plaster group
Exhibitions: Royal Academy 1925; Royal Scottish
              Academy 1927 (400gns).
Literature: *The Builder* May 1925 p795, illus;
              Royal Academy Illustrated 1925 p126,
              illus.

Smoking Casket with Buddha for Sir Stanley
No further information known

Smoking Cabinet
Medium: Ivory, bronze and silver
Locations: Commissioned by Sir Dorabji Tata for
              his board room in Bombay. Still in situ.
Literature: *The Studio* 1925 Vol 89 p197, illus;
              The Artist 1934 Nov p79, illus.

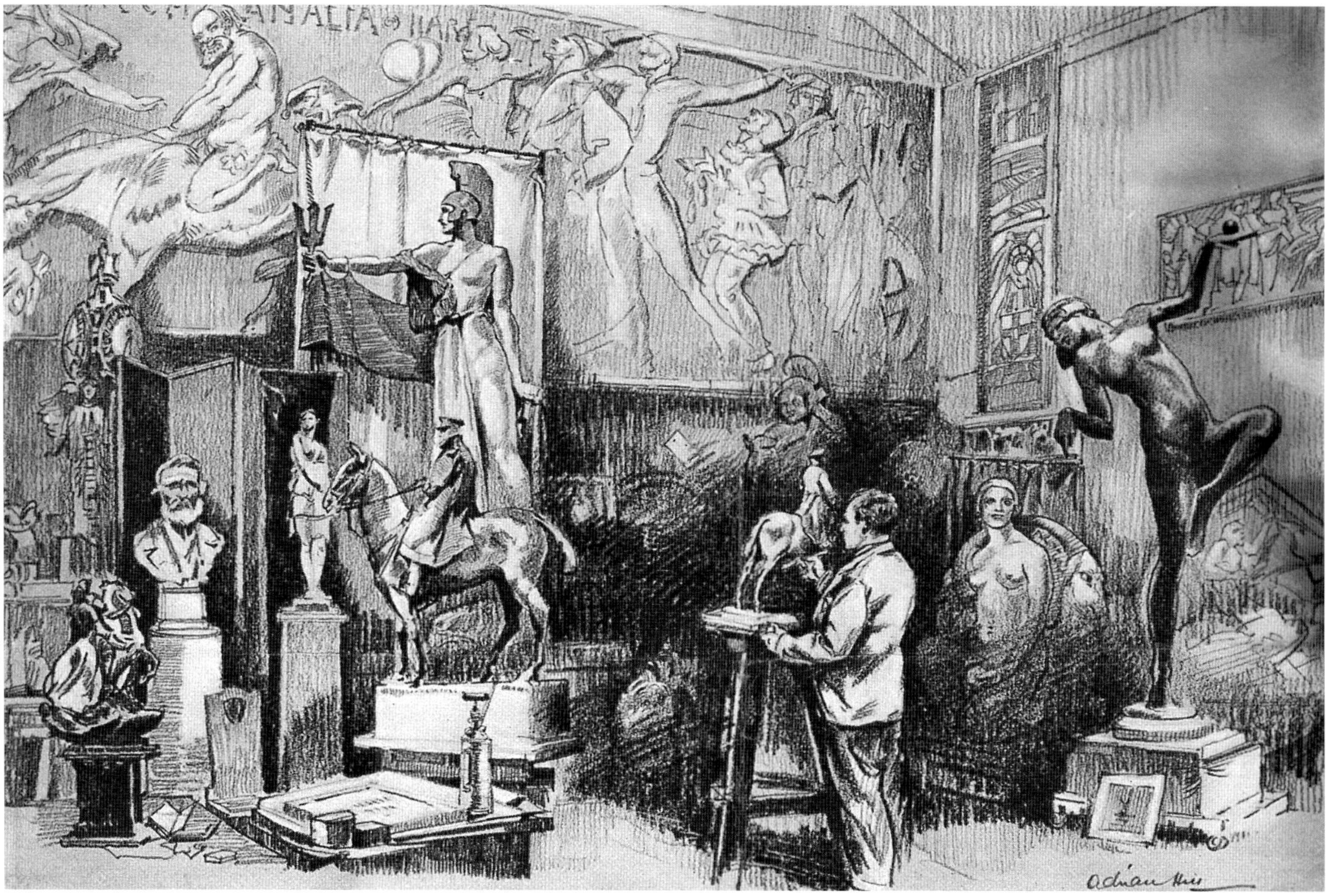

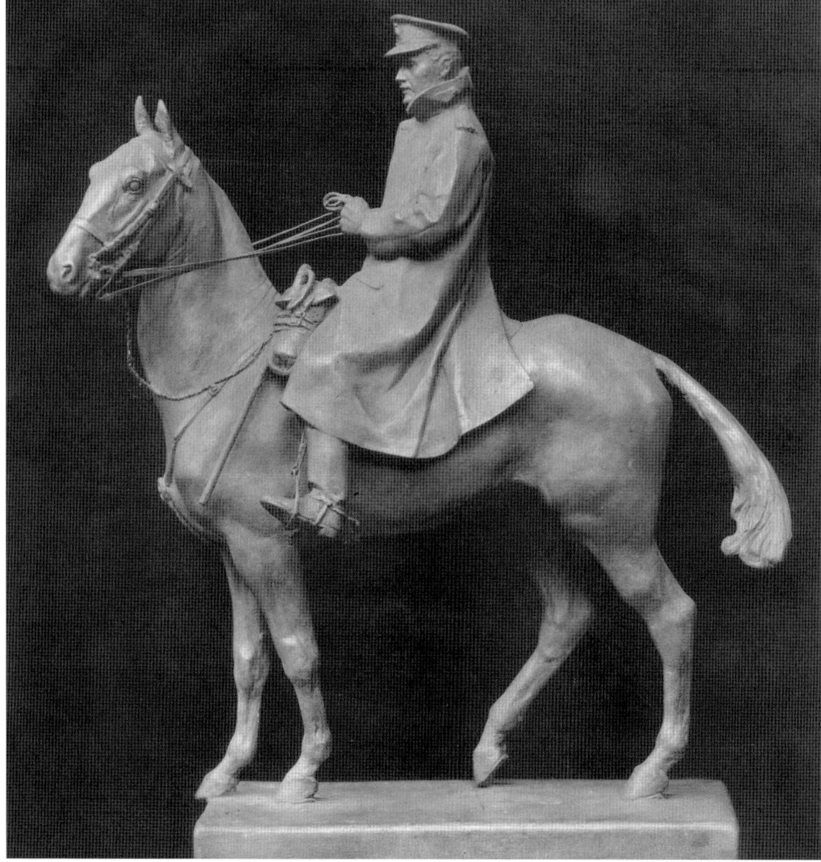

A drawing published in The Sphere in 1933, showing Gilbert Bayes in his studio at Greville Place. He is working on a version of the Haig statue inspired by his Colonel Laurie figure which can be seen to the left. Also identifiable are the Spirit of the Streams, the Frog Princess, the Guardian of the Seas, the Underworld, Diana, Pegasus floor panel, the Selfridge's Clock and part of the Saville Theatre frieze.

Lt Col P.R. Laurie of the Metropolitan Mounted Police

Medium: Plaster maquette for bronze statuette
Size: H 31ins (78cms)
Exhibitions: Royal Academy, Ridley 1926; Institute
                 1929.
Locations: Bayes Trust (plaster)
Literature: The Sphere 1933 Aug p314, illus.
Colonel Laurie's horse was called Quicksilver and he posed for this portrait at Bayes' studio.

1926

Drama, Romance, Adventure and Terpsichore

Medium: Doulton stoneware roundels
Size: D 36ins (91.5cms)
Exhibitions: Arts and Crafts 1928 (*Drama*, £36.15s);
                 Royal Academy Arts and Industries
                 1935 (*Romance*).
Locations: White Rock Pavilion, Hastings.
                 Architect C. Cowles Voysey; formerly St
                 Pancras Housing Association; Bayes
                 Trust (*Drama* and *Romance*).
Literature: Modelling for Sculpture, Gilbert Bayes
                 1930, illus; The Artist Oct 1934 p45, illus;
                 The Connoisseur 1979 Aug p252, illus.

The Outpost

Medium: Bronze statuette
Exhibitions: Glasgow 1926; Liverpool 1927 (£26.5s);
                 Institute 1927; Bristol 1930.

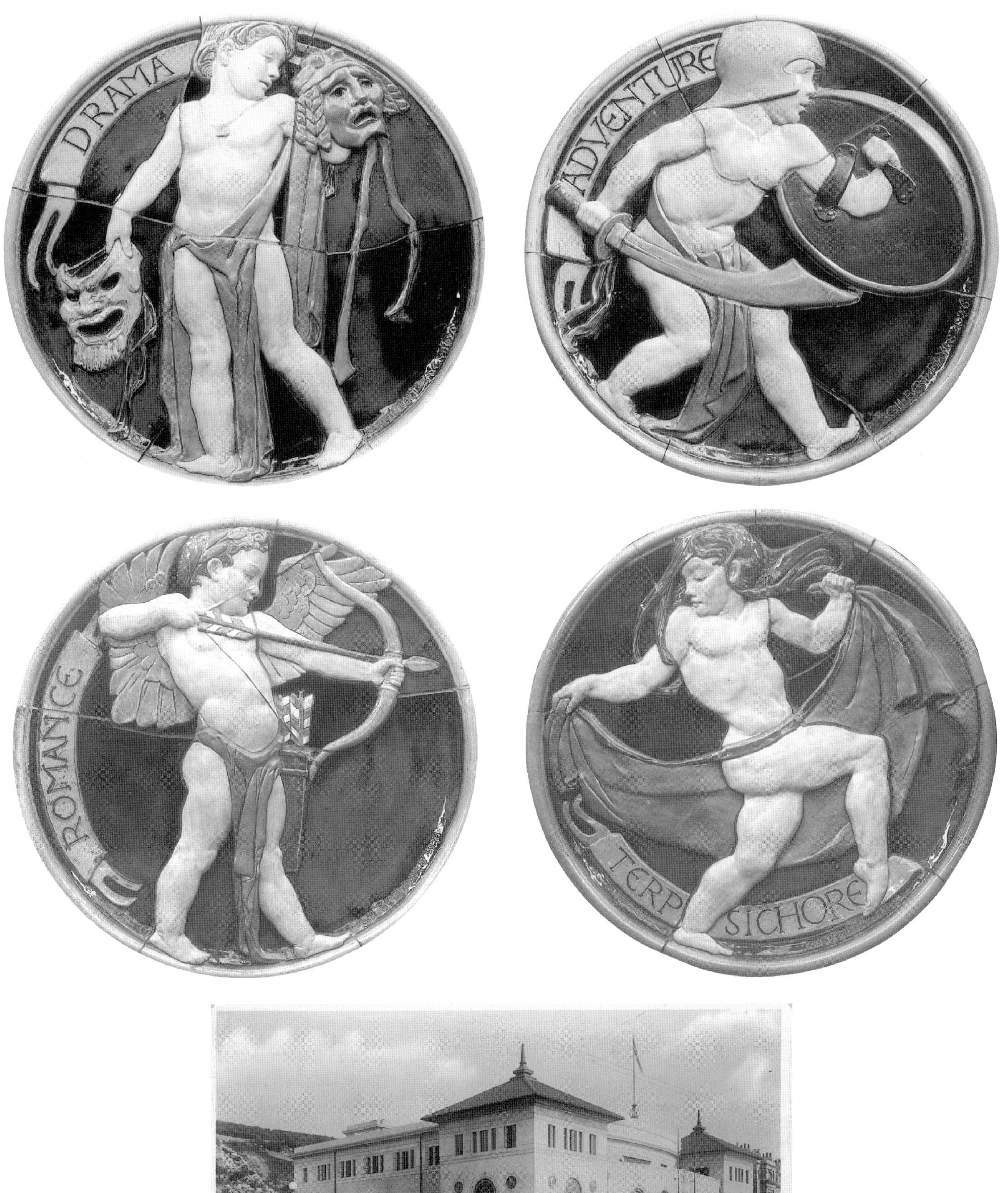

Postcard showing the roundels on the White Rock Pavilion, Hastings, Sussex

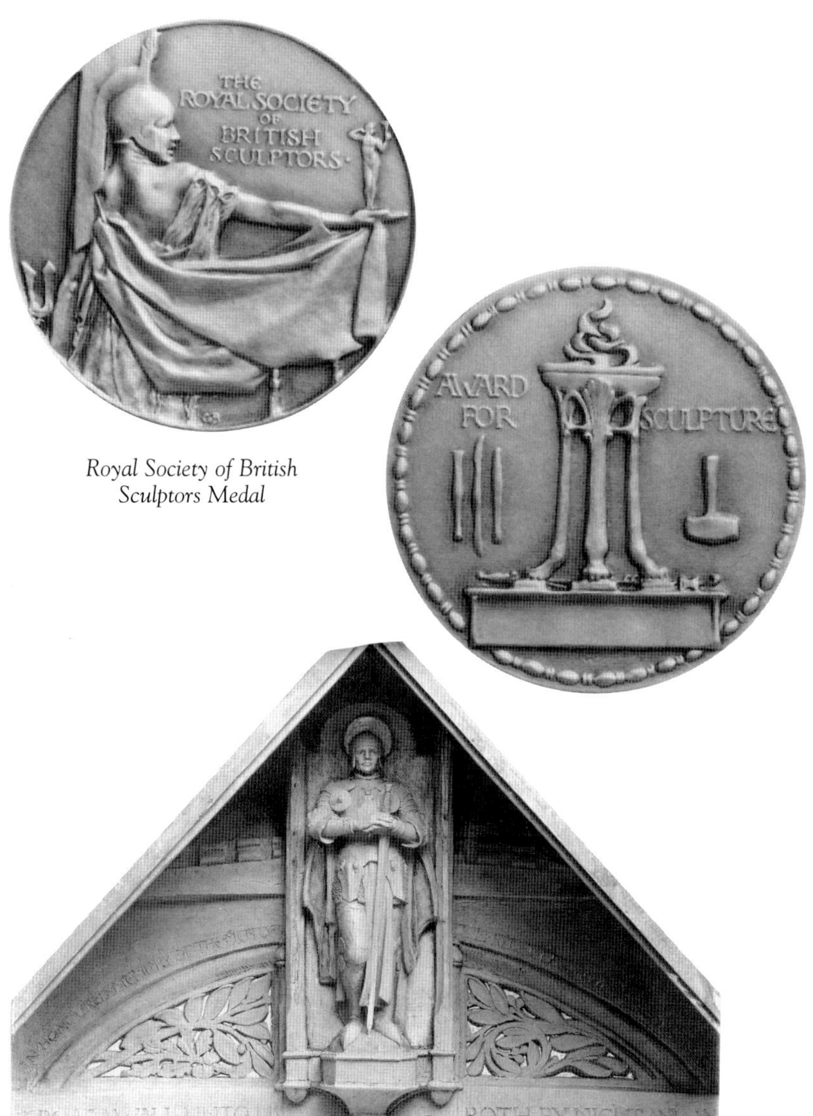

Royal Society of British Sculptors Medal

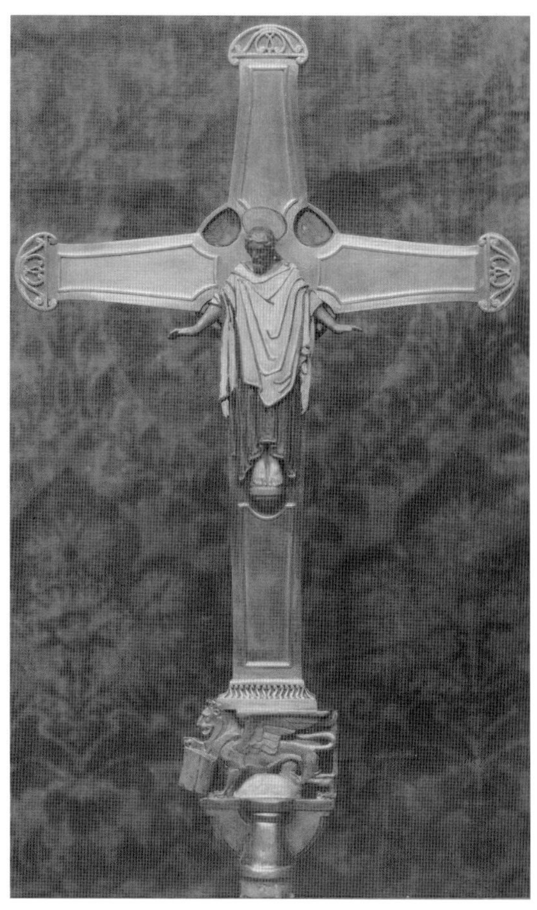

Processional Cross

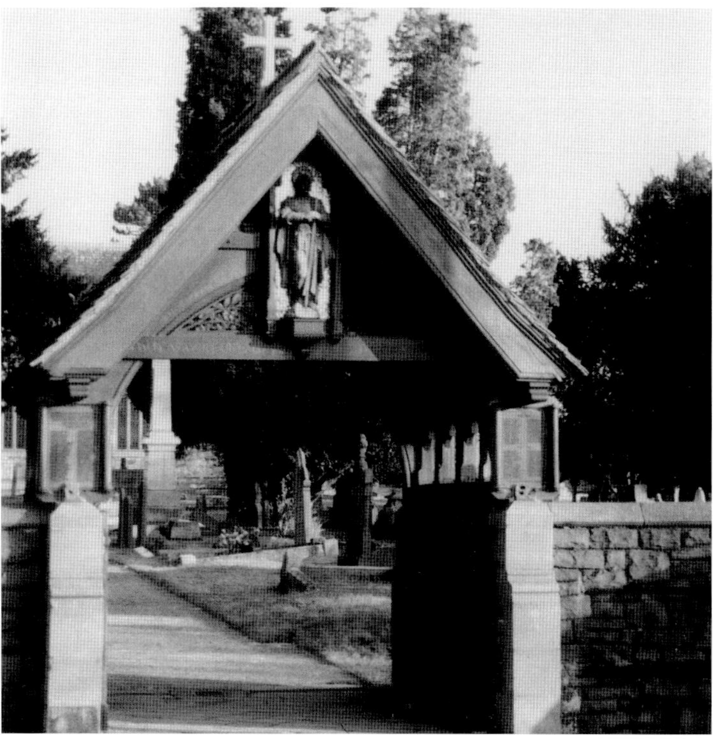

St George figure and lych gate, Rogerstone and Dyffryn Craig War Memorial

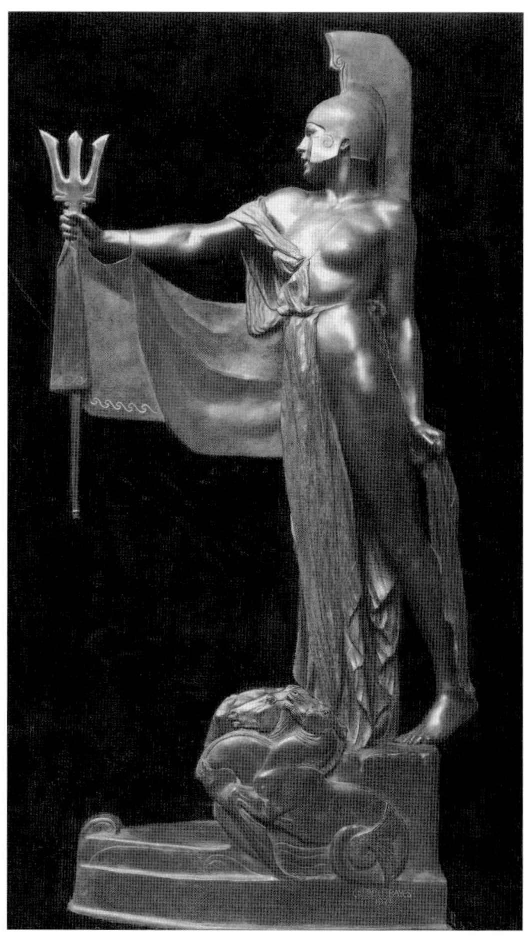

England My Mother, bronze statuette

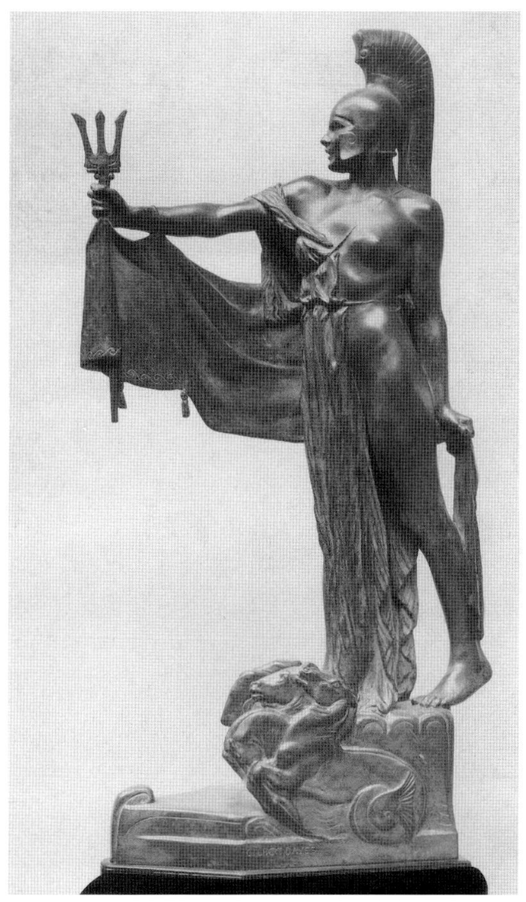

Plaster model for 8ft high statue of England My Mother

Processional Cross
Medium: Silver, bronze and enamel
Exhibitions: Festival of Church Art 1930
Locations: St Mark's Church, Hamilton
               Terrace, London
Literature: *The Artist* 1934 Dec p125,
               illus.
The cross was dedicated at Christmas
1926 in memory of Miss Isabel Bowmar.

England My Mother
Medium: Bronze statuette
Size: H 24ins, 32ins with base
               (61.5cms, 81.5cms)
Exhibitions: Institute 1926 plaster (£105);
               Liverpool 1926 bronze
               (£105); Royal Academy 1927
               bronze (100gns); Glasgow
               1927; Royal Scottish
               Academy 1928 plaster, 1932
               bronze; Bristol 1928; Buenos
               Aires 1928 (150gns); Ridley
               1929, 1932; Aberdeen 1933;
               Bournemouth 1948; Institute
               1952 (200gns).
Locations: Bayes Trust; P & O (ex Fine
               Art Society); formerly in the
               collection of Gordon
               Selfridge.
The title is taken from Kipling 'England
my Mother, Warder of Waters, Builder of
Cities, Maker of Men'.
This figure is known also as *The Guardian
of the Seas*, the *Wardress of the Waters* and
the *Ruler of the Seas*.

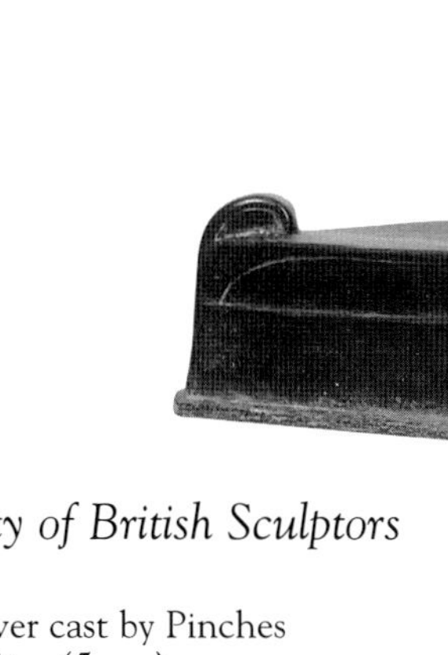

Royal Society of British Sculptors Medal
Medium: Silver cast by Pinches
Size: D 2ins (5cms)
Exhibitions: Royal Academy 1943
Locations: British Museum, Royal
               Society of British Sculptors;
               private collections.
Literature: *The Studio* 1946, illus; *The
               Numismatic Chronicle* 1992 pl
               23, illus.

St George Lych Gate, Rogerstone and Dyffryn Craig War Memorial, 1914-19
Medium: Bronze mosaic and oak
Size: H 18ft (5.5m)
Exhibitions: Arts and Crafts 1926 (lych
               gate figure)
Locations: St Basil's Church, Bassaleg,
               nr. Newport, Gwent

1927

The Guardian of the Seas
Medium: Bronze and enamel
Size: H 8ft (2.5m)
Exhibitions: Royal Academy 1928; Ridley
               1929 and 1932; Edinburgh
               1932; Aberdeen 1933.
Locations: Royal Automobile Club
               swimming pool, London,
               purchased by 6th Earl Howe
Literature: *Royal Academy Illustrated* 1926
               p128, illus: *The Builder* 1926
               Aug p277, illus; *The Builder*
               1928 May p888; *Modelling for
               Sculpture*, Gilbert Bayes 1930,
               illus; *The Artist* 1935 Feb
               p191, illus.
Also known by the Royal Automobile
Club as *Speed*.

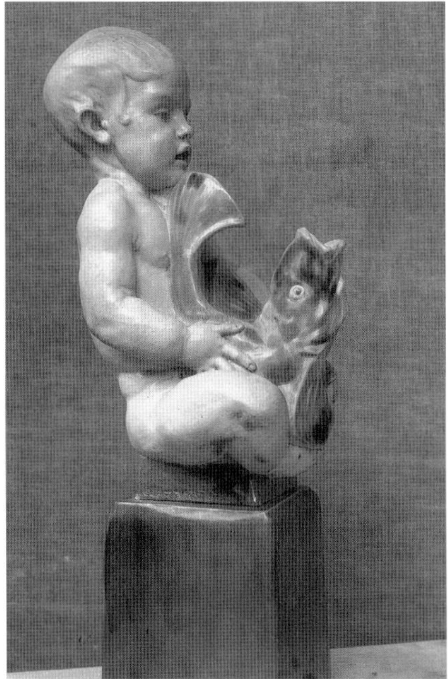

The Water Baby

Medium: Doulton stoneware fountain
Exhibitions: Royal Academy 1927; Waring and Gillows Galleries 1931.
Locations: Formerly nursery school Sidney Street estate, London; Bayes Trust.
Literature: *The Builder* 1931 May p567, illus; *The Architect and Building News* 1934 May p119, illus; *The Artist* 1935 Jan p158, illus.

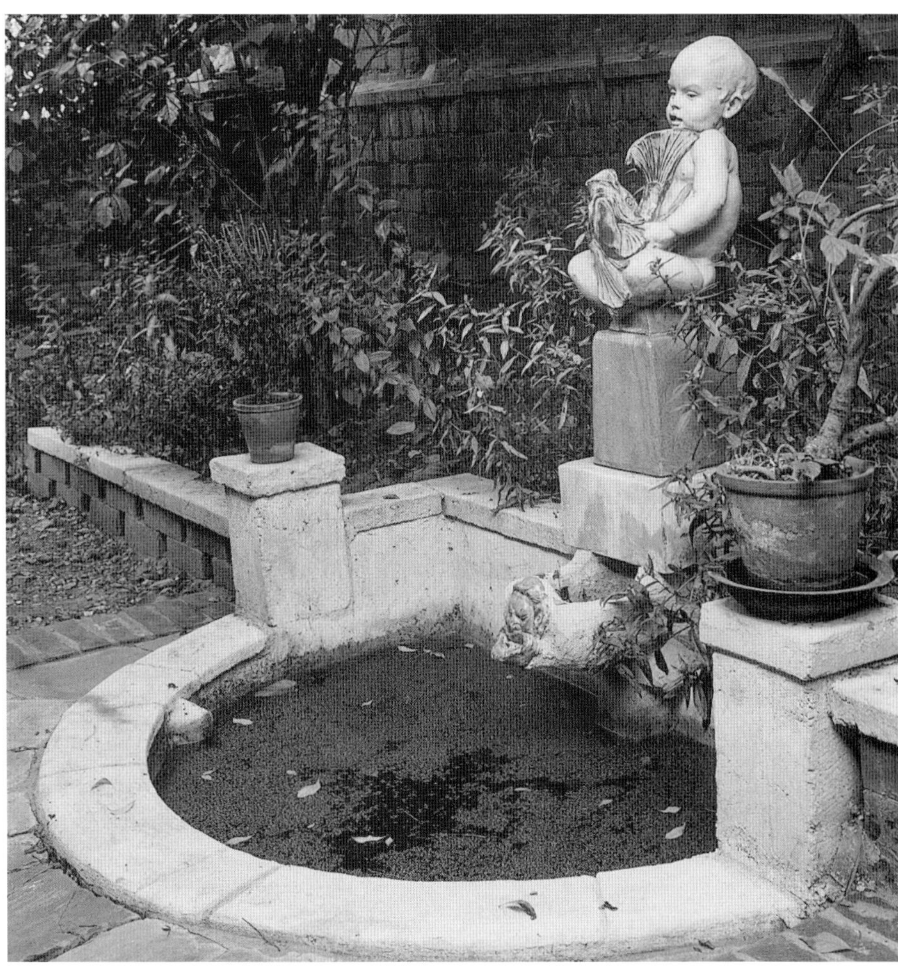

The Water Baby fountain at Boundary Road, London

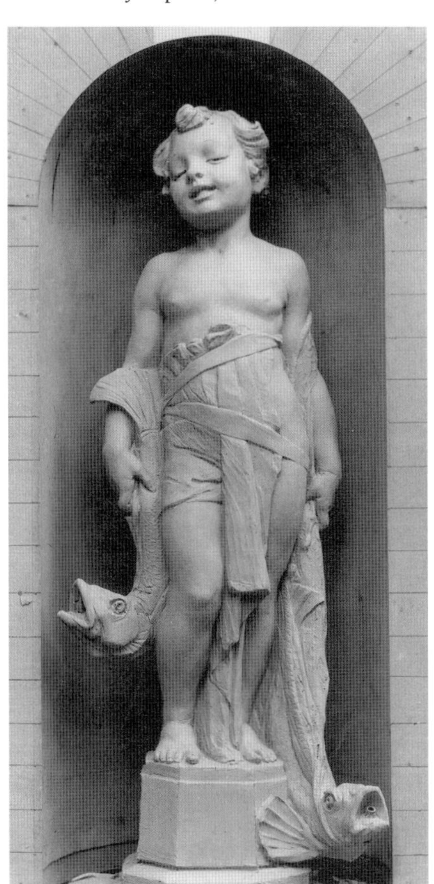

Plaster model of the Fisherman

The Fisherman

Medium: Doulton stoneware fountain
Size: H 3ft 6ins with base (1.05m)
Exhibitions: Ridley 1927 sketch model; Ridley 1939 (60gns); Royal Academy 1941.
Locations: Nursery School, Sidney Street Estate, St Pancras Housing Assoc., London; Christie's 30.4.84 (sold).
Literature: *Glazed Expressions* 1986 Vol 12 p2, illus.

A sketch model was first shown in 1927. Later it was completed in plaster and then made in Doulton stoneware in 1939.

St George, British War Cemetery, Jerusalem

Medium: Bronze figure
Size: H 79ins (2m)
Exhibitions: Royal Academy 1926
Locations: Memorial Chapel, British War Cemetery, Jerusalem, to the Missing of the Egyptian Expeditionary Force. Architects Sir John Burnet and Partners, unveiled on May 1927 by Field Marshal Viscount Allenby; Bayes Trust (plaster).
Literature: *The Architect and Building News* 1927 Mar, illus; *The Artist* 1934 Sep p13, illus.

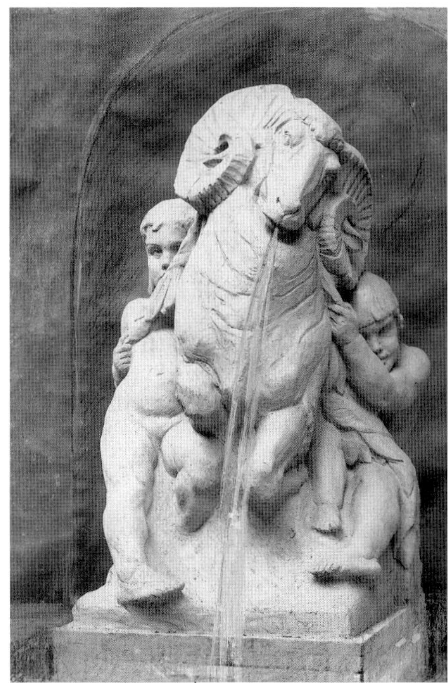

Ram Fountain

Medium: Concrete
Locations: Winterstoke Gardens, Ramsgate. Architect Sir John Burnet and Partners.

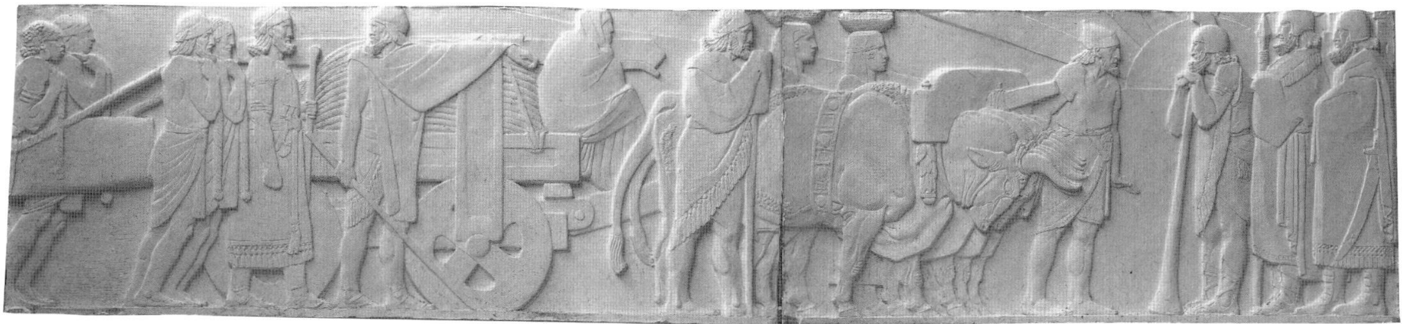

Plaster model for the left hand panel, King Solomon's Temple, former Masonic Temple, Birmingham

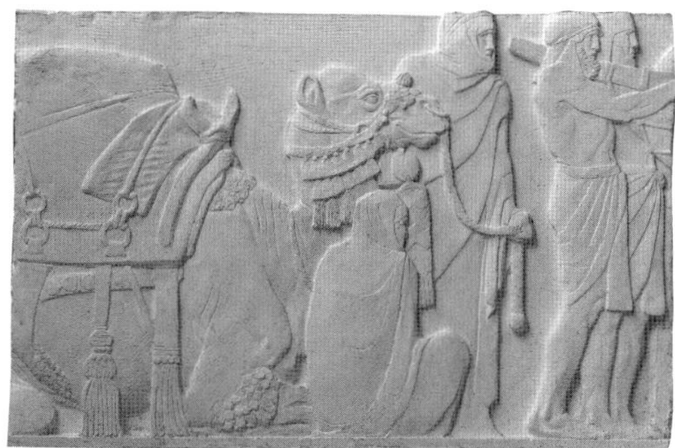

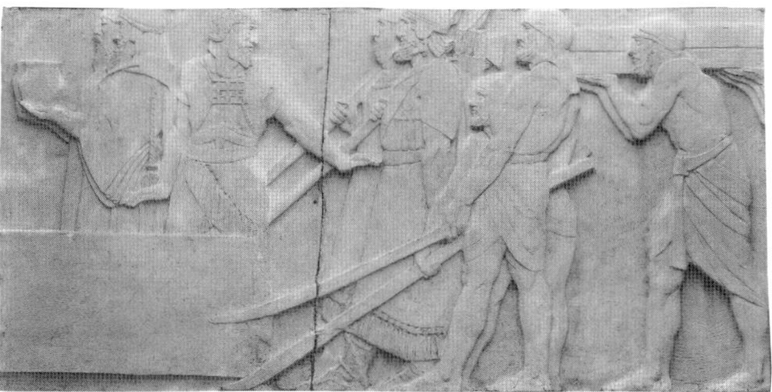

Sections of the plaster model for the right hand panel, King Solomon's Temple, former Masonic Temple, Birmingham

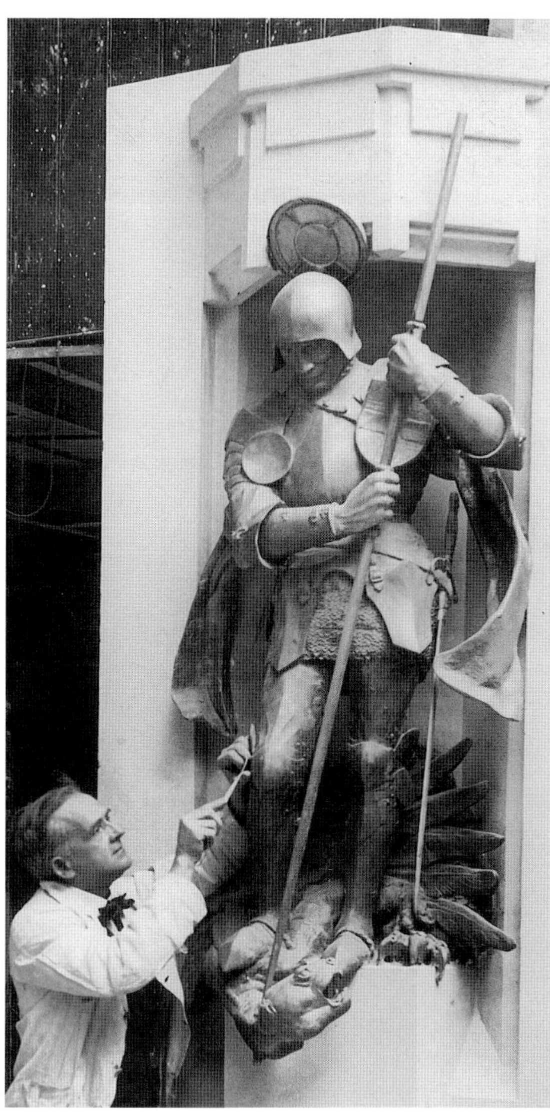

Bayes working on the plaster for St George

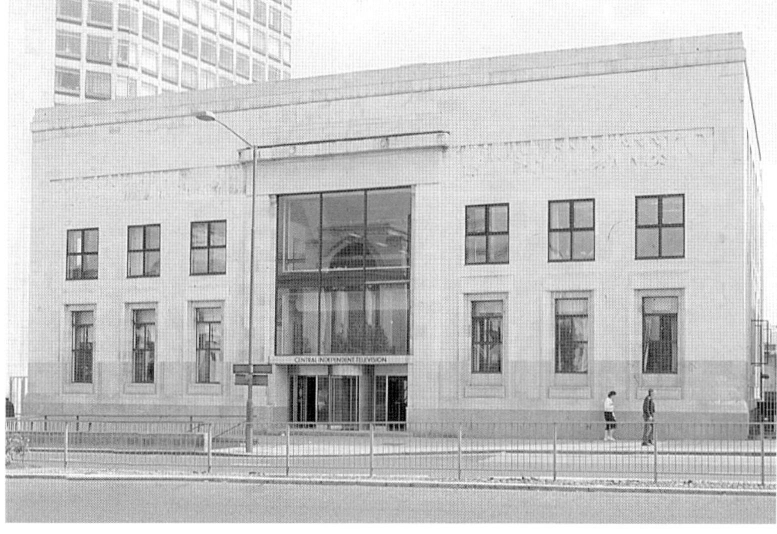

Former Masonic Temple, Broad Street, Birmingham

Building of King Solomon's Temple
Medium: Portland stone frieze
Size: H 4ft L 64ft (1.20 x 20m)
Exhibitions: Royal Academy 1928 (model)
Locations: Masonic Temple, Broad Street, Birmingham (now Engineering and
           Building Centre)
Literature: *The Builder* 1928 May p893, illus; *Modelling for Sculpture*, Gilbert
           Bayes 1930, illus; *The Artist* 1934 Sep and Oct p45, illus.

Stained Glass Window in Memory of Samuel Garrett, 1850-1922
Medium: Glass
Locations: St Peter and St Paul Church, Aldeburgh, Suffolk (window
           destroyed during World War II)
Bayes worked with the stained glass expert, Leonard Walker, on this
commission which led to him becoming a member of the Worshipful Company
of Glaziers. In 1933, he was described as a 'citizen and glazier' when he was
given the Freedom of London.

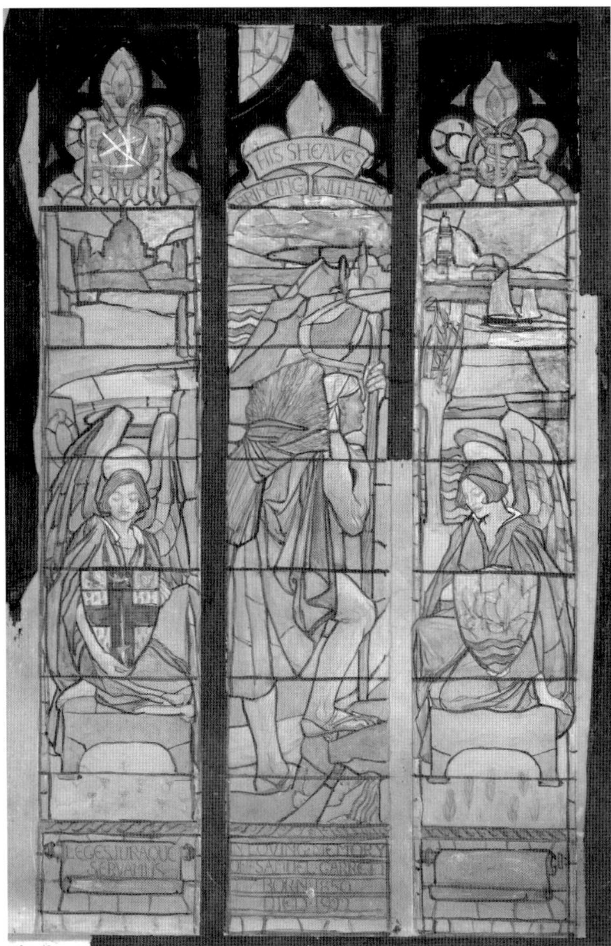

Drawing for Samuel Garrett window, Aldeburgh, Suffolk

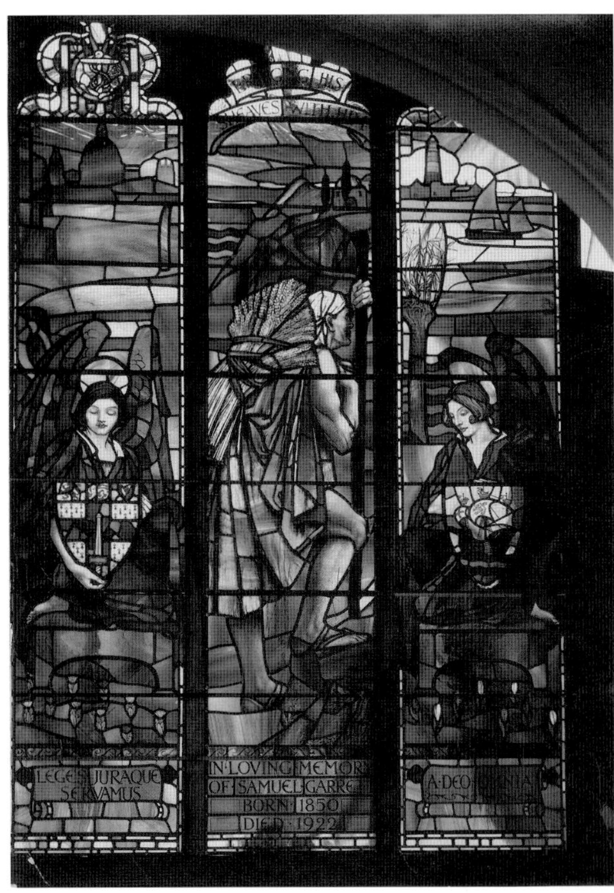

Samuel Garrett window, Aldeburgh, Suffolk

1928

The Hesperides, Diana & Judgement of Paris

Medium: Doulton stoneware and artificial stone
Size: H 39ins W 27ins (99 x 69cms)
Exhibitions: Arts and Crafts 1928 (£26.5s)
Locations: Private collection; Fine Art Society; Bayes Trust.
Literature: *Modelling for Sculpture*, Gilbert Bayes 1930, illus.

The Water Baby

Medium: Bronze statuette
Size: 5¹/₂ins (14cms)
Locations: Bayes Trust; Sladmore Gallery.

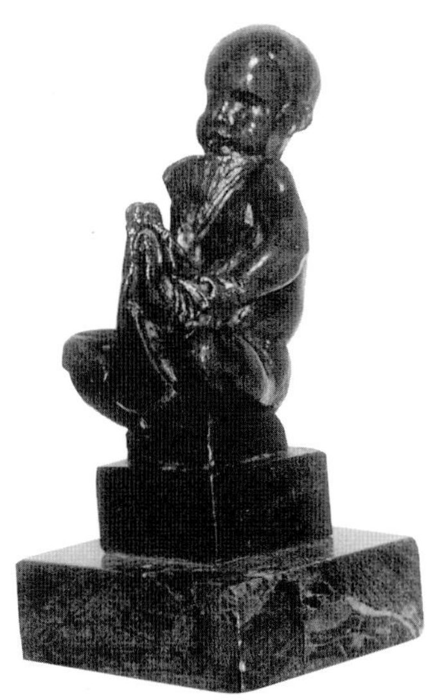

The Water Baby

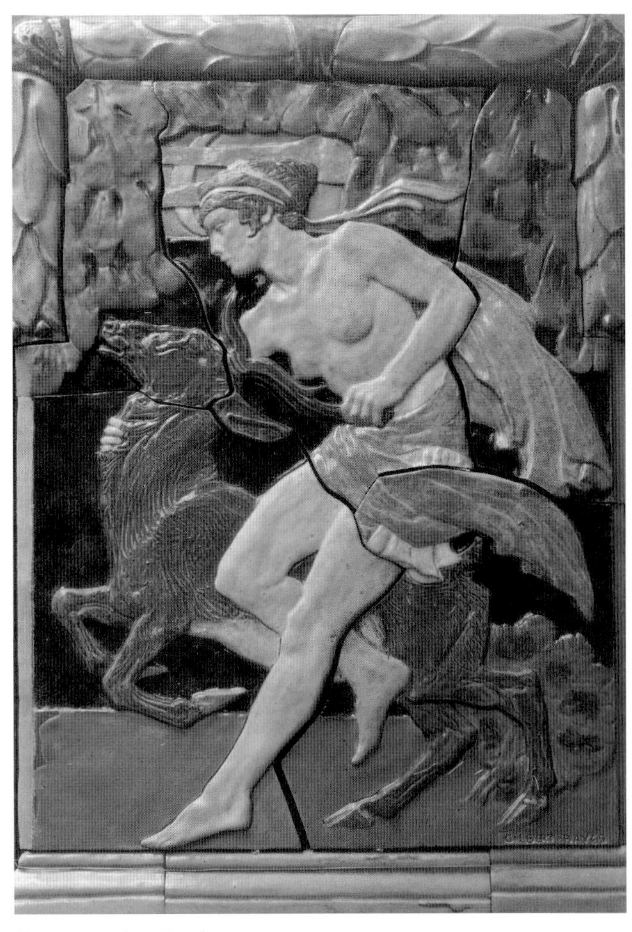

Diana panel in Doulton stoneware

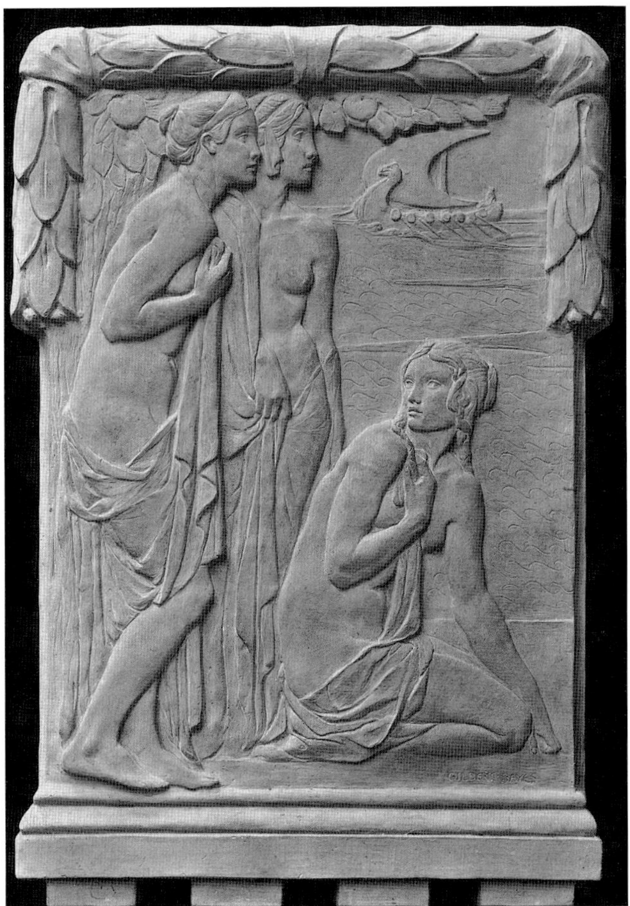

Plaster model for the Hesperides panel

1929

Institute of Actuaries Medal
Medium: Gold
Size: D 2³/₄ins (7cms)
Locations: Bayes Trust; British Museum.
Literature: *The Numismatic Chronicle* 1992, pl 23, illus.
Made in honour of George James Lidstone who was a past President of the Faculty of Actuaries in Scotland and presented by the Institute of Actuaries.

Pan Mask, or Grotesque
Medium: Doulton stoneware
Size: H 12ins (30cms)
Locations: Bayes Trust
Literature: *Modelling for Sculpture*, Gilbert Bayes 1930, illus.
Versions were used in the garden at Greville Place.

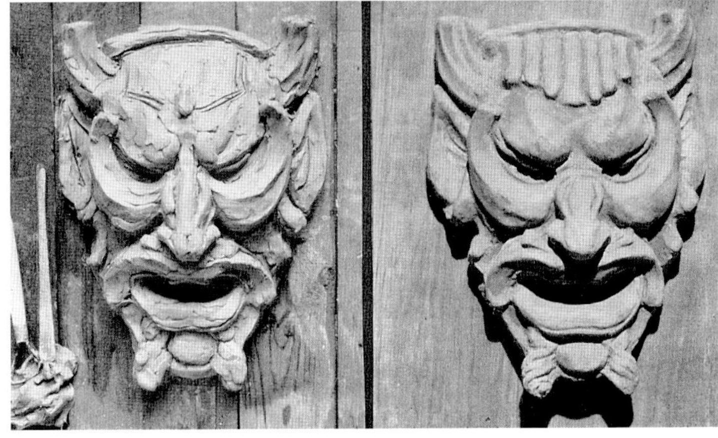

Model of Pan mask

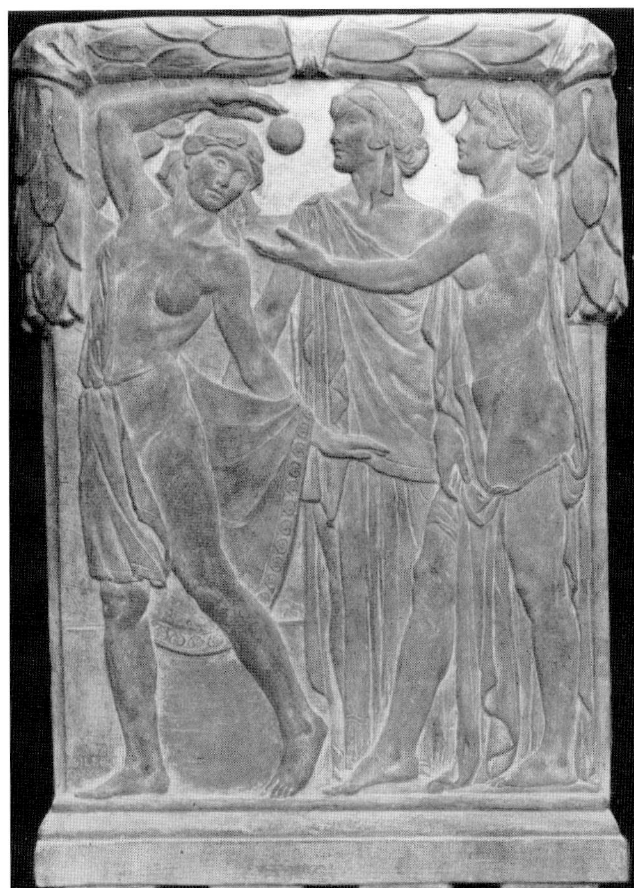

Judgement of Paris panel in artificial stone

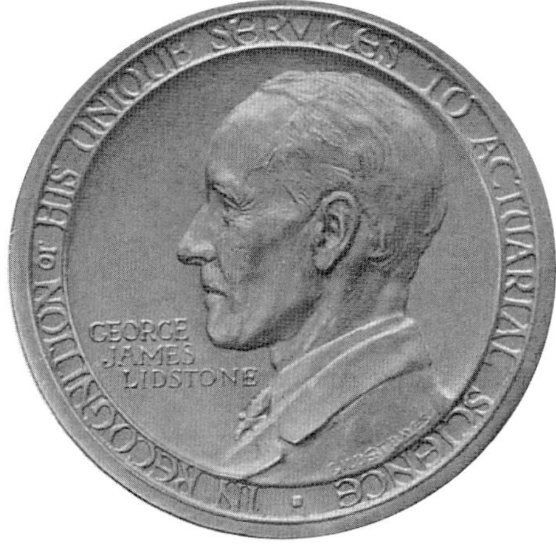

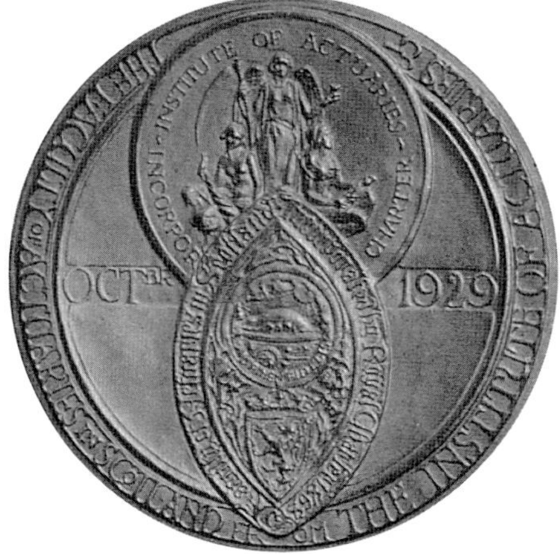

Institute of Actuaries Medal

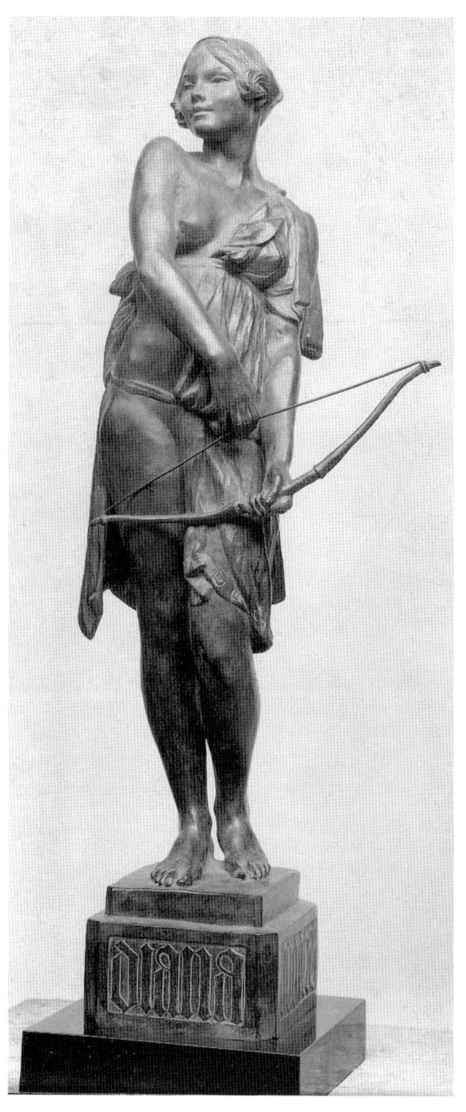

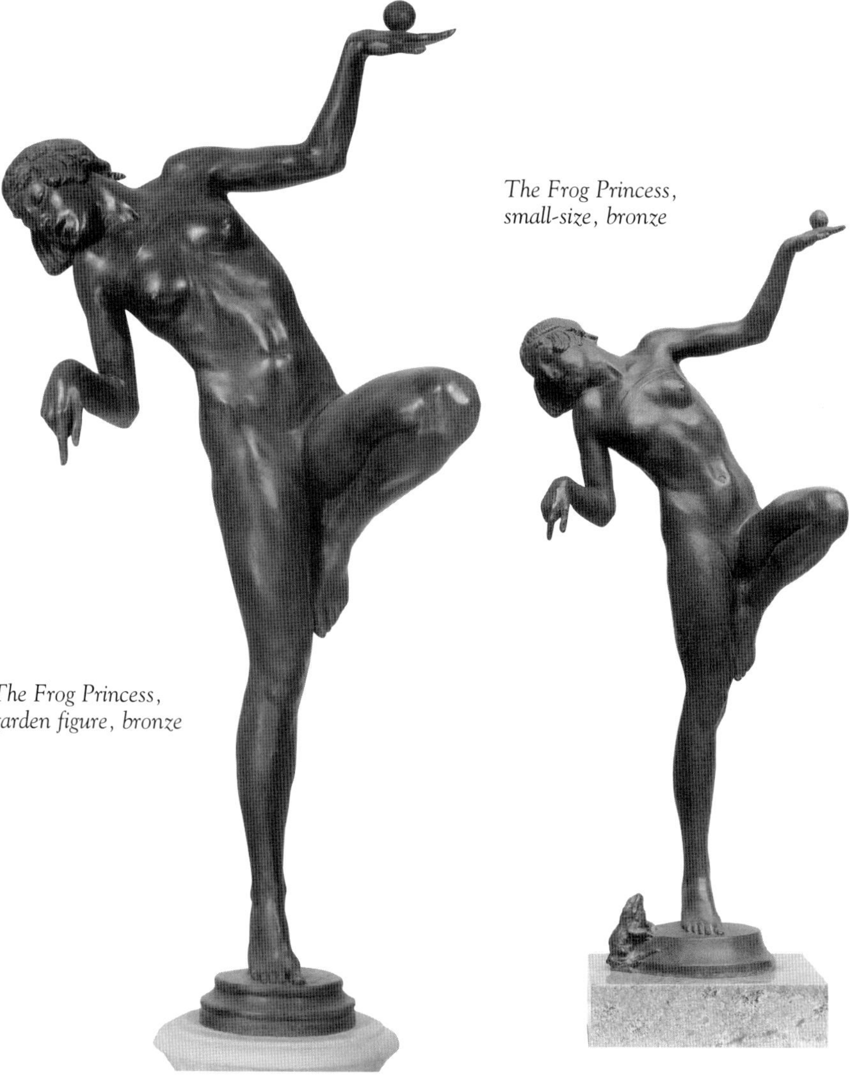

*The Frog Princess,
garden figure, bronze*

*The Frog Princess,
small-size, bronze*

Diana

Medium: Bronze statuette
Size: 29ins with base (74cms)
Exhibitions: Royal Academy, Ridley, Bristol 1929 (100gns); Liverpool (£105),
Institute 1930; Waring and Gillow Galleries 1931; Ridley, Sussex
Artists 1933; Toronto 1935; Aberdeen 1937 (£105).
Locations: Lady Lever Art Gallery, presented in 1931 by Lord Leverhulme; Sir
Francis Bowring purchased the cast at Liverpool in 1930 for £80.5s.
Literature: *The Builder* May 1931 p567, illus; *Modelling for Sculpture,* Gilbert
Bayes 1930, illus; *Royal Academy Illustrated* 1929 p128, illus.

The Frog Princess

Medium: Bronze garden statue
Size: H 6ft 1ins (1.85m)
Exhibitions: Royal Academy 1931 (280gns); British Empire Exhibition, Glasgow
1938; Paris Salon 1939.
Locations: Bayes Trust; bronze formerly in a Chobham garden, Surrey
purchased 1977 from Syon Lodge for the Devonian Gardens,
Calgary; another in a private collection.
Literature: *The Builder* May 1931 p835; *Royal Academy Illustrated* 1931 p97,
illus; *Arts and Decoration* May 1932, illus; *The Artist* Jan 1935 p158,
illus.

The large *Frog Princess* was originally made for Mrs Robert Jones, née Margaret
Huston. It stood in her garden at the Villa Reposa, Montecito, California and
was later presented to the Santa Barbara Botanic Garden in 1952. Having been
sold to a private collector in the US it eventually entered the London art
market and was sold in 1993 for £35,000. Bayes was awarded a Gold Medal at
the Paris Salon in 1939 for this statue.

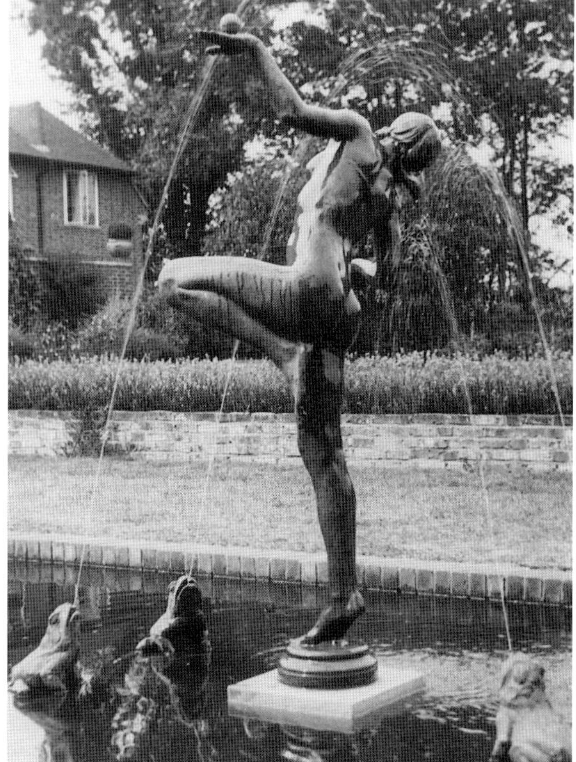

The Frog Princess fountain in a Surrey garden

The Frog Princess
Medium: Bronze statuette on plinth
Size: H 18ins (46cms)
Exhibitions: Rio de Janiero 1930; Bristol, Institute 1931 (£36.15s); Ridley 1933 (33gns); Oldham, Aberdeen 1937; Southport 1939.
Locations: Bayes Trust (plaster maquette); Black Horse Agencies, Leamington Spa 18.10.90 (dated 1929 - sold £3,100); private collection.

Great Pan
Medium: Stone with gilding and mosaic
Exhibitions: Royal Academy 1929; British Empire Glasgow 1938.
Locations: Originally made for a garden in Greenwich USA; Bayes Trust.
Literature: *The Artist* January 1935 p160, illus.

Funerary Casket
Medium: Doulton stoneware
Made for Mary Lawrence, died 28.10.1928, and Basil Edwin Lawrence, died 10.12.1928.

Ship Roundels
Medium: Bronze and mosaic
Size: D 6ft (1.83m)
Locations: Selfridge's, Oxford Street, London
Dated 1927 but inlaid in 1929 in the marble floor at the lift entrances, these are now in archive area.

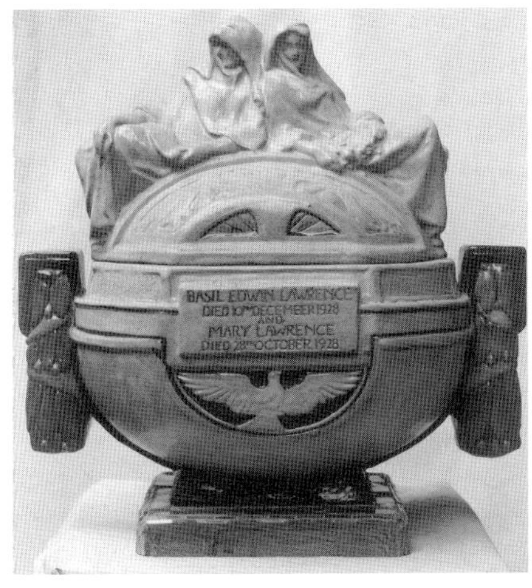

Funerary Casket

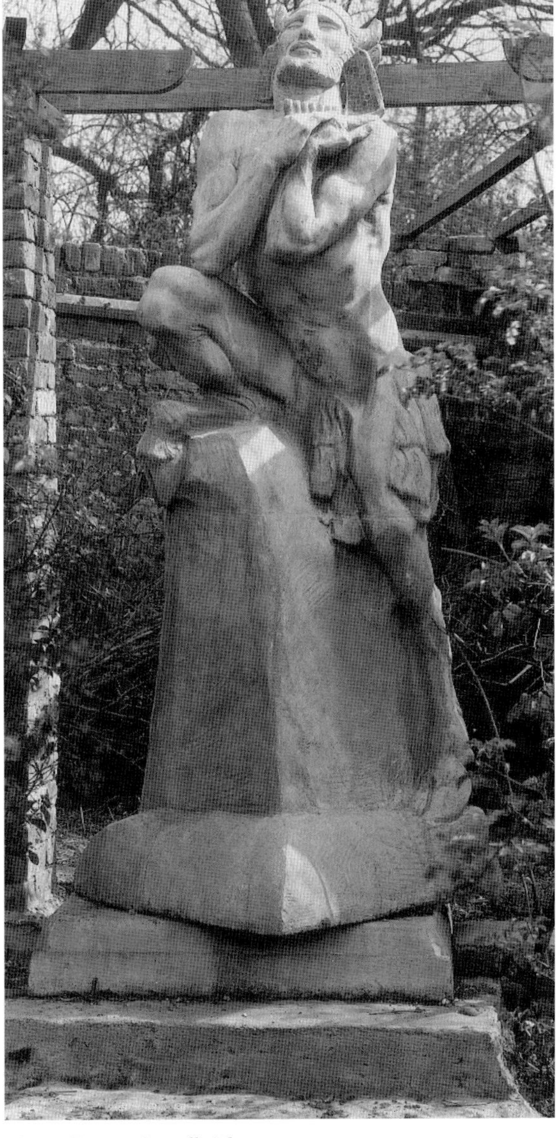

Great Pan at Greville Place

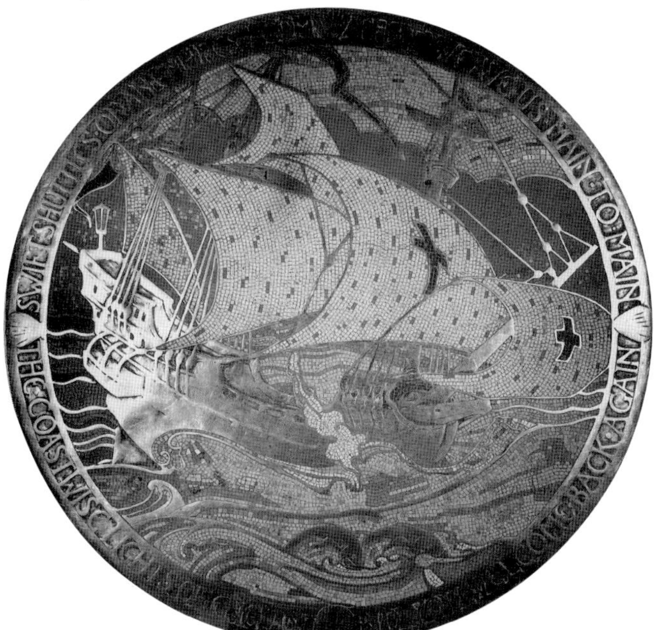

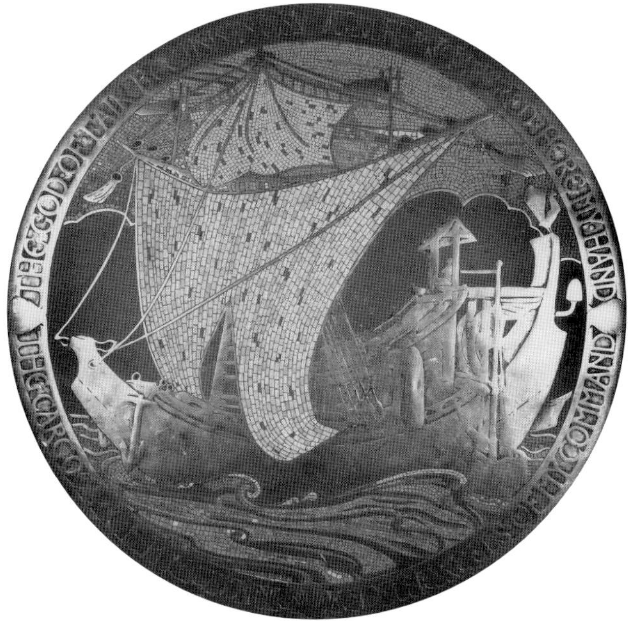

Ship Roundels for Selfridge's, London

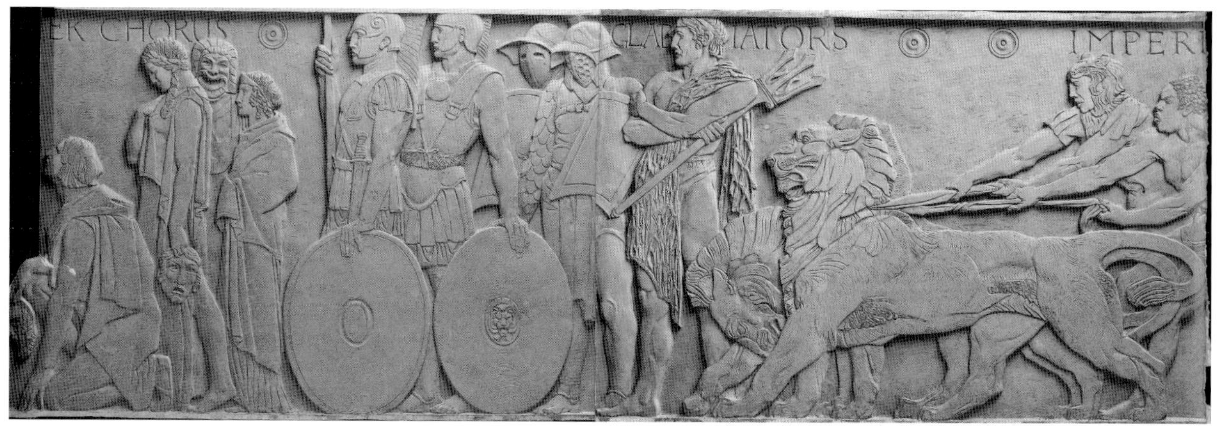

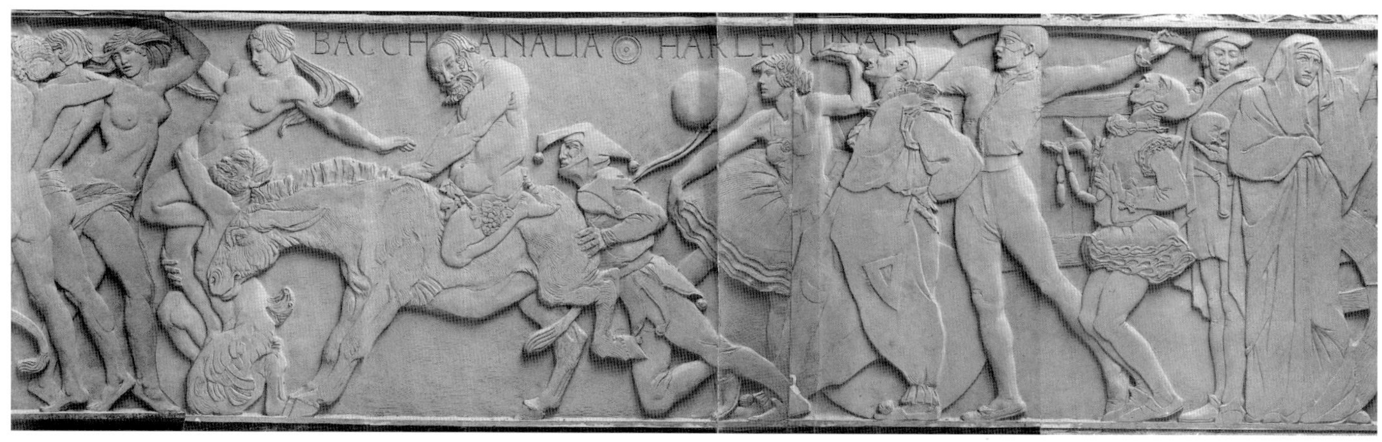

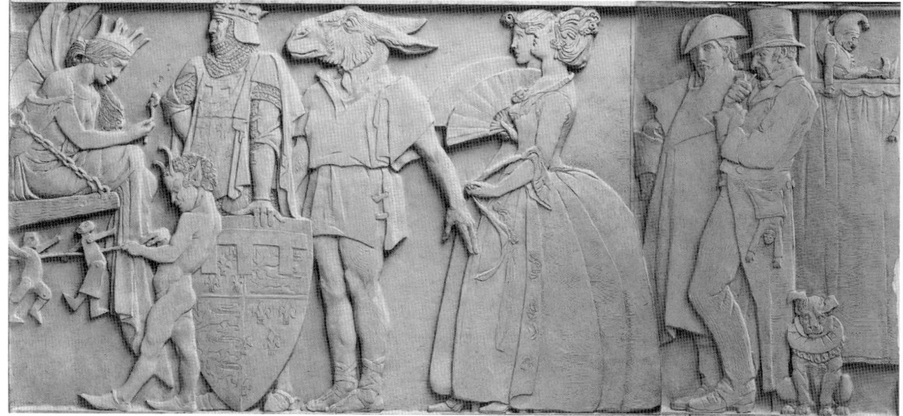

Sections of the full-size plaster models for the Drama Through the Ages frieze, Saville Theatre

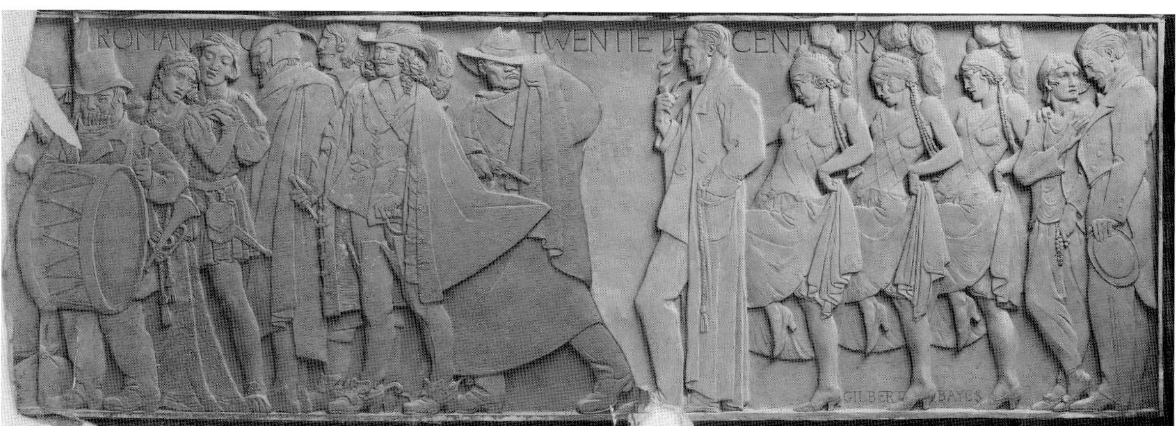

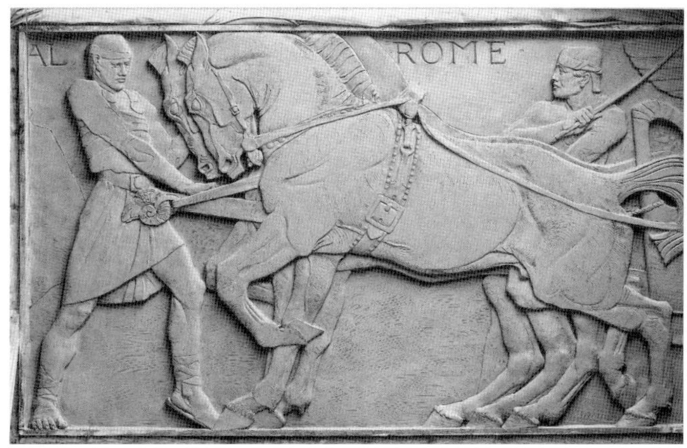

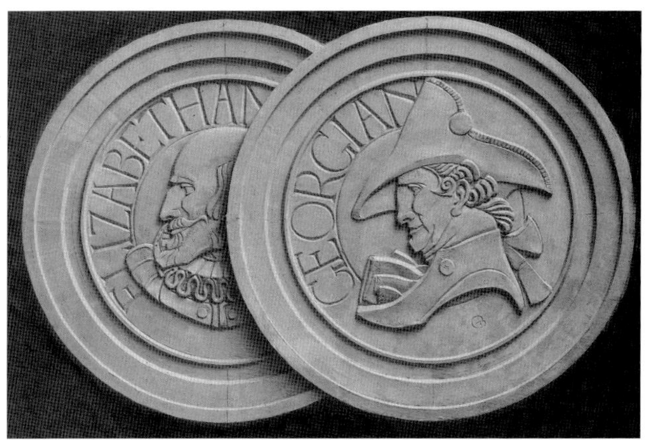

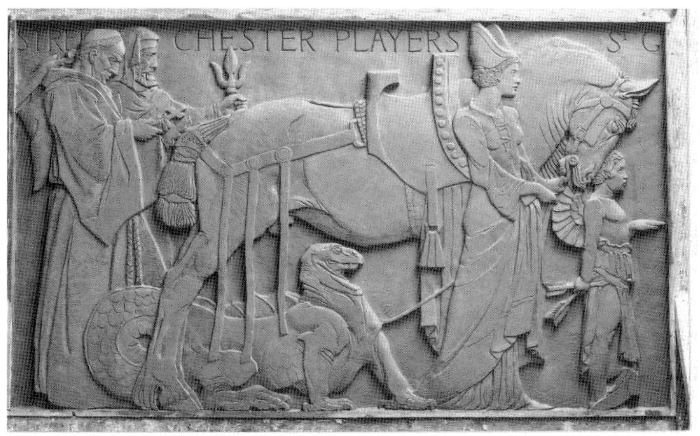

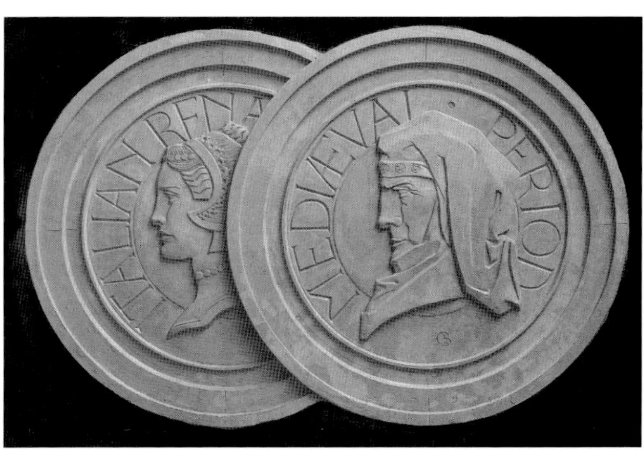

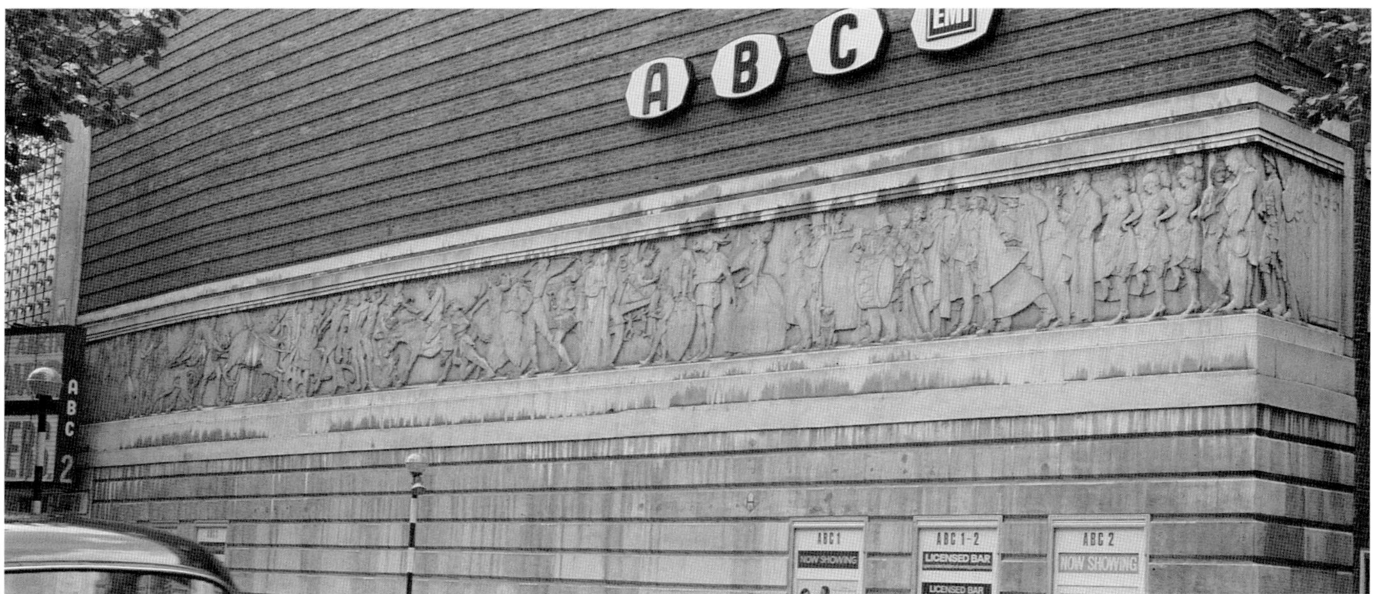

The former Saville Theatre, Shaftesbury Avenue, London

1930

Drama Through the Ages, Frieze and Roundels

Medium: Artificial stone
Size: H 6ft L 120ft (1.83 x 36.5m)
Exhibitions: Royal Academy 1930 and 1931 (models). Bayes was awarded the RBS Silver Medal for this work.
Locations: Saville Theatre, Shaftesbury Avenue, London, now a cinema. Architect T.P. Bennett.
Literature: *Art News* 1930, illus; *The Architect and Building News* 1930 May p601, illus; *The Builder* 1930 May p888, illus; *The Architect and Building News* 1931 Jul p33, Aug p238, illus; *The Builder* 1931 May pp828, 835 Sep pp370, 585, illus; *The Artist* 1934 Sep p12, illus.

Frank Ransome assisted Bayes with this scheme.

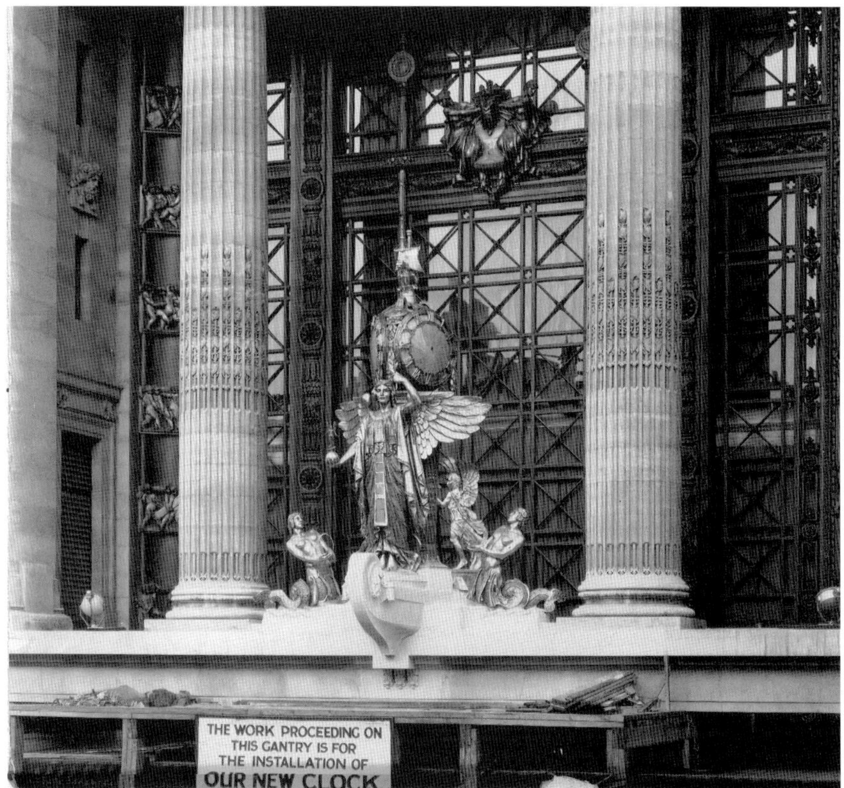

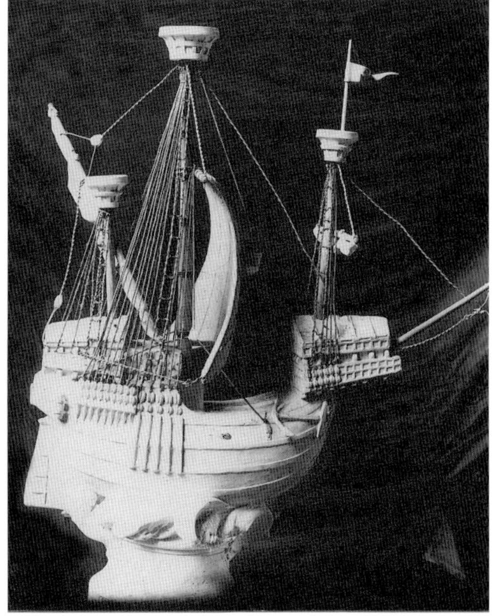

Maquette of ship for the Queen of Time clock

The Queen of Time Clock

Medium: Bronze, gold inlaid with Doulton stoneware
Size: 11ft (3.35m)
Locations: Selfridge's, Oxford Street, London. The clock was included in plans of
1926, approved 1930 and completed in 1931.
Literature: *The Builder* 1931 May p789, illus; *The Artist* 1934 Nov p79 and 80, illus;
Decorative Arts Society Journal 1980 p10, illus.

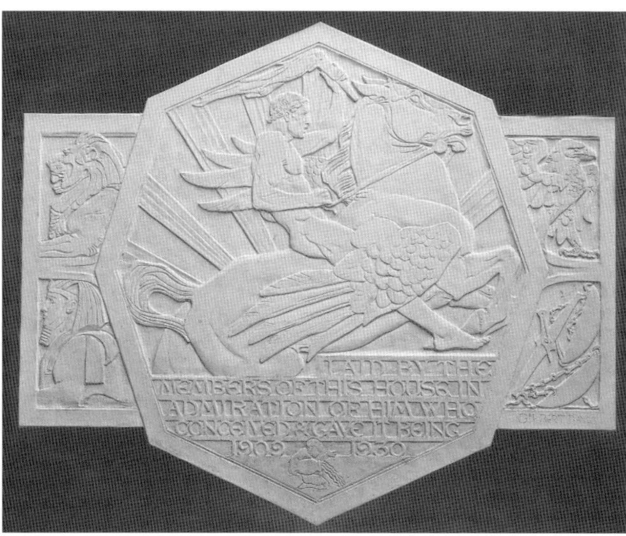

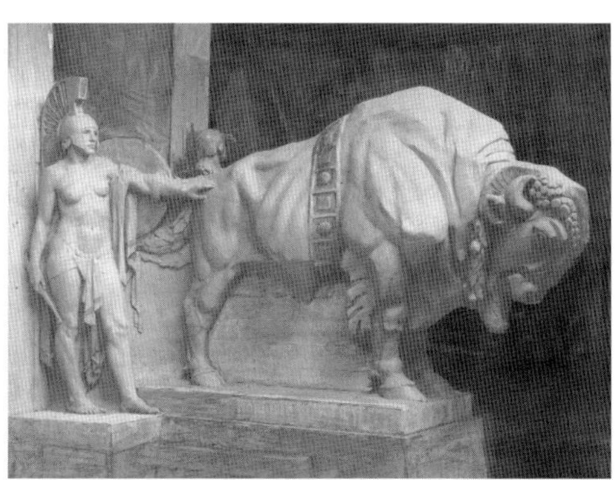

Plaster of colossal Bison

Pegasus Floor Panel

Medium: Plaster model for bronze panel
Size: H 53ins W 62½ins (135 x 159cms)
Locations: Entrance to Selfridge's, Oxford Street, London. Inscribed 'Laid by the
members of this house in admiration of him who conceived and gave it
being 1909-1930'.
Literature: *The Builder* Dec 1930 p103, illus.

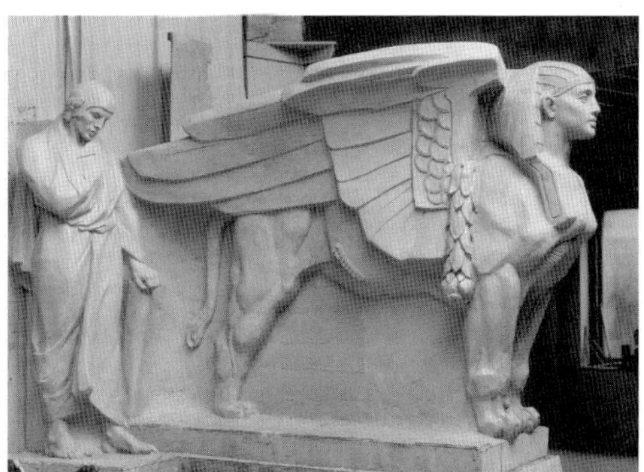

Plaster of colossal Winged Sphinx

The Four Winds

Medium: Plaster
Literature: *The Artist* 1934 October p46, illus., (*Bison*)

These colossal groups were originally designed as part of a scheme for a tower on
Selfridge's store in the 1920s. Owing to planning difficulties, this was never constructed.

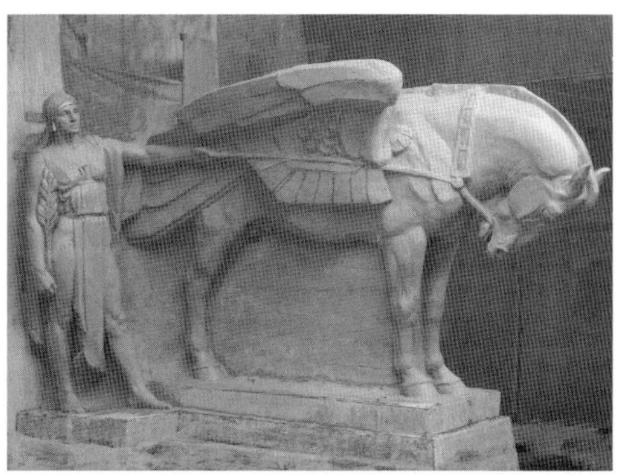

Plaster of colossal Pegasus

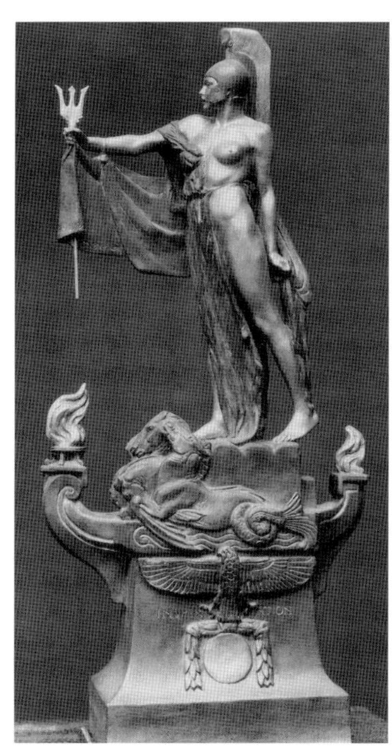

Plaster maquette for Segrave Trophy

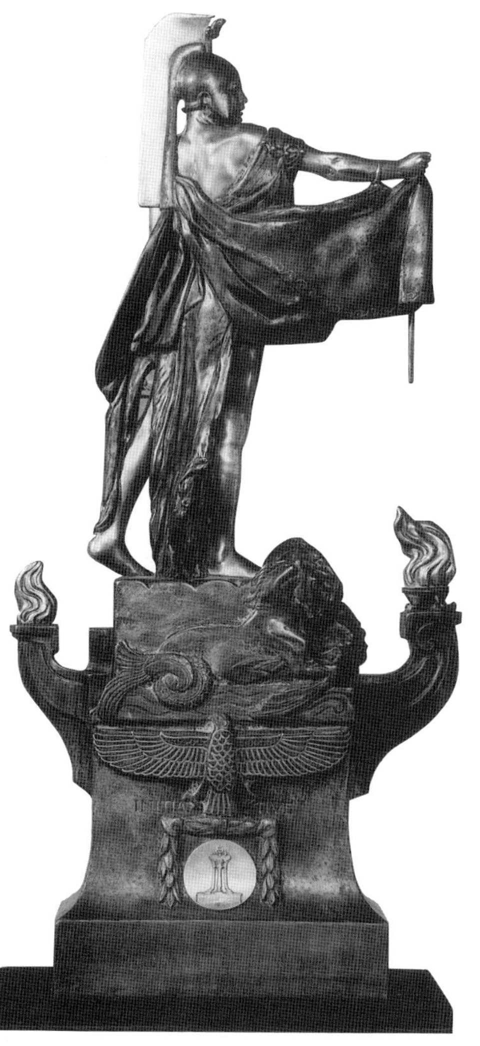
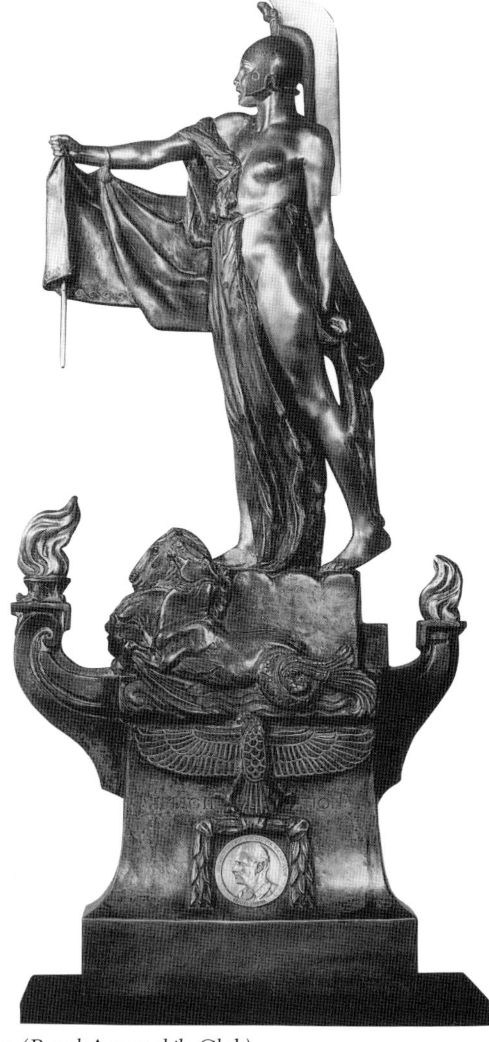

Segrave Trophy back and front (Royal Automobile Club)

Segrave Medal

Medium: Silvered bronze
Exhibitions: Commissioned by the Royal Automobile Club in honour of Henry O'Neil de Hane Segrave (1896-1930) the holder of the land speed record 1927-31.
Locations: British Museum; private collections.
Literature: *The Numismatic Chronicle* 1992 pl 25, illus.

The Segrave Trophy and Plaque

Medium: Bronze and gold
Size: Plaster H 28ins (71cms)
Exhibitions: Royal Academy 1932
Locations: Trophy Royal Automobile Club, Pall Mall awarded since 1930; private collection (polychrome plaster) ex Fine Art Society 1990.
Literature: *Apollo* 1932 Vol 15 p256, illus; *The Builder* 1932 p834, illus; *The Numismatic Chronicle* 1992, pl 24, illus.

This trophy was based on the statue, *England My Mother*. The trophy remains at the Royal Automobile Club and annual winners are awarded a Segrave plaque. Up to six medals are awarded to persons associated with the winner of the trophy in the award-winning performance.

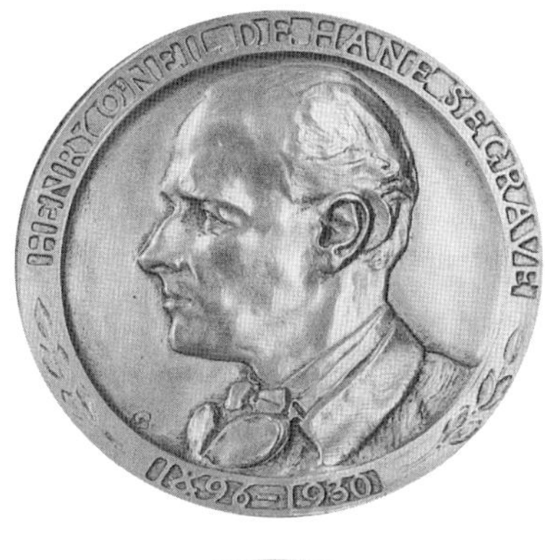
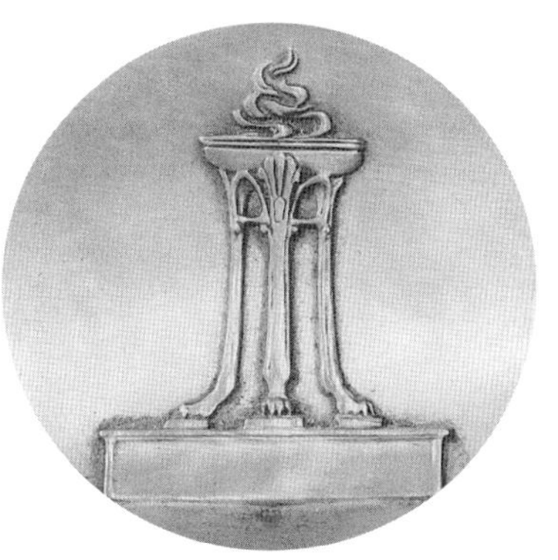

Segrave Medal

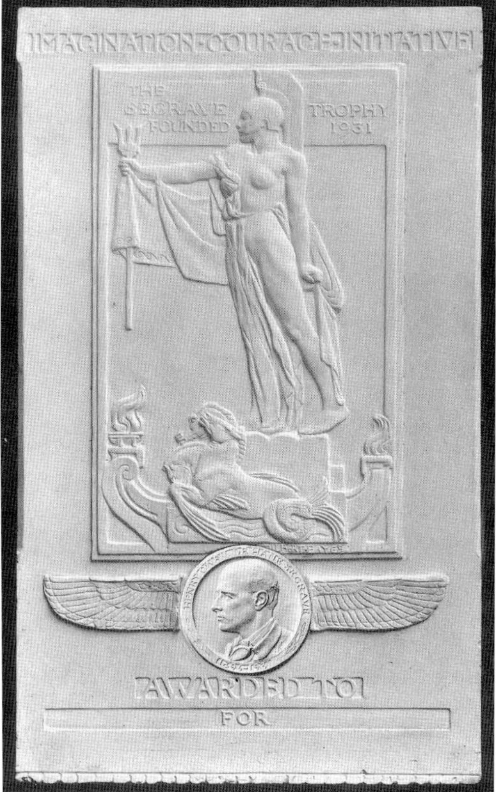

Segrave plaque

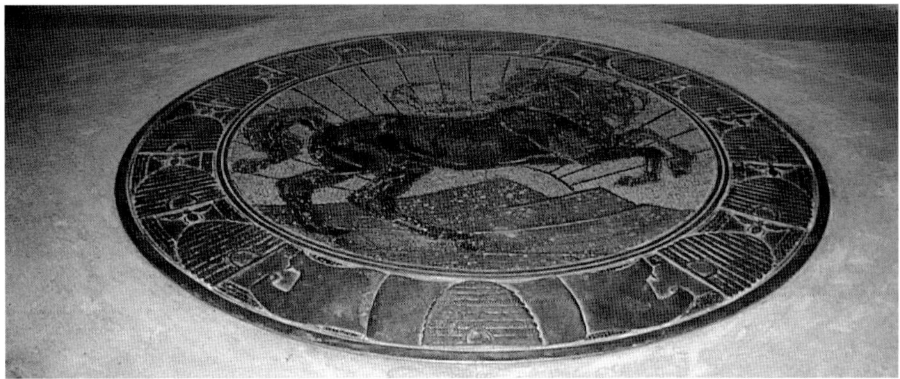

Black Horse floor medallion

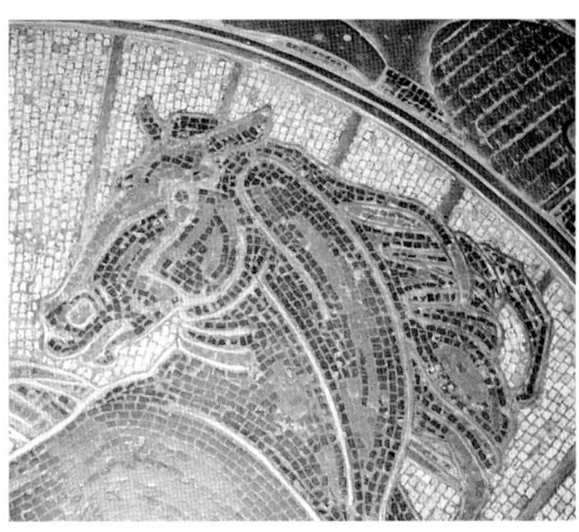

Detail of Black Horse roundel

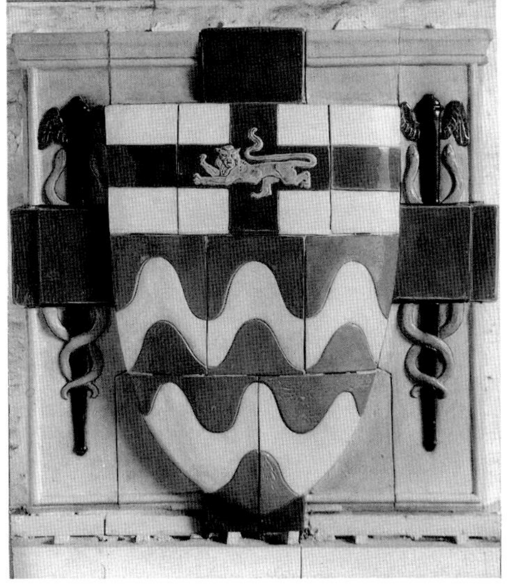

Heraldic panels

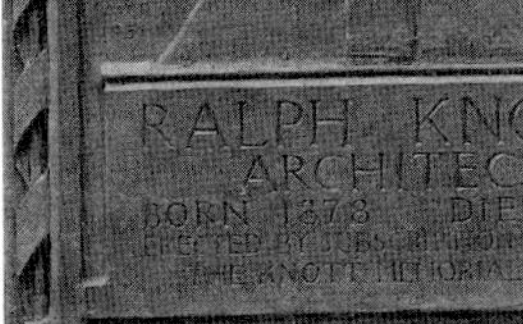

Ralph Knott

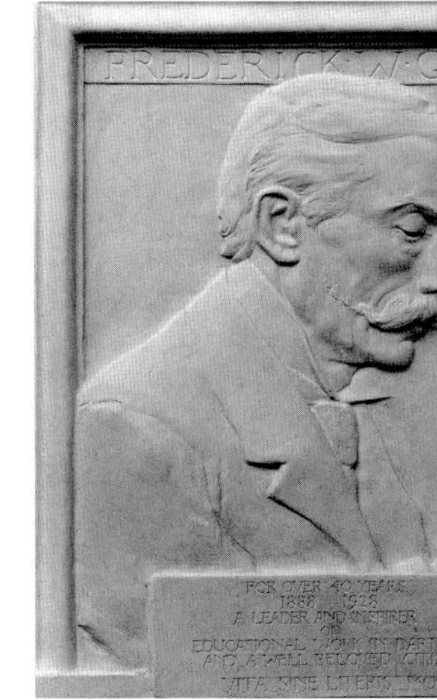

Frederick W. Gill

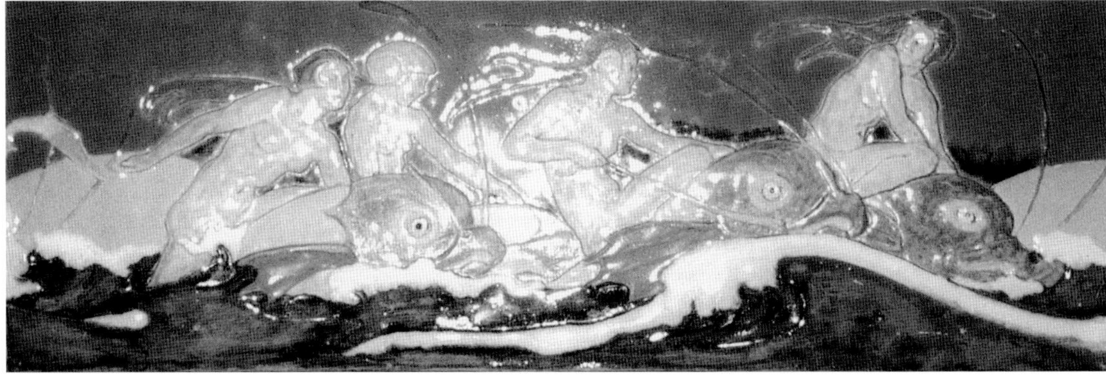

Water Nymphs

Ralph Knott, 1878-1929

Medium: Bronze panel
Exhibitions: Royal Academy 1932
Locations: Courtyard of County Hall, London. Erected by
              subscription through the Knott Memorial Fund,
              (now removed).
Literature: *The Builder* 1932 May p837 and Jun p1042, illus;
              The Artist 1934 Dec p127, illus.
Ralph Knott was the architect of London's County Hall.

Heraldic Panels

Medium: Doulton stoneware
Locations: South East London Technical College, (now
              Lewisham College) Lewisham Way, London SE4.
S. Nicholson Babb also designed some panels for this building.

Frederick W. Gill JP, d.1928

Medium: Bronze
Frederick Gill was an educationalist in Dartford, Kent.

Black Horse Floor Medallion

Medium: Bronze and mosaic
Size: D 8ft (2.44m)
Locations: Lloyds Bank, 17 Lombard Street, London. The
              architects Sir John Burnet and Partners were awarded the
              London architecture medal for this building in 1932.
Literature: *The Architect and Building News* 1930 Aug p142, illus.
The black horse and the beehive are the traditional symbols of Lloyds Bank.

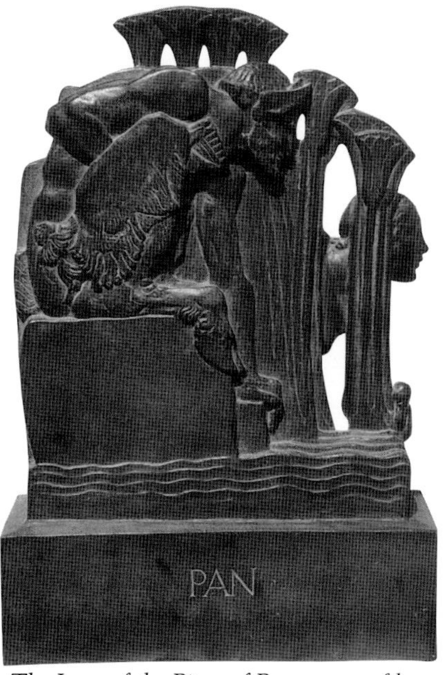

The Lure of the Pipes of Pan, verso of bronze

Water Nymphs
Medium: Doulton stoneware
Locations: Private collection
This was based on an earlier metal relief.

1932
Casket
Medium: Bronze
Locations: Royal Masonic Hospital,
Ravenscourt Park, London,
unveiled 1932
Literature: *The Artist* 1934 Nov p78, illus.
The book of donors was illuminated by Jessie
Bayes.

The Lure of the Pipes of Pan
Medium: Artificial stone statue
Size: H 54ins W 42ins (137 x
106.5cms)
Exhibitions: Royal Academy 1933 (purchased
Cadbury 200gns)
Locations: Birmingham Art Gallery; Bayes
Trust.
Literature: *The Builder* 1933 May p800,
illus; *The Artist* 1935 Feb p191,
illus; *The Studio* 1938 Vol 115
p301, illus; 'Sculpture of Today'
Studio Special Spring 1939 p80;
Modern British Sculpture, RBS
1939 p3, illus; *The Last Romantics*,
J. Christian 1989 p148.

The Lure of the Pipes of Pan
Medium: Bronze statuette on integral base
Size: H 17ins (43cms)
Locations: Bayes Trust (plaster maquette and
bronze)
Although dated 1933, this group was
designed in 1932.

Mother and Child
Medium: Bronze
Size: 9ins (23cms)
Locations: Private collection

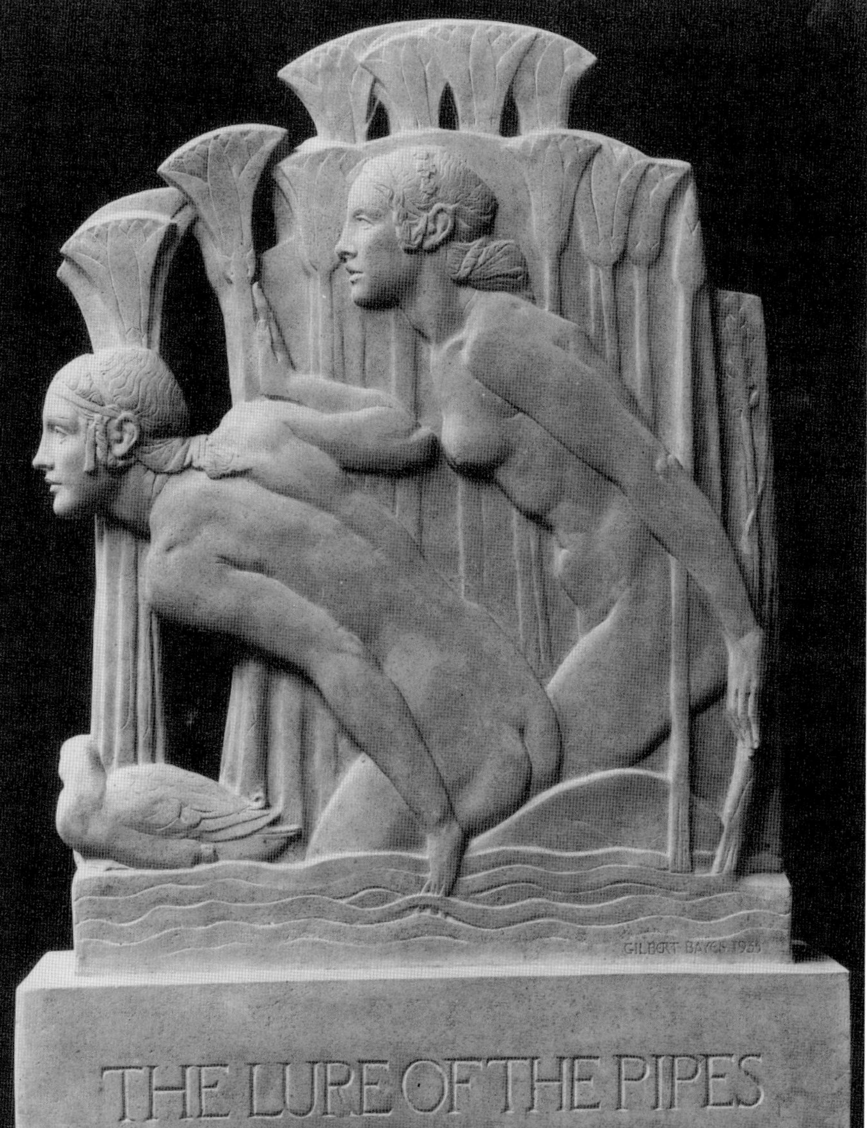

The Lure of the Pipes of Pan

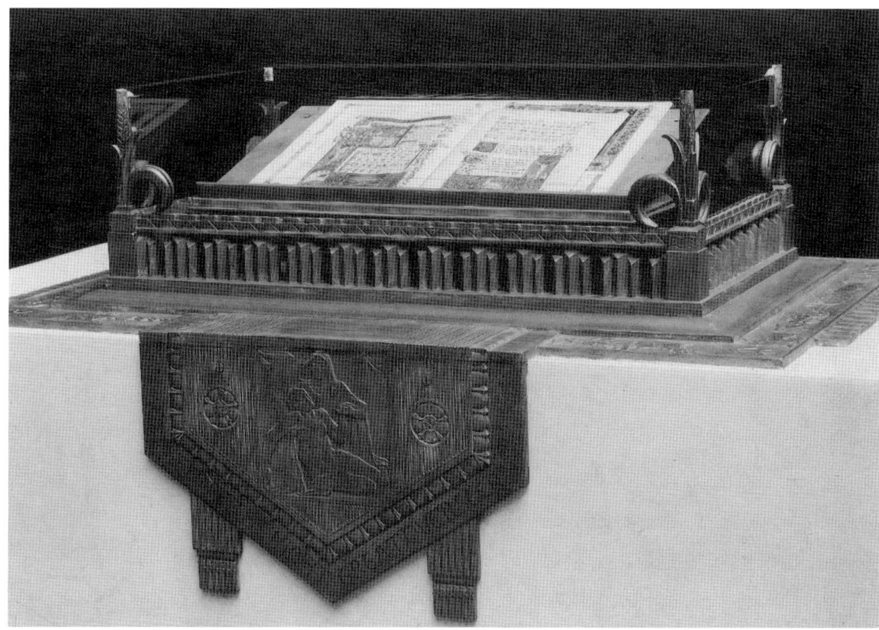

Casket

Gilbert Bayes

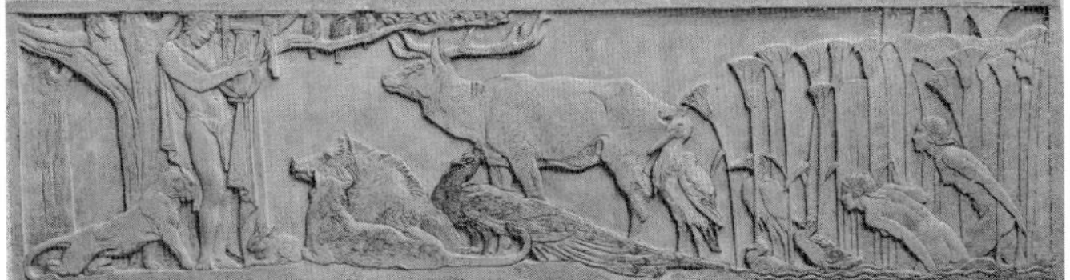

Music

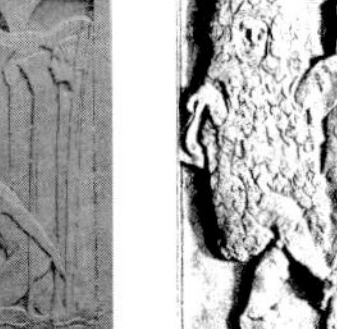

The Country Dance

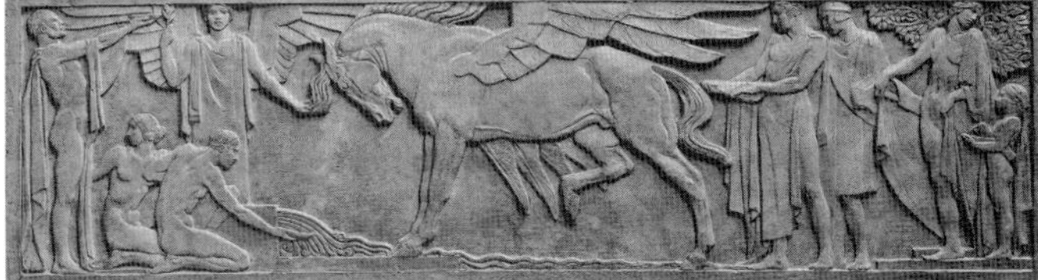

Poetry

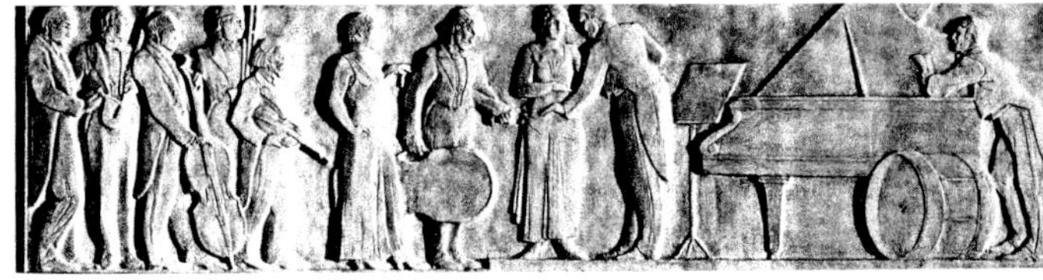

Music

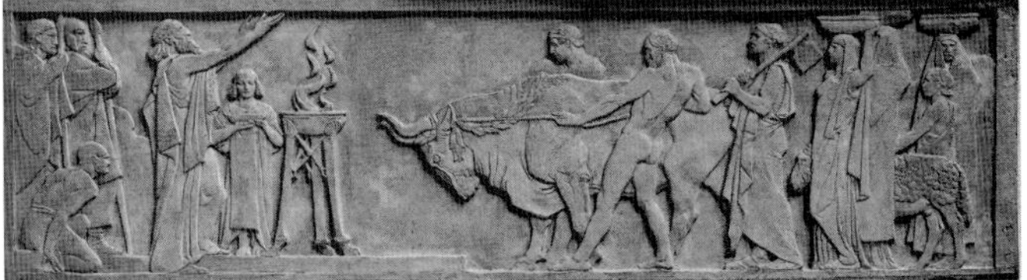

Sacrifice

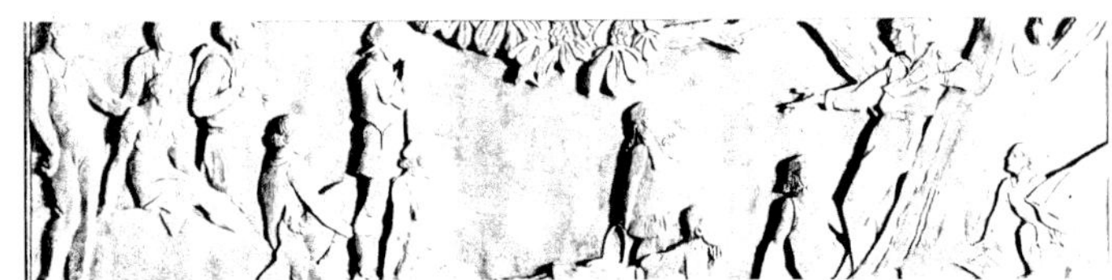

The Spoken Word

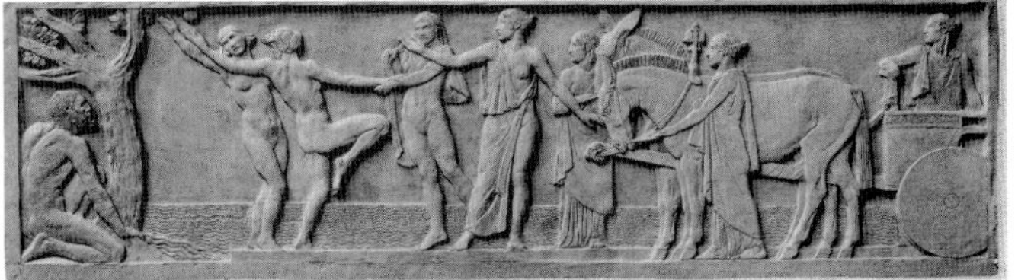

Ball Game

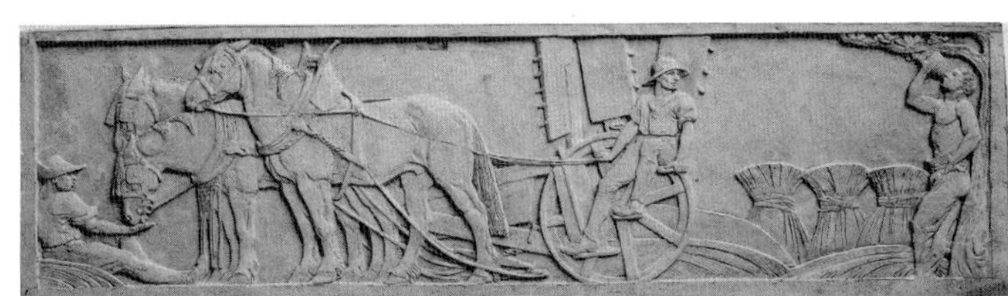

Harvest

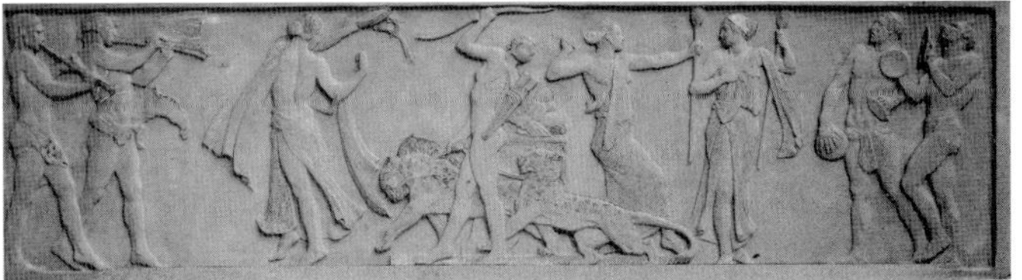

Dance

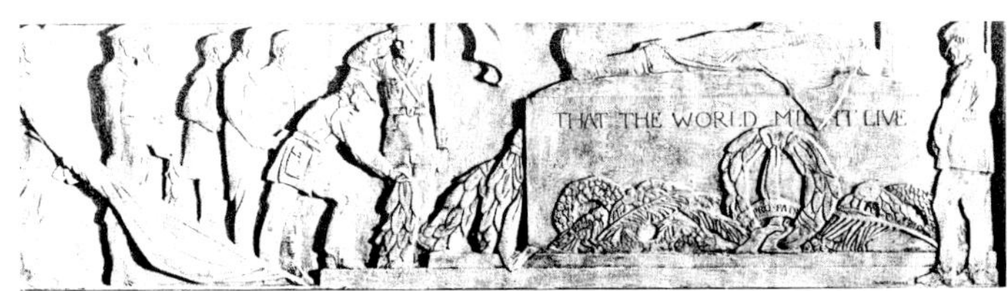

Worship/Sacrifice

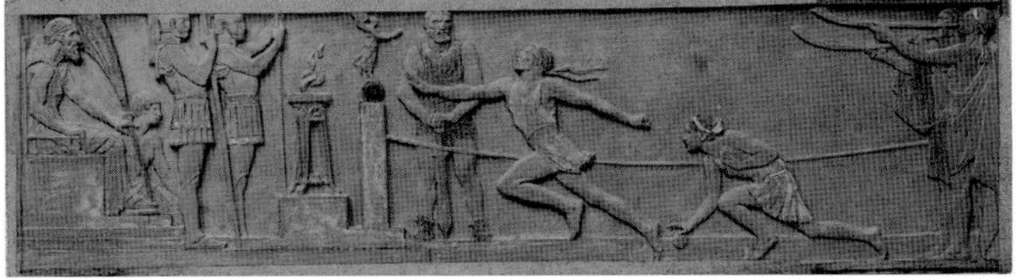

Foot Race

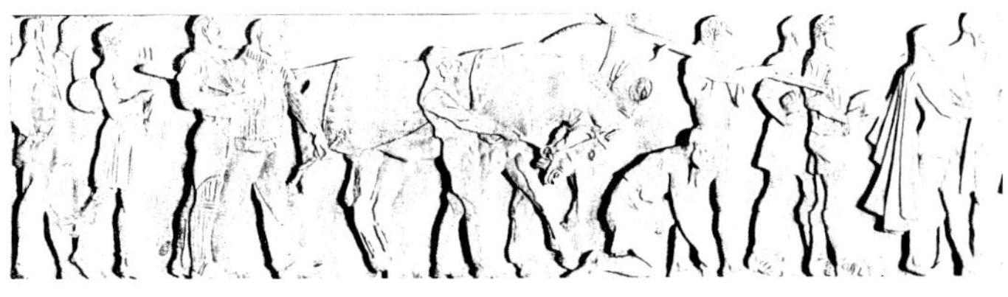

Games

Relief Panels, Classic and Modern Subjects

Medium: Coloured plaster
Size: H 24¹/₂ins W 81ins (62 x 206cms)
Locations: BBC Concert Hall, now Radio Theatre, Portland Place, London; Bayes Trust (plaster maquette of *Music* and *Sacrifice* in artificial stone).
Literature: *The Architect and Building News* 1932 May pp258-266
The first six classic panels were installed in 1932, the second six modern panels in 1934. The classic subjects are: Poetry, Dance, Ball Game, Sacrifice, Foot Race, Music. The modern subjects are Harvest, Country Dance, The Spoken Word, Worship/Sacrifice, Games, Music.

Wisdom

Medium: Doulton stoneware
Exhibitions: Institute (sold), Newcastle, Bristol 1932 (12gns); Sussex Arts, Aberdeen 1933 (8gns); Pastel Society 1934 (12gns); Southport 1934, 1938.

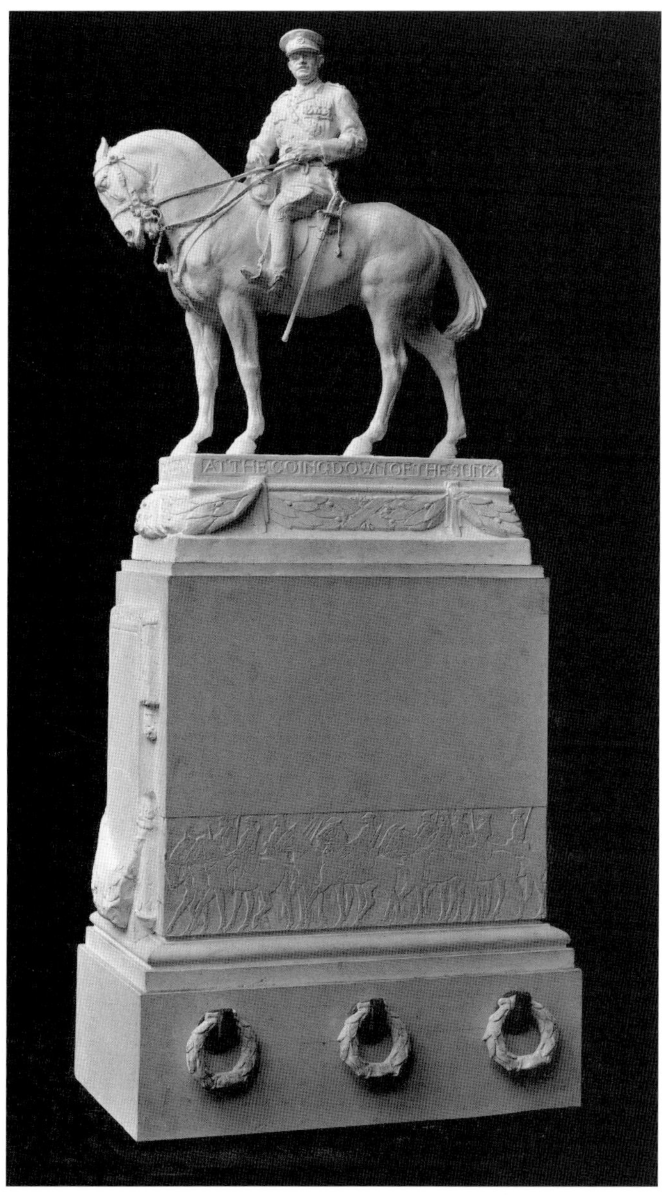

Haig Memorial, first version

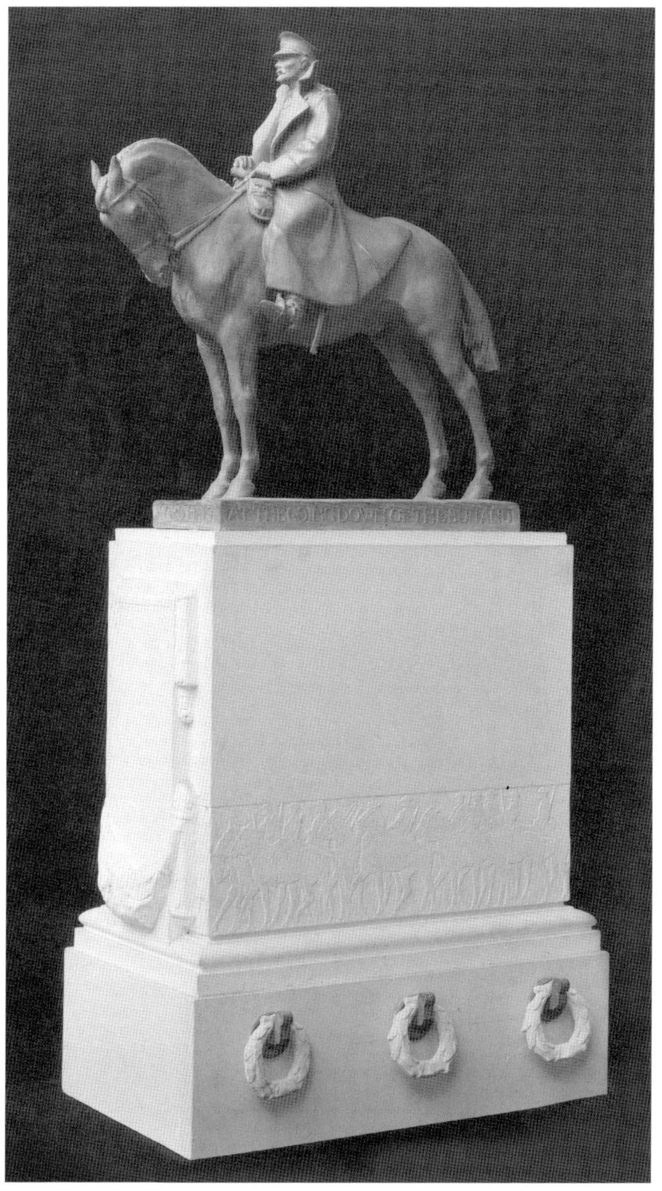

Haig Memorial, second version, with the figure inspired by the style of the Colonel Laurie figure

1933

Earl Haig, 1861-1928

Medium: Plaster
Size: H 2³/₄ins (59cms)
Locations: Bayes Trust

Bayes was not impressed with the horse in the Haig sculpture by Hardiman, the winner of the competition and so modelled his own interpretations. There are two versions of this model.

Royal Fusiliers Memorial

Medium: Bronze reliefs
Locations: Formerly All Souls,
                  Langham Place, London.
                  The church was bombed
                  during the Blitz in 1940 and
                  restored in 1975. The panel
                  was removed then and the
                  figures are now in a private
                  collection.

Dedicated to the 12th Services Battalion. The figures depict David and Jonathan.

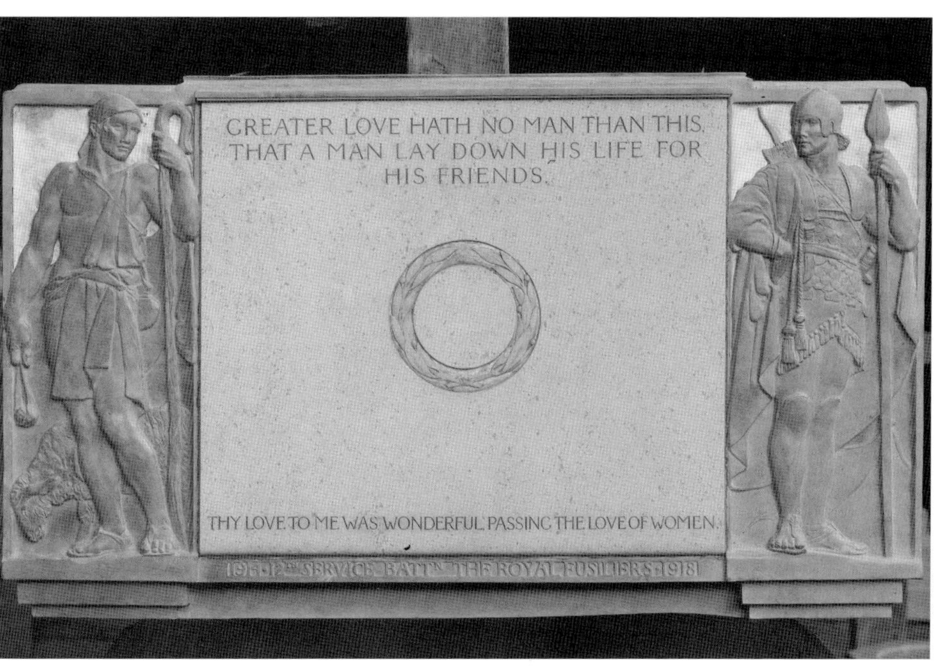

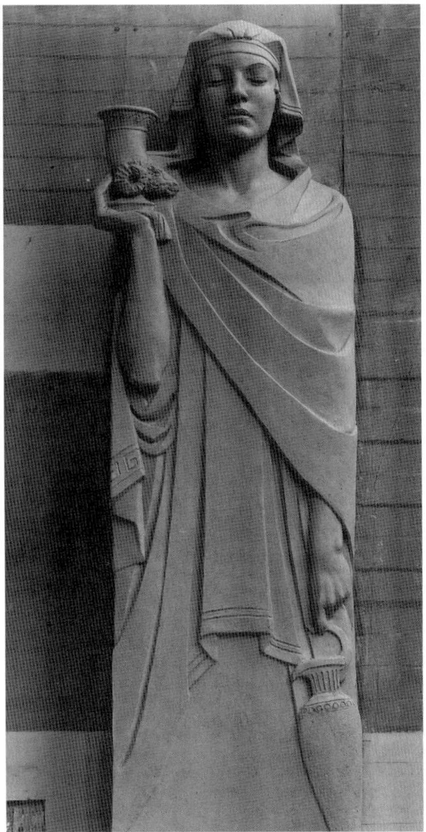
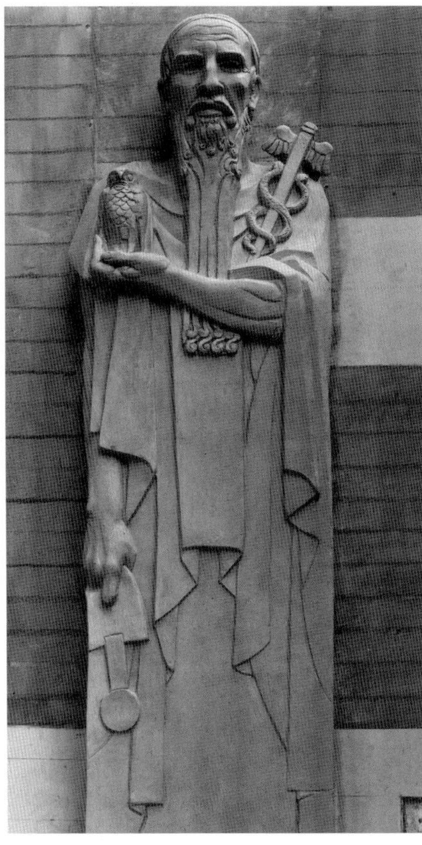

Hebe and Aesculapius

Hebe and Aesculapius
Medium: Carved concrete terminals
Size: 1^1/$_2$ times life-size
Locations: Royal Masonic Hospital, Ravenscourt Park.
             Architects Sir John Burnet, Tait and Lorne.
Literature: *The Builder* 1933 Aug p255, illus; *The Artist* 1934
             p12, illus.

Power
Medium: Bronze statuette
Exhibitions: Royal Academy 1933
Literature: *The Builder* 1933 May p803,
              illus.

Casket for Sir Edward Drummond
Medium: Wood and bronze with
              presentation scroll from
              Carpenter's Hall
Sir Edward Drummond was the first
Secretary General of the League of
Nations. He was granted an Honorary
Freedom by the Carpenter's Company on
11th October 1933.

L. Heath Jones
Medium: Bronze relief
L. Heath Jones was the founder of St
Monica's and was headmistress 1902-27.

A Sea Dream
Medium: Marble statuette
Exhibitions: Institute 1933 (£105); Bristol
              1934 (100gns).

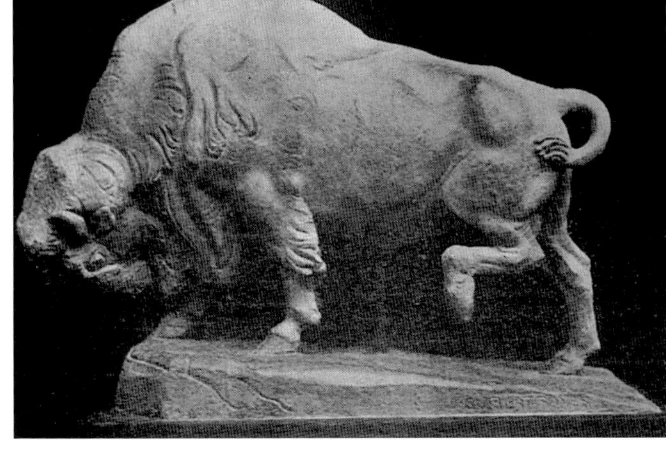

Power

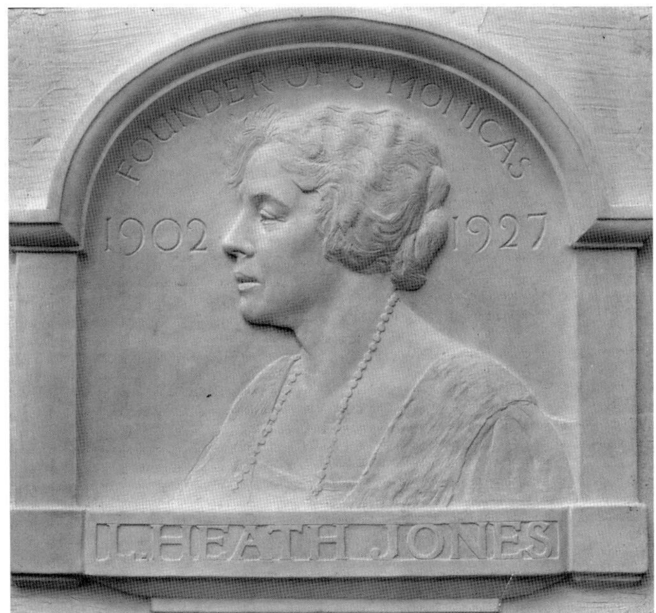

L. Heath-Jones

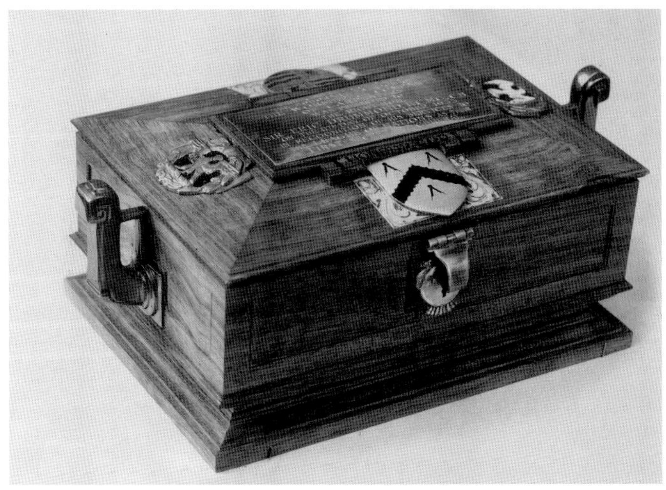

Drummond Casket

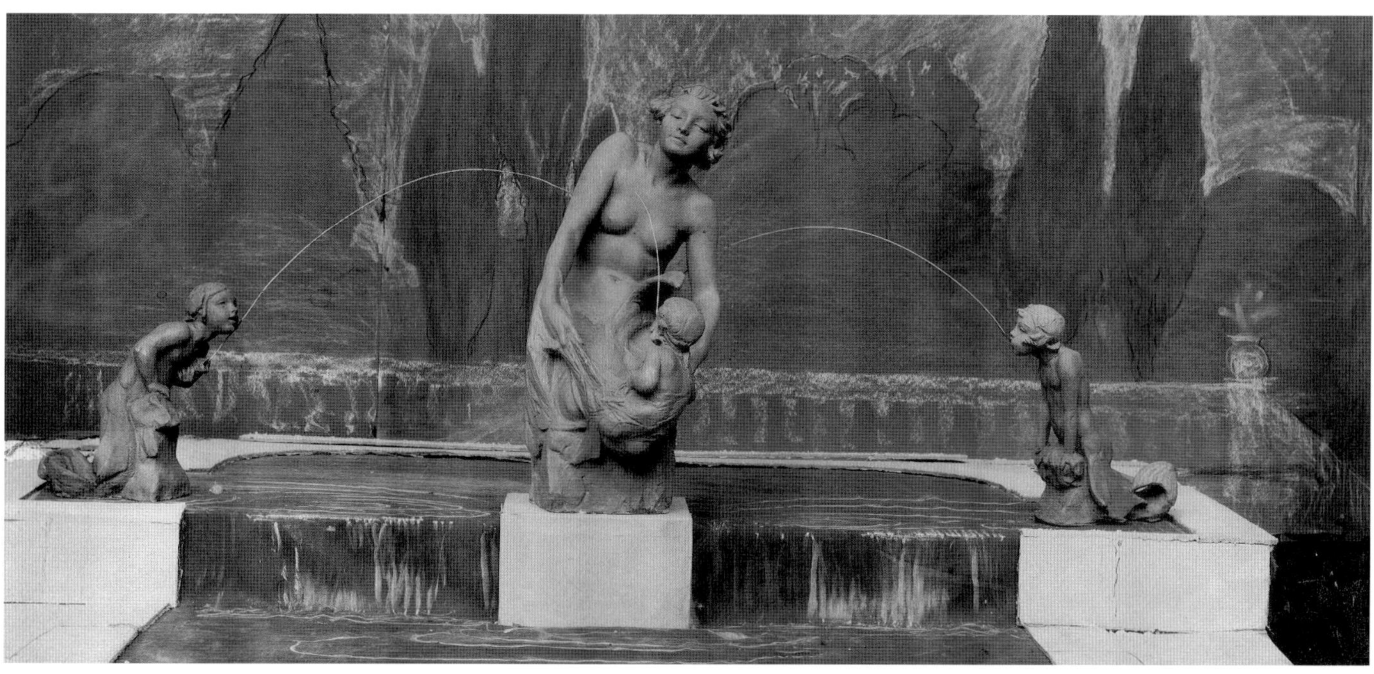

The Sea Urchin, in a typical Bayes invented garden setting

1934

The Sea Urchin
Medium: Plaster for bronze
Size: H 54ins (138cms)
Locations: Bayes Trust
Literature: *The Artist* 1934 Sep ed, illus.
Originally a small statuette, priced in 1934
at £54.10s, this was subsequently reworked
and enlarged as a garden concept.

The Water's Caress
Medium: Empire stone statue
Size: H 70ins (178cms)
Exhibitions: Royal Academy 1934; Royal
                 Scottish Academy 1935;
                 *Sculpture in Britain Between the
                 Wars*, Fine Art Society 1986.
Locations: Bayes Trust
Literature: *The Builder* 1934 Jun p929,
                 illus; *Sculpture in Britain
                 Between the Wars*, B. Read and
                 P. Skipwith 1986 p31, illus.

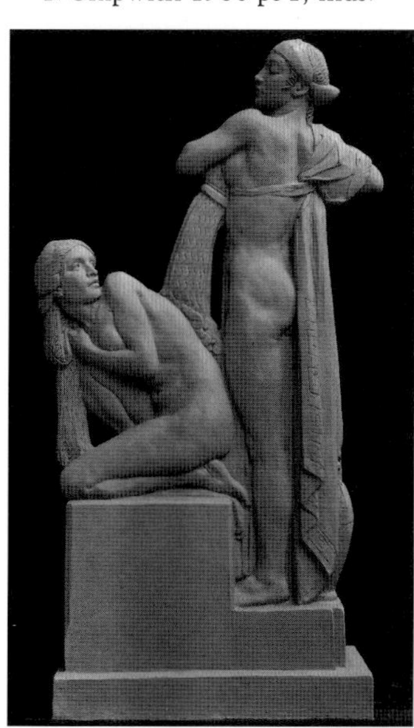

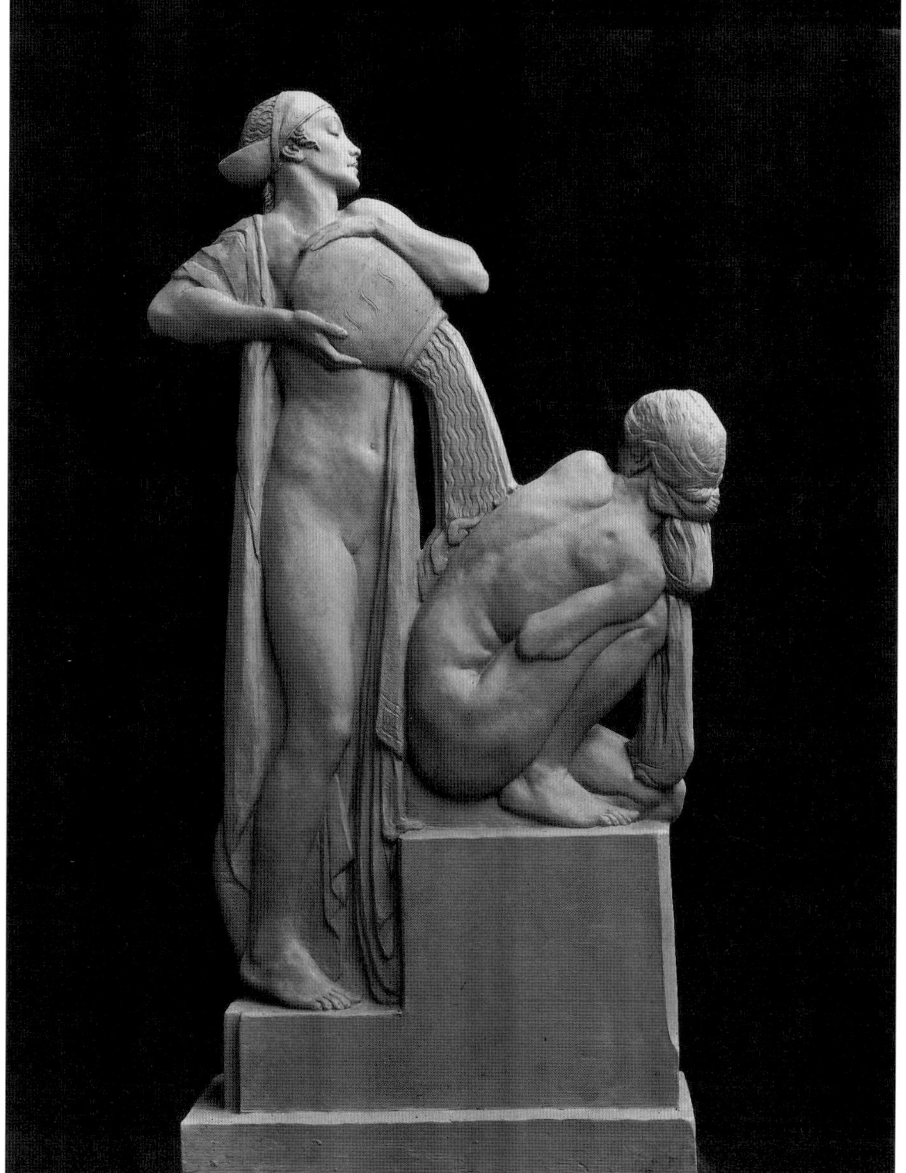

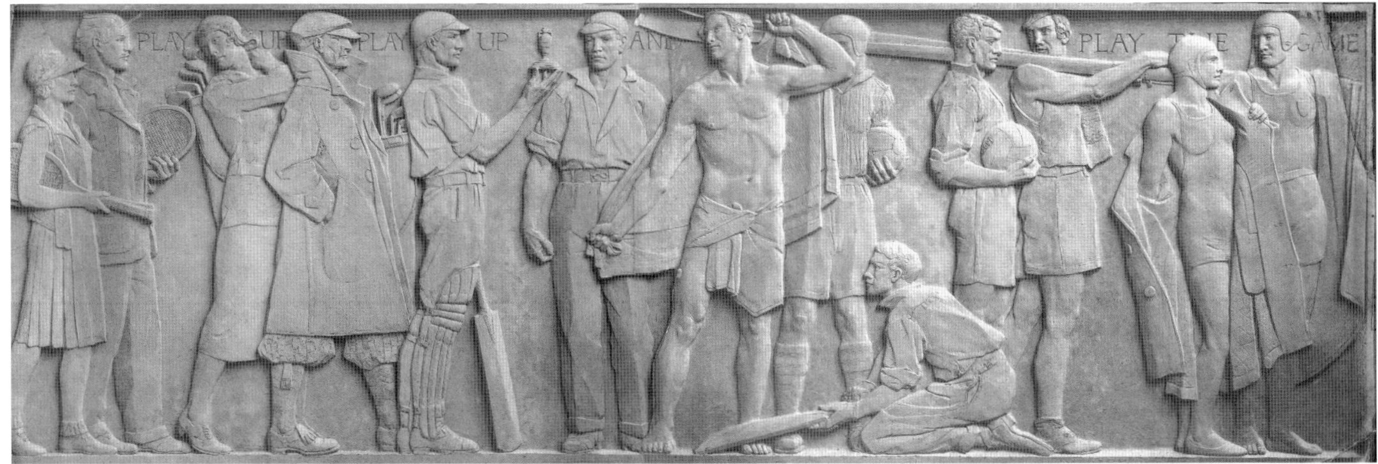

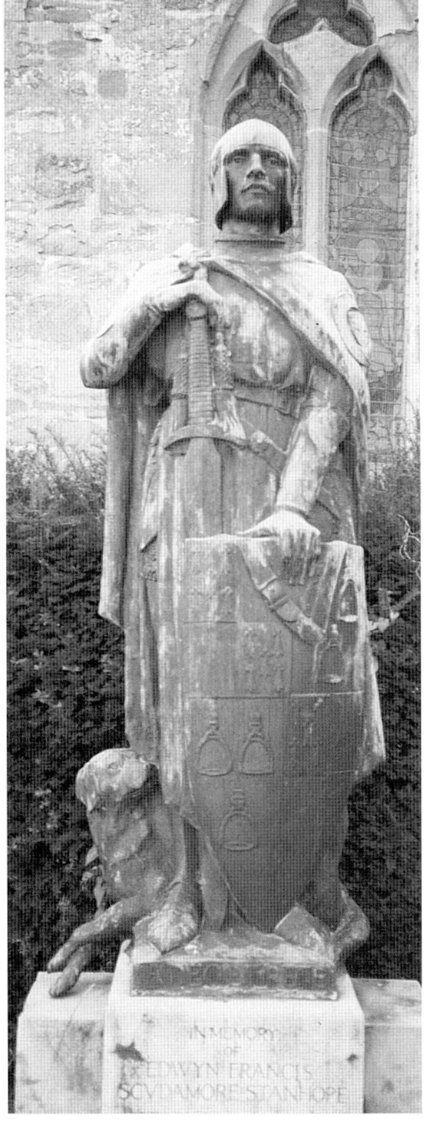

Memorial to the 10th Earl of Chesterfield, E.F. Scudamore-Stanhope, d.1933

Medium: Bronze figure
Size: Life-size
Exhibitions: Royal Academy 1934
Locations: St Cuthbert Churchyard,
             Holme Lacy, nr. Hereford
Literature: The Builder 1934 Jun p929,
             illus.

'Play up! Play up! and Play the Game'

Medium: Stone frieze
Exhibitions: Royal Academy 1934
Locations: Lords Cricket Ground,
             Wellington Road, St John's
             Wood Road, presented by
             Alderman Isaacs and unveiled
             July 1934.
Literature: The Architect and Building
             News 1934 Jul p91, illus.

The quotation in the title is from Henry Newbolt, commissioned as a tribute to all sportsmen.

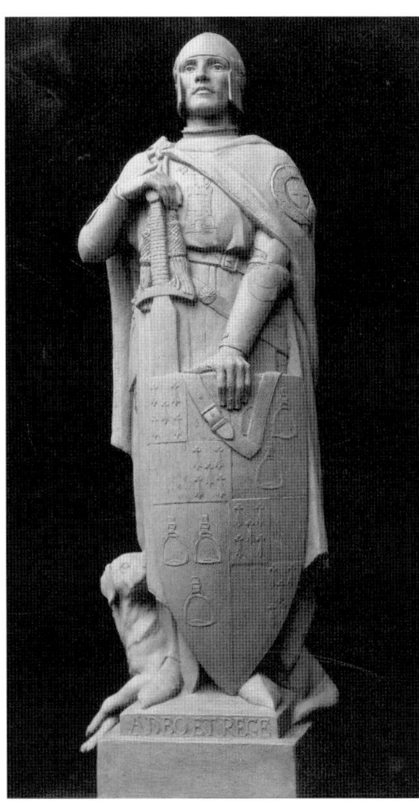

Plaster maquette for the Chesterfield Memorial

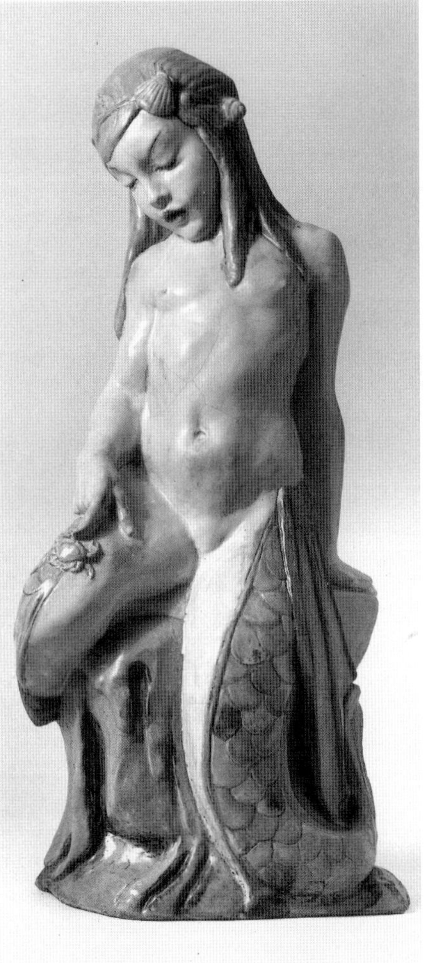

The Mermaid

Medium: Doulton stoneware statue
Size: H 32ins (80cms)
Exhibitions: Royal Society of Arts 1938
             (60gns)
Locations: Bayes Trust; another formerly
             at Sidney Street Estate,
             St Pancras, London.
Literature: The Artist 1934 Feb p192,
             illus; The Doulton Story, P.
             Atterbury & L. Irvine 1979
             p30, illus.

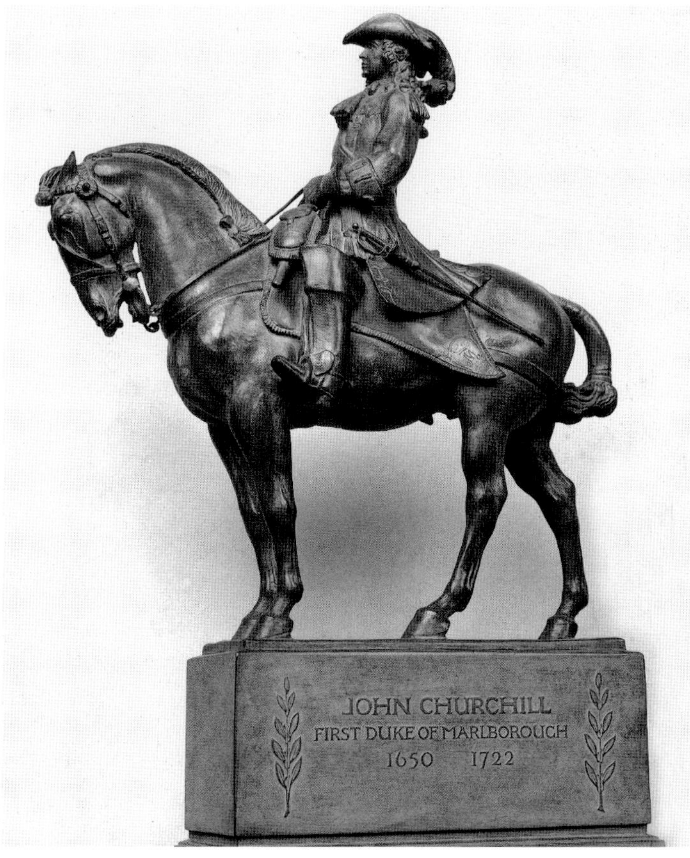

John Churchill, 1st Duke of Marlborough, 1650-1722
Medium: Bronze gilded statuette
Size: H 35ins (89cms)
Exhibitions: Royal Academy, Liverpool 1935; Glasgow 1936; Institute 1939 (150gns); Royal Academy Winter 1940; Russia 1942 (150gns).
Locations: Bayes Trust
Literature: *Modern Sculpture RBS* 1939 p2, illus; *The Studio* 1946 Vol 32 Jul p83, illus.

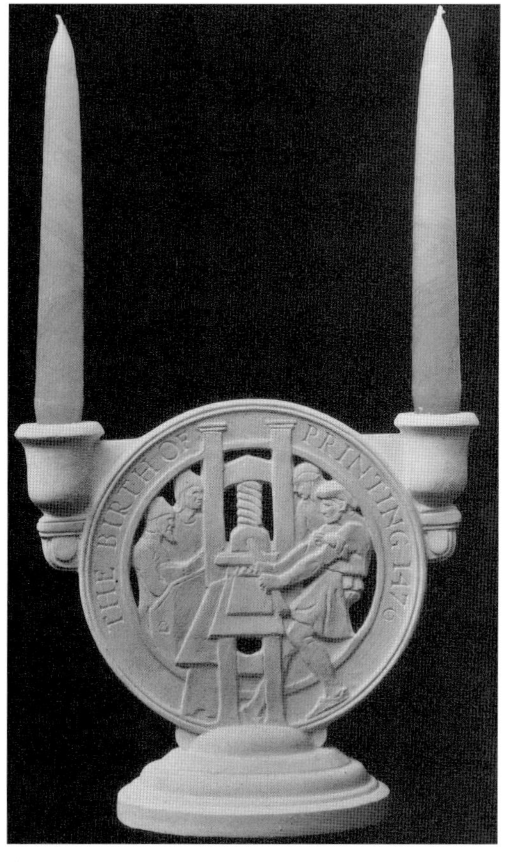

1935
The Birth of Printing, 1476
Medium: Doulton stoneware
Size: H 8ins (19cms)
Locations: Bayes Trust; private collection.
The candlestick was made for Allied Newspapers.

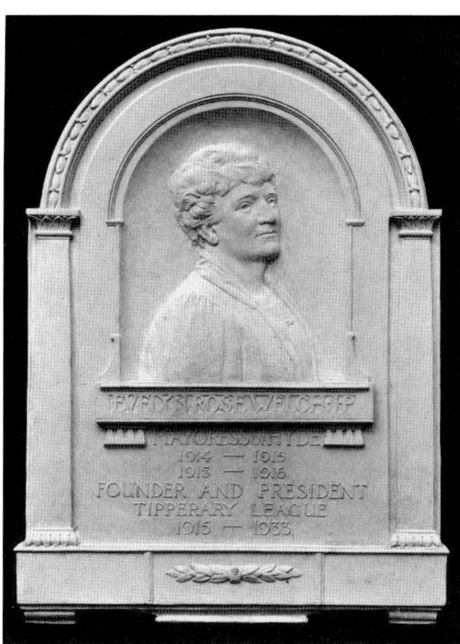

Evelyn Rose Welch JP
Medium: Plaster for bronze panel
Locations: Hyde Town Hall, Hyde
Evelyn Welch was Mayoress of Hyde in 1933 and founder and president of the Tipperary League.

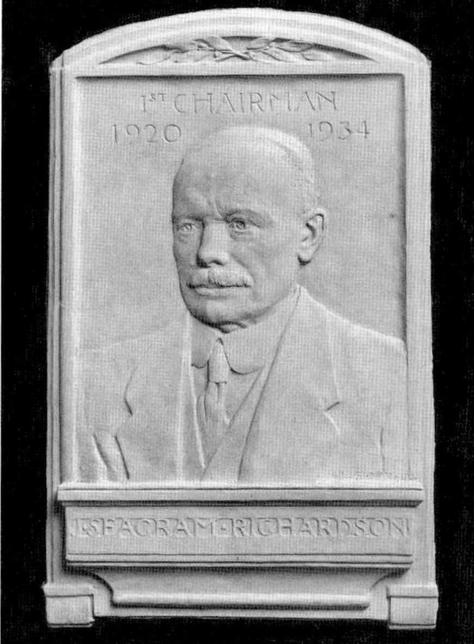

J. Seagram Richardson
Medium: Plaster for bronze
Size: H 30ins W 18ins (76 x 46.5cms)

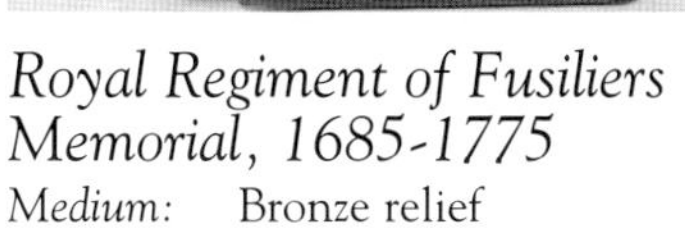

Royal Regiment of Fusiliers Memorial, 1685-1775
Medium: Bronze relief

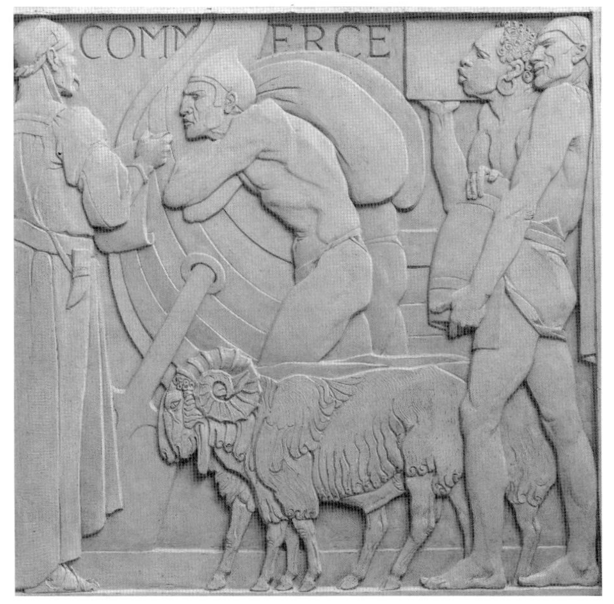

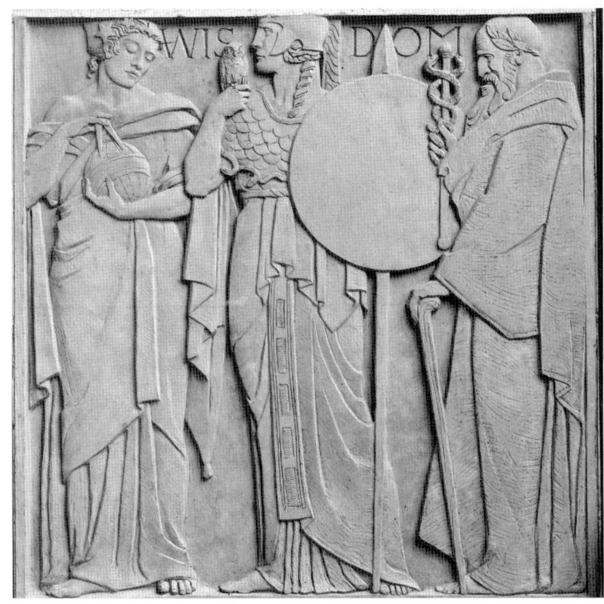

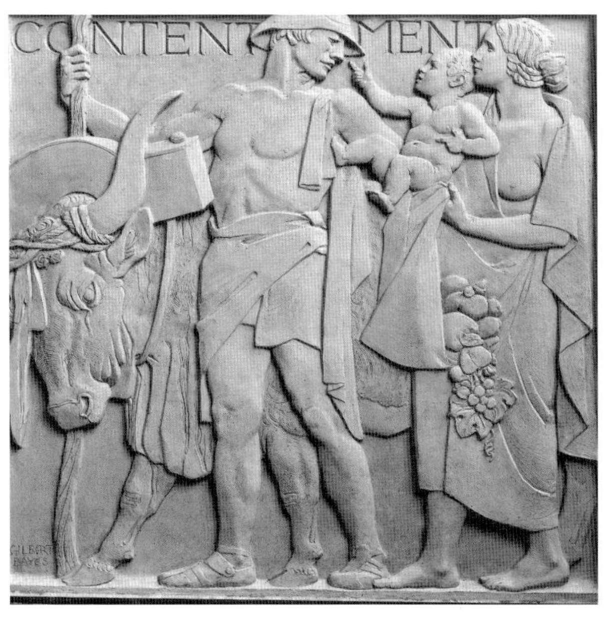

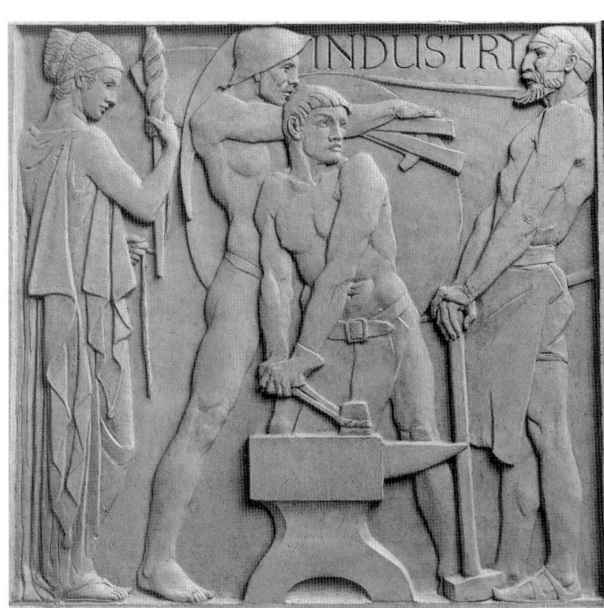

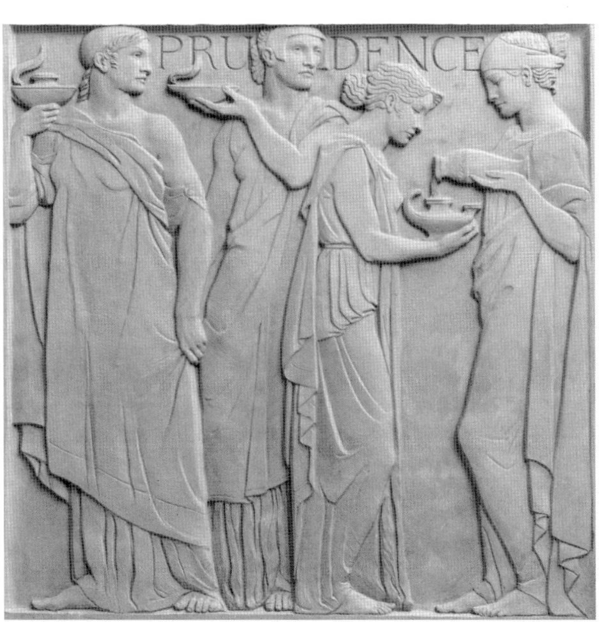

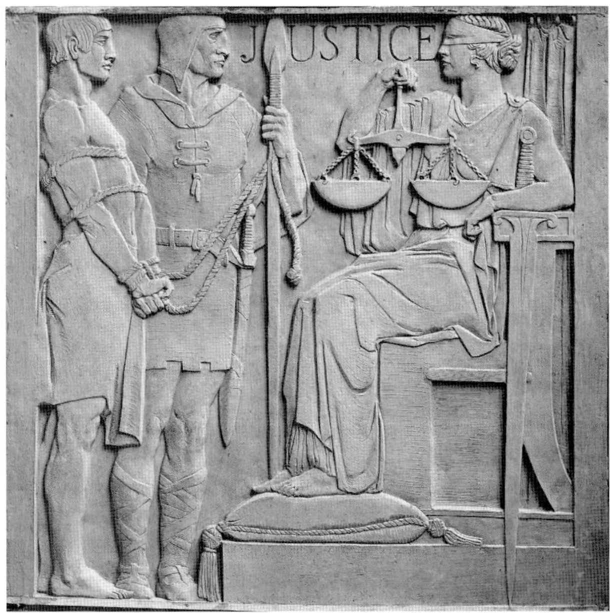

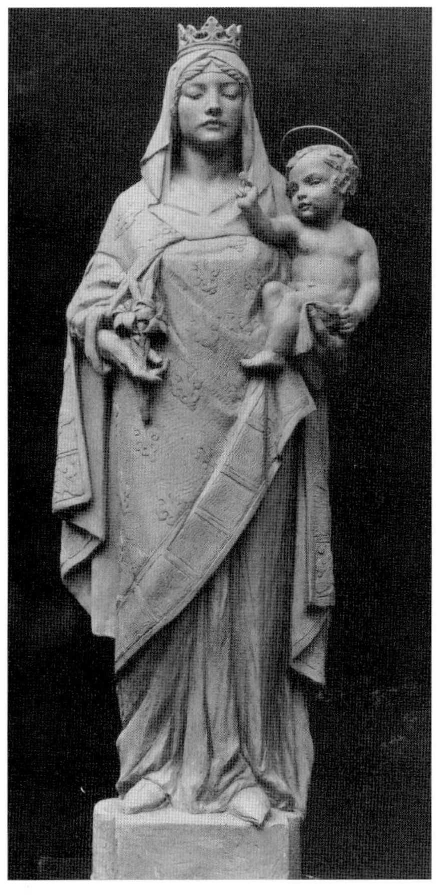

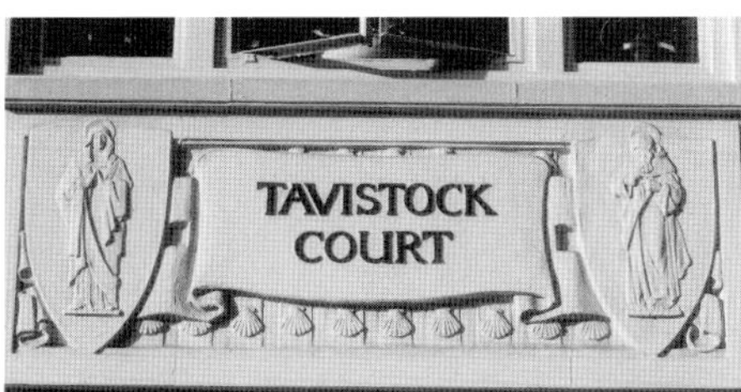

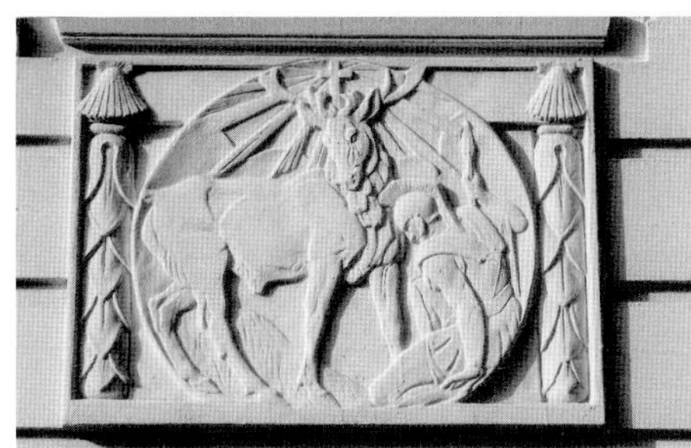

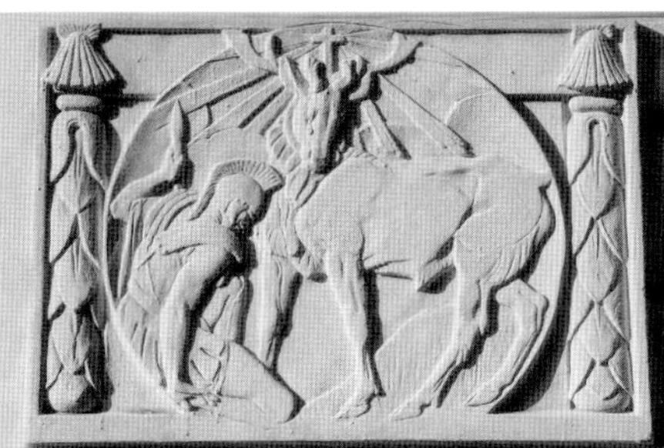

Madonna and Child

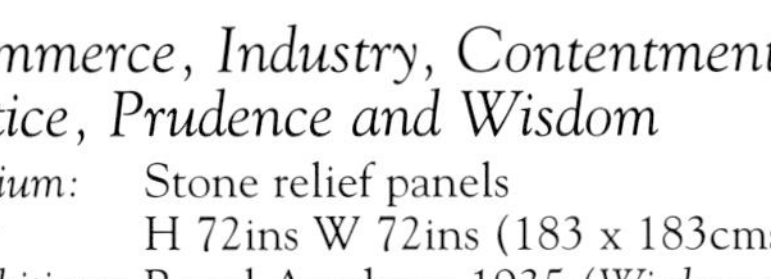

Spread of Christianity Panels

Commerce, Industry, Contentment, Justice, Prudence and Wisdom

Medium: Stone relief panels
Size: H 72ins W 72ins (183 x 183cms)
Exhibitions: Royal Academy 1935 (*Wisdom* and
                Contentment); Royal Academy 1936
                (*Commerce*).
Locations: Originally made for the Commercial
                Bank of Scotland, renamed Royal
                Bank of Scotland, Bothwell Street/
                Wellington Street, Glasgow;
                private collection (plaster of
                Commerce); Bayes Trust (original
                drawings).
Literature: *The Builder* May 1935 p954 and May
                1936 p1, illus.

Queen Mary Medal

Medium: Gold or bronze
Size: D 2³/₄ins (7cms)
Exhibitions: Sculpture in Britain Between the Wars,
                Fine Art Society 1986
Locations: Bayes Trust; British Museum; private
                collections.
Literature: *The Numismatic Chronicle* 1992 pl 26,
                illus.

Five gold medals were struck for special
presentation, 3,000 in bronze for sale at £1 to
commemorate the launch of the ship in 1934.

Panels Symbolising the Spread of Christianity

Locations: The Free Churches Council, Tavistock
                House, 27 Tavistock Place, London.
                Architect Richard Mountford Piggott.

Madonna and Child

Medium: Coloured plaster
Exhibitions: Institute 1935 (£31.10s)
Literature: *The Studio* May 1942 vol 124,
                p92, illus.

Invicta White Horse of Kent

Medium: Bronze statuette, plaque and
                silver table centre

The firm of Aveling Barford was formed
from a merger in 1934. Aveling, a long
established Kent-based engineering
company, used as its trademark the Invicta
horse of Kent. This was based on the steed
of Odin, displayed on the standard of the
Saxon chief who invaded Kent. After the
merger, the device was remodelled by Bayes.

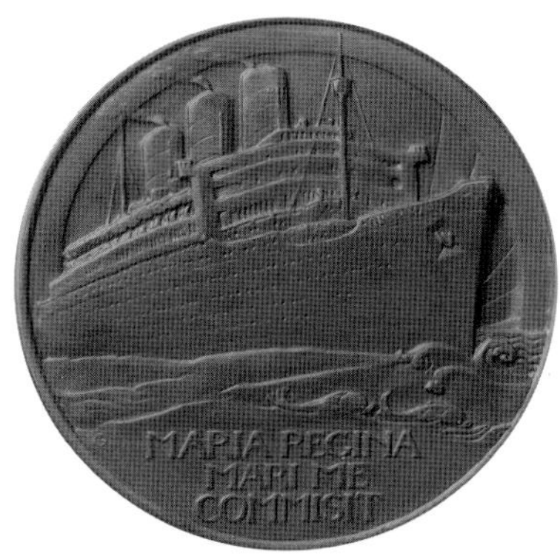

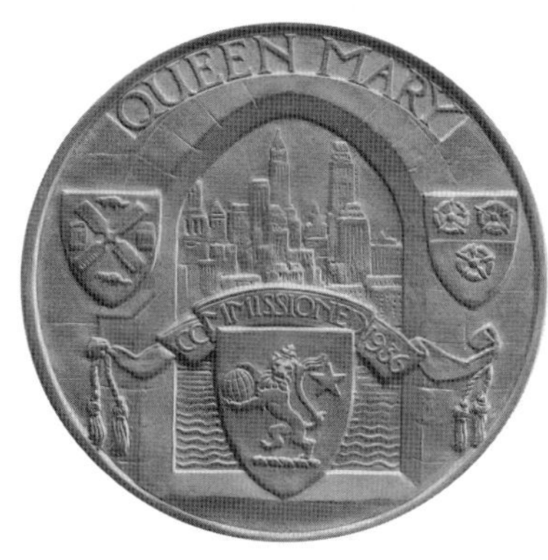

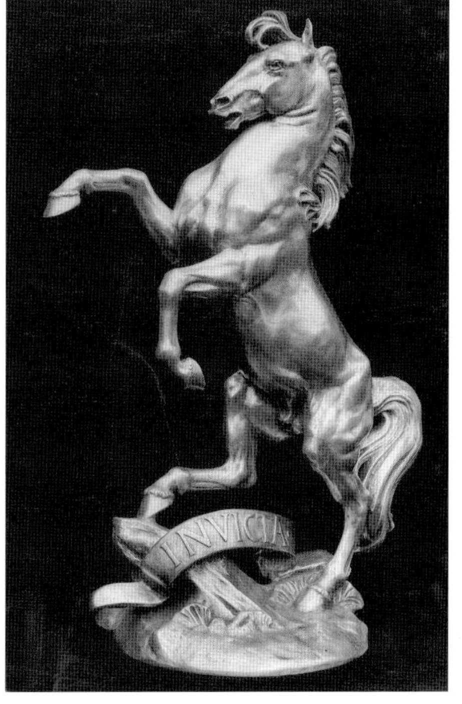

Invicta table centre for Aveling Barford

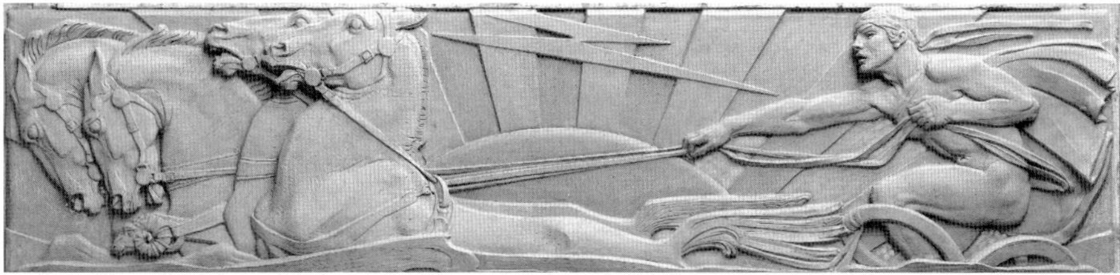

Helios in his Chariot

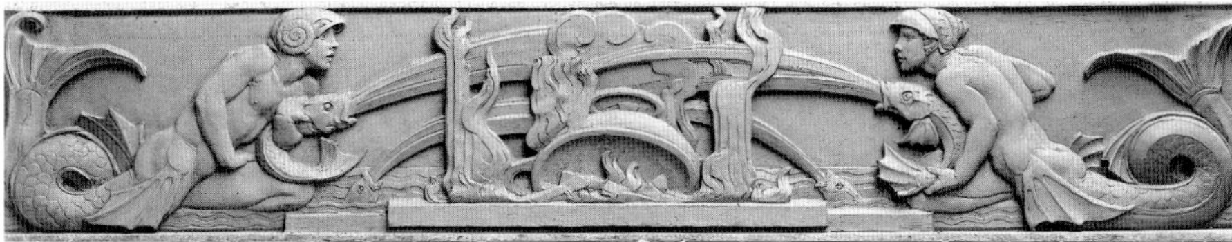

Mermaids Fire Fighting

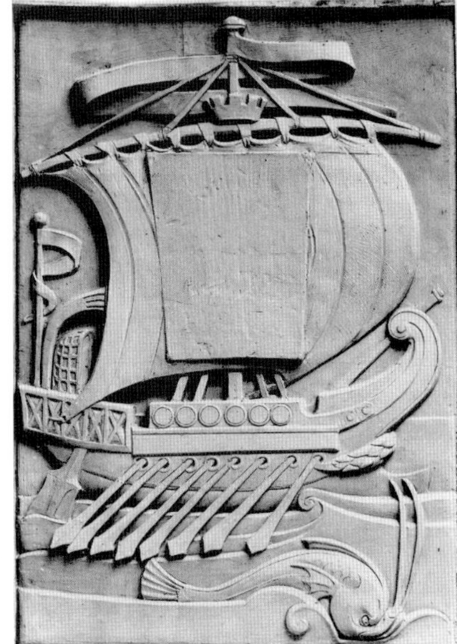

Sailing Boat

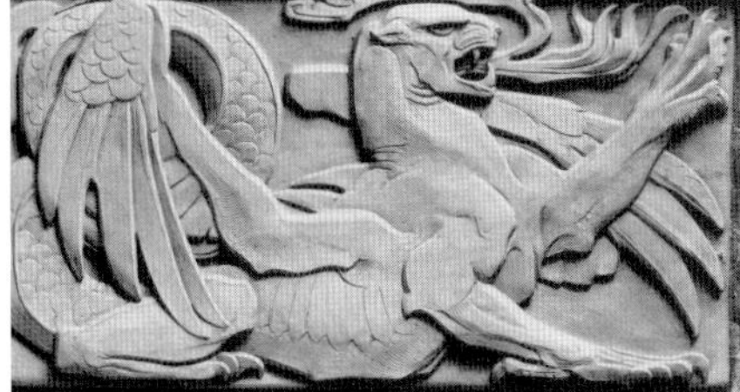

Dragon

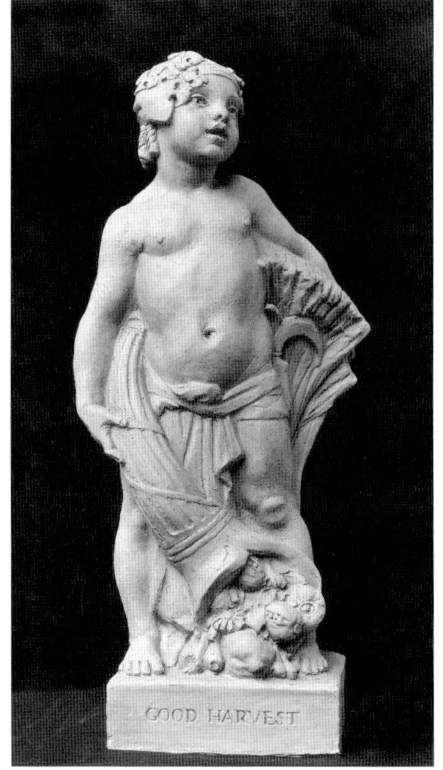

Good Harvest

1936

Dragon, Helios in his Chariot, Mermaids Fire Fighting and Sailing Boats

Medium: Relief panels
Locations: London Fire Brigade HQ,
Embankment, London.
Architect E.P. Wheeler.
Literature: *The Builder* 1937 Mar p560-2,
illus.

S. Nicholson Babb also produced three panels for the facade and F.P. Orton was responsible for the coat of arms.

Good Harvest

Medium: Papier mâché statuette
Size: H 16ins (41cms)
Locations: Bayes Trust
Made for Allied Newspapers.

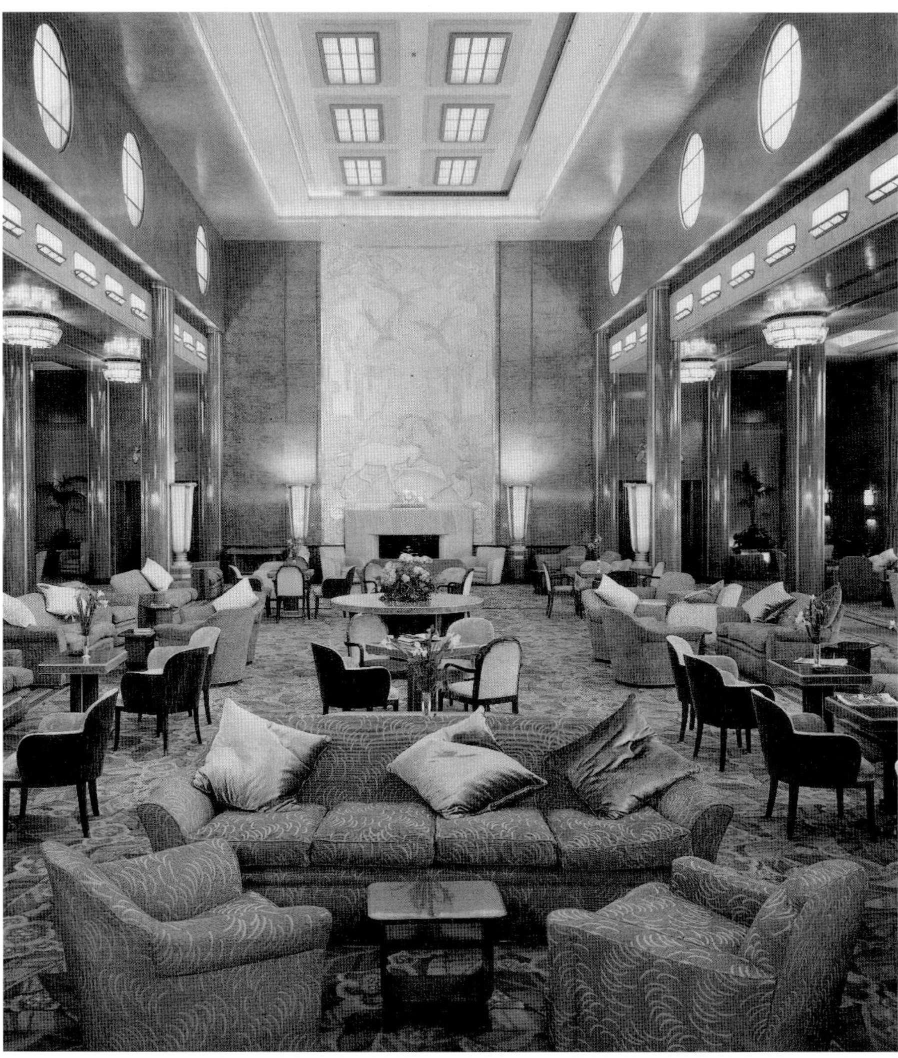

The saloon on the RMS Queen Mary with the Unicorns panel

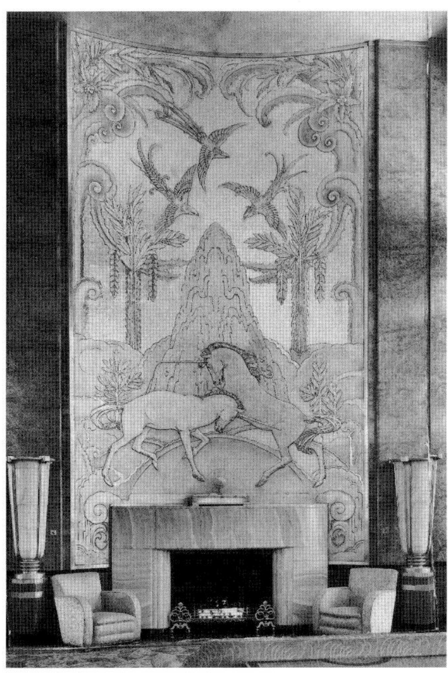

Unicorns in Battle

Medium: Gesso panel
Locations: Made for the RMS Queen
            Mary. Original drawing,
            Bayes Trust.
Literature: *The Illustrated London News*
            Vol 188 May 1936 p903, illus;
            Queen Mary, James Steed
            p99, illus.

Bayes and Alfred Oakley worked together
on this commission, but it was the
Oakley design that was the basis for the
panel.

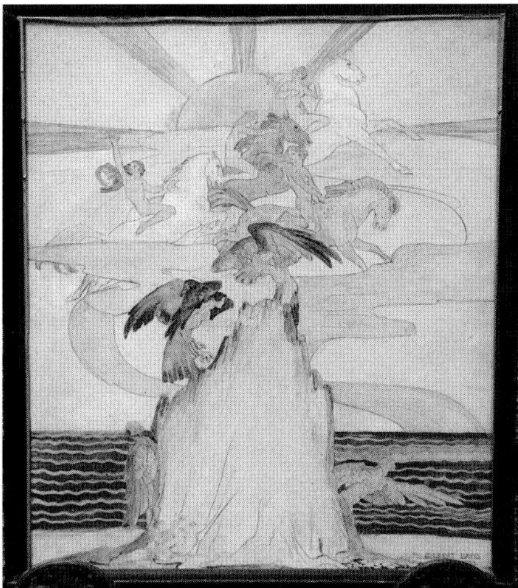

Queen Mary Drawing

Size: H 29 W 22¹/₂ins (73 x 54cms)
Locations: Bayes Trust

This drawing represents Bayes' scheme
for the gesso panel. Later, in 1952 this
was framed by Bayes into an earlier
fire screen.

Tomorrow Will Be Friday

Medium: Fountain figure in Doulton
             stoneware
Exhibitions: Institute (£63), Glasgow (£52)
             1936.

1937

Calvary

Medium: Stone
Size: Over life-size
Locations: Bayes Trust (small scale
            plaster maquette); St
            Saviour's Church, Ealing, cost
            £524. The Church was
            bombed during World War II
            but the calvary survived.
Literature: *Middlesex County Times* 12
            June 1937, illus.

Erected in memory of Father Charles
Buckell, the first vicar of the parish from
1898 to 1936.

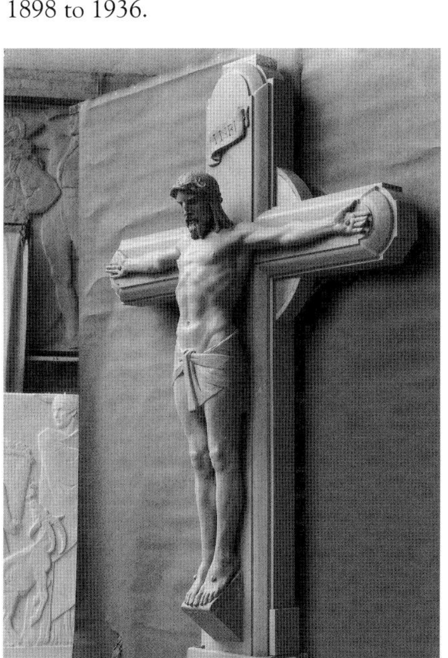

Plaster for the Calvary in Bayes' studio

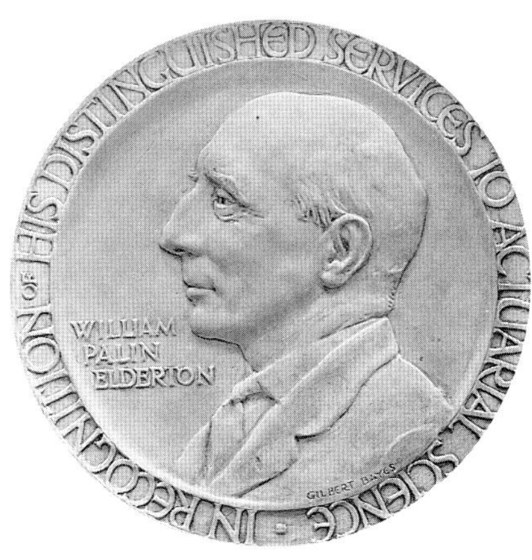

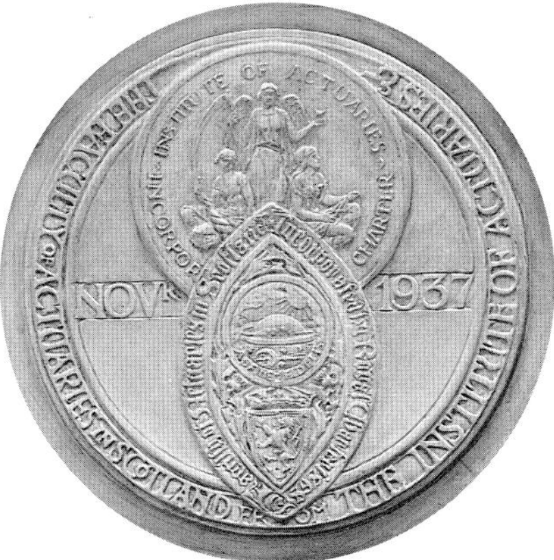

Institute of Actuaries Medal

Size: D 2³/₄ins (7cms)
Exhibitions: Royal Academy 1943
Locations: Bayes Trust
Literature: *Journal of the Institute of
             Actuaries* 1938; *The
             Numismatic Chronicle* 1992.

This medal commemorates Sir William
Palin Elderton.

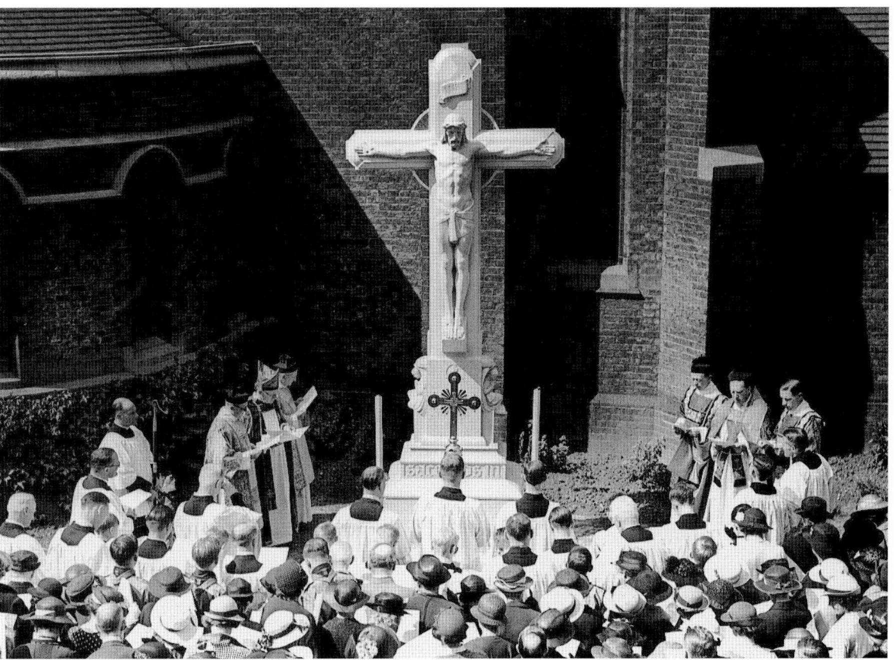

The dedication of the Calvary on 5th June, 1937

Gilbert Bayes

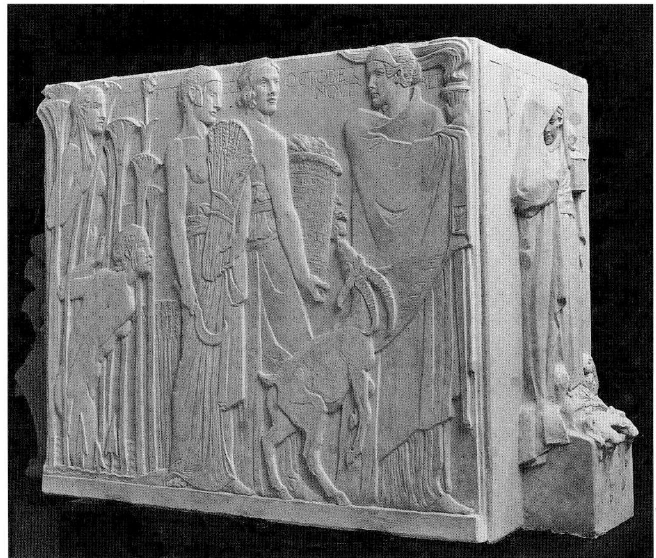

The Fountain of the Months complete, in plaster

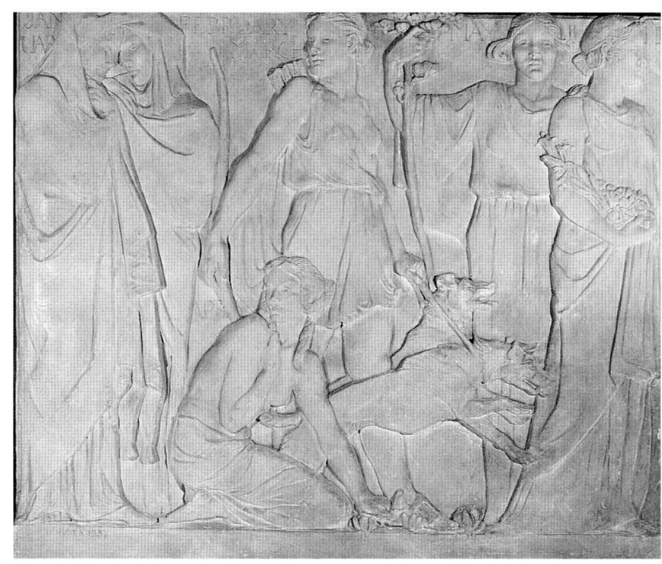

Verso of The Fountain of the Months

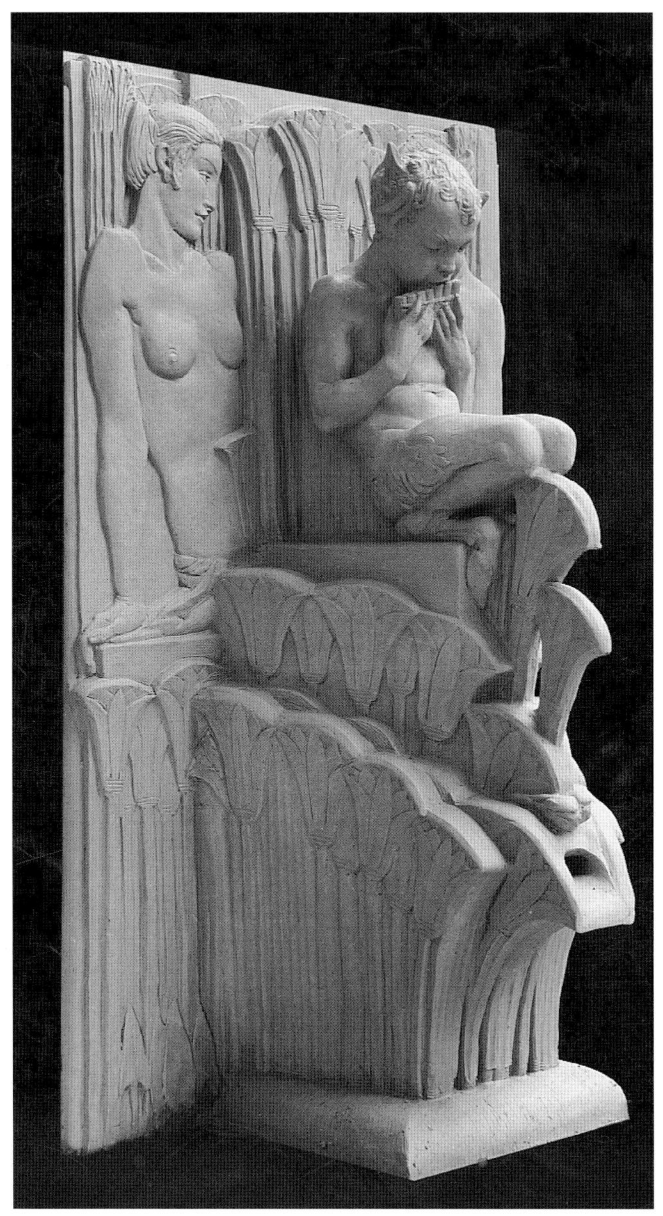

Plaster of the end section of The Fountain of the Months

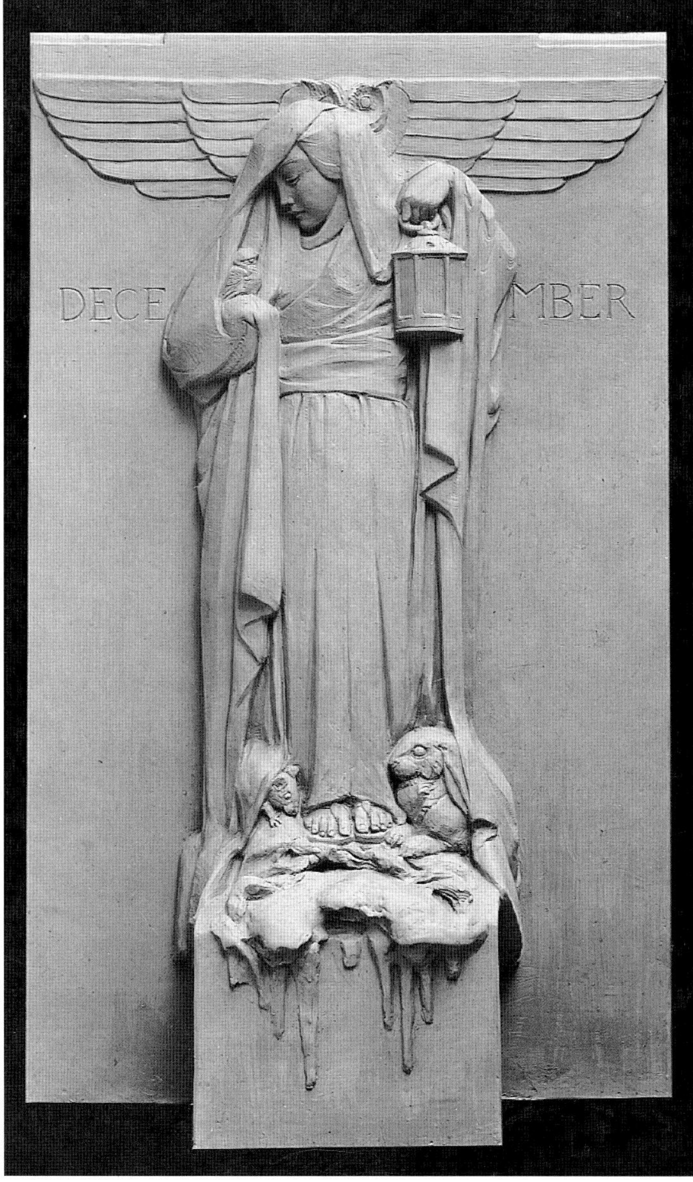

Plaster of the end section of The Fountain of the Months

The Fountain of the Months

Medium: Plaster for artificial stone
Size: H 61ins W 71ins
(155 x 180.5cms)
Exhibitions: Royal Academy 1937 (North and South panels)
Locations: Private collection (North and South plaster panels)

This fountain was made in artificial stone for a London garden setting but it was destroyed by bombing in 1940.

Let Peace Prevail, Selfridge's Coronation Decorations

Medium: Plaster
Locations: Selfridge's, Oxford Street London, temporary decorations. Architect Albert D. Millar, Chief of Sculpture Sir William Reid Dick. None of the decorations survive.
Literature: *Selfridge's Souvenir Portfolio* May 1937, illus.

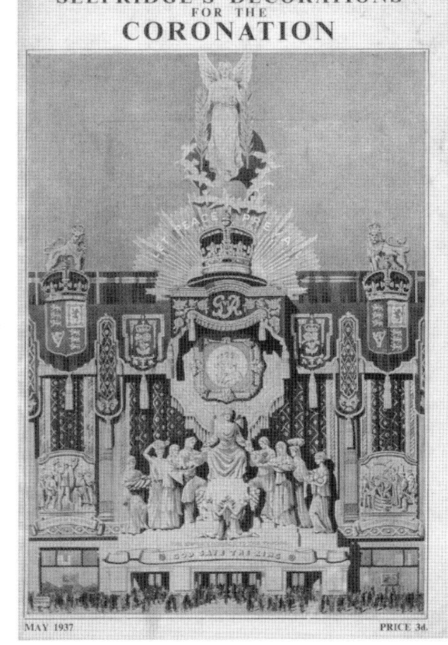

The souvenir brochure for Let Peace Prevail

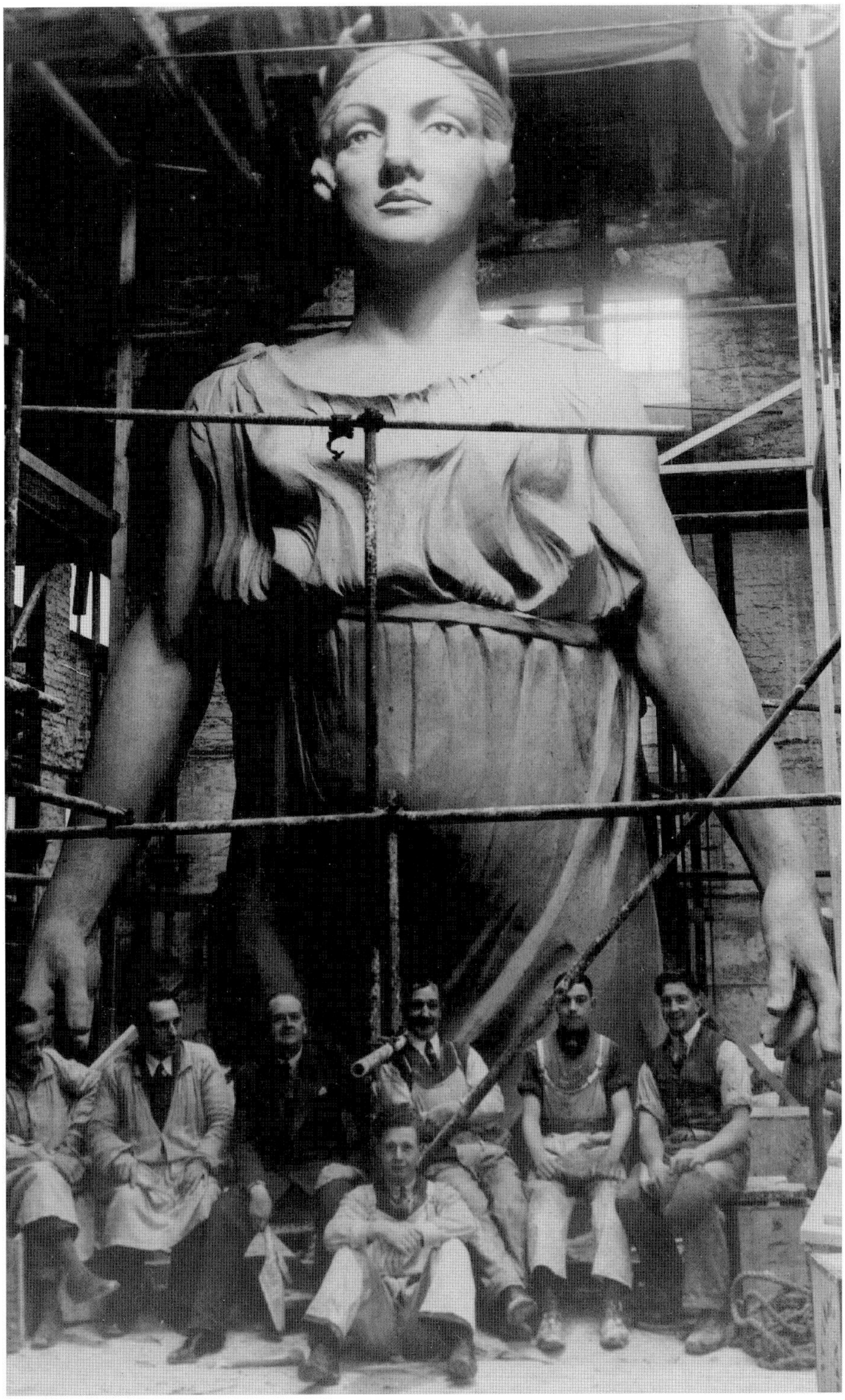

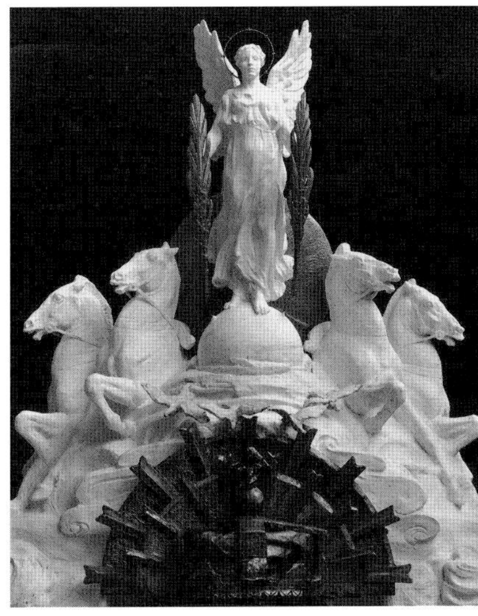

Alternative design for the Peace figure

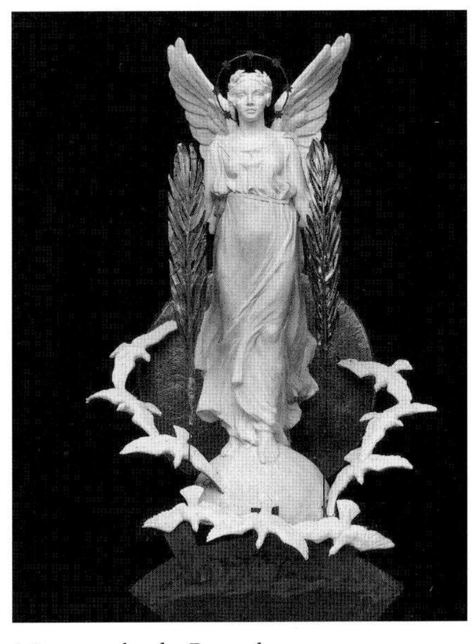

Maquette for the Peace figure

The figure of Peace under construction. Bayes is third from the left.

Gilbert Bayes

Fairy Tale Lunette Panels and Four Seasons Clock

Medium: Doulton stoneware
Size: Panels H 30ins W 60ins (76 x 152.5cms), clock
             H 42ins W 42ins (107 x 107cms).
Locations: Sidney Street Estate, St Pancras Housing Association,
             London. Architect Ian Hamilton.
Literature: *The Doulton Story*, P. Atterbury & L. Irvine 1979 p102,
             illus; *Glazed Expressions* 1986 Vol 12 pp1, 2, illus.

The subjects depicted in the panels are: The Little Mermaid, The
Soldier and the Princess from the Tinderbox, The Princess and
the Swineherd, the Swan Princess and St George and the Dragon.
Related is the cast stone Eagles and Fish panel made for the
Drummond Estate, St Pancras Housing Association.

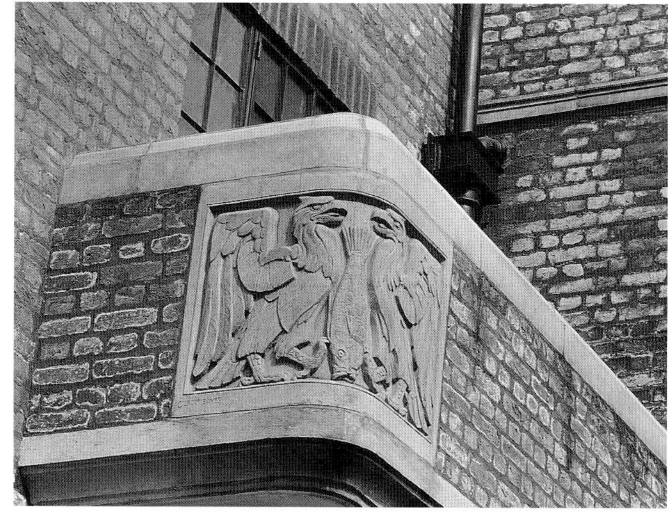

Cast stone Eagles and Fish panel, Drummond Estate, St Pancras
Housing Association

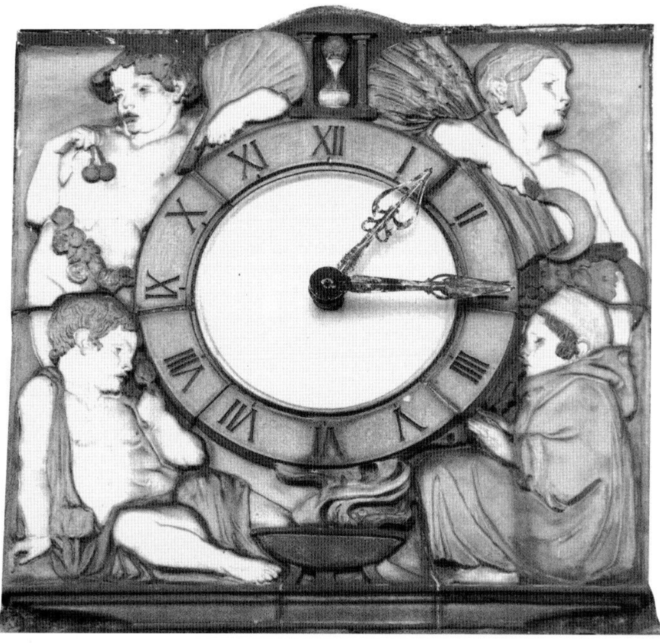

Four Seasons clock, Doulton stoneware

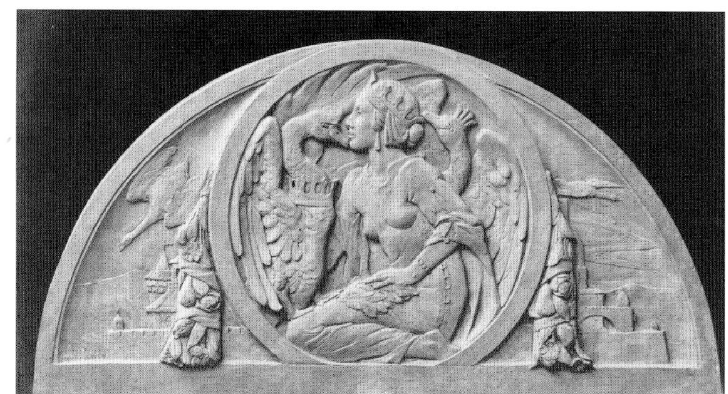

Plaster maquette for the Swan Princess

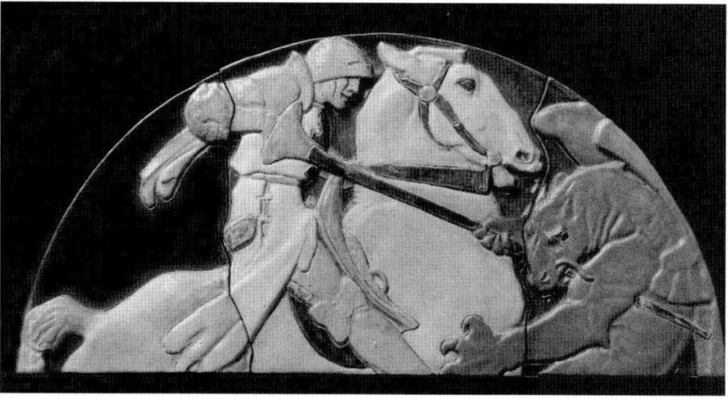

Doulton stoneware lunette, St George and the Dragon

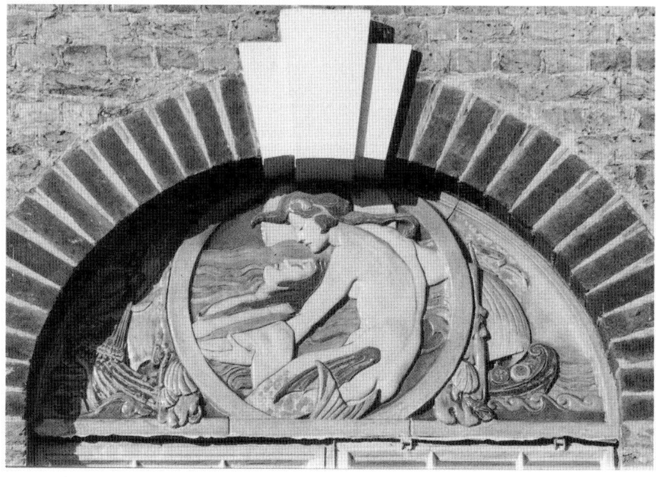

Doulton stoneware lunette in situ, The Little Mermaid

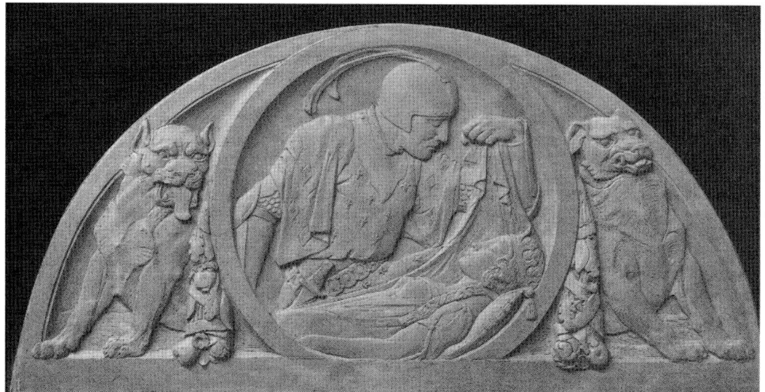

Plaster maquette for the Soldier and the Princess

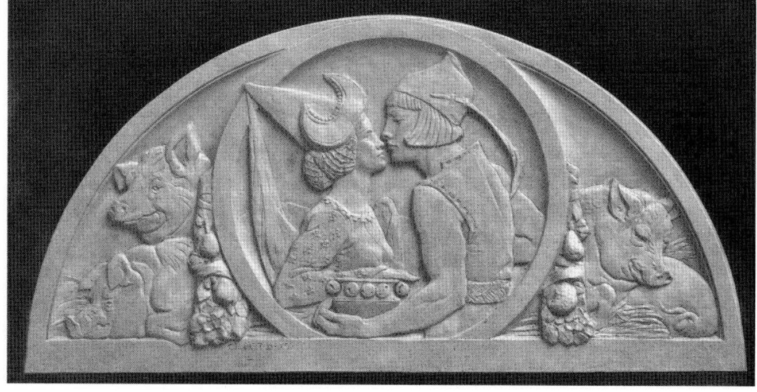

Plaster maquette for the Princess and the Swineherd

Finials for Washing Line Posts

Medium: Doulton stoneware
Size: H 13-19ins (33-48cms) approx
Exhibitions: Some of the finials were exhibited during the 1930s and sold as garden ornaments with different names (5-8gns); Institute 1933, 1937, 1938, 1939 (Tailor, Dove, Ducks); LCC Creative Art 1934 (Blackbird, Ship); Pastel Society 1934, 1940 (Snail, Ship, Rose); Bristol 1937 (Dove, Duck); Ridley 1937, 1938 (Dove, Ducks, Devil); Graphic Arts 1937, 1938 (Blackbird, Duck, Devil); Sussex Artists 1937 (Dove); Southport 1938 (Duck); New Zealand 1939 (Blackbird, Doves, Duck).
Locations: The finials were made for the St Pancras Housing Association between 1931 and 1938 and used on washing line posts at their estates in Sidney Street, Eversholt Street, Drummond Street, Athlone Street and York Rise. They were inspired by nursery rhymes, Christmas carols or the lives of the saints and have now all been removed. The sets were as follows: Wren and Blackbirds (St Christopher's Flats); Snail and Tailors, two models (St Francis Flats); Christmas Tree and Ships (St Nicholas' Flats); St Michael and Devils, two models (St Michael's Flats); St Anthony and Fishes (St Anthony's Flats); St Martin and Ships, different model from above (St Martin's Flats); Carpenter's Bag and Doves, two models (St Joseph's Flats); Ducks, two models (Athlone Estate); Dragon, Roses and Thistles (York Rise). A clay model exists for a Deer finial which does not seem to have been produced.
Literature: *The Doulton Story,* P. Atterbury & L. Irvine 1979 p30, illus; *Decorative Arts Society Journal* 1980 p10, illus; *Glazed Expressions* 1986 Vol 12 p1, illus.

Dog Finial

Medium: Doulton stoneware
Size: H 19¼ins (49cms)
Exhibitions: Pastel Society 1936, (*The Guardian*); Ridley 1936 (sold); Institute 1939.
Locations: Bayes Trust; private collections.

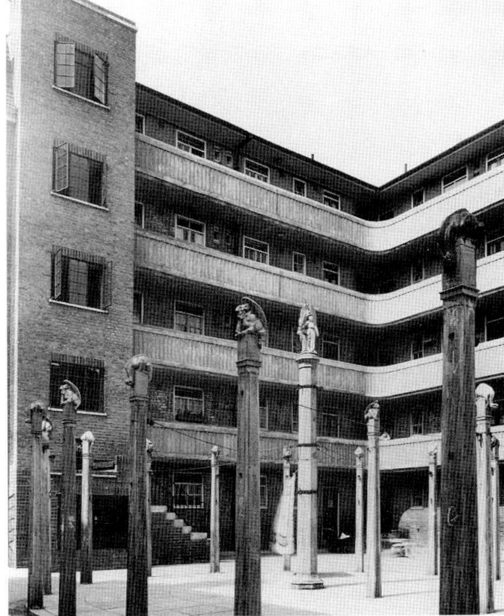

Washing post finials in situ

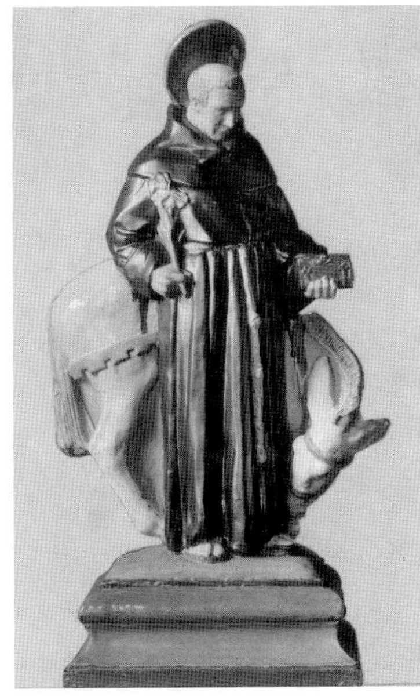

St Anthony

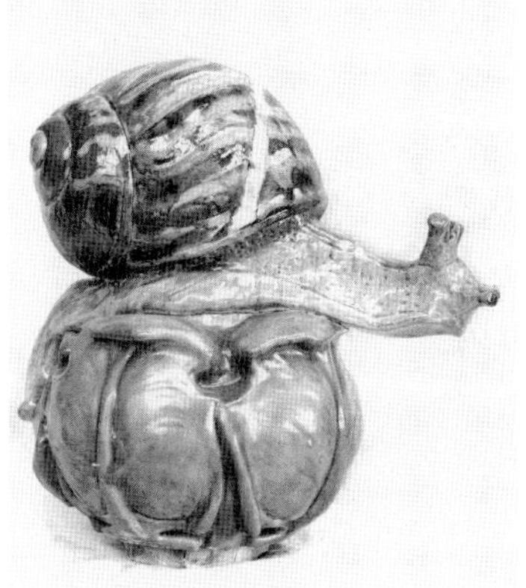

Snail

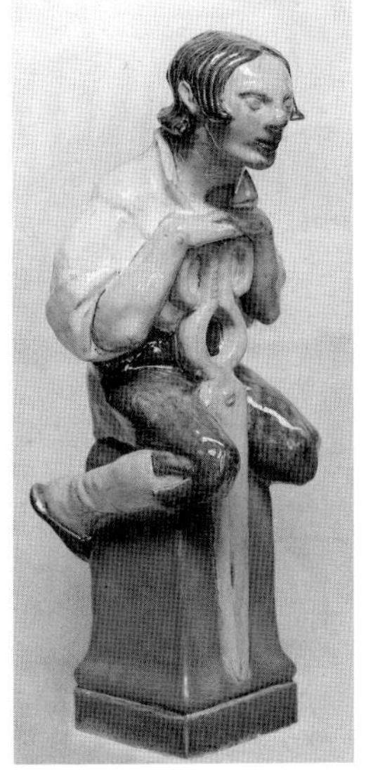

Tailor

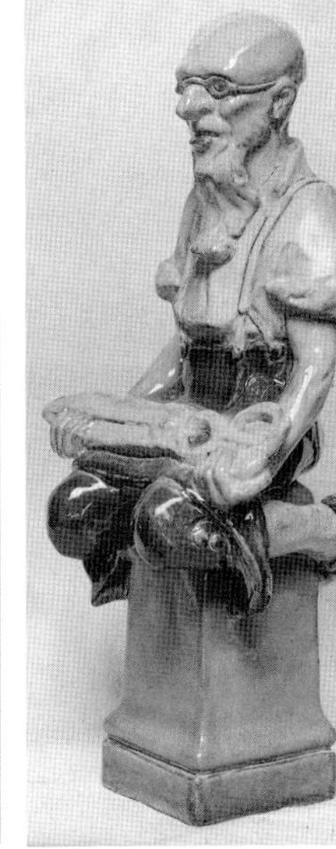

Tailor

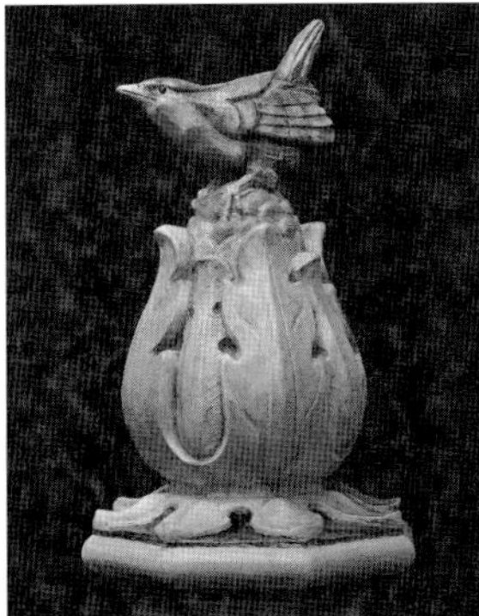

Wren

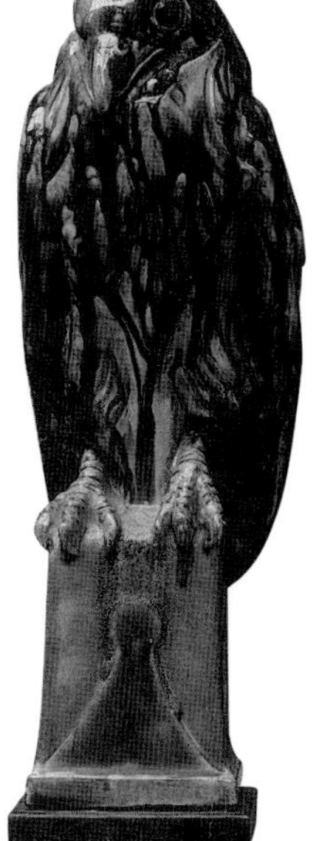

Blackbird

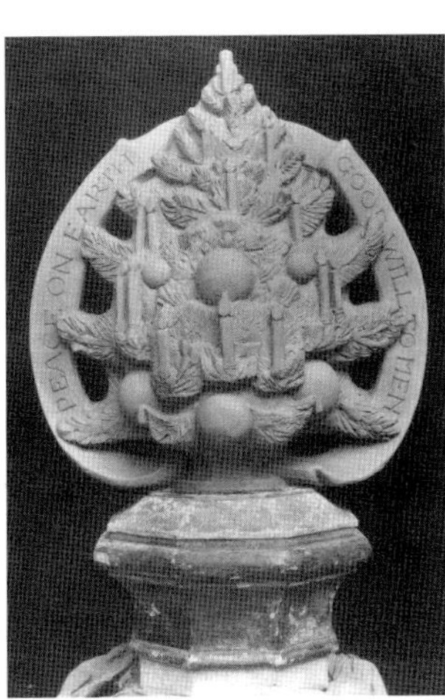

Christmas Tree

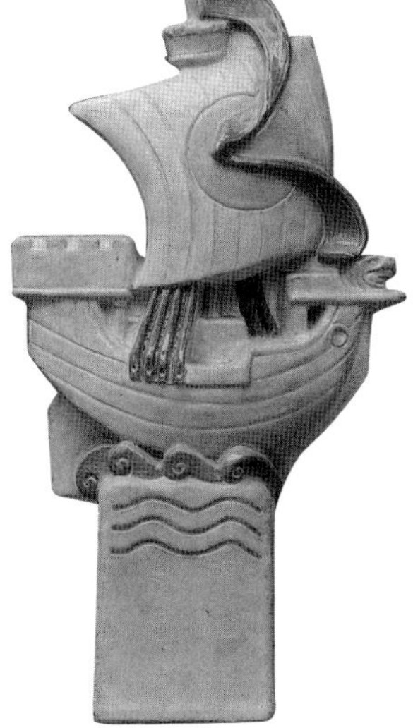

Ship

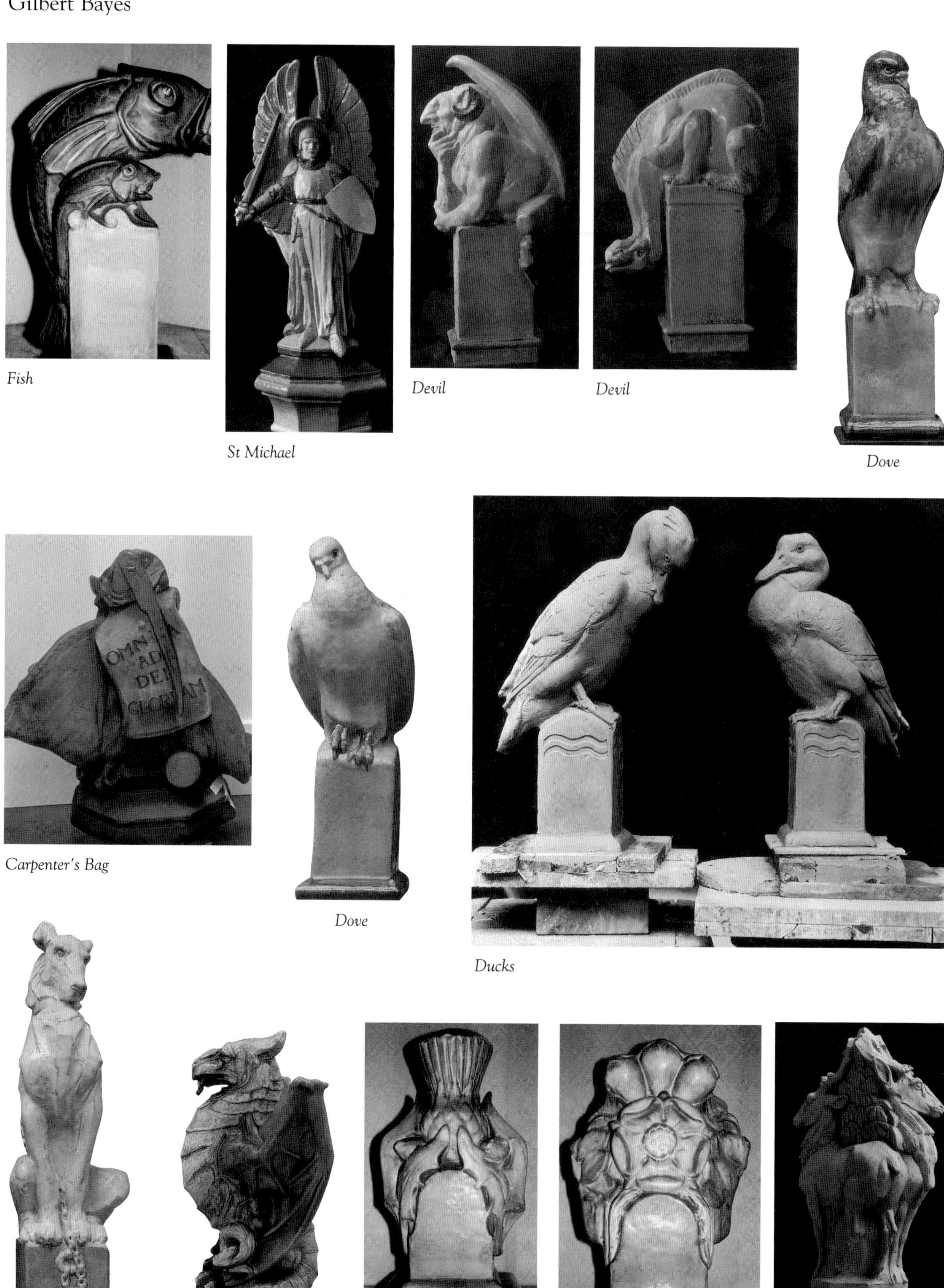

Fish

St Michael

Devil

Devil

Dove

Carpenter's Bag

Dove

Ducks

Dog

Dragon

Thistle

Rose

Deer

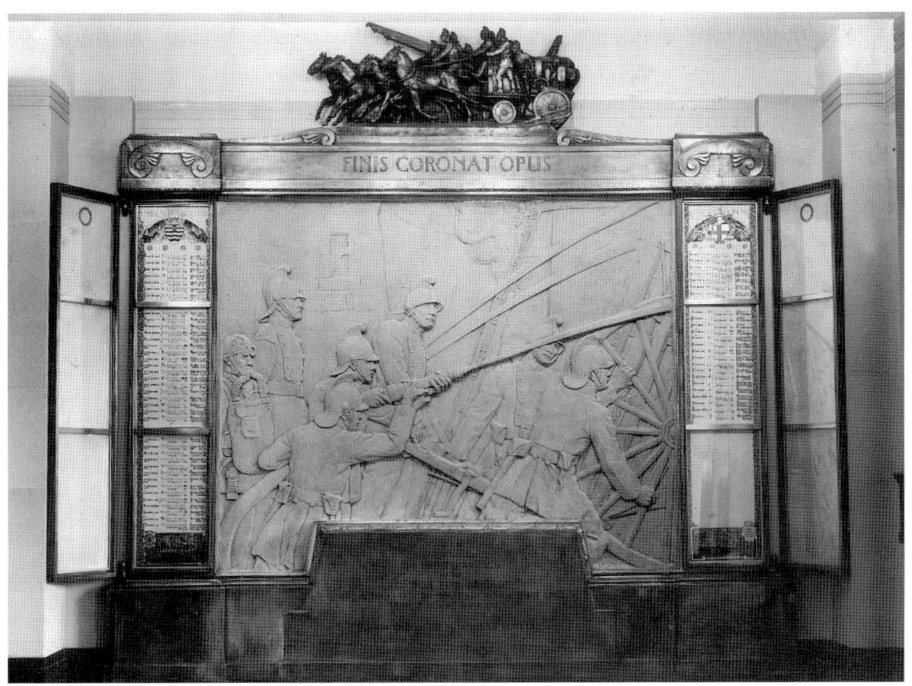

London Fire Brigade Memorial

Medium: Stone and bronze
Exhibitions: Royal Academy 1936 (bronze group)
Locations: London Fire Brigade HQ, Albert Embankment, London. Presented by Lloyds Underwriters 'To the memory of the officers and men of London Fire Brigade who throughout the years laid down their lives whilst doing their duty'.

The bronze panels on either side of the stone relief are inscribed with the names of the men killed on duty, a total of sixty-two when the memorial was unveiled in 1937. Since then many more names have been added including 327 who died in action during World War II. Inscribed Finis Coronat Opus (the end crowns the work).

1938

Dame Ethel Smyth DBE, 1858-1944

Medium: Plaster bust
Size: H 26ins (66cms)
Exhibitions: Bradford 1938; Royal Academy 1939.
Locations: Plaster, Bayes Trust
Literature: Dame Ethel Smyth composed *The March of Women* which became the anthem of the Suffragettes. This bust was made in her eightieth year.

Fame

Medium: Equestrian statuette
Exhibitions: Royal Academy 1938

Bust

Medium: Doulton stoneware
Exhibitions: Institute 1938
This bust was made for an almshouse.

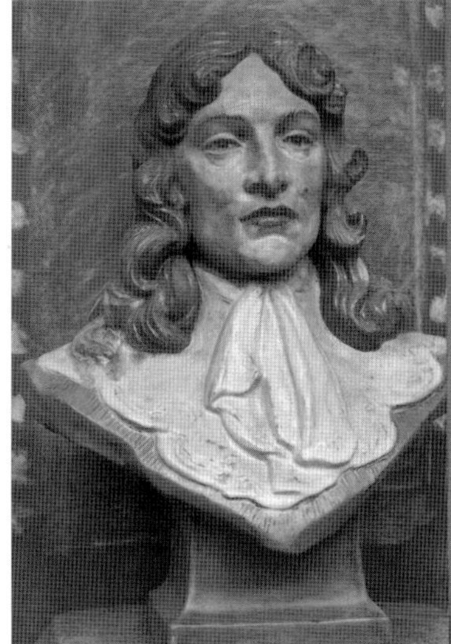

Bust in Doulton stoneware

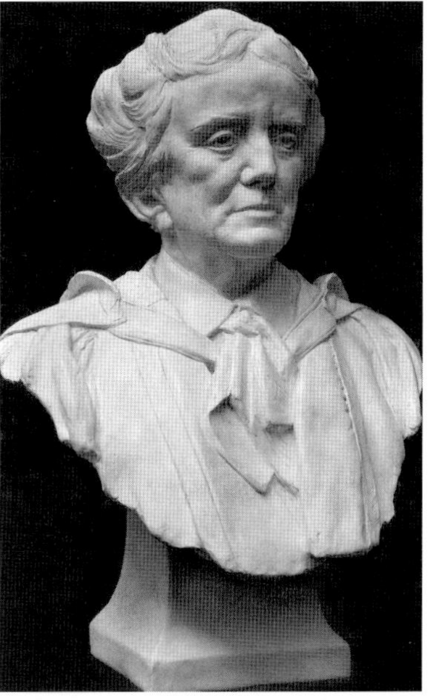

Dame Ethel Smyth

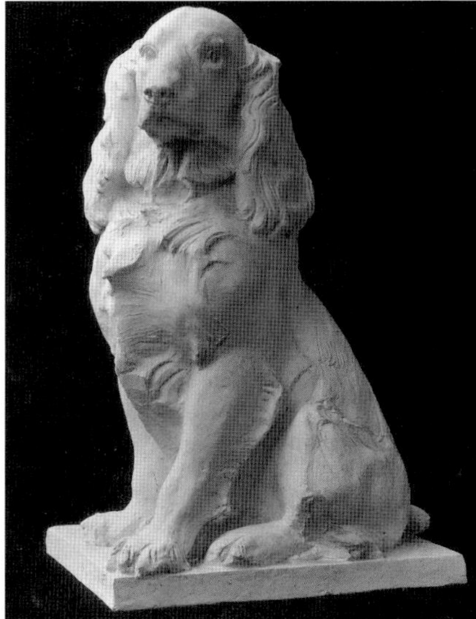

Tweedledum

Medium: Plaster
Size: H 24½ins (62cms)
Locations: Bayes Trust

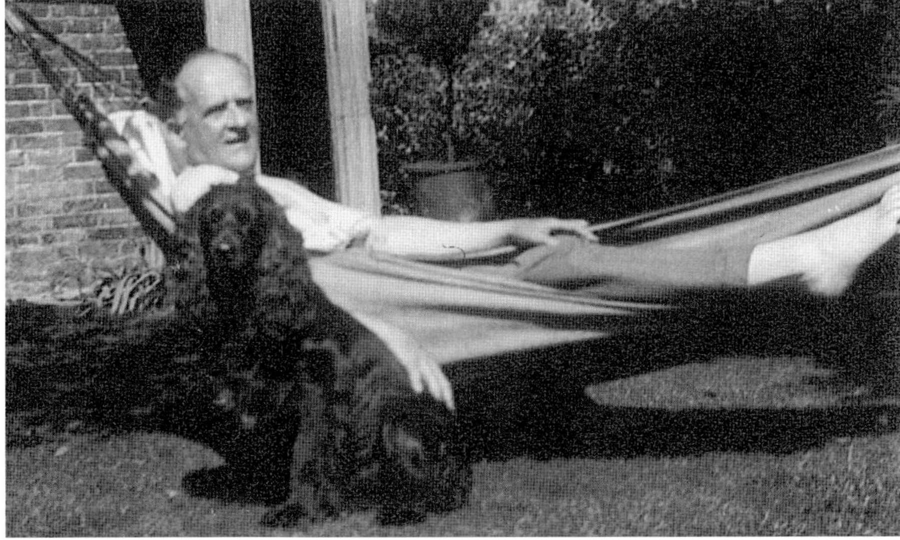

Bayes and Tweedledum in the garden at Greville Place, c.1938

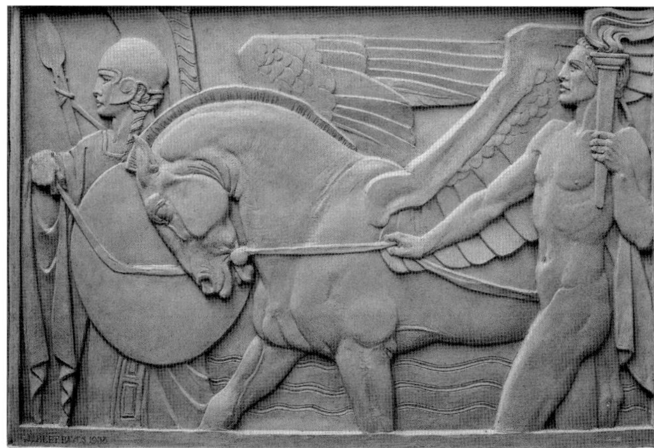

Bellerophon, Pegasus and Pallas Athene Panel

Locations: Cleland House, Page Street, London. Architect
T.P. Bennett (destroyed).
Literature: *The Builder* 1939 Vol 156 p703, illus; *The Architect
and Building News* 1939 Apr p34, illus.

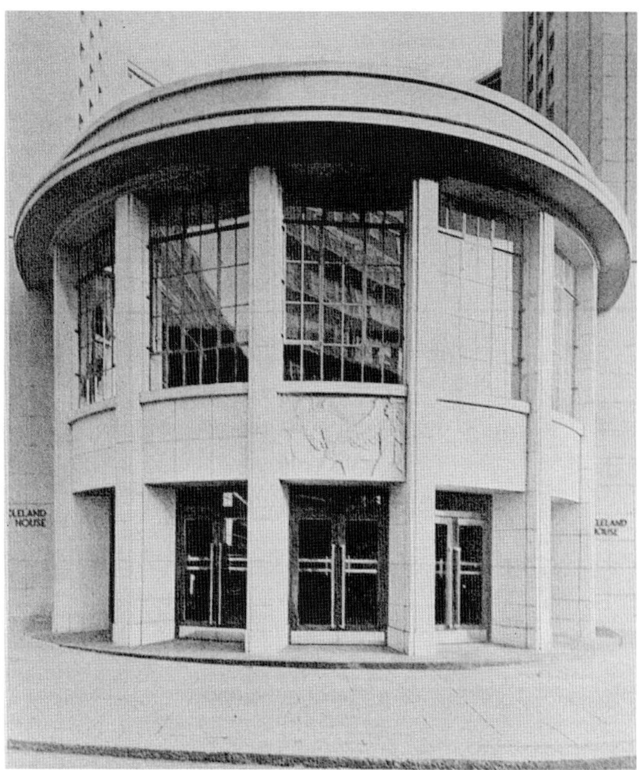

Cleland House, showing the panel in situ

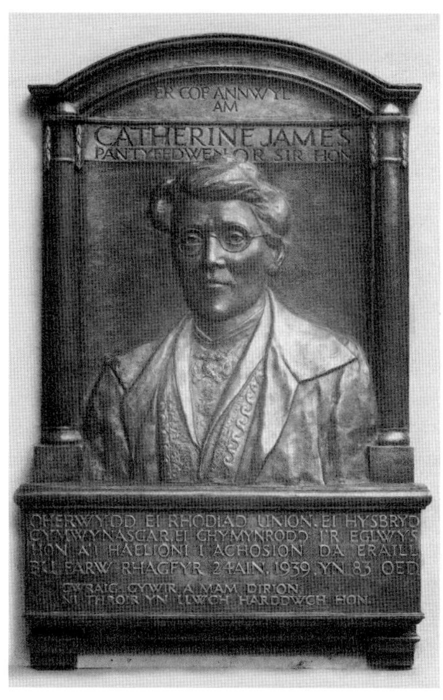

1939

Catherine James, d.1939
Medium: Bronze relief

St George 'He is for England'
Medium: Bronze statuette
Size: H 33ins (84cms)
Exhibitions: Royal Academy 1940 (150gns); Glasgow (150gns); Russia
1942; Bournemouth 1943; Southport 1946; Ealing 1947.
Locations: Bayes Trust

Heraldic Reliefs
Medium: Coloured plaster
Size: H 8ft W 8ft (2.44 x 2.44m)
Exhibitions: British Pavilion, New York World Fair 1939
Literature: *Historic Heraldry of Britain* Anthony R. Wagner 1939, illus.
The subjects depicted are: Owen Glendower; Thomas Wolsey; Simon
de Montfort; Sir William Wallace; Robert the Bruce; Robert Walpole,
Earl of Orford; William Pitt, Earl of Chatham; Horatio Nelson; Arthur
Wellesley, Duke of Wellington; Oliver Cromwell; John Churchill,
Duke of Marlborough; Edward the Black Prince; Richard Neville, Earl
of Warwick; William Cecil, Baron of Burghley, and the Royal Arms.

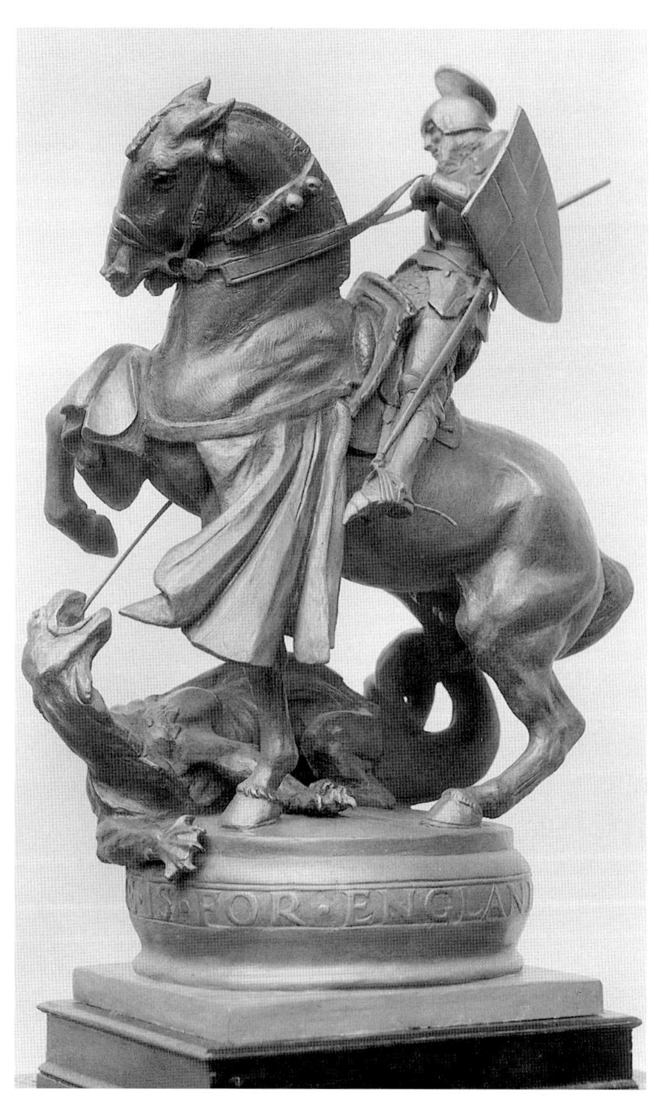

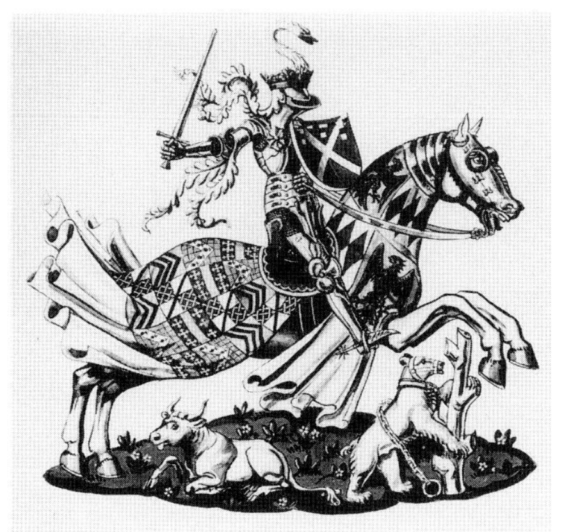

Richard Neville

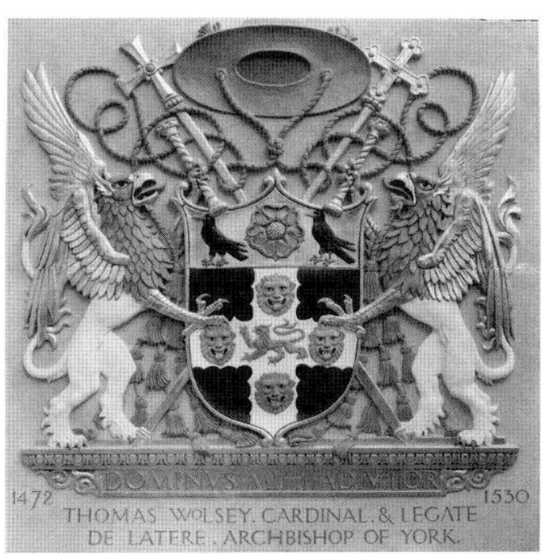

Thomas Wolsey

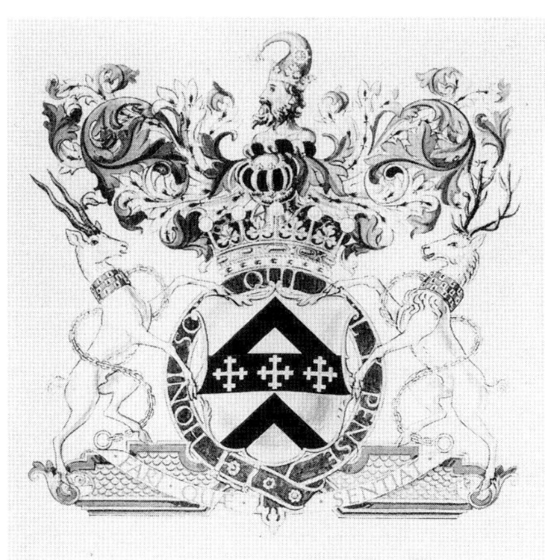

Robert Walpole

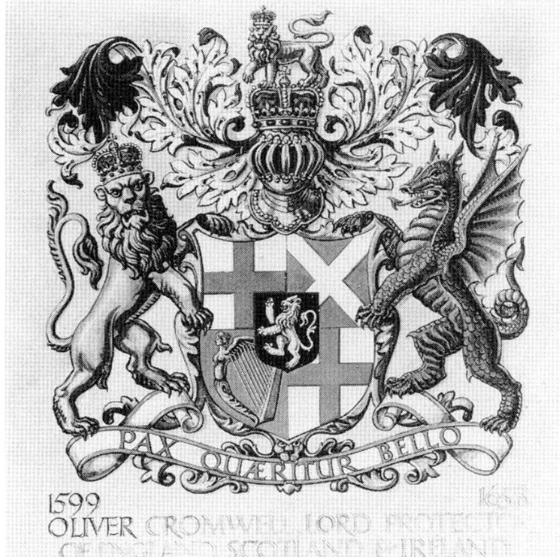

Oliver Cromwell

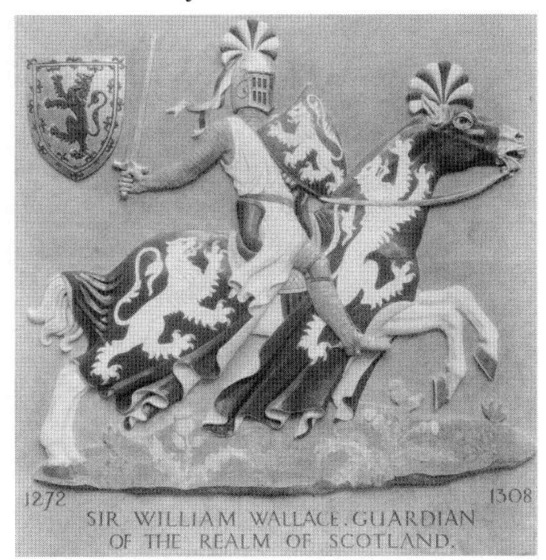

Sir William Wallace

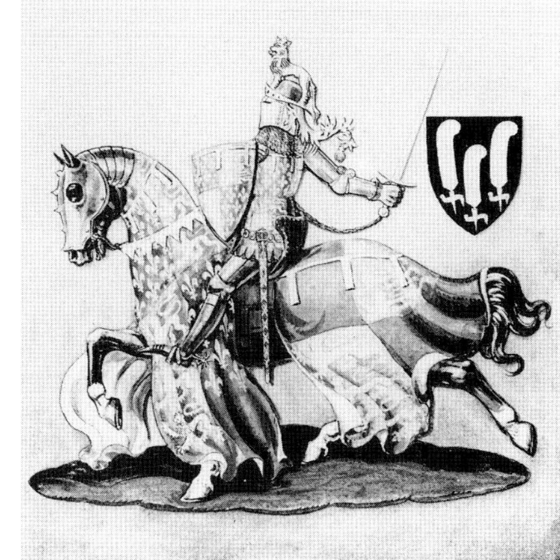

Edward, Prince of Wales

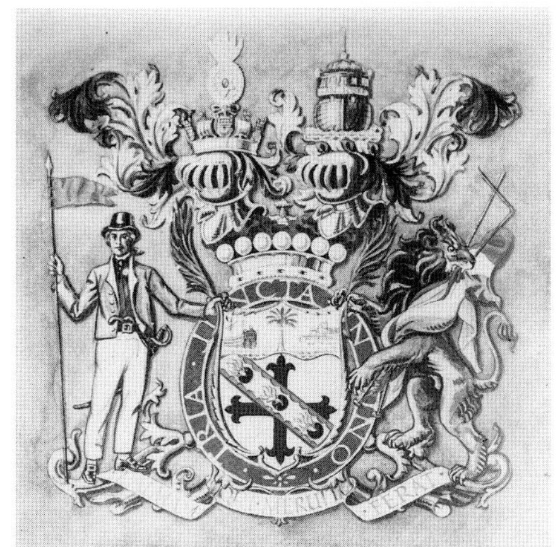

Horatio Nelson

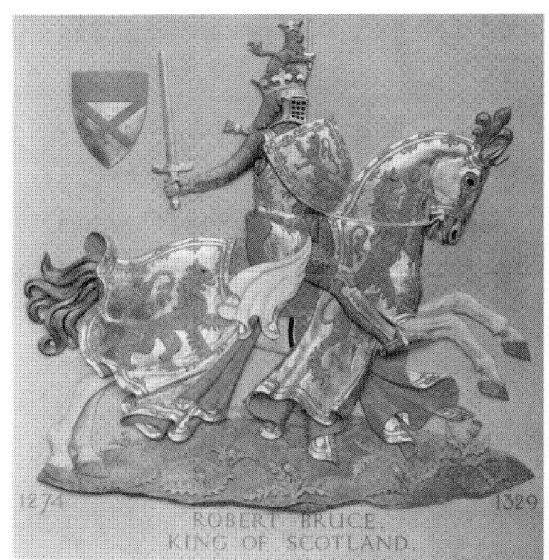

Robert Bruce

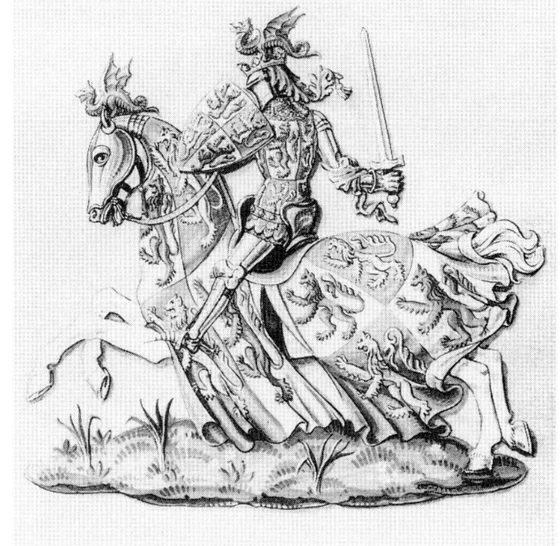

Oliver Glendower

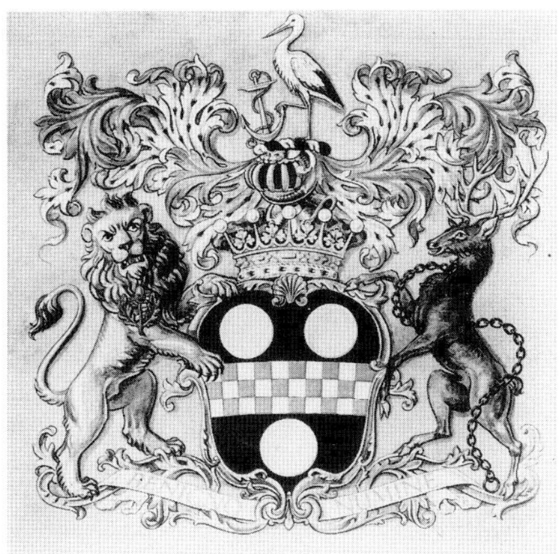

William Pitt

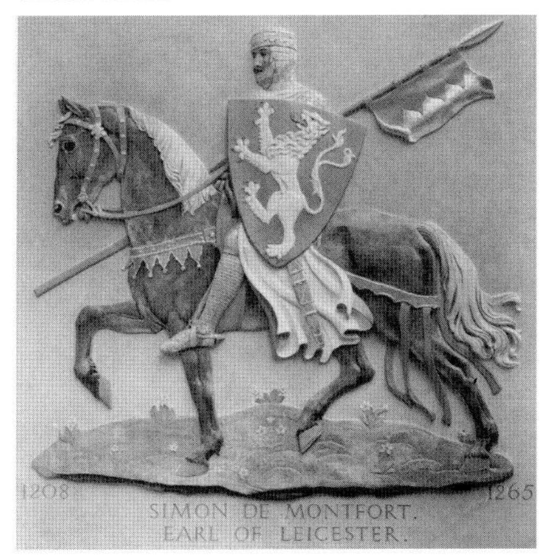

Simon de Montfort

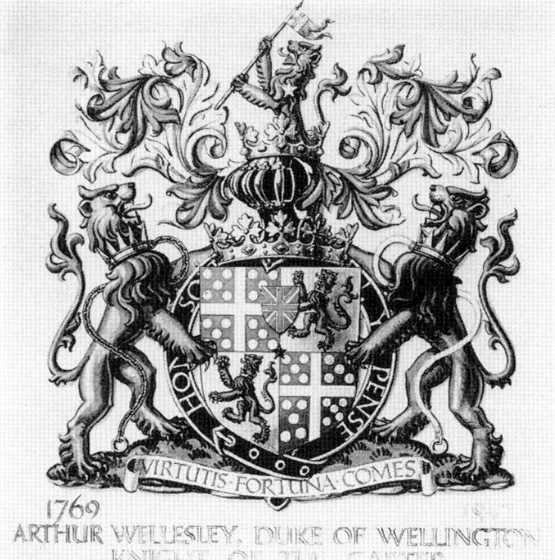

Arthur Wellesley

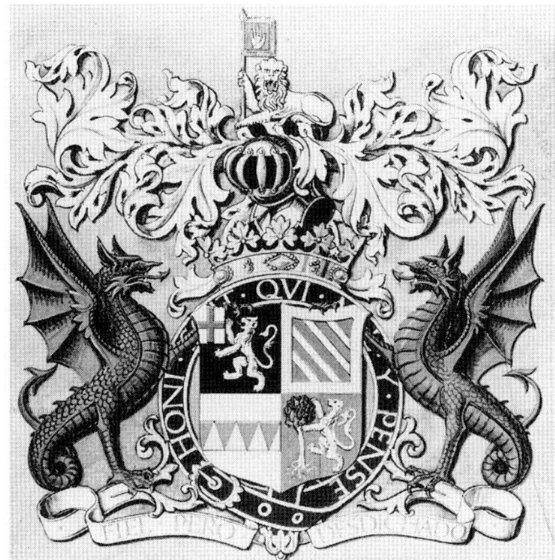

John Churchill

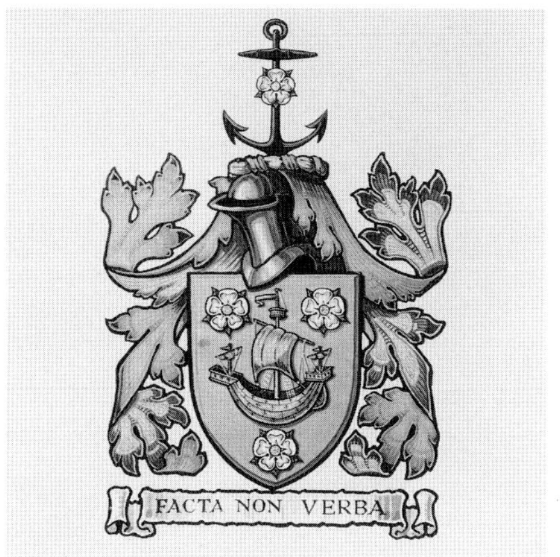

Related armorial panel, probably not used

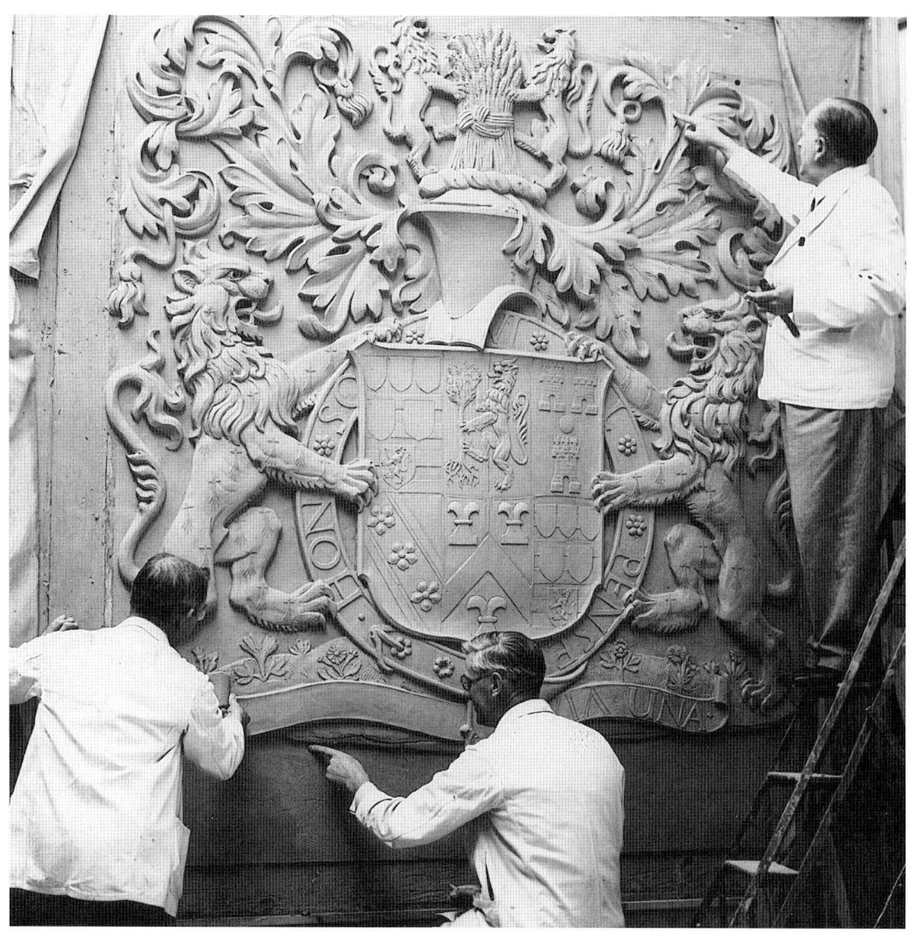

Bayes and his colleagues at work on the Royal Arms panel

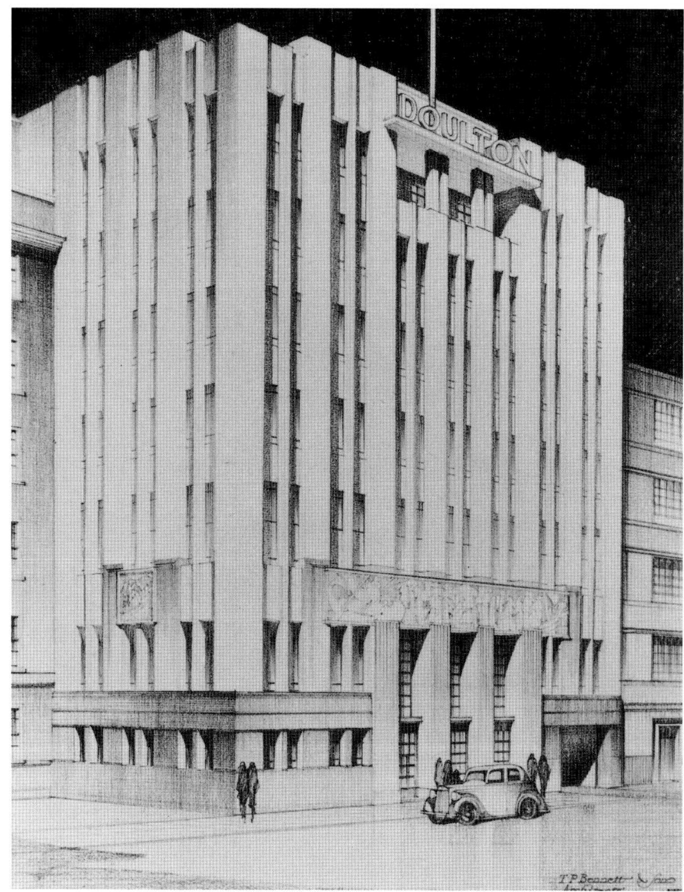

T.P. Bennett's drawing for Doulton House, showing the Bayes panels

Friezes, Pottery Through the Ages and Dutch Potters

Medium: Doulton stoneware
Size: *Dutch Potters* H 78ins W 93ins (198 x 236cms)
Exhibitions: Royal Academy 1939 and 1940
Locations: Victoria & Albert Museum (*Pottery through the Ages*); Ironbridge Gorge Museum (*Dutch Potters*); Fine Art Society (plaster *Dutch Potters*).
Literature: *The Builder* 1940 Feb p185-9, illus; *Pottery and Glass* 1950, illus; *The Connoisseur* 1979 Aug p252, illus.

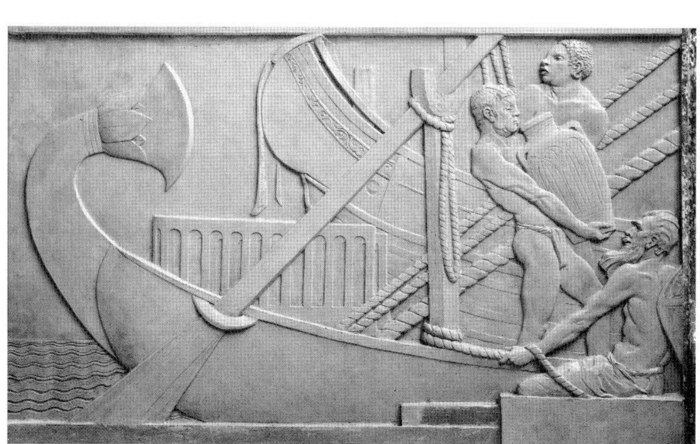

Full-size plaster panels for the Pottery Through the Ages frieze

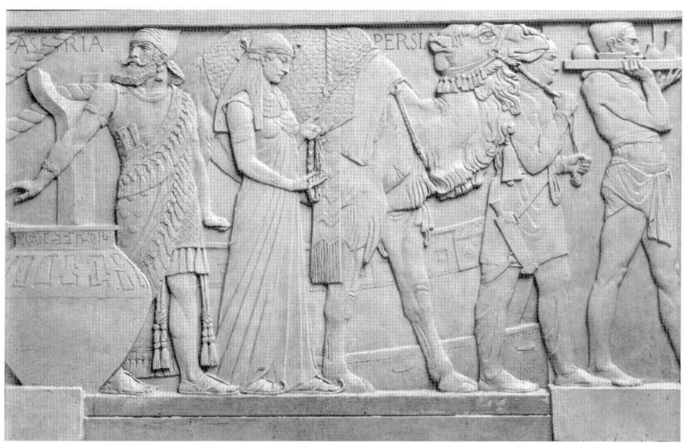

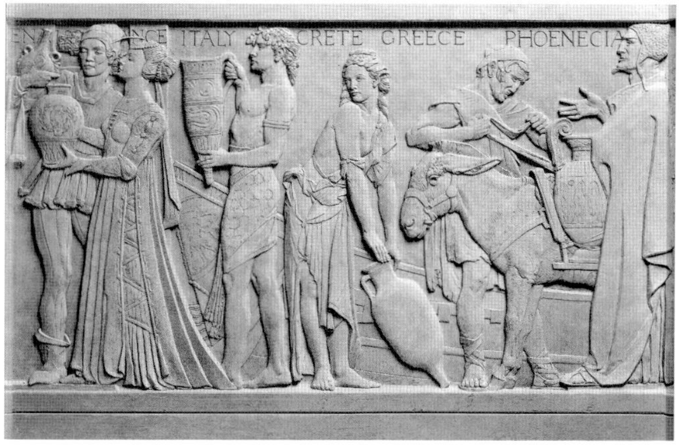

Full-size plaster panels for the Pottery Through the Ages frieze

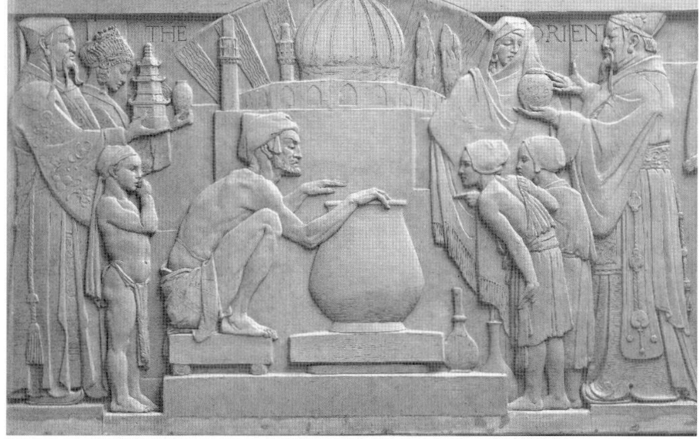

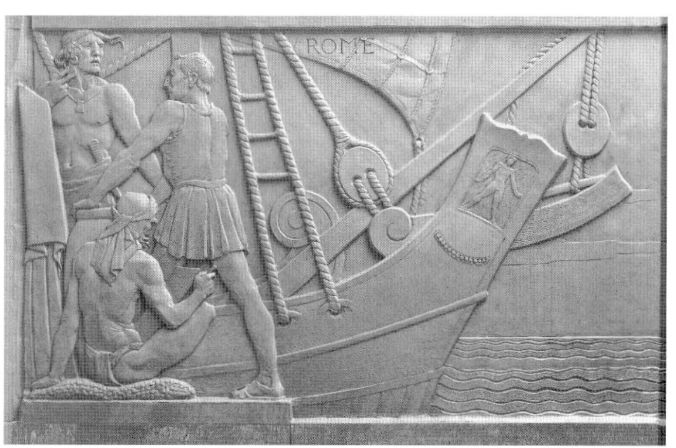

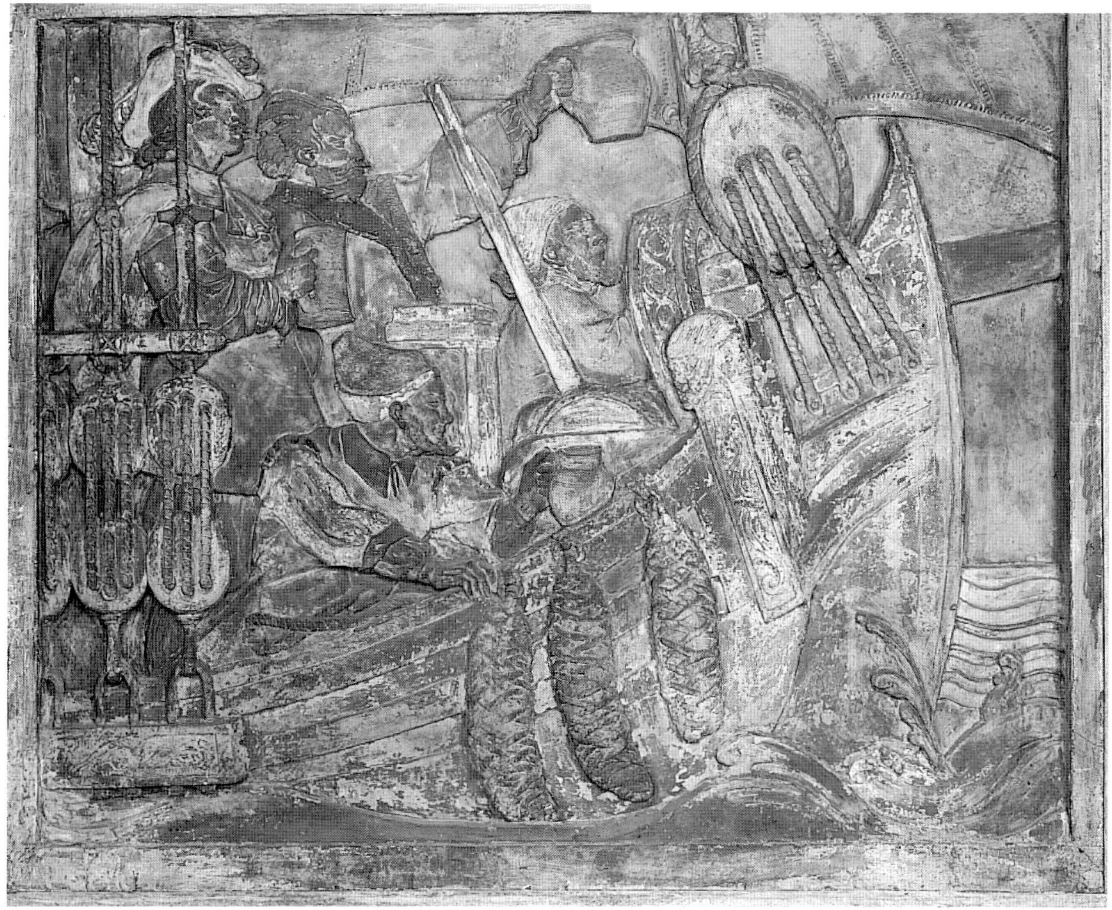

Full-size plaster for the Dutch Potters panel

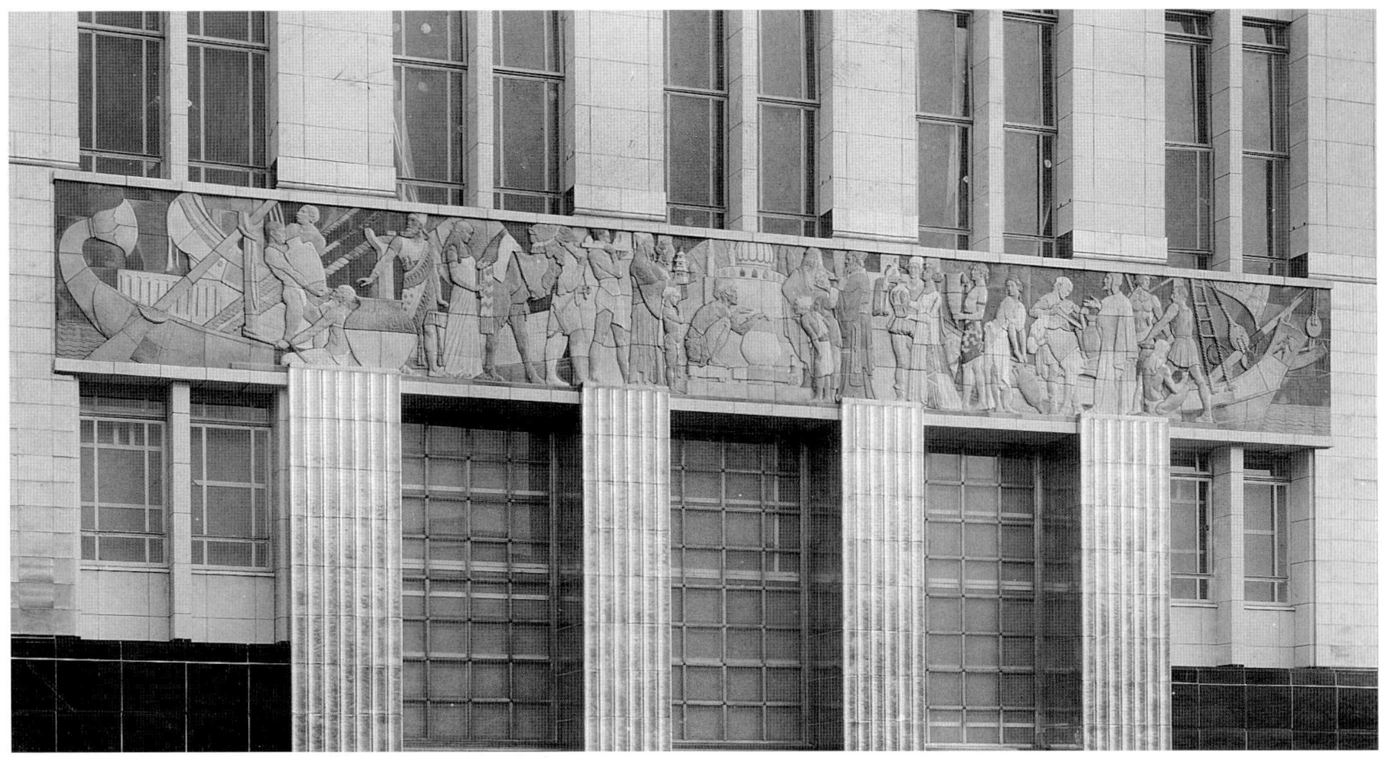

Facade of Doulton House, Lambeth, showing the Pottery Through the Ages frieze (now in the Victoria & Albert Museum)

1940

Maurice Webb FRIBA, 1880-1939

Medium: Bronze
Locations: Originally above the principal entrance, Bentall's department store, Kingston, now in the archive. Commissioned by Leonard H. Bentall, JP and inscribed 'Friend, Collaborator, Architect'.
Literature: *The Builder* 1940 Aug p131, illus; *The Architect and Building News* 1940 Aug p89, illus.

Maurice Webb FRIBA was the architect of Bentall's store, Kingston-upon-Thames, Surrey.

Progress

Medium: Pencil drawing for relief

H. Gordon Selfridge, 1858-1947

Medium: Bronze panel cast by Singer's
Size: H 45 ins W 73 ins (114 x 187cms)
Exhibitions: Royal Academy 1941 (frieze)
Locations: Selfridge's, Oxford Street, London. Originally in the Palm Court restaurant, now in Gordon's Bar. Unveiled by H.G. Selfridge May 1940, the founder of the department store.

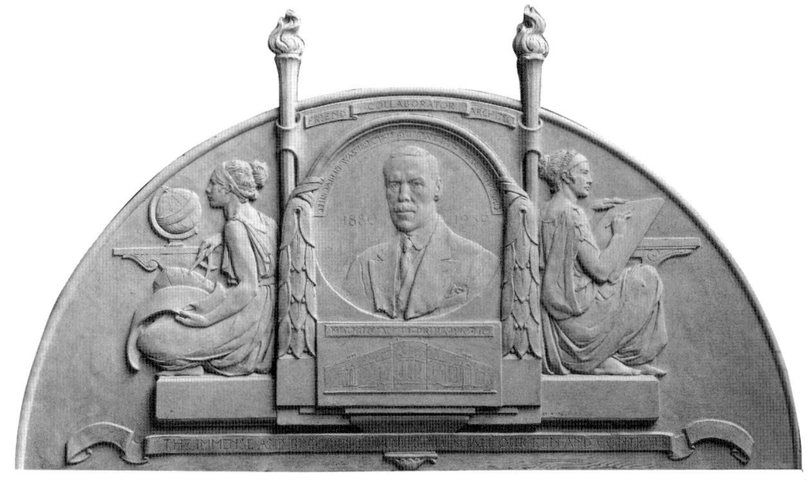

Maurice Webb Memorial

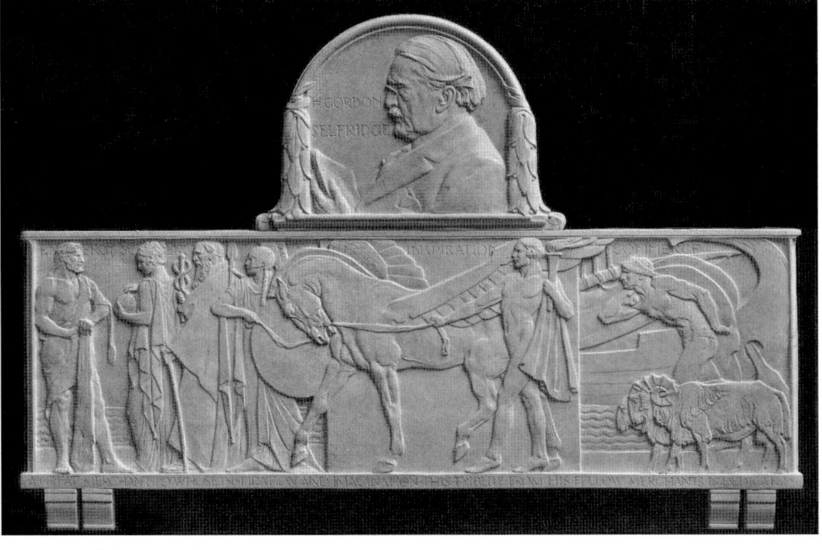

H.G. Selfridge panel

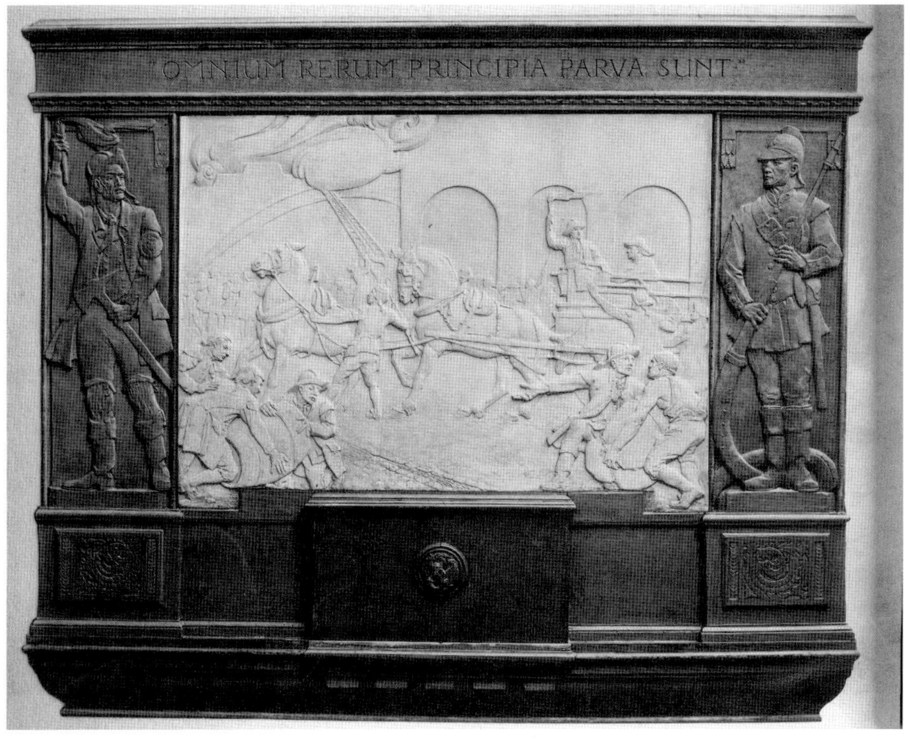

London Fire Brigade Memorial

Medium: Stone and bronze panel
Exhibitions: Royal Academy 1942 (When London Burned Reliefs)
Locations: London Fire Brigade HQ, Albert Embankment, London, presented in 1937 by
               the insurance offices whose brigades were formed into London Fire Brigade in
               1833.

Inscribed Omnium Rerum Principia Parva Sunt (The Beginnings of all Things are Small).

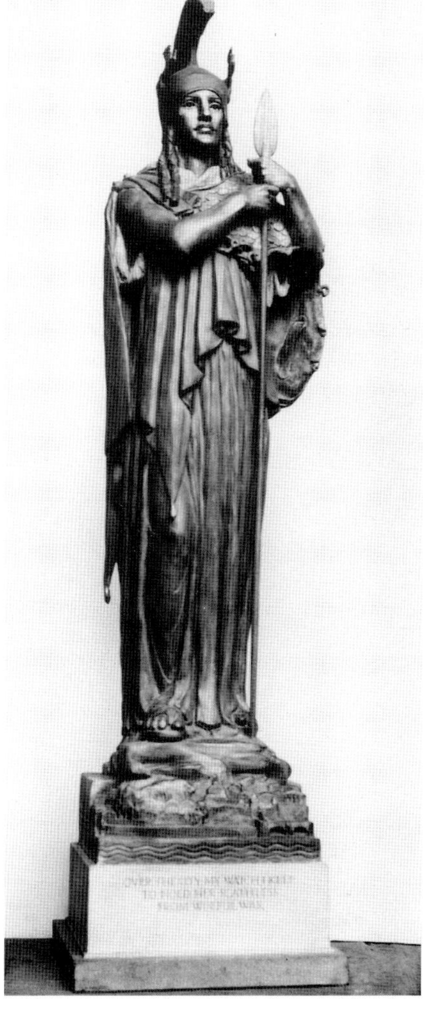

The Vigil

1941

The Vigil or 'Over the City My Watch I Keep', Law Society War Memorial

Medium: Bronze statue
Exhibitions: Royal Academy 1941
Locations: Law Society, Chancery Lane,
               London, (this memorial to
               solicitors and articled clerks
               was dedicated by the
               Archbishop of Canterbury in
               1949); Bayes Trust (half-size
               plaster).

London and North Eastern Railway Medal for Bravery

Medium: Silver
Size: D 1¹⁄₂ins (4cms)
Exhibitions: Royal Academy 1943
Locations: Bayes Trust; Imperial War
               Museum.
Literature: The Numismatic Chronicle
               1992 pl 25, illus.

Twenty-two medals were presented before
the award was discontinued in 1947. The
lettering was by Jean Bayes.

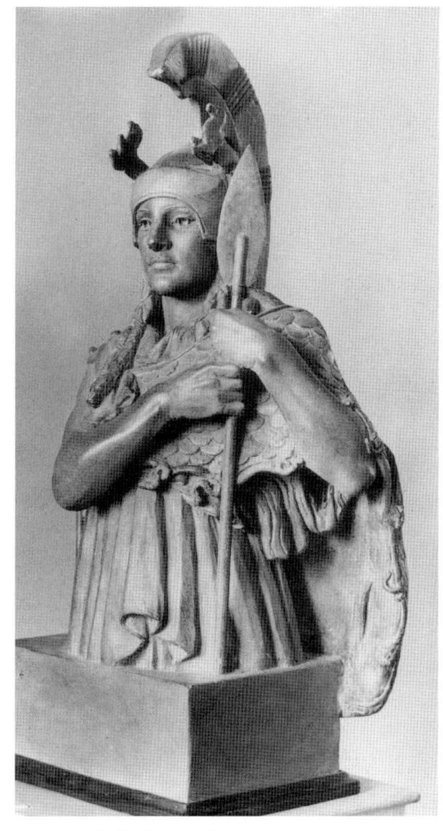

The Vigil, half-size plaster

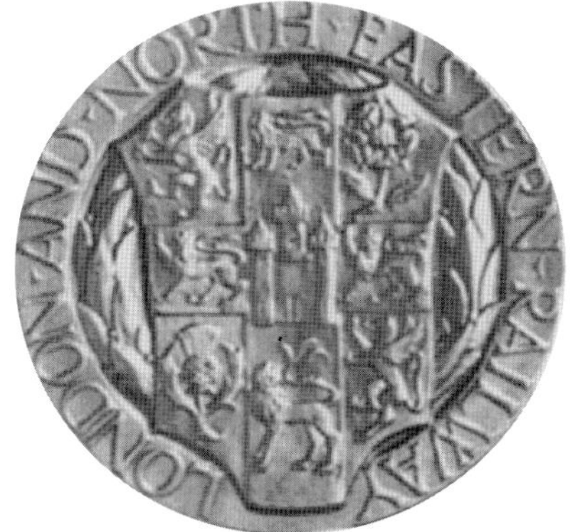

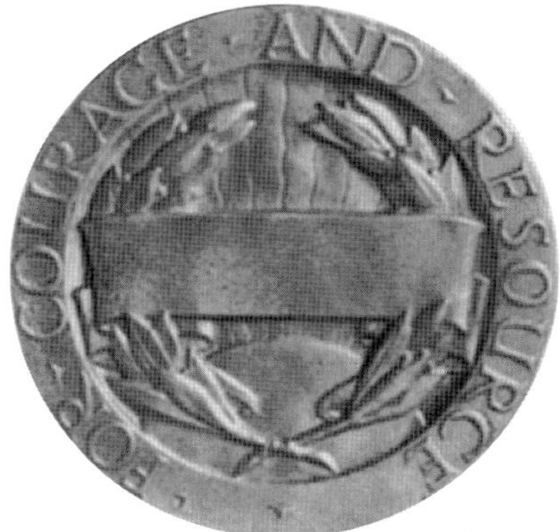

*London and North Eastern Railway
Medal for Bravery*

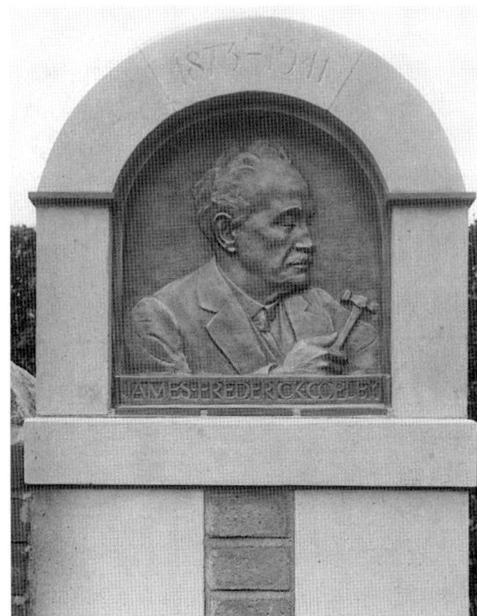

James Frederick Copley

James Frederick Copley, 1873-1941
Medium: Bronze relief
Locations: New Mill Working Men's Club,
Holmfirth, Yorkshire
Five small versions of the plaque were made
for members of the family.

1942

The Goose Girl
Medium: Plaster maquette for bronze cast
by Singer's
Exhibitions: Royal Academy 1942; Glasgow
1942; Bournemouth 1943
(75gns); Southport 1944; Sussex
Artists, Hove 1948; Institute
1949; Ealing 1950.
Locations: Bayes Trust

Captain Glyn Rhys-Williams
Medium: Bronze
Size: H 15ins (39cms)
Exhibitions: Royal Academy 1943
Locations: Private collection
Presented by friends in Glamorgan to mark
his 21st birthday.

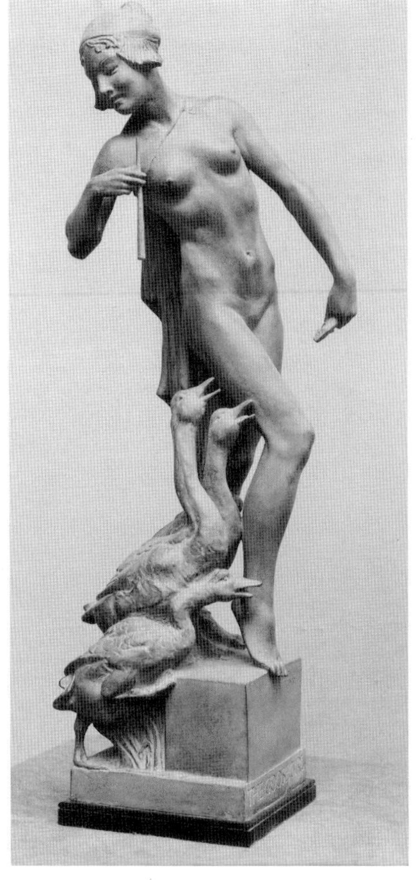

The Goose Girl

Shire Horse Being Groomed
Medium: Bronze

1943

On a Windy Day
Exhibitions: Royal Academy 1943 (200gns)

The Sultana of Champough:
Portrait of Jean Bayes
Medium: Portrait bust
Size: H 25^{1}/$_{2}$ins (65cms)
Exhibitions: Institute 1943
Locations: Bayes Trust

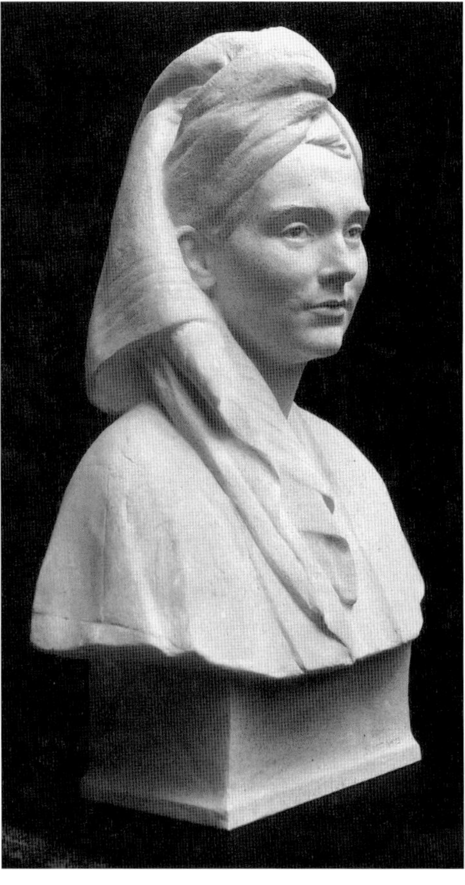

The Sultana of Champough

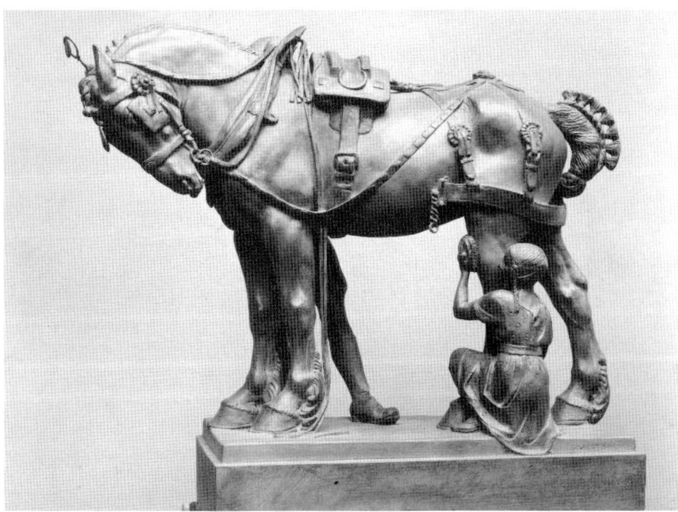

Shire horse being groomed

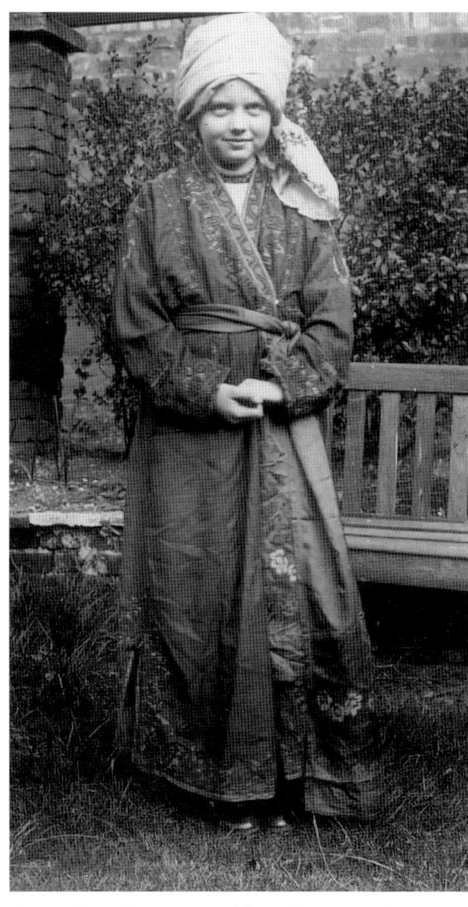

*An earlier photograph of Jean Bayes as the
Sultana of Champough*

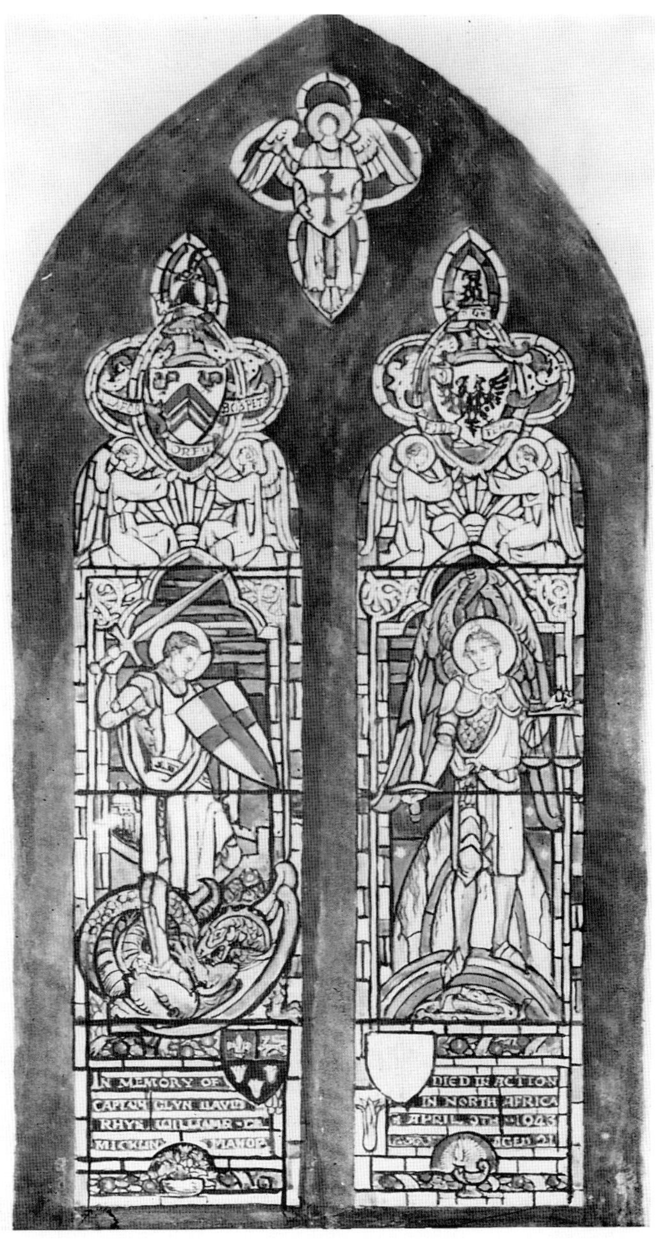

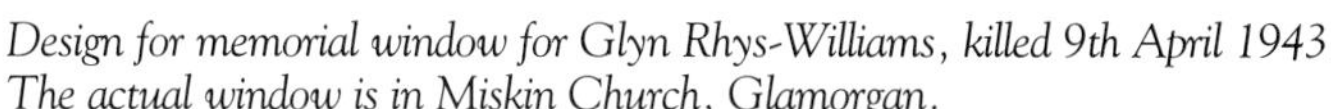

Design for memorial window for Glyn Rhys-Williams, killed 9th April 1943.
The actual window is in Miskin Church, Glamorgan.

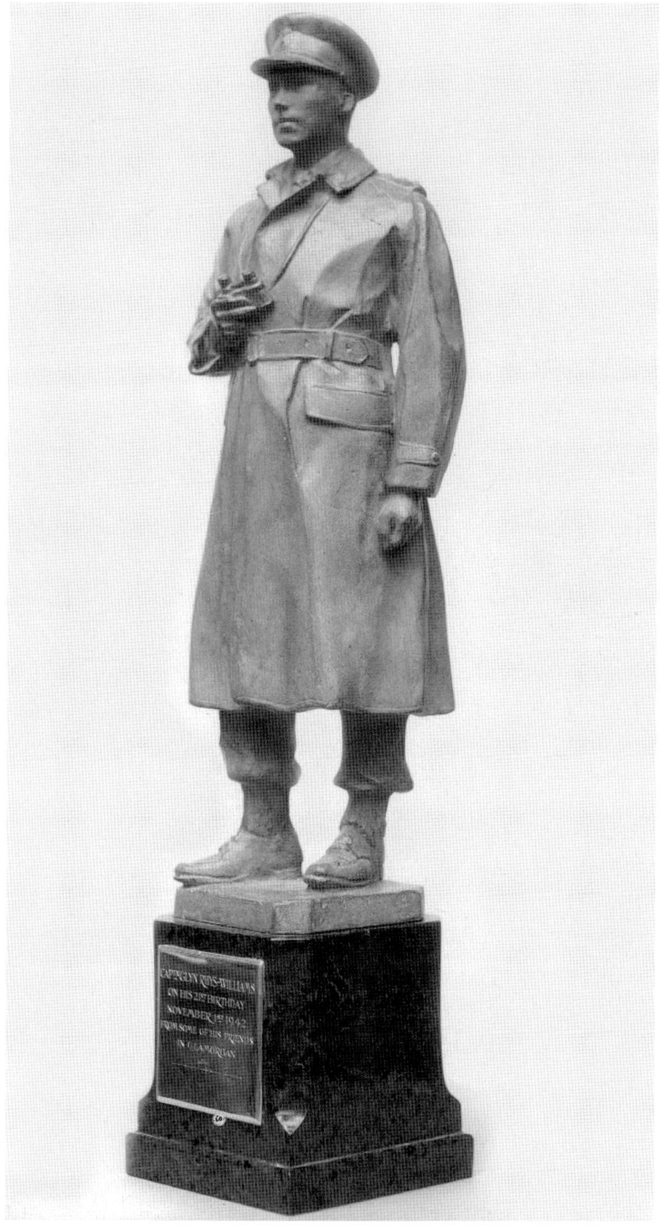

Captain Glyn Rhys-Williams

Young Bacchus

Medium: Bronze relief
Size: H 32ins W 18ins
     (81 x 46.5cms)
Exhibitions: Royal Academy 1944
Locations: Sotheby's Belgravia
     28.5.75 (dated 1943 –
     sold £180)

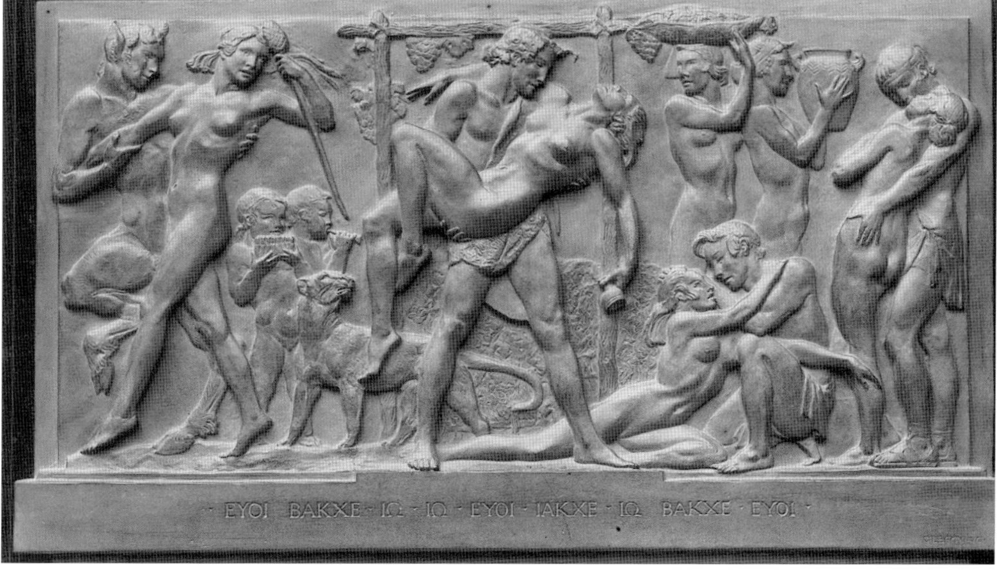

Young Bacchus

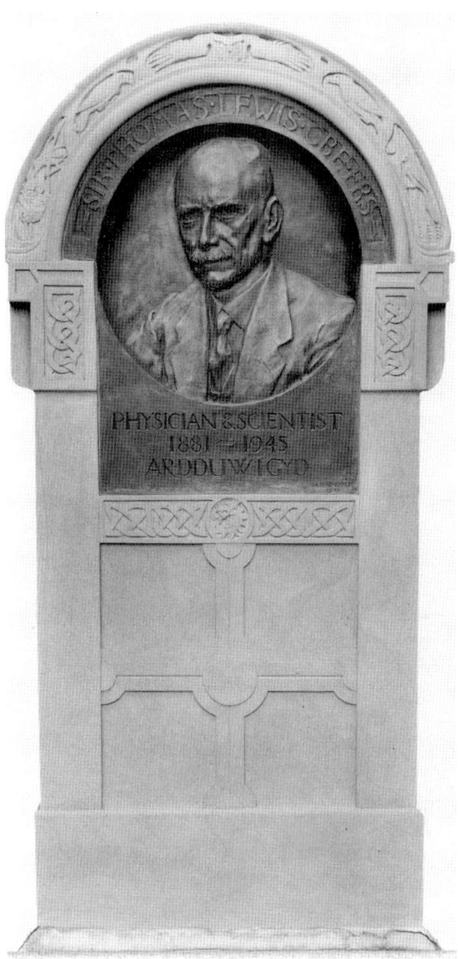

Sir Thomas Lewis

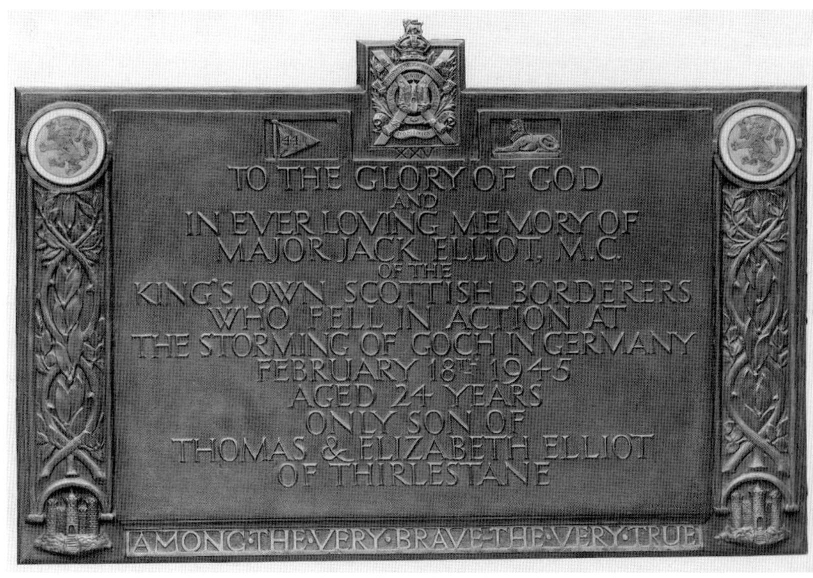

Major Jack Elliott Memorial

1944

The Challenger

Medium: Bronze statuette
Size: H 25¼ins (64.5cms)
Exhibitions: Royal Academy 1944
Locations: Sotheby's 9.6.89 (dated 1944
            – sold)

This is a variation of *The Challenger* from 1914.

Bacchus

Medium: Plaster figure

1945

Major Jack Elliot MC Memorial Panel, d.1945

Locations: Thirlestane

1946

Sir Thomas Lewis CBE FRS Memorial, 1881-1945

Medium: Bronze cast by Singer's

1947

Alice Margaret Douglas BA Memorial

Medium: Stone

The Surgeon

Medium: Plaster
Exhibitions: Institute 1947

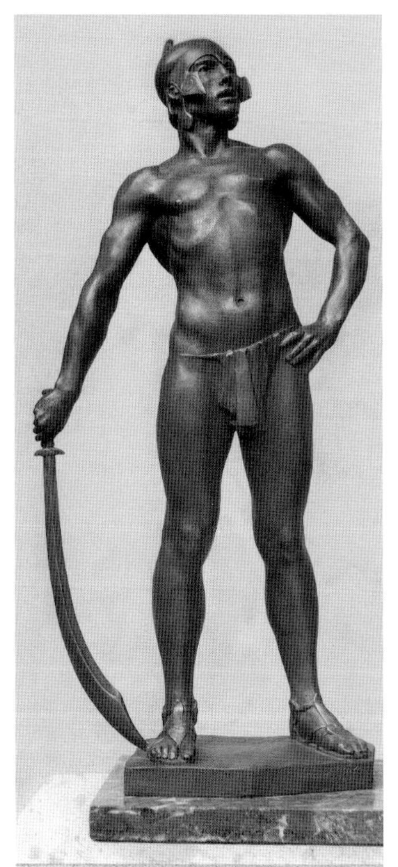

The Challenger

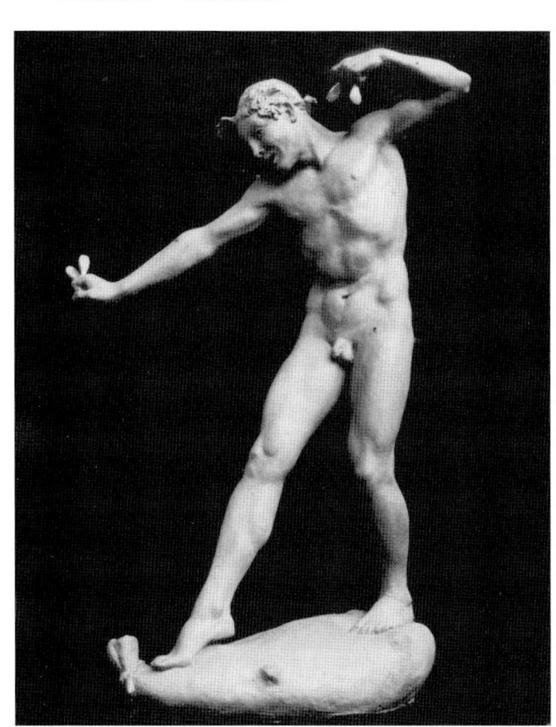

Bacchus

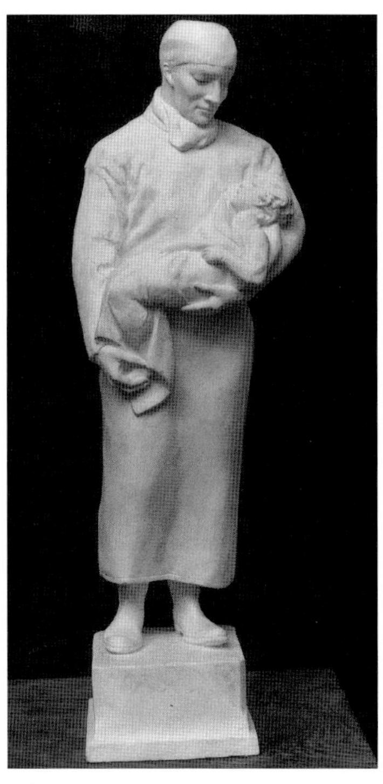

The Surgeon

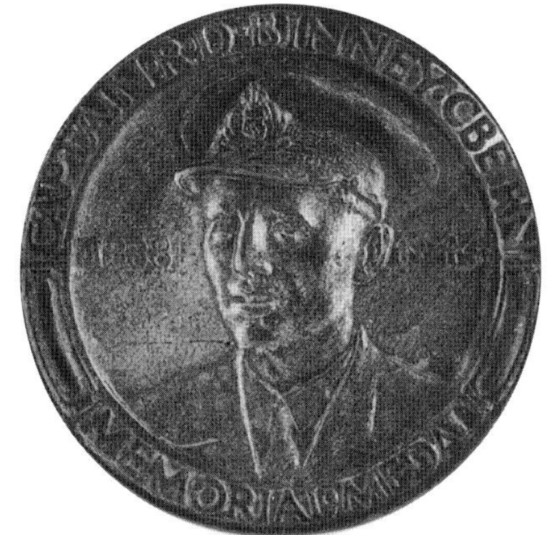

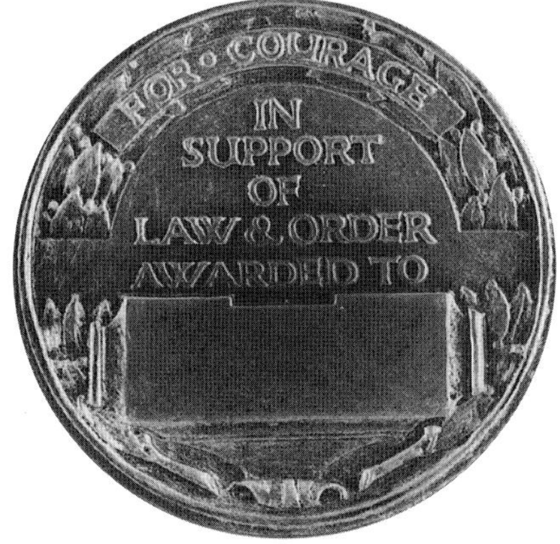

Captain Binney Medal

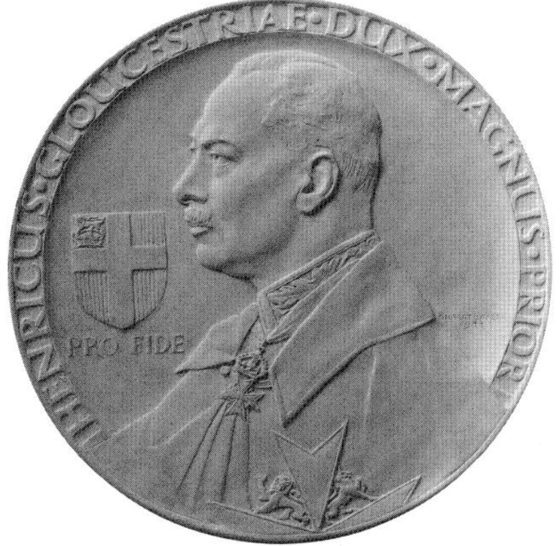

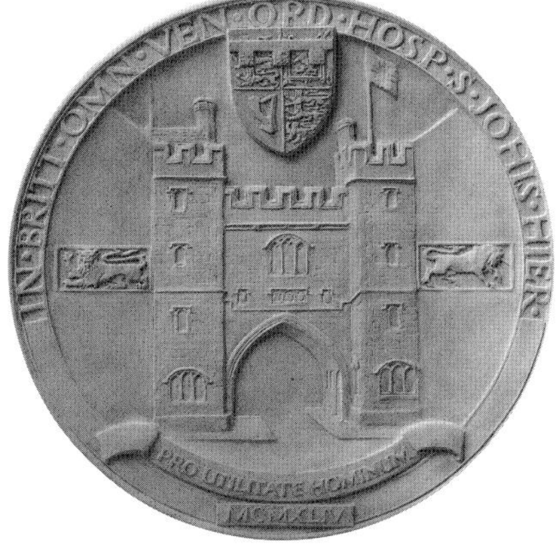

Duke of Gloucester Medal

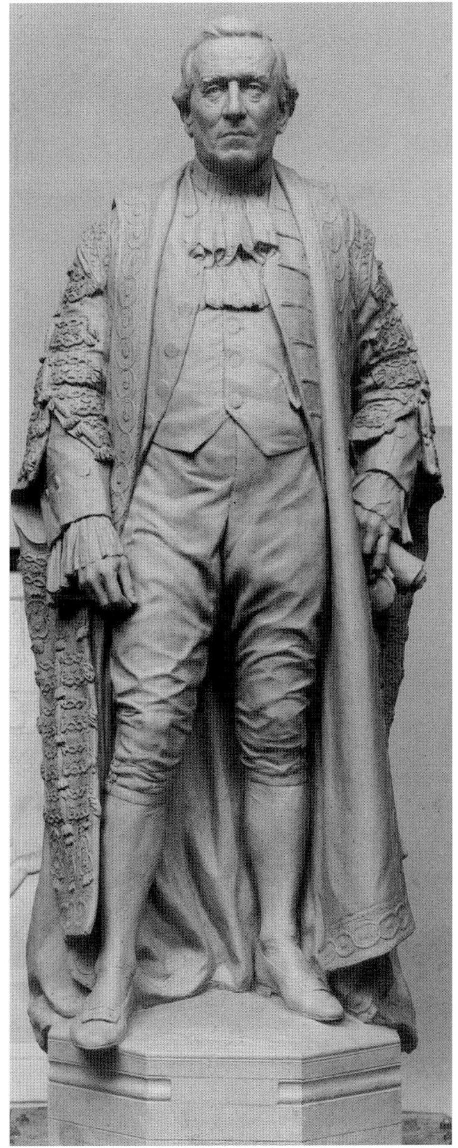

Herbert Asquith

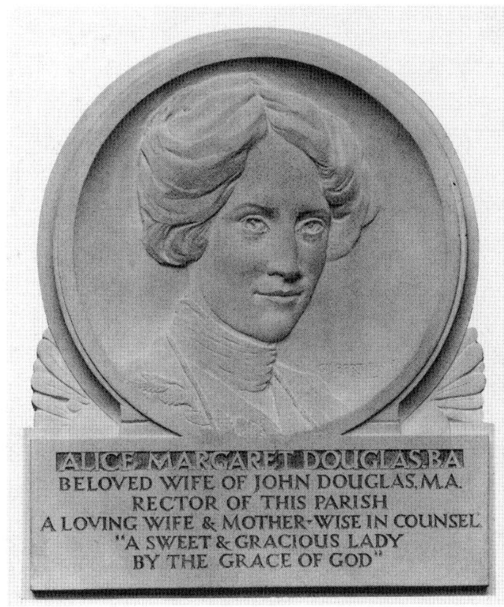

Alice Margaret Douglas

Captain R.D. Binney CBE RN Memorial Medal

Medium: Bronze
Size: D 1³/₄ins (4.5cms)
Locations: Bayes Trust and holders

Captain Binney was killed in December 1944 while single-handedly trying to catch armed robbers in the City of London. The Memorial Medal which was instituted in 1947 is awarded annually to the British citizen who displays the greatest courage in support of law and order in the areas covered by the Metropolitan and City of London Police.

1948

Herbert Asquith, Lord Oxford, 1852-1928

Medium: Marble
Locations: House of Commons, erected 1950

Leonard Merrifield began this commission in 1939 and Gilbert Bayes finished it in 1948. Herbert Asquith, Liberal politician and Prime Minister, 1908-1916.

Order of St John, Duke of Gloucester Medal

Exhibitions: Royal Academy 1950
Locations: British Museum and holders
Literature: *The Numismatic Chronicle* 1992 pl 27, illus.

Martin Bayes

Medium: Bronze portrait head
Size: H 10¹/₂ins (27cms) plus base
Exhibitions: Ealing 1951; Royal Academy 1952.
Locations: Bayes Trust, plaster and bronze

Martin Bayes was Gilbert Bayes' grandson.

War Memorial Panels

Medium: Bronze cast by Singer's
Locations: Originally at St Olave's Grammar School, Tooley Street, London SE1, now at the school in Orpington Kent.

The war memorial was unveiled by Field Marshall, Sir Claude Auchinleck.

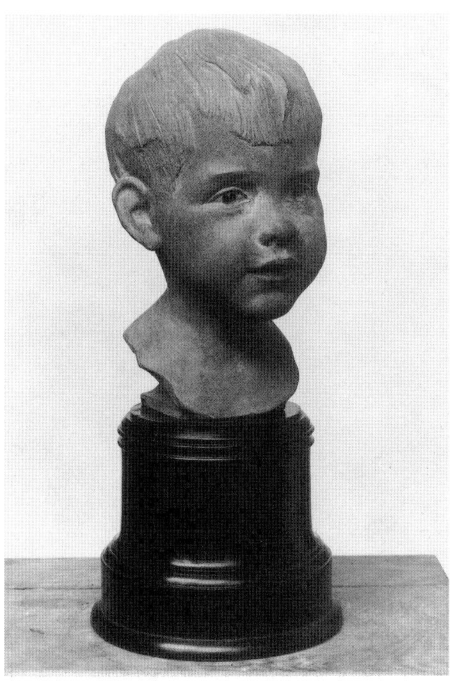

Martin Bayes

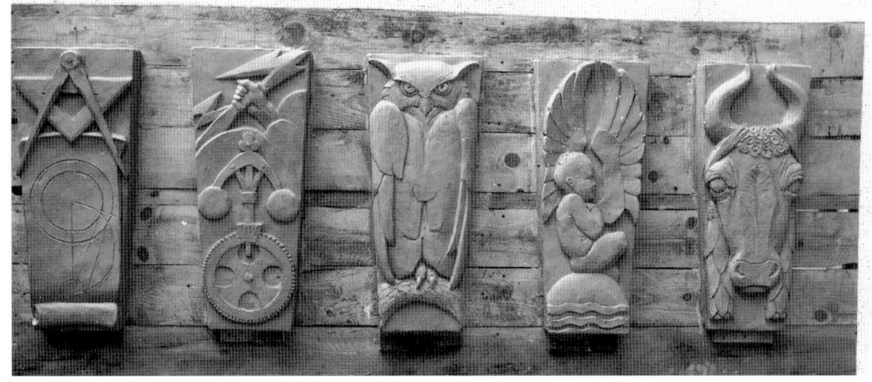

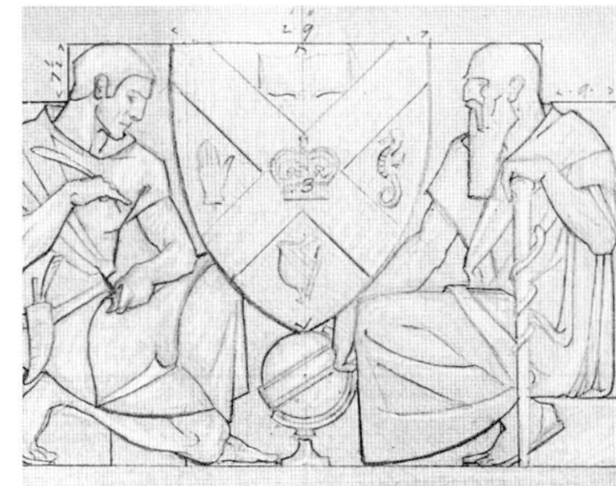

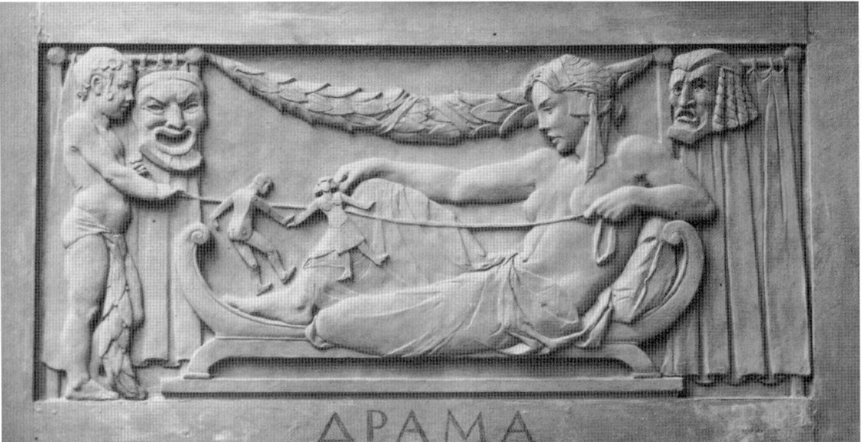

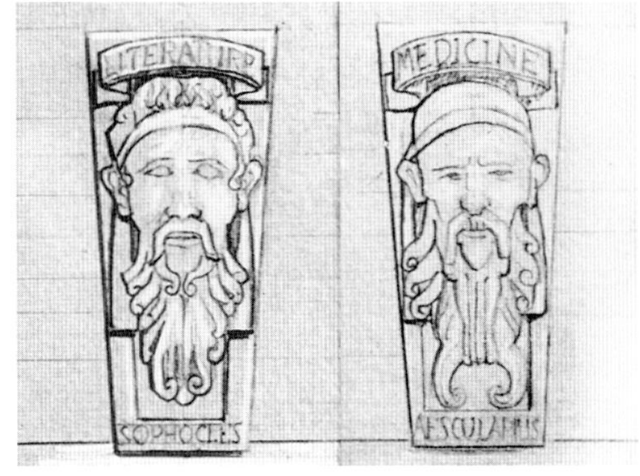

Drawing for panel and keystones

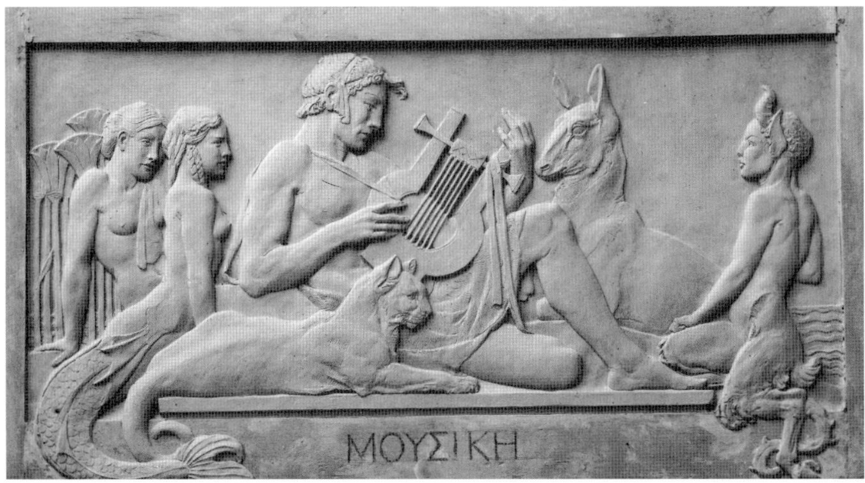

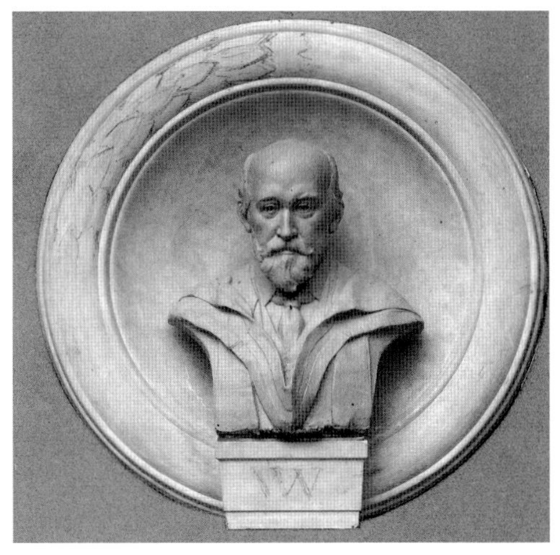

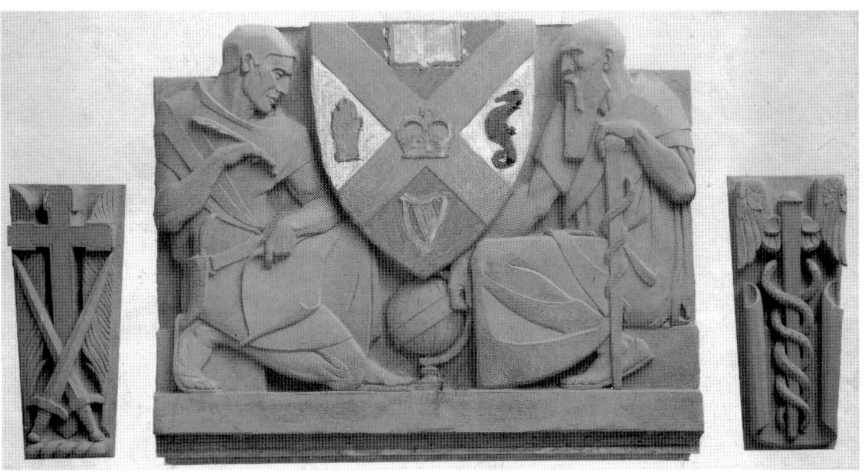

Full-size plasters for the Whitla portrait bust, panels and keystones

Sir William Whitla Hall Portrait Bust, Panels of Music and Drama and Keystones

Medium: Bronze and stone
Locations: Sir William Whitla Hall, Queen's University, Belfast. Fourteen stone keystones with symbols of science and humanities carved by Morris Harding and finished by Bayes; plaster panels of *Music* and *Drama* for entrance halls; University Arms and bronze bust of Sir William Whitla for exterior – total cost £770.

Whitla, 1857-1933, was a physician and professor of medicine at the University. Architect John MacGeach commissioned Bayes in 1939 and the work was finished by 1948.

1950

Goldcoast Forces War Memorial

Medium:	Bronze cast by Singer's
Size:	H 7ft 4ins (1.93m)
Locations:	Accra, Ghana, commissioned 1946, completed 1950

1951

Harvest Panel

Medium:	Empire stone
Size:	H 36ins W 50ins (91 x 127cms)
Locations:	Withersdane Hall, Wye College (originally the School of Agriculture and Horticulture for the University of London)

The panel was given by Miss E.A. Jones, a member of the college's governing body.

1952

Imperial Chemical Industries War Memorial Obelisk and Panels

Medium:	Portland stone and bronze cast by Singer's.
Locations:	Imperial Chemical Industries, Billingham, Stockton on Tees Co. Durham. Commissioned in 1947 at a cost of £1,573. Moved in 1996 to Station Road, Billingham.

Flight Wings

Exhibitions: Bournemouth 1952

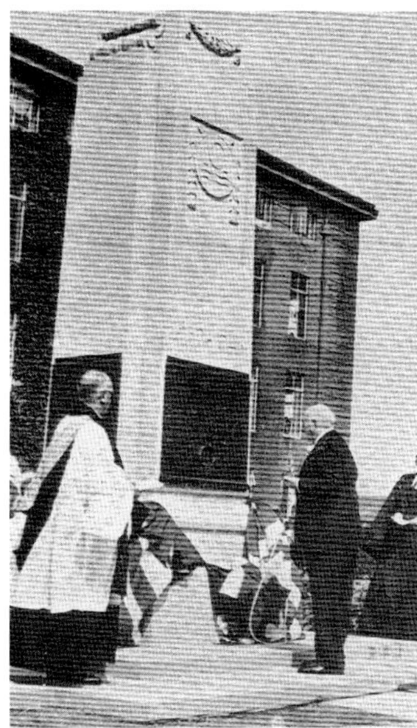

The unveiling of Billingham War Memorial by Lord McGowan, 1949

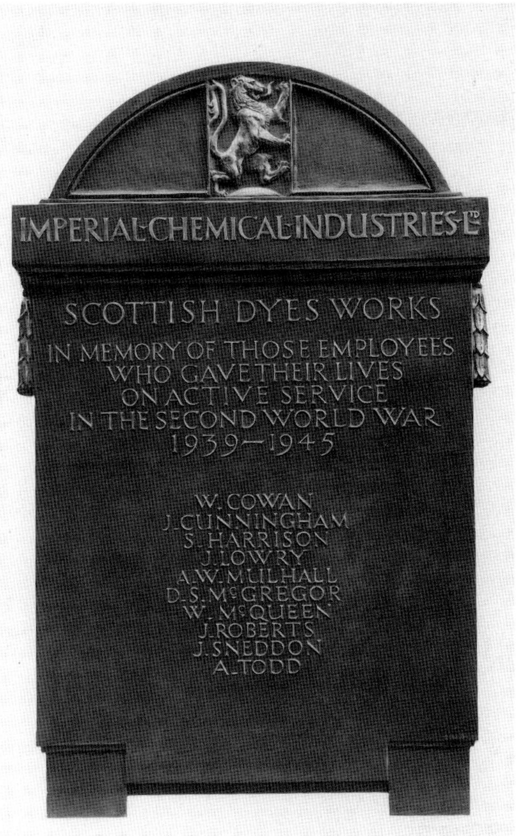

War Memorial panel for ICI's Scottish Dyes Works

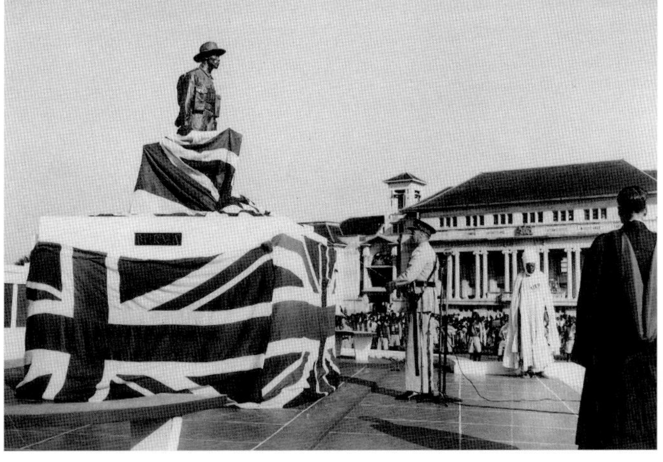

The unveiling of the Gold Coast War Memorial, 1950

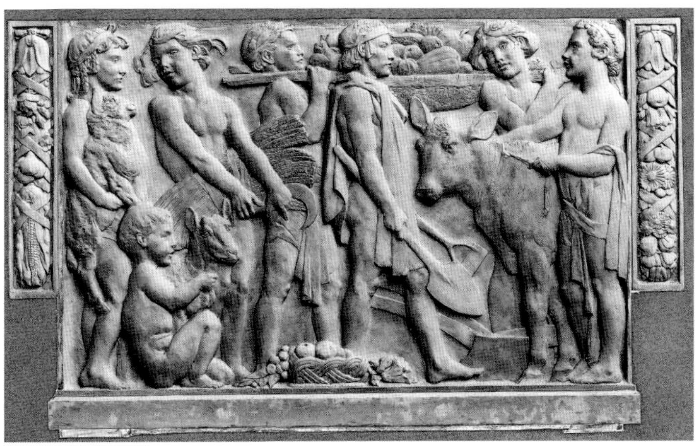

Harvest panel

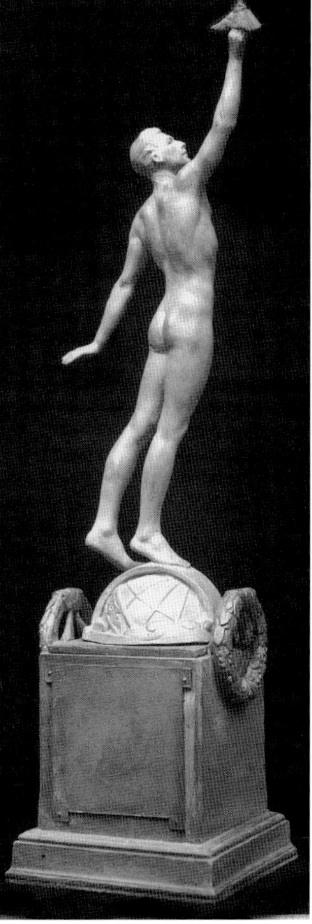

Flight Wings

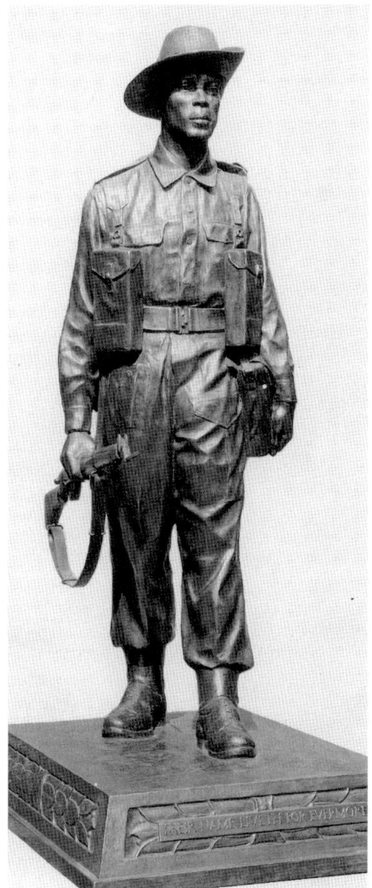

Gold Coast War Memorial

1953

Robert Owen, 1771-1858

Medium: Bronze figure and relief cast
       by Singer's
Locations: Short Bridge Street, Newtown,
       Wales; Bayes Trust (plaster
       quarter-scale figure and relief).
Literature: *The Monument Guide to*
       England and Wales, Jo Darke
       1991 p114, illus.

This memorial to the social reformer and philanthropist was completed by W.C.H. King (1954) after Bayes' death.

St Christopher

Medium: Bronze figure
Size: 16$^{1}/_{2}$ins (42cms)
Locations: Bayes Trust (plaster and
       bronze)

This figure was inspired by the Royal Automobile Club Plaque d'Honneur.

Royal Automobile Club Plaque d'Honneur

Medium: Bronze cast by Pinches
Size: H 3$^{1}/_{2}$ ins W 5ins
       (9 x 12.5cms)
Locations: Society of Motor
       Manufacturers and Traders
       (1975) and other holders

This plaque was awarded by the Royal Automobile Club between 1954 and 1979 to mark anniversaries and other events at motor clubs around the world.

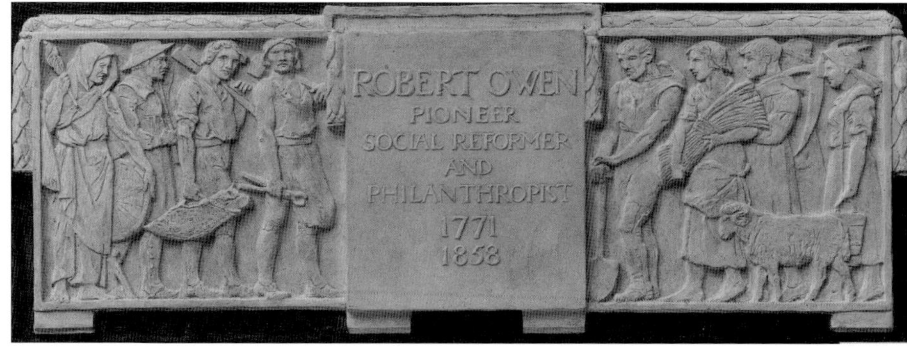

Plaster for the Robert Owen panel

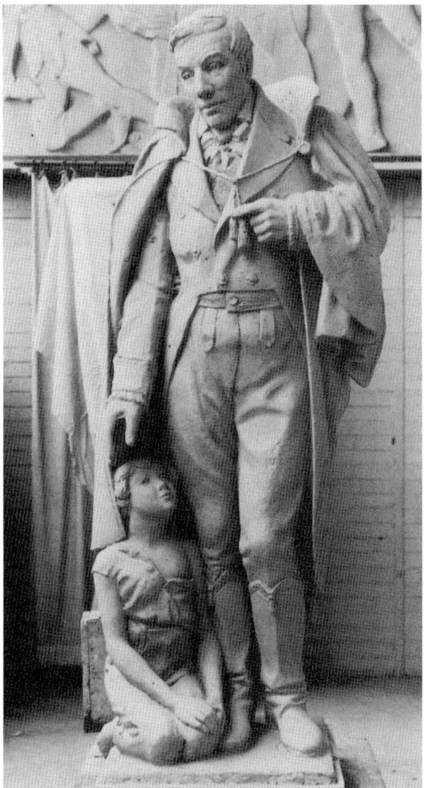

Full-size plaster for the Owen statue

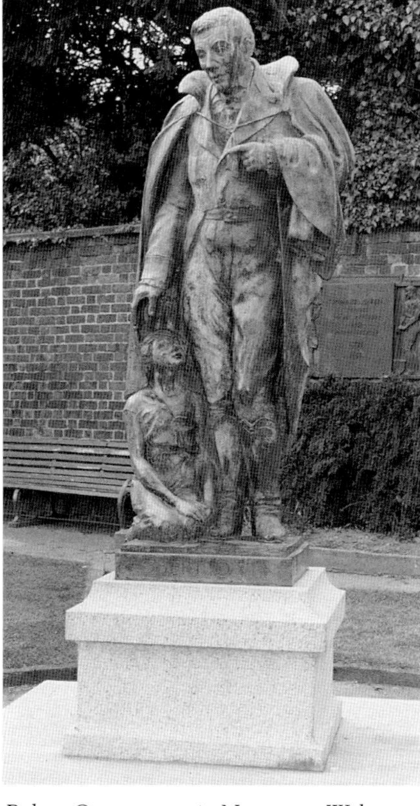

Robert Owen statue in Newtown, Wales

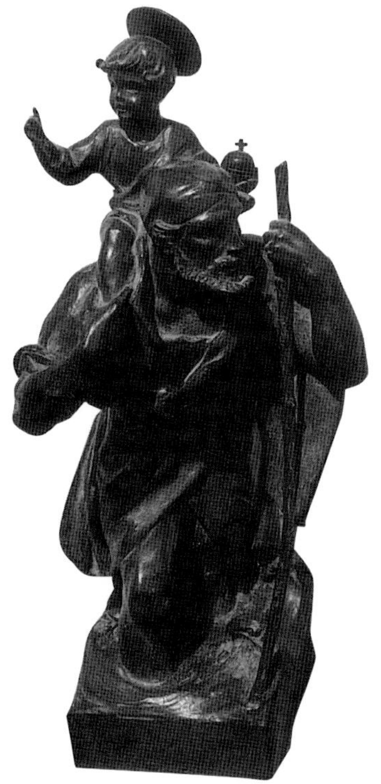

St Christopher

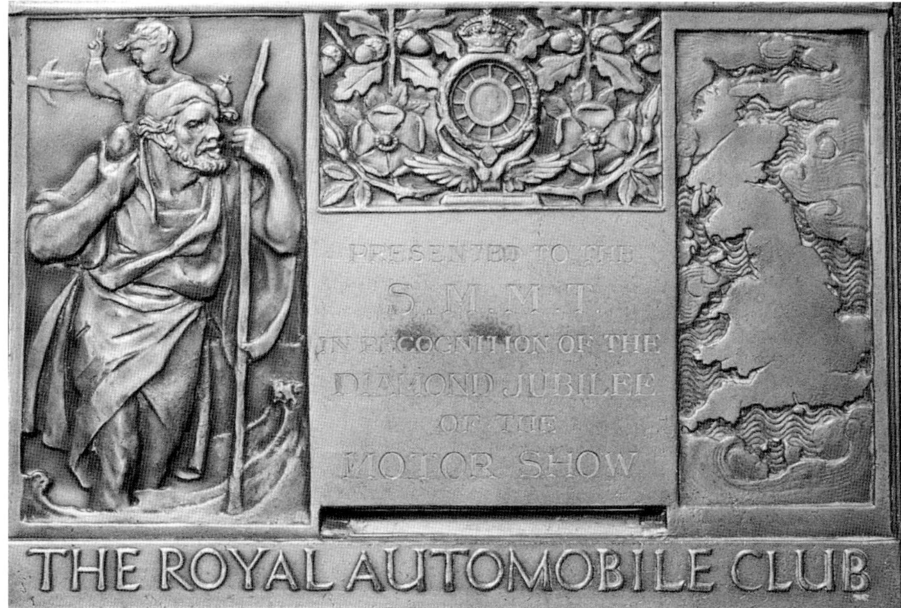

Royal Automobile Club Plaque d'Honneur

MISCELLANEOUS WORK

All the following pieces are known to be by Bayes, but there is no information about them and their present whereabouts is unknown. Most of the photographs come from the Bayes Trust archive. Some of the bronzes have passed recently through the London art market, but no other details are known.

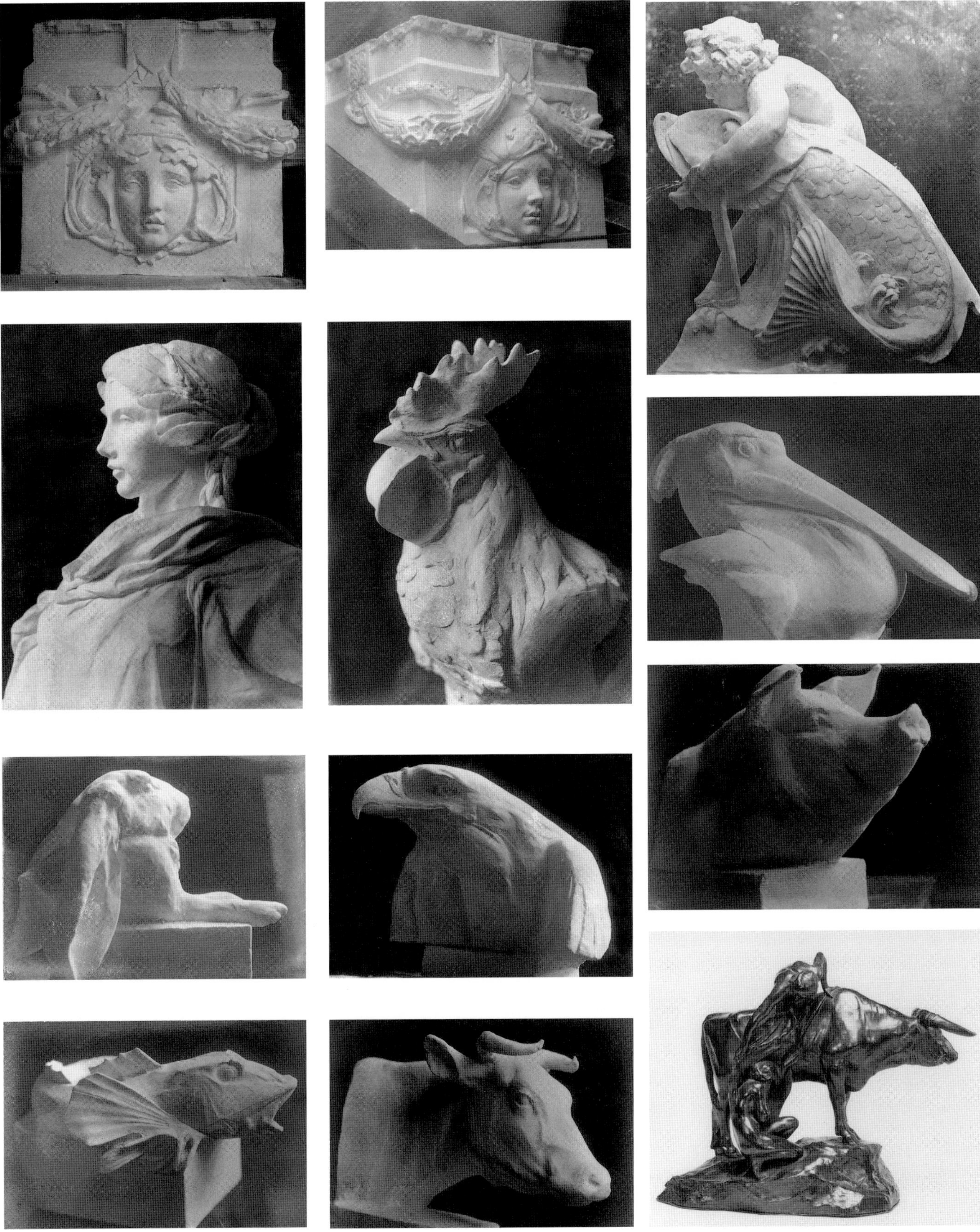

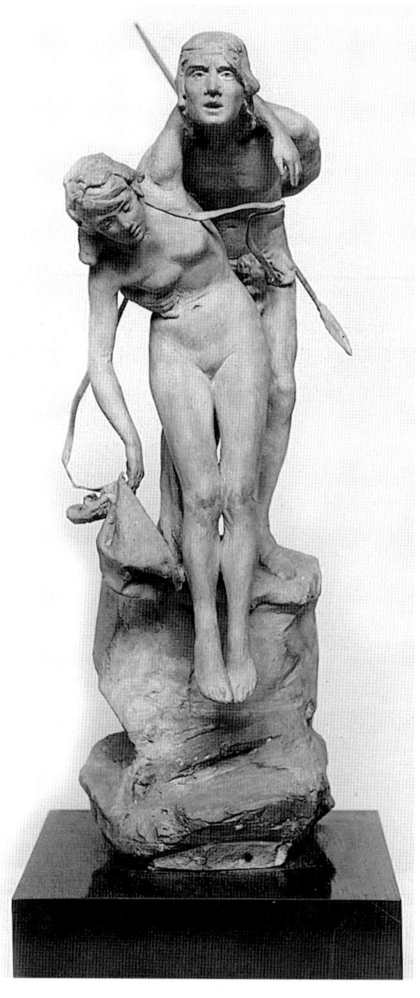

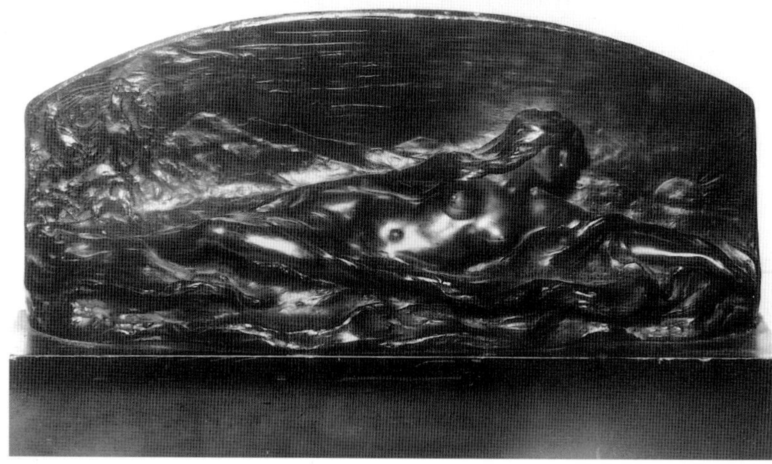

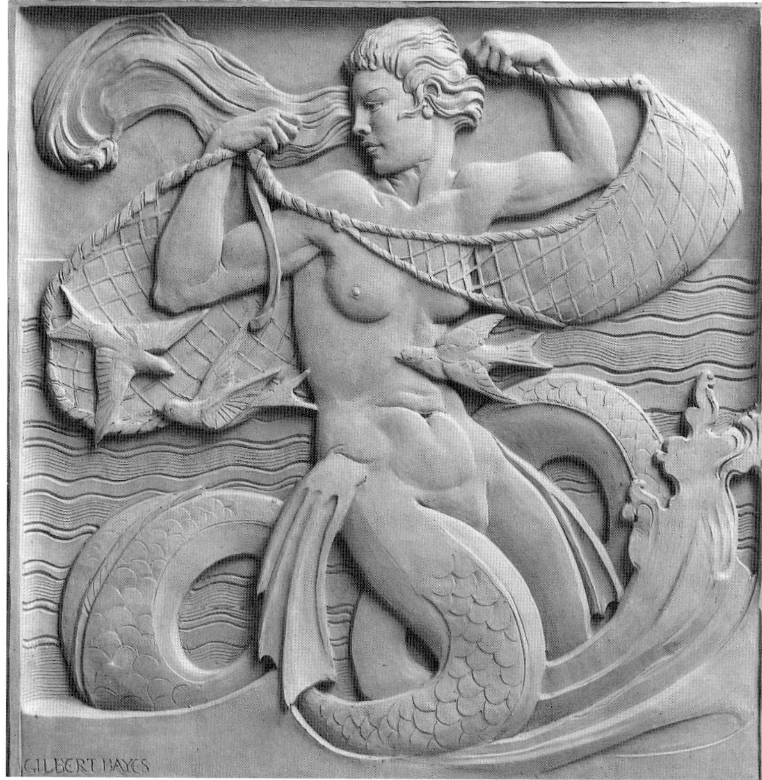

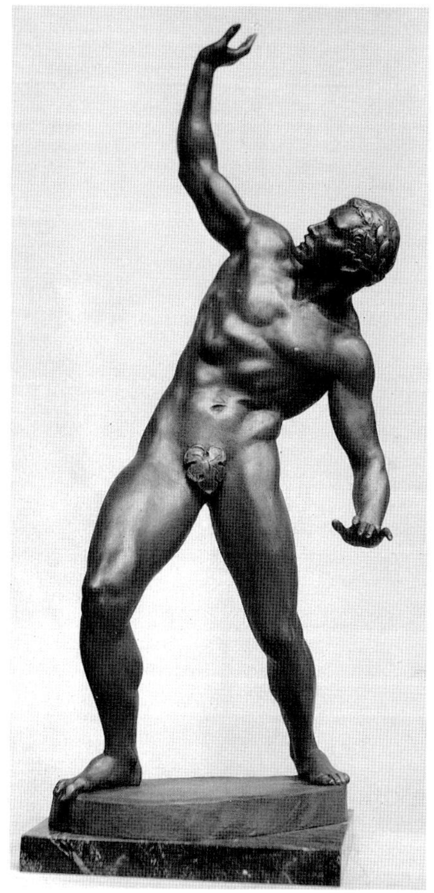

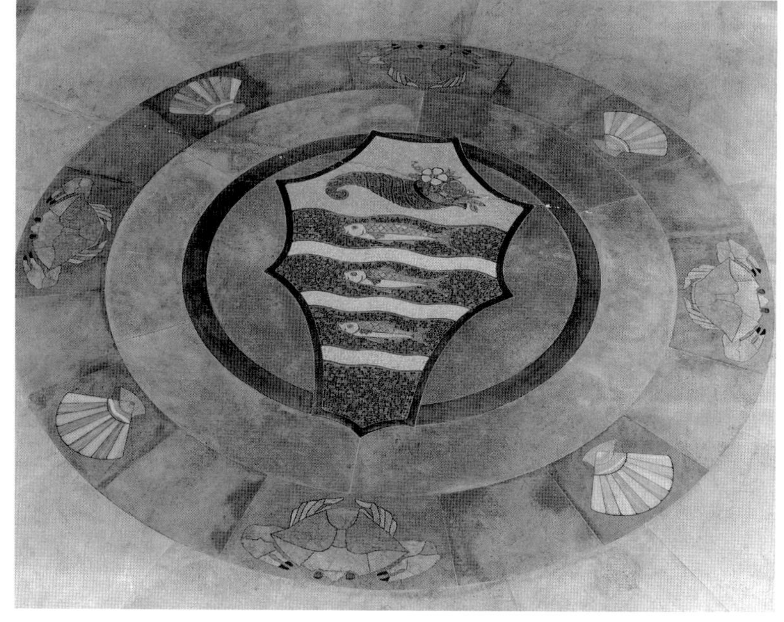

EXHIBITION VENUES

Bayes kept a notebook which gives brief details of the pieces that he sent to art galleries and other venues between 1909 and 1953. Further details have been gleaned from contemporary exhibition catalogues. His more important venues have been listed below with the periods that he exhibited.

ABERDEEN Aberdeen Artists Society, Aberdeen Art Gallery, 1921-1937. This society began in 1885, the same year that the gallery was opened.

BIRMINGHAM Royal Society of Artists 1890-1912.

BOURNEMOUTH Russell Cotes Gallery, 1943 and 1948. These were exhibitions of contemporary sculpture predominantly by members of the Royal Society of British Sculpture.

BRISTOL Royal West of England Academy, Queens Road, 1913-1937. Bayes showed regularly at these exhibitions which began at the Academy gallery in 1858.

GLASGOW Royal Glasgow Institute of the Fine Arts, 1901-1942.

EDINBURGH Royal Scottish Academy, 1913-1939.

LIVERPOOL Walker Art Gallery Autumn Exhibition, 1892-1935. Bayes exhibited regularly at these annual exhibitions which began in 1889.

LONDON Arts and Crafts Exhibition Society, 1888-1931.

LONDON Ealing Arts Club, 1947-1953. This club was established in 1910 and Bayes was their President for a while. He also wrote letters for their journal in the 1940s.

LONDON Fine Art Society, 1902-1920. Bayes showed work at the exhibition of British and French sculptors organised by M.H. Spielman in 1902. Thereafter, the Fine Art Society handled his work sporadically until 1920.

LONDON Goupil Gallery, 1907-1926. The annual salon at the Goupil Gallery was inaugurated in 1906 with a view to bringing together the works of artists of various tendencies.

LONDON Leicester Galleries, Leicester Square, 1914-1918. Several bronze statuettes by Bayes were kept in stock at this gallery, which was founded in 1902 by Ernest Brown and Phillips, formerly of the Fine Art Society.

LONDON New Gallery, 121 Regent Street, 1897-1906.

LONDON Pastel Society, 1933-1936. Bayes showed a few sculptures, mainly coloured Doulton stoneware, at these exhibitions held at the Royal Institute Galleries.

LONDON Ridley Arts Club, 1900-1946. Gilbert Bayes was on the council of this society which was constituted as a sketch club in memory of the late Mathew White Ridley, a well-known art master of the time and a friend of Whistler's. For some years, membership of the club was confined to his students and friends and then the circle was enlarged. The club aimed to be catholic in its ideals but inclined to the conservative rather than the experimental and revolutionary. Exhibitions were held at the Spring Garden Galleries, Trafalgar Square.

LONDON Royal Academy of Arts, Burlington House, 1889-1952. Bayes first exhibited at the Royal Academy at the age of seventeen and continued until he was eighty years old, the year before his death.

LONDON Royal Society of British Sculptors, 1928 and 1947. Bayes helped organise an exhibition of garden sculpture on behalf of the RBS at the Royal Horticultural Society in 1928. An exhibition of children in sculpture was mounted at the Royal Watercolour Society in 1947. Bayes was President of the RBS from 1939 to 1944.

LONDON Royal Institute of Painters in Water Colours, 1911-1953. Bayes was an honorary sculptor member of this society from 1918 and frequently showed statuettes at its exhibitions.

LONDON Royal Society of British Artists, 1890-1892. Bayes exhibited a few early wax reliefs at this society's exhibitions in Suffolk Street.

LONDON Royal Society of British Portrait Painters, 1905-1909. This society was founded in 1891 and included sculptors from 1899 when they exhibited at the New Gallery. Exhibitions were later held at the Grafton Galleries and the Suffolk Street Galleries.

LONDON Sir John Cass Arts and Crafts Society, 1909 and 1913. Bayes was an honorary member of this society which held its first exhibition in 1906. Bayes taught at Sir John Cass Art School briefly after the First World War.

LONDON Society of Graphic Arts, 1931-1938.

LONDON Whitechapel Art Gallery Exhibition of Contemporary British Art, 1929.

SOUTHPORT Atkinson Art Gallery, Southport, 1910-1950. Bayes showed his work regularly at the spring exhibition organised by this gallery which began in 1879.

WOLVERHAMPTON Art Gallery and Museum Special Autumn Exhibition, 1912 and 1920.

INTERNATIONAL EXHIBITIONS AND OVERSEAS VENUES

ARGENTINA
Buenos Aires 1928: *Sigurd, Guardian of the Seas.*

BELGIUM
Ghent Arts and Crafts Exhibition 1913: *Jason Ploughing the Acres of Mars, Newel Post, Amor Victor, Fountain of the Valkyries, Medal Case, Great Seal of George V.*
Ghent Exposition Universelle et Industrielle 1913: Fine Arts section: *Sigurd, Lord Nunburnholme Memorial Angel, Under the Moon.*

BRAZIL
Rio de Janeiro 1930: *Sea King's Daughter, Frog Princess, Wealth of the Earth, Wings of the Wind, Greek Dancer, Young Diana.*

CANADA
Toronto 1912: *Greek Dancer, Top Spinner, Wings of the Wind, Angel of the Off Shore Wind, Reverie, Storm Ride, White Horses.*
Toronto 1913: *The Years at the Spring.*
Toronto 1914: *Door Knocker.*
Toronto 1925: *Door Knocker, The Recorder.*
Toronto, Canadian National Exhibition 1927: *Brynhilde.*
Toronto, Canadian National Exhibition 1928: *Sea King's Daughter, Bacchante.*
Toronto, Canadian National 1929: *Moon and the Lotus Pond, Mask, Water Baby, Philosopher.*
Toronto, Canadian National 1935: *Diana, Moon and the Lotus Pond.*

CHINA
Art to China 1943: *Mermaid, Guardian of the Seas.*

FRANCE
Paris Exposition Universelle 1900: *Jason Ploughing the Acres of Mars* and some door panels (Honourable Mention).
Paris Arts and Crafts 1914: *Fountain of the Valkyries, Greek Dancer, Sea King's Daughter, Monkey Newel Post, Jason Ploughing the Acres of Mars.*
Paris Exposition Internationale des Arts Decoratifs et Industriels Modernes 1925: *Blue Robed Bambino* (Gold Medal), *King Cophetua.*

Paris British Artists Exhibition, 1927: *King Cophetua.*
Paris Salon 1939: *Frog Princess* (Gold Medal).

HOLLAND
Hague 1923: *St George.*

ITALY
Venice 1910: *Greek Dancer.*
Rome, International Fine Arts Exhibition 1911: *Greek Dancer, Sigurd with Ring.*
Venice 1922: *Wealth of the Earth.*
Rome 1923: *Unfolding of Spring, Roman Wine Cart, Sigurd.*
Venice 1928: *Moon and the Lotus Pond, King Cophetua.*

NEW ZEALAND
Christchurch, New Zealand International Exhibition of Arts and Industries 1906-07: *Greek Dancer, Mushroom Sprite, Water Nymphs.*
Dunedin, New Zealand and South Seas International Exhibition, 1925-26: *Wealth of the Earth, St George, Water's Caress.*

UK
London, Franco-British Exhibition 1908: *Amor Victor, White Horses, Knight Roland.*
London Anglo-Japanese Exhibition 1910: *Pegasus, Jason Ploughing the Acres of Mars, Greek Dancer.*
London, British Empire Exhibition, Wembley 1924: *King Cophetua, Anatkh, Fountain of the Valkyries, Blue Robed Bambino.*
Glasgow, British Empire Exhibition, 1938: *Frog Princess, Water's Caress, Pan, Bank of Scotland panels, Saville Theatre frieze detail.*

USA
St Louis, World's Fair 1904: *Jason Ploughing the Acres of Mars.*
International Medallic Exhibition 1910: American Numismatic Society: Selection of plaques and medals.
American Numismatic Society 1924. Selection of medals.
New York World's Fair 1939: *Heraldic Panels.*

BIBLIOGRAPHY

Atterbury, Paul & Irvine, Louise
The Doulton Story The Victoria & Albert
Museum Exhibition catalogue, 1979

Aumonier, W.
Modern Architectural Sculpture, 1930

Biographical Dictionary of Medallists, 1923

Baldry, A.L. (Foreword)
Modern British Sculpture An official record of
some of the works by members of the Royal
Society of British Sculptors, 1921
Modern British Sculpture A record of works by
members of the Royal Society of British
Sculptors, c.1939

Bayes, Gilbert
Modelling for Sculpture, 1930

Beattie, Susan
The New Sculpture, 1983

Bennett, T.P.
Architectural Design in Concrete, 1927

Bluhm, A. & Others
The Colour of Sculpture, 1996

Borg, Alan
War Memorials, 1991

Casson, Stanley
Modern Sculptors, 1928
'Sculpture of Today', *The Studio Special* Spring
1939

Christian, John (Ed)
The Last Romantics Exhibition catalogue,
Barbican Art Gallery, London 1989

Collins, Judith
Eric Gill: The Sculpture, 1998

Compton, Ann
War & Peace Sculpture: Charles Sargeant Jagger,
1985

Cooper, Jeremy
Nineteenth-Century Romantic Bronzes 1830-1915
Exhibition catalogue, 1975

Curcin, M. & Others
Ivan Mestrovic, 1919

Darke, Jo
The Monument Guide to England and Wales, 1991

Dircks, Rudolf
'Mr Gilbert Bayes' *Art Journal*, 1908, pp193-9

Edwards, A. Trystan
*The Architectural Work of Sir John Burnet and
Partners*, 1930

Free, Renée
'Late Victorian, Edwardian and French
Sculptures' *Art Gallery of New South Wales
Quarterly*, January 1972, Vol 13 No.2, pp646-63

Friedman, T. & Others
The Alliance of Sculpture and Architecture, 1993

Gosse, Edmund
'The New Sculpture 1879-1894', *Art Journal*
1894

Handley-Read, L.
British Sculpture 1850-1914 Exhibition
catalogue, Fine Art Society 1968

Irvine, Louise
'Art and Industry' *The Connoisseur*, August 1979

James, Duncan S.
A Century of Statues, The Morris Singer
Foundry 1984

Johnson, D.L.
*Fantastic Illustration and Design in Britain 1850-
1930*: Museum of Art, Rhode Island and
Cooper Hewitt, New York, 1979

Koch, Alex
*Sculptures from Academy Architecture 1904-
1908*, 1908

Marriott, Charles
'The Recent Works of Gilbert Bayes', *The
Studio*, December 1917 Vol 72, pp100-113

Massé, H.J.L.
The Art Workers' Guild, 1935

Nairn, Sandy & Serota, Nicholas
British Sculpture in the Twentieth Century
Exhibition catalogue, Whitechapel Art Gallery,
1981

Parkes, Kineton
Sculpture of Today Volume 1, 1921
The Art of Carved Sculpture, 1931

Physick, J.
*The Victoria & Albert Museum: the History of its
Building*, 1982

Pyke, E.J.
A Biographical Dictionary of Wax Modellers, 1973

Read, Benedict
Victorian Sculpture, 1982

Read, Benedict & Skipwith, Peyton
Sculpture in Britain Between the Wars
Exhibition catalogue, Fine Art Society 1986

Royal Academy
Victorian and Edwardian Decorative Art
Exhibition catalogue, Handley Read Collection,
Royal Academy 1972

Silber, Evelyn
The Sculpture of Jacob Epstein, 1986

Skipwith, Peyton
Architectural Sculpture in London, *Decorative
Arts Society Journal*, 1997 No.21, pp121-9

Sparrow, Walter S.
'A Young English Sculptor: Gilbert Bayes', *The
Studio*, March 1902 Vol 25, pp102-8

Spielman, Marion H.
British Sculpture and Sculptors of Today, 1901
*First Exhibition of Statuettes by Sculptors of Today
British and French*, Fine Art Society, London 1902

Stansfield, H.H.
Sculpture and the Sculptor's Art, 1918

Taft, Lorado
Modern Tendencies in Sculpture, 1921

Underwood, Eric G.
A Short History of English Sculpture, 1933

Wagner, Anthony R.
Historic Heraldry of Britain, 1939

Whittick, Arnold
War Memorials, 1946

Royal Academy Pictures, Magazine of Art 1888-
1915

Royal Academy Illustrated, Magazine of Art
1916-1950

KEY DATES IN GILBERT BAYES' LIFE

1872	Bayes born 4th April.
1888	First exhibit at the Arts and Crafts Society, Regent Street.
1889	First exhibit at the Royal Academy, aged 17.
1890	Joined an office of tie merchants in the city.
1891-6	Attended evening classes at City and Guilds College, Finsbury.
1896	Won County Council Scholarship for two years.
1896	Attended Royal Academy Schools, taught by Thomas Brock, Harry Bates and George Frampton.
1896	Proposed as member of the Art Workers' Guild by George Frampton and A. Finn Brophy.
1897	Won Armitage Prize and £30 for composition.
1898	Won Silver Medal for life modelling and £50. Anatomical figure cast in bronze was purchased by the Royal Academy.
1899	Won Gold Medal, Landseer Scholarship of £80 and travelling scholarship for £200.
1900	Travelled Italy (3 months) France (9 months).
1900	A set of panels exhibited in Dresden National Museum was purchased by the state. 'Best Work of the Year' for 1900.
1900	Received Honorable Mention at Paris International Exhibition.
1906	Married Gertrude Smith.
1906	Taught at Camberwell Art School.
1908	Daughter, Jean, born.
1910	Sigurd purchased by the Chantrey Bequest.
1912	Son, Geoffrey, born.
1918	Exempted from war service because of the equestrian statues for Australia.
1918	Became an Honorary member of the Royal Institute of Painters in Watercolours.
1922	Became an Honorary member of the Société des Artistes Français.
1925	Awarded Diploma of Honour and Gold Medal at the Paris Exhibition of Decorative Art.
1925	Elected Master of the Art Workers' Guild.
1929	Won Bronze Medal at the Paris Salon.
1930	Moved to Greville Place and built new studio.
1930	Published 'Modelling for Sculpture'.
1931	Awarded Royal Society of British Sculpture Medal for Saville Theatre.
1933	Awarded Freedom of City of London.
1939	Won Gold Medal at the Paris Salon.
1939-4	Elected Vice President of the Incorporated Association of Architects and Surveyors.
1939-4	Elected President of the Royal Society of British Sculptors.
1952	Wife, Gertrude, died.
1953	Bayes died 10th July (aged eighty-one).

INDEX

Gilbert Bayes